...rica
WEST AFRICA AND THE SAHEL

The Women Writing Africa Project

A Project of the Feminist Press at the City University of New York
Funded by the Ford Foundation and the Rockefeller Foundation

Women Writing Africa, a project of cultural reconstruction, aims to restore African women's voices to the public sphere. Through the publication of a series of regional anthologies, each collecting oral and written narratives as well as a variety of historical and literary texts, the project will make visible the oral and written literary expression of African women. The definition of "writing" has been broadened to include songs, praise poems, and significant oral texts, as well as fiction, poetry, letters, journals, journalism, and historical and legal documents. The project has been undertaken with the expectation that the publication of these texts will allow for new readings of African women's history.

PROJECT CO-DIRECTORS AND SERIES EDITORS
Tuzyline Jita Allan, Department of English, Baruch College, CUNY
Abena P. A. Busia, Department of Literatures in English, Rutgers University
Florence Howe, emerita, Department of English, The Graduate Center, CUNY, and executive director, The Feminist Press at CUNY

EXECUTIVE COMMITTEE

Anne Adams, Cornell University
Diedre L. Badejo, Kent State University
Ann Biersteker, Yale University
Debra Boyd, Winston-Salem State College
Judith Byfield, Dartmouth College
Frieda Ekotto, University of Michigan
Thomas A. Hale, Pennsylvania State University
Peter Hitchcock, Baruch College, CUNY

Nancy Rose Hunt, University of Michigan
Marjolijn de Jager, New York University
Eileen Julien, Indiana University
Judith Miller, New York University
Angelita D. Reyes, University of Minnesota
Joyce Hope Scott, Wheelock College
Marcia Wright, Columbia University
Louise Allen Zak, Marlboro College

BOARD OF ADVISORS

Jacqui Alexander, Barbados
Belinda Bozzoli, South Africa
Boutheina Cheriet, Algeria
Johnnetta B. Cole, United States
Carolyn Cooper, Jamaica
Fatoumata Sire Diakite, Mali
Nawal El Saadawi, Egypt
Aminata Sow Fall, Senegal
Wanguiwa Goro, Kenya
Asma Abdel Halim, Sudan
Charlayne Hunter-Gault, United States
Adama Ba Konaré, Mali
Joy Kwesiga, Uganda
Françoise Lionnet, United States
Marjorie Oludhe Macgoye, Kenya

Fatma Moussa, Egypt
Mbulelo Mzamane, South Africa
Lauretta Ngcobo, South Africa
Kimani Njogu, Kenya
Asenath Bole Odaga, Kenya
Mamphela Ramphele, South Africa
Sandra Richards, United States
Fatou Sow, Senegal
Filomena Steady, Sierra Leone
Margaret Strobel, United States
Susie Tharu, India
Nahid Toubia, Sudan
Ngugi wa Thiong'o, Kenya
Aminata Traore, Mali

◆

Volume 1: The Southern Region (Botswana, Lesotho, Namibia, South Africa, Swaziland, Zimbabwe)

Volume 2: West Africa and the Sahel (Benin, Burkina Faso, Côte d'Ivoire, Gambia, Ghana, Guinea-Conakry, Liberia, Mali, Niger, Nigeria, Senegal, Sierra Leone)

Women Writing Africa

WEST AFRICA AND THE SAHEL

The Women Writing Africa Project, Volume 2

Edited by Esi Sutherland-Addy and Aminata Diaw

ASSOCIATE EDITOR: Abena P. A. Busia

CONTRIBUTING EDITORS: Tuzyline Jita Allan, Antoinette Tidjani Alou,
Diedre L. Badejo, Rokhaya Fall, Fatimata Mounkaïla,
Christiane Owusu-Sarpong

TEXT EDITORS: Florence Howe and Judith Miller

The Feminist Press at the City University of New York
New York

Published by The Feminist Press at the City University of New York
The Graduate Center, 365 Fifth Avenue, New York, NY 10016
www.feministpress.org

First edition, 2005

12 11 10 09 08 07 06 05   5 4 3 2 1

Library of Congress Cataloging-in-Publication Data
  Women writing Africa. West Africa and the Sahel / edited by Esi Sutherland-Addy
  and Aminata Diaw.— 1st ed.
     p. cm.—(The women writing Africa project ; v. 2)
     Includes bibliographical references and index.
       ISBN 1-55861-501-6 (cloth: acid-free paper) — ISBN 1-55861-500-8 (pbk: acid-free paper)
    1. West African literature—Women authors. 2. Folk literature—Africa, West.
  3. Oral tradition—Africa, West. 4. Women—Africa, West—Literary collections.
  5. Women—Africa, West—History—Sources. 6. Africa, West—Literary
  collections. 7. Africa, West—History—Sources. I. Sutherland-Addy, Esi. II.
  Diaw, Aminata. III. Series.
  PL8014.W372W66 2005
  896'.082--dc22
                              2005050708

Publication of this volume is made possible, in part, by funds from the Ford Foundation and the Rockefeller Foundation.

Text and cover design by Dayna Navaro
Cover art: Sous-verre. India ink and lacquer paint under glass. Senegal. 4 1/4″ x 6″.
Private collection, New York, N.Y.
Printed in Canada on acid-free paper by Transcontinental Printing

CONTENTS

*A bracketed date signifies the date of collection of a text that either bears a long historical tradition or describes a historical occurrence or activity.

LULLABIES AND SONGS OF YOUNG WOMEN

SONGS AND TALES OF SOCIAL NEGOTIATION

THE 1990S AND THE NEW CENTURY

A Note on the Women Writing Africa Project

The first conversation about this project took place when Tuzyline Jita Allan spoke with Florence Howe at the 1990 meeting of the Modern Language Association. Allan was responding to the recent publication by The Feminist Press of the first volume of *Women Writing in India: 600 B.C. to the Present,* edited by Susie Tharu and K. Lalita. Referring to this landmark publication as a striking example of the untapped potential of international feminist scholarship, Allan pointed to the need for a similar intervention in Africa. Both Allan and Howe knew that a project for Africa like one that the Press had begun for India could testify to the literary presence and historical activity of African women. While Howe did not want to assume responsibility for such a project, she agreed to discuss it at a meeting of the Publications and Policies Committee of the Feminist Press held in February 1991. All present understood that so massive a project would need funding. Howe expected that the Africans interested in such a volume would prepare a grant application, organize the work, and, when it was ready for publication, offer it to the Feminist Press.

Later that year, when Howe was delivering the volume of *Women Writing in India* to the Ford Foundation to thank it for its small grant in support of that project, Alison Bernstein said, "Africa has to be next." A small group—Abena P. A. Busia, Chikwenye Ogunyemi, Peter Hitchcock, Allan, and Howe—met with Bernstein to discuss the possibility of and support for a planning meeting to follow the meeting of the African Literature Association (ALA) in Accra, Ghana, in April 1994. We are grateful to Johnnetta B. Cole, then president of Spelman College, who opened that meeting and testified to the need for such a project and to the commitment of The Feminist Press to publishing women's lost voices. Susie Tharu, who grew up in Uganda, Abena P. A. Busia, and Florence Howe also spoke with enthusiasm about the importance of such a project. They were joined by Margaret Busby and Bella Brodsky, who shared their experiences of editing individual volumes on women in Africa and around the world. In addition, some forty members of the ALA attended these two-day meetings, including Judith Miller, who has been an important member of the committtee for the West/Sahel region ever since.

Three primary considerations guided the preliminary discussions of the project. First, in spite of their overlapping agendas, Women Writing Africa could not be an exact replication of *Women Writing in India*. Africa's entrenched oral traditions called for a different response to the discursive modes of expression on the continent. To this end, reconceiving the notion of "writing" marked a conceptual breakthrough in determining how to name a project aimed at capturing African women's creative landscape.

"Writing" in *Women Writing Africa* metonymically suggests a blend of verbal and written forms of expression embodying the experience of African women in envisioning their lives in relation to their societies. The project's matrix of spoken and scripted words represents the creative interaction between living women in the actual world and the flux of history: in short, African women "making" a world.

Women Writing Africa, therefore, became a project of cultural restoration that aims to restore African women's voices to the public sphere. We are publishing several volumes documenting the history of self-conscious expression by African women throughout the continent. This expression is both oral and written, ritual and quotidian, sacred and profane. We are as interested in dance songs and private letters as in legal depositions and public declamations. We hope to foster new readings of African history by shedding light on the dailiness of women's lives as well as their rich contributions to culture. In the end, seeing through women's eyes, we expect to locate the fault lines of memory and so change assumptions about the shaping of African knowledge, culture, and history.

A second consideration focused on the establishment of a framework for conducting research on the continent, and here two hard questions presented themselves: how to think of Africa regionally rather than nationally, and how to set up working groups in those regions and also in the United States. We originally projected five volumes, but conditions in the countries of central Africa led to the decision to produce four representative, rather than all-inclusive, volumes—from West Africa and the Sahel, from Southern Africa, from East Africa, and from North Africa.

Following the Ghanaian planning conference, Abena P. A. Busia joined Allan and Howe as co-directors of the project. Together we formed an Executive Committee of U.S.-based Africanist scholars to serve as a resource and review board for the project's articulated goals, and an Advisory Committee of prominent scholars and writers in the field. Together we planned how to organize both regionally and nationally in the field: Allan would find the scholars in the Southern region; Busia would do the same in the West/Sahel region. For their help with this phase of the project, thanks are due to Debra Boyd and Joyce Hope Scott, who attended the Accra meeting and have continued to make contributions to the project. Then, with Africa-based colleagues, both Allan and Busia began the work of developing research teams in their assigned regions, first by locating national coordinators who would work as a team with their regional counterparts. Later, we would proceed in a somewhat similar manner in the East and the North.

The third consideration essential to realizing the project's promise was funding. The three co-directors wrote the first grant proposal to the Ford Foundation, and within two years, another to the Rockefeller Foundation. At Ford, we wish to acknowledge specifically the instigating interest of

Alison Bernstein and the support of our several program officers—Janice Petrovitch, Margaret Wilkerson, and Geraldine Fraser. At Rockefeller, we wish to acknowledge the interest and support of Lynn Szwaja, our program officer. We would like to thank both Lynn Szwaja and Morris Vogel for their support of the French edition of this volume. We are also grateful to the Rockefeller Foundation for three Team Awards to its Bellagio Study and Conference Center, where we worked with the editorial team and translators of the Western volume, and where we wrote drafts for this Note. We want to thank especially Susan Garfield, for her administrative support, and Gianna Celli, the director of the Rockefeller Foundation's Bellagio Center, for her special interest in our work. This time spent in Bellagio was invaluable for editors and consultants who live in different countries and who were working toward a volume destined to appear both in French and in English.

Without the commitment of the staff and Board of Directors of The Feminist Press, we could not have done this work. Florence Howe wants to acknowledge the whole staff during the years 1997 to 2000—and again in 2005—when she was also the publisher/director of The Feminist Press, especially for their support during the weeks when she was holding meetings in Africa. We want also to acknowledge the extraordinary talent and energy of the team of people essential to the final production of the volume. We want to thank Jean Murley, who for more than three years has been Florence Howe's skilled assistant, mastering many of the steps toward producing a published book. We are also grateful for the work of several project assistants: Alyssa Colton, Kim Mallett, Rona Peligal, Sandra Vernet, and Deidre Mahoney. We want to thank Jean Casella, former publisher/director, and Livia Tenzer, former editorial director, as well as other Feminist Press staff and consultants for their work on this volume. In particular, we want to acknowledge Phoebe St. John for her painstaking work seeking permissions, Nancy Johnston for her detailed work on the bibliography, and Sierra Van Borst for her careful editorial work, which has seen this volume through some of its final stages; also, Anjoli Roy and Marion Valladares Smith, who worked on the index. While Dayna Navaro designed the volume's cover and the series's interior, Lisa Force has creatively revised the design to suit the particular needs of this volume. We are thankful also for the marketing work of Franklin Dennis and Jeannette Petras, and for Paul Pombo's careful attention to the myriad financial details of this project. We appreciate the continuing faith in this project of The Feminist Press's Board of Directors, and, finally, we wish to express our thanks to friends and colleagues in the African Literature Association for their continuing interest and support.

Tuzyline Jita Allan would like to thank the friends, acquaintances, and strangers throughout Southern and Eastern Africa who became part of a great wave of kindness and support during her travels. Malcolm Hacksley, Paulette Coetzee, and other members of the National English Literary

Museum (NELM) in Grahamstown were at once generous and efficient. She sincerely thanks the following individuals for dispensing generously the famed African hospitality: Nobantu Ratsebotsa, Leloba Molema, Austin Bukenya, Susan Kiguli, Sheila Meinjies, Fulata Moyo, Saida Othman, Naomi Shitemi, Sheila Ryanga, Amandina Nihamba, Shebo Meebelo, and Jane Bennett, former director of the Gender Institute at Cape Town University. Allan also acknowledges the important contributions of Carol Sicherman, who traveled with her to East Africa in 1999 to set up the project and to help recruit scholars in the region, and Adam Ashforth, whose intimate knowledge of South Africa proved invaluable. She thanks Chikwenye Okonjo Ogunyemi, Jane Marcus, and Rashida Ismaili for their intellectual and moral support, and she is especially grateful to Hawa Allan, who used the periods of her mother's absence to develop her own creativity. Allan and Busia wish to thank Irene Asseba D'Almeida, Carol Boyce Davies, Peter Hitchcock, Nancy Rose Hunt, Brenda Berrian, Ketu Katrak, Angelita Reyes, and Mete Shayne for their wisdom and sincere interest in the project. Both Allan and Howe would like to thank the Zimbabwe Women Writers and the organizers of the Zimbabwe Book Fair for their enthusiastic embrace of the project. And all three owe a debt of gratitude to Delia Friedman for her diligence and professionalism in handling travel plans for scores of women from all corners of the globe to attend our regional meetings through the years.

Abena Busia wishes to acknowledge the support of the Department of English at Rutgers University, especially chairpersons Barry Qualls, Cheryl A. Wall, and Richard Miller for flexible teaching schedules that allowed for extensive travel in Africa. In addition, she is grateful for the support of several Rutgers University graduate students: Carol Allen, now in the English department at Long Island University, for her work planning the ALA meeting in Accra at which Women Writing Africa was launched; Ronald Tyson, Kimberly Banks, Shalene Moodie, and Nia Tuckson for assistance of various kinds over the years, including teaching and monitoring classes during her absences for editorial board meetings; and Krista Johnson, who, after graduating from Northwestern, spent time in Ghana and helped with the preparation of the second Bellagio meeting. Her special thanks go to Jessica Fredston-Herman, for her diligence in decoding the "notes" and "arrows" in the revision of an early version of the introduction, and to her entire family, for being, as always, a safe haven in a storm. Finally, a debt of gratitude is owed Anita Ake, her personal assistant since 2003, for her exemplary equanimity in the face of chaos.

Florence Howe would like to thank Feminist Press Board members Helene D. Goldfarb, Mariam K. Chamberlain, and Shirley L. Mow for their extraordinary support of her work. She would also like to thank Marcia Wright, Judith Miller, and Albert and Christiane Owusu-Sarpong for their friendship, counsel, and hospitality.

With regard to the production of the introduction to this volume, we want to acknowledge the contributions of all involved. Volume editors Aminata Diaw and Esi Sutherland-Addy provided outstanding writing and scholarship for the individual sections of the introduction, as well as determining its overall shape. Diedre Badejo and Christiane Owusu-Sarpong gave generously of their time in the summer of 2004 to travel to New York, and dedicated additional time at home to add supplemental material to the introduction. We have made Judith Miller's helpful editorial contributions to the introduction and volume as a whole visible by naming her as text editor of the English as well as the French volume. Along with our names on the French volume will be that of Christiane Owusu-Sarpong, who will translate the introduction and all the headnotes, as well as many of the texts. Finally, we want to say how supremely grateful we are to Aminata Diaw and Esi Sutherland-Addy for their editorial wisdom and unfailing determination to see this project into a published book.

We are aware that Women Writing Africa represents the largest undertaking of our lives, a responsibility to set the reality of African women's lives in history and in the present before a world that is only just waking up to their importance. It is our continuing hope that these volumes will give birth to hundreds of others.

> Tuzyline Jita Allan
> Abena P. A. Busia
> Florence Howe
> Series Editors and Project Co-Directors

PREFACE

This is a welcome space in which to place on record the working history of the West African and Sahelian volume of Women Writing Africa. The project aspires to produce an overarching introductory text and to provide an alternative channel for West African women's voices. Our process has championed equity between scholars of the global North and the South. In the following paragraphs, we will set out the highlights of our enriching and complex experience, which has also raised some conceptual issues influencing the shape of the volume.

From its inception, the West African and Sahelian volume took on the intense richness and complexity of the West African region it represents. Situated between the Sahelian expanse and the Gulf of Guinea, this region is a mosaic of ethnic groups, languages, cultures, histories, and countries. In our volume, we represent twelve nations: Benin, Burkina Faso, Côte d'Ivoire, Gambia, Ghana, Guinea-Conakry, Liberia, Mali, Niger, Nigeria, Senegal, Sierra Leone. Togo and Guinea Bissau are absent for logistical reasons. Instead of tackling the more contemporary reality of postcolonial national diversity, it seemed more pertinent to attempt an appreciation of the cultural specificities relevant to the area as a whole. The story of West Africa is a story of indigenous and migrant populations traversing a terrain as vast and diverse as that which encompasses the whole of Europe, from the Republic of Ireland to the Baltic Sea, including Spain and Portugal, the whole of Scandinavia, and the new Balkan states up to Latvia, Lithuania, and Belarus. The unity of this space is borne out by archeological evidence, oral traditions, magnificent artworks, and the number of languages with wide coverage throughout the region. Among these languages are Fulfulde/Fulani, Hausa, and Mande, whose distribution often coincides with the influence of extensive precolonial trade links, as well as kingdoms and empires of the thirteenth through the nineteenth century, which were in a constant process of amalgamation and resurgence.

Added to this complexity are the layers of two major external influences: the advent of Islam from the eleventh century and the arrival of Europeans in the middle of the fifteenth. Both influences were spread through trade and conquest. Although Islam brought with it Arabic language and culture, one of the striking aspects of this region is the way Islamic elements have been effectively indigenized by existing cultures. European languages and culture permeated the fabric of West African society not only through trade and imperial conquest but also through the infrastructure of colonialism. While French and English influences predominate, traces of the earlier Dutch, German, Danish, and Portuguese may be found. Out of the sixteen countries in West Africa, four were colonized by the English, nine by the French, and two by the Portuguese. Liberia was never colonized but looked to the United States as its metropole.

Because of the diversity of cultural and colonial influences, we originally felt that the region would have to be covered by more than one volume. Ultimately, however, the underlying similarities, particularly in women's circumstances and evolution, convinced us not to separate the Sahel from the rest of West Africa. We believe that it is possible to see the whole region as one life-zone through the recurring themes and tropes—both historical and literary—of women's experience: most saliently, women as organizers and the glue of their communities; women as subject to recurrent migrations, amalgamations, and fragmentations, including the colonial emphasis on women as central to the physical work of sustaining lives and families economically; and women as crucially defined by their status as mothers. We have thus chosen to illuminate women's knowledge of and involvement in the dynamics of the region by working simultaneously in two European languages, French and English. This, we expect, will make the West African and Sahelian volume a rare publication, conceived in a truly multilingual context and available throughout the region.

The team that contributed to putting the volume together eventually consisted of over 150 researchers, translators, and editors working in eleven countries and twenty-six languages. Each country had a national committee and/or a coordinator who took the responsibility of interpreting the evolving requirements of the project and selecting a body of appropriate texts. Each national committee devised its own strategies for achieving this goal. Often, scholars involved in the project had already come across appropriate texts in their own research, but many committees had to undertake research specifically for the project.

Five regional meetings were critical for interpreting the objectives of Women Writing Africa in the West African and Sahelian contexts. The first was held in 1997 in Dakar, Senegal, where we discussed theoretical issues and made the decision to merge West Africa and the Sahel. We were then ready for the collection of texts to begin. In 1998, representative members of the national committees met in Bamako, Mali, where a vigorous discussion of texts defined and refined the scope of the volume. Three more regional meetings were held: in Fez, Morocco, in 1999 (following the African Literature Association meeting); in Accra, Ghana, in 2000; and in Dakar in 2001.

During the 1998 meeting in Bamako, the group agreed on two bilingual (French/English) editors for the volume. Speaking personally, our first meeting as editors sparked a wonderful coming together of minds and souls that has sustained us through the monumental task of editing this volume. Since then, each time the self-confident little Mamie Cisse, Aminata Diaw's daughter, has walked into our presence to demand her mother's attention, we have been reminded of how much of our lives are invested in the project, for Aminata was pregnant with Mamie in 1997.

After the Bamako meeting, literally hundreds of texts poured in, based on criteria that had been set for their collection. A review of these caused us to reassess our criteria with regard to issues of dating and situating the texts as part of a history of women. Such issues were a matter of serious negotiation. The bulk of the texts first offered had been produced in the course of women's daily social and working lives. They raised the question of what constitutes "history." It became clear that, for this region, it would be necessary to undertake a reading of texts that also recognized history as a decoding of the quotidian. We had to engage, for example, in the tricky process of dating oral texts—one of the exciting aspects in the development of African historiography. We were able through content analysis to place a set of Mossi maiden songs from Burkina Faso in the colonial period, although they were recorded recently. This shows how history endures but also reminds us that the reception of such songs will change according to historical contexts.

Work on this project brought home to us the difference between tracing the voices of women through writing and through oral performance. Nineteenth-century African women left more written records than had been anticipated, but their ancestors also left far more in sacred chant and song for far longer than we had expected to be able to verify. Tracing these voices, whether in songs that have come down from sixteenth-century Igalaland in Nigeria or in legal depositions unearthed from the archives of early-twentieth-century colonial courts in Senegal, has empowered us to claim a countertradition, a history of West Africa and the Sahel that focuses on women's lives and work. It has also uncovered the enormous importance and variety of spoken texts, which far outnumber written pieces.

The relatively limited availability of written texts was a grim reminder that, especially since colonial times, West African women—for all their vibrancy—had been denied access to official channels of communication and of economic and social development. This volume therefore contains a large number of oral texts; even today, the only mode of self-expression for most West African women is speech. At the African Literature Association meeting in Fez in 1999, when those of us working on West Africa and the Sahel met with scholars working on southern Africa, the southern team was struck by the extent to which our research had yielded oral texts, while our team became acutely aware of the value of archival research. The types of texts unearthed and gathered in both regions spoke volumes about the different histories of colonization in the southern and western parts of Africa.

We should have liked to share the richness of texts in indigenous languages alongside translations into French or English. Translation always poses a challenge for an anthology such as ours with texts originating in various languages. In this respect, the project received invaluable support from national committee members who provided the editorial team with an initial translation into French or English depending on which was their official language. Since the majority of countries in West Africa and the

Sahel are officially French-speaking, the translations of texts originally in African languages were made initially into French. These were subsequently translated into English in close consultation with either national committee members and/or fluent speakers of the relevant African languages. To ensure that there is no ambiguity about the fact that particular texts were translated from the French rather than the original African language, these texts have been so marked in the English volume.

As research brought in more and more oral texts, we tried not to be despondent about our inability to convey their texture and spirit. Many members of the team felt compelled by the desire to experience these texts in performance. As adult members of our respective societies, all of us had very personal experiences of our own ethnicities. Many of us are also trained specialists in the area of oral performance. This made it easy for us to break into performance to demonstrate the sheer aesthetic power of the texts. In fact, we created short performances at two separate meetings. The first was that of the chairs of the national committees in Accra in 2000, where country representatives presented sketches based on our texts, accompanied by Ghanaian performers. The second was at an editorial meeting in Bellagio, Italy, where our group did a reading for other scholars in residence at the Rockefeller Foundation's Bellagio Study and Conference Center. We still dream of producing an audio disc.

The two of us, as primary editors, held a number of editorial meetings in Accra and Dakar. Florence Howe, the codirector and series editor of the project, attended two of them. Abena P. A. Busia joined us whenever she could; she also worked regularly with Esi Sutherland-Addy in Accra several times a year. Through the efforts of Florence Howe, two team residency awards gave her and us the opportunity of working with our consulting and associate editors at the Rockefeller Foundation's Bellagio Center in 2001 and 2002. At various times Tuzyline Jita Allan, Antoinette Tijdani Alou, Diedre Badejo, Abena P. A. Busia, Rokhaya Fall, Florence Howe, Tobe Levin, Judith Miller, Fatimata Mounkaila, and Christiane Owusu-Sarpong joined us. Our interaction generated a wealth of information, expertise, and camaraderie, which has contributed to the shape of the volume and been a source of personal joy.

The table of contents was the subject of the final meeting of representatives of the national committees in Accra in 2000. These meetings were robust and rigorous, and they revealed the tensions between the pre-established objectives of the project and the patterns emerging from the texts coming in from the field. National committees were to have ownership; they were in control of prioritizing items. They had, on that premise, gone out and found what mattered to them, but at times they found their decisions at odds with the requirements of a large, continent-wide project being published by an American and a French press. Indeed, we may have consequently lost some participating researchers. This meeting, however, clarified a number of issues and revealed gaps in the research that had to be addressed in order to achieve the goals of the project.

Of course, the diverse group of people shaping this project did not always share the same vision of Africa or of the project. African-born women and women of African descent, living in exile in the diaspora among other émigrés and exiles and teaching in the academies of the West, were eager to voice their concerns. The largest group, West African scholars and feminists residing in the region, desired to shape a volume that addressed issues internal to the area's history and needs. A third group, made up of Euro-American scholars, some of whom were Africanists, was aware of the lacunae in knowledge about Africa and the needs of the U.S. publishing market. All, however, were committed to redressing the absence of integrity in the presentation of images of African women and the places they come from. Working on the West Africa volume sorely tested the core principles of Women Writing Africa as a project: that the authority of African women scholars should be presumed primary in shaping the intellectual parameters of the project; that egalitarian partnerships between African and non-African scholars should be maintained; that collaborative feminist work should be promoted. We have kept these goals before us throughout our work on this project; we believe we have served them well.

The process we adopted made visible a rich array of perspectives of "living feminism" that testified to the realities and complexities of global feminism. The multiple demands forced us to accept the challenge of negotiating the power and agency of African women and could only be resolved through painful compromise. Nevertheless, we believe that the significant contribution of this project lies in confirming the overarching value of global sisterhood, which found expression in the project's genesis: it was conceived when a West African feminist scholar in diaspora, Tuzyline Jita Allan, shared her heartfelt need for viable records of home with a dedicated American feminist and publisher, Florence Howe. The project now involves over two hundred women in nearly two dozen countries on two continents.

The editors also had problems agreeing on a definition of African writers when it came to contemporary women of the West African diaspora who had spent a good part of their lives abroad. The question of formal citizenship became a contentious matter during editorial discussions but was finally resolved by ceding space to women still in Africa. On the plus side, the team of editors and translators has understood translation as a sacred duty—and often an agonizing one. There were, indeed, many days during which we and our associate and consulting editors could be heard whooping with joy at having found just the right turn of phrase to accommodate the cadences and spirit of a particular text.

A project of this magnitude necessarily evolved according to the difficulties it encountered. The state of official records and archives in various countries, for example, made it difficult to track written records. This necessitated searches elsewhere in the world. Given the gaps in the materials sent us, we needed to buttress these materials with texts found in archives by African and Africanist scholars working in American and European institutions. We were once again struck by the reality that some of the most spectacular information about Africans can now only be found in archives in Europe and America. The many librarians and archivists the world over who responded with enthusiasm to our requests cannot go unmentioned. Their timely intervention made possible the inclusion of some of our most prized historical texts. For example, we would not have been able to place Sarah Forbes Bonetta's letters with those of her daughter, Victoria Davies, without the support given to Abena P. A. Busia by several librarians: Jackie Lewis of the Local Studies Library of Brighton and Hove, Janet Johnstone of The Cheltenham Ladies College, and Jean Bray, archivist at Sudley Castle. We are most grateful to all of them.

The Nigeria committee faced particular problems due to the sheer size of the country and a poor communications infrastructure. Indeed, even holding committee meetings proved to be a major feat. Nigeria had to appoint three coordinators rather than one—one each for the north, east and west. The other committees, such as the one in Côte d'Ivoire, had trouble sustaining a team of women in high demand elsewhere for the length of time demanded by the project. Some countries were never able to hold a committee together for more than a few months. We recall the heroic efforts of the Liberians and Sierra Leoneans, who were able to pull texts together despite armed conflicts occurring in those countries.

Along the way, we encountered problems directly connected to the colonial legacy. Formal borders, such as those of Ghana with Cote d'Ivoire to the west and Togo to the east, represent imperial and colonial history. Different official systems, based on the English in the case of Ghana and on the French in Togo and Côte d'Ivoire, have led to separate trajectories and significant mutual exclusions. For example, even in places with a common indigenous language and culture, we had great difficulty coming up with a uniform orthography for language groups: is it Dioula or Djula? Songhai-Zerma or Songhay-Zarma or Songhai-Djerma? We eventually selected the most commonly used version of the name.

The process of putting the volume together revealed that even what texts are celebrated and which writers are well known is complicated by questions of language and modes of expression and exposure. Women's work songs, almost unknown in Europe and the United States, were familiar to the women across the region. However, pieces celebrated in the West by writers such as Buchi Emecheta and Mariama Bâ were unknown to women from the same region and even from the same ethnic group. Different colonial heritages have affected language and education policies. It is possible for literate women of French-speaking Côte d'Ivoire, thoroughly familiar with Francophone luminaries such as Veronique Tadjo, to grow up ignorant of the works of their English-speaking Ghanaian neighbor Ama Ata Aidoo. The same is true for literate Ghanaian women. Yet the writing of both these authors reveals that they have been quite influenced by the storytelling traditions of neighboring cultures.

We also had to deal with the question of separations created by trans-Atlantic and trans-Saharan slavery and emigration from West Africa. We had no doubt that the voices of women subject to slavery would provide the volume with a more nuanced and complete story of the West African experience. Here also, we faced a number of dilemmas in terms of finding appropriate texts. The inclusion of a text by the early diasporan slave Madlena Van Poppos, a Benin woman sent to the Caribbean island of St. Thomas in the early eighteenth century, helps palliate the absence of texts speaking to the experience of slavery. We were also happy to include a letter by a twice-displaced ex-slave who returned to Liberia in the mid-1880s.

We hope that as editors we have been able to distill the essence of the massive collections submitted from the field and remain true to the hundreds of researchers we represent. We also wish to thank here those who have contributed immensely to this volume. Throughout the editorial process, associate editor Abena P. A. Busia worked very closely with us. She became the archivist of the project, painstakingly keeping records of the dozens of revisions of the table of contents. She devised classificatory systems to keep track of the many versions of texts and the information on documents submitted, as well as helping to shape the anthology as a whole.

The writing of the introduction went through a number of phases. The first organization was provided by us and modified substantially by a team of people who wrote additional text: Christiane Owusu-Sarpong, Diedre Badejo, Tuzyline Jita Allan, and Abena P. A. Busia. Perspectives were juggled and negotiated in order to provide an essay contextualizing this anthology historically, culturally, and theoretically.

We wish to acknowledge especially the support of two institutions: the Institute of African Studies of the University of Ghana, Legon, and the West African Research Center (WARC) in Dakar, Senegal. The Institute of African Studies accepted Women Writing Africa as an official research project, which permitted Esi Sutherland-Addy and other members of the African Languages, Literature, and Drama section of the institute to dedicate their time and energies to the project. The institute will also establish a repository for the records of the project. WARC not only provided excellent support to Aminata Diaw and served as hub for the Senegal Committee, but also for four years opened its doors and facilities for the long, intense editorial meetings required for the project. We thank former WARC director Wendy Wilson-Fall for her hospitality and perceptive leadership and for the insightful brainstorming sessions held there.

The volume would not have been possible without the research and painstaking translation and selection processes that took place at the community and national level. There were also those who offered invaluable support services from all over the world. We list them here by country and trust that all listed will accept our sincere gratitude in proportion to their contribution:

Benin: Fafa Hazoume, Hortense Mayaba

Burkina Faso: Denise Badini-Folane, Fatoumata Kinda, Burkina Faso WWA Committee

Côte d'Ivoire: Chantal Ahobaut, Georgette Dick, Helen N'gbesso, Bernard Zadi Zaourou

Europe and the United States: Debra S. Boyd, Judith Byfield, Sven Ehrilich, Marjolijn de Jager, Tobe Levin, Joyce Hope Scott, Louise Allen Zak

Gambia: Baba Ceesay, Dusu Naba Cham, Hanna Foster, Aji Lala Hydara, Siga Fatima Jagne, Kajiatou Jallow Baldeh, Matilda Johnson, Beatrice Prom, Patience Sonko-Godwin

Ghana: The Gender Studies and Human Rights Documentation Centre; Kate Abbam, Kofi Baah Acheamfour, Dede Addy, Korkor Addy, John Budu Afful, Agatha Akonnor-Mills, Misonu Amu, Akosua Anyidoho, Helena Asamoah-Hassan, Eric Asare, Theresa Ashaley Armah, Cosmas Badasu, Frederika Dadson, Audrey Gadzekpo, Christina Kissiedu, Mary-Esther Kropp-Dakubu, Edward Nanbigne, J. H. K. Nketia, Irene Odotei, Naana Jane Opoku-Agyemang, Harriet Tachie-Menson, Rita Yankah, Robert Yennah, Dzifa Zormelo, Fafa Zormelo

Liberia: Medina Wesseh, Hester Williams

Mali: Odette Ba, Anna Dao, Fatoumata Siré Diakité, Mamadou Diallo, Mariama Keita Diallo, Aïcha Fofana, Fatimata Maiga, Bintou Sanankoua

Niger: Diouldé Laya, B. Saley, Jacques Sille, Manou Zara Villain

Nigeria: Nancy Achebe, Helen Bodunde, Helen Chukwuma, Nkoli Ezumah, Mary Kolawole, Patience Mudiare, Christine Ohale, Sr. Maria Keke Oluchi, Marie Umeh, Ladi Yakubu

Senegal: Sarani Bodian, Awa Cissé, Mamie Cissé, Thierno Cissé, Awa Cissé Ba, Bassirou Dieng, Mariétou Diongue Diop, Souleymane Faye, Dior Konaté, Katiatou Konaté, Mariawa Mbaye, Mariama Ndure-Njie, Aïssa Niandou, Astou Touré

Sierra Leone: Edith Tatoh Kpendema, Josephine Isabella Nicol, Abator Medwin Thomas, Kate Thomas, Christiana Thorpe, Gracie Anne Williams

The West Africa and Sahel team had a distinctive relationship with the Rockefeller Foundation's Bellagio Study and Conference Center. We would like to thank Gianna Celli and her team for their efficiency, thoughtful care, and friendship. The time spent in Bellagio helped us engage with particularly intricate aspects of teamwork, such as translation and the writing of the first drafts of the introduction. We are also grateful to those who contributed to the difficult task of creating the introduction through critical readings, notably Anne Adams, Eileen Julian, Marcia Wright, and Frederick Cooper.

The work of Florence Howe, co-director and cotext editor of Women Writing Africa, in raising the funds to sustain the project cannot go unmentioned. She brought to the West African and Sahelian volume the resources necessary to produce a publishable piece of writing from countries with minimal financial resources and infrastructure. She also offered freely the benefits of a lifetime of expertise in scholarly writing. Beyond this, we engaged with Florence Howe, more than with anyone else on the project, in strong debates around issues such as the presentation of the West African experience and perspective and the inclusion of Africa-centered scholarly thought. We have since heard of so many dramatic stories of relationships between African authors and non-African publishers that we consider our experience a badge of honor in an old struggle.

We are especially mindful of those who have generated a sound factual and theoretical base for self-knowledge and global feminist theory. We wish to mention some representative scholarly forerunners and contemporaries who have greatly inspired us: Filomina Chioma Steady, Bólánlé Awé, Ifi Amadiume, Margaret Busby, Alice Walker, and Oyeronke Oyewunmi.

The process has been very important for us, and we have learned a great deal from and bonded in many ways with our colleagues in the national committees and with the consulting and associate editors. Our initial commitment to the ideals of the project and our experience in the academy would not have been adequate to the task without the almost uncanny complementarity that has developed between our two personalities. Juggling professional demands, social pressures, and the legitimate requirements of our accommodating families, we kept each other going. When we had delicate decisions to make, we made them with trust, mutual respect, and confidence. We feel our sisterhood stands in part as a testimony to the legitimacy of the project, rising above the superficialities of ethnic, religious, and national differences. We hope that this volume, as incomplete as it now feels to us, will take a firm place in a movement to give multivalent representation to the voices of African women. And we fervently wish that others will take up the challenge where we have left off.

Esi Sutherland-Addy
Aminata Diaw

INTRODUCTION

> Where to find the proper word
> For the door of silence . . .
> To open the story's dance
> Close to my woman's skin
> Which the good Lord created
> As an instrument of unpublished music
>
> —*Tanella Boni, 1997*

Opening the doors to new stories, participating in new thinking about African women in the current postcolonial moment, means filling in gaps in the epistemologies and histories on the continent as well as in the European discourses of Africa's "invention." The historiography of West Africa and the Sahel, a vast expanse of land lying between the Sahara Desert and the Gulf of Guinea, reveals that women were often absent from the official record. During the last fifteen years, however, notable research by Niara Sundarkasa, Bólánlé Awé, Claire Robertson, and Martin Klein, among many others, has produced various historical accounts of women in West Africa and the Sahel. The work of E. Frances White and Sandra Greene emphasizes economic change in the positioning of African women, while Ann Stoler examines gender relations within colonialism and Adame Ba Konare surveys forms of women's power in contemporary times. Hence, this volume of the Women Writing Africa project provides a timely intervention that can be situated within the abundance of recent vibrant scholarship about the region, all of which constitutes the strong beginnings of a revised historiography of African women.[1] The myriad voices in this volume establish a clear artistic perspective on the lives of women in the region and correlate with a subtext that both challenges former European assumptions about African women and adds information to newly reconstructed histories.

European presence in the region dates back to the era of exploration initiated in the fifteenth century by the Portuguese and expanded in the sixteenth with the entry of the British and the French, joined later by the Dutch, the Danes, and the Germans. The intervening centuries covered various phases of commerce, the Atlantic slave trade, the so-called Scramble, colonization, and its aftermath. By the nineteenth and early twentieth centuries, the entire region, except for U.S.-dependent Liberia, was under European control, with France and Britain overseeing the lion's share. Of the various periods of contact with Europe, those of the Atlantic slave trade and colonization probably had the greatest impact on Africa's peoples, because of the ideological effects of European invasion and conquest. In particular, colonialism's discourse of race and gender was aimed at a predominantly settler-free region to extract maximum subservience from the population.

The popular image of West Africa as a seductive woman casting a "spell" on Europeans through "its strange and unfathomable charm," to quote from Princess Marie Louise, granddaughter of Queen Victoria, in an account of her official visit to the Gold Coast, later known as Ghana, in 1925, perhaps best represents the Western ideological perspective. "It lays its hand upon you," the princess continued, "and having once felt its compelling touch you can never forget it or be wholly free of it" (1926: 233). Another observer claimed that "Africa is a woman, a dark witch of a woman, coiling herself around you like a snake, making you forget everything but her burning breasts" (Steen [1941]: 319). The feminization of Africa is a familiar trope in late Victorian discourses of empire, used with double effect to explain Africa's lure for Europeans and to maximize its denigration through the conflation of two devalued identities. The metaphor had a special resonance in western Africa, because it expressed the contradictory attitudes of desire and anxiety underlying imperial control in the part of Africa known as "the white man's grave." European conquest and colonization of the region took a heavy toll in life and money on the colonizers abroad and the metropolitan centers at home.

Critics generally associate the oversexualized images of African women with repressive Victorian sensibilities seeking distant zones of rapture in the outposts of empire, but there are graver implications in the way the fantasy worked to displace the reality of African women. In West Africa, the stereotype painted a picture of women as an undifferentiated mass, lacking individuating markers of ethnicity, class, or creativity. More importantly, the focus on women's bodies drew attention away from the female mind, resulting in a preponderance of images of women as serial childbearers in colonial topography and a reluctance to associate women's oral art forms, such as song and performance, with the creative imagination.

Colonial indifference to female traditions of power in West Africa was especially staggering. The inevitable result of diminishing the political importance of secret societies, paramount chieftaincies, and spiritual leaderships was to perpetuate the perception of women as voiceless outsiders in the public arena. In general, colonial administrators preferred to form alliances with African men, thereby tightening patriarchal control of women. The British colonial policy of indirect rule, which aimed to establish an indigenous surrogate system of governance, was a backhanded way to strengthen male hegemony. Its French counterpart— although not fully official and called variously "assimilation" or "association"—tended to remove local cultural structures to facilitate ascent into French civilization. Male chiefs stepped in as intermediaries, trained in a school for the sons of chiefs and interpreters established in Senegal in 1922.

Efforts by postcolonial historians to deconstruct received knowledge about Africa prompted the expectation that women would be rehabilitated in the emerging epistemologies, especially in the wake of a renewed interest in exploring the past cultures of empire in West Africa and in recognizing the influence of Africa and Africans in the making of transatlantic modernity. The results, however, have only recently begun to be encouraging. Until the outbreak of feminist-inspired scholarship on African women in the last few years, established Africanist historians have been reluctant to engage the idea of women as subjects of history. This is due in large part to the longstanding opinion that history is the study of laws and wars, all promulgated by men. But, as Jacques Le Goff points out in his book *History and Memory*, this definition has yielded to the more flexible idea of the "historicity of history," which "links an interpretive practice to a social praxis" (1992: 102–103), thereby opening the door for the recognition of other views of African women and men. The stakes for African gender studies are high, given the subaltern state of women in the canon of African history. To cite a well-known example, Basil Davidson, a pioneering and respected writer-scholar of Africa's historical rehabilitation, claims that his book *West Africa before the Colonial Era: A History to 1850* is a broad-based history. It is, indeed, an account of the dynastic empires of Songhai, Mali, Benin, and Ghana, a fascinating narrative of wars, conquest, political and religious rivalries, migration, trade, wealth, and power. But it also depicts a phallocentric social order in which women's lives are oddities or ignored entirely. Davidson acknowledges as much when, in reference to the self-governing framework of early Igbo society, he writes, "The village governments of the Igbo, and others like them, were popular governments. Every grown-up man (and women in some but not all cases, *feminism in Africa being for a distant future*) could and did have a say at village assemblies where matters of common interest were decided" (1998: 127, emphasis ours). Davidson's observation about feminism rightly cautions against any attempt to interpret the period anachronistically, since the gender ideologies that helped to organize that world are clearly different from our own. Yet some of the issues he raises could have been expanded to shed light on women's social standing.

First published in 1967, Robert William July's *Origins of Modern African Thought: Its Development in West Africa During the Nineteenth and Twentieth Centuries* provides an early example of an intellectual history of the region that shows little interest in the contributions of women. July sets out to trace the influence of "western scientific-technological thought" on "the institutions and ideas of the modern states of mid-twentieth-century Africa" (15); in the process, he errs measurably toward the standard Eurocentric view of a static Africa awakened from a dreary past by its contact with the West. His predominantly internationalist and class-based representation of the transforming events and ideologies of West African modernity ignores local trends of populist reform, and his foregrounding of male achievement results in a nearly complete erasure of women. Contemporary scholars argue for a remapping of the region's modern trajectory to locate and define the intercultural and gendered spaces in this era of revolutionary change.

A series of recent pertinent studies of women writers indicates that women of West Africa and the Sahel have been instrumental to the conception of modern Africa. Stephanie Newell, for example, reasserts female authority in the idea of West African modernity in her book *Literary Culture in Colonial Ghana: "How to Play the Game of Life."* This analysis of the domesticating influences on the colonial culture of literacy in Ghana between 1880 and 1940 shows that women were not peripherally situated in the emerging modern traditions, even though "female literacy levels remained low throughout the colonial period, and women formed a tiny portion of the small percentage of literate Africans" (2002: 60). Newell adds the strong and dominant voice of Mabel Dove-Danquah to a range of views expressed by the local elite on the menacing effects of colonialism, particularly the threat posed by the loose morality of "desperate" European men, who threatened to ruin the lives of young Ghanaian women by destroying "their prospects of attaining positions of respect as married women in African society" (120). Journalist, playwright, fiction writer, and cultural critic, Dove-Danquah wrote extensively about the sexual exploitation of women at the hands of expatriates and local men. By amplifying the record of her contribution to the society, Newell in effect puts her on the same scale as the men who are prominent in Robert July's book.

This volume of Women Writing Africa represents a significant attempt to reappraise the coinage of history to include, as Newell's perspective illustrates, women as producers of knowledge and catalysts for cultural renewal. Our archive of oral and written narratives debunks the notion of African women's unsuitability to make history. The book's repertoire of individual and collective identities evokes both experiences determined by a specific course of events and artistic quests for self-reflection. Simultaneously representing the self-histories of women and the achievement of community, the volume evokes a stream of artistry ranging across the ritual spaces of orality through various stages of negotiations with colonial and patriarchal power to literary reflections on the social order. The enveloping presence of orature attests to the dynamic authority of women's verbal art to act at once as a reservoir of history, a mode of cultural validation, and an arena of protest. Stylistically free forms such as songs, lullabies, and folktales, as well as their formulaic counterparts like dirges, praise songs, incantations, elegies, and proverbs, are vehicles of knowledge creation, preservation, and transmission, which provide tangible and symbolic ways for women to legitimate and critique the social system. Orality supports the traditional structure of women's lives, but as the poetry and prose in the volume illustrate, it also provides the inspirational underpinnings for their writing.

Equally significant is the recovery of the female voice in the tradition of modern writing, which grew out of the social and political transformations in the region following the Atlantic slave trade and European colonialism. Not only in journalism, such as that of Dove-Danquah, but also in petitions and letters of protest, African women make their opinions heard and their difficulties clear. Later, just as a significant number of colonial-trained African men began to produce fiction, African women—Ama Ata Aidoo, Aminata Sow Fall, and Mariama Bâ, for example—also began to produce both short stories and novels, using elements that recall aspects of the oral tradition. Contemporary African women writers experiment with form in ways similar to contemporary writers all over the world, the borders having come down and intercultural projects abounding. Nevertheless, even as they flourish, African women writers do not lose sight of the social, political, and economic conditions that influence their lives, nor have they diminished the inspiration of their oral and literary heritage.

Throughout the following pages, we will effect a complicated "pas de deux" between the writings (understood here in the broadest possible sense) and the history of women in West Africa and the Sahel. In the first part of this introduction, we will explore the question of orature. We will examine how women's songs, dirges, praise poems, and other works both celebrate and subvert the enshrined social order. We will suggest how orality can redefine history, and vice versa, for orature is directly dependent on the context of its reception and on its performance. In the second part of the introduction, we will situate women's writing within a historical continuum from the eighth century, through the period of the great West African empires, to the early twenty-first century. Along the way, we will see how rewritten tales, poetry, autobiographical essays, and prose fiction, as well as songs of social negotiation and other forms of writing, make known the many places of women in West African and Sahelian cultures. Almost all of the texts we will mention foreground women's defiance and self-assertion and demonstrate their skill at managing tensions imposed by social organization and external pressures.

To return to the Tanella Boni poem that serves as the epigraph to our introduction, we hope here to find our own "proper word" with which to "open the story's dance" of African women. In this introduction, we will contextualize, characterize, and make our way through a formerly occluded history of women in West Africa and the Sahel. Four scholars and two editors, all engaged in re-visioning the history and culture of women in Africa, have written the pages that follow. While they emphasize different aspects of that history and culture, they all agree that the orature and written texts collected here illuminate the strategies of adaptation, resistance, and invention that West African and Sahelian women have used to survive and shape the organization and material conditions of their lives.

ORATURE

Mikhaïl Bakhtin has described textual "genres" as "the drive belts from the history of society to the history of language" (1986: 66). West African societies have created a multiplicity of literary genres to answer specific political, social, and individual needs. These genres have long been misread by Europeans, in particular by colonial anthropologists who presented them from a purely static point of view and disregarded them as art forms because they were "oral." Successive schools of thought, including ethnolinguistics, structuralism, folklore, communication studies, and (literary) semiotics have led to creative approaches to African languages and literatures, both oral and written.

Contemporary research on "oral literature," "verbal art," "textorature," or—to avoid a sterile controversy—simply orature has, in particular, gone a long way toward recognizing that orally performed West African texts do not merely provide "folksy, domestic entertainment,"[2] but rather represent a "domain in which individuals in a variety of social roles articulate a commentary upon power relations in society and indeed create knowledge about society" (Furniss and Gunner 1995: 1). In that context, orature not only illuminates power structures but also constitutes a power in itself. Those "in power" (religious and political leaders, elders, and, often, men in general) have over the centuries used various performance events (such as rituals and festivals) to reassert their authority and to exclude the socially dominated from the sphere of public speech and from knowledge itself. Yet, as is made visible in this anthology, oral genres have also sprouted through in ways that permitted socially dominated women to exert "compensatory or counter powers" (Derive 1995: 129) and often to break verbal taboos.

Clear gender divisions generally instituted and determined the use or misuse of genres. These divisions presumably reflected the gender divisions of work and power in specific cultures. For instance, among the Dyula established in Kong, in the northeastern part of Côte d'Ivoire, men were usually in charge of the *ko koro*, or "chronicles," and a great portion of mask songs and war songs were hidden from women. On the other hand, women were in charge of wedding songs and songs for female circumcision (*kenekene donkili*), and "when they [had] a grievance to air with their close relations," they sang *kurubi* songs (Derive 1995: 123). (See, for example, "Songs of Insult," from Niger and Senegal, p. 259.) Where catharsis was possible through the performance of songs, women seized upon these as openings for verbal rebellion.

Artistic expression
Among the Igbo people of southeastern Nigeria, folktales (*akuko-ala*, or "the tales of the land," and *akuko-ifo*, or "the tales of the imagination") appear to have been a most powerful form of artistic expression, both forms "reflect[ing] and serv[ing] to perpetuate [the] fascinating tension [that

exists in Igbo culture since time immemorial] between monarchical power and democratic values" (Azuonye 1995: 65). Veronika Görög-Karady notes that the Malinké-Bambara stories, just like the Akan *anansesem*, or "spider-stories," often end in a "nonconformist" manner because narrative fiction has always been, in West Africa, "a field of social space where ... controversial issues may find legitimate expression" (1995: 91). (See, for instance, "The Man Who Dug Up Yams," p. 335.)

Creativity in West African orature can be found first and foremost in the constant creation of genres, which, over the centuries, have forced dialogues and opened up social negotiations, even where doors were usually tightly closed to protect those in power from losing face. Alongside "reversal rituals" such as the Brong *Apo* (see Rattray 1923; Turner 1977), during which gender roles are actually reversed for short periods of time and lampooning is officially allowed, the existence of the Abe *Eyidi*, or "Naming," from Côte d'Ivoire (see p. 340), the Nzema *Avudwene* festival songs (Agovi 1995), and *Ayabomo*, or "maiden songs" (see p. 154) provide evidence that neither husband nor king is ever above insult, even within the most tenacious forms of patriarchy.

In oral cultures, the art of orature moves far beyond the skillful choice of words. The "power of the Word" in orature emerges from the appropriate use of cultural metaphors and from indirect speech or "pro-verbiality" (Owusu-Sarpong 1995, 2000). Thus meaning is first transferred and deferred in polysemic images, before being altered, once again, in performance. These poetic texts, ambivalent and ambiguous in themselves, are performed in an expressive, rhythmic manner, enhanced by a play on intonation that, combined with theatrical gestures and mime, opens up the meaning of the "text in context" and reinforces the double entendre, thus producing a subtle connivance between the speaker or singer and the listeners, who might respond to or choose to ignore the message. Meaning—especially when it is provocative—can further be wrapped up in total theatrical silence or simply rewritten and transformed through various nonverbal codes, such as the drum, the xylophone, the flute, or the horn, or even through "textile and color rhetoric." During daily interactions, "textile rhetoric," along with proverb creation, constitutes a tool to which women along the West African coast can resort. Akan women, for instance, can use such tools when they want to make a sarcastic argument within a polygamous marriage. Proverbial textile prints such as *Ahwene pa nkasa* ("The precious bead does not talk") can be worn by a teasing senior wife who might well feel like proclaiming loudly and clearly, but still proverbially, that "Man [is] not a pillow upon which to rest one's head" (Yankah 1995: ch. 5).

In what follows, we will investigate, using representative oral texts from our collection, how women, by linking words, images, and rhythms, continue to transmit knowledge and aesthetic norms as well as insights about the complexity of relationships in society and the family. We will see how orature provides a forum for the power struggles between men and women and for the exploration of the boundaries of public and private spheres. We will also suggest how the magic of the spoken and chanted words allows women to reconfigure venues of power for themselves by rolling back the boundaries of the forbidden.

Early scholars

Ruth Finnegan intended that her 1970 seminal work *Oral Literature in Africa* breach a gap in the field. At a time when "the popular myth of Africa as a continent devoid of literature" was still very much alive, she correctly underlined that research had started in earnest in the field and that "some of the most original work [had] come from the growing number of Africans carrying out scholarly analyses of oral literature in their own languages. These writers," Finnegan continued, "have been able to draw attention to many aspects which earlier students tended to overlook either because of their theoretical preconceptions or because they were, after all, strangers to the culture they studied" (1970, rpt. 1976: 43).

Finnegan quotes Kwabena Nketia as having been "outstanding" among even the most remarkable African pioneers. She elaborates particularly on Nketia's acclaimed study of southern Ghanaian dirges (1955, rpt. 1969), which were and occasionally still are "sung or intoned by women as part of public mourning during funerals" (see "Three Lamentations: Nyaako," p. 110). In them, Finnegan quotes Nketia, "'speech [is] inlaid in music, sobs and tears and conjoined to bodily movement'" (1970, rpt. 1976: 153). Not only had Nketia, half a century ago, underlined various important facets of orature, but he had also demonstrated that the art of dirge singing was both a fixed *and* a flexible genre, and that if it had "its own complex and sophisticated conventions," it was "a tradition at the service of the individual composer" (1970, rpt. 1976: 166).

Nketia's study hinted at major contemporary semiotic concerns with intratextuality, inter- or trans-textuality, and literary re-creativity. It also prefigured Simon Battestini's concepts of "text" and "texture," which apply to both oral and written cultures. "Every culture," Battestini writes, "possesses this capacity to generate texts, which it uses to produce the types and quantities it feels it needs, both functionally and aesthetically. . . . Writing in the semiotic sense, which includes all signifying sets of social signs, points to the notion of texture, social fabric, web of experienced and accepted constraints, claims of possible imaginative pulsions in a given culture" (2000: 361).

Women's historical and genealogical knowledge

Women across West Africa have managed to infiltrate all zones of their regional "textures," despite perceptible boundaries imposed by the dominant power structures upon their verbal expression. For instance, although many women may have had rich historical and genealogical knowledge, in many cultures they were excluded from the oral performances about the official history of their social groups or family lineages, and so the transmission of history often lay in the hands of male poets and professional court historians. Raphaël NDiaye, Thomas Hale, and Aissata Sidikou, among others in recent years, have studied the very significant yet long-ignored achievement of female professional oral historians and praise-singers, or *griottes*, particularly in Senegal and Mali. Lucy Durán turned to the phenomenal rise in popularity of the *jelimusow*, the "superwomen of Mali music," and concluded that "women singers in Mali are debating social conventions through their music and are involved in maintaining a sense of tradition in their musical innovation" (1995: 207). The Malian *jelimusow* of today, while continuing to remember the history of the past, now use their art to comment on contemporary events, thus contributing to change in contemporary Mali.

Trained female specialists—whether called *jelimusow* in Mali, *gewel* in Senegal, or *iyalosa* or *oloriki* in Nigeria—are represented in this collection by several texts. Indeed, the *griotte*[3] is one of the most important personalities of a host of West African and Sahelian cultures: Wolof, Mende, Songhay, Bariba, Fulbe, Mossi, Dogon, Hausa, and Dagomba. The *griottes'* work, as is true in general of oral texts, is marked by a sophisticated use of language. It is codified by specific methods for the articulation of theme and style. Other professionals of the "literary class" to which *griottes* belong, as well as their patrons, appreciate their work for its ability to conform to the tenets of the genre while also displaying originality in subtle embroideries of language, voice, and style of performance. All professional singers are judged according to the beauty of their singing voices, the quality of their memories, their sense of artistry, and their cultural knowledge and literacy. They usually benefit from their professional training by accruing power and privilege through their sociocultural positions. They should not, however, be confused with the elite women who are their patrons, nor with the non-guild-affiliated and non-elite women who form the greatest group of "commoners" who also create and perform orature.

Praise-singing

Representative of praise-singing, and performed by the priestesses of the Osun shrine, the praise poem from the Yoruba people in this collection ("Praise Poem for Osun," p. 89) was performed for Diedre Badejo in 1981, by Sangotundun Asabi, in Osogbo, Nigeria. She is a valued praise-singer, and her commitment to Osun, the "Good Mother," who opens the portals of human existence, legitimates the rulership of the Ataoja of Osogbo. Asabi, one of the custodians of the sacred history of Osun, began her training as a praise-singer during her childhood. She continues today to be a notable performance artist and presence at the Osun festival, the Osun shrine, and of course the Osun River. Asabi notes that during her early childhood training, she mastered the knowledge and stylistics of the critical Osun texts while perfecting her style, voice, and performance. She states that Osun worship permeates her daily life and that chanting testifies to her beliefs. Like the goddess herself, Asabi also lives as wife, mother, and market-woman. As a professional praise-singer, or *oloriki*, she exudes the confidence of a master artist. Her voice intones the warbling, honeyed sound of the Osun River in phrases that recall its flow. Modulating her voice to accentuate the tonality of the Yoruba language, Asabi enhances the ethereal ambience of the praise poem. The language and musicality of the Oriki Osun highlight the meaning of Osun's many cognomens and chronicle the towns once known primarily for their female rulers and their loyalty to Osun. During festival performances of Osun's orature, Asabi's chants in concert with a gathering of female and male devotees, artists, and performers heighten the sacredness of the space where the deity is worshipped. Asabi's mellifluous voice, coupled with her superior knowledge of the *oriki*, or praise names of Osun, and her mastery of the structure of Osun chants, makes her a most gifted singer (Badejo 1996).

The Ede Court Historians, or *olorikin*, who chant the Nigerian text "Oya, the Wind Behind the Lightning" (p. 87) also invoke a powerful goddess of the Yoruba. These unusual female court historians are responsible for the political history of Ede's royal ancestral lineage. They have been trained from childhood to master the mnemonic techniques that make it possible to hold on to and reproduce lengthy and complicated verse stories. Their ritual performance of "Oya" reinforces the notion of balance, which maintains Sàngó, the principal male deity, in check.

For a long time, West African societies described as "stateless"—such as the Gurunsi or Lela of Burkina Faso and Northern Ghana—were regarded as having no history. Yet we now know that historical knowledge existed in the memories of "earth priests" and of women.[4] According to Emmanuel Bayili, elderly Lela women had an appreciable knowledge of the history of their lineage, and this placed them in the middle of marriage negotiations and funeral rites. In addition to such specialized artists and craftsmen as singers, drummers, and blacksmiths, the group of "professional women singers who mourned the dead throughout the night of wake-keeping" had the greatest genealogical knowledge in the society (1989: 23). This, of course, emerged through their songs. Even today, the *Woyei* or priestesses at Ga shrines in Ghana are custodians of the esoteric Klama songs, which carry the history of the Ga people.

Knowledge has always constituted power. Amid a matrilineal society such as that of the Brong people of Wenchi, knowledge of the catastrophic events that took place around 1712, during the Asante wars of conquest by King Osei Tutu, rests in the mind of the political leaders of the polity—the chiefs, their spokesmen, and one single woman. The Queenmother, or *Ohemmaa*, whose stool-name, *Sraman Gyedua a oto asuo* ("Divine Lightning That Strikes the Shade Trees of Kings, Threatening Floods"), retells the glorious heroism of her predecessor on the stool, three centuries earlier, who alone saved her people from total disgrace when the chief and his men had fled the town. She alone can mention this side of her people's history, since she is the only woman who can pronounce the forbidden words recalling the infamous defeat, whenever she takes part in the funeral rites of a chief (see "*Ntam*, an Oath," p. 114). While singing the praises of the dead chief and reminding him of his part in the development of his polity, the Queenmother will use the opportunity to remind her audience of the power she holds as the descendant of her magnificent predecessor. Such a performance, especially the poetic allusions to the hidden past, redeems the women in this male-centered culture. Even the most dramatic performances of funeral laments by the *atumpan* and the royal *fontomfrom*, both "talking drums" to which only the chief and his male relatives are allowed to dance, cannot erase this historical truth or kill the Queenmother's pride.

Analogical condensation, or the creation of metaphors and metonyms, as well as allusions, are fundamental for the creation of praise names, since the poetic act of praising consists of addressing an important figure (dead or alive) by inventing a long list of praise names mixed with proverbs and other cultural tropes. This traditional art, often linked to royalty, has found new expression in the churches of Ghana today. Afua Kuma's text "Jesus of the Deep Forest" (p. 310) beautifully exemplifies this form of contemporary "inculturation." "Jesus of the Deep Forest" is today's "King of Kings":

> We shall announce his many titles:
> They are true and they suit him well. . . .
> Jesus you are a solid rock! . . .
> Jesus you are the Elephant Hunter. Fearless One!
> You have killed the evil spirit, and cut off his head.

The Akan art of praise poetry has been borrowed by the churches of contemporary Ghana. In fact, among the coastal Ga who live in southern Ghana, the art of libation pouring accompanied by prayers for the chiefs is very similar to this now generalized "Ghanaian" art of praise giving:

> He should be like a great Umbrella,
> That we may stay under it,
> That the rain should not beat us,
> That the sun should not scorch us,
> He should be an Elephant.
> If you follow an elephant you do not suffer from the morning mist.
> (Kropp-Dakubu 1987: 518)

We have here the perfect example of intertextuality, of the manner in which words, images, and texts move over time and space. Praise-singing also enables us to witness the changes that may occur when cultural groups that were once separate West African polities and have been "unified" under foreign influence as one nation seek their own "textural" roots to reassess themselves.

Other specialized genres and history

Communal or regional "troubadours," who ritually mark major moments in women's lives, differ from praise singers. Bété singers of Côte d'Ivoire, for example, perform "*Maïéto*, or the "Battle of the Sexes" (p. 91) as part of a funeral held following the death of a woman in childbirth. In "*Maïéto*," a piece of total theater, the references to female leadership are subtly veiled beneath the very real sorrow and anger expressed by women after one of them dies giving birth. The war of the mythical Mahié is based on the primordial myth about how men came to dominate women. Through the structure of the work and its allusions to war and vengeance, the women singers challenge the legitimacy of male authority and its inability to protect them. The community of women assumes the guise of warriors and sings war songs as they march in military fashion, carrying symbolic weapons. In most West African and Sahelian communities, such an affront to male authority can occur only in exceptional periods, through this form of ritualized performance and cultural practice.[5]

Women artists have made extensive contributions to the aesthetics of orature in West Africa and the Sahel. Those who perform the Senegambian Wolof *cossaan*, or mythical and historical narratives, and those who perform the Ghanaian Akan *abodinsu*, or funeral dirges, create, within culturally specific genres, maps of the region's historiographic terrain. Women praise-singers in the Yoruba tradition, dirge-singers in the Akan tradition, and *jelimusow* or oral historian/musicians in the Mandinka tradition all practice specific genres that may claim a place among the best of West African orature.

Orature and family life

While specialists hold forth in the courts, sacred groves, and family or guild shrines—and may also be called to serve elite families—many other areas of daily life become arenas for the performances of less formalized songs and narratives of "ordinary" women, who use them to voice social commentary. The centers of towns and marketplaces, as well as women's quarters and spaces—including kitchens, bedrooms, children's playgrounds, and areas reserved for manufacturing household items—lend themselves to performances before audiences intimately familiar with the genres concerned. Within such contexts, the audience becomes both critic and part of a particular cultural engagement (Okpewho 1990; Badejo 1996). Because women dominate most of these spaces, lead singers, choruses, dancers, musicians, storytellers, and proverb users engage in a dialogue with other women, as well as with their communities and deities.

Women often use their artistic talents and cultural literacy to document their daily lives and entertain themselves and their families. As age-mates, cowives, new wives and mothers, friends, and family members, they are vital to the development of the region's oral literary heritage. These women return to themes that speak about their work or their relationships, or assert onto-logical principles, even as they also capture ordinary daily life and its trials, disappointments, and joys. Most frequently, songs and tales address the changes in women's lives as they move through various rites of passage. Their overarching frame is the complex West African and Sahelian social and political structure.

Many songs and narratives in our anthology address marriage, birth, nam-ing ceremonies, and other areas of social negotiation, the most important contexts for oral literary performance in which women function. When the more ceremonial areas of life are the focus, orature is structured and guided by precise parameters. But when these oral performances accompany such daily tasks as trade and marketing activities or collecting firewood and cook-ing, for example, they are often more spontaneous and communal—although every literary genre functions according to precise rules of composition. On formal ritual occasions, the objective of the performance is usually to strengthen the bonds among members of a group, to reaffirm the sanctity and authority of the leadership, and to consolidate particular religious or associative relationships. Daily objectives may be more wide-ranging and may help to facilitate cooperative work, to release interpersonal tension, or to engage in a controlled form of social criticism. These less formal oral literary performances allow and applaud an appropriate infusion of innovation and spontaneity in order to embellish a given performance.

Women, birth, and death

Lullabies are, according to the *Oxford English Dictionary*, "songs or sooth-ing refrains to put a child to sleep." The West African "lullabies" presented in this collection hardly suit the Western representation of this genre. The Senegalese or Tuareg mother, for example, uses the opportunity of the birth of her child to produce a text whose message is not really addressed to the one she is soothing with her soft singing voice. The quiet tone and melody may disguise a deep melancholy: The mother may use the "pretext" of her child's birth to produce a "text" in which she expresses her most pro-found anxieties as an adult woman, seemingly subdued by the hard condi-tions of her life, in the cultural "context" of her song. This is, again, how "texture" evolves when women emerge from behind the walls of their homes and enter "social discourse."

Fatimata Mounkaïla has described the lullaby as an African woman's soliloquy, responsive to the pressures of family life and motherhood, and consciously performed for ears other than those of the baby she is holding. Using the lullaby as a vehicle, women analyze their own situations and speak of attendant problems, including the pain of being rejected by their husbands for cowives. In "*Ayo*, My Baby" (see p. 152) and "Lullaby" (see p. 152), the procurement of proper nutrition as a major worry for mothers features in the subtle references to salt and corn. Suggesting an exchange of a baby for salt may allude to the possible death of the child or its mother from dehydration. It might also recall the slave trade, in which children could indeed be exchanged for valuable commodities. Similarly, the allusion to a child who steals corn reflects a mother's desire to teach her child appropriate moral behavior, despite hunger and poverty. In "Who Did My Baby Wrong?" (see p. 153) and "Hindatou" (see p. 153), each woman sings of her dependence and that of her child in her husband's household. These songs suggest that, in West African and Sahelian households, women are often more dependent on the success of their children as a means for survival in old age than on their husbands or their natal families.

While premenopausal women often gain visibility through membership and status in a particular family, postmenopausal women gain visibility in their own right as they progress toward old age. Geneviève Calame-Griaule's psychoanalytic and comparative study of Dogon folktales illuminates this point. She notes that fertility is an essential value in Dogon patriarchy. In fact, among the Dogon of Mali, she writes, "It is only at the time her first child is born that a woman is introduced into her husband's home" (1993: 9). Yet Calame-Griaule postulates that because fertility alternates with highly infertile periods in a woman's early life, women may be seen as fearfully ambiguous figures. Male-performed proverbs, tales, or mythical narratives, therefore, often describe women as "sorcerers" and "eaters of men" (see Paulme 1976). Such unconscious fears could have often prevented young and fertile women from being granted access to public speech. When they reach menopause and have performed their procreative duties, however, elderly women become the intercessors between life and death. They help women in labor and "deliver" them, aided by herbal medication and incantation. Awaiting delivery, young women sing their own songs, celebrating, expecting, or rejecting motherhood.

Two Igbo songs from Nigeria entitled "Celebrating Birth" (see p. 105) present motherhood as a powerful icon and source of women's power, evoking the exclusive power of women to reproduce themselves and the men who attempt to control them (Benton-Rushing 1979). In this light, fertility features prominently in the battle of the sexes. As Ifi Amadiume says, "Whether in the past or today, women are essentially seen as producers, be it in the management of subsistence production or in biological production" (1987: 69). In proclaiming possible only through birth the various male-dominated occupations named in the song, the singers of "Where Is It From?" accentuate women's power, and also express their joy in giving birth:

> Where is it from? It is from the womb.
> A policeman—he is from the womb.
> A lawyer—he is from the womb.
> A doctor—he is from the womb.

While women may see birthing as elevating their social status, the singers of "If Not for Childbirth" also see it as an opportunity to get what they need:

> If not for the power of giving birth,
> Who will give me?

Not surprisingly, given the importance of motherhood, childlessness is tragic in most West African and Sahelian societies. A narrative from the Gambia, "*Kanyeleng*, or Childless" (see p. 106), describes not only a ritual success in conquering childlessness but also aspects of the social stigma infertile women must endure: All through her long-desired pregnancy, Binta Bojang, a Malinke woman from the Gambia, had to bear the taunts of women who did not believe that she was really carrying a child.

In a complementary example, the narrator of the Diola song "The Torments of Labor" (see p. 354) refuses to comply with the conventional silence about the difficulties of the birth process. She refuses to suffer the pain quietly and acknowledges, "All I wanted was delivery." To be delivered from obligatory motherhood—as well as of the child in her womb—is the subtext complicating the depiction of motherhood as triumphal.

At the time of death, elderly women will proceed to the "verbal release" of the dead into a new life; their prayers and songs of lament will liberate both the living and the dead from the burden of death. In Diola, Akan, Sereer, and Bété cultures, women control essential aspects of funeral rites, including the acts of public, stylized mourning. As is true of birthing, they watch over the final rites of passage. The Akan lament "We Offer You Condolences" (see p. 112) uses tonal rhyme, onomatopoeia, and alliteration to convey the sense of anguish and primordial chaos created by death. Our translation has attempted to duplicate the original Akan by repeating verbal patterns and sibilants. In societies in which women are expected to be self-effacing in the public sphere, ululation—a loud, high-pitched trill, which can be a special feature of mourning female voices—provides a piercing indication of women's presence and opinions.

Singing marriage rites

A momentous event, and an essential rite of passage, marriage is also an important occasion for song, anticipated in a genre we can call "maiden songs." In three of these from Burkina Faso, young girls express various anxieties about arranged marriages. The playful songs allow young women to voice their concerns without appearing disrespectful of their parents' wishes. In these instances, songs function both as discursive social commentary and as entertainment. Comparing a girl's mother to the mother of her future husband alludes to the custom of carrying the bride to her in-laws' home to learn the ways of her new family from her mother-in-law.

The marriage song cycles from contemporary Nigeria and Côte d'Ivoire (see p. 96) illuminate the elaborate rites of weddings. Both wedding cycles fill several days, during which the bride is coaxed to leave her former life by friends and family members and to enter her new home. Some of the singing is playful and foregrounds the singer's modesty and reserve. In jest, for example, one Dyula song (from Côte d'Ivoire) suggests that the married women and their age-mates mock the young bride by singing:

> Women of the village, oh, please go home, please go to bed
> So you'll be fast asleep before my beloved comes to me.

With much pampering and preparation, brides learn through song and various ceremonies how to be wives and mothers. They are expected to spend time with their in-laws, learning their songs, dances, behavior, culinary arts, and other customs. In a Hausa song from Nigeria ("*Shimbidi*, or Opening Day," p. 99) for example, a daughter-in-law will have to learn about cooking rice balls (*tuwo*) and porridge (*fura*):

> If marriage could escort marriage
> I would have accompanied you so that we'd go together
> If only to learn to stir *tuwo*
> Even if it is *fura* I will learn.

Often the tone and language of these songs are gleeful, romantic, and optimistic, as the brides and their entourage allude to the intimacy of married life. The persona of a confident Hausa bride, for example, sings of her own beauty ("*Ahaiye Yaro*, or No Way, Boy," p. 100):

> When it comes to beauty, someone is more beautiful than another.
> When it comes to beauty, I too am more beautiful than another.

Songs may also express sorrow about leaving behind age-mates and the world of youthful abandon. Another Hausa song feigns a tussle between the natal and marital families for possession of the young woman whose value lies in her reproductive years. Although it is not explicitly stated in the songs, we can deduce that this mock battle alludes to the negotiation about her bride wealth as well ("*Mai da Aro*, or Returning The Borrowed Bride," p. 100):

Here is the loan given to us.
Here is your daughter we've returned.

In contrast to the cheerful tone of many of these songs, other women remind young brides that marriage is burdensome, and that their lives will change radically when they become the person who must "bring me" whatever the new husband and his family want. The Dyula cycle from Côte d'Ivoire (p. 97) even mourns a woman's loss of freedom in marriage:

I got a letter from Majuman Baro
Let all those of her age-group weep for her.
A sorrowful day has come for her.
Let all those of her age-group weep for her.

Class and caste in polygamous households

In a study of two modern female *griottes*, Edris Makward (1990) makes a distinction between one who chronicles contemporary society and one who transmits the history of the ruling class. It is indeed necessary to read certain women's songs through the lens of class and caste. The language and imagery of professional *griotte* Dior Konate's "She Who Destroys Her Harp" (see p. 101) celebrates the morality of the young bride in an elite Wolof household. Konate's song, set in an intimate bedroom, in the presence of the bride's mother and other female relatives, chronicles the status as well as the cherished virginity of the bride:

When they send me to seek the hand of a good woman's child,
I never get weary
When you're sent to seek for a bride, you choose a girl of good repute
For with a virgin for a bride, a man has no trouble.

On the other hand, we hear in "Xaxar" (see p. 104) the lampooning and verbal abuse that greets a new bride, probably from a less elite Wolof family, when she enters a polygamous household for the first time:

Will she stay, the new bride, will she stay?
Look at her, this new bride, her skin's dull and ugly,
She's snotty and dirty, and lousy in bed.
Will she stay, the new bride, will she stay?

Similarly, in "Welcoming the Bride," a Zarma welcoming song (see p. 105), there is no concern for the bride's virginity. Instead she is greeted as an intruder, a laborer, or a "slave"—evident from references to her as a "donkey" and a "dog." This ritual welcome depends on the accumulation of derogatory metaphors. However distasteful, such language signals the realities of female rivalry. Mothers, aunts, cowives, and sisters not only sing these songs but also frequently collude with the patriarchy to place constraints on female sexuality and equality.

Such insulting welcoming songs can, however, be cathartic, functioning to soften the realities of polygamy. The crude language and the dramatic hostility expressed toward the new wife may be experienced as directly in opposition to polite female discourse, kindness, and self-control. If a patriarchal familial organization forbids direct challenges to husbands, women may still attack other women, especially if they are newcomers. Rivals are never to be directly confronted but are to be challenged through their friends, their age-set, who may stake out respective territories in a husband's affections through duels sung and danced. The verbal texts, on such occasions, are collective productions, constructed as the protagonists take turns before the drummer or on the dance floor, accompanied by sharp, modulated shouts, clapping, and each group's choruses.

Orature for morality and the reality of excision

Throughout the West African and Sahelian region, brides enter marriages and cross the boundary that separates them from adulthood with the support of other women, who perform maiden and bridal songs. Girls have generally prepared for this dramatic access to womanhood, motherhood, and all the other changes that accompany marital life by a period of initiation that, in some societies, includes female circumcision. As soon as girls reach nubility, they are taken aside by respected elderly women of their community, who become their initiators. To supplement the skills they have acquired in their mothers' homes, the young girls receive sex education and are taught to become responsible women in their homes and communities.

During initiations, and in fact throughout life, the moral and religious values that constitute the foundations of their culture are conveyed to young girls through narratives followed by discussions of the often enigmatic meanings hidden behind proverbs and tales, such as the ubiquitous story of "two girls," represented in this volume by "The Poor Orphan" (see p. 347). In most of these tales, the protagonists—a "good" and a "bad" girl—are sent off into an unknown forest or across a river to find an object each has lost. Symbolically, these tales are said to represent the ambiguous relationship of mother and daughter at the moment the daughter enters womanhood and the mother (or, as in our text, the older and still unmarried sister) approaches menopause. The initiatory quest allows the young girl to acquire the tools she needs to survive in the world of adults: She must conquer the unknown and master the art of survival in her community. The mother must release her daughter, despite her own pain in doing so. Frequently, these adventures occur in the context of a polygamous home, where a stepmother might treat her own child and her adopted daughter differently. Such tales obviously not only address the general topic of marriage and separation from the maternal home but also prepare young girls to behave appropriately in polygamous homes. The treatment of such themes as rivalry, jealousy, and competition aims to prepare a young girl to accept situations she might not find pleasing in her marital life. The performance may be seen as anticipating or even preventing crises to come.[6] Although recounted by women, these narratives may still be seen as serving a patriarchal system under which the narrators have themselves lived and suffered.

Where circumcision is practiced, tales exist to legitimate the custom. Female circumcision is a psychologically and often physically harmful and painful experience, yet elderly women who have been circumcised themselves still continue to circumcise their daughters. As Sylvia Wynter has noted, in circumcising communities, that act, most often part of an elaborate ritual, serves as a "symbolic birth," a means through which young women are made legitimate members of the body of their society through the "civilizing" marks made on their bodies. And the practice will perhaps continue, as Geneviève Calame-Griaule explains to Praline Gay-Para (2002: 64), until a new symbolic gesture comes to replace the old one.[7] Thus Wynter's succinct observation—"There are profoundly different conceptions of the human at work here" (1997: 507)—refers to profound differences that undergird and support, for example, the conversation in this volume between the two midwives, the Western-trained Aoua Keïta and the traditionally informed Sokonna Diaouné. Diaouné, oblique and guarding her esoteric secrets, admires Keïta's skills but calls into question the cultural nature of her vision (see "Conversation with Midwife Sokona Diaouné," p. 281).

Almost everywhere in the world, formal education, rural exodus, and the changes brought about by modernity have led to the birth of feminist movements. In Africa, many such movements search for a more acceptable modus vivendi for women in their communities that would not require them to break with their indigenous values. Aoua Keïta is a trailblazer in this movement, and it may well be that traditional narratives have helped to integrate this rebellion. Even though the art of storytelling is itself endangered, it is also being transformed as young girls now take up their own pens and write poetry, short stories, and essays.

Social significance of language in greetings and work songs

In West African and Sahelian society, the use of language is not regulated only during ritual events. Daily happenings, which involve face-to-face verbal exchanges, are also surrounded by strict dialogic rules. No encounter between two human beings is considered insignificant. Numerous West African proverbs focus on speech and, more particularly, describe the various organs humans use to make their thoughts heard through their voices. They serve as a metalinguistic commentary on communication, on the manner in which a speaker speaks or hears, and indirectly suggest what kind of personality hides behind the smooth, sweet, tender, slippery or hard, rough, itchy tongue.

Among the Dogon of Mali, it was forbidden to speak loudly or to whistle in the night, because, according to Ogotommêli, Marcel Griaule's informant, "Words fly away. We do not know where they go. They get lost. Strength gets lost" (1966: 134). Speech should never be in vain. It should not be excessive either. The Sereer of Senegal, for instance, used to be extremely scared of "big mouths" because, according to Raphaël NDiaye, "They say that an enormous mouth is not even tolerated by a tree. For, according to a saying, 'If you transplant a tree along a roadside, and if everyone passing by speaks about the tree, if the mouths catch the tree, then the tree eventually dries up and dies'" (1985: 23).

Restrained and contained, as well as diplomatic and possibly embellished with imagery, somehow enigmatic—that is how speech should always be. It should also be truthful, brief, and well prepared, for, as an Akan proverb says, "If you speak into a hole and cover up your words, they will escape. Once spoken, words cannot be swallowed up again." Speech should be thought-provoking.

In "Greetings and Praise" (see p. 251), the Hausa *lugude*, a specialized genre, testifies to the cultural significance of greetings. Indeed, in West African and Sahelian societies, passing people by without a greeting— whether they are acquaintances or strangers—epitomizes rudeness and a lack of home training. Some greetings, like the example below ("You of the House"), are elaborate interlocutions, expressing a simple joie de vivre and interest in the general well-being of others:

> Hey, you over there, you over there,
> You people of Mallam Audu's house,
> Mallam Audu's first wife
> And his favorite,
> The one with henna on the palms of her hands,
> Good afternoon.
> I wish you a very good afternoon.
> This is Hawa greeting you.
> Did you sleep well?

The language here, even in translation, is direct. In a few short lines, we learn that the greeting is extended to the senior and favorite wife of a Muslim man, and that the wife uses henna to decorate and beautify herself. Hawa, the name of the woman who initiates the greeting, asks after the other woman's health and, in a later line not included here, congratulates her for "good work pounding," most likely grain for the afternoon meal. The setting for this greeting would be the outdoor kitchen or cooking area, the purview of women.

In some cases, greetings are social acts that transmit tidbits of information. In "One Single Measure" (see p. 254), for example, the song conveys the news of a successful planting and harvesting of rice. The title also offers a double entendre, for it names both a measure of rice for sale in the market, thus suggesting profit, and a measure of work to procure the proper result. The singer narrates succinctly how she has selected good seeds, waited for the best planting time, and harvested the crop. Since others have recognized her industrious farming skills, she has obviously won the cultural right to sing her own praises.

Language serves the most conventional needs of politeness and respect of the other in social discourse. But as we mentioned at the start of this section, it is also "misused" and turned upside down to achieve other elocutionary ends. Several texts we have collected are witty, oblique, or even deeply sardonic. For example, the insinuating repartee made up of pithy couplets improvised by two Abe women from Côte d'Ivoire (see "*Eyidi*, or Naming," p. 340) can deride a rival publicly without ever having to confront her directly. Women-on-women violence is exercised and exorcised through sarcasm in this particular social arrangement. Humor, in the form of satire, is also used to make strong ethical arguments. The Zarma *griotte* Salle-Ka-Ma-Kani regales her audience with her typologies of wives and husbands (see p. 344). The suspense created by the incremental layers of caricatured spouses makes the ideal all that much more evident at the end.

The tyranny of the mother-in-law, the complicity of the father-in-law, the aggressive spite of the sisters-in-law are targeted through register and tone, as a woman sings or chants while washing, pounding, preparing meals. Because she is "the thing in which money is invested," a woman is often under the authority not only of her husband but also of his family. Since she is obliged to respect and obey her husband's family, a singer must make use of indirection, as in the pounding song "*Seybata*—My Backside—Insult Her!" (see p. 262). Because the speaker and addressee are both disguised, possibilities arise for language unencumbered by social constraints. What rule, taboo, or prohibition can be imposed on insulting buttocks? One cannot even reply to such a song without exposing one's identity and risking the loss of one's dignity and hence authority. The objective of such singing is not to provoke conflict but rather to externalize intimate realities in search of relief. The gaining of such relief is also a goal of the plethora of work songs in this volume, especially those from the Sahelian region.

From the point of view of performance, the pounding song "*Seybata*—My Backside*" can be classified as an aesthetic, even theatrical act. There may, indeed, be ten or more closely coordinated performers.[8] The blatant exploitation of the highly provocative movement of the well-formed bottom of a young woman pounding grain with a cloth tied around her body is a potent weapon with which to duel other family members. Even a father-in-law or another female family member may enter the exchange as a character in the song. The communal nature of this performance indicates clearly that the stance of protest and defiance is not an individual gesture but rather part of an enduring ethos of a community of women, which each generation may reinterpret and reinforce.

Dance, drums, clapping, and other accompaniments to orature

Women may use not only words but also dance to convey subversive messages, often amplified by the rhythm of drums. In many West African cultures, music is made from a rich blend of drums and percussion instruments, including bells and rattles, and such wind instruments as horns, flutes, and trumpets, as well as xylophones and a variety of string instruments, especially lutes and the kora. Some of these, however, are forbidden to women, except under rare conditions, since instruments are often associated with male spiritual or political power. Not surprisingly, therefore, women have had to be creative. They have turned their bodies, their everyday utensils, and even their clothes into instruments to accompany songs and chants. In Igbo, Toucouleur, and Akan societies, for example, a popular instrument women play is the water drum, either a pot filled to a certain level with water and then beaten over the opening with a fan, or a large bowl of water covered by a calabash; the water level may be deftly raised or lowered to provide various levels of sonority. Other sorts of cooking utensils feature in certain ceremonies and in funeral rites of the Diola. Akan women strike a hoe head with stone in their performances, as in "The Warring Hosts" (see p. 133). For work songs, including pounding songs, the mortar and pestle act as accompaniment. As Frafra women of northern Ghana sing, they pull their clothes tightly across their thighs, turning them into drums on which they play a complex rhythm. Clapping is also an advanced art in many West African female genres of performance. It can be observed in women's traditional rhythm games and in highly complex rhythmic patterns accompanying songs and chants. Finally, women may also resort to imitating the sounds of instruments. This is what the Ghanaian Zegbulo of Loho does with the sound of the Dagaare xylophone in her "Praise Song" (see p. 254).

Songs and tales offer routes into the complex realities and challenges of women's lives. They express both joy and suffering. They help women survive while serving their families and communities. Throughout the region, women's orature expresses as much anxiety about the change from girlhood to womanhood to motherhood as about marriage itself. The high incidence of mortality in childbirth, coupled with the possible violence of husbands, endangers women's lives. No wonder women celebrate their womanhood with passion and conviction. But first and foremost, the performance of songs or tales by a good singer or storyteller opens avenues for discussion, for argument, for protest, for debate. The skillful use of indirection has made it possible for women to be heard on the most delicate issues of concern to them, and to fight for change. Performance events in the traditional oral West African context favor responsiveness and force the deaf to hear.

KINGSHIP, KINSHIP, AND GENDER

The Nzema of Ghana approach history through proverbs and metaphors linked to the kola nut (*eresele*) and medicine (*ayile*). When they say that "the monkey who has stayed in the forest long enough knows where to find the kola nut," they mean that "the elders know the family history" and can be trusted. When they add that "the chick that stays close to its mother gets to eat the thigh of the grasshopper," they caution young people who do not follow the elders that they will be responsible for losing their history. Indeed, according to an Nzema narrator, "The 'words' of the ancestors may well correspond to a historical truth [that the Nzema of today] have [already] renounced; repeating the ancestors' words, then, helps to re-establish this very truth" (Pavanello 2000: 33). Historical knowledge becomes, thereby, a continuous quest: Those searching for it constantly attempt to reconnect the present to the past and to the future, to create an uninterrupted chain between the dead, the living, and those who have not yet come to earth. The knowledge of the past cannot be static: "History is what we say about what we have heard about what is ahead of us: what the ancestors left behind" (Pavanello 2000: 36). History is always a story retold.

Telling the story of the West African and Sahelian past, particularly the period of overlapping empires—the immensely long era from the eighth century to the end of the nineteenth—while attempting to find women's place in that story is the goal of this section. Our research leads us inevitably to describe and reflect on the institution of slavery, which helped structure internal and external relationships during this time. As in all societies, forms of servitude have marked social organization in West Africa and the Sahel. We must also focus as well on the real power that certain women had, corresponding to the rise and fall of ruling groups. First, though, it will be useful to sketch a history of the region to attempt to illustrate its complexity.

A view of historical complexities

Recent strides in African historiography have begun to elucidate the extreme layering of the various important empires that regrouped territories and peoples from the Atlantic coast and the Sahelian countries through West Africa to Central Africa. From the early Empire of Ghana in the eighth century to the fall of the Asante Empire in 1900, powerful empires moved farther and farther east, all greatly influenced—since the eleventh century—by contact with Islam and—since the fifteenth—by contact with Christianity.

To suggest the layers and complexities in the progression of this history, one has only to look at the development of the fabled city of Timbuktu.

This ancient city of scholars and notables, which, from around 1400, was controlled by a "patriarchate of wealth, learning and descent" (Saad 1983: 20), had by the sixteenth century become the emporium for West Africa. Timbuktu was situated at the crossroads where traders exchanged salt from the Sahara for gold arriving from Begho, and grain from the southern states with cattle brought down from the north. Timbuktu formed part of the Mali empire from 1325 to 1433 and was then integrated into the Songhai in 1468, before being invaded and occupied by the Moroccan Ruma military from 1591 to 1737. Thereafter, from 1825 to 1844, it was ruled by the caliphate of Massina. The empire then suffered an internal counterjihad led by one of its own scholars in 1862 and finally fell into the hands of the French in 1894.

It is instructive to know that this multiethnic western Sudanese city, which, from the twelfth century on, had begun to accommodate Tuareg, Berber, Soninke, Songhai, Arab, Malinke, and Fulani settlers in its quarters, managed to keep its balance and even prosper amid the political turmoil. This was so, claims Elias N. Saad, thanks to the influence and authority of its large erudite and dignified elite. A real "tradition of learning" was probably mature by the fifteenth century, by which time solid chains of educational transmission (*silsilas*) and numerous *madrasa* (Qur'anic schools) had been set up (Saad 1983: 60–61). Timbuktu should be remembered as a model city where, beyond prosperity and political leadership, citizens were encouraged to find their happiness in the quest for truth and knowledge.

From the earliest period to the present, official keepers of oral traditions, including the Mande *jeli,* the Fon *kpanligan,* the Yoruba *babalawo,* and the Akan *okyeremma,* continued their own systematic work as professional inscribers of history through their creation of panegyric and epic genres. In contrast, from as early as the tenth century, foreign intruders began to impose their own idealized or distorted views of what was called, in Arabic, *bilal-al-Sudan,* literally "the Land of the Blacks." Most of these Arab observers described the lands they had visited through the lens of Islam. Their reports of West African women, in particular, tell us very little about the daily lives of women encountered, but rather initiate—beginning with the Arab chronicler Ibn Battūta's description of unclothed females, for example (Levtzion and Hopkins 1981: 296–297; Cuoq 1975: 311–312)—the misogynist view of Africans still prevalent today.

In addition, there were the Christians. The first Portuguese "discoverers" of the coastal regions arrived in the 1460s, followed by others from Holland, Denmark, France, and England during the following centuries, all offering their own presumptuous descriptions of these "pagan" countries, considered rich in gold and slaves and ready to be colonized and Christianized. Such nineteenth-century European explorers as Mungo Park and especially René Caillé produced texts in which one must carefully separate the interesting observations of daily life from the impassioned statements of the authors (Chevrier 2004). Caillé, who traveled to the "mysterious city of his dreams" by impersonating a freed slave, proposed an image of Timbuktu's "ornamented" women totally at variance with Ibn Battūta's portrait.

The views of the West African past sketched above changed as the forms of intrusion changed. A growing awareness of West African abundance sparked competition within the sprouting kingdoms themselves (Coquery-Vidrovitch 2003). The historical reality of competition, growth, takeovers, and amalgamation was nuanced, sometimes even paradoxical or contradictory. El Fasi and Hrbek recount a version of what happened, including the intelligent negotiation with Islamic power at the time of the Muslims' arrival in the western Sudan between the eighth and the eleventh century. A series of states were already in existence or in formation, including the complexly structured polities of old Ghana or Wagadu (eighth to eleventh century), Mali (thirteenth to sixteenth century), and Songhai (fifteenth to seventeenth century)—each of which developed into an important empire. Mohammed El Fasi and Ivan Hrbek quote A. G. Hopkins's suggestion that these states welcomed Islam because it had, by that time, become the way to economic power in the region:

> Islam helped maintain the identity of members of a network or firm who were scattered over a wide area, and often in foreign countries; it enabled traders to recognise, and hence to deal readily with, each other; and it provided moral and ritual sanctions to enforce a code of conduct, which made trust and credit possible. (Hopkins 1973: 64, quoted in El Fasi and Hrbek 1990: 96)

At the same time, most newly converted sub-Saharan states did not fully embrace the religion. They tended to remain rooted in their own religious beliefs and, for a long period of time, continued to practice a sort of hybrid religion. It was in the interest of the royal elite of those days to offer an Islamicized image of themselves, and so the Malian *mansa* and the Songhai *askia*, who had welcomed Muslim clerics and scholars into their cities and who sometimes even made holy pilgrimages, often only embraced the new faith in a mostly official manner. They frequently continued to perform pre-Islamic ceremonial rituals, which clearly indicates that syncretism was at work. Several centuries passed before some Mossi people became Muslims, while the Bambara resistance could never be broken. In other words, the process of assimilation of and conversion to Islam was gradual and cautious, inflected by indigenous systems and movements. Islam had perhaps its greatest impact on the structures of the family and the distribution of political power and authority.

Because of prolonged periods of contact between the North African

Islamic world and the sub-Saharan western Sudanese world, a cultural dialogue still evident today opened all along the trans-Saharan trade routes. The *Wangara* (Dyula traders), for example, who sometimes settled in such northern Akan market towns as Begho, were important disseminators of the art of weaving. This eventually led to the production of the Asante *kente* cloth, as well as to the adoption by the Akan of gold-weights cast in brass, a metal the Akan thereafter continued to import for centuries through the two main routes to Kumase. The northern route opened markets across the Sahara and up to the Mediterranean Sea and the Indian Ocean; the southern one later linked them to the transatlantic trade. Yet this was not a one-way exchange: According to Garrard (2003: 153), cities like Jenne and Timbuktu could not have reached their high degree of economic development without the vast amount of gold they imported from the Akan forestland. Everywhere across the vast expanse of successive and overlapping empires, people in communities wove together strands from various cultures, in a process that permits us now to speak of the entire area as a life-zone.

However one may describe the history of the region, one sees people moving goods, other people, and themselves across tremendous distances. The Fulfulde/Pulaar language, for example, can be found in present-day Guinea, Benin, Nigeria, Cameroon, Senegal, Mali, Côte d'Ivoire, and Niger, indicating a migration pattern that covers the entire area of West Africa and the Sahel. The history of the region, inside and outside empires, offers a dynamic history of evolving new allegiances and syncretizing systems of belief.

On the nature of enslavement

The practice of enslavement varied greatly across Africa, and the word "slave" carried different connotations and described different human conditions in the various West African languages. For example, the passing remark made by C. H. Armitage in 1898 that the domestic "slaves" he had seen among the Gonja were "kindly treated and more like family members" than slaves is a far cry from the way enslaved peoples en route to the Americas were herded into ships and held in chains.[9] Moreover, the confusion between the words "women" and "slaves" in Gen. Eugène Daumas's mid-nineteenth-century account of enslavement among the nomadic Tuareg people draws our attention to the subtle and very ambiguous semantic variations of the word "slave."[10]

To understand how the ideas of "slavery," "caste," and "class" can be nuanced and layered, we might consider aspects of the kinship and labor systems, which, in tightly structured monarchies, came to mold the daily lives of all the members of western Sudanese societies. This is especially true of the lives of women, whose roles as wives, cowives, mothers, sisters, and concubines, and as favorites guarded by the ruler's eunuchs, all fell under the umbrella of a generalized and commonly accepted situation of "servitude." Up to this day, in Asante, for example, the newly enstooled chief swears, in a solemn oath, not to remind anyone of his or her origin; he is to be a father of all, a shelter in times of storm or scorching sun, an umbrella and a shade tree (*gyedua*) to his subjects, wherever their ancestors originally came from.

Ivor Wilks has recently argued that the "openness of texture" of the Asante matriclans (*abusua kese*) probably dates from the time of the clearing of the forests in the fifteenth century and functioned to "facilitate the assimilation of strangers" into the process of empire building, so much so that "no slave caste [arose] in Asante society" (1993: 18). In this flexible social arrangement, erasure of "slavery" became state policy. By contrast, along the border between Senegal and Mauritania, freedom had to be earned, sometimes through the forms of ultimate self-sacrifice that have been memorialized in several epics from the area. In all of these poems, as individuals and as community members, women appear fully aware of the harrowing experience of slavery and are frequently willing to risk even their lives to save their communities from entering slavery or remaining slaves.

Joseph Inikori warns against using the terms "slave" and "slavery" with "terminological looseness." "Slavery and serfdom," he writes,

> under the socioeconomic conditions of medieval Europe provide better comparative insights for a precise and disciplined study of servile institutions in precolonial Africa than the New World comparisons that have hitherto been conducted. This is because the societies of medieval Europe were closer in all respects to those of precolonial Africa than were the New World slave societies that were specifically organized for large-scale production of commodities for an evolving capitalist world market. (2001: 50–51)

Inikori concludes that his comparative study of medieval Europe and precolonial Africa "shows unequivocally that, while there were slaves in late-nineteenth-century Africa, the bulk of the people hitherto so described were approximately serfs." He further explains,

> The phenomenon of what scholars refer to as intergenerational mobility among slave populations in Africa—the tendency for the children of slaves to become free people or nearly so—meant that the slave class in Africa could not reproduce itself, not only because its rate of reproduction was low in the context of Meillassoux's theory, but largely because the children of slaves normally did not remain in slavery. They either became free or became serfs. (67)

With Inikori's warning in mind, one must nonetheless mention that the practice of slavery in Africa existed as early as the seventh century. The human beings captured, bought, sold, or used for heavy military, agricultural, mining, or domestic tasks may have been war captives, slaves, or serfs, depending on the circumstances. Some of these people were moved far from their birthplaces, some as distant as the Red Sea. They may have traveled or stopped along the Arab-Muslim trans-Saharan trade routes in existence since the seventh century, or along the Euro-Christian transatlantic routes that emerged during the fifteenth century. While some remained on the African continent to serve in the North African and Egyptian armies, most were taken across the Mediterranean Sea, all the way to Arabia, to the Persian Gulf, to India, and, from the fourteenth century on, toward Spain, Italy, and Portugal (Murano and Atti 2003).

One of the texts included in our volume provides evidence that even the sacred rules forbidding slavery in an Islamic society were disregarded. During the eighteenth-century jihads in Futa Jallon, Futa Toro, and northern Nigeria, Muslims were, against the rules, captured and sold to slave ships. This is how the first Muslims arrived in the Americas (Hunwick 2005; Saad 1983: 101). Nana Asma'u Shaykh Uthman D'an Fodioyo (known in our volume as Nana Asma'u), the erudite daughter of the founder of the Sokoto Caliphate, alludes in "Give Us Victory" (1827) to the breaking of Islamic rules she had been brought up to believe in (see p. 125):

> When the army is victorious
> Slaves are taken, including some for the leader.
> But some men act illegally
> They fall on the women, disregarding all sanctions.
> They will fall in the Fire, Be sure of God's truth.

In this poem, we see a disregard for women's safety and physical integrity. A practicing Muslim woman expected such behavior to be condemned.[11]

The allegorical story "*Makori*, or the Triumph of Slaves" (see p. 129), which comes from the Sahel, may shed light on concerns about integrating slaves. It recounts the myth of the integration of Pular slaves into the Futa kingdom, which was structured in a particularly rigid manner. A legendary female slave jumped into a well of fire and symbolically transformed fire into milk, just after giving birth to her own child. After the ritual cleaning of her body, the proud mother went on, so says the story, to liberate the slave caste into which her child was born from the emotional stigma of bondage. She, the female slave and young mother, had done what neither a young man on his horse nor any male or female member of the Futanke community had been able to do. She is described as having disturbed, through her miraculous achievement, the certainties that had been, until then, written in the minds of the members of "higher" castes.

Through Farmata Kamara's exploit, which is kept alive in Fulfulde oral tradition, those of servile condition have been psychologically redeemed; their caste has been given the pride that goes with the knowledge of a "noble" ancestry—a nobility of the spirit, that is, not of blood. All members of Farmata Kamara's caste can now rejoice and clap whenever the *wambabe* (guitar players) start their own song of praise, called *Makori*:

I have earned Makori for the slaves from now on until the end of my line.
Every slave who hears Makori should offer money.
If he/she has none,
He/she should snap his fingers to be heard.
If he/she cannot snap
He/she should shout "Yes!"
If he/she cannot do that, however poor he/she is,
He/she can grab a handful of soil.
And offer it to the guitar player!

Slavery and "freedom" in the Americas and elsewhere

The demand for human labor to support sugar plantations in the West Indies and cotton plantations in the United States opened trans-Atlantic trade, thus forcing millions of captives—men, women, and children of the western Sudan—to become "human cargo" shipped perilously across the Atlantic Ocean in the most infamous journey of no return. On the other side, they entered a far more radical and inhumane form of enslavement than the kind of bondage and serfdom that had been practiced in their own lands. Women again suffered the most. As Mary Kolawole has written, "Although domestic slavery in Africa predates the trans-Atlantic slave trade, it is essential to reiterate that there is a wide gap between the motive, nature, practice and implication of the two forms of enslavement. Domestic slavery was not racially constructed, nor did it involve the repugnant scope of degradation, geographical dislocation, cultural disorientation or forced acclimatisation and attendant devastation and death" (1994: 29).

During the eighteenth century, the slave trade fostered competition among British, French, Danish, and Dutch companies. Slave ships took off from Liverpool and Bristol, from Nantes and Le Havre, from Middleburg and Amsterdam. They carried iron bars, arms, alcohol, cloth, and other shoddy goods, which were exchanged for slaves on the island of Goree, Senegal; along the Sherbo coast of Gambia; and along the Gold Coast (now Ghana), to the south of what is now Angola. Upon arrival in the Americas, slaves were sold to plantation owners and exchanged for already-produced goods such as tobacco, rice, indigo, and sugar cane, and later cotton and coffee. These new "necessary goods" were thereafter transported to the point of departure of the ships, thus closing what was called the "triangular route" among the American colonies, the West Indies, and Africa.

A few texts in this volume were written by or about slave women during this highly troubled period from the mid-eighteenth to the mid-nineteenth century, when internal wars of competition and expansion led to the demise of many African kingdoms. These interwoven events, often exacerbated by the involvement of African rulers in the trans-Saharan and transatlantic slave trades, ultimately weakened the region sufficiently to usher in colonialism.

With the advent of the "triangular trade," the commerce of human beings took on new proportions, and an important part of Africa's population was transported forever across the Atlantic Ocean, into what would become the black diaspora in the New World. Some legal prohibitions and a generalized practice forbidding the education of slaves silenced the protests of the exiled population. Slaves were mostly prevented from becoming literate. In addition, although unscrupulous "masters" sometimes used verses from the Bible to encourage a spirit of acceptance and humility in the slaves, their Christian and egalitarian values were absent, as we can see from a petition written in 1739 by Madlena Van Poppos, a slave woman living on St. Thomas in the Caribbean. As part of a Negro congregation established by a missionary, Friedrich Martin, who taught slaves how to read the Bible for themselves and to write, Van Poppos writes her "Letter of Petition" (see p. 122) to the queen of Denmark. Her letter's subtext suggests that, as soon as female slaves were educated, they joined the revolutionary banner of the freedom of the mind. In the words of her creolized African language, she took it as duty to become the "fighting arm" of those who had not yet learned how to hold a pencil. She managed, with the simple words at her disposal, to write a provocative and even sarcastic missive to the queen whose representatives had cut off her African "brethren" and "sisters" from their religious and cultural roots. She further argued that these same people were now preventing the slaves from integrating into their new society, whose members only preached but rarely practiced their own faith: "If the Whites do not want to serve the Lord, be that as it may. But if the poor Black brethren and sisters want to serve the Lord, they have to behave as if they were Maroons." Here Van Poppos equates the slaves' Christian faith with freedom from slavery.

In her book of *Slave Women in Caribbean Society, 1650–1839* (1990), Barbara Bush underlines the particular hardships of female slaves and their efforts to defy the sexual harassment and oppression they were forced to suffer. For persistent insolence, they were punished by solitary confinement and chained in stocks. The most famous woman rebel was probably "Nanni of the Maroons," who stands out as the only Jamaican national heroine today. A recent publication, *A History of Queen Nanny*, describes the "Leader of the Windward Jamaican Maroons" as a fearless Asante warrior who fought the British during the First Maroon War from 1720 to 1739 (Gottlieb 2000). Songs and legends depict her as "Granny Nanny," a small, wiry woman with piercing eyes whose influence over the Maroons had become so strong that it seemed supernatural. She continues to be cherished because, at the same time that she led her people to fight for their freedom, she encouraged the continuation of customs, music, and songs that had come with the people of Africa. She knew how to instill a sense of pride and confidence in her deprived people's hearts.

When in the course of the nineteenth century manumission was instituted, it did not, by any means, offer immediate happiness for Africans in the Americas. Between 1820 and 1861, the American Colonization Society sent liberated slaves from northern states to settle in Liberia. The pain of separating from beloved friends who had been left behind was only one of the harrowing features of their experience. Ultimately, the project of decently relocating these people proved a tragic failure. The letter written by Malinda Rex in 1839 (see "Letter from a Former Slave," p. 135 vividly testifies to the endless battles these once more abandoned people had to fight, not only for their survival but also for the fulfillment of broken promises. In the end, with her son's help, Rex was able to carry her legal argument across the Atlantic. She could not write, but he, as her "master's" son, had received an education. Disillusionment and anger seep through the lines of a woman who had always been an "Obedient Servant," and who had "found nothing as *they* said" in this place of which she had dreamed. "Truly," she declares, "*I* am in Africa where *I* cum [*sic*] to be free. *I* am well satisfied on that," but "*we* should be treated just[ly]." Most of her companions in misery endured their fate in silence.

"Saved"

The letters of Sarah Forbes Bonetta and her daughter Victoria Davies (see "Letters of Queen Victoria's Wards." p. 138) describe another kind of acculturation, which they share with other displaced and exiled women from West Africa. At about the same time as abolition in the United States, the liberation of slaves was also going on in Africa itself. Bonetta's dramatic life story may be summarized through the successive names she was given. Her original Yoruba name has been lost, yet it must have been a royal name, for she was born to the ruler of the town of Okeadon, near Ketu, where she was captured by King Gezo's army and taken to the palace of Abomey. In 1850, Captain Forbes of the British Royal Navy arrived in his ship, the *Bonetta*, and opened the palace's walls. He thought of himself as the "liberator," and when he noticed the young child, offered to care for her, naming her after himself and his ship. When she married, she became Sarah Forbes Bonetta Davies. Throughout her youth, she was Queen Victoria's special protégée. She received a "proper" education, both in England and in Freetown. She learned how to speak "the Queen's English" and could write letters in a purely Victorian style, concerned with "black silk dresses," "velvet buttons," and "black kid gloves." The difficulties of her life really began when she was forced into marriage with a Yoruba merchant, against her heart's desire—although seven years later, in a letter dated 22 April 1868, she wrote:

> The fact is James is infinitely too good & kind to everybody, & he is not appreciated, & when he does anything, people detract him as a matter of course, & i think it his duty—to labor for the benefit of others but because they are all jealous of his position & influence they are only too ready to cry him down & abuse him.

Her first response to his marriage proposal had been quite different, as expressed a year before they married in a letter to her foster mother, Elizabeth Schoen: "I don't feel a particle of love for him and never have done so." Was this pressure for her to marry a conscious move on the part of her "benefactors" to keep her "under control" and to prevent her from crossing the racial barrier? She was, we know from her correspondence, moving in highly noble European circles.

Sarah's daughter Victoria, more self-assured and assertive in her letters, maintained a precarious balance between two worlds. She lived most of her early life in elite Nigerian circles, the daughter of a prominent couple. She married a man who would become an early African graduate of the University of Edinburgh, and who was, at the time of their marriage in 1891, an assistant colonial surgeon. When she wrote her second letter, to Lord Stamfordham, in 1916, both he and his son were serving with the allied troops in the protracted campaign to defeat the Germans at Douala. Like Sarah, she could assume the privileges of British royal connections, for she was Queen Victoria's goddaughter, educated by her at what is still one of the most elite schools in England. She was a guest of aristocrats at Sudeley Castle where, on each occasion, she signed the visitor's book with a proverb in Yoruba, a gesture that would be unusual even today. We can see this act as signifying a conscious claiming of Africa that must have been part of her upbringing. At the same time, she was steeped in elite English culture and education, all of which made possible a strategic self-fashioning in European terms. She thus speaks of her mother's life in terms that might make an African story comprehensible to a European audience. Is this a deracinated mentality pandering to European prejudice, or a proud African finding ways of claiming cultural as well as social equality?

It is interesting to note that, during Victoria Davies's lifetime, women from the Gold Coast felt that they had to refrain from committing their own names to the letters they wrote to the editors of a local newspaper (see "Two Letters to the Editor," p. 147). Much ahead of their time, in 1886, their feminist words claimed for women rights still often denied them: the right to disagree with men openly; the right to express an opinion publicly; the right to dress according to foreign fashions; the right to be educated and liberated; the right to deviate from the "norm."

Slavery in fiction, memory, life

During its long history, slavery has worn many faces and has spawned lasting legacies, casting a deep shadow over the region's women. The zeitgeist
of the region includes contradictory social norms and priorities, which are
inevitably part of a labor-intensive economic system dependent on slavery
and other forms of indentured servitude. This volume includes a chapter
from Buchi Emecheta's 1977 novel *The Slave Girl*, depicting an urban
Nigerian market woman's purchase of a rural girl child from her destitute
parents (see "A Necessary Evil," p. 294). Buchi Emecheta leaves her readers no doubt that child-labor in Nigeria today is a continuation of an age-
old practice:

> Many of the market women had slaves in great number to help
> them with the fetching and carrying that went with being a full-
> time trader—and also in the vain hope that one day the British
> people at the coast would go and some of these house slaves could
> be sold abroad, just as their fathers and grandfathers had done, so
> profitably that the abundance of capital and property they had
> built could still be seen in many families round Onitsha and Bonny
> and Port Harcourt.

Emecheta, like other contemporary African writers and like traditional storytellers, holds a mirror to her own society, in this case revealing the responsibility of some women for perpetuating a pernicious form of child labor.

Like Emecheta's fictional account, Carolyn A. Brown's oral history project "Memory as Resistance" seeks "to document the ways that slave experiences are remembered by communities in an area that was intensely
involved in the slave trade" (Brown 2003: 219–220; 223). Brown's interviews, conducted in the Biafran region of Nigeria, reveal not only "the cen-
trality of the slave trade in the collective memory," but also new insights
about women's enslavement:

> While the interviews revealed that widows and their children were
> most likely to be enslaved, they raised complex problems both about
> the historical trajectory of the trade as well as women's acceptance of
> gender ideologies. First, because we are unable to determine with
> sufficient accuracy the time period within which these sales
> occurred, we cannot say if this practice coincided with the erosion of
> family ideologies of kinship or if it was considered by the majority of
> the rural community to be an antisocial practice. . . . Some of the
> accounts suggest that enslavement was a reaction to a more wide-
> spread expression of social resistance by women. There were
> instances of a particularly "troublesome" girl or a transgressive
> woman who broke gender taboos. (Brown 2003: 219, 229)

Perhaps the seeds of social resistance can be found amid the excesses of women's enslavement. On the other hand, the crucial importance of the work of market women, the political and spiritual leadership of many women in transcultural and transnational social organizations, have distinctly marked West Africa and the Sahel as a region where women wield far-reaching and distinctive forms of power.

Exceptional political women

The exemplary coastal Fante woman Adwoa Kwadua, a legendary widow, decided to compensate families for the loss of men in a battle led by her husband's Asafo company, who fought along with British allies against the Asante army in the early 1820s. She gave each family a measure of gold dust. Metaphorically, in "The Warring Hosts" (see p. 133), she is remembered for her closeness to Governor Charles McCarthy:

> Know that however pale your skin
> You can be to the Whiteman no closer kin
> Than Adwoa, daughter of the Whiteman.

The governor, who was killed on the battlefield in 1824, is still portrayed by a traditional Adzewa singing group as having admired this exceptional woman, who, instead of lamenting her dead husband, continued to support him in death by offering financial security to her sisters in distress. This incident is remembered as a painful episode in the long-standing alliance between the British forces and the Fante people on the coast, who were under constant threat of being overrun by their previous masters, the Asante, and had thus become part of the British Protectorate. Kwadua no doubt saw in the British governor a hero who helped the Fante fight the "arrogant" Asante and their overcentralized state machinery.

Powerful Queenmothers

Under British indirect rule along the Gold Coast, when "chiefs" (*ahene*) were sometimes appointed against all rules of succession, popular movements of resistance were led by the *ahemmaa* or Queenmothers against chiefs who had been installed by the government or who were "traditionally legitimate but unpopular" (Owusu-Sarpong 2005b). An Akan Queenmother was the keeper of peace in the family; she further served as the role model for young girls, teaching them—in part through folktales (see, for example, "The Poor Orphan," p. 347)—how to become adult women. Her political authority rested on her knowledge of history, for she was the trusted repository of royal genealogies and pedigrees (see "Kapro, the Royal Gift," p. 417). At all times, the Queenmother was to sit beside her male counterpart, so that she might whisper words of wisdom into his ear.

Her proximity to him validated the chief's rule. In one case (Agogo 1917), a group of commoners called for the removal of Kwabena Tandoh, who had not been approved by the Queenmother, Adjuah Jiawah. The rebellion failed, however, and the British instead removed the Queenmother in question, accusing her of being of a "relentless, revengeful and vicious disposition" (Owusu-Sarpong 2005b; Allman and Tashjian 2000: 21).

Even today, Akan orature is replete with allusions to powerful Queenmothers and their glorious deeds. The Asante oral tradition remembers with particular joy the powerful Queenmother of Edweso, Nana Yaa Asantewaa, the first woman to have been appointed war-leader (*Osahene*) or commander of the Asante fighting force, which fought the last battle against British troops, now celebrated as the 1900 "Yaa Asantewaa War" (Arhin 2000). Various oral poetic genres sing the praises of other Queenmothers and refer to their important historical and social functions. We find them in Akan stories of origin (*atetesem*), texts related to state building (*abakosem*), and in particular in drum texts or royal funeral laments, including the "*Ntam*, or Oath" (see p. 114), pronounced by the Queenmother of Wenchi at a chief's funeral in 1989.

In a recent publication, *Nigerian Women in Perspective*, Sa'ad Abubakr takes the view that in Hausaland, as among the Akan, "women appear to have been the early political masters." Quoting the example of the Daura in the ninth century, Abubakr argues that the *Magajiyas*, or Queens, were once dynastic rulers. "But," he adds, "following the advent of alien elements, probably Arabs or Berbers, this dynasty came to an end." For instance, the oral tradition of Katsina, now northern Nigeria, recalls the sixteenth-century queen Amina, who is said to have led the military expansion of the territory up to Nupe, to have received tribute from powerful chiefs, and to have introduced the kola nut into the region. Queen Amina is also remembered as an astute administrator "who never relied solely on information about events and developments in the kingdom reaching her through messengers and courtiers." She has become, in the collective memory of her people, the image of a truly effective and independent leader (1992: 11–25).

The powerful women behind Sunjata

The Mande epic of Sunjata is one of the most often discussed cases in debates about the validity of using poems and stories as historical documents. Our inquiry about women's power finds a place in this debate as well. At the Malian empire's apogee in the fourteenth century, under Kankan Moussa, its area of influence extended well beyond its Manden core: from west to east it stretched from present-day Senegal to Aïr in Niger; from north to south, it reached from the Sahara to the southern edges of the Sudanic zone. The history of Mali and its founding hero, Sunjata, has had a profound impact throughout the Mande cultural world. Local chroniclers have adapted the elements of their common heritage in the production of locally marked stories. All variants of the tale, however, involve the heroic male figure of Sunjata, who is remembered as the founder of the Malian empire, and include a series of legendary female figures described as having directly or indirectly affected the wondrous story of Sunjata and his government.

In "The History of the Sunjata Epic: A Review of Evidence," Ivor Wilks invites the reader to concentrate on old Mande songs, which, he postulates, most certainly constitute a faithful rendering of the original composition. Wilks believes that these short texts, which mention "outstanding incidents" of the past, have been transmitted with accuracy, thanks to the Mande metric pattern of composition that introduces rhythm into the text and, at the same time, serves as a mnemonic device. He reminds us of Ibn Battūta's fourteenth-century testimony from Mansa Suleyman's court. Battūta reports, "Dougha the interpreter (the *jeli*) comes with his four wives and his slave girls [to sing and commemorate]. There are about a hundred of these, with fine clothes and on their heads, bands of gold and silver adorned with gold and silver balls." According to Wilks, Battūta's chronicle authenticates the existence of Sunjata and places him in the "second antecedent generation" to the fourteenth-century ruler Mansa Musa (Wilks 1999: 47). He affirms that the songs we still hear and record today were most probably those Battūta heard (Wilks 1999: 25–27).

The Sunjata songs reproduced in this volume (see "Two Songs for Sunjata," p. 119) may well belong to this "original" corpus of short but pungent Mande songs. The corpus as a whole encapsulates the successive states of the story of Sunjata, each song referring to a striking episode of the hero's childhood, exile, return, or reign. Each is to be read as a metaphor describing the making of a revered ancestral figure. The two songs anthologized here recall the triumphant words supposedly uttered by Sunjata's mother and sister on the day of his "waking up." On that day, after seven years of crawling, Sunjata is said to have finally stood upright with the help of a specially made iron bar. This symbolic act, through which the child vindicates his mother's power, becomes the signal of an extraordinary destiny in the making. The mother's song of praise is followed by the sister's song of expectation for even better things to come.

We know that the legendary founder of the Mali empire is thought to have been able to surpass his foe—known for his control over occult forces—only because the powerful spirit of Sogolon, his mother, coursed through his blood. Sogolon, whose name meant "able to avoid all pitfalls," was considered to have extraordinary occult powers. She was regarded as a woman who had crossed gender lines; she was described as a "monstrous" being. Sunjata's sister, "who [had] taken over the occult duties of the female line at the death of Sunjata's mother during his exile," seduced and destroyed Sumamuru, Sunjata's enemy (Johnson 1999: 20–21). Indeed, Sunjata's name—"Son-Joro" or "Sogolon Jara" (Sogolon's Lion)—praises both the hero and his mother. That alone is "an acknowledgement that men derive their power from their mothers and that human existence and survival depend on the strength of women" (Conrad 1999: 190). In epic narratives about the foundation, salvation, or restoration of states, the heroine through whom the "miracle" happens reenacts her most revered social function as a woman, that of a "giver of life." By giving her own life away, the martyr becomes the Mother of the Kingdom in eternity.

Heroic women martyrs

Thus, in the most tragic representations of state creation in the western Sudan, the heroine willingly sacrifices herself to save her people and to open the way to her father's, husband's, or brother's success. For example, the story of the Baule people's migration away from Kumase in the eighteenth century—a time of political unrest—to a region that is now part of Côte d'Ivoire tells of Queen Abraha Poku, who "threw her son into the river to save her people." And a miracle occurred: "All the majestic trees along the riverside then bent down and formed a bridge made of branches and lianas across the river" and let the people go.[12] Inikpi, the daughter of Ata Ayegba—who was, in the sixteenth century, the first dynastic ruler of Igalaland—is forever celebrated in a shrine dedicated to her as the martyr of Igala. Her self-sacrifice is believed to have saved her father from the dangerous threat of an invasion (see "Elegy for Inikpi," p. 120).

While powerful women officially share credit for the success of the male rulers they have supported—through their control of the natural forces of life and death or through exemplary acts of courage—acknowledgment of their active political work has been rare. Recently scholars have recovered the histories of some "powerful and influential women" from the empire-building period, through recording and comparing multiple variants of epic narratives and panegyric poetry. These women formed alliances by marriage. Some of them mediated quarrels between major rulers in times of political upheaval or fed crowds in times of crisis. Some participated directly in battles or in running governments. Nevertheless, male "traditionalists" continue to talk about the "powerful women of old" only with reluctance. This reluctance underlines their own attachment to a tradition that has, over the centuries, systematically kept women in subordinate positions in the family, the community, and the state.[13] Women's supposedly unstable nature, which oscillates between periods of "pure" fecundity and "impure" infertility, has led to specific social habits and to the formulation of many proverbs on this fundamental dichotomy, which seems forever to have puzzled men. As the Dogon proverb goes: "It is through the woman that all forms of evil and of good come into the world" (Calame-Griaule 1993: 9).

Ruling women

Research has finally begun to unearth the probable historical shift from female to male rule or to dual systems of governance in various West African societies, a change that took on different forms in patrilineal and matrilineal groups but that still often resulted in the surrender of female power. Rather exceptionally, the social life of the Sherbro remained organized in ancestor-focused corporate descent groups, which represented themselves indifferently as having descended from named male or female ancestors. Some *mano*, or "aristocratic," Sherbro women have, therefore, become significant "elders" with rights over people and land. Their status was also validated by the Sande religious society to which they belonged, which controlled their biological reproductive power. Carol MacCormack reports on the story of a "very important woman," Ya Ndama, who became one of the most prominent "paramount chiefs" in the history of Sierra Leone. She assisted traders and later became a successful trader herself (1997: 271).

Yoko Gbanhnyer of Senehun, born in 1849, whose cosigned letter to the colonial government in Freetown (see "Letter from the Women of Senehun," p. 145) appears in this volume, was another renowned member of the Sande society of "noble descent." She became head of Mowoto before succeeding her husband as ruler of the Kpa Mende confederacy on his death. In keeping with her high social status, she was at the time of her marriage elevated to the rank of "senior wife" above her husband's other wives. The documents kept in government archives show how shrewd a negotiator she was and how much she had mastered all levels of power.

Fighting women

One of the most puzzling cases of "powerful women" during the period of empire building in the western Sudan is that of the "captives" who once lived behind the walls of the Simboji palace in Abomey. Among them, tradition most particularly remembers the famous women fighters, or Dahomean "amazons," and the Queenmothers, or *Kpojito*. During the nineteenth century, from five thousand to eight thousand *ahosi* were kept in the palace: They were either "wives" or dependents of the king. Some were captives and slaves purchased abroad (*kannounnon*). Others were daughters or female descendants of the king's lineage, who were considered *ahovi* (royal). There were also *anato* (commoners) recruited from all the lineages of the Dahomean state. In the kingdom of Dahomey, one's status or class never changed, but rank could change, and a woman of slave origin could sometimes rise to the level of Queenmother (Bay 1997: 342). Some Dahomean Queenmothers were very wealthy. For their outstanding service and loyalty, kings rewarded them with titles and gifts. They enjoyed a great amount of prestige and were extremely influential, so much so that the palace in Dahomey became the "political and economic nerve centre of power." Labor-intensive industries, including the processing of palm oil and the manufacture of pottery, as well as preparations for war, were carried out mostly inside this gigantic place of perpetual servitude. A few women were sent out to be used as spies or to "seduce men, [and] denounce them for having intercourse with an *ahosi* and then see that they were enrolled in the army as punishment" (348).

Beginning in the 1720s, women fighters were part of a permanent force. Under King Gezo (1818–1858), some women fighters were drawn from among young captives, others from among the so-called "criminal" elements of the palace. The famous amazons of Dahomey are still remembered as having fought in battle without fear, in particular in Abeokuta, an Egba town, on 3 March 1851. Here is how a recent radio broadcast reconstructed their activity:

> The Dahomey Amazons are in the first line of fighting. Originally meant to parade and to guard the king, these women warriors have become over the years one of the elite battalions of the Dahomean army. They're armed with rifles, lances, and razor-sharp sabres. For the siege of Abeokuta, 6,000 of them were mobilized.[14]

In their lifetimes, western Sudanese women like Sogolon or Yaa Asantewaa were not silent witnesses of troubled times, but active participants in historical events, even though today we often hear *of* them or read *about* them in documents written by "outsiders." Although the actual words they used to influence important matters of state have not, in most cases, been recorded by the male traditional recorders of their societies exactly as they once uttered them, their names and their deeds have been kept alive in the allusive style of orature. Sometimes, as in the rare texts of this collection, women's voices sing their ancestors' proverbial names and tell of their heroic deeds on ceremonial occasions. On an even rarer occasion, a Muslim woman, Nana Asma'u, much loved by her father, was able as early as 1827 to participate directly in the scriptural recording of her times (see p. 124).

Although outstanding women do appear in several epics that record their immeasurable contributions to political and military life, these epics are performed—and the women's words are spoken—by men. What makes these texts valuable to us, however, is that many conserve a considerable amount of direct speech, thus giving agency to women. Although each epic as recounted by an individual *griot* tells the tale slightly differently, the words of the women appear consistently unchanged. One of these epics is "The Battle of Ngangaram or Ngone Latyr." The nineteenth-century conflict between the Kajoor/Bawol kingdom and the Trazza Moors remains famous in Senegal because of the courage of Ngone Latyr, daughter of King Lat Sukaabe. She distinguished herself by bravely leading the troops, replacing her father, who was ill—a singular occurrence never repeated in the history of the region. She fought the battle of Ngangaram, wounding the most intrepid of Moorish warriors and thus saving her father's kingdom. In the epic she sings of wishing to lead her men exactly as her father would:

Bring all the horses around
I will be any man's equal
I will wear father's clothing
I will mount father's horse
I will brandish father's guns.

Another epic poem celebrating the sacrifice of "The Women of Nder" describes an event in the nineteenth-century Walo Kingdom of northern Senegal. When the French took the colony of Senegal, the situation of Walo as a center of colonial agriculture led the rulers of the kingdom to attempt to keep off envious neighbors. When the Trazza Moors and the Tukuleur carried out an offensive in the absence of the kingdom's sovereign, the *Lingeer*, or first wife of the king, asked all women of Nder to burn themselves in the *tata*, a fortified building, rather than become slaves of the victors. At the same time, she asked one of their number, Seydani Maa Fatim, to escape, so that Fatim might tell their story and thus memorialize their bravery:

Agree to leave with the Moors
We will burn ourselves in the *tata*
For if the Moors take us
They will turn us into slaves.

Talatay Nder, or Nder Tuesday, the day of the glorious act of the Nder women, has moved beyond the borders of Walo to be inscribed today in the collective memory of the Senegalese as the very expression of the refusal to submit.

GENDER AND CHANGE IN THE COLONIAL SITUATION: 1900 TO 1940

Before 1880, the rulers of most parts of Africa were African kings, queens, earth priests and divine officers, clan and lineage heads, governing empires, communities, and polities of various sizes and shapes. By 1900, the colonizing powers of France, Britain, and Germany had partitioned West Africa and the Sahel. Internal problems and political disarray had weakened the once powerful West African states of the interior—Benin, Oyo, Dahomey, and Asante. The power of ruling chiefs, inherited through descent, was more and more contested by a new generation of entrepreneurs acquiring personal wealth. In Africa, by the start of the First World War, only Liberia, the empire of Ethiopia, and the tiny sultanate of Darfur remained independent.

Several complex elements disrupted African life, not necessarily in unison: colonial conquest and the consequences of legal and political changes,

Christianity and the attendant Westernization of education, and further and more complex integration into an Atlantic world economy that changed the rules for trading. All of these took firm root between 1880 and 1920. In what follows, we will focus on the Christian missions' delivery of Western education for girls as well as boys and on the ways Western ideas and law changed Africans' lives. We will also note the tensions of those torn by dual cultures in the decades before the long struggle for independence.

The first Christian missionary expeditions were launched early in the nineteenth century. In the early 1800s, Catholics came to Senegal; in 1804, Protestant missionaries began to work in Sierra Leone. Outlawing slave-owning and converting freed slaves became a powerful motive for setting up missions along the West Coast after 1834. Large settlements of freed and repatriated slaves traveled from the United States and Britain to Sierra Leone and Liberia, countries that became important centers of Christian practice in West Africa. In Freetown, the Christian Mission Society (C.M.S.) established the Fourah Bay College in 1827 for the training of young mission teachers. Its first pupil, Samuel Ajayi Crowther, became the first African Anglican bishop. He was followed a generation later by another powerful African churchman, the Nigerian Rev. I. O. Ransome-Kuti, whose wife, originally a teacher, soon became a dynamic political figure and a founder of the Abeokuta Ladies Club in 1944.[15]

By the middle of the nineteenth century, the French—who first came to Africa in 1659—had established themselves fully in the region of the Senegal river, and the British had taken control of the fortified trading posts on the Gold Coast. Both the French and the British had long histories of direct and intimate contact with Africans, many of whom lived in the somewhat Westernized urban communities of Cape Coast, Dakar, Freetown, St. Louis, Monrovia, Accra, and Lagos. Children of African and European descent born on the Sherbro coastland, on Gorée Island, or in Fanteland benefited at a very early stage from Western education. European merchants (Danish, Dutch, and English) made initial attempts to introduce formal education for the children born of European men and African women by arranging classes in the forts and castles along the coasts. The first castle schools for boys were established on the Gold Coast as early as 1600; in 1766, Philip Quaque returned from England to become the first African headmaster of the Colonial School at Cape Coast. By the 1870s and 1880s, a number of African elite men had returned from Europe, armed with professional qualifications gained abroad, to work all along the region's coasts.

In some cases, coastal people readily agreed to participate in the planned annexation of the interior to the colonial territories and thereby take advantage of the new opportunities political change might offer them. The military conquest of the interior was undertaken with the support of those who wished for change. Despite the fierce movements of resistance by the once unconquerable warrior states—some of which had been triggered by defiant female rulers (for example, the 1900 "Yaa Asantewaa war" in Asante)—the superior quality of their arms led the European conquerors to victory on the battlefields (Edgerton 1995). Nevertheless, for the Europeans, a much more challenging battle had yet to be won: ensuring the psychological surrender of the people and their traditional rulers to the newly established authorities, who knew little about the customs and the culture of their subjects. This marked the beginning of the ambivalent relationship between the colonial administration and Christian missions.

Colonialism did not, in Stephanie Newell's words, "spread across and submerge entire regions like a steadily expanding flow" (2002: 7). Its influence was "disaggregated—episodic and uneven, gendered and generational" (Allman and Tashjian 2000: 222). The missionaries' writings on local cultures and languages provided colonial administrators with valuable information, but the colonial powers also depended, to some extent, on the type of Western education offered to Africans by Christian missions (Ajayi and Crowder 1973). A number of committed Christian missionaries, such as the Scottish Mary Slessor, who fought in Calabar against the cultural habit of throwing twins into the bush to die and who may have inspired Ezumah, the Igbo "Champion of Twins" (see p. 182), engaged in humanitarian crusades against outmoded customs that needed to be eradicated in the name of human rights. Some preachers, on the other hand, supported colonial administrators by preaching obedience or by encouraging adherence to a Westernized way of life, which helped keep rebellious elements under control and promoted new commercial ventures, such as the importation of manufactured goods.

Young, educated West African men were needed to uphold the colonial bureaucracy and act as office clerks and court interpreters. The coastal middlemen who had long been the only direct commercial contacts between European traders and the African leaders in the interior, in particular during the slave trade, thus became a class of native agents of the colonial administration. But no one could ever predict where education would lead the newly constituted literate elite, who began to organize Anglophone West African clubs and literary societies and were quick to learn how to "interpret and utilize Western education, English literacy, mission Christianity and colonial power structures to their own ends" (Newell 2002: 43).

From the start, the colonial policies "seemed in a sense an attempt to create a chaotic situation" (Ajayi and Crowder 1973: 536) by encouraging missionaries to start converting first the class of African outcasts and underprivileged who had long been oppressed by their own rulers or by those of a higher class. Thus split, the communities found their opposition to colonial rule weakened. At the same time, colonial authorities took control of the appointment of chiefs, who gradually became their auxiliaries, both under British indirect rule and under the more centralized French policy. The authorities appointed willing "collaborators," who helped to reinvent customs that often led to the corruption of traditional rule and to the abuse of power by chiefs who accumulated wealth and forgot about the well-being of their people. Whereas men sometimes capitulated to seemingly colossal colonial power, West African women stood up against the defeatist and immoral stand adopted by some of their chiefs, and "malcontents" led Queenmothers to overthrow the most illegitimate among them (Allmann and Tashjian 2000: 21).

In fact, there was, throughout the colonial period, and especially during the decades that led to decolonization and independence, a constant "effort by African people to retain some control over their destinies" (Ajayi and Crowder 1973: 536). These struggles, though, were not engaged in merely to re-create the precolonial situation. West African men and women at the beginning of the twentieth century spoke out against the hardships brought about by the new economic order: Mining and the cultivation of cash crops (cocoa, timber, rubber, cotton, coffee, groundnuts) led to the collective migration of the poor; these industries required the construction of roads and railways, which had to be paid for by heavy taxes; at the same time, few new technologies were imported to ease the labor of agricultural workers or miners. West Africans and Sahelians protested the taxes decreed by the new so-called fathers of the nation. (See "Satire from the Women's Corner," p. 174.)

African soldiers who survived their participation in the First World War came home knowing that Europeans were not invincible, an awareness that opened the door for rebellion, resistance, and opposition, and for making gains within colonial systems. Progress in literacy unavoidably led to the multiplication of written petitions, to the emergence of a politically and socially committed West African press, and to the publication of literary works written by West African "patriots." In all these areas, women entered the debate, despite the fact that the new male elite would keep them at the fringes of public affairs.

Women's education

Christianity also became an agent of change for women in the non-Islamized West African territories. In 1847, the Anglican Church Missionary Society in Sierra Leone opened one of the earliest girls' schools in the region, renamed the Annie Welsh Memorial School in 1878. In Cape Coast, the Wesleyan mission established the first girls' school in 1836 and upgraded it in 1884 to the first girls' secondary school of the Gold Coast, just after the Methodist mission had set up the first boys' secondary school in 1876. The progress was slow and uneven: Not until 1907 was the first girls' school established in Lagos. In addition, as Stefanie Newell writes, "Young women and men did not [simply] gain literacy from mission schools: they gained *Christian literacy*" (2002: 60). Mission schools imparted a gender-differentiated education: In "vocational" classes, girls were taught European domestic skills and received a thorough "bride-training" based on biblical models, which urged them to enter monogamous marriages as subdued and devoted wives.

Female literacy remained low throughout the colonial period, and even when girls received a basic education, they were often withdrawn from school at an early stage. The bias against educating girls not only came from the missionary perspective described by Sylvia Leith-Ross (1939) but also conformed to a more profound prejudice, especially among rural Africans, that remained alive throughout the pre-independence period. This volume includes a prize-winning piece of fiction published in 1947 by the Nigerian Pheban Ajibola Itayemi Ogundipe that illuminates the conflict between mission education for females and a family's expectation of a daughter's future. In "Nothing So Sweet" (see p. 189)—the title's metaphor refers to education—parents arrange a marriage between their daughter (when she is six) and a well-to-do but illiterate middle-aged neighbor. The groom-to-be expects and pays for a bride educated enough to help him in his business. In the following dialogue, the girl's mother understands the possible conflict to come, probably because of her own life's denials.

> "Will you not send my 'wife' to school?" he asked in our language.
>
> My mother seemed surprised.
>
> "To school?" she asked. "Surely you do not want her to be sent to school? If she goes to school, she will soon scorn you as an illiterate farmer, and an old one too.
>
> "I do not mean that she should be sent to school to get up to Standard Six," explained Ogongo. "I just want her to receive enough Christian education to enable her to read the Bible . . . and to read any letters that may come for me. She will also learn about weights, so that I can be sure that these Produce Buyers who buy my cocoa do not cheat me when they weigh it. . . ."
>
> "I am warning you, Ogongo, that the girl will probably become unmanageable if you send her to school. She is obstinate and proud enough as it is. Besides she would not help me much at home," objected my mother.

Women writing

The writing of women during the early years of the twentieth century reflects the desire of the independent-minded to take their lives into their own hands, an opportunity offered to them by the ambiguous political situation. Their words express a profound awareness of the complexity of the shifting new world they lived in. Their writing reveals their power to deride an already vanishing world and to greet with sarcasm or irony a prediction of better days to come. Perhaps they also fear that they might still have to pay the price of their increasing freedom.

One of the prices women have always paid under colonialism is tied to sexuality, in this instance the tensions created by white "gentlemen" arriving in coastal cities without spouses. Some of the temporary relationships imposed on pretty young girls wreaked havoc in communities. For example, "Poko" (see p. 165), an anticolonial song from Burkina Faso, warns young girls of the danger of losing one's place in society, in other words, of becoming an outcast. On the other hand, the *signares* of the coastal city of St. Louis, in Senegal, built their wealth on the profit they realized from the French "husbands" with whom they had children. But not all women living in this sophisticated, creolized city could boast of a happy life. N'Della Sey's petitions to the governor in 1919 and 1920 (see "A Mother's Plea," p. 161) draw a line between the nouveau riche, allegedly degenerate Senegalese women "who give their children total freedom" and spoil them, and honest women like the author herself, a widow without means, whose eldest son has now gone astray in an already polluted society where money can be acquired more easily through dubious means than through hard work. She pleads with the governor for her son's early release from prison, putting part of the blame on the moral depravation brought about by these new circumstances and on her son's painful adolescent awareness of the hopeless poverty that characterized the society of migrant workers and abandoned wives in shantytowns. Her letter, which she may have dictated—we cannot be sure she was literate—is subtle in its implications and decidedly clever. She appeals to the governor "in the name of humanity," to which he belonged, just as she did, just as her son did, and just as other women and their sons did—all in a new world that was imposing its fast-changing laws on all.

Similarly, the petition of Houleye Diop in 1923 (see p. 165) testifies to a woman's courage and resourcefulness at a time when both the judicial system and Islamic practices were being revised. This widow's petition for her cows—which meant her financial independence—underlines not only the dishonesty of her stepson, who was one of her husband's heirs and who refused to return to her the money her husband had lent him, but also the malpractices of the court. She protests forcefully, using Islamic law to assist her, declaring, "I stand firmly behind my right to protest the verdict of the subdivision's court and that of the Sedhiou circle." This was a bold statement, which she supported with rational and convincing evidence, ending her plea with "Let justice be done."

The existence of these letters of petition calls for further comment about the colonial law courts, which were foreign elements established by the French in their territories and by the English in theirs. Alien to African culture was the idea of imprisonment, commonplace in a Western world that used jails and penitentiaries. Especially for her financial security as a widow, N'Della Sey needs the possibility of her son's employment. The

Ghanaian K. A. Busia once remarked, in a conversation with his daughter, Abena P. A. Busia, that he understood that the aspect of the British legal system that most baffled the elders of his rural community when he was a young man was the notion that restitution could be made to anyone for anything by removing a working person from his or her dependents and community. The conversation had arisen over the issue of a stolen sheep. Under customary law, the thief would have had to find a means of returning the sheep or its equivalent value, whether by returning the meat if the animal had been slaughtered or by working for the offended party until the value of the sheep had been paid. In this particular case, the British authorities had intervened, and the culprit had been sentenced to a prison term. The victim was still sheepless, and the perpetrator's family found itself not only without a breadwinner but also under the stigma of having a family member in prison.

Widowhood

N'Della Sey's maturity and knowledge of legal clauses finds its match in this volume in other texts and testimonies on the vulnerable position of widows in African society. This volume contains the testimony of Lucie Traoré Kaboré (see "My Name Is Lucie Traoré," p. 207) about her founding of a Widowhood Association in Burkina Faso in the early 1970s, almost at the same moment that Kate Abbam in Ghana was writing an editorial about the oppression of widows (see "On Widowhood," p. 227). Even as late as 1994—seventy years after the petitions of the Senegalese widows discussed above—Abbam wrote a strong speech condemning both the Christian church and the Ghanaian legal system for allowing the continuing, systematic abuse of widows.

In recent years, the complexity of law surrounding widows has been debated throughout the continent, and women's groups have continued to work for solutions, acknowledging that the contest rests on the definition of family itself. For the most part, an African perspective would see family as the kinship group, however defined, whereas the laws of modern nation-states are built on the assumption of a male-headed nuclear family. On the death of a spouse, these two ideas come into competition. As Christine Dowuona-Hammond suggests, the symbolic success of Ghana's 1985 Intestate Succession Law protecting the rights of widows may in the end have been pyrrhic, for the law makes widows and *all children*—whether born in or out of wedlock, to the ordinance wife or another woman—equal partners in the share of the estate with the natal family, effectively superimposing a layer of legality over entrenched customary practices without really dealing with the complex issues at stake (1998: 133).

The introduction of ordinance marriages in the latter part of the nineteenth century offered elite urban women greater security as legal partners in marriage with the right to initiate divorce.[16] But even at the end of the century, such ordinances had no impact on the fundamental ethic of West African society, which regards women as perpetual insiders with inheritance rights in their natal families and perpetual outsiders in their marital families. Thus, laws meant to protect them as wives could at the same time threaten their security and that of other women, as sisters and aunts, without in the end securing their protection. Under customary law, most women retain the right to the fruits of their labor, but European law and banking and lending systems, for example, frequently give authority to husbands, or to married persons jointly, leaving a wife vulnerable to having her property, in particular the marital home, taken from her by customary law at her husband's death.

Journalism

As early as 1826, the *Liberia Herald* appeared, published by Charles Force and marking the beginning of an African press critical of European presence. Charles Bannerman's *Accra Herald*, the first African paper produced on the Gold Coast, opened its doors in 1858. In 1926, the popular *Daily Nigerian Times* also began publishing, and the *West Africa* magazine, which originally came out in London in 1917, quickly became an open forum for the discussion of all questions affecting the welfare of people in the region, both African and European. *West Africa* remains in print today. It published contributions from expatriates and from the African urban elite, including the famous Gold Coast nationalist Kobina Sckyi. French West African journalism began in the 1920s with the birth of several papers such as *Le Paria* and *La Voix du Nègre*—all published in France by such precursors of the Négritude movement as Marc Kojo Towalou Houénou, who, in 1924, founded *Les Continents* as well as the Ligue Universelle de Défense de la Race Nègre, a movement designed to fight against French colonies and their ubiquitous "African lackeys." On the African continent, *La Voix du Dahomey* (1927) was followed by many other vibrant newspapers. As the recent work of Audrey Gadzekpo makes clear, these newspapers reflected the ideology, biases, preoccupations, and agendas of the educated elite who were both its producers and consumers. In their pages, one can see the social attitudes toward gender of their time (Gadzekpo 2001).

Women's involvement in newspaper work has a long history in this region. Kate Abbam, for example, ran her own magazine in Ghana for thirty years at the end of the twentieth century, but more than one hundred years earlier, in 1886, women were writing letters to the editor of a newspaper in Ghana (see "Two Letters to the Editor," p. 147). By the mid-1930s, prominent women writers, led by Mabel Dove-Danquah, wrote satires ranging from irony to invective for daily Ghanaian newspapers, to be published in assigned spaces that were usually called the "Women's Corner" or the "Women's Column." These spaces became a primary locus for the feminization of public discourse. What may have seemed to be insignificant space reserved for the public expression of women's opinions often took on unexpected magnitude. Women had become critical observers of their time, and no single individual or social "misbehavior" escaped the sharpness of their eyes. They wrote no gossip, sentimental vagaries, or other forms of insipid prose. Rather, their essays were replete with serious observations and critical views, presented with a masterly sense of humor acquired over the centuries as they practiced metaphorical storytelling and satirical song. Now they could use the journalists' weapon of caricature to critique contemporary life and self-serving politicians:

> Editors of and contributors to women's columns acted as gatekeepers of the female world and adjudicated over social change. Women columnists set the agenda, policed the bounds of their columns and the boundaries of their discourse by highlighting certain concerns. They also exerted power over their readers by conferring status on some issues and recommending certain feminine interests, by validating certain feminine experiences, advocating a particular course of action, asserting women's intellectual capabilities and potential equality, and recommending ways that they could achieve prescribed aims and goals. (Gadzekpo 2002: 2)

To make her point about the moral ugliness of a "Father of the Nation" who could sign harmful "Water and other Seditious Bills" and therewith sign the death warrant of his "children" (see "Satire from the Women's Corner," p. 174), Yaa Amponsah (a pseudonym) narrates a story inside a story and introduces a dialogue in which she creates a "true" father—her own—who cries before his daughter and says, "Yaa, have you ever, since you first saw light, seen me weep? And is my cause for weeping unjust?" It was culturally unheard-of for a man or a father to cry and lament before his children, and even more unusual for a daughter to talk about it. But satiric essay writing allows transgressions. The distorted use of biblical or literary quotations out of context allows Odarley Koshie (probably a pseudonym for Dove-Danquah) to point an accusatory finger at "the English [who] brought the Bible" and who have, seemingly, forgotten the lesson of neighborliness therein. This writer introduces the persona of a converted African mother who implores "the kindly light" of the hymn so often sung in church, but who ends up shedding tears "as hot and bloody almost as Christ's in Gethsemane," for the colonial "fathers" will not listen to the concerns of their "dark-skinned kiddies." (See "From the Women's Column,'" p. 208.) Thus, women were prepared to take on a whole range of adversaries, from the colonial governor on down.

This volume also includes a piece of journalism by Efwa Kato, a woman about whom we know nothing except that her essay—the only one by a woman—appeared in 1934 in the *Journal of West African Students in Great*

Britain and Ireland, the official organ of the West African Students' Union.[17] Even without her biography, her essay alone suggests that she was an important part of the African national movement of the period. In the first lines of "What We Women Can Do" (see p. 178), Kato uses the most patriarchal of all Christian symbols of women's deviance, the Genesis story of the forbidden fruit, to challenge her readers. "I think," she postulates, "that the world owes a lot to Eve for tempting Adam to eat of 'the tree of knowledge of good and evil,' for it is in the eating thereof that man owes his subsequent development." The key word for the future, "development," is thrown onto the paper like a challenge, and there follows a daring set of paragraphs in which the author confidently deconstructs previous representations of family structures and upgrades areas where women are to be especially responsible—in particular the duty to rear their children as politically conscious beings. The most striking part of her text is probably the one in which she addresses women themselves, challenging them to urge their husbands to give up social climbing for patriotism, which would mean that both partners were ready for sacrifice. All that this newborn ideal African woman would need, according to the ardent author, is a "passion for souls." Then she would become another Mary Kingsley, another Emmeline Pankhurst.

From the early nineteenth well into the middle of the twentieth century, essays and editorials in newspapers and journals debated the question of education for women. The predominant view in the early years was that appropriate education would create intelligent, socially and culturally informed women who would become good domestic partners to their husbands. While Efwa Kato writes from this context, her essay may also be seen—like Marjorie Mensah's, and others—as offering a significant challenge to the notion of "companionate marriage," one that sees women as partners in the building of a new nation.

Early literary production

Francophone West African literary production as a tool toward political consciousness and self-determination started among poets, most particularly among the generation of students like Léopold Sédhar Senghor and David Diop, who were studying in Paris and meeting African American poets like Langston Hughes. Contacts with poets and painters of the French Dada and Surrealist movements influenced the African poets, helping them to break linguistic constraints. In the Parisian "melting pot," where a new generation of artists and thinkers mixed, Africans crossed borders of race and nation to dream of an egalitarian world. Away from their homeland, they were able to consider the decisive act of demolishing long-standing ideological partitions. From Paris, this West African intelligentsia looked homeward with annoyance, with bitterness, and with clairvoyance, and felt torn between the claims of direct confrontation and the desire for reconciliation.[18]

The Négritude movement and its production of poetry, such as the poems that appear in the *Anthology of the New Black and Malagasy Poetry in the French Language* (edited by Senghor in 1948), held a torch to freedom and independence, even beyond the first Francophone novels, which had appeared on the West African continent, written by such 1930s Senegalese writers as Ahmadou Mapaté Diagne or Ousmane Socé. (Women at this point were chiefly muses and helpmates to their writer-husbands.)[19]

Anglophone Africa's literary production at the beginning of the twentieth century was famously in prose. Such writers as J. E. Caseley Hayford and R. E. Obeng of the Gold Coast expressed early political consciousness in works such as Caseley Hayford's *Ethiopia Unbound: Studies in Race Emancipation* (1911), which paved the way for a most prolific and now renowned literary production in the second half of the century. To such later writers as Chinua Achebe, Ayi Kwei Armah, Wole Soyinka, and many others, we can add especially four women: Efua Sutherland and Ama Ata Aidoo of independent Ghana and Flora Nwapa and Buchi Emecheta of Nigeria.

A few exceptional women entered higher education during the first half of the twentieth century, aware that formal education would be needed to reshape West Africa in a complex, multicultural world. Often they chose careers in education. This was true, for example, of Mariama Bâ, who grew up in a Muslim environment in Dakar and was sent by her progressive father to schools established by the French in Dakar and Rufisque for formal Western education. Likewise, Adelaide Casely-Hayford, who grew up in a Krio family with a long-standing interest in culture and education, was sent to Germany to study music. She spent a lot of time traveling and searching for ideas for the establishment of a vocational school for girls and tried to impart the same dream to her daughter Gladys, who was better known as a poet.

Mariama Bâ's talent as a writer can already be discerned in "My Little Country" (see p. 186), a short essay she wrote in 1943, while a student at the Teacher Training School in Rufisque. In a transparent, open style, she portrays "life before" with a few touches of childhood memories: the "nourishing song of the pestle in the mortar," the "intoxication of drinking the water that falls from the sky," and the "warm, grilled meat with pepper and a pinch of salt" prepared during Tabaski festive days. She also suggests her early tomboyish ways, which, even after her transformation into an "educated" young lady, made her join the Négritude outcry and claim her African heritage in words as sharp as the blades of a razor (heralding David Diop's *Hammer Blows* of 1973): "They whitened my mind, but my head is black. . . . The blood in my civilized veins remains pagan. It revolts and rises up at the sound of black drums" (see p. 188).

We have already seen, in the texts of Sarah Bonetta and Victoria Davies, the complexities of mother/daughter relationships. During periods of intense social change—having to do both with the changing status of women and with the movements for independence—family relationships could only grow more difficult to sustain. Even when talented intellectual women had claimed their right to speak out alongside their husbands, even when they were ready to support the efforts of their male companions, marriages between such independent-minded women as Adelaide Casely-Hayford and her prominent lawyer husband (see p. 213) could not survive the pressures of an African world in which existing patriarchal attitudes seemed to blend so well with complementary European forms. In many respects, Caseley-Hayford's husband was exemplary of this blending. J. E. Casely-Hayford, a celebrated writer and activist, was part of that "small group of early educated indigenous males from coastal families who had a double heritage that was traditional African and Anglo-Saxon. These men were the founders of Gold Coast nationalism and at the same time the upholders of Victorian mores and lifestyles in the Cold Coast colony" (Gadzekpo 2002: 3).

For women, the blending of this "double heritage" was fraught with particular contradictions. The gap between women's destinies on both sides of the colonial world had begun to narrow, and disillusionment grew with the awareness of the magnitude of a common battle still to be fought by women—black and white, in Europe and in West Africa—to obtain equal access not only to education but also to academic and highly qualified scientific work, to entrepreneurship, to political activism, and to the rights to vote, to hold party membership, and to enjoy political appointments. Writers and speakers in the first half of the twentieth century debated the range of women's rights, possibilities, and responsibilities, reflecting the coexisting and contradictory ideological positions "that underscore[d] simultaneously the enthusiastic acceptance of change and its positive impacts on lifestyles, and the loss of traditional values and the corruptive nature of modernity" (Gadzekpo 2002: 3). In West Africa and the Sahel, as elsewhere in the world, even if unacknowledged, women were at the center of the storm.

As the century advanced, women's resistance to the status quo intensified, and many women's lives ended in lost dreams. For Gladys Caseley-Hayford, having to split her days between a mother and a father who were living apart, inside a shaken society struggling for independence, the price was high. The acceleration of change set generations apart, and mothers did not understand daughters driven into depression. Only after Gladys's premature death was her mother able to realize "what a place she had made for herself in the affections of her community." Only then did she see that "life did not seem quite fair" to her daughter because of her "daddy's empty chair" in the house. Despite her sorrow and pain, the hypersensitive daughter of Adelaide and the Honorable Casely-Hayford had become a patriot, calling upon all black hands to "Beat, beat, beat . . . beat distrust and bloodshed out of Africa," to "Clean, clean, clean . . . clean away the scales that hide true Africa from view," and to "Grind, grind, grind" in order to "guide and comfort Africa, when passing through life's mill" (see "Mother and Daughter," p. 211).

POLITICS AND GENDER AT THE END OF COLONIAL RULE

For centuries, elite West African and Sahelian women organized their lives through a variety of cultural and social associations. As Gwendolyn Mikell notes, African women have had "a quixotic relationship to tradition and modern political systems." She identifies three "indigenous models of gender, polity, and state" that existed in various forms throughout much of the continent: first, the "corporate" form, based on kinship that emphasized the group identity as more important than the individual; second, the "dual-sex" form, based on occupational and ritual organizations that emphasized "sex-complementarity" and age-group status; and third, the gender-based form of women's royal authority, which slowly eroded over time. From the late nineteenth century forward, colonialism transformed African sociopolitical structures—especially those dominated by elite males—in part by co-opting the authority of the region's cultural elite, thus undermining and diverting their accountability to their diverse constituent populations. Perhaps the most egregious intrusion into previous polities resulted from the collusion between colonial authorities and African patriarchal systems that weakened women's control of institutions, a process described by Mikell as "benign female exclusion" (1997: 16).

Although British colonialists, for example, viewed the very notion of African women's institutions as unfathomable, Akan, Yoruba, and Igbo rulers, among others, knew full well the extent of women's authority and power within their respective cultures. Similarly, although men fought colonialism side by side with women, many men at the same time manipulated colonialism's sexist tenets to suppress their own women. In the process, West African women found themselves fighting both African and European patriarchy with few of their former "corporate" or "dual-sex" resources and tools of resistance intact. Nevertheless, as Christiane Owusu-Sarpong (2005a) and LaRay Denzer (1997) have said, colonialism's impact on West African and Sahelian women and women's institutions was different in different places, for although the Akan *ohemmaa* system weakened, the Yoruba *iyalode* system grew and evolved as realities changed.

The Akan *ohemmaa* (Queenmother) and the Yoruba *iyalode* (Mother of the Outer/Public Spaces) provide us with regional models of traditional elite women's sociopolitical and economic organizations that challenged and were challenged by colonialism. Dating back to the founding of the Asante empire in the seventeenth century, the *ohemmaa* experienced the collusion between African and colonial sexism throughout the nineteenth and twentieth centuries. Grounded in a matrilineal "dual-sex gender system," the Queenmother, as an institution, led Akan women's organizations and also had significant power to name the king and advise about the behavior of local rulers. This institution maintained its own network and organization of female as well as male patrons, all of whom wielded considerable power throughout the empire.

Similarly, among the patrilineal Yoruba, the *iyalode* commanded an equally complex organization of patrons that influenced and controlled a regional network of traders and warriors. Although it is difficult to date its origins, we can surmise that the *iyalode* institution existed by the sixteenth century, at the height of the Oyo empire. Where the Ghanaian Queen-mother was chiefly a sociopolitical, rather than economic, institution, the Yoruba *iyalode* was also an economic institution, for she controlled the women residing within her polity. She usually owned her own farms and laborers, and organized a network of local and long-distance traders. After the disintegration of the Oyo empire, some *iyalode* took the opportunity to strengthen their positions, especially in and around Abeokuta and Ibadan (Denzer 1997; White 1999). These women and their organizations were critical to the development of nationalist and independence organizations.[20]

Whereas the *ohemmaa* and *iyalode* institutions represented ruling-class women, Igbo women's organizations, following their own cultural norms, represented local non-elite women's interests. Ultimately, Igbo women's tactics provided one of the greatest challenges to British imperialism led by women (Amadiume 1987; 1997). Like their Akan and Yoruba sisters, Igbo women organized around motherhood and marketplace, and developed institutions to confront patriarchal oppression. They conceived of motherhood as empowering, fluid, and interweaving multiple responsibilities. The marketplace, associated with adult women's dual responsibilities as daughters and wives to their lineage and kin groups, is independent of men and provides non-elite Igbo women with a locus of power (Sudarkasa 1973; Amadiume 1987; Steady, 1981; White 1999; Badejo 1998a).

Motherhood

In this volume, women often speak through their common identity as biological, surrogate, and communal mothers. When motherhood is associated with power and the mystery of transformation, as well as with the authority to activate or suspend life, it is esteemed as the gateway to lineage, rule, and personal immortality. It may also be used as a metaphor for communal organizing and as a catalyst for familial, social, economic, and political transformation. As Filomina Steady (1981) has argued, motherhood was and is still as much a socioeconomic institution as a political one. It signifies more than the responsibilities of childbirth and child rearing; it also signals identification within a network of similarly obligated females and, by extension, their male relatives and their dependents. In certain environments, motherhood controlled large numbers of workers—including slaves—on farms, in the marketplace, and within the domestic sphere.

As an institution, motherhood enabled women to function as an interest group through a network whose members provided services for one another. This is particularly true of elite women, whose marriages usually enhanced the positions of their respective families as well as themselves. For non-elite and enslaved women, marriage as a social contract could be either a blessing or a curse. In spite of class distinctions, however, motherhood remained a unifying element in the symbiotic relationship between reproduction and immortality, which meant that women were both feared and respected (Amadiume 1997).

As the texts in this volume and other research demonstrate, African motherhood is not purely idyllic. As an icon of cultural discourse, motherhood operates through a system of institutions that work for, as well as against, women themselves. Despite lofty maternal symbolism, motherhood has been a source of social discontent and upheaval, not to mention outright oppression, as in the case of forced marriage, cowives, lineage disputes, and the treatment of widows. Moreover, women are constantly reminded that motherhood resides at a crossroads of life and death where a woman risks her own life as an arbiter of immortality. In texts like "*Maïéto*, or the Battle of the Sexes" (see p. 91), for example, the death of a woman during childbirth rallies other women in mock opposition to a community of men, who are viewed as the source of their suffering.

Similarly, Nwayeruwa's reaction to the census-taker in the 1929 text we have included about the Nigerian "Aba Women's War" (see p. 169) illustrates the deep bonds that tie women to childbirth: "He asked me to count my goats, sheep, and people. I turned to look at him. I said, 'Are you still counting? Last year my son's wife who was pregnant died. What am I to count? I have been mourning the death of that woman. Was your mother counted?'" How does one count the life of a woman lost in giving birth? Will the census-taker also insult his own mother and by extension his own family?

Nwayeruwa continues, "I raised an alarm," she says, as Emeruwa, the census-taker "ran away." Raising an alarm was a call for the women to organize against the imposition of both internal and external abuse. Nwayeruwa's cowife urged the townswomen to organize against what was perceived as a collective insult and threat to their well-being. The notion of "counting human beings," a religious taboo, offended many, and the demand for taxes based on a head count would double the insult, since it would weaken women's primary responsibilities to their families by submitting them to the demands of colonists and their corrupt local lackeys.

In her testimony, Nwayeruwa recalls as the next step the women's age-old practice of "sitting on a man," meaning demonstrating, perhaps with bare breasts, before his house. She recalls that "the women inside Emeruwa's compound begged him to get rid of the protesters, for the women in his own compound knew its potential consequences for them." They could face sanctions in the marketplace and exclusion from certain rituals.

Organizing for independence

Ifi Amadiume, Gwendolyn Mikell, Niara Sudarkasa, and other scholars have described how West African women's customs and training encoded institutions that allowed them to organize quickly, whether in opposition or in support. In their own communities, women's ability to act or organize politically was expected. Barring an offending husband or lover from the kitchen and the bedroom was a common model of women's protest, all the more effective in polygamous households, where several wives might participate simultaneously. Furthermore, a fear of women's ritual prerogatives might limit the extent of men's misbehavior.

In Anne-Marie Raggi's recounting of the march on Grand Bassam (see "That Is How the Women Woke Up," p. 205) in 1949, women tied the membership card of the Organization of African Democracy/Democratic Party of Côte d'Ivoire (RDA-PDCI) in their wrappers, signaling to their men that nationalist political action was more important to them than sex. Like the Igbo women in Nigeria and the Wolof and Bambara women in Senegal and Mali, respectively, these women in Côte d'Ivoire organized grassroots support for the anticolonial movement. The march, a landmark event, included women like Lucie Kaboré of Upper Volta (now Burkina Faso), Célestin Ouezzin of Dahomey, and Aoua Keïta of Mali, as well as Raggi from Côte d'Ivoire. For all of these women, the march was a defining moment of political consciousness. Unfortunately, as politics became institutionalized, via elections and the formations of governments, politics also became both more public and more masculine.[21]

Both the French and the British reduced the status of women to a par with women in their own countries. In addition to thus exacerbating regional forms of African sexism, colonial policies also tore into class distinctions by manipulating social inequities. Outcasts, barren women, mothers of twins, and slaves were drawn to, and recruited by, missionaries who promoted Western education as a vehicle for social mobility. Culturally elite women were also drawn to these opportunities, as much for themselves as for their sons, brothers, and husbands. In all cases, elite and non-elite educated women found ways to ensure that their voices would be heard. To meet the new challenges, some women were able to restructure some of their institutions and use their organizational skills to address collective and specific needs. Women used both the spoken and the written word to comment on and often protest aspects of the changing conditions of their indigenous and contemporary lives.[22]

An especially notable *iyalode* was Alhaja Rukayat Orogunbodi Ajisomo of Ibadan, Nigeria, who ruled from 1935 to 1951. She was active in Ibadan politics, and in addition to protesting a rather suspicious scarcity of salt, like her Igbo counterparts she mobilized women to demonstrate against the Ibadan chief Olubadan and the colonial regime. She also prohibited trade with members of the household of Olubadan, thus causing personal embarrassment and extensive damage to his authority. Her leadership and authority, supported by the protests of other women, grew so strong that the "colonial government required their material and moral support for the smooth running of price control, market distribution and produce collection" during the World War II years. Through the activism of such women, the title of *iyalode* became part of the British administration, thereby ensuring that women's voices were heard (Denzer 1997: 20).

Such scholars as Marcia Wright, in her detailed overview of gender and power in Africa, are documenting the enormous economic power of women traders in West Africa, as well as women's specific creativity in inventing subcultures to sustain other forms of power. According to LaRay Denzer, for example, market women—as "corporate" entities—were especially astute in their observation of the ways of imperialists. They sent their young daughters to schools, which turned them into "young career women" who defended the women's institutions that had provided for their education. These younger women bridged the worlds between their mothers' organizations and "evolving modern political associations" (Denzer 1997: 20). One such modern bridge was the Abeokuta Ladies Club, founded in 1944 and reestablished as the Abeokuta Women's Union in 1946 by Funmilayo Ransome-Kuti, the great-granddaughter of Yoruba slaves who were repatriated to Nigeria through Sierra Leone. She called the organization a "social welfare club for market women" (Mba 1992: 138) and dedicated her early years to teaching market women to read and write in what was the first adult education program for women in the country. In the process of teaching them skills, she learned about their struggles against taxation and African rulers then serving the interests of British colonialists. As a founding member of the National Council for Women Societies (NCWS), she brought together the common interests of Western-educated Nigerian women and market women. According to Nina Emma Mba, Ransome-Kuti thus gained credibility as a successful organizer of women and became an invaluable asset to the struggle for Nigeria's independence: She served as the only woman on the Nigerian delegation to the 1954 constitutional conference in London. E. Francis White tells us that Ransome-Kuti was an educated nationalist who identified more with market women than with the British elite (1999: 110–112). Her memoir in this volume suggests a similar conclusion (see p. 238).

Independence

Between the end of the 1950s and the end of the 1960s, most West African territories colonized by European countries became independent nations. Inspired by Ghana's example in 1957, many felt the intoxication of independence so strongly that so-called negative ideas were not to be heard. As the Ghanaian Efua T. Sutherland declares in her 1961 preface to *The Road*

Makers (see p. 219), "We shall build the land with our strength." A year later in her drama *Foriwa* (see p. 220), Sutherland's Queenmother questions the hegemony of empty cultural norms and urges self-examination and the inclusion of women in leadership positions to build the new African nation.

Still, there had been hopes beyond the creation of individually independent nation-states. A pan-African movement had for a decade envisioned and worked toward something more. In May 1963, African heads of state met in Addis Ababa to create the Organization of African Unity (OAU). In practice, the OAU fell short of launching the pan-African dream of a continental government and joint military command within and across the frontiers of existing states. Indeed, over time the OAU evolved into "an Assembly of African heads of state, many of whom were part of an anti-democratic trend in their own country" (Cooper 2004: 184). Needless to say, such leaders were not interested in extending rights and power to women.[23]

A document of the African Party for the Independence of Guinea and Cape Verde (PAIGC) written in the 1960s by women leaders in the midst of "fighting two colonialisms" expresses women's own vision of their role in independent Africa:

> By a liberated woman I mean a woman who has a clear consciousness about her responsibility in the society and who is economically independent. By a liberated woman I mean one who is able to do all the jobs in the society without being discriminated against, a woman who goes to school to learn, and can become a leader. While women are fighting for their freedom at present, a new system is evolving which is preparing the young people of the next generation. And this new system is trying to change their idea of liberty, their idea of freedom and their idea of coexistence between the elements of the family and within the society in general. (White 1999: 113)

While such goals may also reflect a long history of women's activism in West Africa and the Sahel, ironically, women who led the march on Grand Bassam were among those who in the 1960s found themselves on the margins of national political life. For example, the Women's Committee of the Democratic Party of Côte d'Ivoire (PDCI) had worked to organize non-elite and elite women throughout the nationalist movements for independence. Women worked within this organization because of their shared belief in the separation of male and female domains, but after independence, the Women's Committee lost much of its power as men took charge of the nation. Subsequently the Ivorian Women's Association (AFI) sought to create an apolitical women's organization to focus on social and cultural matters, specifically in women's domains. Many women resisted the attempt to limit their hard-won political influence in the nationalist movement, but they were eventually forced to comply with the leadership's iron-fisted paternalism (Dei 1997: 208–211).

The women's texts from this period are not uniformly exhilarating, since innumerable tensions in women's lives and in the national politics of what were mostly one-party states still needed to be resolved. For example, when Funmilayo Ransome-Kuti, whose active political career in the 1940s and 1950s helped realize Nigeria's independence, writes in 1961 a long essay about the status of women in Nigeria, she notes that, despite many gains, women are still considered inferior by Nigerian men. They suffer from divorce and rejection if they behave too independently. Her own ambivalence is apparent, moreover, when she also declares that women must be tolerant of men accustomed to being masters (Mba 1997: 137–140).

Constance Cummings-John, the mayor of Freetown in Sierra Leone, was one of the few women in the region to hold political office shortly after independence. Educated not only in Sierra Leone and Ghana but also in Britain and the United States, she was a pan-African thinker and activist. Her work as mayor focused chiefly on the education of the next generation. She developed youth centers and schools for all, including orphans. She functioned remarkably well in a "man's world," naming her sister-in-law the mayor's "wife," an obligatory complement to the mayoral position, and she mobilized many other women to head committees and to explore questions of tolerance in the city. But Cummings-John also learned that politics is a dangerous business. One of her own bodyguards later became the military head of state, a state that Cummings-John had to flee to protect her life.

Post-independence—the mid-1970s and the 1980s

By the mid-1970s, the high ideals of independence had begun to slip away under increasingly bad economic news, in part a result of the loss of national control over the falling prices of raw materials. Years of drought in the early 1970s, a crisis in the production of cash crops, and increasing national and personal debt drained the economies of West Africa and the Sahel.[24] Governments used corruption, political vote-buying, and restraints on freedom of expression to control civil society. Their promises evaded or forgotten, political leaders stood fixed in positions that no longer breathed the ideology of hope and opportunity for all. Several perspectives on the decline in personal and political morality are reflected through texts in this volume spoken or written by women to allay their personal suffering or to inform a whole nation in turmoil.

In "Nawa's Lament" (see p. 317), for example, we hear the voice of a young woman describing the tragic trajectory of her life in rural Côte d'Ivoire. She and her new husband leave her home to become migrant laborers in the cash economy in another part of the country. Beyond the reach of the social controls of their own community, the young husband sacrifices his wife's life for material wealth and a new partner. This true story turns the clock back for a woman who has no recourse beyond the clandestine recording of her travail, meant originally only to inform her family but made famous by public distribution.

While Ellen Johnson-Sirleaf seems to have little in common with Nawa—Johnson-Sirleaf is an educated woman, a Liberian politician, and a human rights activist—ultimately, like Nawa, she is powerless to do more than suffer and tell her story. Because of her honest reporting on the failures of the Liberian government in the 1960s, she had to be spirited away to the United States to protect her life. After her return and a decade of governmental service in the 1970s, she was removed from office in a coup and, later, in the 1980s, arrested and nearly executed for her political activities. Still a remarkably courageous opponent of undemocratic governance in Liberia, she continues to shudder "at the tremendous cost which we pay under righting the wrongs of the past" (see p. 326). Democracy, she adds, must *not* be a luxury in Africa.[25]

LATE TWENTIETH CENTURY: BAD NEWS AND GOOD NEWS

Women at a loss, still resisting . . .
Bravo to our ingenious grandmothers,
Who carded cotton into *jalam* and *deru,*
Wood and clay that made up distaff and ash.
They had no cash to use; they bartered,
Importing what they could not find,
Exporting what they had in abundance,
Trading, bartering, and doing all they wanted.

Adja Khady Diop's poem, written in 1998 (see p. 279), is part of the collection of African "oraliterature" (Wilentz 1992: 118) that aims at uncovering a positive African heritage, at reconstructing a history in which women played a glorious part. It bears testimony to the fact that the production of goods, crafts, and long-distance trading had been part of the economic life of West African women for centuries before the colonial era. Without money, women exchanged products that each specific region needed most: salt and textiles, for instance, for gold and kola nuts.

Economic equilibrium had also, then, been ensured in the microcosm of social and family life, through an ideology of communal support. In the hard times of drought or during the rich moments of harvest, a group spirit reinforced individual efforts, often through the performance of songs and tales that systematically condemned individualism. In the Senegalese tale "The Man Who Dug Up Yams" (see p. 335), a selfish husband who refuses to share his yams with his wife learns that lesson: "When it's a famine, you have to think about each other. If somebody goes out, everything he finds should be brought back and shared by all." Those were also the days when a husband's and wife's agricultural and industrial work ideally complemented one another. Among the Baule of Côte d'Ivoire, for instance, husbands used cotton thread produced by their wives to weave cloth. Among the Sehwi of Ghana husbands prepared their wives' lands for the cultivation of subsistence crops (Berger and White 1999: 103).

At the peak of the colonial era, however, family structures shifted, in part because of Christianity's protection of women against forced marriages (see, for example, "Nothing So Sweet," p. 189). Kinship ties were loosened as young women began to follow young men of their choice to places where their "Darlings" were engaging in waged labor. Nawa, the young Senufo woman whose song of lament was recorded by her brother (see "Nawa's Lament," p. 317), chose this "ambiguous adventure." The kin she had run away from could not protect her from her husband's determination to sacrifice her to his newly gained ambition in the contemporary era of competitive cotton and cloth production in Côte d'Ivoire. This autobiographical song and its like have been widely circulated (often without their authors' permission) because they help to break the taboo of ritual sacrifice, which continues to plague the West African region despite its legal abolition. Nawa recorded her song in 1986 to let her kin know about her sufferings in the cotton fields, "trapped among vultures, . . . trapped among snakes." She sang in total despair, lost in a world in which she had no bearings: "I am just trying to know how all this came about."

International organizations and women's conferences, including the major 1985 United Nations meeting in Nairobi and the 1995 one in Beijing, attended by West African writers, activists, and politicians, have openly condemned such practices as the forced marriages of girl-children, ritual murders, genital mutilation, and harsh widowhood rites. Many West African countries have signed various United Nations protocols and charters on human rights. They have also adopted laws that officially declare these practices illegal and punishable. Yet laws and good intentions have not, on their own, achieved cultural revolutions. Effective transformation of cultural norms and social practices is a long process, requiring uncompromising dedication to implementation by many people, including judges and lawyers, as well as community leaders of the church and family elders.

From the 1970s forward, Kate Abbam fought with her pen for the rights of women, including the rights of widows. In 1972, as editor of an important women's magazine, she wrote an editorial (see "We Shall Overcome," p. 229) denouncing the abusive treatment of Ghanaian widows, a cause important to her for twenty years and one of the remaining paradoxes of West African life. At her husband's death a year later, the militant writer experienced the very trauma she had battled against. She looked on, in some bewilderment, as her in-laws, including those of an "intellectual class" that had benefited from Western education, suddenly "turned around in a chameleon fashion and, hiding behind a mantle of *what they called 'tradition'* [rushed] to her house soon after her husband's death . . . to take inventory of his personal effects." She was particularly stunned when she saw that "the church sat and looked on with apathy." In 1994, when she was made Queenmother, the traditional leader of her community, she accepted an invitation from the Methodist conference (see "Christianity and Widowhood Rites," p. 230) to assert her opinion even more strongly than she had in print. She spoke publicly, as a formally named leader of women, about the need to revise "traditions." She appealed to the "conscience of the churches as well as the Law makers in Ghana," and she called on the women of Ghana to work for significant change.

Probably one should not be surprised that men in powerful positions have not been especially concerned about the rights of women. Such advances as women have made in education, for example, have usually served to threaten the patriarchy and to cause disturbances in the status quo (see Berger and White 1999: 104). Male Ewe intellectuals and politicians, including poet Kofi Awonoor, for example, were not pleased with an internationally supported campaign against the "Trokosi" institution, wherein girls and women are still being imprisoned within religious shrines. The campaign is attempting to break this practice of ritual atonement, which continues to plague certain parts of West Africa despite its legal abolition. Awonoor accused those leading the battle against "Trokosi" of inappropriate involvement in the internal and regional affairs of a nation.[26]

Female rebellions have sometimes led young girls to desperate life decisions. In the Cross River Basin of Nigeria, for example, prostitution as a means of survival increased in cities to which unmarried young women fled. As men and machines took over agricultural production, women also left rural areas to search for work. Uneducated, they could try various forms of petty trade, often learning from a successful market woman. From the account of her life that Afua Kobi, an Asante trader, gives to the American anthropologist Gracia Clark in 1994 (see "A Trader Caught in Ethnic Violence," p. 393), we catch a glimpse of the changing economic world of women traders. We see that new forms of competitive trading in single food crops depend on the accumulation of capital, and that without capital, one can only accumulate debt. We also see that major economic changes in the region affect political stability for the Gonja and the Dagomba living in areas where competition over land and water repeatedly turns into violent confrontation, including armed conflict between those who declare themselves the "owners of the land" and those who settled there centuries ago.

Throughout her simple, straightforward argument, Afua Kobi proves herself a lucid analyst of her time. She understands that, in the global marketplace, everything has become an instrument of political exploitation. Her images of the intimidation and actual molestation by soldiers and of the brutalities and false promises of electoral campaigns are characteristic of the era of West African post-independence military dictatorships. To return alive from her trip to the north of Ghana, Afua Kobi, now disillusioned and bed-ridden, had to cry and beg cold-blooded soldiers who were holding guns and threatening not only to steal her goods but even to kill her. "The money was all gone," she says, "It has all become a debt." And she concludes, "I will sit down for God himself to show me the way."

We have gathered specifically for this volume several kinds of oral texts, a few from successful Senegalese women whose families were supportive of their professional lives. Their stories are relatively optimistic and provide a counterweight to what Afua Kobi has endured. For example, Adja Dior Diop, who had no more than a grammar-school education, now holds a seat on the Economic and Social Council of Senegal and has organized a credit and loan system for female Senegalese entrepreneurs, which has allowed more than a hundred of them to develop small-scale businesses. We are privileged to fulfill the wishes of a non-literate Ghanaian Queenmother, Nana Adwoa Anokyewaa (see "Kapro, The Royal Gift," p. 417), who wanted to see that the history of her stool be recorded for posterity. To this end, she sought out a known and trusted scholar who was also a member of the Ghana committee of Women Writing Africa, and who, with permission, gave the text to us. The Queenmother's testimony bears witness to a superior memory, a profound sense of dignity and belonging, and a kinship system that has protected and nurtured her and allowed her to occupy the position of crucial responsibility that she holds in Asante culture as Queenmother of Kapro.

In a reported conversation between two midwives from Aoua Keïta's autobiography, we have caught a portrait of two Africas (see "Talking with Midwife Sokona Diaouné," p. 281) that both still exist today. Profoundly influenced by years of training in indigenous medical practice, Diaouné confidently discussed her methods and philosophies but could not bring herself to reveal all the "secrets" of her esoteric knowledge in conversation with her Westernized friend Aoua Keïta. Although she admires the modern midwife's ability to save mother and child in difficult childbearing situations and is open to new medical techniques, the Soninké *magnamagan*, who looks after birthing mothers and acts as young brides' initiator, only meets her Westernized counterpart half-way. She refuses to let her hear the "magic words" she pronounces during the future brides' ritual preparation, for "such words are only passed on from mother to daughter." She also continues to hold on to the idea of predestination, to explain cases of death among girls during the difficult period of the traditional Soninké preparation for marriage and the sacred act of procreation: "Naturally," she says, "there are girls who fall ill and are cured during the initiation period. Some die: everyone has her destiny. If it is written that a girl should go to God rather than to her marriage bed, then that's what happens." Something of this kind of thinking also permeates the resistance to revisiting female circumcision, still practiced in Mali, as in other parts of the region.

Literary texts

The first generation of educated elite West African women often became the leaders of women's associations and the educators of their less favored sisters. They served to connect senior representatives of various oral traditions with literate members of multicultural and multilingual nations inside of which shifting values have needed constant reexamination. Feminist writers, working in the interface between the oral and the written, often represented a past they were not simply restoring to memory but rather renegotiating into contemporary times. For literature, in Julia Kristeva's words, is necessarily a *futur antérieur*. It talks to us, backward and forward. West African women have developed various styles and used different genres to achieve their literary goals: the redefinition of their African selves and the awakening of a West African consciousness. Their literature, of course, carries them beyond the imaginary borders they had drawn for themselves.

When Bernadette Dao Senou, a Burkinabé writer who was born in Mali and later became the minister of education in Burkina Faso, addresses the topic of marital relations in Muslim homes (see "A Decent Woman," p. 373), her tone vibrates with sarcasm and the dialogue in her poem borders on the grotesque. The politician speaks through her literary skill, and one hears the poem as a diatribe played on a xylophone whose gourds resonate loudly with a woman's annoyance with husbands who persist in closing their ears to the new marriage "Code," which offers married women protection against abuses. "A Decent Woman" is a witty invitation to indecent behavior, an incitement to rebellion against all *kalifas*, or prototypical "husbands," who still expect their wives to "leave everything to [them] / to [them] alone / and wait / enraptured / for [them] to bring life / and the world to [their wives]!" The poem is a passionate call for action, particularly addressed to those who, like the poet, have learned the art of using their "paper and pen" and who cannot possibly "forget" what they learned in school.

In the past, women who felt they were being treated unfairly had their own ways of putting communal pressure on their disgraceful spouses. Written poetry is now partly substituting for orature aimed at mocking unacceptable behavior. We recall the performances of the proverbial Eyidi (see "*Eyidi*, or Naming," p. 340), found in Abe culture in Côte d'Ivoire, which allowed two friends to spread their complaints through the village: "I love the man" (offended party), "but the man does not love me" (her ally), thus forcing the offender's "hard ears" to open. The contemporary poet who redefines "masculinities" and writes from personal observation for an unknown and large readership may function on a different scale but in the same manner as the Songhai-Zarma *griotte* who makes use of parody that invites all men and women present to laugh—and possible to identify themselves—with the types caricatured (see "Types of Wives and Husbands," p. 344). While oral poets and singers sometimes still have a direct impact on the social and family lives of their own communities, the poet-writer, who reaches beyond her immediate surroundings, may be more "delocated" but may also reach a broader audience.

According to Susan Stanford Friedman, geographical migration is at the origin of "cultural grafting," and new "mappings" determine "cultural geographies of encounter" (Friedman 1998: 24). Or as James Clifford has put it, emerging feminisms develop in "travelling cultures," the title of his 1992 essay. Thus, a globe-trotter like Anna Dao, a writer of Malian ancestry, born in Paris, partly educated in Canada, and settled in the United States after a temporary stay in her homeland, reworks her grandmother's teaching on "ancestral traditions" into her own short stories. As Friedman puts it, "New patterns of relating across difference" can be analyzed in the literary works of women who, like Dao, were "born between two heritages" and today are "walking in two worlds" (67). Thus, African women living outside Africa continue to be inspired by their ancestors as well as their sisters on the continent, as they draw attention to difficult cultural issues.

Although her grandmother taught her that "nothing was really black or white" and that "each side had its 'rotten apples,'" Anna Dao's intense search for her West African roots leads her to invent a West African past *she* wants to remember as the place "where she came from." In "A Perfect Wife" (see p. 430), she indicates that she is paying tribute to her grandmother by creating two female characters, cowives in a polygamous household, each of whom carries some of her grandmother's qualities. Thus, they appear as the "perfect cowives," their "sisterly" attitudes conforming to models often praised in folktale orature. The ideal that Dao presents stands in strong contrast to customary polygamous households, in which women have to negotiate their own space and that of their children with their in-laws, while confronting possibly deadly jealousies of "rivals" (see, for example, "I Am Not a Cow," p. 357).

Anna Dao's short story contains still another layer of history, in an effort common to her generation of writers, for whom "reconstructing history has been involved with . . . a laying bare of the original material culture as well as a layering of emergent cultural traditions which oppose Eurocentric hegemony" (Wilentz 1992: 117). Her story allegorically portrays, in a flashback, the historical drama of the coerced enrollment of West African men into the French army during World War I. These soldiers' letters back home never told wives of "the daily horror that their lives had become." The truth, therefore, remained long hidden to their closest family. The writer's "duty to memory" drives an angry hand on the paper:

Condemned to endless hours of toil in the trenches, they spent days in the icy rainwater with swollen and chafed feet confined to boots designed just for them. . . . To escape flying bullets, they piled up dead bodies as barriers and hid behind them. There were so many bullet-ridden, mangled bodies.

Today, images of disaster appear frequently on television screens everywhere in the world, and the daily sight of bloodshed may no longer horrify those watching in comfort. Still, West African women writers continue to describe the impact of such national cataclysms as the Nigerian civil war or the Rwandan genocide on the lives of humans caught in the conflict. Two Ivorians, Tanella Boni and Véronique Tadjo, were part of a contingent of African writers who went to Rwanda and then wrote about what they saw. Tadjo describes the pain of a daughter (see "Regrets for Rwanda," p. 412), who has already lost her "destroyed and broken" imprisoned mother before the mother's actual death. "In this place," Tadjo writes "there are no mothers and no daughters," and the inescapable horror has abolished chronological time: "Consolata has already mourned the future." All remembrances of happiness have gone and there is no possibility for hope, wish, or dream while living in a present where the living do not even "exist."

One cannot help wondering whether the person who watches the evening news can imagine the tearing apart of a mother's heart when she is unable to stand in the way of her eleven-year-old son who is driven into "Child Soldiering" (see p. 441) by the rebel militia of their country. Only a poet such as Issatou Alwar Cham-Graham can imagine the words of regret such a child could write, on a dying bed, to his mother, when her "milk has spilled before it fermented, like the fig tree never to be fruitful."

As writers uncover a devastated world, and as women from many nations experience the similarities among literatures depicting rape—see, for example, Tadjo's "Anastasia and Anastasio" (p. 412)—writers in Africa are joining others interested in the "utopian dream of coalition and connection," described by Susan Stanford Friedman, who notes,

> As the globe shrinks, as racially and ethnically inflected confrontations increase worldwide, as weapons become even more deadly, and available, as transnational economies further polarize wealth and poverty . . . our survival as a species depends on our ability to recognize the borders between difference as fertile spaces of desire and fluid sites of syncretism, interaction, and mutual change. (1998: 66)

CONCLUSION

In Mariama Ndoye's short story "En Route to the Twenty-first Century" (see p. 445), we read of the broken promises of West African politicians in a text somewhat muted by humor. She depicts various slices of shattered lives without heroes, juxtaposed higgledy-piggledy with no logic, but expressive of various individual survival strategies necessary to cope daily. Beyond the broken promises, the wars and mutilations, the absurdity and horror of daily life, however, West African writers at the beginning of the twenty-first century may also offer visionary perspectives. Paradoxically, even if the myth of the year 2000 no longer holds its former significance—and has been replaced by failed policies—women remain the bearers of hope.

Ama Ata Aidoo's essay "Speaking as a Woman" offers a dynamic of defiance capable of restructuring relations between women and men, and thus reorganizing the political world. The texts of Ghanaian Aidoo, Côte d'Ivoire–based Cameroonian Werewere Liking, and Malian Aminata Traore all portray women coming to terms with their lives, their personal ambitions, and their aspirations for a continent that has both history and future. They have all had ample opportunities for international experiences, work, and relationships. The trajectory of their very different lives in search of personal and political development for themselves and a far wider community than sometimes even their nations has led them to several similar conclusions. As Aidoo makes clear, the first of these is that Africans must know their history, warts and all, if they are to move productively into the future.

Werewere Liking speaks for Africans who have moved several times to improve the conditions of their lives. A Cameroonian, she has founded and managed and continues to support a large theater group in Côte d'Ivoire, from whose productions Africa appears as a panorama of cultures and ethnic origins, joined by music, drums, dance, and ritual story. She works to educate her students and her audiences about the richness of African cultural traditions, and she seeks the possibility of making professional artists central to the refashioning of an African identity.

Aminata Traore spent the early years of her life working to transform cotton into beautiful fabric, and then she worked further to organize the manufacture and distribution of well-designed cloth. This work experience, common to many girls and women in West Africa, formed for Traore the basis of a view of economic development that sees Africa as resource-rich and full of untapped creativity. The experience also allowed her to organize a thriving business, on the basis of whose success she insists that "Africa is not poor" and offers direction for development:

> It is time for us to make a go of ourselves and to claim our right to make our own mistakes. Africa is not poor; it has been impoverished. As such, and despite enormous difficulties people have been confronted with, there is an enormous potential for hope, a will to live

which is absolutely resistant to all odds. And that is why I believe in the power of culture. I believe that culture has the power to generate transformation from within, to negotiate, to renegotiate our destiny as African people. Nobody can teach us what we should aspire to become in the twenty-first century, in the third millennium.

Ama Ata Aidoo's analysis of the history of African women brings her to a similar conclusion: "It is high time African women moved onto center stage, with or without anyone's encouragement. Because in our hands lies, perhaps, the last possible hope for ourselves, and for everyone else on this continent."

Tuzyline Jita Allan
Diedre L. Badejo
Abena P. A. Busia
Aminata Diaw
Christiane Owusu-Sarpong
Esi Sutherland-Addy

ENDNOTES

1. Historical and sociological perspectives on women in West Africa and the Sahel appear in collections of edited books on African women. See *Women and Work in Africa*, ed. Edna G. Bay (Boulder: Westview, 1982); *Women in Africa: Studies in Social and Economic Change*, eds. Nancy J. Hafkin and Edna Bay (Stanford: Stanford University Press, 1976); *African Women and the Law: Historical Perspectives*, eds. Margaret Jean Hay and Marcia Wright (Boston: Boston University, African Studies Center, 1982); *Women and the State in Africa*, eds. Jane L. Parpart and Kathleen A. Staudt (Boulder: Lynne Reiner, 1989); *Widows in African Societies: Choices and Constraints*, ed. Betty Potash (Stanford: Stanford University Press, 1986); *Women and Class in Africa*, eds. Claire C. Robertson and Iris Berger (New York: Holmes and Meier, 1986); *Women and Slavery in Africa*, eds. Claire C. Robertson and Martin Klein (Madison: University of Wisconsin Press, 1983); and *Patriarchy and Class: African Women in the Home and the Workforce*, eds. Sharon B. Stichter and Jane L. Parpart (Boulder: Westview, 1988). More recent works include *Women in African Colonial Histories*, eds. Jean Allman, Susan Geiger, and Nakanyike Musisi (Bloomington: Indiana University Press, 2002); *"Wicked" Women and the Reconfiguration of Gender in Africa*, eds. Dorothy L. Hodgson and Sheryl A. McCurdy (Portsmouth: Heinemann, 2001); *Engendering African Social Sciences*, eds. Ayesha Imam, Amina Mama, and Fatou Sow (Dakar: CODESRIA, 1997); *Gender in African Prehistory*, ed. Susan Kent (Walnut Creek: AltaMira Press, 1998); and *African Words, African Voices: Critical Perspectives in Oral History*, eds. Luise White, Stephan F. Miescher, and David William Cohen (Bloomington: Indiana University Press, 2001). For a focus on women in Western Africa, see, for example, Ifi Amadiume, *Male Daughters, Female Husbands: Gender, Sex in an African Society* (London: Zed Books, 1987); Diedre Badejo, *Osun Seegesi: The Elegant Diety of Wealth, Power and Femininity* (Trenton: Africa World Press, 1996); Karin Barber, *I Could Speak until Tomorrow:*

Oriki, Women and the Past in a Yoruba Town (Edinburgh: Edinburgh University Press, 1991); Gracia Clark, *Onions Are My Husband: Survival and Accumulation by West African Market Women* (Chicago: University of Chicago Press, 1994); Nina Emma Mba, *Nigerian Women Mobilized: Women's Political Activity in Southern Nigeria, 1900–1965* (Berkeley: University of California, Institute of International Studies, 1982); *Female and Male in West Africa,* ed. Christine Oppong (London: Allen and Unwin, 1983); Audrey Smedley, *Women Creating Patriliny: Gender and Environment in West Africa* (Walnut Creek: AltaMira Press, 2004); and E. Frances White, Sierra Leone's *Settler Women Traders: Women on the Afro-European Frontier* (Ann Arbor: University of Michigan Press, 1987).

2. Sylvain Meinrad Xavier de Golbéry describes storytelling as a form of domestic entertainment among big (adult) "children": "C'est là (dans la grande case de réunion) que se réunissent des coteries de nègres qui y passent des journées entières à fumer, à jouer, mais surtout à causer, et à faire des contes et des histoires. . . . Car les contes les plus absurdes, les histoires les plus mensongères sont le souverain délice et le plus grand amusement de ces hommes, qui parviennent à la vieillesse sans être sortis de l'enfance" (*Fragments d'un voyage en Afrique,* 1802, quoted by Marcelle Colardelle-Diarassouba, *Le Lièvre et l'Araignée dans les contes de l'ouest Africain,* UGE-10/18, Paris, 1978, p. 347).

3. *Griotte* is an approximation and a modern, "invented" term used to describe female oral performers. We have used it frequently in this volume, but each culture has a specific name and place for its oral artists.

4. "Earth priests," such as the Tallensi *tendaana,* are men recently recognized as having been keepers of history in chiefless—or "acephalous"—societies once considered to have no history.

5. We can also read this ritual of inversion as potentially reinforcing gender roles, as the rituals could only occur in bounded contexts. Breaking verbal taboos certainly has a cathartic effect.

6. Most African tales that feature human characters have few prominent female characters. The stock secondary female characters are a study in notoriety, including the jealous cowife, the wicked stepmother, the unfaithful wife, the unreasonable wife, the spoiled sister, and the wife/woman who cannot keep a secret. Other female characters provide the protagonist with a "typical" family, such as the long-suffering wife (e.g., Okonore, the wife of Ananse, the Akan trickster-spider).

7. In Dogon mythology, a human being (male or female) is represented as having been born ambivalent—both male and female—before circumcision. Thus, the act of cutting the sexual part of the flesh was conceived as a necessary transformation of the young person's body into that of a perfect young man deprived of femininity or that of a perfect young woman deprived of masculinity. Many tales warned rebellious adolescents that refusing to accept the custom would lead to the impossibility of marriage—a totally unacceptable consequence, since, until very recently, people could not imagine living unmarried.

8. Pounding is usually done within homesteads by members of the family, but there are occasions on which it may be done in the larger community. The most striking of these are extended sessions held to pound grain for a woman with a newly born child, particularly the first-born. Not only will individuals volunteer to do the pounding for the new mother, but others will also bring their mortars, pestles, and grain either to the compound where she lives or to the village square. The

air will fill with rhythmic pounding and singing. Nor is such activity confined to rural areas. In cities and towns such as Dakar, Senegal, or Niamey, Niger, this form of pounding may occupy a whole street taken over for the purpose. Such pounding sessions may include as many as thirty women singing to the rhythm of pounding, orature that has been developed into a distinct genre with subgenres.

9. We are most grateful to Ivor Wilks for alerting us to this "note." It comes from the British National Archives, Kew, CO 879/52, African West 549. In January 1898, C. H. Armitage, who was then the assistant inspector from the Gold Coast constabulary in Dagomba and Salaga, wrote, "Many slaves are brought down yearly by the Moshis [sic] and are sold to the Gonja people, who put them on their farms. They are kindly treated and more like members of the family than slaves to it. The female slave, as a rule, either marries her master or becomes his concubine. The price paid for a slave is from £2 to £4."

10. We are very grateful to John Hunwick for having allowed us to read his essay "Islam and Slavery in Africa," which will constitute a chapter in a forthcoming four-volume history of slavery from the fifteenth to the early nineteenth century, to be published by Cambridge University Press under the title *Slavery in the World*. This is the opening of Daumas's description of a Tuareg caravan: "In a superior nomadic tent, the inside work is confined to Negro slaves who are cheap and numerous. The Négresses fetch water and wood and prepare meals."

11. The poem by Nana Asma'u has not been quoted in relationship to the transatlantic slave trade. It serves, rather, as a testimony to the forms of slavery practiced in Muslim West and Sahelian Africa, begun before the transatlantic slave trade.

12. Extracts from "La Reine Pokou fondatrice du Royaume Baoulé," Globe Access Internet: *La Côte d'Ivoire Profonde*, based on archives consigned in the *Mémorial de la Côte d'Ivoire* (http://www.globeaccess.net/globe3/ciarch16.htm). Our translation.

13. In most indigenous West African cultural views, femininity is seen as powerful and, likewise, power exercised by women is seen as feminine. Consequently, powerful women dress in the most feminine style they can muster. They also share more than "credit" for male empowerment. Through ritual and organization, indigenous women demonstrate an inherent power that most men revere, albeit often in silence or through ritual expression.

14. Jacqueline Sorel, "Femmes de l'ombre: Tinubu, la dominante du marché d'Abeokuta" (http://www.rfi.fr/fichiers/MFI/CultureSociete/646.asp), a story retold on the basis of Ibrahima Baba Kaké, *Journal de l'Afrique* ([Paris?]: Editions AMI, 1989), vol. 2. In the same series of radio programs, Jacqueline Sorel introduced listeners to a Mossi amazon who is remembered as the ancestor of the Mossi people who arrived in the region of Wagadugu somewhere between the eleventh and the fifteenth century. Hers is the story of Yennaga who used to follow her father, Naba Nedega, the chief of Gambaga (in Dagomba), on his warlike expeditions. When she was of age to marry, she ran away on her horse and married a hunter named Ralié, who became her host in the forest. Her son Ouedraogo, according to tradition, was to become the founder of the Mossi state in the Boussansés region of today's Burkina Faso. Louis Tauxier told the story in *Le noir de Yatenga* (Paris: Larose, 1917).

15. Samuel Ajayi Crowther officiated at the wedding of Sarah Forbes Bonetta and James Davies, both of whom, like him, were graduates of the first Christian

mission schools. Crowther set up the Niger mission, that of Badagry and Abeokuta, and published many works, including the first written grammar of the Yoruba language and the first Nupe grammar. The first West African Catholic bishop, Joseph Faye in Senegal, was appointed in 1939.

16. The Marriage Ordinance, first passed in the Gold Coast in 1884 and revised in 1951, required marriage licenses and the registration of marriages.

17. This text was contributed by Tuzyline Jita Allan; it forms part of her ongoing archival research at the British Library.

18. Whether we are talking about the founder of "Présence Africaine," Alioune Diop, or Léopold Sédar Senghor, or Kwame Nkrumah, their nationalism was in large measure formed by their experiences of the West. The arrival in Paris of young African students or Members of Parliament, the creation of the FEANF or the West African Students' Union—all opened up perspectives for nationalist discourse. These emerging African nationalists were galvanized by the influence of leaders of African descent, including Marcus Garvey, W. E. B. DuBois, and George Padmore. The fifth pan-African Congress in Manchester, England, organized by DuBois, Nkrumah, and Padmore, was a defining moment in the struggle against colonialism, calling for immediate independence.

19. For a true picture, however, we must look beyond the colonial prism. The state of Sokoto in Nigeria, for instance, a product of Fulani Holy War (*jihad*) in the nineteenth century, was the site of a highly developed literary society based on the Arabic culture of letters. Here, women were not generally excluded from intellectual discourse or Islamic study. The Fulani Jihadist leader Ousmane Dan Fodio's daughter, Nana Asma'u Bint, his mother, Hawa, and his grandmother, Rukiyya, were all teachers and recognized women of letters. In the context of making Islamic teaching accessible in order to promote religion, Nana Asma'u Bint wrote religious poetry in the Fulfulde language. Another Islamic scholar living thousands of kilometers away and in the modern era, Mariame Niasse, who was interviewed in Senegal for this volume, speaks of the greatness of Nana Asma'u Bint and her immense contributions to literature, scholarship, and evangelicalism in the expansive Islamic universe of the subregion.

20. As the original Akan Queenmothers functioned in significant sociopolitical ways, so in recent times market women in Ghana have organized themselves in similar fashion. They have now given themselves "market queens," who defend their rights, set rules, organize fair trade, and so on. See Gracia Clark, *Onions Are My Husband: Survival and Accumulation by West African Market Women* (Chicago: University of Chicago Press, 1994).

21. The impact of the march of the women on Bassam and especially the mobilization that made it possible are particularly significant because these women, educated or uneducated, wives of politicians or not, came from different social and ethnic groups, even from different countries. The account of Anne-Marie Raggi, who, despite her old age when recalling the march, seems to have kept intact the sequence of the events, restores the place and initiative of women in an anticolonial struggle usually attributed by historians to men—Léopold Sédar Senghor, Sékou Touré, Kwame Nkrumah, and Félix Houphouët-Boigny, for example. *La March des Femmes sur Grand-Bassam* (The March of Women on Grand-Bassam) by Ivorian historian Henriette Diabaté makes an exceptional contribution to the history of nationalism in the subregion.

22. It is appropriate here to recall the differences between the *indirect rule* of British colonialism and the *direct rule* of the French. If men like Senghor, Lamine Gueye, or Houphouët-Boigny could accede to positions of power in French political parties and parliament with the support of French socialists and communists, such was not the case in the British-ruled colonies, where they made greater use of the press to communicate their ideas. The African women in the French-speaking territories articulated a different anticolonial voice. The narratives of the lives of Anne-Marie Raggi, from Côte d'Ivoire (p. 205), and Lucie Traoré Kaboré, of Burkina Faso (p. 207), and journal articles in the *Accra Evening News* by Adjua Mensah ("The Blackman's Burden," p. 209) and Akosuah Dzatsui ("I Have Tamed My Wife," p. 210) illustrate different modes of African nationalist expression in colonial contexts.

23. A Constitutional Act that went into effect on 11 July 2000 formally replaced the OAU with the African Union (AU) and provided it with instruments intended to strengthen the organization politically and economically, including specific provisions for the protection of the rights of women and children.

24. As a solution to the near collapse of many states in the subregion, international institutions like the International Monetary Fund (IMF) and the World Bank have been trying for years to apply various structural adjustment programs (SAPs), all of which take the form of huge budget cuts for social services such as education and health care and bring in their wake increased impoverishment, especially of women and children. Generally, these crises and the proposed solution, the SAPs, have made the lives of women and children more and more insecure.

25. The field of liberalization is widening with the growing number of political parties and seems to be turning away from the Liberian realities of the decade described by Ellen Johnson-Sirleaf. These gains are delicate and could easily be reversed. New wars undermining the stability of Liberia, Sierra Leone, and Côte d'Ivoire, for example, could escalate, leaving in their wake forced exile and thousands of refugees—who would then flee to Guinea, for example. These wars and conflicts are a reminder that, at the beginning of the twenty-first century, Africa's mineral wealth is once again whetting strong appetites, and the continent is once again subject to a potentially injurious process of globalization.

26. Trokosi, which means "wife of the gods" in Ewe, is a practice found among the southern Ewe and part of the Dangme people of Ghana. According to custom, if someone commits a serious crime or social infraction, traditional leaders order that a young girl from that family be sent to the shrine as a form of atonement. She is expected to serve the priest for three to five years, after which the family may redeem her. This injunction, claimed by its adherents as a mechanism for social order, in reality results in lifelong servitude to the male priest, whose status is enhanced by the productive and reproductive labor of the bonded women (Ameh 1998).

WORKS CITED AND SELECTED BIBLIOGRAPHY

Abubakr, Rashidah Ismali. 2001. "West African Women in Exile: City, University and Dislocated Village." *Jenda: A Journal of Cultures and African Women Studies* 1. www.jendajournal.com/jenda/voll.1/abubakr.html.

Abubakr, Sa'ad. 1992. "Queen Amina of Zaria," in Bólánlé Awé, ed. *Nigerian Women in Perspective*. Lagos: Sankore/Bookcraft. 11–25.

Ade Ajayi, J. F., ed. 1996. *L'Afrique du XIXe siècle jusque vers les années 1880*, vol. 6, *Histoire générale de l'Afrique*. Paris: Editions UNESCO-NEA.

Ade Ajayi, J. F., and Michael Crowder, eds. 1973. *History of West Africa*, vol. 2. New York: Columbia University Press.

———. 1988. "La Traite négrière atlantique jusqu'à 1810," in *Atlas Historique de l'Afrique*. Paris: Editions de Jaguar.

Afigbo, A. E. 1985. "The Social Repercussions of Colonial Rule: The New Social Structures," in A. Adu Boahen, ed. UNESCO *General History of Africa*, vol. 7. Paris: UNESCO/NEA. 487–507.

Agawu, Kofi. 2001. "African Music as Text." *Research in African Literatures* 32(2): 3–16.

Agovi, Kofi. 1995. "A King Is Not Above Insult: The Politics of Good Governance in Nzema Avudwene Festival Songs," in Graham Furniss and Liz Gunner, eds. *Power, Marginality and African Oral Literature*. Cambridge: Cambridge University Press. 47–64.

Ahmad, S. B. 2002. *Narrators, Interpreter Stability, and Variation in Hausa Tales*. Ibadan: Spectrum Books Limited.

Ajayi, S. Omofolabo. 1998. *Yoruba Dance. The Semiotics of Movement and Body Attitude in a Nigerian Culture*. Trenton: Africa World Press.

Alldridge, T. J. 1901. *The Sherbu and Its Hinterland*. London: Macmillan.

Allman, Jean. 1996. "Adultery and the State in Asante: Reflections on Gender, Class and Power from 1800 to 1950," in John Hunwick and Nancy Lawler, eds. *The Cloth of Many Colored Silks: Papers on History and Society, Ghanaian and Islamic, in Honor of Ivor Wilks*. Evanston: Northwestern University Press. 27–65.

Allman, Jean, and Victoria Tashjian. 2000. *I Will Not Eat Stone: A Women's History of Colonial Asante*. Portsmouth: Heinemann.

Amadiume, Ifi. 1987. *Male Daughters, Female Husbands: Gender and Sex in an African Society*. London: Zed Books.

———. 1997. *Reinventing Africa: Matriarchy, Religion and Culture*. London: Zed Books.

Ameh, Robert Kwame. 1998. "Trokosi (Child Slavery) in Ghana: A Policy Approach." *Ghana Studies* 1: 35–62.

Anyidoho, Kofi, and James Gibbs. 2000. *Fontomfrom: Contemporary Ghanaian Literature, Theatre and Film*. Amsterdam: Rodopi.

Arhin, Brempong. 2000. "The Role of Nana Yaa Asantewaa in the 1900 Asante War of Resistance." *Le Griot* 8: 49–68.

Arndt, Susan. 2002. *The Dynamics of African Feminism: Defining and Classifying African-Feminist Literatures*. Translated by Isabel Cole. Trenton: Africa World Press.

Austen, Ralph A., ed. 1999. *In Search of Sunjata. The Mande Oral Epic as History, Literature and Performance*. Bloomington: Indiana University Press.

Avorgbedor, Daniel K. 2001. "'It's a Great Song!' Halò Performance as Literary Production." *Research in African Literatures* 32(2): 16–43.

Awé, Bólánlé, ed. 1992. Nigerian Women in Historical Perpective. Lagos: Sankore.

Azuonye, Chukwuna. 1995. "Igbo Ewe Ewe: Monarchical Power Versus Democratic Values in Igbo Oral Narratives," in Graham Furniss and Liz Gunner, eds. *Power, Marginality and African Oral Literature*. Cambridge: Cambridge University Press. 65–82.

Ba Konaré, Adame. 1993. *Dictionnaire des femmes célèbres du Mali.* Bamako: Editions Jamana.

Badejo, Diedre L. 1989. "The Goddess Òsun as a Paradigm for African Feminist Criticism." *Sage* 6(1): 27–39.

———. 1996. *Òsun Sèègèsí: The Elegant Deity of Wealth, Power and Femininity.* Trenton: Africa World Press.

———. 1998a. "African Feminism: Mythical and Social Power in the Orature and Literature of Women of African Descent." *Research in African Literatures* 29(2): 94–111.

———. 1998b. "Icons of Yoruba and Akan Women's Spirituality and Social Autonomy." Unpublished public lecture, College of Wooster, Ohio.

———. 2001. "Authority and Discourse in Orin Odun Osun," in Joseph Murphy and Mei Mei Sanford, eds. *Osun Across the Waters.* Bloomington: Indiana University Press. 128–141.

Bakhtin, Mikhaïl. 1981. *The Dialogic Imagination.* Translated and edited by Mikhael Holquist. Austin: University of Texas.

———. 1986. *Speech Genres and Other Essays.* Translated by Van W. Megee. Austin: University of Texas Press.

Bame, Kwabena N. 1991. *Profiles in African Traditional Popular Culture: Consensus and Conflict.* New York: Clear Type Press.

Barnes, Sandra T. 1997. "Gender and the Politics of Support and Protection in Precolonial West Africa," in Flora Edouwaye S. Kaplan, ed. *Queens, Queen Mothers, Priestesses, and Power: Case Studies in African Gender.* New York: Annals of the New York Academy of Sciences. 1–18.

Battestini, Simon. 2000. *African Writing and Text.* Translated by Henri G. J. Evans. Ottawa: Legas.

Bay, Edna G. 1997. "Servitude and Worldly Success in the Palace of Dahomey" in Claire C. Robertson and Martin Klein, eds. *Women and Slavery in Africa.* Portsmouth: Heinemann. 240–368.

Bayili, Emmanuel. 1989. "Les accès à l'histoire dans une société sans état: les Lela-Gurunsi (Burkina Faso)," in Claude Hélène Perrot, ed. *Sources Orales de l'Histoire de l'Afrique.* Paris: CNRS. 19–28.

Belcher, Stephen. 1999. "Sinimogo, 'Man for Tomorrow': Sunjata on the Fringes of the Mande World," in Ralph A. Austen, ed. *In Search of Sunjata. The Mande Oral Epic as History, Literature and Performance.* Bloomington: Indiana University Press. 89–110.

Benton-Rushing, Andrea. 1979. "Comparative Study of the Idea of Mother in Contemporary African and African American Poetry." *Colby Library Quarterly* (Autumn).

Berger, Iris, and E. Frances White, eds. 1999. *Women in Sub-Saharan Africa: Restoring Women to History.* Bloomington: Indiana University Press.

Berrian, Brenda, and Art Broek. 1985. *Bibliography of African Women Writers and Journalists: Ancient Egypt–1984.* Washington, D.C.: Three Continents Press.

Boahen, Adu A., Emmanuel Akyeampong, Nancy Lawler, Thomas C. McCaskie, and Ivor Wilks, eds. 2003. *"The History of Ashanti Kings and the Whole Country Itself" and Other Writings by Otomfuo, Nana Agyeman Prempeh.* Oxford: Oxford University Press.

Bobo, Jacqueline. 1995. *Black Women as Cultural Readers.* New York: Columbia University Press.

Borgomano, Madeleine. 1989. *Voix et visages des femmes dans les livres écrits par les femmes en Afrique francophone.* Abidjan: CEDA.

Boston, J. S. 1968. *The Igala Kingdom.* Ibadan: Nigerian Institute of Social and Economic Research.

Boyce Davies, Carole, and Anne Adams Graves. 1986. *Ngambika: Studies of Women in African Literature.* Trenton: Africa World Press.

Brown, Carolyn A. 2003. "Memory as Resistance: Identity and the Contested History of Slavery in Southeastern Nigeria, an Oral History Project," in Sylviane A. Diouf, ed. *Fighting the Slave Trade: West African Strategies.* Athens: Ohio State University Press. 219–226.

Bruner, Charlotte H. 1994. *Unwinding Threads: Writing by Women in Africa.* London: Heinemann.

Brydon, Lynne, and Karen Legge. 1995. "Gender and Adjustment: Pictures from Ghana," in Gloria T. Emeagwali, ed. *Women Pay the Price: Structural Adjustment in Africa and the Caribbean.* Trenton: Africa World Press. 63–86.

Burton, Annie L. 1909. *Memories of Childhood's Slavery Days.* Boston: Ross Publishing.

Bush, Barbara. 1990. *Slave Women in Caribbean Society, 1650–1839.* London: James Currey.

Busia, Kofi A. 1951. *The Position of the Chief in the Modern Political System of Ashanti: A Study of the Influence of Contemporary Social Changes on Ashanti Political Institutions.* London: Frank Cass.

Caillé, René. 1979. *Voyage à Tombouctou.* Paris: Maspero. Reprint of *Journal d'un voyage à Tombouctou et à Jenné, dans l'Afrique centrale, précédé d'observations faites chez les Maures Braknas, les Nalous et autres peuples: pendant les années 1824, 1825, 1826, 1827, 1828.* 1830. Paris: Imprimerie Royale.

Calame-Griaule, Geneviève. 1965, rpt. 1987. *Ethnologie et Langage: La Parole chez les Dogons.* Paris: Gallimard.

———. 1970. "Pour une étude ethnolinguistique des littératures orales africaines." Languages 18: 21–47.

———, ed. 1993. "Le Pouvoir de la femme." *Cahiers de Littérature Orale* (34): 7–17.

———. 2002. *Contes tendres, contes cruels du Sahel nigérien.* Paris: Gallimard.

Calame-Griaule, Geneviève, and Praline Gay-Para. 2002. *La Parole du monde: Parole, mythologies et contes en pays Dogon, Entretiens.* Paris: Mercure de France.

Camara, Seydou. 1999. "The Epic of Sunjata: Structure, Preservation and Transmission," in Ralph A. Austen, ed. *In Search of Sunjata: The Mande Oral Epic as History, Literature and Performance.* Bloomington: Indiana University Press. 59–68.

Cazenave, Odile. 1996. *Femmes Rebelles: Naissance d'un nouveau roman africain au féminin.* Paris: L'Harmattan.

Charry, Eric. 2000. *Mande Music: Traditional and Modern Music of the Mininka and Mandinka of Western Africa.* Chicago: University of Chicago Press.

Chevrier, Jacques. 1984, rpt. 1999. *La littérature nègre.* Paris: Armand Colin.

———. 1986. *L'arbre à palabres: Essai sur les contes et récits traditionnels d'Afrique noire.* Paris: Hatier.

———. 2004. "Tombouctou, la cité mystérieuse: du mythe à l'utopie." *Notre Librarie, Revue des Littératures du Sud* 153: 72–77.

Chrétien, Jean-Pierre, and Jean-Louis Triand, eds. 1999. *Histoire d'Afrique: Les enjeux de mémoire*. Paris: Karthala.

Christaller, Rev. J. G. 1881, rpt. 1933. *Dictionary of Asante and the Fante Language Called Tshi (Twi)*. Basel: Basel Evangelical Missionary Society.

Clark, Gracia. 1994. *Onions Are My Husband: Survival and Accumulation by West African Market Women*. Chicago: University of Chicago Press.

Clifford, James. 1992. "Travelling Cultures," in Lawrence Grossberg, Nelson Cary, and Paula A. Treichler, eds. *Cultural Studies*. London: Routledge. 96–116.

Conrad, David C. 1999. "Mooning Armies and Mothering Heroes: Female Power in the Mande Epic Tradition," in Ralph A. Austen, ed. *In Search of Sunjata. The Mande Oral Epic as History, Literature and Performance*. Bloomington: Indiana University Press. 189–230.

Cooper, Frederick. 2002. *Africa since 1940: The Past of the Present*. Cambridge: Cambridge University Press.

Cooper, Frederick, and Ann Laura Stoler. 1997. *Tensions of Empire: Colonial Cultures in a Bourgeois World*. Berkeley: University of California Press.

Coquery-Vidrovitch, Catherine. 1994. *Les Africaines: Histoire des femmes d'Afrique Noire du XIXe au XXe siècles*. Paris: Desjonquières.

———. 1965, rpt. 2003. *La Découverte de L'Afrique: L'Afrique Noire Atlantique des origines au XVIIIe siècle*. Paris: L'Harmattan.

Coussy, Denise, ed. 2000. *Notre Librairie: Revue des Littératures du sud: Littératures du Nigeria et du Ghana*, vol. 14. Paris: CLEF.

Cromwell, Adelaide M. 1986. *An African Victorian Feminist: The Life and Times of Adelaide Smith Casely Hayford, 1896–1960*. London: Frank Cass.

Cuoq, Joseph M. 1975. *Recueil des sources arabes concernant l'Afrique Occidentale du VIIIe au XVIe siècle-(Bilal-al Sudan)*. Paris: Editions du CNRS.

D'Almeida, Irène Assiba. 1994. *Francophone African Women Writers: Destroying the Emptiness of Silence*. Gainesville: University Press of Florida.

Daniel, Yvonne. 2001. "Embodied Knowledge in African American Dance Performance," in Sheila S. Walker, ed. *African Roots / American Cultures: Africa in the Creation of the Americas*. Lanham, Md.: Rowman Littlefield.

Daumas, Eugène (Général). 1857. *Le Grand Désert: Itinéraire d'une caravane du Sahara au pays des nègres (Royaume de Haoussa)*, 4th ed. Paris: Michel Lévy Frères.

Davidson, Basil. 1998. *West Africa before the Colonial Era: A History to 1850*. New York: Longman.

Dei, Carlene H. 1997. "Women and Grassroots Politics in Abidjan, Côte d'Ivoire," in Gwendolyn Mikell, ed. *African Feminism: The Politics of Survival in Sub-Saharan Africa*. Philadelphia: University of Pennsylvania Press. 206–231.

Denzer, LaRay. 1997. *The Iyalode in Ibadan Politics and Society, c. 1850–1997*. Ibadan: Humanities Research Centre.

Derive, Jean. 1975. *Collection et traduction des littératures orales*. Paris: SELAF.

———. 1995. "The Function of Oral Art in the Regulation of Social Power in Dyula Society," in Graham Furniss and Liz Gunner, eds. *Power, Marginality and African Oral Literature*. Cambridge: Cambridge University Press. 122–129.

———. 1999. "De L'héroïque au lyrique: La poésie orale africaine." Notre Librairie, Revue des Littératures du Sud 137: 12–25.

Diabaté, Henriette. 1975. *La Marche des femmes sur Grand-Bassam*. Abidjan: Nouvelles Editions Africaines.

Diawara, Mamadou. 1999. "Searching for the Historical Ancestor: The Paradigm of Sunjata in Oral Traditions of the Sahel (13th–19th Century)," in Ralph A. Austen, ed. *In Search of Sunjata: The Mande Oral Epic as History, Litterature and Performance*. Bloomington: Indiana University Press. 111–140.

Dieterlen, G., and S. Diarra. 1992. *L'Empire de Ghana: Le Wagadou et les traditions Yerere*. Paris: Karthala / Association ARSAN.

Diop, Majhemout, et al. 1993. "Tropical and Equatorial Africa under French, Portuguese and Spanish Domination, 1935–1945," in Ali A. Mazrui, ed. UNESCO *General History of Africa*, vol. 8. Paris: UNESCO. Ch. 3.

Dolphyne, Florence Abena. 1991. *The Emancipation of Women: An African Perspective*. Accra: Ghana Universities Press, pp. 132–168.

Dowuona-Hammond, Christine. 1998. "Women and Inheritance in Ghana," in Akua Kuenyehia, ed. *Women in Law in West Africa: Situational Analysis of Some Key Issues Affecting Women*. Legon: Human Rights Study Centre, Faculty of Law, University of Ghana.

Dupuis, J. 1824, rpt. 1966. *Journal of a Residence in Ashantee*. London: Frank Cass.

Durán, Lucy. 1995. "Jelimusow: The Superwoman of Malian Music" in Graham Furniss and Liz Gunner, eds. *Power, Marginality and African Oral Literature*. Cambridge: Cambridge University Press. 197–207.

Edgerton, Robert B. 1995. *The Fall of the Asante Empire. The Hundred Years War for Africa's Gold Coast*. New York: Free Press.

El Fasi, Mohammed, and Ivan Hrbek. 1990. "Etapes du développement de l'Islam et sa diffusion en Afrique" in Mohammed El Fasi and Ivan Hrbek, eds. *Histoire générale de l'Afrique Vol. III: L'Afrique du VIIe au XIe siècles*. Paris: UNESCO / NEA. 81–116.

Euba, Akin. 1990. *Yoruba Drumming: The Dundun Tradition*. Beyreuth: Eckhard Breitinger.

Falgayrettes-Leveau, Christiane, and Christiane Owusu-Sarpong, eds. 2003. *Ghana Yesterday and Today*. Paris: Editions Dapper.

Ferera, Lisette. 2000. *Women Build Africa*. Quebec: Musée de la Civilisation.

Finnegan, Ruth. 1970, rpt. 1976. *Oral Literature in Africa*. Oxford: Clarendon Press.

Friedman, Susan Stanford. 1998. *Mappings: Feminism and the Cultural Geographies of Encounter*. Princeton: Princeton University Press.

Furniss, Graham. 1996. *Poetry, Prose and Popular Culture in Hausa*. Edinburgh: Edinburgh University Press.

Furniss, Graham, and Liz Gunner, eds. 1995. *Power, Marginality and African Oral Literature*. Cambridge: Cambridge University Press.

Gadzekpo, Audrey. 2001. "Gender Discourses and Representational Practices in Gold Coast Newspapers." *Jenda: A Journal of Culture and African Women's Studies* 1(2) (http://www.jendajournal.com/jendavol1.2/gadzekpo.html).

Garrard, Timothy F. 2003. "Akan Metal Arts," in Christiane Falgayrettes-Leveau and Christiane Owusu-Sarpong, eds. *Ghana Yesterday and Today*. Paris: Editions Dapper. 151–184.

Görög-Karady, Veronika. 1994. *Le mariage dans les contes africains*. Paris: Karthala.

———. 1995. "Tales and Ideology: The Revolt of Sons in Bambara-Malinké Tales," in Graham Furniss and Liz Gunner, eds. *Power, Marginality and African Oral Literature*. Cambridge: Cambridge University Press. 83–91.

Görög-Karady, Veronika, and Gérard Meyer, eds. 1988. *Images féminines dans le conte.* Paris: CILF/EDICEF.

Gottlieb, Karla Lewis. 2000. *The Mother of Us All: A History of the Queen Nanny, Leader of the Windward Jamaican Maroons.* Trenton: Africa World Press.

Greene, Sandra. 1996. *Gender, Ethnicity and Social Change on the Upper Slave Coast: A History of the Anlo-Ewe.* Portsmouth: Heinemann.

Griaule, Marcel. 1966. *Dieu d'eau: Entretiens avec Ogotommêli.* Paris: Fayard.

Grosz-Ngate, Maria, and Omari H. Kokole. 1997. *Gendered Encounters: Challenging Cultural Boundaries and Social Hierarchies in Africa.* New York: Routledge.

Hagan, George P., and Irene Odotie, eds. 2000. *The King Has Gone to the Village: The Death and Burial of Otumfuo Opoku Ware II.* Accra: Ghana Universities Press.

Hale, Thomas A. 1999. *Griots and Griottes: Masters of Words and Music.* Bloomington: Indiana University Press.

Henige, David. 1974. *The Chronology of Oral Traditions: A Quest for a Chimera.* Oxford: Oxford University Press.

———. 1982. *Oral Historiography.* London: Longman.

Herskovitz, M. J. 1967. *Dahomey. An Ancient West African Kingdom.* Evanston: Northwestern University Press.

Hopkins, A. G. 1973. *An Economic History of West Africa.* London: Longman.

Hopkins, J. F. P., and Nehemia Levtzion. 1981. *Corpus of Early Arabic Sources for West African History.* Cambridge: Cambridge University Press.

Horton, Robin. 1976. "Stateless Societies in the History of West Africa" in J. F. Ade Ajayi and Michael Crowder, eds. *History of West Africa,* vol. 1. New York: Columbia University Press. 78–119.

Hunwick, John. 1985. "Notes on Slavery in the Songhay Empire," in John Ralph Willis, ed. *Slaves and Slavery in Muslim Africa.* London: Frank Cass. 16–32.

———. 1999. *Timbuktu and the Songhay Empire.* Leiden: Brill.

———. [forthcoming]. "Islam and Slavery in Africa," in *Slavery in the World.* Cambridge University Press.

Hymes, Dell. 1962. "The Ethnography of Speaking," in Thomas Gladwin and William C. Sturtevant, eds. *Anthropology and Human Behavior.* Washington, D.C.: Anthropological Society of Washington. 15–53.

———. 1964. "Introduction: Towards Ethnographies of Communication," in John J. Gumperz and Dell Hymes, eds. *The Ethnography of Communication.* Washington, D.C.: American Anthropological Association. 1–34.

Ifemesia, C. C. 1965. "The Peoples of West Africa around AD 1000," in J. F. Ade Ajayi and Ian Epsie, eds. *A Thousand Years of West African History.* Ibadan: Ibadan University Press. 39–54.

Inikori, Joseph E. 1996. "Slavery in Africa and the Transatlantic Slave Trade," in Joseph E. Harris, ed. *The African Diaspora.* Arlington: University of Texas Press. 39–72.

———. 2001. "Slaves or Serfs: A Comparison between Slaves and Serfs in Europe and Africa," in Isidore Okpehwo, Carole Boyce Davies, and Ali Mazrui, eds. *The African Diaspora.* Bloomington: Indiana University Press. 49–75.

Irele, Abiola F., ed. 2001. "The Landscape of African Music." *Research in African Literatures* 32(2): 1–2.

Isichei, Elizabeth. 1997. *A History of African Societies.* Cambridge: Cambridge University Press.

Johnson, John William. 1999. "The Dichotomy of Power and Authority in Mande Society and in the Epic of Sunjata," in Ralph A. Austen, ed. *In Search of Sunjata: The Mande Oral Epic as History, Literature and Performance.* Bloomington: Indiana University Press. 9–24.

Johnson-Odim, Cheryl, and Nina Emma Mba. 1997. *For Women and the Nation: Funmilayo Ransome-Kuti of Nigeria.* Urbana: University of Illinois Press.

Jones, Durosimi, and Marjorie Jones. 1987. *Women in African Literature Today.* London: James Currey.

———. 1992. *Orature in African Literature Today.* London: James Currey.

———. 1996. *New Trends and Generations in African Literature.* London: James Currey.

Julien, Eileen. 1992. *African Novels and the Question of Orality.* Bloomington: Indiana University Press.

July, Robert William. 1967. *The Origins of Modern African Thought: Its Development in West Africa during the Nineteenth and Twentieth Centuries.* New York: Praeger.

Klein, Herbert S. 1999. *The Atlantic Slave Trade.* Cambridge: Cambridge University Press.

Klein, Martin A. 1997. "Women in Slavery in the Western Sudan," in Claire C. Robertson and Martin Klein, eds. *Women and Slavery in Africa,* 2nd ed. Madison: University of Wisconsin Press. 67–88.

Kolawole, Mary E. Modupe. 1994. "An African View of Transatlantic Slavery and the Role of Oral Testimony in Creating a New Legacy," in Anthony Tibbles, ed. *Transatlantic Slavery: Against Human Dignity.* London: HMSO. 105–110.

Kropp-Dakubu, Mary-Esther. 1987. "Creating Unity: The Context of Speaking Prose and Poetry in Ga." *Anthropos* 82:507–527.

de La Fosse, Eustache. ca. 1520; rpt. 1897. "Voyage à la côte occidentale d'Afrique." *Revue Hispanique* 4: 174–201.

Larrier, Renée. 1998. "Discourses of the Self: Gender and Identity in Francophone African Women's Autobiographies," in Anne V. Adams and Janis A. Mayes, eds. *Mapping Intersections: African Literature and Africa's Development.* Trenton: Africa World Press. 123–135.

Larson, M. Pier. 2000. *History and Memory in the Age of Enslavement: Becoming Merina in Highland Madagascar, 1770–1822.* Portsmouth: Heinemann.

Le Goff, Jacques. 1992. *History and Memory.* Translated by Steven Randall and Elizabeth Claman. New York: Columbia University Press.

Lebeuf, Annie M. D. 1963. "The Role of Women in the Political Organisation of African Societies," in Denise Paulme, ed. *Women of Tropical Africa.* Berkeley: University of California Press. 93–119.

Lee, Sonia. 1994. *Les Romancières du continent noir.* Paris: Hatier.

Leith-Ross, Sylvia. 1939, rpt. 1965. *African Women: A Study of the Ibo of Nigeria.* London: Routledge.

Levtzion, Nehemia. 1972. "The Early State of Western Sudan to 1500," in Michael Crowder and J. F. Ade Ajayi, eds. *History of West Africa,* vol. 1. New York: Columbia University Press. 120–157.

Lindfors, Bernth. 1991. *Popular Literatures in Africa.* Trenton: Africa World Press.

Lovejoy, Paul E., ed. 1983. *Transformations in Slavery: A History of Slavery in Africa.* Cambridge: Cambridge University Press.

MacCormack, Carol P. 1997. "Slaves, Slave Owners and Slave Dealers: Sherbo Coast and Hinterland," in Claire C. Robertson and Martin Klein, eds. *Women and Slavery in Africa.* Portsmouth: Heinemann. 271–294.

Mack, Beverly B. 1997. "Authority and Influence in the Kano Harem," in Flora Edouwaye S. Kaplan, ed. *Queens, Queen Mothers, Priestesses, and Power: Case Studies in African Gender.* New York: Annals of the New York Academy of Sciences. 159–172.

Makward, Edris. 1990. "Two Griots of Contemporary Senegambia," in Isidore Okpewho, ed. *The Oral Performance in Africa.* Ibadan: Spectrum Books. 23–41.

Marie Louise (Princess of Great Britain). 1926. *Letters from the Gold Coast.* London: Methuen.

Mazrui, Ali A. 1986. *The Africans: A Triple Heritage.* Boston: Little, Brown.

Mba, Nina E. 1992. "Olufumilayo Ransome-Kuti," in Bólánlé Awé, ed. *Nigerian Women in Historical Perspective.* Ibadan: Sankore Publishers.

M'Bokolo, Eliaka. 1985. *L'Afrique au XXe siècle: Le continent convoité.* Paris: Seuil.

McCaskie, Thomas C. 1995. *State and Society in Pre-Colonial Asante.* Cambridge: Cambridge University Press.

de Meideros, François. 1990. "Les peuples du Soudan: Mouvements de populations," in Muhammed El Fasi and Ivan Hrbek, eds. *Histoire générale de l'Afrique III: L'Afrique du VIIe au XIe siècles.* Paris: UNESCO / NEA. 143–163.

Mikell, Gwendolyn. 1997. "Introduction" in Gwendolyn Mikell, ed. *African Feminism: The Politics of Survival in Sub-Saharan Africa.* Philadelphia: University of Pennsylvania Press. 1–50.

Milbury-Steen, Sarah L. 1981. *European and African Stereotypes in Twentieth-Century Fiction.* New York: New York University Press.

Mounkaïla, Fatimata. 1985. *Le mythe et l'histoire dans la geste de Zabarkâne.* Niamey: Centre d'études linguistiques et historiques par tradition orale.

Mouralis, Bernard. 1994. "Une Parole autre, Aoua Keïta, Mariama Bâ et Awa Thiam." *Notre Librairie, Revue des Littératures du Sud* 117: 21–27.

Mudimbe-Boyi, Elisabeth, ed. 1993. "Post-Colonial Women's Writing." *L'Esprit créateur* 33(2): 1–136.

Murano, Maria R., and Francesca Degli Atti. 2003. "Les traites négrières" in Maria R. Murano and Paul Vandepitte, eds. *Pour une histoire de l'Afrique.* Lecce: ARGO. 143–166.

Murano, Maria R., and Paul Vandepitte, eds. 2003. *Pour une histoire de l'Afrique.* Lecce: ARGO.

Nasta, Susheila. 1992. *Motherlands: Black Women's Writing from Africa, the Caribbean and South Asia.* New Brunswick: Rutgers University Press.

———. 1997. *Writing African Women: Gender, Popular Culture and Literature in West Africa.* London: Zed Books.

NDiaye, A. Raphaël. 1985. "La Parole chez les Sereer." Notre Librairie, *Revue des Littératures du Sud* 81: 18–23.

———. 1986. *Archives Culturelles du Sénégal: La place de la femme dans les rites au Senegal.* Dakar: Les Nouvelles Editions Africaines.

Newell, Stephanie. 2002. *Literary Culture in Colonial Ghana: "How to Play the Game of Life."* Bloomington: Indiana University Press.

Niane, Djibril Tamsir. 1960. *Sundiata: An Epic of Old Mali.* London: Humanities Press.

———. 1985. "Le Mali et la deuxième expansion manden," in *Djibril Tamisir Niane, ed. Histoire générale de l'Afrique IV: L'Afrique du XIIe au XVIe siècle.* Paris: UNESCO / NEA. 141–196.

Nketia, J. H. 1950, rpt. 1969. *Funeral Dirges of the Akan People.* New York: Negro Universities Press.

Nnaemaka, Obioma, ed. 1997. *The Politics of (M)othering: Womanhood, Identity and Resistance in African Literature.* London: Routledge.

————. 1998. "Introduction: Reading the Rainbow," in Obioma Nnaemeka, ed. *Sisterhood, Feminisms and Power: From Africa to the Diaspora.* Trenton: Africa World Press. 1–35.

Nwapa, Flora. 1998. "Women and Creative Writing in Africa," in Obioma Nnaemeka, ed. *Sisterhood, Feminisms and Power: From Africa to the Diaspora.* Trenton: Africa World Press. 89–100.

Ogede, Ode. 1997. *Art Society and Performance, Igede Praise Poetry.* Gainesville: University Press of Florida.

Ogundipe-Leslie, Molara. 1998. "Literature and Development: Writing and Audience in Africa," in Anne V. Adams and Janis A. Mayes, eds. *Mapping Intersections: African Literature and Africa's Development.* Trenton: Africa World Press.

Ojaide, Tanure. 2001. "Poetry, Performance and Art: Udje Dance Songs of Nigeria's Urhobo People." *Research in African Literatures* 32(2): 44–73.

Okpewho, Isidore. 1979. *The Epic in Africa: Towards a Poetics of Oral Performance.* New York: Columbia University Press.

————. 1983. *Myth in Africa: A Study of Its Aesthetic and Cultural Relevance.* London: Cambridge University Press.

————, ed. 1990. *The Oral Performance in Africa.* Ibadan: Spectrum Books Ltd.

Olajubu, Chief Oludare. 1981. "Yoruba Oral Poetry: Composition and Performance," in Uchegbulam N. Abalogou, Garba Ashiwaju, and Regina Amadi-Tshiwala, eds. *Oral Poetry in Nigeria: Selections from the Papers Presented at the Seminar on Traditional Oral Poetry in Some Nigerian Communities.* Lagos: Nigeria Magazine Special Publications. 71–85.

Ong, Walter J. 1982. *Orality and Literacy: The Technologizing of the World.* New York: Methuen.

Opoku-Agyemang, Naana-Jane. 1999. "Gender-Role Perceptions in the Akan Folktale." *Research in African Literatures* 30(1): 16–40.

Owusu-Sarpong, Christiane. 1993. "L'altération des proverbes akan," in *Mélanges offerts à Jean Peytard.* Paris: Diffusion Les Belles Lettres.

————. 1995. "Akan Funeral Texts. Classification, Interrelation and Altercation of Genres." Paper presented at the 2nd International Conference of Oral Literature in Africa, Legon, 24–30 October.

————. 1996. "L'écriture métissée de Marie-Joseph Bonnat dans son journal (1868–1874)." *Journal des Africanistes* 66(1–2): 225–254.

————. 1999. "Retelling the History of Wenchi: Intertextual and Typological Study," in Esi Sutherland-Addy, ed. *Perspectives on Mythology.* Accra: Goethe Institute.

————. 2000. *La Mort akan: Etude ethno-sémiotique des textes funéraires akan.* Paris: L'Harmattan.

————. 2003. "From Words to Ritual Objects," in Christiane Falgayrettes-Leveau and Christiane Owusu-Sarpong, eds. *Ghana Yesterday and Today.* Paris: Editions Dapper. 25–92.

————. Forthcoming, 2005a. "'Afin que les noms demeurent'—Les Akans du Ghana et le traçage de leur histoire," in Simon Battestini and Olabiyi Yaï, eds. *De l'écrit africain à l'oralité.* Paris: Présence Africaine.

————. Forthcoming, 2005b. "The Predicament of the Akan 'Queenmother' (Ohemmaa)," in Donald Ray, ed. *Reinventing Chieftancy in the Ages of AIDS, Gender and Development.* Calgary: University of Calgary Press.

Owusu-Sarpong, Christiane, ed. 1998. *Trilingual Anthology of Akan Folktales.* Vol. 1. Kumasi: Department of Book Industry, KNUST.

————. 2001. *Trilingual Anthology of Akan Folktales.* Vol. 2. Accra: Woeli Publishing Services.

Oyewumi, Oyeronke. 1997. *The Invention of Women: Making an African Sense of Western Gender Discourses.* Minneapolis: University of Minnesota Press.

Paulme, Denise. 1976. *La mère dévorante: Essai sur la morphologie des contes africains.* Paris: Gallimard.

————, ed. 1963. *Women of Tropical Africa.* Translated by H. M. Wright. Berkeley: University of California Press.

Pavanello, Mariano. 2000. "Le concept d'histoire dans les traditions orales nzema." *Le Griot* 8: 17–40.

Pemberton, John, III, and Funso S. Afolatan. 1996. *Yoruba Sacred Kinship: "A Power Like That of the Gods."* Washington, D.C.: Smithsonian Institution Press.

Perrot, Claude-Hélène, and Albert van Dantzig, eds. 1989. *Sources orales de l'histoire d'Afrique.* Paris: Editions du CNRS.

————. 1994. *Marie-Joseph Bonnat et les Ashanti—Journal (1869–1874).* Paris: Mémoires de la Société des Africanistes.

Rattray, Robert Sutherland. 1917, rpt. 1952. *Ashanti Proverbs.* Oxford: Clarendon Press.

————. 1923, rpt. 1969. *Ashanti.* Oxford: Clarendon Press.

————. 1927, rpt. 1959. *Religion and Art in Ashanti.* Oxford: Clarendon Press.

————. 1929, rpt. 1969. *Ashanti Law and Constitution.* Oxford: Clarendon Press.

Ray, Donald I. 1998. "Chief-State Relations in Ghana: Divided Sovereignty and Legitimacy," in Emile Adriaan Benvenuto van Rouveroy van Nieuwaal and Werner Zips, eds. *Sovereignty, Legitimacy, and Power in West African Societies: Perspectives from Legal Anthropology.* New Brunswick: Transaction Publishers. 48–69.

Reindorf, Carl Christian. 1889, rpt. 1966. *The History of the Gold Coast and Asante.* Accra: Ghana University Press.

Ricard, Alain. 1995. *Littératures d'Afrique noire: Des langues aux livres.* Paris: CNRS Editions, Karthala.

Robertson, Claire C. 1997. "Post-Proclamation Slavery in Accra: A Female Affair?" in Claire C. Robertson and Martin Klein, eds. *Women and Slavery in Africa,* 2nd ed. Madison: University of Wisconsin Press. 220–245.

Robertson, Claire C., and Martin Klein. 1997. "Women's Importance in African Slave Systems," in Claire C. Robertson and Martin Klein, eds. *Women and Slavery in Africa,* 2nd ed. Madison: University of Wisconsin Press. 3–25.

Saad, Elias N. 1983. *Social History of Timbuktu: The Role of Muslin Scholars and Notables, 1400–1900.* Cambridge: Cambridge University Press.

Sardan, Jean-Pierre Olivier de. 1997. "The Songhay-Zarma Female Slave," in Claire C. Robertson and Martin Klein, eds. *Women and Slavery in Africa,* 2nd ed. Madison: University of Wisconsin Press. 130–143.

Sarpong, Peter Kwasi. 1977. *Girls' Nubility Rites in Ashanti.* Accra: Ghana Publishing Corporation.

————. 1990. *The Ceremonial Horns of the Ashanti.* Accra: Universal Printers and Publishers.

————. 1998. *Dear Nana: Letters to My Ancestor*. Takoradi: Franciscan Publications.

Sidikou-Morton, Aissata. 2000. *Recreating Words, Reshaping Worlds: The Verbal Art of Women From Niger, Mali and Senegal*. Trenton: Africa World Press.

Steady, Filomina Chioma. 1981. *The Black Woman Cross-Culturally*. Cambridge: Schenkman.

Steen, Marguerite. 1941. *The Sun Is My Undoing*. New York: Viking Press.

Stoeltje, Beverly J. 1997. "Asante Queen Mothers: A Study in Female Authority," in Flora Edouwaye S. Kaplan, ed. *Queens, Queen Mothers, Priestesses, and Power: Case Studies in African Gender*. New York: Annals of the New York Academy of Sciences. 41–72.

Stoler, Ann Laura. 2002. *Carnal Knowledge and Imperial Power: Race and the Intimate in Colonial Rule*. Berkeley: University of California Press.

Struck, B. 1923. "Geschichtliches über die östlichen Techi—Länder (Goldküste)." *Anthropos* 18: 465–483.

Sudarkasa, Niara. 1973. *Where Women Work: A Study of Yoruba Women in the Marketplace and in the Home*. Ann Arbor: University of Michigan Press.

Tashjian, Victoria. 1996. "'It's Mine' and 'It's Yours' Are Not the Same Thing: Changing Economic Relations between Spouses," in John Hunwick and Nancy Lawler, eds. *The Cloth of Many Colored Silks, Papers on History and Society, Ghanian and Islamic, in Honor of Ivor Wilks*. Evanston: Northwestern University Press, 205–222.

Terborg-Penn, Rosalyn, Sharon Harley, and Andrea Benton Rushing. 1987. *Women in Africa and the African Diaspora*. Washington, D.C.: Howard University Press.

Turner, Victor. 1977. *The Ritual Process: Structure and Anti-Structure*. Ithaca: Cornell University Press.

Vansina, Jan. 1985. *Oral Tradition as History*. Madison: University of Wisconsin Press.

Webb, Vic, and Kembo-Sure, eds. 2000. *African Voices: An Introduction to the Languages and Linguistics of Africa*. Oxford: Oxford University Press.

Weigle, Marta. 1998. "Women's Expressive Forms," in John Miles Foley, ed. *Teaching Oral Traditions*. New York: Modern Language Association. 298–307.

White, E. Francis 1987. *Sierra Leone's Settler Women Traders: Women on the Afro-European Frontier*. Ann Arbor: University of Michigan Press.

————. 1999. "Women in West and West-Central Africa," in Iris Berger and E. Frances White, eds. *Women in Sub-Saharan Africa: Restoring Women to History*. Bloomington: Indiana University Press. 63–129.

————. 2001. *Dark Continent of Our Bodies: Black Feminism and the Politics of Respectability*. Philadelphia: Temple University Press.

Wilentz, Gay. 1992. *Binding Cultures: Black Women Writers in Africa and the Diaspora*. Bloomington: Indiana University Press.

Wilks, Ivor. 1975, rpt. 1989. *Asante in the Nineteenth Century: The Structure and Evolution of a Political Order*. Cambridge: Cambridge University Press.

————. 1993. *Forests of Gold: Essays on the Akan and the Kingdom of Asante*. Athens: Ohio University Press.

————. 1999. "The History of the Sunjata Epic: A Review of Evidence," in Ralph A. Austen, ed. *In Search of Sunjata: The Mande Oral Epic as History, Literature and Performance.* Bloomington: Indiana University Press. 25–57.

———. 2003. "Glimpses into Ghana's Past," in Christiane Falgayrettes–Leveau and Christiane Owusu–Sarpong, eds. *Ghana Yesterday and Today.* Paris: Editions Dapper. 185–213.

Willis, John Ralph, ed. 1985. *Slaves and Slavery in Muslim Africa.* London: Frank Cass.

Wright, Marcia. 2004. "Gender, Women, and Power in Africa, 1750–1914," in Teresa A. Meade and Merry E. Wiesner–Hanks, eds. *A Companion to Gender History.* Malden: Blackwell. 413–429.

Wynter, Sylvia. 1997. "'Genital Mutilation' or 'Symbolic Birth?' Female Circumcision, Lost Origins, and the Aculturalism of Feminist/Western Thought about Symbolic Birth," in *Case Western Reserve Law Review.* 501-522.

Yai, Olabiyi Babalola. 1994. "In Praise of Metonymy: The Concepts of 'Tradition' and 'Creativity' in the Transmission of Yoruba Artistry over Time and Space," in Rowland Abiodun, Henry J. Drewal, and John Pemberton, eds. *The Yoruba Artist: New Theoretical Perspectives on African Arts.* Washington, D.C.: Smithsonian Institution Press. Ch. 5.

Yankah, Kwesi. 1989. *The Proverb in the Context of Akan Rhetoric: A Theory of Proverb Praxis.* New York: Peter Lang.

———. 1995. *Speaking for the Chief: Okeyeame and the Politics of Akan Royal Oratory.* Bloomington: Indiana University Press.

Zak, Louise Allen. 2001. "Writing Her Way: A Study of Ghanaian Novelist Amma Darko." Ph.D. dissertation, University of Massachusetts, Amherst.

Zelaza, Tiyambe. 1997. "Gender Biases in African Historiography," in Ayesha Imam, Amina Mama, and Fatou Sow, eds. *Engendering African Social Sciences.* Dakar: Codesria. 81–115.

RITUAL AND CEREMONIAL WORDS

Ede Court Historians
OYA, OR THE WIND BEHIND THE LIGHTNING
Nigeria [2001]*   Yoruba

The female *arokin*, or court historians, at Ede palace are the designated keepers and raconteurs of royal ancestral lineage. During the annual Sàngó festival, they chant the names of all the kings who have ruled the city. The story of Oya, Sàngó's wife, forms part of Sàngó's lore, although it is not usually recounted during his festival. When the women performed it upon my request, they did so simply, without drawing any conclusions.

On an immediate sacred level, the story illustrates the relationship between the elemental phenomena and the environment represented by the two òrìsà (deities), Sàngó and Oya. Both are primary òrìsà of the ancient Oyo empire, situated in the northern part of Yorubaland. Unlike the later Oyo empire that emerged farther south, the ancient Oyo empire was located in the savannah region, an area highly susceptible to wildfires, especially during the *harmattan* or dry season, which follows the rainy season around September. It is marked by a stormy combination of thunder, lightning, and high winds that produces very little or no rainfall. The lightning often sets the dry grassland ablaze during this period. Furthermore, during a dry spell of rainless, stormy weather, the river Oya (Niger River) is often turbulent.

The story in essence also illustrates the significance of complementarity between male and female powers in Yoruba society. Like the two sides of a coin, each is unique but neither is complete without the other. The Yoruba say, *"t'ibi t'ire ni won jo nrin"* (the bad and the good are traveling companions), an expression that emphasizes the importance of balance in Yoruba thought. With respect to gender in the context of the story, we are reminded that female and male both have their spheres of authority. Nonetheless, the story recognizes the patriarchal structure of the society. Hence, on the one hand, Oya is reluctant to justify her objections to Sàngó's plans, thereby showing respect for his power. But when Sàngó forces her to reveal her reasons, he feels affronted. On the other hand, Oya maintains confidence in her own authority, and at the appropriate moment claims it. In acknowledgment of her authority, the elders retreat, thereby indicating to Sàngó that he is overstepping his bounds. That the contest happens at all ensures that when men misuse patriarchal power and infringe on women's sphere of authority, they will be criticized. However, in keeping with the philosophy of *t'ibi t'ire ni won jo nrin*, the outcome is not totally unfavorable to Sàngó: The dry season he heralds completes the seasonal cycle and ensures agricultural continuity. Many farm products, such as yams and some fruits, need the dry spell to complete their growth season.

Unfortunately, today this story is almost forgotten, its significance rarely mentioned in the repertoire of either Sàngó or Oya's sacred dogma. The pieces of the story that have survived in the shrines and made their way into contemporary society often convey the wrong message about gender relations in Yoruba society. One such example is the commonly quoted contemporary Yoruba phrase *"Sàngó l'oko Oya,"* meaning "Sàngó is Oya's husband," without the preceding *"Oya n'iyawo Sàngó,"* "Oya is the wife of Sàngó." When the phrase is uttered partially, it may still indicate triumph over an adversary, but in the mouths of most men, it is used to silence women into submission and to suggest that women are secondary in the social structure. Without the phrase naming Oya as Sàngó's wife, the sacred intent and context is lost. Sàngó is the husband of Oya, but Oya is the wife of Sàngó, and without the wind of her power in support, Sàngó cannot be a husband.

Omofolabo Ajayi

✦

"Oya is the wife of Sàngó and Sàngó is the husband of Oya. Their marriage began in heaven before they descended to earth."

While still in heaven, Sàngó woke up one morning to inform his wife he was coming to earth as rain but Oya was against the idea. When pressed for her reasons, she replied she did not think it was a great idea but would not elaborate any further. Sàngó could not decide, which annoyed and baffled him more, whether it was this very unsatisfactory explanation or her refusal to support him in his adventure. After days of trying in vain to get her to change her mind, Sàngó asked some *òrìsà* (deities) elders to intervene on his behalf and talk sense to Oya. The *òrìsà* elders tried their best to plead Sàngó's cause, but Oya was unyielding. She neither changed her mind nor offered any further explanation beyond what she had earlier told her husband. She claimed she was right to oppose any unsound plans and that her judgment should be trusted.

Indeed, the Elders agreed with Oya and advised Sàngó to forget the whole idea of going to earth either as rain or anything else as long as Oya was against it. They agreed that Oya must indeed have valid reasons for her decisions and urged Sàngó to respect her views. Sàngó thanked them but could not abide by their verdict. Most of all, he wanted Oya to give him a reason and he pestered her until she finally gave in. She told him his idea was not sound because it would pit his power against hers and since she was more powerful than he was, he would be disgraced. No answer could have infuriated Sàngó more. He could not accept Oya's analysis and he was determined to prove who was the more powerful.

The following day found Sàngó getting ready to fall on earth as rain. As he gathered his energy and the clouds together, Oya too called the winds around her ready to stop him. As soon as the clouds started to form, Oya blew them away. Undaunted, Sàngó tried several times more, exerting even more energy with each attempt, but all his efforts were in vain. Oya was so successful that Sàngó could not form enough rain clouds to darken the sky. The more energy Sàngó expended, the more heat he generated; the more he failed, the angrier and more desperate he became. Try all he could, Sàngó could not descend as rainfall. Rather, the heat from his energy became the sparks of fire darting across the sky as lightning while his cries of frustration echoed through the skies in the form of thunder. Sàngó failed to withstand the power of Oya's winds. Oya's affirmation of her authority became the whirlwind that funnels down to earth from the heavens.

Translated by Omofolabo Ajayi

Olorisa Osun
PRAISE POEM FOR OSUN

Nigeria 1981   Yoruba

In Yoruba cosmology Osun is often depicted as the only female among the *Irunmole,* those deities assigned by Olodumare, the Creator, to organize the world. When the sixteen other deities—who are male—exclude her from their planning sessions, Osun uses her talents and powers to disrupt their plans. When the male Irunmole complain to Olodumare, they are rebuffed and required to beg Osun for forgiveness. They comply, and she demands the inclusion of powerful women like herself in all worldly affairs. The Irunmole agree, and she releases the covenant that binds their works.

The priestesses at the shrine of Osun chant *"Oriki Osun,"* or "Praise Song for Osun," in three sections, a cappella, during both sacred and secular occasions in honor of the deified founder of Osogbo, the goddess Osun. Section One presents Osun's many appellations and attributes, and names the townships historically associated with her or her worship. Section Two elaborates on her prowess and those characteristics that attract people to celebrate her as *YeYe,* the Good Mother. Section Three captures her spiritual essence and cosmological authority from which Osun worshippers derive their own authority and strength.

This *Oriki Osun* is significant for many reasons. First, it signals the possibility of an aboriginal past that is both matrifocal and dual-gendered in its leadership structure. This is a clear departure from the universal view of gender inequity and female oppression as the dominant paradigm in traditional West African cultures. Second, although both women and men worship Osun, the *Oriki Osun* are maintained and intoned by women who are trained as professional praise singers. These women maintain the oral texts, the stylistic integrity, and the performance aesthetics of the Osun oral literary corpus.

The section of the chant published here is replete with complex metaphors and layered meanings. In its oral recitation, the highly stylized chanting evokes images of the power and "coolness" for which Osun is celebrated. In this section, Osun's sacred and secular metonyms allude to her as a giver of life, a healing mother, a wealthy woman, a ruler, and a wife of Sàngó, another powerful deity. Osun's ability to "deliver" townspeople and women from life's challenges is signified by references to the majestic flow of her body, which is the river Osun, and to her co-rulership with the Ataoja, the traditional ruler in Osogbo. In the poem, Osun conquers many challenges with ease and grace while remaining vigilant as well as energetic. For the women and men who worship Osun, she is the epitome of female power and femininity, and her characteristics suggest central aspects of a feminine ideal in Yoruba culture.

In addition, this section of the poem also provides historical as well as political allusions that suggest that Osogbo as well as other Yoruba towns may have had matriarchal origins. For example, one of her praise names or cognomens, Solagbade, refers to a wealthy person who wears a crown. Since only rulers or those who have the authority to rule wear crowns, her praise name signifies her rulership of Osogbo, and ties female rulership to such towns as Ara, Ijesa, Efon, and Anke, which are identified in the poem. References to extinct towns such as Anke indicate that the poem and its origins are rooted in antiquity. These references also name towns where Osun is worshipped and/or through which her river flows. It is important to note that the breadth of Osun's characteristics and Osun worship suggest a cultural perspective that values abundance and variety among human beings.

Diedre L. Badejo

✦

Osun Osogbo ooo
The child is secretly created, Osun Osogbo!
The one who in flowing majestically along hits her body against the grass.
The one who in flowing majestically along hits her body against the rocks.
Praise-worthy owner of the secrets of life.
The wealthy one who wears a crown! The effervescent one!
I again salute the Great Mother Osun, Osun Osogbo.
My Mother, Osun Osogbo,
Who gives birth like a female animal with ease and grace,
My mother, please deliver and rescue me!
The wealthy one who wears a crown! The effervescent one!
I cried "deliverance" through the water,
Osun Osogbo, please deliver me!
I cried "deliverance" to you!
Osun Osogbo ooo!
My Mother is the giant cock
Who climbed to the top of the palm nut tree to build her house.
Yes, it is from there that she calls the King of Ara with a loud voice.
I stand to wait for Osun's blessings, my hands are not deep enough.
Osun Osogbo!
Osun Osogbo greetings, I spread my clothes,
I will certainly receive more.
Solagbade, she who scoops sand, and scoops sand to hide money!
Come and look at Osun Osogbo!
My Mother, Owner of the medicinal healing pot.
Oloro, Ruler of Ijesa!
In the dead of night, please do not sleep!
I salute the Great Mother, Osun!
The spirit of King Adenle, I salute the Great Mother,

People who quickly salute the Great Mother Osun!
The spirit of King Adenle, I come again to greet the Great Mother Osun!
I receive money, I receive children.
The wealthy one who wears a crown! The effervescent one!
I salute the Great Mother Osun!
The spirit of King Oyewale, I salute the Great Mother Osun!
All the people of Okeya, north of the River Niger,
I Salute the Great Mother Osun!
My Mother who hails from Efon town, from Anke town, the land of
    kola nuts.
The wealthy one who wears a crown! The effervescent one!
I salute the Great Mother Osun!
Who does not know that it is Osun who helps the Oba to manage and
    rule Osogbo?
Osun Osogbo is the one who will help me
Accomplish my goals.
Osun Osogbo is the one who will definitely help me
Accomplish what I cannot accomplish on my own!
Because of children she eagerly listens to noise!
Because of Sàngó she masters the art of cooking amala!
My father of the house, my husband!
Because of children she cultivates nutritious spinach!
The wealthy one who wears a crown, the effervescent one!

Translated by Diedre L. Badejo

Béatrice Djedja
MAÏÉTO, OR THE BATTLE OF THE SEXES

Côte d'Ivoire [2000]*   Bété

Every time a woman dies in childbirth, the event is seen in the Bété region as
the manifestation of a struggle between men and women that has existed
since the beginning of time. The women's community comes together and
performs a war dance, the only one of this kind that women are permitted to
dance. On that day, the wives, who have suddenly become terrifying, chase
the men away from the village and take over. When the men return, for three
consecutive days they are forced to perform the duties ordinarily reserved for
women: They must haul water, grind rice, and cook, under the strict supervi-
sion of their wives, who hold court and give orders, each one of them in imitation of the customary quirks and whims of her husband. On these days, no
man has the right to enjoy sexual pleasures.

The Bété justify the rite through a myth of origins, the essence of which follows. In the beginning of time, women and men lived in two separate cities. The men were governed by a man, Gnali Zagô. The women were governed by a woman, Mahié. One man alone, of whom all the women were extremely fond and whose name was Zouzou, lived among them. Now, the men fervently desired the women and wanted to conquer them. Unfortunately for them, Mahié kept watch over the grain and thwarted every one of their attempts, crushing all of the men's attacks. In order to overpower this strange female city, the men used a subterfuge and succeeded in poisoning Zouzou. With Zouzou dead, the vanquished women gave in to the men. But in the eyes of the women, the men, having killed Zouzou, now had a blood debt. Mahié formulated this and etched it into the memory of each of her co-citizens. Before handing themselves over to the men, Mahié taught the women sorcery so that they could make all future husbands pay the blood debt incurred upon the destruction of the city of women.

Every time a woman dies, three particularly remarkable songs, stemming directly from the myth, are included in the funeral dance, known as the *logbo digbeu*, performed by women. Since these songs and dances awaken wicked instincts in women, the sensible man should distance himself when unbridled female mourners come near him. Béatrice Djedja, singer of the village of Yacolidaboudy in the Soubré region, sang the following ceremonial songs for us. They are usually performed as the women return from burying the deceased. They enter the village with their faces blackened with charcoal, the bellies of the pregnant women also blackened. They wear men's clothing and hold bludgeons, machetes, and spears.

Helen N'gbesso

✦

Song One

Will the day of vengeance ever come
For he who killed our dear Zouzou?
Oh, see, Zouzou, that day is here!
Here within your very city!

Song Two

We are coming for Zagô.
We are coming for Gnali Zagô, the ruler of the village.
You cannot run away from us!

Song Three

We shall avenge you
Waging war, waging war.
We shall avenge you
Declaring war, declaring war.

We shall avenge you
Unleashing war, unleashing war.
We shall fight
And avenge you.

We shall avenge you
Waging war, waging war.
We shall avenge you
Waging war, waging war.
We shall avenge you.
Hear the click of our rifles!
We women are now like men.
Hear the click of our rifles!
Hear the click of our rifles!
We nippled women are just like men.
Hear the click of our rifles!

Here we are on the pond.
Let the otter dare come out.
We are panthers!
Here we are on the pond.
Let the otter dare come out.
We are panthers!

I say let us greet Naki.
Oh Naki
Such fine mourning tears we weep.
Tell him I greet her.
We are greeting Naki.
We shall avenge you.
Waging war, waging war.
We are deaf to men's cries.
We shall avenge you.
Warrior shrub, go and fight.
Armored shrub, go and fight.
Go and fight!
We shall avenge you.
We shall fight for you.
Rest where you are.
Rest, where you are lying down.
For we shall fight.
Do not avenge yourself.
We shall avenge you.
Do not avenge yourself.
We shall avenge you.

I seek my husband.
Yes, I seek the husbands.
I seek my husband.
Yes, I seek the husbands.
Just watch me seek my husband!
Yes, seek our husbands.
I seek the husbands of misfortune.
Yes, I seek our husbands.

Translated into French by Bernard Zadi Zaourou
Translated from French by Marjolijn de Jager and Judith Miller

Communal
THE PLUMP WOMAN'S SONG

Niger [1972]*   Songhai-Zarma

"The Plump Woman's Song" is the opening air of *Mani Foori,* a festival that celebrates plumpness, which takes place in rural Songhai-Zarma societies. Based on a clearly articulated sense of the feminine aesthetic, the festival is a grand beauty and fashion pageant that takes place after the harvest. The underlying perceptions are those built around the woman as representing for the society a sense of well-being and fulfillment. The woman who is able to evolve into a state of majestic plumpness also reflects the prosperity of her family and/or her husband. A woman who has just had her first child is considered to be at her most beautiful.

A few months before the day of the pageant, the previously crowned queen of plump women distributes grilled chicken parts to all of the young women in the community. In the spirit of this playful festival, each woman accepts a chicken part meant to correspond to her body. Thus, for example, white meat goes to those with well-developed breasts, thighs to those whose lower body is well developed, feathers to those with a lot of hair, and the chicken back to the very thin ones. Women perceived as running around the village rather than caring for their own homes receive chicken feet.

Then women go into seclusion for forty days to fatten up. If a woman has received a bony piece of chicken, the whole family, including the husband, want to meet the challenge of making her attractive. Women eat particular foods, which may even include foreign dishes such as *gari* (a grainy, toasted cassava flour), from Nigeria and Ghana.

On the day of the festival, the dance arena becomes a space of intense competition. Women emerge from their fattening seclusion, radiant and beautifully dressed, to preen before the public. The drummers are at their disposal as they enter the arena. "The Plump Woman's Song" is of the genre of rhythmic poetry, chanted at the request of the reigning *Waymonzon,* queen of plump women, as the drummers beat out the dance rhythm. Those who have not been fattened will not escape mockery should they enter the dance arena.

The first two lines of the last stanza mention the Kebbi and Zamfara armies respectively. These are two powerful Hausa states that rose in the early sixteenth century. Kebbi indeed defeated the formidable army of the powerful Songhai empire of the western Sudan. In the shared memory of the Songhai-Zarma, this allusion is an apt metaphor for the exclusion of thin women from this celebration. Amid the poetry, dance, and music, another woman will be elected Waymonzon, queen of the plump women until the next harvest.

Fatimata Mounkaïla

✦

When the bony woman hears the drum beat the *komkom-no-aci* air,
she springs up, then collapses on her bed.
Her men-folk cry, Hide her! hide her!
The grandmothers cry, Let us hide her.
The mothers cry, Hide her! hide her!

The drums repeat, No hiding place today!
Let her heart burn like a campfire!

When a Zarma girl hears the plump one's air, the *komkom-no-aci,*
When a scrawny woman hears this air,
Her heart burns like a campfire.

As if the whole Kebbi army had swooped down on her,
As if the whole Zamfara army had swooped down on her,
Her heart burns like a campfire.

When the skinny woman hears the drums play *komkom-no-aci* for the
    plump woman,
She springs up from her sleep.
She runs to her men-folk.
She runs to their children.
She cries, Hide me! hide me!

Her co-wife retorts,
No hiding place, today!
The drums keep beating
No hiding place today for a woman who is so meager
You could lodge a *balanites,* an entire date palm and its roots,
In the empty space between her two buttocks!

Translated by Aïssata Niandou and Antoinette Tidjani Alou

MARRIAGE SONG CYCLES

In many West African and Sahelian communities, marriage ceremonies span a number of days during which a bride prepares for a radical break with youthful life and familial shelter and initiation into marriage. Female members of her family and the most important of her friends surround her. During the rituals, song is the medium that conveys advice, comfort, and warnings about various aspects of married life. Many songs retain a wistful banter about the last days of the young bride as a playful maiden. Dyula marriage songs from Côte d'Ivoire, called *Konyon Bondolon Donkili,* and the Hausa marriage song cycle from Nigeria offer some startling revelations about the themes and forms of the ritual.

The *Konyon Bondolon Donkili*—marriage songs of the Dyula—form part of the marriage ceremonies of Dyula society in the Kong region of southern Côte d'Ivoire. The weeklong ceremonies begin on a Sunday evening with ritual songs of young women the age of the bride, usually her close friends. The same set of songs is repeated on Monday, Tuesday, and Friday evenings. The songs mention the name of the bride frequently, and that of the groom on some occasions (see Song Six). More significantly, they enjoy the nostalgia of idyllic adolescent love, set in direct opposition to the relationship that the young woman is about to enter. These songs challenge assumptions about restrictions on the sexuality of young African women. They tacitly recognize that the young woman has had a teenage sweetheart, quite independent of future marriage prospects. In a ritual of collective fantasy, the young women bring to life through song a mysterious suitor, and through him the young girl relives the joys of young love. She must now abandon such joys, in view of the inevitable consummation of marriage—described as "the Thursday war" (because it occurs on the Thursday of the first week). The songs often express either the point of view of the bride or her secret lover.

The songs describe the secrecy of this nostalgic love, fiercely guarded and powerfully palpable. They juxtapose personal choice and sensuality with the ominous, impending marriage, which is out of the hands of the young woman and involves considerations beyond her emotional happiness. The bride may become an actual persona in the songs.

If the general tenor of the songs is melancholic, many of them also bear the playful, lilting tonality of youth. The refrain *"Féfé, filerifé"* in Song Twelve is like singing "tra la la" in the European musical tradition. Song Forty-two, which always comes last in the cycle, is a collective lamentation on behalf of bride Majuman Baro, for "she has been struck by a calamity." The songs provided below were recorded at the marriage of husband Balamini Baro and wife Majuman Baro on the evening of Sunday, 1 February 1976. Many of the lines or whole stanzas are repeated from three to ten times.

The songs of the Hausa cycle are more formally connected to particular rituals on specific days. Each day's name addresses an activity meant to transform the maiden into a wife: Days one, three, and five, for example, address the domestic and conjugal responsibilities of the new bride with references to cooking, body adornment, and health care; days two and four dramatize the uncertainty of both the bride, who "runs away," and her family, who must return "the borrowed bride." Senior women enact the secrets and stories of their lives as married women to the newcomer. On day six, when the new bride is escorted to her husband's house, she has moved beyond the days of her childhood. On the seventh day, unveiled before her in-laws and new husband, she seals their union and her transformation. She has now joined the league of married women whose lives center on the needs of their husbands and families.

The seven poems here illuminate each day's ritual. On the opening day, the song names two staple foods of the Hausa—*fura,* a combination of millet and milk, and *tuwo,* corn, rice, or millet dumplings—that all women are expected to prepare. On the second day, the bride runs away from her parental home and goes into hiding with her friends for the last time, perhaps into the "bush," where they dance circle dances. From noon until evening, a special search party consisting of the groom's friends and relations searches for the bride. In the song "Laula," the maidens comfort the bride, who cries because the songs remind her of the past. The maidens console her, telling her that she is only being taken to the school of marriage. In this school, patience, tolerance, and hard work are watchwords, qualities she needs to survive as a wife.

On the night of the third day, the bride's body, particularly her feet and hands, is dyed in *lane* (henna). This is done in the house of the bride's maternal aunt. On the fourth day, the bride returns to her father's house briefly, usually carried home on the back of another woman. There, her companions dramatize their anxiety over the rebellious behavior of the precious daughter for whom they have been caring.

On the fifth day, an old woman bathes the bride. She places two large kola nuts into the bride's mouth, on either side of her jaw, so that the gaping mouth cannot swallow the water. As the old woman bathes the bride, she prays for her, while her friends sing and place money on her forehead. The bride weeps all through this period. On day six, the song reminds the new bride that she no longer belongs among the companions with whom she used to sell her wares on market days. She has now graduated. On the seventh day, the maidens advise their friend that she no longer belongs to their group but now belongs to a man. From now on, they sing, she will be at the beck and call of her husband. He will say, "Bring me my cap, my gown, or water for my ablutions," and the wife will obey.

Patience Mudiare, Helen N'gbesso, and Diedre L. Badejo

✦

Young Women of Kong, DYULA SONGS

Côte d'Ivoire 1976   Dyula

SONG ONE

Women of the village, oh, please go home, please go to bed
So you'll be fast asleep before my beloved comes to me.

Song Two

Let's take a walk, my guest, let's go for a walk.
O, let's go for a walk.
Besides myself, who will discover this?
Except my mother, except my father,
No one will know, but God alone.

Song Three

Master of the Koran, pray to God,
For if you do not pray, our maidens will not marry.

Song Four

I will send someone to the mother of my beloved
To ask her to forgive me
That I ever spoke to her son.

Song Five

They are talking about next Thursday's war.
Didn't little Majuman Baro know anything about it?

Song Six

Duo: Féfé, filerifé
Chorus: Féfé, filerifé
Duo: Majuman has no salt
Chorus: Féfé, filerifé
Duo: To put in Lamini's soup.
Chorus: Féfé, filerifé
Duo: Féfé, filerifé
Chorus: Majuman has no salt
Duo: Féfé, filerifé
Chorus: Féfé, filerifé
Duo: Lamini has no salt
Chorus: Féfé, filerifé
Duo: To give to Majuman.
Chorus: Féfé, filerifé
Duo: Féfé, filerifé
Chorus: Lamini has no salt
Duo: Féfé, filerifé
Chorus: To give to Majuman.
Duo: Féfé, filerifé

Song Seven

I have kept it secret.
I have kept my beloved's name secret,
But how long will I keep this secret?

Song Eight

Oh, young girls who have come out to dance, come out in your numbers.
Oh, young men who have come out for the dance, come out in your
    numbers.
I got a letter from Majuman Baro.
Let all those of her age-group weep for her.
A sorrowful day has come for her.
Let all those of her age-group weep for her.

Translated into French by Jean Derive
Translated from French by Antoinette Tidjani Alou and Marjolijn de Jager

Communal, HAUSA SONGS

Nigeria 1979   Hausa

SONG ONE: *SHIMBIDI*, OR OPENING DAY

Aye, mama ye iye
   mama ye iye
Aye mamula bolabo
   mama ye iye
If marriage could escort marriage
   mama ye iye
I would have accompanied you so that we'd go together
   mama ye iye
If only to learn to stir *tuwo.*
   mama ye iye
Even if it is *fura* I will learn.
   mama ye iye

SONG TWO: *LAULA*

Laula, new bride, Laula
Laulay, Laulaye, Laula,
Stop crying my friend, Laula,
I'm not getting you married, Laula,

I am only taking you to school,
The school of those who own the town.

SONG THREE: *AHAIYE YARO,* OR NO WAY, BOY

"A haiye" "boy"
"A haiye," "no way," "A haiye," no doubt about it.
When it comes to noses, someone is better than another.
When it comes to noses, I too am better than another.
When it comes to eyes, someone is better than another.
When it comes to eyes, I too am better than another.
When it comes to cooking, someone is better than another.
When it comes to cooking, I too am better than another.
When it comes to work, someone is more hard working than another.
When it comes to work, I too am more hard working than another.
When it comes to beauty, someone is more beautiful than another.
When it comes to beauty, I too am more beautiful than another.

SONG FOUR: *MAI DA ARO,* OR RETURNING THE BORROWED BRIDE

Aye, here is the borrowed one returned.
Here is the loan given to us.
Here is your daughter we've returned.
She refused to eat, she refused to drink,
She rejects guinea-corn dumplings,
She just cries some more.
Here is your daughter, owners of the house.
Here is your daughter, we've returned her.
Here is your daughter, we've returned her.
The one who cries all the more,
Cries like a statue,
Red eyes like a buffalo.

SONG FIVE: *WANKA,* OR BATHING THE BRIDE

Old woman with small pot,
May Allah kill you next month,
The month after next so that we drink
Ayyiraye, here is the bastard,
The bastard wrapper *tsalala.*
Don't you allow it to be worn around the waist.

SONG SIX: *BAKYARAYA BA,* OR FAREWELL SONG

You will not stay, you won't stay.
You will stay in front of your house.
You will stay with your husband.
You will not stay [with us].

From this year on, you won't be with us on Tuesday.
From this year on, you won't be with us on Tuesday.
Monday, Tuesday, Wednesday,
You won't stay with us.
Your mother-in-law owns the garage.
You won't stay with us.
Your father-in-law owns the garage.
You won't stay with us.

SONG SEVEN: *BUDAR KAI,* OR UNVEILING THE BRIDE'S FACE

You have become "bring me gown"
You have become "bring me trousers"
You have become "bring me cap"
You won't give me water for prayer?

Translated by Ladi Yakubu, Rabi Garba, and Patience Mudiare

Dior Konate
SHE WHO DESTROYS HER HARP

Senegal 1998   Wolof

As in many other Senegalese ethnic groups, the marriage ceremony in Wolof society lasts several days. One of the most important moments of the ceremony occurs the morning after the wedding night, when the bride's family members express their joy at discovering that their daughter had remained a virgin until her marriage. At dawn, the bridegroom alerts the paternal aunt and the family *griotte,* who had spent the night posted at the door of the bridal chamber. They carry away the blood-spotted white wrapper while exclaiming their joy in a noisy *sarxole,* or ululation. The good news travels around the neighborhood, and little by little, as neighboring women and female friends fill up the house, the paternal aunts, the *griottes,* and the neighbors sing songs of praise for the girl who has been wise enough to save herself for her husband. The bride's mother, ecstatic on this day, which is glorious for her as well, offers money and presents to everyone, to her sisters-in-law, who must admit that she has been an excellent wife to their brother, and to the *griottes,* who will also sing the good mother's praises.

Marriage is not simply an affair between private parties: two families, two lines, unite and contract a relationship. Thus, as we can see in the second stanza of the song included here, the choice of the bride requires the greatest of care by the bridegroom's family. His sisters especially carry out secret inquiries to make sure that the potential bride has good morals and that her ancestry is likewise irreproachable. It is obvious why *griottes* play such an important role in these ceremonies. As the memory of the group, they witness and keep alive the family histories that make future unions possible.

The praise songs sung at this time form part of the socialization process for girls of marriageable age. They remind the girls of the values and rules of their society, among which is the all-important chastity. The song compares the irreversible consequence of breaking the chastity rule to breaking one string of a harp. It brings dishonor not only on oneself but also on the family and even the children to come. Preserving virginity determines the quality of life the wife and mother will experience. It foreshadows especially progeny who can also expect to have prestigious marriages.

A day after the wedding night, on the day known as *labaan*, the assembled women sing to the marriageable girls. The *labaan* ceremony demonstrates how Islamic Wolof society builds and maintains control over female sexuality. Paradoxically, *labaan* also allows for a moment of controlled subversion. A ceremony exclusively for women, *labaan* permits them to ignore social conventions and speech codes and to speak frankly, even vulgarly, about sex—and all this in the presence of the youngest women.

Aminata Diaw

✦

She who destroys her harp, pluck as she will, she'll make no music.
She who destroys her harp will never see this beautiful day.
She who destroys her harp will never deserve a feast like today's.

When they send me to seek the hand of a good mother's child,
                    I never get weary.
When they send me to seek the hand of a good mother's child,
                    I never get weary.
When they send me to look for a pure maiden to marry,
                    I never get weary.

When you're sent to seek for a bride, you choose a girl of good repute
For with a virgin for a bride, a man has no trouble.

Happy is she who finds her match in good time,
For endless waiting is full of snares,
Which lead girls astray from the way of virtue.

Translated into French by Souleymane Faye
Translated from French by Antoinette Tidjani Alou

ARRIVAL OF THE NEW BRIDE

The welcoming of the new bride into her home by her cowife constitutes a celebratory moment for the family and a time of great creativity for women. One must welcome the new wife appropriately, to the sound of drumming. During the course of the ceremony, the women relatives and friends of the first wife participate in oral jousting, satirical songs, insults, and gibes that often stun by the violence they contain. This paradoxical welcoming ceremony would seem to have a cathartic function for the first wife, allowing her, with the help of her friends, to endure a difficult occasion.

The two texts selected here offer glimpses into two different sociocultural contexts in which polygamy is accepted through African tradition and Islamic law. *Xaxar*, the name Wolof people in Senegal give to satirical songs during the welcoming ceremony for the new bride, highlights the oratorical prowess of the first wife's friends and supporters. The song uses all possible poetic resources to denigrate the new wife physically and morally, to destabilize her psychologically in order to encourage her not to stay. The comparisons to a donkey and especially to a dog—given the Islamic context in which they take place—are particularly cutting. The vulgarity of the language contrasts sharply with the qualities of moderation, politeness, and courtesy normally expected of the Wolof woman.

In the second text, Zerma women of Niger offer another kind of oratorical contest. Two groups of antagonists, one supporting the first wife, the other supporting the new bride, confront each other, raising the level of verbal violence. Nevertheless, as soon as the jousting ends, the two groups offer to both wives the usual congratulations and advice. Representatives of both groups remind the women that they are henceforth sisters who will give birth to children linked by blood.

The verbal vigor, the rawness amplified by the sound of drums—which provide a particular rhythm to the festivities—reproduce aesthetically the emotions of the cowives. In both Wolof and Zerma cultures, the performance of the welcoming ceremony for the new bride functions to reduce the pressures of potential conflict. The ceremony suggests that such conflicts must not imperil domestic peace.

Aminata Diaw and Fatimata Mounkaïla

Communal, XAXAR, OR SATIRICAL SONG

Senegal [1998]*   Wolof

First Wife:
My greetings to you, new bride, like one greets a donkey.
My respects and honor to you, but you're worse than a bitch.

Chorus of Her Friends:
We greet you, new bride, as we would greet a donkey.

We respect and honor you, but you're worse than a bitch.
We greet you, new bride, as we would greet a donkey.
We respect and honor you, but you're worse than a bitch.

First Wife:
Will she stay, the new bride, will she stay?
Will she stay, the new bride, will she stay?
Look at her, this new bride, her skin's dull and ugly
she is snotty and dirty, and lousy in bed,
Will she stay, the new bride, will she stay?

Chorus of Her Friends
Will she stay, the new bride, will she stay?
Will she stay, the new bride, will she stay?

First Wife:
A good wife must keep calm, or she cannot stay.
A good wife must show poise, or she'll have to go.
A good wife must be upright, or it shatters all to bits.

Chorus of Her Friends:
A good wife must keep calm, or she cannot stay.

First Wife:
Will she stay, the new bride, will she stay?
Will she stay, the new bride, will she stay?

Chorus of Her Friends:
Will she stay, the new bride, will she stay?
Will she stay, the new bride, will she stay?

First Wife:
Look she's dull and ugly, really rotten and repulsive,
She's edgy and dirty and bad in bed
She irritable and dirty and useless in bed
Will she stay, the new bride, will she stay?

Chorus of Her Friends:
Will she stay, the new bride, will she stay?
Will she stay, the new bride, will she stay?

Translated into French by Souleymane Faye
Translated from French by Antoinette Tidjani Alou and Abena P. A. Busia

Niger [1997]   Songhai-Zarma

Group of First Wives:
  The second wife is worthless.
  May God curse the woman who is worthless.
  The second wife is a stork of misfortune.
  Who heralds winter but cannot stay.

Group of Wives in Second Position:
  Have they gone mad,
  These first wives with their empty heads?
  You were brought here.
  We were brought here.
  Stop the assault.

Translated into French by Aïssata Niandou
Translated from French by Marjolijn de Jager

CELEBRATING BIRTH

Among the Igbo of southeastern Nigeria, the birth of a child gives rise to a celebration by women in the community. A day is set aside when they go to the home where the child has been born not only to rejoice with the new mother but also to reaffirm themselves as a community of mothers. Underlying the joy is the relief that the new mother has escaped the fate of a woman denied her personhood and fulfillment because of her inability to procreate.

In producing a child, the new mother vindicates all mothers. In this spirit, the mothers of the community sing and dance. While all may join in, the songs are usually begun and sustained by those with special proficiency. The dancing of some women may even be described as frenzied, marking the deep emotion associated with the ritual of birth.

Most of the songs are of vintage origin, although performers may embellish them. This does not preclude the coining of new songs in performance. The songs bear an air of cockiness, pride, and defiance.

Although the texts cover a range of themes, they generally extol womanhood and especially the exclusivity of maternal fulfillment. In this mood, women remind themselves and others of their accomplishments, making themselves, in this respect, superior to men as agents of procreation and therefore of perpetuity. Childbirth thus provides a guarantee against oblivion.

While the ritual is communal, it is also individual and private. Two prominent Igbo womanist intellectuals collected the texts below.

Nkoli Ezumah and Esi Sutherland-Addy

Communal, WHERE IS IT FROM?

Nigeria 1986   Igbo

Where is it from, eh? It is from the womb.
Where is it from, eh? It is from the womb.
A policeman—he is from the womb.
A lawyer—he is from the womb.
A doctor—he is from the womb.

Translated by Helen Chukwuma

Communal, IF NOT FOR CHILDBIRTH

Nigeria 1987   Igbo

If not for childbirth!
If not for the power of giving birth,
Who will give me?
Buy white fowl, who will give me?
Bring white palm-wine, who will give me?
If not for the power of giving birth,
Who will give me?

Translated by Ifi Amadiume

Binta Bojang
KANYELENG, OR CHILDLESS

Gambia [2000]   Malinke

In the tradition of the Malinke people of Gambia, *Kanyeleng* is a barren woman or a woman who loses her children during childbirth or at an early age. Women who are *Kanyeleng* usually group together and undergo certain rituals to enable them to bear children or help their children survive by overcoming the evil spirits that some believe responsible for their deaths. Many people of West Africa believe that a bad child enters a mother's womb and is born only to die and be born again. (See the concept of *abiku* among the Yoruba of Nigeria.) Many believe that this process of coming and going will continue until rituals are performed to end it. One way to stop the process is to make a mark on the body of the dead baby, for instance by cutting off a finger. The child born to a woman who has been through *Kanyeleng* may be given a nickname indicating her or his ritual origins.

Binta Bojang was childless for twelve years. When she got pregnant, no one really believed she was with child. When she delivered, she sang the song that is featured in the narrative to embarrass the people around her. Because she has felt rejection, the formerly childless woman sings with rebellious irony and defiance. She suggests that she has had sexual relations with men from various ethnic groups and she makes derogatory remarks about her child. Indeed, Binta Bojang, whose life story appears here, has confessed to editing the song to remove its more racy aspects.

Like other women saved from the crushing social and emotional burden of childlessness, Binta Bojang feels eternally drawn to the circle of spiritual power and emotional strength in the hope of helping other women to overcome the odds. *Kanyeleng* is also known as *Fouraafen* in the adjoining Casamance region of Senegal where the Diola live.

Patience Sonko-Godwin and Esi Sutherland-Addy

✦

I know that the *Kanyeleng* ritual works.

I got married at Talinding Dembakunda and for ten years after I was unable to have a child. People told my husband, Yusupha, to divorce me because I would never have children. I tried all different ways of getting pregnant and having a child but to no avail.

There is a big baobab tree at Talindingkunjang. This tree has been there for years and is linked with the history of the first residents of Talinding. Women who are childless are taken there and prayers are offered at this spot to implore Almighty Allah to grant them children. Prayers are also offered on behalf of women who have had a number of stillbirths or who have had a number of children die during childhood. If a child is taken there and bathed at the site of the tree, by God's grace the child sometimes survives and grows up to be an adult. A woman who suffers frequent miscarriages also seeks prayers there.

One day a lady traveled from Jarra Sankwia and came to ask for prayers to be said on her behalf. She said it had taken her a long time before she had had her first child and that all her children had died young. She mentioned this to a woman called Satounding Badgie, wife of Jaeling Suwareh, who prayed for her and washed her at the site. After these prayers, she had a child and then she was told to bring the child to the site for the usual Kanyeleng ceremony and bathing. At the time, as part of the ceremony, rice porridge was cooked. In the past, the Diolas used to cook a Diola dish known as *serreng*, as well as rice porridge. Cola nuts and snuff were also sometimes used for the ceremony, even though the spot is not a magic one. It is a place where people entreat Almighty Allah to help those who have come there to pray, so that they may have children.

Those who used to bathe the women were Mariama Amangkawu, Sally

Colley, who is now dead, Yayending Jatta, as well as Penda Badgie, who is also no longer alive. Satounding Badgie has also died.

One day, Satounding Badgie asked a lady called Mariama Sanneh to go to my compound and ask me to come. I was cooking at the time and I was worried and asked what I had done that had warranted Satounding's summons. I wanted to know why they were asking for me. Mariama said, "You have not done anything. I have just been told to come and ask you to go to Satounding." I then accompanied Mariama and we walked on and on until we came to the baobab tree. At the time, that area was very dark. When I arrived, the *Kanyeleng* were all lying down and as soon as Satounding Badgie saw me she pointed her finger at me and all the *Kanyeleng* got up and took hold of me and asked, "Why have you not had a child up to now?" They then took the porridge and rubbed it all over me; others started to pinch and punch me. Then they put me down on the ground and started asking me, "Will you have children or not?" I was crying all the time and my grandmother Wassa Saidy and other relatives who were present were also crying. At the end of the ceremony, the *Kanyeleng* women conveyed me back to my grandmother's home and asked me not to take a bath that day. The following day they washed me, and by Allah's grace soon after I became pregnant.

When I informed my grandmother that I had missed my period, the old woman asked me not to reveal this to anyone. Some people even approached my husband to suggest that I was not pregnant. But he just told them, "Let us wait and see what Allah will do." Many people did not believe that I could have a child, and some even said that I had an illness in my stomach. Others attributed my bulging stomach to a bundle of clothes, though some people acknowledged that I had been washed at the site of the baobab tree where prayers are held for barren women. On the day I was being taken to the hospital to deliver, some people continued to mock me, "What did I tell you, she was just stuffing her stomach with clothes and is not pregnant or maybe she has an illness." At the hospital, I had my first child, a girl, and she was called Mbassey Colley. Others called her "Diolamuso" since she had been bathed by the Diolas, who also prayed for her to have children.

I had a very close friend residing at Bakau, Mariamanding, who has now passed away. When she heard that I had delivered, she came to the naming ceremony and asked to be introduced to the *Kanyeleng* women, Satounding Badgie and the others. She told them that their bathing had been very good for me and she said, "Today is your day but I beg your indulgence to allow me to sing for Binta, because even when I was at Bakau I used to hear people say that Binta was not pregnant, but had stuffed her stomach with clothes." She sang as follows:

One child nine fathers; Dala is a bastard
She said the society [of *Kanyeleng*] accepts the child
The Manjago are there

The Kassinko are there
The Diola are there
The Fula are there
The Balanta are there
All ethnic groups are there

She asked those present at the naming ceremony to echo her words and then sang on:

One child nine fathers Dala is a bastard
I am telling you that she is a bastard
One child nine fathers Dala is a bastard
Yusufa Demba is there
Basiru Demba is there
Njanko Demba is there
The Fula are there
The Balanta came
Diola came
I say the Kassinko were also there
The Serahuli are there
The Fula are there
The Aku are there
One child nine fathers Dala is a bastard
All the Fula are there
The Diola came
The Balanta came
The Kassinko were also there
The Fula are there
All the Aku were there

After singing the song several times, Mariamanding took some *Kanyeleng* beads and put them on me while my baby was on my back, and asked me to sing this song at any ceremony I attended. So I sang this song even when I stopped carrying my child on my back.

For me, the *Kanyeleng* ritual worked because I had a child after I was bathed by Satounding and the *Kanyeleng* group.

I want to repeat the warning given to me at the time of my bathing that I should not sleep with anyone else's husband, except my own. All those who are bathed and participate in this ceremony are told that if they do not sleep with someone else's husband, and if it so happens that they have a child by their own husband, the child will survive by Almighty Allah's grace. I am grateful to the Almighty that my prayers for a child have been answered. The *Kanyeleng* ceremony has been with us for a very, very long time and our elders used to offer prayers to Almighty Allah for those without a child, those for whom most of their children died during childhood, and those women who miscarried frequently. Through the prayers of the *Kanyeleng* women and the ritual, the Almighty has granted me five children. That is why today I still practice the *Kanyeleng* ritual, and whenever the women have their ceremony, I try to attend.

Translated into French by Kombo Sanyong Koringkunda
Translated from French by Aminata Deme and Judith Miller

LAMENTATIONS

In many African societies, death is a time of collective mourning and celebration, for it signifies a transition from this world into that of the ancestors. Funeral and burial ceremonies, meant to usher the deceased into their next abode, are therefore of great importance. During such ceremonies, women speak the grief of the entire community. They also function as historians by celebrating the dead person's life achievements. In many societies, including the Akan of south and central Ghana, songs, chants, and recitatives express grief aesthetically in funeral dirges and laments. These are performed at different points during the burial ceremony, some at such dramatic moments as the opening of a wake or upon the return from the cemetery. Women may dress in costume and perform short dramatic skits. It is a moment for exaggerated gestures of distress, such as laying hands on heads or stomachs or stretching arms to indicate their emptiness.

The three dirges that follow suggest some of the diversity of this form. The first two are Ghanaian. Like all traditional Akan dirges, "Nyaako" deals with the themes of the ancestor, of the place of origin of the deceased, following a well-known, prescribed pattern. The verbal skills of the solo performer, the daughter of the deceased, allow her to prolong the lament in an endlessly repetitive style, as she rhythmically interweaves names, appellations, proverbs, messages to the dead, and praise-singing. The performer poetically creates a mythic figure of her dead, idealized mother through praise epithets. She also attempts to reach out to the silent world through laments and messages. The text expresses the Akan philosophical approach to death, a declared belief in the survival of the dead in *Asamando,* the world of the dead, where they can be consulted through libation and sacrifice. In addition, the song hints at the strong ties between an Akan mother and her daughter in a matrilineal society whose motto is *wo ni wu a, wo abusua asa,* "when your mother dies, you have no more family."

"We Offer You Condolences" comes from the repertoire of *Manhyia Tete Nnwonkoro,* a group of Kumasi women in the Asante region of Ghana. For approximately fifty years, organized and predominantly women's groups have sprung up in many Akan communities, which perform *nnwonkoro,* a form of singing, at funeral celebrations. In response to modern demands, such songs have both the air of ancient tradition and a vital contemporary quality. The composer in this song highlights the loss as she engages in "crying and wailing" and a continuous search for the obliterated and unrecoverable "footprints" of "Grandfather," as she remembers his magnanimity and military prowess. The text emphasizes the Akan belief that both the physical and the metaphysical worlds are thrown into disarray when death occurs: "Ancient God *Kwaframoa* [Eternal] thundered. He also brought lightning." In addition, this song provides information on some activities performed at the funeral of a royal, including the firing of guns: "At the sound of the gun, we offer condolence."

The third song, "Dry Your Tears Little Orphan Doe," is a lament improvised by Sereer women of Senegal during a procession to the cemetery of one of their age-mates. They emphasize the crucial loss to the deceased's children, now orphans, to her sisters, and to themselves. The song is meant to comfort the youngest daughter of the deceased, who is affectionately called "Ngaay" or "Little Doe." "Seen," the name joined to "Ngaay," tells us immediately that we are in the Sereer world, where every family has a totem animal. The Seen family's totem is the deer. The composer emphasizes that dignity should hold sway over suffering in the face of death. Part of the beauty of the text resides in its repetitive rhythm.

Akosua Anyidoho, Rokhaya Fall, Christiane Owusu-Sarpong, and Aminata Diaw

✦

Afua Siaa (Fofie), NYAAKO

Ghana 1955   Akan-Twi

Grand-daughter of Nana Kwaagyei of Hwedee, who drinks the water
of Abono,
Kyeame ba, Kyeamewaa, spokesman's daughter, of a spokeswoman's
calling,
Mother, all looks well with me, but it's a battle.

Nyaakowaa of Anteade and grandchild of Osafo Agyeman,
Oh, mother, all looks well with me, but it's a battle.
Mother, when you send food, send it with a munificent cooking pot,
grand enough for feasting strangers.

The god Opem has seen red, the palm oil of failure,
and the gourd of spells wears the white clay of success.
Oh, mother, there is no branch within reach that I can grasp.
Mother, when you send your presents, send parched corn
Then even without cooking fire, I'll eat it raw.
Mother, pestiferous common fowl can kill a glorious parrot!
Grand-daughter of Nana Kwaagyei of Hwedee, who drinks the water
of Abono,

Nana, mighty pot, succor of strangers,
Appearances are really deceiving, for the battle is overwhelming.
Mother, generous gift-giver, when you find a voyager give them a gift
    for me.
Mother, this deserted dwelling has no fire to provide a lighted brand
    for me.
My Sustaining-Wicker-Basket that rescues me with rocks of salt,
O, mother, Otire's child doesn't cry, or I would weep blood for you.

Nana, the crab that knows the hiding places of alluvial gold,
What ails you, Kyeameba?
Oh, Mother! The shock of your death has ambushed me so.
Mother, all looks well with me, but it's a battle!

Translated by J. H. Kwabena Nketia
Translation revised by Abena P. A. Busia

Manhyia Tete Nwonkoro Group, WE OFFER YOU CONDOLENCES

Ghana 1994   Akan-Twi

Indeed, we offer condolence
At the sound of the gun, we offer condolence
In the silence we offer condolence
Your children are crying and wailing
We call the immutable one
Bonsu, the man, offspring of Nana Kwaku Yiadom Adusa
His wife and children are searching for him
Just as the rainbow searches for early morning mist
Oh, Nana,
His children are searching for him
    Alas!
Queen-Mother Dwomo's brother, the royal one
    Alas!
Queen Mother's child
His children are calling for him.
Ancient God Kwaframoa thundered, Kurudu!
He also brought lightning, Krada!
Had we known, we would have gone with grandfather
He is from Osenema
One who labors and succeeds
We have lost sight of your footprints, grandfather
The great one is gone
    Alas!

We search for him but cannot find him
   Alas!
Queen Mother's brother
Nana is no more
   Alas!
Intrepid warrior who led his own battles
If he had had his way, life would be a game of ceaseless warfare
He who could hit several men with one bullet
And yet would sport with several shots and hit nothing
Making others wish the game of war were over.
Bonsu, the man, grandson of Mother Earth
It is grandfather I am calling
At the sound of the gun, we offer condolence
In the silence we offer condolence
Orphan
Orphan
The sun has set
I am crying and searching for my father
I am privileged to be his offspring
Nana
I am crying and calling for him
The Valiant One
   Orphan
   Orphan
The sun has set
I am crying and searching for my father

Translated by Akosua Anyidoho and Abena P. A. Busia

Communal, DRY YOUR TEARS, LITTLE ORPHAN DOE

Senegal 1998   Sereer

Oh, my little doe, dry your tears!
Look, Thiab is crying! Oh, my little doe, dry your tears!

Tening Thiab's mother! Oh, my little doe, dry your tears!
Look, Thiab is crying, Oh, my little doe, dry your tears!

You are so forlorn, but oh, my little doe, dry your tears!
Look, your mama's here, Oh, my little doe, dry your tears!

Ndiague Dibor's mother! Oh, Thiab Diome, dry your tears!
Comfort your sister, Dibor, don't let her cry. Oh, do dry your tears!

You're not frightened, you're just feeling lonely, dry your tears!
Ngouma Mane Diome, my sister! Oh, Mane Diome, dry your tears!

You're not frightened, you're just feeling lonely, dry your tears!
Only Siga Ndour came back with the orphans. O Mane Diome, dry
  your tears!

So, your mama's home, Mane Diome! Oh, Mane Diome, dry your
  tears!
You're so forlorn, but Oh, Mane Diome, dry your tears!
Who will you confide in tomorrow? Oh, Mane Diome, dry your tears!
Oh, please comfort Mane Diome! Mane Diome, dry your tears!

Waly Diome's sister! O Mane Diome, dry your tears!
Dibor Ngoumba, do not cry! Mane Diome, dry your tears!

Where is Tening Diome's mother? O Mane Diome, dry your tears!
Show me Tening Diome's mother! Mane Diome, dry your tears!

Oh, my little doe, dry your tears!
Oh, Ngaay Seen, my little doe, dry your tears!

Translated into French by Souleymane Faye
Translated from French by Antoinette Tidjani Alou and Marjolijn de Jager

Nanahemmaa Toaa Ampofo Tua III
NTAM, AN OATH

Ghana 1989   Akan-Twi

Among the Akan of Ghana, funerals of chiefs are of particular cultural
importance. In the past, the death of a royal was considered a calamity, a
major threat to communal peace and continuity. Very structured rituals were
put in place by the elders to lead the endangered society to symbolically
break the "road of death" and to reopen the "road to life."

Among the most powerful speeches pronounced during such ceremonies
were those mentioning forbidden words referring to dreadful historical
events of the past. The speakers were few, carefully selected and trained; they
were either members of the royal family, occupying ancestral stools, or court
functionaries who had committed the history of the people to memory,

among them drummers, horn-blowers, or spokesmen. The only woman to occupy a high position in this tradition was, and still remains, the "Queenmother," known as the "mother of all royals." She is not necessarily the chief's mother but is nevertheless always related to him through the maternal lineage. In Akan society, the Queenmother participates significantly in the selection of the male leader, and also in the "matters of the house." She has her own court and officers, and she participates, as the only woman, in various functions usually reserved for men.

Hence, on 3 August 1989, Nanahemmaa Toaa Ampofo Tua III was the only woman to take part in a major ritual event, the funeral of Nana Abakumahene Asumadu Yeboah III, one of the subchiefs of the Wenchi traditional area in the Brong-Ahafo region of Ghana. The time for lamenting was over, and the time of separation—burial—was approaching, the high point of the funeral, since the dead had to be pacified and sent away willingly, through praises and good wishes. All the chiefs of the Wenchi traditional area, their spokesmen, as well as the Queenmother of Wenchi, stepped forward amid the congregation to address the dead chief one last time, in a manner both proverbial and diplomatic. Some of these poetic texts were reminiscent of the history of Wenchi. All ended with the famous forbidden words (*ntam*), which called to mind the disastrous period of Asante raids during the eighteenth century, in the Bono region northwest of Asante.

The only glorious moment during those old tragic events was an episode during which the Queenmother of Wenchi, Nanahemmaa Toaa Ampofo Tua I, predecessor of the current Queenmother, escaped from the hands of the *Asantehene*, the powerful Asante King Osei Tutu. Around 1711, Osei Tutu had gone on a campaign against the Domaa, whose chief, Kyereme Sikafo, had refused to enter into an alliance with Asante. On King Osei Tutu's way to Domaa, the beautiful Queenmother, who was performing a ritual by the riverside, was captured by Osei Tutu's army and taken to the Asante empire's capital city, Kumase, where the king wanted to make her his wife without having performed the customary rites. She was soon to be released, for the Gods who were protecting this most powerful woman nearly destroyed Kumase, causing a terrible rain to flood the streets, destroying the king's shade tree—hence her praise-name, *Sraman Gyedua*, Divine Lightning That Strikes the Shade Tree of Kings, Threatening Floods.

This is the glorious historical episode remembered by Nana Wenchihemmaa Toaa Ampofo Tua III, whose duty it was always to serve the chief and the royal family as others had before her. She started her text with pacifying praise words and ended by reminding him of the glorious past of his illustrious ancestors. The present battle—his journey to *Asamando*, the abode of the dead—would also be won by the "departing," with the support of all the royals. Most of all, the battle against death, the survival of the community of the living, would be achieved through the pronouncement of the most forbidden words by the most powerful people in the community as a general catharsis against evil and death.

Christiane Owusu-Sarpong

Firebrand, flinty bullet reeking of gunpowder,
youthful sage,
dependable emissary,
maturity of the elders in the form of a child—
I say, condolences!
Worthy lancer—
I say, bravo, for a fight well fought!

Were it not Odomankoma, Almighty Death, that had claimed you,
Were it not that fierce beast that had cast you out,
Would I, Nanahemmaa Toaa Ampofo Tua,
Sraman Gyedua,
  Divine Lightning That Strikes the Shade Tree of Kings, Threaten-
  ing Floods,
Would I have turned my back on you?
Invoking our Unspeakable Taboo, I swear!

Translated by Abena P. A. Busia and Christiane Owusu-Sarpong

THIRTEENTH CENTURY TO 1916
THE AGE OF AFRICAN EMPIRES

Communal
TWO SONGS FOR SUNJATA
Mali [1993]*   Malinke

These two songs were composed in honor of Sunjata Keïta (1235–1255), emperor of Mali. Both academic and traditional historians attribute the first song to Sogolon Kondé, Keïta's mother, and the second to his sister. According to oral history, King Gnankouman Doua gave Sogolon Kondé to hunters who had managed to kill a buffalo that was threatening the Do country. They, in turn, gave Sogolon Kondé, who was an ugly hunchback, said to be the buffalo's alter ego, to King Maghan Fon Katta, who married her. She gave birth to a first child, Sunjata Keïta, whose praise-name became the Lion-Child. Sogolon became Maghan Fon Katta's favorite wife. According to predictions, the child was to become ruler of the Manding and would immortalize its people.

Sunjata was, however, handicapped from birth. When his father died, he was seven years old and had not yet walked. His half-brother, Dankara Touman, the son of Maghan's first wife, Sassouma Bérété, was declared king through his mother's intrigues. That was when Sunjata, his mother, and his sisters, Kolokan and Djamarou, began to experience hardship and humiliation. One day, Sogolon asked her cowife to give her some baobab tree leaves to prepare a sauce. Sassouma complied but not without letting her know, in a vicious manner, that when Dankara Touman was seven years old he used to be the one to collect the leaves for her. Sassouma Bérété's mocking laughter profoundly exasperated Sogolon. She felt so humiliated that, when she got back home, she could not help but turn her anger against Sunjata. In order to avenge his mother and fulfill her wish, Sunjata decided not only to walk but also to uproot a whole baobab tree and plant it in front of Sogolon's house, so that all the children of Dakadyalan would have to go there to collect their leaves from that day on.

Sunjata asked for a cane. Balla Fasséké, the *griot*, had it made at the royal blacksmith's. Farakourou, the master blacksmith, who was a soothsayer himself, immediately knew that the day had come. He instantly ordered his apprentices to carry an iron bar to the palace. That bar had been made by his father, and its purpose had been a mystery to everyone. Sunjata then used it to get himself off the ground, making it bend under his weight, to the amazement of all who lived in the palace, particularly Sassouma Bérété and Balla Fasséké.

On seeing this feat, Sogolon Kondé sang her thanksgiving to God, celebrating her son's ability to walk. She also sang to force her malicious cowife to witness the event. Sunjata's youngest sister, Sogolon Kolonkan Konaté, sang the second song on the same occasion.

Both these songs date from the thirteenth century. They have been remembered throughout the ages and are part of popular culture of contemporary Mali. We are grateful to historian Adama Bâ Konaré for their preservation.

Aminata Diaw

✦

ONE

Come out, women, come out of your huts!
Sunjata has walked!
Women, you Witches!
Sunjata has walked!
Today is a sweet day!
Today is the most beautiful day Allah ever made!

TWO

My sterling brother, the eldest of us all,
The day you call me to celebrate with you,
I will strut about, preening among your crowd of guests
With the majesty of a vulture,
My base older brother, so much hated by all,
The day you call me to celebrate with you,
I will crouch in my corner,
Like a tree frog.

Translated into French by Adama Bâ Konaré
Translated from French by Christiane Owusu-Sarpong

Communal
ELEGY FOR INIKPI

Nigeria [2000]*   Igala

A simple six-line song that immortalizes Inikpi, the martyr of Igalaland, is part of a performance at an annual land festival in Nigeria. A complex series of founding myths begins with a ruling clan founded by Ebele Ejaunu, daughter of Abutu Eje, who first established an Igala kingdom and dynasty. Ebele Ejaunu married a handsome stranger who, though said to have been born a slave, rose through merit and marriage to become the first *Ashadu*, or principal king-maker, of the clan, and in fact the *Ata* (king) is ritually referred to today as the Ashadu's "wife." After the death of Ebele and her brother, her brother's son Idoko became the first Ata of Igala. Idoko, a renowned hunter and magician, was the father of Ata Ayegba, the first dynastic ruler of the consolidated kingdom, from whom all the royal clans of Igalaland trace their descent. Ata Ayegba was the father of the legendary martyr Inikpi.

In serious difficulty with a powerful neighboring people, Ayegba consulted Ifa, a Yoruba oracle, whose advice called for the sacrifice of his beloved virgin daughter. When Inikpi heard what had been divined and understood the source of her father's suffering, she begged him to save himself by sacrificing her. She is said to have offered herself willingly, and to have pressed her father nine times before he finally consented. A large hole was dug in the marketplace, and she went down into it with nine slaves and with all her jewels and charms. To this day her statue stands above the site where she was buried alive along with her slaves, at Ega market, near the bank of the Niger River, at Idah.

Today, two main cults underpin state rituals in Igalaland. These are the cult of the ancestors and the cult of the land. Inikpi is worshiped as part of the rituals associated with the land cult. This is significant because the commemoration of her sacrifice serves as a solemn reminder to the king that, given the history of the establishment of the kingdom, he has no automatic claim for the control of the land. The sacrifice of Inikpi restores balance following the disruptions of bloodshed.

Since the time of Inikpi (generally estimated to have been in the middle of the seventeenth century, though some scholars place it a century earlier), at the conclusion of the yearly *Ocho,* or land festival, the Ata makes a round of various sacred sites that culminates at Inikpi's shrine. As the Ata dips his bare feet into the river Niger, the priestess of the shrine makes ceremonial offerings to Inikpi. She and other women sing the song below, calling to Inikpi for guidance through difficult times. They invoke her to avert witchcraft and all misfortune from the kingdom for the next year so that the land may be fertile, the numbers of children increase normally, and the king rule in peace. The annual and necessary rite of restoration is held sacred to this very day.

Patience Mudiare and Abena P. A. Busia

✦

Inikpi, father's beloved daughter
Inikpi, father's beloved daughter
The Igalaland you fought for
Is no longer progressing
So, we plead with you, to open the way for us
Inikpi, father's beloved daughter.

Translated by D. L. Obieje

Madlena Van Poppos
LETTER OF PETITION
Benin 1739   Dutch Creole

This entry's significance stems from its being first written, in 1739, in an African language, by one "Marotta, now Madlena from Poppo in Africa," and then translated into Dutch Creole. *A History of the Moravian Church,* written by J. E. Hutton in 1909, contains the only information on record about this woman. From that book we can learn something about the origins of this text.

The Moravian church established a mission in St. Thomas in the Caribbean in late 1732, making it the first organized church mission to the New World. In 1736, master missionary Friedrich Martin, "the Apostle to the Negroes," referred to as "Bas Martinus" in Madlena Van Poppos's letter, took over and advanced the work of the mission, despite fierce opposition from the planters and the Dutch Reformed church. He established several native congregations, opened a school for Negro boys, and helped to form groups for Bible study and prayer.

On 29 January 1739, Count Nikolaus von Zinzendorf, usually held responsible for the revival of the Moravian church at the beginning of the eighteenth century, arrived to monitor the work of the mission; he stayed for three months. Hutton records that, to crown Brother Martin's work, the count appointed one "Peter" chief elder of the brethren, and "Magdalene" chief elder of the sisters. Both were slaves who were apparently literate. Zinzendorf returned to Europe with two letters, one from the male slaves to the king of Denmark and the other from the female slaves, addressed to the queen. These two letters thus represent early diplomatic correspondence in a Creole language.

The letter from the male slave, Peter, was written in Dutch Creole, but the one from the female slave, Madlena, had first been written in a now unidentifiable African language, arguably an ancient version of Mina, Phla, or Ewe languages spoken today on the stretch of the Gulf of Guinea between the Volta region of Ghana and present-day Benin. Her letter was then translated into Dutch Creole for the purpose of transmission to the queen of Denmark. Both the African and the Dutch Creole versions were later published in the 1742 volume of the "Periodical Accounts Relating to the Missions of the Church of the United Brethren Established among the Heathen."

The Danes had established a trading post in St. Thomas in 1666. In 1685, they signed a treaty with the Duchy of Brandenburg to allow the Brandenburg American Company to establish a slave-trading post there, and slavery remained the focus of commerce until its abolition in 1848. Even though by 1739 the island of St. Thomas was owned by the Danes, Dutch was then the lingua franca of the planters. Hence, it is not surprising that the slaves spoke it. Danish, however, remained the official language for records, documents, and public signs. The language of the slaves, Dutch Creole, was preserved in oral folktales originating in West Africa, and in missionary translations of the Bible and liturgical texts. Thus, the written record of this letter in Dutch

Creole is extraordinary; that the letter exists as well in Madlena's African language is exceptional.

The letter seems occasioned by a problem confirmed elsewhere in the church history, as well as in other sources: The conditions under which the slaves were living in St. Thomas was wretched. The Moravian mission to St. Thomas had been inspired by a chance encounter at the court of King Christian VI of Denmark in 1731 between Count Zinzendorf and a West Indian Negro slave named Anthony Ulrich, who pleaded for someone to come to St. Thomas to preach the gospel to the suffering slaves. His pleas persuaded the Moravians.

It is noteworthy that Madlena is clearly establishing her right to be heard by emphasizing her conversion from worship of "The Lord Mau" in her unconverted state. In the Dahomean pantheon of gods, MawuLisa is the dual-aspect, male-female creator deity. Despite the fact that in Dahomey, it is the female aspect that is generally referred to as Mau or Mawu, in this letter Madlena refers to her as "the Lord Mau." The expression "*A Niba*" comes from the Mina expression "*anyi gban*," which means master of the earth (*anyi* means "earth" and *gban* means "master" in the sense of governing god or spirit). We have not been able to confirm the exact derivation of "*Neacanda*," translated here from the 1742 Dutch Creole version as "Great Queen."

Abena P. A. Busia

✦

The eldest [*sic*]of the community of the Negroes in St. Thomas write [*sic*] to the Queen of Denmark in 1739.

Great Queen:
At the time I lived in Poppo in Africa, I served the Lord Mau. Now that I have come to the Land of Whites I don't want to serve that Lord. I do not have reason to serve that Lord; my heart is saddened, because Negro woman cannot serve the Lord Jesus on St. Thomas. If the Whites do not want to serve the Lord, be that as it may. But if the poor Black brethren and sisters want to serve the Lord, they have to behave as if they were Maroons. If it pleases you Great Queen, you have to pray to the Lord Jesus for us, and also pray A Niba, the Master of the Earth, to let Brother Martinus remain and preach the word of the Lord, because we have to learn to know the Lord, and also to baptize us Negroes, in the name of the Father, the Son, and the Holy Ghost. May the Lord keep and bless sons and daughters, and the whole family, and I shall pray to the Lord Jesus for them.

In the name of more than 250 Negro women who love the Lord Jesus, written by
Marotta, now Madlena from Poppo in Africa

Translated from Dutch Creole by Cefas Van Rossem and Hein Van Der Voort
Translation revised by Abena P. A. Busia

Nana Asma'u
POEMS

Nana Asma'u Shaykh Uthman D'an Fodiyo was born a twin with a brother named Hassan in 1793 in Degel, a small Torankawa Fulani settlement northwest of Sokoto. She died in 1863, leaving a collection of about eighty poems in Arabic and Ajami—a localized version of the Arabic script—and was buried in the family's mausoleum beside her father, who died in 1817, the same year as Hassan. Her father was a nineteenth-century Islamic revivalist leader and the founder of Sokoto Caliphate, an area that today forms the northern states of Nigeria and other parts of formerly French-occupied Cameroon, Niger Republic, Benin Republic, and Burkina Faso, thus making it the largest empire in Africa since the fall of Songhai in 1591.

Her descent from a family of learned Islamic teachers and scholars of Sufi Qadriyya brotherhood is crucial to her extraordinary contributions to Islamic women's scholarship and literature. Her father promoted women's education, and her paternal great-grandmother, grandmother, mother, aunts, and other sisters were all scholars. From some of them Nana Asma'u received her early training.

The relevance of Nana Asma'u's place as a historical figure of sub-Saharan African literature stems from the female imprint she stamped on Jihad literary production and theory, reflected in the thematic versatility of the poetry aimed to integrate new female converts. Nana Asma'u used her literacy in classical Arabic and her abilities in such local languages as Fulfulde, Tamajaq, and Hausa to transform the works of her father and her brother Ahmadu Bello. Thus, the new Islamic ideology could reach both the unlettered Fulani brethren and the Hausa women converts who were deeply immersed in Bori, spirit possession healing practices, and cosmological views of the universe. As Beverly Mack and Jean Boyd have pointed out, the integration of a heterogeneous new constituency into a religiously homogenous Islamic Caliphate, especially through women, the primary transmitters of the ethos of culture and cultural traditions, rested heavily on, and benefited from, Nana Asma'u's intellectual genius. Using African languages, she feminized the classical Arabic Jihad literature, and in the process, shifted its masculinist formulation.

Written in 1827, "Give Us Victory" is an urgent and impassioned plea to God to come to the aid of the Caliphate forces facing armies on two fronts. To the south and east they were hard-pressed by a rebellion, and to the north and east they faced a massed army of Hausa rulers, furious at their overthrow and trying to reassert their control. In this powerful work, Asma'u calls on a variety of "Holy Allies," who are marshaled as reinforcements. The line "For the Honor of the board and the pen" in this poem is a reference to the writing board and pen, the instruments that create the holy word. In addition, the poem contains several terms that refer to the holy works of the "people of the book": "Tawra" is the Torah, "the book" given to Moses; "Zabaura" is "Zabur" or the Psalms; and "Lanjiyla" is the New Testament. Muslims recognize all the Jewish prophets including Jesus of Nazareth, but they do not accept the interpretations, such as the Acts of the Apostles or the letters of the Apostles. The poem is unfinished; the concluding few couplets that would have provided the closing doxology were lost at some time. No other copy has been found.

"Be Sure of God's Truth," written in 1831, illustrates how, through translation and cultural adaptation of the works of her father and her brother Ahmadu Bello, Nana Asma'u's texts now stand as a challenge to any "individualist" analysis of authorial voice in Afro-Islamic literature. At play here is the distinction between Western norms that seek to establish the absolute individuality of an author and the dual African-Islamic aesthetic tradition that gives room for improvisation built on others' work.

The African side of this heritage draws from the oral tradition in which texts of the collective imagination are continuously recrafted by individual narrators and performers in response to the audience and the functional imperatives of the moment. The Islamic dimension of the heritage, on the other hand, is tied to the Islamic principle of Ijthihad, a search for truth to achieve a higher order of meaning and understanding, by building on and/or transforming prior works collectively or individually produced. In spite of the collective essence of the "final" works, however, comparative textual analysis may reveal individual genius and creativity. *Hakika*, though a word with special Sufi significance, is also used in everyday speech to mean "undoubtedly." It has been retained by the translators to provide the sense of its mantric effect. It is clear from the word used that the "sanctions" referred to as being violated by victorious armies include the mandatory period of three menstrual cycles during which women may not remarry if widowed or in this case permanently separated from their husbands. It was, however, lawful for soldiers to have sexual intercourse with a female captive after waiting for one menstrual cycle.

In "Elegy for Zaharatu," Nana Asma'u celebrates Zaharatu for her specialized knowledge as a midwife and her kindness as a volunteer mortician who prepared the dead for burial. This celebratory poem describes a supportive group of "beloved women friends."

Ousseina D. Alidou

✦

GIVE US VICTORY

Nigeria 1827 Fulfulde

I begin with God, the Beneficent, and the noble Prophet, bringer of
    the Qur'an
May the blessing and peace of Allah be upon him;
    he was taken to heaven and greatly rewarded
And upon his Relatives and Companions who exceeded their
    contemporaries, also those known for their piety and generosity who
    followed
I beseech God to give victory to the Muslims. It is right to make
    requests to Him,
    for He is omnipotent.

And has other wonderful attributes, Almighty Merciful and Beneficent.
Oh God I beg you to unite and reconcile all Muslims wherever they
 may be
And give them victory. Destroy unbelief and fortify religion until it
 reaches
  to the very throne of God.
For the sake of the matchless Prophet who is our rightful mediator.
And for his sake quell the rebellion which engulfs Hausaland and its
 borders:
  it is right to cleave to him.
Oh God destroy Gandi, Maradi, and Talata. Bring them to utter ruin.
For the Honor of the board and the pen and what was written.
For the Honor of the Qur'an, the most excellent of books, and the Old
 Testament Books of Psalms and the words of Jesus.
For the Honor of all the Holy Books of God, religion, and insight of
 precious Belief.
For the honor of the Prophet and other Envoys of God; I rely on them
 and pray that God
For the honor of the Assembly of His Angels.

BE SURE OF GOD'S TRUTH

Nigeria 1831 Hausa

Let us praise the King, *hakika*, in Truth,
Who is merciful and generous, *hakika*, in Truth.
Mankind is fully aware of this, *hakika*, in Truth.
Thanks be to God the Sovereign, *hakika*, in Truth
 One God sufficient for all, Be sure of God's Truth.
Kinsmen, let us pray ceaselessly for the Prophet
With attention to detail let us beseech the Prophet
Let us pray and invoke blessings on the Prophet
 Ahmadu who excelled all, Be sure of God's Truth
Let everyone consider and reflect.
I will give you good advice: be respected
Let us continue to follow the Path, and escape retribution.
Listen to my song and repent
 And so find salvation, Be sure of God's Truth. . . .

If you join the Jihad, give heed—
You fight for God's sake, do not forget.
Those who cheat their companions using evil charms,
And those who use brute force to wrest things illegally,

Will be exposed, Be sure of God's Truth
When a town is captured wreak no vengeance
Wrongdoing is unworthy of us.
Yet some of us are always defaulting:
Those who steal booty from those who first captured it.
    Will be seized by the Fire, Be sure of God's Truth
Captured booty must definitely not be hidden:
War trophies must be taken to the leader.
There are those, without doubt, who conceal booty.
Those who deny the poor their rightful share
    Will receive the Fire as their share, Be sure of God's Truth.
When the army is victorious
Slaves are taken, including some for the leader.
But some men act illegally
They fall on the women, disregarding all sanctions
    They will fall in the Fire, Be sure of God's Truth
Be fair in all your dealings, even about the smallest thing
Do not dupe people headed to the market to sell.
It is wrong, like reclaiming gifts you have given away.
Those who are untrustworthy, Hereafter,
    Will have no trust left, Be sure of God's Truth
You have been warned to practice no oppression
So that you will receive the pardon of God the Bountiful
Anyone who refuses will eat the bitter fruit of Hell
And he who robs with violence, including Muslims,
Or breaks faith, will burn, Be sure of God's Truth. . . .

I have set forth my warnings, kinsmen,
to make you wake from slumber,
to make you repent. Do you hear Muslim friends?
Everything I have said in this song is true,
    As are forgiveness and salvation, Be sure of God's Truth
I have finished, kinsmen, hear the Truth
take it into your hearts, it is the truth
the truth is what the song is about, hear the Truth.
All of us, let us repent, for anyone who in Truth
    repents will be saved. Be sure of God's Truth.
I shall praise the Prophet all my life
Until the time when I shall die.
Because of him God made forgiveness possible,
let us give thanks to Him and pray
For Muhammadu who excelled, Be sure of God's Truth.
Shehu composed the original version of this song
Nana translated it into Hausa

Isa wrote the *takhmis*,
In Hausa, and the reason was
> To bring this warning, Be sure of God's Truth.

ELEGY FOR ZAHARATU

Nigeria 1857   Fulfulde

I give thanks to God, Who never dies, only He can
> put right the misfortune which has occurred.
He is Omnipotent, He alone has power, His
> authority is limitless.
I pray for the Prophet who dwelt in Mecca.
I pray for his Kinsmen and Companions
> and all those who followed the Sunna
My friends with this song I sympathize with you
> over the death of Zaharatu.
She was a fine person who benefited the Muslim Community.
She gave religious instruction to the ignorant and helped
> everyone in their daily affairs.
Whenever called upon to help, she came responding
> to lay out the dead without hesitation.
With the same willingness she attended women in childbirth.
> All kinds of good works were performed by Zaharatu.
She was pious and most persevering: she delighted
> in giving and was patient and forbearing.
I grieve for her in this song: I weep because unhappiness
> fuels my burning heart.
And I am sorrowful because the world is being
> depleted by the deaths of my beloved women friends
Help me, Muslims, with this elegy
> I composed for Zaharatu.
I bow before the authority of God, for nothing can
> deflect His intentions.
O God forgive her and be merciful for
> Your mercy is infinite.
May God help her to answer the questions
> of Munkari and Nakiri.
May she have comfort in the grave,
> knowing that she will be saved.
May she be united with the Shehu, and redeemed
> by the Prophet, the Exalted.
On the Day of Judgment may she be sheltered
> from the sun and shielded from the Day's terrors.

May she be given her papers in her right hand
    and on the scales, may God assist her.
May she be helped on the Bridge, and drink at Kausara,
    for all who drink there thirst no more.
May she be saved from Hellfire and taken to Heaven,
    the place all Muslims long for.
Unite her with those who will see Your Holiness,
    then every desire will have been met.
May we be united with her in Paradise
    where joy is unceasing.
Together with all other Muslims, for the sake of
    the Prophet of Medina
O God receive these requests. I thank you
    and pray for the Prophet.
And his Kinsmen and Companions and all those
    Who have followed the Sunna.
In the year of the Hajira 1274.

Translated by Jean Boyd and Beverly B. Mack

Nditi Ba
MAKORI, OR THE TRIUMPH OF SLAVES

Senegal [1998]*   Fulfulde

The original date of *"Makori,* or the Triumph of Slaves" cannot be deter
mined, but its composition can be inserted into the historical sequence that
covers the eighteenth through the mid-nineteenth century. It is set in the
Puular community in northern Senegal.

The slave trade had a tremendous impact on this region. During the eighteenth century, its consequences began to be felt internally, for it disrupted
all social structures. Social and political institutions underwent profound
changes. New military aristocracies established reigns based on violence and
the search for slaves through raids. Such turmoil in the entire northern
region of Senegambia continued through the early nineteenth century until
France abolished the slave trade in 1848.

"Makori," a traditional tune, is, in fact, a legend that is recounted in the
Fuuta region in northern Senegal. It establishes and consecrates the integration of the slaves as a social group into the Fuutanke community. The text
sets out all of the social components of the Fuuta kingdom: the *torodos*
(nobles) who have political power; the fishermen who are important here
because the river Senegal crosses the region of Fuuta; the *sebbees,* foreigners
of Wolof origin; the *diawandos* who are the courtiers; the *wambabe* who are

the musicians; the cobblers and blacksmiths who are the artisans; and finally the slaves—at the bottom of the social ladder.

Each of these constituencies occupied a well-defined place in society that was assigned by "tradition." According to the legend, "social standing comes with mother's milk." It is obvious that one cannot talk about social standing for slaves; they have none. Their integration into the community could come about only by another means, and the development of the Makori legend, attributing a glorious feat to them, was the opportunity. The significance of the text is that it shows, beyond the issue of the liberation of the slaves and through the character of Farmata Kamara, the importance of women in this society. If it is through mother's milk that each individual achieves social standing, then it is still through the exploits of one woman that one can shatter restrictive social structures. What Makori ultimately comes to mean, therefore, is the unheard-of, the impossible, the music of total freedom beyond our dreams.

The text was performed by Nditi Ba, in the village of Bogo, which is located in the department of Podor. *Ndeyssane* means "it is so." *Sallifana* and *tiisbar* are afternoon prayers.

Renée Larrier

✦

Ndeyssane! A child cannot play with the lizard that captures a python.
  This is Makori.

Hear me: Possessing nothing is unfortunate. Happiness is not for
  everyone.
Poverty keeps one from being happy. Poverty is bad.
It may not determine your fate
But it prevents you from doing what you want.

This is the story of Makori.
Let me tell you its origins.
Makori can always be played with pleasure.

The Peuls said Makori was for them.
The *torodos* said it was theirs.
The *diawandos* said it was theirs
The fisherman said it was theirs.
The *sebbees* said it was theirs.
The cobblers said it was theirs.
The blacksmiths said it was theirs.
The slaves said it was theirs.
Kalilou Bourema pronounced: "Social standing comes with mother's milk
But glory can be earned.
We must earn Makori.
We must dig a well whose depth is seven times a man.

We must light a fire for a week.
We must play the music of Makori.
The caste that braves the fire in the well will earn Makori as its own."

Ndeyssane! For a week, they lit a fire in the well.
The drums resounded.
The *wambabe* brought out their guitars.
They sat around the well.
They began to play.
They began to play.
They played Makori from morning until *sallifana*.
Whoever leaned over the edge of the well
Quickly backed away.
The music rose and fell.

A young man attired himself carefully, then mounted his horse.
He arrived to see what was happening.
He was told that if he entered the well
He would earn Makori.
He got off his horse.
He reached the edge of the well
And thought the game wasn't worth it.
A young woman slave was about to give birth.
She was in labor.
Her name was Farmata Kamara.
She was in labor until *tiisbar*.
In the village, the guitars were playing loudly.
God granted her wish.
She gave birth.
Her mother gave the child its first bath
And threw the water behind their dwelling.
Farmata bathed herself.
She opened her baskets and took out her clothes and her finery.
She left her dwelling and went towards the crowd.
She was wearing a cowry headband and holding a rod.
She was quite fair-skinned.
The young slave told her mother to watch over the child
So that he would not be taken by evil spirits.

(When the world was the world, if a woman had a baby and needed to go out, the child had to be watched. Now no one thinks about it and that's why there are so many idiots.)

The young slave approached the assembled people.
Her husband asked her, "Where are you going?"

She did not answer.
She went towards the well
While the guitars played more intensely.
When she reached the well, the fire rekindled
As if expecting the young woman's arrival.
The heat increased.
The guitarists had to leave their places.
She was not dissuaded. She arrived and looked into the well.
And then she laughed!
She said, "Wambabe, play Makori!"
They played Makori. She listened.

She said: "Wambabe, where there is no witness, there is nothing."
I will earn Makori for all the slaves.
Slaves, here is what I have to tell you:
If Makori is played in the presence of a man,
He must give something if he can.
If he has nothing to give,
Let him take in a breath and let it out.
If he has nothing to give,
Let him flinch and show how bad he feels.
If he has nothing to give,
Let him be silent and sad.

If Makori is played in the presence of a woman,
If she has something to give
Let her give.
If she has nothing to give,
May she not mourn me if I die.
A slave with rain-drenched face
Must not cry for me,
Nor the woman who ladles couscous out of a pot
And takes a handful to keep,
Nor she who is awakened roughly
And must calm her body,
Nor she on whose foot the lizard sits all day long.

She attached a white scarf to her head.
She jumped into the well.
And God transformed the fire into cold milk.
The well was filled with cold milk.
She began to swim
Some came up to the well.
They pulled her out

And saw that her clothing was wet.
She went back to the assembled people.
They said it was magic.
Others said she had secret knowledge.
The well began to blaze again.
She jumped back in three more times.
She said, "This is Makori.
I have earned Makori for the slaves from now until the end of my line.
Every slave that hears Makori should offer money.
If they have none
They should snap their fingers and be heard.
If they cannot snap
They should shout 'Yes!'
If they can't do that, however poor they are,
They can grab a handful of soil
And offer it to the guitar player."
As far as I know, that's where Makori comes from.
That's why slaves only know true pleasure when they listen to Makori.
That is how I heard the old ones tell it.

Translated into French by Omar Ndongo
Translated from French by Judith Miller

Ola Bentsir Adzewa Group
THE WARRING HOSTS
Ghana [1996]*   Akan-Fante

Every Fante community in Ghana has at least one militia or Asafo group, which once defended the community. Today Asafo remains a strong ritual institution, with every man automatically belonging to his father's Asafo, and with women taking charge of the ritual and celebratory occasions. The Adzewa group, an association of women, learns about and passes on the history of the Asafo, particularly through a sacred core of texts, always sung first during formal performances. The Adzewa group also has license to compose songs expressing frank opinions on current events.

"The Warring Hosts" forms part of the sacred core of texts from the Bentsir Adzewa group of Cape Coast. The song was composed in honor of Adwoa Kwadua, who is best known for responding bravely to the wartime death of her husband and ninety-nine other men. In an alliance with the British Governor Charles MacCarthy, they had lost a campaign against the Asante kingdom. Adwoa Kwadua assumed the onerous burden of redeeming the lives of these dead men by paying each of the surviving families a measure of gold dust. News of this brave act reached the governor, who personally offered his condolences.

Since MacCarthy arrived on the Gold Coast in 1821 and died in a campaign against the Asante in 1824, the song can be dated as composed during that period. MacCarthy is the "Whiteman" in the song, given the Fante name "Kwesi," thus acknowledging the family bond between him and Adwoa, as father and daughter. The word *"enyaado"* is a gracious greeting of respect offered to Adwoa Kwadua by the governor.

Esi Sutherland-Addy

✦

Call	In this situation, what am I to do? The warring hosts have destroyed my most precious treasure. Ayee. Adwoa, daughter of Asebu ancestors.
Response	The warring hosts have destroyed my most precious treasure. Ayee.
Call	Adwoa, Daugher-of-Kwesi-the-Whiteman.
Response	The warring hosts have destroyed my most precious treasure. Ayee.
Call	Adwoa, daughter of Kofi Dadzie.
Response	The warring hosts have destroyed my most precious treasure. Ayee.
Call	Know that however pale your skin You can be to the whiteman no closer kin Than Adwoa, daughter of the whiteman.
Response	The warring hosts have destroyed my most precious treasure. Ayee.
Call	Ayee! Pitiable one.
Response	Pity, *enyaado,* ee. The whiteman says, "What a pity." Pity, *enyaado,* ee. The warring hosts have destroyed my most precious treasure. Ayee.
Call	What is it? Aaaahhhh! It is my most precious treasure, Adwoa, Daughter-of-Kwesi-the-Whiteman.
Response	The warring hosts have destroyed my most precious treasure. Ayee.
Ensemble	Ayee! Pitiable one. Pity, *enyaado,* ee, such a pity. The whiteman says, "What a pity." Pity, *enyaado,* ee, The warring hosts have destroyed my most precious treasure.

Translated by Esi Sutherland-Addy and Abena P. A. Busia

Malinda Rex
LETTER FROM A FORMER SLAVE
Liberia 1839   English

Between 1820 and 1861, some twelve thousand people were transported from the United States, under the protection of the American Colonization Society, to form what became the West African country of Liberia. More than half of these émigrés were freed slaves. While the American Colonization Society provided some amount of housing, food, and other necessaries during the early months, for the most part people had to find their own way. The 273 letters collected by Bell I. Wiley in *Slaves No More: Letters from Liberia 1833–1869* express the unhappiness and pessimism of some as well as the contentment, relief, and optimism of others. Many describe severe illnesses and the deaths of their loved ones. Some of the writers change their views over the years, as their circumstances improve or worsen. In many letters, the themes of religion and education remain dominant, as do the continuing ties to former masters and the deep and abiding interest in the fate of relatives left behind. We are very fortunate to have these letters, many of them from literate slaves.

The letter from Malinda Rex to Duncan Cameron, like others in the volume, describes hardships and asks for aid. She arrived in Caldwell, Liberia, in September 1839, on the ship *Saluda*, and wrote her letter to Duncan Cameron, one of the executors of the estate of her former master, John Rex, a tanner and property owner from North Carolina, within a few months of her arrival. She is not happy to be in the colony, she wants what was promised to her, and she is not optimistic about the future.

The history behind her arrival in the colony, however, makes it clear this is not merely Malinda Rex's pique or discontent. She arrived with fifteen other people, including a son named Alexander, as a result of being manumitted by their former master John Rex. In his will, Rex had made a provision for the manumission of his slaves and for their transportation to North Carolina. There, manumission was legal but remaining in the state as a free slave was not. Rex's will made two major bequests from the sale of his substantial estate, one to go to the building of a hospital for the poor and needy—Rex Hospital in Raleigh, which still stands today. The other was for the transportation and settlement of his former slaves in Liberia. As Malinda's letter makes clear, these former slaves were transported with the expectation of having their needs met and provision made for them to establish themselves in their new homes. William Thompson, the man who made those assurances, was the agent employed by the executors, including Cameron, to see to the details of the execution of Rex's will. He made the promises in good faith. Nevertheless, it took eighteen years for Rex's wishes to be carried out, and had it not been for the persistence of the agents of the American Colonization Society and the integrity of Cameron as executor, the freed colonists might never have realized a penny beyond the fare for their passage.

In a complex case that went to the Supreme Court of North Carolina, the executors first deposited the value raised by the estate with the courts until certain aspects of the will could be clarified, and then, when the decisions had been made, had to fight the court for the release of the funds. Much of the delay rested on two issues: whether the considerable amount of leather left by John Rex, who was above all a tanner, should be considered "stock" like his livestock and therefore part of the bequest to his slaves; and whether people who had been slaves at the time of the bequest were legally able to inherit at all. In the end, the court, presided over by antislavery judge William Gaston, ruled in favor of the slaves on both counts. Having decided that the leather belonged with the livestock, the court then decided that though slaves could not inherit, they could receive the funds nonetheless, as money left to free and settle slaves could be seen as a "charitable purpose."

Nevertheless, partly because of the resistance of lawyers and others on behalf of the state, the matter took eighteen years to resolve. It is unclear what happened to Malinda in later years. She is recorded in one place as being forty years old and another as being fifty at the time of her departure for Liberia, so if she was still alive eighteen years and much hardship later, she would have been fifty- or sixty-eight. It is known that she was not among the slaves listed as having assembled eighteen years later to receive their long-awaited and welcome bequest. What is known, however, is that she was the mother of the unmarried John Rex's mulatto son. This son, who first traveled with the others to Liberia—the only literate one among them—was probably his mother's scribe.

He returned to the United States to settle in Buffalo, New York, within a year. On his return, he was given preferential treatment and awarded a sum of $140 against his share of his father's estate before the final settlement was made. It seems clear that Alexander Rex never claimed any money beyond what was advanced to him, since the funds kept in trust for him remained unclaimed when the bank went bankrupt following the Civil War. In the end, in addition to their transportation and initial expenses, those former slaves still alive received bequests of approximately $650 each to ease their way in their new land, but it was a long time coming.

Abena P. A. Busia

✦

Caldwell, Liberia, November 3, 1839
Dear Sir: I have met with the oppitunity of writing to you to inform you that I have arrived safe in Africa. We all had a safe passage here but we all have not enjoyed our health since we been here. Benjamin has been very sick but he is getting on the mend. I am not satisfied. I have not found nothing as they said and never will like [?] it. My Dear Sir if you had of known that this place was as poor as it is you would not [have] consented for us to come here. If I had of known myself when you was telling me I would not of been so willing to come. But I thought I could git along like I could there but I fond it to the contrary. Dear Sir, we understood from you that all our provision were paid for but I find it to the contrary. Our

Governor Buchanan says that we must pay for all our provision, likewise all the expenses. I would wish to learn from you if thos are facts. If it is so, such [h]as never been known in the colony before. I did think you was not aware of them. If you were I thought that you would not suffer it to be so. You [are] aware if we have to pay for all our expenses it will consume all. If we do [not get] all what is coming to us we shall never be enable to pay all expenses. My respects to you, Your Obedient Servant, and if I have to pay for all of the expenses and all the provision, you will please to inform me by writing by the Ship Saluda. We [are] informed she will return as soon as she gits there and gits in her load. It was understood here at the decease of my Master there was some quantity of money left to be divied. I never was able to understand how many thousand dollars it were. After the Governor understood this they then say they expenses shall come out of that money as I was aware my self that there was some money left. I was sorry to hear this. I met with a friend and he told me that I had better inform you of this and if it were not left in the will, though you are a great way off from us, I hope you will not suffer this to be. You are all my dependance at this time to receive information, [therefore I write] this letter. William Thompson said that all our provision were paid for. Now they say it is not so. They have multiplied how many pounds it takes to serve one one week. They have [al]low one three pounds as they may know what quantity of our money to take to pay for it, flour twelve and half cent per pound, pork 25. You know if we have to pay for all of this it will mount to a great sum of money. Sweet potatoes [are] one dollar per Bushel. Truly I am in Africa where I cum to be free. I am well satisfied on that head but I beg you to write me as quick as possible by the [next] vessel. Our vice Agent, namely Anthony Williams, he is willing that we should be dealt by just[ly], but Sir they low him no privaleges. He is treated so ill he says he intend to leave in december wich [means] my friend is gone. We have been bless with friends by the orders of Mr. Williams. Ellick [sends] respects to his wife, namely Jane. Please to inform him if she is coming out. My respects to your wife. I have not been sick since I arrived here. Nothing More remains at present, But remains your obedient servant,

Malinda Rex

The facts about Sarah Forbes Bonetta's life are startling. In early 1850, at the age of seven or eight, she was liberated from Abomey, the capital of the ancient kingdom of Dahomey, by Commander Frederick Forbes of the British Royal Navy. She was of noble birth, from a neighboring Yoruba principality, and by all accounts had been in captivity for approximately two years at the time of her liberation. Most dramatically, she became a ward of Queen Victoria. At the queen's express desire and consent, she was educated in Freetown and later married to James Pinson Labulo Davies, a Yoruba merchant also probably educated in Freetown, on 14 August 1861, in Brighton. This marriage produced three children, the eldest of whom, Victoria, was a goddaughter to the queen and was subsequently reared as the queen's ward, for Sarah Forbes Bonetta, her mother, died on the Island of Madeira in August 1880.

The most influential account of Sarah Forbes Bonetta's early life comes from Commander Forbes. The names "Forbes" and "Bonetta" are his name and the name of the ship he was commanding at the time. The daughter of a Yoruba chief defeated by King Guezo of Dahomey, Sarah was brought to the Court of St. James as a child. Her letters are remarkable for two reasons—their very existence and how acculturated they sound. Between her arrival in court in 1850 and the date of her first surviving letter in 1855, when she was only twelve years old, she had become a young Victorian lady of noble class, but with an African education behind her. Concerned about the young child's health and well-being, the queen sent her to spend four years at the female institution established by the Anglican Church in 1816, in Freetown, Sierra Leone.

Two letters addressed to "Mama," her foster mother, Elizabeth Schoen, the wife of the renowned missionary and African linguist Rev. James F. Schoen, testify to her familiarity with and access to royal people and places. In the first letter, she writes vividly, and yet underneath the self-assurance and concern for propriety and decorum, we hear the tone of youthful affection and a girlish concern for correct behavior and dress.

The second letter, written only four months later, contrasts with the first. She has received an offer of marriage from an older, widowed Nigerian merchant, educated, like her, under the aegis of the Church Missionary Society (CMS). Clearly she does not wish to marry him. She had been "banished" to Brighton to act as a companion to an elderly lady of royal connections, to "finish" her education, and to reflect on the proposal. The letter reveals the feelings of a young girl torn between duty and inclination, writing to someone she feels she can trust. We know that Sarah did indeed marry James P. L. Davies in August of that very year. The accounts of their wedding in the Brighton newspapers report that the event caused a sensation.

From what can be learned from the records of the CMS, the couple returned first to Freetown, then to Lagos, to "do their duty" at a difficult time. Her husband was for a time a successful businessman, though it seems that by the time of Sarah's death, they were facing some troubles. The couple named their first child Victoria, and the family remained in touch with the queen until her very last days. Sarah Forbes Bonetta continued the relationship with her surrogate parents, the Schoens, all her life.

The letter from her daughter, Victoria Davies, to Emma Dent represents the only extant account of Sarah's early life other than the official record from Commander Forbes. Victoria wrote the first letter in spring 1882, after her first visit to Dent's home at Sudeley Castle, Winchcombe, in the Cotswolds between Oxford and Cheltenham.

Victoria Davies visited Sudeley many times during her life, the first time while she was still at school at Cheltenham Ladies College a few miles from the castle. On each occasion, she signed the visitor's book at the castle with a proverb in Yoruba, a gesture that would be unusual even today. We see the act as signifying a conscious claiming of Africa that must have been part of her upbringing by her mother. Her comparison of the Yoruba kingdoms with Germany under the old regime shows the level and sophistication of her education and her ability to make the African condition explicable to a European audience. Her grandfather was chief of the Egbado, her mother's people. At the time of her mother's capture at the height of the wars between Dahomey and its Yoruba neighbors, the Egbado lands lay between Abomey, the capital of the Dahomey empire, and Abeokuta, which had become the new capital of the Egba kingdom after the destruction of the old Oyo empire. The struggle in Yorubaland, which had been waging in different ways for the entire century, encompassed the lives of both mother and daughter.

Davies's second letter, to Lord Stamfordham, the influential private secretary to George V, was written thirty-four years later, when she was fifty-three years old. This letter reveals an interesting nexus of connections that sheds light on the situation in Britain and her colonies at the time. Of first significance is the date, August 1916—the middle of the First World War. Victoria Davies (now Randle) had come to a court intimately involved by marriage and diplomacy with a host of significant world events, such as the Easter uprising in Ireland and the threatening revolution in Russia.

This letter establishes Randle as both a current and past member of royal circles, with access to their royal homes. Since arriving in London she had seen Queen Alexandra, the queen consort to the late King Edward VII, with whom her mother would have grown up. The reigning king with whom she wanted an audience was the elder brother of the Princess Alice, who had been mentioned in one of her mother's early letters. Alice had married the Grand Duke of Hesse only one month before Davies's mother herself married, and Alice's daughter, Victoria of Hesse, the Princess Louise of Battenberg (grandmother of the current Duke of Edinburgh), was born the same year as Davies. In reestablishing intimacies, Davies makes a point of referring to memories of "the old days" at Osborne House, a reference few people, even of the British aristocracy, could make. Windsor Castle was Queen Victoria's primary residence, and some of Sarah Forbes Bonetta's early letters were written while in residence there. Osborne House, on the Isle of Wight, was where Queen Victoria's extended family spent their vacations. This family clearly included Bonetta and her family. Osborne House was also where Queen Victoria died, and we know Victoria Davies was one of her last visitors.

All these places and people are familiar to her through a childhood spent with her mother as Queen Victoria's ward, but by 1916 the people who remembered her mother were largely dead or dying, and Queen Victoria herself had passed away fifteen years before. Davies now styles her mother "Princess Bonetta," and it is clear that she wishes it remembered not only who her mother was, but also who Davies herself is. Unlike her mother, who was born the daughter of a prince and became a valuable prisoner of war and then a distinguished royal British ward, Victoria Davies had grown up in elite Nigerian circles, initially the daughter of a successful businessman. Here she presents herself as an emissary coming on behalf of "the people of my country," as she had promised the Prince Eleko, the traditional ruler of Lagos. She brings greetings and gifts for the royal children, of whom she mentions the eldest three.

Finally, it is striking that she took the trouble to write a postscript to mention that her husband and son could not accompany her as they were "special constables as our soldiers have been fighting at Douala and elsewhere." This is an important aside, since it again established her also as a loyal part of the imperial family, with a husband serving with the West African troops fighting the Kaiser's German troops on the African front in the German colony of the Cameroons. The significance of this footnote would not have been lost on Lord Stamfordham.

Abena P. A. Busia

✦

LETTERS OF SARAH FORBES BONETTA

Benin/Nigeria/London 1860–1861   English

LETTER ONE

Windsor Castle
November 22, 1860
My dear Mama,
I am now writing to you at 10 o'clock at night in haste to ask you to get my black silk dress altered and retrimmed as the Court is in mourning and I dare not appear before the Queen in colours. I go to Mrs. Brown's before on Saturday & do not in the least know when the Queen will send for me, not before Sunday I am sure as she knows that Lady Phipps is not well. Could you possibly get Mrs. Foster to alter & retrim my dress & have it sent to Windsor by Wednesday morning early or Tuesday night which would be best I think. *Do try* if you can possibly manage it. I should like the skirt lengthened by 2 inches at the back & 1 in front. The bottom of the dress I should like bound with black velvet nice & deep, nearly as deep as this envelope. The body will want something done to it under the arms and the sleeves a little more trimmed with some of the bows down the front.

Bye the bye, I should like some velvet buttons all down the whole dress (though it is not *absolutely necessary*). I should not in the least like to borrow a dress from Harriet to see the Queen in. She would not like it at all. Please send me a pair of black kid gloves. I should have written for my dress before but thought I might borrow one. Since I've seen her my mind's altered. I am so sorry to hurry you so much (but Lady P. ought to have told about the Court being in mourning before I came). I'll pay for the gloves. The dress had better come in a paper parcel (being a plain skirt it won't hurt) to me directed. My name, Dr. Brown's, Windsor. It will be sure to find me there.

Harriet & Col. P. came home this evening. She enquired after you & is very kind. With best love to all, yourself of course included.

Yours affectionately,
S.F. BONETTA

[P.S.] I have been writing this in my bedroom when everyone else is asleep. Please send in the parcel the black lace off my green bonnet & the black trimming off the one I brought with me. Don't forget them please.

LETTER TWO

Clarence House
East Bognor
Sussex
Mar 16th /61
My dearest Mama,

I have been in a state of mental misery & indecision ever since your 2nd letter arrived yesterday. I should have sat down to write to you the moment it arrived, but remembered that you would have said "take time to consider." I shall now tell you truly what my thoughts & feelings are, with regard to Mr. Davies. You remember perhaps when he proposed a year ago, I said I could never either love or marry him, and I thought it impossible for us to make each other happy. Had I cared for him, age would never have come in the way of my decision. It would be wicked I think, were I to accept him, when there are others that I prefer. It is useless expecting perfection, but at the same time I do not feel that our two dispositions would mix well together. I don't feel a particle of love for him & never have done so, though now it is a year since he last asked me. What am I to do? Please tell me dear Mama & don't say "decide as you feel." I have prayed & asked for guidance but it doesn't come, & the feeling of perfect indifference to him returns with greater force. I am quite stupid & don't know what to do, because I know that there are many of my friends who would say accept him, as then you would have a home & protector & not be obliged to stay at Miss Welsh's for an indefinite time. Others would say "He is a good man

& though you don't care about him now, will soon learn to love him." That, I believe, I never could do. I know that the generality of people would say he is rich & your marrying him would at once make you independent, and I say "Am I to barter my peace of mind for money?" No—never!

Yours affectionately,
Etta

LETTERS OF VICTORIA DAVIES

Benin/Nigeria/London 1882–1916   English

LETTER ONE

Easneye, Ware.

My dear Mrs. Dent

It has been rather a trouble to me to decide in what way I should write my narrative; I have however arrived at the conclusion that it would be best told in a letter to yourself.

But first permit me to thank you for the pleasant day spent at your beautiful home, the remembrance of which will always afford me the greatest pleasure.

I think you wished to know how my mother came to be adopted and so kindly treated by the Queen?

My mother came from the Yoruba country which is one of the most important kingdoms of West Africa. Its constitution rather resembles that of Germany under the old régime; being divided into states ruled over by princes or chiefs who will scarcely acknowledge the head chief as their liege lord.

My grandfather was one of those princes and he owned the town of Ketu including the adjacent country. He was a good ruler & much loved by his subjects. The Prince's palace was made of mud I think and habited by his wife & the youngest and only surviving child of a family of eight. Some little cousins & friends lived with mama as her companions. The other inhabitants were composed chiefly of rather distant relations, attendant servants and soldiers.

When Mama was about five years old, the King of Dahomey with a large force appeared before the town gates and attempted to storm the town, but it was too strong and its defenders were too brave to submit tamely to such an act. After several days spent in a vain endeavour to attain his object, the king baffled and angry was obliged to retreat into the woods. The Katuans were naturally elated with their success for Dahomey is the most powerful kingdom of West Africa & its ruler the dread of all surrounding nations. This unpremeditated attack had been made in consequence of no quarrel, but from the kings desire to obtain riches enough for his great yearly & triennial religious festivals at which men women and children were slaughtered with a refinement of cruelty and in such a wholesale manner that the Dahomians were disliked & avoided by those unfortunate enough to be their neighbours.

At Abomey, the capital, there are various places of torture & execution situated near enough to be seen from the stand where the king & his friends are assembled to enjoy these fearful sights as much as the Spaniards enjoy their bull fights & the old Romans enjoyed their wild beast shows & martyrdoms. Women, children, & men muster in great force attired in the gayest & richest of clothing.

The unhappy victims are placed, some in the street of Blood, to be shot at by the Amazons, others in little canoes held by two men on a large and high platform whence they are precipitated below; others are hewn to pieces; & others stand at the brink of a precipice & are hurled into the dark abyss below at the king's signal.

These and many other atrocities are committed, which the shouts & laughter of the spectators & the monotonous tom toms drown the shriek & cries of the victims. It was from slavery or from such a fate as this that the Katuans believed themselves freed. The gates were reopened three days after the departure of their enemies a fact ascertained by the scouts.

The same night owing to the oversight of the guards the gates were forced open by the Dahomians who had overpowered half the inhabitants before their presence was discovered.

The chief and his warriors appeared half armed and half dressed on the scene. They had been awakened from their slumber by the din of the unequal conflict, & they fell bravely fighting for their homes & dear ones. The town was taken; many prisoners were made, many more were killed, & a few escaped into the woods including the wife & niece of the chief, but they mostly came to an untimely end. The former died of a broken heart caused by the death of her husband and the capture of her child. My mother was kept in the king of Dahomey's palace at Abomey for two years; she was kindly treated but the sights she witnessed were not calculated to inspire her with any affection for the murderer of her parents & destroyer of her home.

The king had not determined whether he would sacrifice her or adopt her himself. He is said to have embraced [her] as the last remnant of a noble and extinct house during their first interview, I do not think the embrace was enjoyed or returned however.

About this time Capt. Forbes of H.M.S. Bonetta was cruising along the coast. He landed at Wydah the chief port of Dahomey & proceeded to the capital to negociate the abolition of the slave trade. He was unsuccessful and narrowly escaped with his life; but my mother was sent by him as a present to the Queen of England. Her majesty was delighted with her little protégée who became one of the companions and play-mates of the royal princesses, during her holidays when at Windsor but principally before going to school. Her chief friend was Princess Alice whose marriage took place a month before her own and whose eldest child Victoria, was born a month before myself. We have a daguerreotype of my mother in her first English made dress. I have told you all I know except that there is a report that my grandfather with his wife and child escaped to Abomey and there hid themselves until betrayed by a chance expression uttered by the lips of their own child. They were executed and she was taken to the palace. But I imagine the first version is the true one. My [m]others after life proved almost as interesting as [her] early childhood.

> With all good wishes
> Believe me
> Yrs. sincerely
> Victoria Davies

LETTER TWO

4, Broadhurst Mansions,
Broadhurst Gardens, N.W.
August 24th 1916
Dear Sir
Miss Knollys has no doubt written to ask you to inform His Majesty of my arrival in England.

Queen Alexandra told me on Monday when I visited Her Majesty at Marlborough House that the King is already at Windsor and that I would find His Majesty there. Miss Knollys therefore gave me your name and address in order that I may be able to communicate with you.

Will you please ask His Majesty to have the goodness to grant me an interview in order that I may do homage as the daughter of Princess Bonetta and deliver a message from the people of my country as I promised the Prince Eleko.

I have also a message from them for Her Majesty Queen Mary.

My late mother spoke often of the kindness of the late Duchess of Teck Her Majesty's mother. Queen Alexandra reminded me of the old days at Osborne and Windsor where my mother and I stayed with my beloved god-mother Queen Victoria. Unfortunately when I came to pay my homage to King Edward—shortly after the coronation, I did not see the Prince & Princess of Wales; they were in the Ophir of which he showed me a painting.

I shall be leaving London about the middle of next week after which my address will be my guardian's c/o his wife Mrs. Christie. Castle Hill. Tonbridge, Kent.

The curios which I took to Queen Alexandra for the royal children I was requested to send to your care and I shall be glad if you will kindly let me know where to send them. They are in a wooden case. I conclude that the ring for the Prince of Wales and the ebony & ivory walking stick for Prince Albert had better go to Sir Sidney Greville at St. James Place. Unfortunately some things were stolen on board so I am obliged to send Princess Mary a big Narragoota basket for work instead of her hair ornament.

Faithfully yours
Victoria Randle.

P.S. Unfortunately my husband Mr. Randle and Jack were unable to accompany me they are special constables as our soldiers have been fighting at Duala & elsewhere. I hope they will do so later V.R.

Mame Yoko and Others
LETTER FROM THE WOMEN OF SENEHUN

Sierra Leone 1882   English

Yoko Gbahnyer of Senehun (ca. 1849-1906) governed the largest territory and was probably the most influential woman in the history of Sierra Leone. The region over which Yoko exercised political authority, a group of chiefdoms south and east of the Freetown colony, had been carved out by Mende warriors during the 1840s and 1850s as part of their expansionist drive from the interior toward the coast. Yoko's husband, Gbahnya, brought together these polities, known as the Kpa Mende Confederacy, through his aggressive war-making and state-building strategies. Upon his death in 1876, he reportedly asked that Yoko be named his successor, a final request that was recognized as a fait accompli by the colonial government in Freetown in 1885. Yoko ruled the confederacy from 1885 until her death in 1906. Under her leadership and after the 1898 war, the territory known as Kpa Mende expanded dramatically. Her skill in keeping its diverse elements united is noteworthy, since the confederacy quickly split into fourteen chiefdoms after her death.

Yoko was born around 1849 in Gbo to a warrior who was part of the effort for Mende expansion. She was initiated into the women's society, the Sande (also known as Bundu), and there gained a wide reputation as an excellent dancer. She was married twice before contracting a marriage to Gbahnya, the best known of the war leaders of that region. Although Yoko was only in her twenties and junior to Gbahnya's other wives, her status became elevated to that of senior wife through her own personality and intelligence. She first came to the attention of the British when, in 1875, she negotiated the release of her husband, whom they had arrested for permitting an attack on one of the coastal treaty chiefs. She is described as having brought gifts to the British governor at his up-country outpost and having confidently assured them that her husband was innocent and that she would personally make sure the true ringleaders in the disturbance were captured.

One of Mame Yoko's methods of influencing both the British and the subchiefs of the confederacy was to mobilize the young and beautiful women of the region. As the *sowei,* or head, of the main Sande society chapter, Yoko could organize Sande dancing for the entertainment of visiting dignitaries. Furthermore, Yoko personally sponsored many beautiful and talented young women, and could arrange their marriages as they graduated from Bundu. As she contracted good marriages, she also forged alliances, which proved to be particularly valuable to establishing familial ties with resident Creole traders and colonial policemen assigned to her town.

This letter was sent by Mame Yoko; Mammy Maroogbah, her cowife; and Mammy Bandawa, her husband's sister, to the colony government in Freetown on 13 September 1882. It was received by George Lawson, the government interpreter for the Freetown colony. At the time, Mame Yoko was officially only the head of Mowoto, a town about two hours from Senehun. In the letter, the three women express their determination to settle the case of a Creole trader who had been wounded in their area. A sword-wielding youth had hurt the woman, Peggy Coker, and the other traders living in Senehun had complained to colonial officials about the incident. A letter written on the same day by several male regional chiefs suggests that the matter had been brought before a large meeting of assembled chiefs who believed that the crime could have negative repercussions for their country.

In their letter, Yoko and the two other high-ranking women declare that they will resolve the matter by sending armed men to arrest the "boy who did the wounding." Preserved in the Sierra Leone Government Archives, the letter attests to the authority and influence wielded by high-ranking women in late nineteenth-century Mende country. The letter indicates that, in the social hierarchy of chiefdom politics, these senior women exercised authority over their own sons and other junior men.

Lynda R. Day

✦

13 September 1882

The women of Senehoo, desire to show the interest they have always taken in the affairs of the country since the death of the Chief. We have not forgotten the kindness shown us by the Government and the many presents received.

The present affair was not brought to our notice till the receipt of your letter. Since then, we have bound ourselves to give ourselves no rest till the matter is brought to an end. We are sorry that the matter was not shown us all. Had they done so the case would have come to your notice only after it was settled. We are women but Gbanyer left us with his sons and men. With these we could not fail in fighting for our strangers here, if anyone should offend them. We don't want any trouble here, we don't want you to send any one to settle this or any other matter. Only be patient and the women of Sennehoo will do what they can. We will send our sons with Commander to get the boy who did the wounding. As we have always done our duty when the country was in danger, so will we do now. Only give us time.

Yoko	X	Gbahnyer	wives of late Chiefs
Mammy	X	Maroogbah	
” Bandawah	X	Sister to Chiefs	

Anonymous
TWO LETTERS TO THE EDITOR
Ghana 1886   English

The last quarter of the nineteenth century was a dynamic period in the history of the Gold Coast and an era in which indigenous newspapers provided the platform for well-articulated rumblings of discontent with the colonial status quo. *Western Echo*, one of the earliest Gold Coast newspapers, carried the first regular "Ladies Column," which was signed with the pseudonym "Cancoanid," a male persona who spoke on behalf of women and who solicited contributions from his female readership. Many of these contributions came in the form of spirited letters, typically written in response to sexist male correspondents and readers. In the first example, from a letter in the 20 November 1886 issue, "Rosa" is responding to a column in which "Monsieur Loquor" suggests that Gold Coast women are "apathetic."

In the second example, from 3 January 1886, the writer signs herself "One of Them," meaning "one of the ladies of Cape Coast," which is how her letter begins. This woman's language is boldly caustic, and like Rosa's letter, an attempt to challenge the trivialization of women by male contributors.

The identities of both letter writers remain unknown, although their choice of words and the framing of their letters are meant to convince readers of their female gender. Anonymity in the early Gold Coast press appears to have been a fairly entrenched convention practiced by both female and male newspaper contributors.

Some scholars have suggested that female contributors in particular may have preferred to conceal their identities. Perhaps women were thus able to circumvent the notoriety that full authorial attribution might have conferred upon them while still speaking out on social issues.

Audrey Gadzekpo

✦

LETTER ONE

November 20, 1886

We the young ladies in this part of the world do not take any pleasure in showing ourselves off in print and without my assertion, common experience would have pointed out this fact to you. Altho' as I have stated above we find no glory in appearing in print, yet, I for one have never failed to peruse all printed documents that have come across me. I was too much surprised in reading the letter addressed to you in the last issue of this journal, and I must confess that I was very sorry to find one who claims to be a gentleman exhibiting his crass ignorance to the world in such a way. . . .

—Rosa

LETTER TWO

January 3, 1886

The ladies of Cape Coast are much obliged to Cancoanid for his zeal in the vindication of our causes. It is true that we Ladies of Africa in general are not only sadly misrepresented but are made the foot-ball of every white seal that comes to our Coast. . . . The gentleman or we should rather say biped (for we cannot call him by any other name and whom we believe is a Just Ass of P's) we say the biped, who said he could not "perceive why we should seek to be clothed in European habiliments or desire to be mentally trained in the education of Europe," is only fit to be Just Ass of P's to the Boobies in Fernando Po. . . . We would like to ask that Donkey Clown what habiliments did his ancestors who worshipped the mistletoe and wood and stone wear? . . . We have been sadly abused by people of such description, and because we have said nothing they continue to abuse us with impunity. . . . It is true had we the advantages of European ladies we should not be a whit behind and although we have not white or angelic faces we are capable of as high a degree of culture as any white lady. . . . Such clownish gentlemen would wish that we were still in our ignorance that they may take advantage of us. . . .

—One of Them

LULLABIES AND SONGS OF YOUNG WOMEN

LULLABIES

The lullabies presented below were originally sung in Sereer, Tuareg, Hausa, and Wolof. While these songs function primarily to calm, celebrate, and affirm a child, other themes suggest a wider adult audience. The Sereer poem "Ayo, My Baby," for example, alludes to the exchange of a person for salt. Here, a lullaby carries elements of history, for salt was a precious commodity, even more valuable than human slaves. Such chilling historical realism may seem eerie when chanted during the mundane peace of child minding. "Lullaby" embodies a mother's fear of being responsible for her child's shameful behavior. Hence, she prays for delivery from such a fate. "Hindatou" reveals an aspiration for higher social status, as well as the deep-seated fear of married Hausa women that their husbands might suddenly repudiate them and leave them destitute. To avoid this and guarantee a stable home, the singer's daughter Hindatou must be healthy and strong. *Koudoudou* is a term of endearment.

"Who Did My Baby Wrong?" is more celebratory in tone and rejoices in the birth of baby Mademba, whose mother, Fatou Kasse, has one of the most beautiful voices of the Youth Circle of Louga, a theatrical group in Senegal that has won many awards. The original words were inspired by Mariam Gaye and then revised by Mademba Diop, the artistic director of the group at the time. Fatou Kasse has managed to give this lullaby a very special sound that always arouses unrivaled emotion in those who hear it. The poem asks, "Why is my baby crying?"—a question that expresses the mother's fear that something might harm her child, since, as the rest of the poem repeats, her future depends on the child's well-being. The poem elaborates with two epigrams, both in the form of proverbs that depend on imagery from the cultural or natural environment: "The drum does not cry if it is not beaten" and "The euphorbia does not weep if it is not broken." (The euphorbia, also known as spurge, is a shrub with an acrid milky juice that can function as a laxative; the juice would, of course, not be apparent as long as the branch was intact.) Both proverbs use the same syntax to indicate the same meaning: on the first level, that no action occurs unprovoked and, on the second, that a disturbed present will upset the peace of tomorrow. They thus suggest, among other things, that the mother must take good care of her child now if she wants him to be well in the future. The use of these proverbs or metaphors gives the lullaby a more profound message than a song for a child might be expected to have. *Ndaayaan,* in the opening lines, refers to the Atlantic Ocean, which represents the farthest possible horizon.

Esi Sutherland-Addy and Fatimata Mounkaïla

◆

Samba Tew Sew, AYO, MY BABY

Senegal 1998   Sereer

Ayo, my little one
Keep on crying

And I'll swap you for salt
The salt will be seized
And I'll come back in tears.

Ayo Aay!
Ayo Aay!
Kuroo—Kurr. . . .
Ayo, my little one
Keep on crying and I'll swap you for salt
The salt will be seized
And I'll come back in tears.

Ayo, aay
Ayo, hush
Ayo, my little one, hush, be still
Ayo, my little one.

Translated into French by Souleymane Faye
Translated from French by Antoinette Tidjani Alou and Abena P. A. Busia

Communal, LULLABY

Niger 1999   Tuareg

Oh, my sweet baby, my *koudoudou*
Whom I bounced upon my knees
And rocked in my arms till I was weary

Oh, my beloved baby
May God keep you from all shame
May you never be like that woman's child

He grew up to be a thief
And stole an ear of corn
And when his cousin saw him
She spat on him
And when his cousin saw him
She threw sand in his face.

Translated into French by Manou Zara Villain
Translated from French by Antoinette Tidjani Alou and Abena P. A. Busia

Maman Ibrah Hinda, HINDATOU

Niger 1998   Hausa

Hinda, Hinda, Hindatou
Father can drive a car,
Father can pilot a plane,
Please stop crying.
Never mind, never mind,
Hinda, Hinda, Hindatou.

Please stop fussing, Hindatou.
Please stop crying, Hindatou.
You're growing like a well-watered sprout, Hindatou,
Even the sea can't harm you, Hindatou,
Hinda, Hinda, Hindatou.

So, please stop crying, Hindatou.
Let them shun us, let them chase us,
Our roots here get deeper day by day,
Hinda, Hinda, Hindatou.

Oh, don't cry for me, Hindatou,
Daughter of Moussa, daughter of Fassouma,
Balki's child, Fassouma's child,
Hinda, Hinda, Hindatou.

Ay, ay, Hindatou,
O, my daughter, Hindatou,
Please stop crying, Hindatou,
Hinda, Hinda, Hindatou.

Translated by Antoinette Tidjani Alou and Abena P. A. Busia

Mariam Gaye, WHO DID MY BABY WRONG?

Senegal 1950   Wolof

Who did my baby wrong?
The drum is far away in *Ndyaan*
Oh, but the drum does not cry if it is not beaten!
Who did my baby wrong?
The euphorbia does not weep if it is not broken.
Oh, my baby, my dear child,
Long may you live

May Allah hear my prayer
Then my future will be bright
For you'll be there to comfort me

Oh, Mademba,
Long may you live, as long as your father
So, all your life your work will honor me
And you'll be there to dry my tears

Oh, my son, honor your parents above all
And you'll reap God's richest blessings
In this life and in the life to come
A grateful child reaps God's richest blessings
In this life and in the life to come.

Oh, be humble, be thankful
Seek after the affection of your kinsmen
Do not stir their ire
For such is the path of wisdom, the road to salvation
Oh, Mademba
Cry not, my baby
Do not cry. . . .

Translated into French by Mariétou Diogue Diop
Translated from French by Marjolijn de Jager

MAIDEN SONGS

On moonlit nights, and on the afternoons of market days, girls and young women in rural Burkina Faso play their clapping and dance games. A girl in the group begins a song, and all the others clap their hands, sing the refrain in chorus, and invent couplets as they go along, depending on the inspiration of the moment. In this manner, the girls improvise in a "dancing circle."

Despite the recreational context, the girls' songs resonate with a sense of impending doom about the next stage of their lives, marriage. Even from the two different languages, the songs offer either a strong reluctance to enter into marriage, resistance to the social control over it, or encouragement to avoid it altogether.

The heart-wrenching plea of a girl in the first song recounts with certain knowledge the details of the fate that awaits her. The second song suggests a young girl expressing her disappointment about being married off to an old man, since such a marriage is synonymous with early widowhood and all its attendant problems. Linking the theme of marriage to that of emigration, the song imagines a young migrant worker who could fulfill a young girl's dreams of adventure and escape, perhaps on the newly built trains. The third song encourages young girls to enjoy their freedom before marriage, when their lives will change radically.

Fatoumata Kinda and Denise Badini-Folane

◆

Communal, I'D LIKE TO STAY

Burkina Faso 1974   San

I'd like to stay by my mother,
I say, I'd like to stay by mother,
Near mother there's peace!

Why would I go to a man's house?
Why would I go to a man's house?
He'll keep me up all night,

Why would I go to a man's house?
Why would I go to a man's house?
He'll lie to me all day!

He'll leave me in the care of his Ma,
and the woman's a witch;
He'll leave me in the care of his Pa,
And papa's a pompous peacock

So, I'd like to stay by my mother,
I'd like to stay by my mother,
Near mother there's peace!

Translated into French by Andre Nyamba
Translated from French by Abena P. A. Busia

Communal, AN OLD MAN

Burkina Faso 1988   Mooré

Give me an old man, I'll surely sit on a tomb and cry:
Find me a young man, I'll dance on a train with joy.
 Papa gave me to the old man, I'll surely sit on a tomb and cry,
Find me a young man, I'll dance on a train with joy,
Give me an old man, I'll surely sit on a tomb and cry
Find me a young man, I'll dance on a train with joy.

Communal, CARRY ON AND HAVE FUN

Burkina Faso 1997   Mooré

Carry on, hang on to those boys and have fun,
for one day it'll all be gone
give it three years, it'll all be gone
give it two years, it'll all be gone
So hang on and have fun with those boys, girls,
in two years, it'll all be gone
give it three years, it'll all be gone.

Translated into French by Oger Kaboré
Translated from French by Abena P. A. Busia

CIRCLE SONGS

Ayabomo is a genre of female recreational performance in which women comment, especially on marriage, and in the process express social solidarity with one another. In a given performance, young women participate in a closed circle, in which their singing is accompanied by clapping and significant gestures. Everyone in the circle is expected to lead the singing in turn with a verse that she individualizes in some subtle manner. The audience, in a designated public area in the village, consists of the women themselves, though others may attend. The appropriation of a closed circle in a public space bonds the participating women, as do their clapping and their spontaneous short shouts.

The three texts that follow all express the rebellious feelings of women who have found themselves in unacceptable unions with men. They sing of their mental and spiritual longings for escape. They are clear about their own aspirations for love as well as for social and material status. Song One employs saucy, defiant indirection to refer to a system of marriage in which young girls are betrothed to old men. It also conveys a young person's longing to be joined to a partner of her own age, especially an educated partner. The imagery is powerfully defiant; the singer wants to escape from her marriage bonds. Song Two expresses a woman's seemingly unrequited love for her migrant lover, on whom she is prepared to spend all her resources. "Your danger sweetheart" refers to the young man's other lover, probably in town, who might beat this village maiden, were she to know of her existence. A special song, such as Song Three below, may be introduced at the opening of the performance to encourage bonding.

Esi Sutherland-Addy and Mary-Esther Kropp-Dakuta

Communal, EVEN IF YOU BEAT ME

Ghana 1998   Nzema

Even if you beat me mercilessly,
And drag me in the mud,
Or turn into a cobra
To block my path,
I will follow him
Wherever he is abroad.

If you turn into a python
To watch the only path,
I will climb over its head.

Communal, I WILL BUY YOU A SHIRT

Ghana 1998   Nzema

I will buy you [a] shirt.
I will buy you men's cloth.
If I buy you all these,
And your *danger* sweetheart
Does not beat me,
I will continue to buy you more things.
So send me something too in return,
If you get someone coming my way.

I will buy you a trunkful of things.
I will buy you gold chains.
My young boy sweetheart,
How dearly I love you.
I will buy you gold chains.
So send me something too in return,
If you get someone coming my way.

I will buy books for you.
I will buy you a pen.
My own dear one,
I love you so much.
I will buy you books.
So send me something in return,
If you get someone coming my way.

Communal, MAIDENS IN A GROUP

Ghana 1998   Nzema

i

Maidens, maidens in a group,
We are only singing Ayabomo songs.
We are not in a group war!

ii

Maidens, maidens, youthful maidens,
I bid you all a fine evening!

iii

Mothers of the household,
I have come to lure
Away your husbands!

iv

If you don't leave him alone,
I will hit you with something!

v

An erect object: there's nothing to it;
Only a piece of half-cut bread!

vi

Yes, we are singing Ayabomo songs.
No fight[ing] is allowed.

vii

We are only playing.
There is to be no fighting here.

viii

Maidens, maidens, yes,
We are only singing Ayabomo songs!

Translated by Kofi E. Agovi

1916 TO 1970
THE RISE OF NATIONALISM

N'della Sey
A MOTHER'S PLEA: TWO LETTERS

Senegal 1919, 1920   French

N'della Sey, the woman who composed these letters, lived in Saint Louis, Senegal, one of the first cities Europeans established in West Africa. Toward the middle of the seventeenth century, the French opened a trading post there, and the town has not stopped developing since. This city has a particular history and culture that explain N'della Sey's awareness of the workings of the colonial administration.

For a long time, Saint Louis was a symbol of the French presence in Senegal, due to the manner in which it had evolved, integrating elements of Western culture with the indigenous culture that had itself already been highly influenced by Islamic civilization. Consequently, Saint Louis could, until the end of the First World War, be considered a creolized city famous as much for its *signares,* eighteenth-century sophisticated mulatto women, as for the refinement and *savoir vivre* of its people generally. Indeed, blacks, whites, and mulattos lived together in two quarters: the South and the North.

It is therefore not strange that in 1919 and 1920 N'della Sey, who lived in the South, one of the oldest quarters of Saint Louis, would appeal to the political and administrative authorities of the colony of Senegal for the conditional release of her imprisoned son.

While the letters presented below may have been dictated by N'della Sey, the consistency and clarity of her statements suggest that she was familiar with the administrative procedures of the day. Even if we do not know whether she was an educated woman, we know that she lived at an address indicated on the letter, which situates the house within the Kertian neighborhood in the southern quarter, a very old residential section of the city, originally home to white settlers and later inhabited by mulatto and a few black families. (The word *Kertian* is a Creolization of the French word *chrétien,* which means Christian.) The grammar, syntax, and punctuation follow the style of the French original.

Aminata Diaw

✦

19 rue Repentigny Saint-Louis
To the Governor of the Colonies
Lieutenant Governor of Senegal
Officer decorated with the "Légion d'Honneur"
Dear Sir,
This comes to you from a mother whose suffering has plunged her into mourning, who finds herself in a great state of misery, who is kneeling at your feet to appeal to your kindness for the release on parole of her son Saliou Ndiaye; her son has been condemned to three years' imprisonment

by the criminal court of Saint-Louis and he has been kept prisoner in the Civil Prison of this same town for about two years. Not that, Mr. Governor, I am one of those women who give their children total freedom, no, but I am only a woman and my child's father who was a chief supervisor of Post and Telegraph and had been transferred to Gabon where he died in 1908, after a terrible illness he had caught in that country, leaving me with four children and insufficient resources to look after them. I had to work very hard to feed them and it is behind my back that the eldest among them who realized the state of poverty he was living in (he had had a bit of education) allowed himself to be influenced by bad friends. My son lost his way Sir Governor and I am sure that he regrets it very much because he is somebody that I never had to complain about.

This is a mother of four children who are still young who is asking you to forgive the eldest among them. I remarried but unfortunately this marriage which was a consolation for me and which helped me to support my own life and that of my children did not last my second husband died also and left me a very young child and so here I am alone without a father nor a mother nor even a friend, I am old my son who was to work and feed me and raise his brothers is in prison. Please Sir Governor have pity, do not condemn me to die of hunger, of cold, do not let my sons like who are unable to work also to be pushed toward wrong doing.

You alone can save me and this would be a humanitarian act. If you let my son be released from prison it is a whole family you will relieve and save. If you release him I will not be able to find words strong enough to prove my gratitude toward you. If you release him I will try to make him follow a path completely different from the one which led him over this precipice and I am convinced Sir Governor that nothing will stop him from doing good.

Thousand and thousand times thank you Sir Governor and no respect is as big as the one I have for you as your devoted servant.

> Saint Louis this 29-12-19
> N'della Sey 19 rue Repentigny
> Sud Saint-Louis
> You can investigate on all that I am saying here.

Saint-Louis this 7th June 1920
From Ndella Sey 19 rue Repentigny Sud Saint-Louis to
Mr. Governor of the Colonies
Lieutenant Governor of Senegal Saint-Louis
Dear Sir,
I have been cruelly troubled since my husband's death and Saliou Ndiaye, my eldest son's imprisonment. He has been condemned to three years' imprisonment during the year 1918, and I am allowing myself to respect-

fully remind you, Sir Governor, of your promise that you made to me in your letter No. 70 of 16th January 1920 and in which you regretted that you could not give me satisfaction because my child had not served the minimum period of imprisonment required by law.

Today he has served the period required that is 28 months of imprisonment which he has now completed. I have four children, the second one has just been recruited by the army, the two others are still young.

I find myself all alone and I must support my family with no other support than my neighbors' charity and they cannot always help me because of the famine that we are experiencing now.

It is in consideration of this difficult situation and in the name of humanity that I appeal to your great kindness and ask you to grant my child the favor of his conditional release so that he can help his brothers and his mother.

No honor or respect, Sir Governor, are as big as the one I have to express the happiness of being your most humble and most devoted servant.

N'della Sey

Translated by Esi Sutherland-Addy and Aminata Diaw

Women of Passoré and Ladre
ANTI-COLONIAL SONGS
Burkina Faso 1988   Mooré

In the years immediately following the First World War, French colonial policy included gigantic construction programs, meant to provide the infrastructure necessary for the exploitation of French West Africa. To get the work done, the French colonial administration instituted forced labor, using an old decree promulgated on 25 November 1912. It was structured in the form of a tax obligation that one could settle by working at a public construction site. These works were varied in nature, and they could be carried out in various places belonging to the vast territory that constituted French West Africa.

This situation generated a body of songs whose main theme is that of colonial exploitation. In singing about such subjects as forced labor, military recruitment, and sexual abuse, women illuminate the impact of French colonialism on daily life.

These songs are popular songs, and it is therefore difficult to identify their actual composers. Most of the time, the songs were improvised, spontaneous reactions to particular situations, and they quickly spread throughout a whole area that may have been exploited in the same manner. The three songs included here were recorded in the Passoré province of Burkina Faso. "The White Man Has Come" and "Poko" were recorded by women from the Passoré region in the villages of Tãosgo and Samba on 8 and 9 April 1988. "Bamako" was recorded on 6 April 1988 by women from the village of Ladre.

"The White Man Has Come" denounces the hardships imposed by the white colonists. It compares the labor to a stone hanging above, ready to fall on the heads of those providing the services. "Bamako" was the capital city of the old French Sudan, today Mali. With scarcely a trace of accusation, we hear the women wailing as their lovers depart for Bamako. In the eyes of the women of Upper Volta, this city was close to hell. It meant hard labor, exile, and the sufferings of those who had to toil on dehumanizing worksites. The song "Poko" refers to a practice that applied only to girls, especially to young and pretty ones. Poko and Pogbi are names usually given to twin sisters among the Moore. Most civil servants came to the colonies without their spouses. They would recruit young girls on their arrival, officially for the purpose of learning the language and the customs of the country. In fact, these young girls were recruited for sex against the girl's will, for young girls of marriageable age were often already betrothed. The girl's future was thus endangered, because, as soon as she showed signs of pregnancy, she was instantly sent away and replaced. This often meant that she would also live a marginal life in her own society.

Fatoumata Kinda and Denise Badini-Folane

✦

THE WHITE MAN HAS COME

The white man has come,
A basket for each woman.
The lady is transformed into an early rising rooster.
The white man has come,
The white man has come to Yako,
A basket for each woman.
Here she is, the tool, ready when the rooster sings,
Here is a stone suspended.
If you don't know the suspended stone
You do not know the white man.

BAMAKO

Bamako!
I do not bemoan my mother.
I do not bemoan my father.
I bemoan my lover who has no clothes
To go to Bamako
And that is tough!

POKO

Poko! Oh! Oh!
What has become of Pogbi, Poko?
Pogbi is the mistress of the white man
Pogbi's hair is nuzzling the white man.

Translated into French by Samuel Salo
Translated from French by Marjolijn de Jager

Houleye Diop
A PETITION
Senegal 1923   French

After the creation of French West Africa in 1895, France attempted to define a coherent governing policy for the vast regions encompassed by its colonial holdings. How to administer numerous territories of culturally divergent populations? Only at the end of the First World War did France put into effect an administrative, political, and legal apparatus to ensure the maximum exploitation of the colonies.

By 1923, when the so-called Houleye Diop affair began in Sedhiou in the south of Senegal in the middle of the Casamance region, the colonial governor, William Ponty, had been exercising for some years an indigenous colonial policy in Senegal. This policy, adapted to local customs and constraints, practiced a "policy of races," including the use of local chiefs when they could be helpful to the administration as well as to the people of the jurisdiction. In 1912, Ponty had proposed a reorganization of the local judicial system. He wrote the 16 August 1912 decree to which most of the documents concerning the Houleye Diop affair refer.

The claim brought by Madame Houleye Diop against her husband's heirs points clearly to many Senegalese problems during that period. In the first place, one can see the impossibility for a woman alone to have won her case, even when she was in the right. It seems incomprehensible that the court would not hear those persons who would have been able to substantiate Diop's claim, to wit, that her adversaries had indeed leased her cows and that they knew very well that the cows in question belonged to her. Likewise, there is the attitude of the person who represented her before the court: He was so outraged by her pugnacity in defending herself that he abandoned her to her fate. In the second place, we see how a wife occupied a position as a foreigner in the midst of her husband's extended family and how insidiously she was made to feel her otherness. Finally, we see how indigenous justice operated and how easy it was for those meant to apply it to manipulate the system.

Diop clearly saw this too, and she herself underscores the fact that one of the men who judged the case was related to her husband, which should have disqualified him from the tribunal. Here we see one of the maneuvers of the indigenous court system: Because Diop was not of the region originally and thus not necessarily held to the same customs or conditions as her adversary, the French West African administration required that she have an ad hoc assessment. However, instead of selecting someone who would have been fully conversant with Diop's culture and practices, the tribunal called upon an ally of the adversarial party, a practice that should have rendered all decisions null and void. In examining all the documents relevant to this trial, we see that not only was Diop fully aware of all the texts governing the local justice system—she does not hesitate to address, in addition to the Sedhiou tribunal, the special chamber of the Dakar Court—but also that she was competent to muster her arguments methodically and forcefully. For example, she uses to great effect the dishonesty of her stepson, who cheated the Manjaque people by extorting money from them, supposedly to help them evade being drafted into the French army. If Diop did not entirely win her case, it is not because she did not defend herself intelligently and with gusto, despite having to do so with no help.

Aminata Diaw

✦

Sedhiou, October 14, 1923

Sir,

At the time of my marriage to Abdou Konaté the following conditions were laid down and accepted by common consent between the representatives of Abdou Konaté and my own:

1. Mandinka customs set aside in favor of Fuuta customs, deemed to be the only acceptable ones.
2. Dowry of seven cows reduced to five on the request of Abdou Konaté's representatives in light of economic hardships at the time. Five hundred francs in compensation to the bride's father and mother as required by Fouta custom. All this, including the dowry, to be returned in the case of a divorce demanded by the wife.

With these conditions accepted by Abdou Konaté himself, I took my place in the family compound.

A few months after my arrival—about two or three months in all—certainly pleased with me, my husband took me into his confidence. He taught me everything about his business and made sure I knew about everything he owned. From that time on until his death, I functioned as his right hand, and he did nothing without consulting me first, even though I was his fourth wife.

Meanwhile, in the course of things, he asked for the cows back that he was meant to give me as a dowry and which would have been sent to Fuuta to my parents, just as all my cowives had sent their cows to their parents. He wanted me to keep these cows nearby, for people were apt to ask him, in his capacity as Head of the Canton, for milk. In that case, he would lease cows out, and as time went by he would see that my cows got preference—because [mine] were the best in his herd.

That's how my animals were placed as rentals at the Nosoco doctor's and at the French West Africa Company. When my husband asked for payment, he always brought me along and told the lessors to pay me because the animals belonged to me. (I have the receipts.) That's how the cows he'd promised for my dowry were duly assigned to me.

As his salary as Canton Head was insufficient to take care of his large family and as he was of delicate health, I wanted to help by practicing my trade as dyer. That way I saved some money with which I paid his debts and built up his strength. That's how I came to lend him 500 francs to complete the payments to the French West Africa Company of a debt he had contracted to snuff out a scandal which would have led to the imprisonment of his eldest son. During the recruitment period for the occupying troops, this son had insisted upon and received from the Manjaque people of his father's canton the sum of 1000 francs. This was supposedly to keep them from being drafted. This is public knowledge. But the affair went no further, the Manjaques having gotten their money back.

Still working at my trade, I gave him, and at sale price, 500 francs worth of dyed goods. In order to reimburse me, my husband had to place his daughter-in-law's cow—the wife of the son of whom I've just spoken—at the Nosoco Company, where I was able to take in exchange 300 francs worth of stamped cotton cloth. Of the above debt, then, he still owed me 200 francs.

After having given about 200 francs worth of milk products, the cow wouldn't milk anymore, but was kept at Nosoco as a guarantee of what remained from our exchange. She's still at Nosoco, even to this day. Thus, to sum up, I loaned my husband 1000 francs: or 500 francs to help with the Manjaque business and 500 francs of dyed goods. Of that sum, 300 francs were reimbursed, which reduced what was owed me to 700 francs.

During his last and fatal illness, my husband asked and obtained for me from his eldest son a sum of 400 francs which I gave to my cousin who had come to place his daughter with me in Sedhiou. But after my husband's death—he died on April 1, 1923—while I was constrained by a four month and ten day mourning period, this same son took my accounts book and collected 1000 francs of which he subtracted 400 francs that his father had had him give to me. So, what was owed to me was again 700 francs.

At the end of the mourning period, in order to get my dowry and my loan back, I related all these facts to the court of our subdivision whose members already knew the case. But after a series of tricky deals, I was only able to obtain from the jurisdiction five heads of cattle: a cow, bull calves, and bulls. The compensation was eliminated—because of "nonconformity" to Mandinka custom (which misrepresents the agreement)—as well as my husband's debt to me—for lack, they said, of sufficient proof. I appealed this verdict; but the third jurisdiction maintained the verdict of the first.

I am thus seeking recourse in you, sir, the Chief Administrator, to ask you to transmit my complaint to the Attorney General who is still in a position to determine the truth or falsehood of my claim. I stand firmly behind my right to protest the verdict of the subdivision's court and that of the Sedhiou Circle.

1. The first violated the agreement undertaken between Abdou Konaté's representatives and my own at the time of his asking for my hand in marriage, an agreement ratified by Abdou Konaté himself. And even though the Wolof expression ("*nao*") was the one used to designate the 5 animals making up my dowry, everyone knows that *nao* in such agreements means "cow" and not "bull calf," "bull," or "steer," which would have meant using the following terms: "*velou*" for bull calf, "*yengue*" for bull, "*khabane*" for steer. As for the 500 francs of compensation imposed by Fuuta custom and freely accepted by Abdou Konaté, as well as the 700 francs which were left to be paid back from the debt contracted by him, I think I've clearly enough established their existence so as not to have to restate the matter.

2. I object, furthermore and for the same reasons, to the verdict delivered by the Circle, which repeats that of the subdivision—so much the more so because one of the members of the Circle is my deceased husband's brother-in-law. This family relationship normally forbids a member from sitting in judgment. Thus, even were the verdict a good one, it should still be deemed null and void.

I insist, then, that my rights be respected:

1. I want the 5 cows that are neither lost nor dead that my husband gave as a dowry and for which I collected rent, and not the sterile cow which belonged to a cowife that the heirs substituted for one I am asking for, nor do I want a bull or a bull calf. I furthermore ask from the heirs payment of the 500 francs of compensation that were an integral part of the same dowry, just as I would have given back cows and money if there had been a divorce.

2. I demand the reimbursement by these same heirs of the 700 francs left of the debt contracted, a debt which I have sufficiently proven in the preceding discussion.

I am prepared to swear to the above, as is required by Muslim law.
  Let justice be done.
        Signed: Houleye Diop
        c.c. Head of the Political Bureau

Translated by Judith Miller

Nwanyeruwa
THE ABA WOMEN'S WAR

Nigeria 1930   English

On 18 November 1929, a mission school teacher, Mark Emeruwa, acting as a census taker on behalf of his local warrant chief Okugo, walked into the compound of a woman named Nwanyeruwa, wife of a man named Ojim, in Oloko, Bende division, Owerri province, in eastern Nigeria, and insisted on counting the wives and livestock in the compound. The ensuing demonstrations sparked off by Nwanyeruwa's resistance to this request spread throughout Owerri and Calabar provinces and lasted approximately six weeks, until the end of December, when British troops restored order. By that time, fifty-five women had been killed, ten native courts destroyed, several others damaged, and the houses of court personnel and six factories attacked, and chief Okugo had been tried, convicted of corruption, and dismissed from office. The incidents were so severe that a commission of inquiry was held in the months following.

The immediate context of the disturbances in and around Aba township was the complex situation in Iboland in the 1920s, which resulted from an unstable combination of the rise of colonial administrations in that area, the economic situation in eastern Nigeria of the late 1920s, and the impact both of these had had on local issues, including governance and local and household management. In their attempts to "pacify" the peoples of the Lower Niger, the British had attempted to impose indirect rule through local authorities such as the emirs, a system that had been quite successful in northern Nigeria. However, in southern Nigeria, especially in Iboland, where systems of autocratic chieftaincy did not exist, the attempt to address the situation through the imposition of a system of warrant chiefs caused a great deal of unrest. In some cases there had been no chiefs of that kind, and in other cases the British had chosen their warrant chiefs from outside the customary families. In almost all cases, the people viewed these chiefs as illegitimate. In the case of Okugo, the warrant chief in the locality where the disturbances first broke out, court testimony reveals the number of autocratic impositions he had made on women and their labor, which underlay their objections in his village. If there were anxieties that the "native authorities" were becoming simply British administrative agents in traditional disguise, Okugo seems to have been a case in point. In Nwanyeruwa's words, before he was appointed by the British and became abusive, "he was an ordinary man."

In many places, the source of the problem was the extra power given to the warrant chiefs, in particular the economic power of taxing. Nwanyeruwa's testimony clarifies Okugo's abuses. She reports that a rumor claimed that the idea of taxing women came not from the government but from the warrant chiefs themselves. And the women were already angry about the taxation of their husbands.

The conflation between census taking and the imposition of taxes had its source in the taxes imposed in 1926, which a census of male heads of household had preceded. These taxes had proved burdensome to all concerned, and families were having difficulty meeting the taxes already imposed on the men. In addition, a period of rapid inflation had forced a sharp and rapid decline in the price of palm oil.

Nwanyeruwa, like many women in her area, was a small farmer specializing in palm-oil trading. She was preparing palm oil when the census taker entered her compound. Since many women were also farmers who produced palm oil as a cash crop, these women governed the economic health of the communities and were anxious to keep the regulation of the trade in their own hands. But the British administration and foreign companies were introducing new quality control inspections and different buying standards, all of which affected the women's control of their trade. Hence, the economic threat of further taxation was a very serious issue.

In addition, the process of census taking violated many taboos. Throughout the region of West Africa and the Sahel, the counting of people, especially of women, is considered abhorrent. Animals can be counted, but fruit-bearing trees and women cannot.

The resistance that ensued had a specifically feminist nature. In fact, one of the reasons this particular war has become so celebrated is that it put women's agency and power on display, and the British authorities simply failed to recognize the significance of the traditional and gendered symbols of the war. Nwanyeruwa's reference to "singing and dancing" against the chief is a reference to a very specific form of women's protest called "sitting on a man." To "sit on a man" involves women congregating in front of his compound, dressed in war apparel and carrying the pestles and palm fronds that symbolize women's power and discontent, to bare their breasts as a ritual signal of war and to sing sometimes scurrilous songs making clear exactly the offense that the man needs to redress. Thus the choice of dress, the use of body language, and song all draw attention to their role and status as women, in particular as women acting in protection of the "good of the land."

Part of the British authorities' perplexity also lay in the spread of the rebellions, covering several hundred square miles. Again, they had failed to appreciate the powerful influence of women's associations, based on both kinship and trade, and the ability of these groups to communicate with one another in both concerted and independent action. In Iboland, traditional social structures led to the formation of associations of wives and daughters in the regulation of affairs and issues of trade. The testimony of the reports makes it clear that they had already organized a series of meetings to discuss their growing discontent; one was in process at the time of Nwanyeruwa's agitation, which became their call to arms.

Nwanyeruwa was an elderly woman at the time of the war; she had one grown son, whose wife had died the year before. Some sources say she was not a Christian, though her own evidence explains that she took her oath on the sword and not the Bible because, as an unlettered woman, she could not be baptized, since the ability to read the Bible was a prerequisite for baptism. Other evidence suggests that she was a traditional nurse and circumciser. Her travels as a circumciser made her privy to the rumors about the pending taxation of women.

In those places where women objected to warrant chiefs on the bases of oppression and corruption, the government acceded to their demands, dismissed the chiefs, and institutionalized mechanisms for getting women involved in the selection of chiefs. The British also, for the first time, appointed women to the native courts. The report of the commission of inquiry, with all its attendant notes and appendices, served as the basis for recording and assessing the women's grievances and for the remedial actions subsequently taken. Although the language of the report is English, readers must always remember that, for the most part, the African people questioned were speaking Igbo. Consequently, their words, simultaneously translated and taken down by a court reporter, come to us with all the implications for mediation that such a process involves.

Nwanyeruwa's opening testimony was given before the commission of inquiry sitting at Umudike on Wednesday, 12 March 1930. She is responding—after being sworn in by the sword—to the question from the chairman: "Will you tell us what you know about these occurrences at Oloko?"

Abena P. A. Busia and Diedre L. Badejo

◆

Nwanyeruwa's Testimony before the Commission of Inquiry

I will tell you what transpired between me, Okugo, and Emeruwa. I was in my house pounding palm nuts in the morning. I was then squeezing oil. Emeruwa came to my house. He asked me to count my goats, sheep, and people. I turned to look at him. I said: "Are you still counting? Last year my son's wife who was pregnant died. What am I to count? I have been mourning for the death of that woman. Was your mother counted?" He held me by my throat. One's life depends on her throat. With my two hands covered with oil I held him also by the throat. I raised an alarm, calling a woman—another wife of my husband—by name. This woman has the same husband with me. She lives in a house quite close to mine. She came to the spot. I asked her to help me to raise an alarm, as I did not know what I had done. In the meantime, Emeruwa ran away. As he ran away, I followed him shouting. This woman, my husband's other wife, asked me to come back. Emeruwa went to Okugo and reported to him saying, "Look at me, see how I have been treated." Okugo then ordered that I should be brought before him. They came and dragged me out of my house. When I came before him, I said, "My father, what have I done?" he said, "Woman, dare you assault my messenger and soil him with oil? If you have yams, you had better go and eat them, as your own matter is over. That is, you will get into trouble. When the District Officer comes, he will take charge of you." He said that I had dared to assault his messenger and soil him with oil.

There and then I shouted and went to the square. On that day, there was a meeting at Eke market. I went to the meeting and told the people there as follows: "Hear what Okugo has told me—he said that I would get into trouble. I was in my house when Emeruwa came there and told me to do counting. Now Okugo has told me that mine is over and that I will get into trouble." The women then said that I should show them the person who directed me to count people. I took them to Emeruwa's house. They said to him, "Why have you said that a woman should pay tax?" The women then sang and danced outside Emeruwa's house. Other women who were living in Emeruwa's compound advised him to devise a means of getting rid of them, as they did not know what he had said to the women to cause them to come to his house.

Emeruwa then led these women to Okugo's house. I advised the women not to go to Okugo's compound but to remain in Emeruwa's compound and sing and dance for him. In the meantime, we went home to prepare food and drink and brought them to those women who were at the meeting. We then heard women shouting and some of them were wounded, blood was coming out of them, they were bleeding. We put down the food we were carrying. We saw that one woman was wounded, that Okugo had used a spear to wound a woman in her foot. Another woman who was pregnant had an arrow pierced in her side. The arrow was taken out. As a result of this injury the woman miscarried. The child was a male. Okugo then set fire to his house and destroyed it; he did this just to show that the women had burned his house, but he did it himself. One woman attempted to put out the fire, but she was wounded on the right side of her neck. Somebody shot an arrow at her. Okugo then gave orders to his people— men and women—to beat these women and to forbid any of them to go free. One woman was wounded in the back of her neck (indicating by hand) with a machete. Eight people altogether were wounded. The women became furious on account of this treatment and went to the Native Court and reported to the Clerk what had happened.

We sent for the District Officer who came himself and saw what had taken place. It was said that the women were to be brought to Bende so that the matter might be gone into there. Okugo sent to the market place where the women had eaten and drunk to collect the materials they used there in order that he might make juju with them to poison them. The materials they used for preparing their food were taken away by Okugo's people. Certain Aro people who were present at the place where the juju was being made came and gave information about it, as they wished the women to be protected. The District Officer, upon receiving this information, sent for the medicine men. Three of them were apprehended and the materials they had used in making the medicine were also brought before the District Officer. We all went to Bende for the matter to be settled.

The District Officer questioned us as to why we had assembled in large numbers. We replied, "You have seen the treatment that Okugo has given us and some of us have been wounded." We demanded that Okugo's cap should be taken away from him before the case against him was tried, as he had ill-treated us. His cap was taken away from him and handed to us (the women) and we kept it. Emeruwa was called and he made a statement. We said to him, "You came and said women were to be taxed. We told you that men had already been taxed and that the amount paid by them was so large that it was unnecessary for women to pay tax. Men had to provide for our food and clothes. We had no money to pay tax.[11] We sang and danced, saying that Okugo became a rich man because of the money he got from us. If he had not got money from us, he would not have been able to provide for himself. On one occasion he called both men and women together and told them that the District Officer had ordered that money should be collected for him to build a house. We collected £20 and handed it to him. He made use of the money in conjunction with his women and did not build a house as he told us he was going to do. On another occasion he told us that the District Officer had been worrying him for a young wife—that the District Officer wanted a young wife—and that both men and women should collect money to pay the dowry of a young wife for the District Officer. We collected the sum of £20 and gave it to him as a dowry for the young woman required for the District Officer. Altogether, he has had three wives by means of the money collected among us. One of them is dead. We are sure these three women were not given to the District Officer. At the time people were planting yams, Okugo came to us to say that the District Officer had ordered that men and women should collect yams for him. We collected yams and gave them to Okugo, but he did not give them to the District Officer. He used them in his farms. I paid for my own share and the share of my only son. These yams were taken away by Okugo to his house and he subsequently planted them. He did not take them to the station [i.e., the District Officer].

Okugo on this occasion came to me—a poor woman—and wanted to ill-treat me, hence this trouble. Okugo is now in prison. If anyone had a case he wished settled in Okugo's house, Okugo would demand from him, £1 on some occasions, and £2 on other occasions. Okugo would use this money without going into the matter. He would not give the complainant any satisfaction. He would beat his drum to call upon men and women to repair his house and those of his women. He would call upon us to repair the court building, but he would not do it himself, nor allow his women to do their share of the work. He would simply let them go and do ordinary work. Emeruwa told me that Okugo had sent him to my house to do the counting first and that he would do the counting in the houses of the other women later. On one occasion, Okugo said that people should not allow their sheep to stray about. My sheep strayed to his house and he kept it. My sheep used to have two kids at a time. He knew I had some means and that is why he sent his boys to my house to do the counting first. I told him that I was once a rich woman, but that as he had been taking money away from me I had now no money to pay tax. When we went with Okugo before the District Officer, Okugo told him that the women had destroyed his house. The District Officer sent police to find out whether this statement was true. The police found that Okugo's house was not destroyed in any shape or form. The thatch was not touched at all. Okugo had nearly twenty cows. The women did not touch them at all. He had nearly four hundred goats in his compound. None of them were touched by the women. None of the fowls were killed by the women. Okugo had assaulted the women who came to answer the alarm that I raised. I advised these women not to do any damage to Okugo's compound.

Okugo had made it a rule in the town that, if two persons had a dispute, one should not spit on or make any row with the other. He also made a rule that persons should not fight one another in town. Another rule he made was that no one should use a machete for fighting another. But he has contravened all these rules he made. He has done the very things he made rules against. When we considered all this treatment we had been receiving at his hands, we felt quite fed up with him and thought that we should not pay tax. Okugo told us that, if a woman owns a fowl or goat she has to pay 5s. for it. He said to us, "Where would you run to? Would you run to Heaven? Wherever you go, you have to pay tax this year." As we were disputing with him, women from other towns heard of it and encouraged us not to agree to women paying tax. That is my case. I told the District Officer that Okugo must be imprisoned and that, if he were not imprisoned, we should not be satisfied. I am a poor woman to pay tax.

SATIRE FROM THE "WOMEN'S CORNER"
Ghana 1934   English

In the absence of elected representatives, educated Ghanaians came to value the press as an important vehicle through which they could express opinions publicly. From the 1930s forward, women's voices were part of important national debates, especially through a regular feature of the *Times of West Africa* called "Women's Corner," by Marjorie Mensah. A persona rather than a real person, Mensah was usually the pseudonym of Mabel Dove-Danquah.

Dove-Danquah was the indisputable doyenne of Gold Coast journalism, having first entered the field as a columnist for the *Times of West Africa* from 1931 until the paper closed in 1935. A mistress of disguise, she wrote for several other newspapers under various pseudonyms as well as in her own name. In her forty years as a journalist, she corresponded for the *African Morning Post* (1935-1940), Nigerian *Daily Times* (1936-1937), Accra *Evening News* (1950-1960s, on and off), and *Daily Graphic* (1952). She also wrote short stories, some of which were published in the *Times of West Africa* and the *Daily Graphic*. Later in life, she contributed short plays and poems to the British Broadcasting Corporation (BBC). Her prolific literary output ceased after she went totally blind in the 1970s. She died on 21 July 1984 at age seventy-nine.

"Women's Corner" was an important gendered space originally constructed to deal with "women's issues" but expanded by Dove-Danquah and others into social and political commentary. Yaa Amponsa's letter "To Miss Bridget Thomas" and Odarley Koshie's "Stupefied" responded to two unpopular bills—the Waterworks Ordinance and the repressive Criminal Code Amendment Ordinance, known locally as the Sedition Bill. The "obnoxious" bills, as they became known in local newspapers, were introduced in 1934, during the governorship of Sir Shenton Whitelegge Thomas, whose daughter Bridget is addressed in the letter. The letter is, however, primarily aimed at the colonial governor and his administrators.

Written on 14 March 1934, in the week before both bills became law, the letter explores the impact of the bills from the viewpoint of marginalized Gold Coast women and children. This "woman-to-woman" discourse, asking the governor's daughter to draw on her filial connections to intercede on a major political matter, is couched in a style suggestive of indigenous mediation strategies.

"Stupefied" continues the protest against the bills shortly after they were passed by the Gold Coast Legislative Council. Again the column draws attention to the effect of the bills on the vulnerable, particularly children. Like Yaa Amponsa's letter, Odarley Koshie's article adopts a style that is personal, colloquial, and derisive of the governor and the colonial establishment.

Audrey Gadzekpo

✦

TO MISS BRIDGET THOMAS

To Miss Bridget Thomas,
Christiansborg Castle
Dear Miss Thomas,
May it please you, noble and fair Miss Thomas, to give me this fine opportunity of telling you of what we little African girls in the distant fields of the Gold Coast Colony and Ashanti, feel about your kind father's WATER and SEDITIOUS BILLS.

All over the length and breadth of this country, are to be found mothers and fathers weeping over the bills your noble father, the Governor, is determined to pass into law for us and our weep-little sisters and brothers yet unborn.

I happened to ask my father this evening, why a grown up man like him should be weeping. "Yaa . . . hm! I have just come from an extra-ordinary Mass Meeting where I heard clearly explained to me by members of the Asante Kotoko Society, and many learned lawyers and laymen, all that your grand Daddy,—the Governor in whom we all have reposed and registered our confidence, has determined to do—to muzzle local presses and make us thirsty and victims of fatal diseases for want of water.

"Surely my daughter," continued my poor father, "if the Governor, Sir Shenton, does pass these laws as he seems strongly determined to do, you and generations after you, were better not to be born at all. The laws doom you to eternal slavery.

"I am of some age now, and undoubtedly before the 14th March, 1934, when the bills would have been dragged against the country's vehement protest, into the law book of this country, I would be your dead father—dead and gone, and you know, Yaa, dead men surely don't bite.

"What fate would fall upon you and hundreds of thousands of girls like you, after these bills have been laws of the land is that which leads me and the country into lamentation and bitter sorrow.

"When I am dead and buried with all my poverty as your dear mother was only three days ago, who will help pay for your clothing, and housing and schooling and your food and in addition, pay for the common water you drink and wash the dirt off your slimy skirt?

"Yaa, have you ever since you first saw light, seen me weep? and is my cause for weeping now unjust?"

Dear Miss Thomas, that is the internal state of my home in particular, and similarly that is the condition of the homes of the other sisters, in the Gold Coast and Ashanti.

Believe us as we believe you and your father that even in distant Ashanti, our fathers have not the slightest idea of malice and war against the white race. Our fathers and mothers—of course I have no mother now,—as well as we and our brothers are perfectly loyal to your King in England and your noble father our Governor.

It is my sincerest hope that you will continually plead and help us [as] in the distant and remote ages, the Princess Ariadne did for the salvation of the children of Athens.

In the name of all Gold Coast and Ashanti girls I ask you, sweet and thoughtful Miss Thomas, to advise your noble father in chambers to withdraw the bills.

> I am,
> Your most humble maid servant.
> Yaa Amponsa
> The Wicket-Gate Villa
> Kumasi

STUPEFIED

Wednesday, March 14, came with fear and hope in my tender heart. Legislative Council was to be opened, and very many Bills, some good, some bad, others worse, were to be passed into laws. Laws that tend to make me, my family, and my descendants something lower than slaves.

My heart bled to think that my darling little kids—I am married and have some kiddies to care for—will some day labour under these yokes now being prepared by one who is a father, and says he is the father of my poor little Gold Coast.

The tower clocks in Accra struck ten in the forenoon. My feelings became tense, almost feverish, when the thought glided into my memory that this was the day of days, the historic day, when the fate of my poor and powerless Gold Coast was in the balance.

Hon. H. E. appears. Splendour and glamour preceded his entourage. Can this be the very father who proposes to make me and my poor dark-skinned kiddies lose all freedom? I may die before my kiddies become men and women but the Labour Ordinance may still be operating unrepealed in their time. What if they unluckily come under the tentacles of that law? Jail, and nothing but jail, stares them in the face. They cannot all of them be public servants when they grow, to be exempt from its pall. Is there not a little of sympathy in Father Thomas? I doubt it. He has a daughter, and a lovely one too. We have daughters too, though black but comely, and sure Father Thomas knows we have some of the love for ours as he for his.

Some of my kiddies may turn out to be newspaper men or women and human nature being what it is all the world over, black, white, or yellow, they may have the love of their Gold Coast at heart. What if that love becomes intense? Jail; and nothing but jail, awaits the true Gold Coast patriot. The more pity it is for our patriots, if they dare defend their poor country.

I pity my husband the more as he is a man and may love his country as tenderly as he loves me. For loving our country there is the jail, or even the gallows for him who dares.

Sedition here may be what treason in England is. The Legislative Council opened. H. E. went to his noble seat. The prayers were read. Good! Love of God, and love of neighbour—the best law Christ gave us. I was hopeful then. My heart started to beat more rapidly. The English brought the Bible to us.

They know and practice its teachings. "A Christian come to judgment" (apologies to the shades of Shakespeare).

This very hopefulness brought the following lines of that pathetic, imploring hymn fleeting across my mind—

"Lead kindly light,
Amid the encircling gloom
Lead thou me on;
The night is dark,
And I am far from home;
Lead thou me on."

My soul jubilated in my hopeful environs. The "kindly light" was implored to lead the deliberations in the Chamber.

Ha-a-a-a! A sign, a gloom on all African faces. S-t-u-p-e-f-i-e-d!! My ears deceived me? What! Is the Governor determined to pass the three Bills into law? After all? Have our menfolk sacrificed sleep only to forge out a broken cutlass.

The Water Bill. Everywhere [one] pays for water that enjoys pipe-borne water. The Labour Bill!! It followed convention adopted by the International Labour Conference, and it must be applied here although no forced labour exists. The Sedition Bill!! It won't take away our liberty. Plausible excuses all.

A lump came into my throat; sights swam before me; my tear gland overflowed—I wept. Tears as hot and bloody almost as Christ's in Gethsemane. I controlled myself and avoided a sob. What can I do more? I am a woman, and can only weep away my lassitude and disappointment; I can only weep away my sorrows, although weeping saves no one. Weeping by women sometimes breaks the most stony hearts of men. It calls forth tender and sublime language from poets. It excites to pity.

Odarley Koshie

Efwa Kato
WHAT WE WOMEN CAN DO
Ghana 1934   English

Efwa Kato published "What We Women Can Do" in March 1934 in *WASU*, the journal of the West African Students Union of Great Britain and Ireland. By the 1930s, Paris and London, the capitals of the largest colonial empires of the time, had become hubs for anticolonial and pan-African nationalism. Traveling to these centers for further education, a small but growing number of students from around the colonial territories in Africa and the Caribbean arrived in unprecedented numbers. Their strong sense of solidarity within informal networks led to the formation in 1925 of the West African Students Union, originally an amalgamation of the Gold Coast's Students' Union and the Nigerian Progress Union. Established in London, WASU at its peak had many branches on the African continent, including the WASU Society of Enugu and the WASU Society of the Belgian Congo.

In the literature documenting the period, scant evidence exists of women's participation in the vibrant discourse within these circles or in the incipient political activity upon which many leaders of independence movements on the African continent launched their careers. Thus, Efwa Kato's essay offers a unique glimpse of the political consciousness of one woman inside WASU. We know nothing more about her, but her name tells us that she was a Fante from Ghana. We know also that her use of a Fante first name—rather than a "Christian" or "English" name—was unusual for the time. Only rarely did educated Ghanaians use their traditional first names in official correspondence or publishing. As in the case of Kobina Sekyi, another Fante nationalist intellectual who used his first name, we believe that the act of calling herself "Efwa" speaks to her strong African consciousness, affirmed in her essay.

Esi Sutherland-Addy

✦

The influence of woman for good or evil, particularly the latter, has been recognised throughout the ages. In the role of a tempter or seducer of man her reputation is world wide. Was it not Eve who was first seduced and through her man fell from primeval innocence? I think, however, that the world owes a lot to Eve for tempting Adam to eat of "the tree of knowledge of good and evil"; for it is in the eating thereof that man owes his subsequent development. I admit that it is idyllic to pass one's life in keeping a garden and making pets of the animals. But who will deny that, in spite of its evils and sufferings, the world is far more interesting and exciting than it would otherwise have been but for Eve? And man loves to have it so. He finds in such a topsy-turvy world an opportunity for his initiative and of moulding it to his heart's desire. But we live in a thankless world. Instead of being grateful to Eve and her daughters, man has held woman in servitude for her alleged natural depravity. However, there has not been wanting, here and there, an acknowledgment of her greatness and nobility of character. Many a man has had to confess that but for his mother, sister, wife or—shall I say it?—lover, he would not have become the great man he became. And now the influence of woman for good has become an axiom.

It is on the influence of woman for good that I wish to direct the attention of my readers. Looking at the sufferings which our race has had to endure and is enduring, I have often asked myself the question which I daresay every other thinking woman of the race has asked herself, namely, What can we women do? The answer to the question depends on so many factors which need not detain us here. Assuming, however, a woman endowed with health, and education of some sort and a modicum of intelligence—all of which I am fortunate to be blessed with—I venture to suggest that the answer is to be found along the following lines:—

In order of importance, I would mention what we women can do as mothers. It has been truly said that the hand that rocks the cradle rules the world. It is those lessons which a child learns in the cradle, or, to put it graphically, on its mother's knees that invariably lead it in the direction it should go. It is therefore important that we women should be aware of our influence as mothers. At the threshold of life the child is dependent on its mother, not only for its physical needs but also for its moral training. I am assuming that every woman who is capable of understanding this article will take the trouble of acquiring, at least, an elementary knowledge of child rearing. I am here concerned with the moral as opposed to the physical welfare of the child. As soon as the child can understand, I suggest that the history of the race be unfolded to him. Our history is an epic in itself, capable of stirring even the dullest imagination. Such passive virtues, for examples, humility and patience, should be relegated to the background, if at all taught. Such virtues are gratuitous in a subject-race. What have we to be humble for? Are not our circumstances humiliating enough? Such positive virtues as courage, manliness, and, above all, that divine restlessness, the impetus of adventure and achievement, should be paramount in the child's moral training.

The mother's interest should not flag even when the child begins to attend school. There is the tendency, all too prevalent, I am afraid, of leaving the moral training of the child to the professional teacher. Admittedly, the teacher helps to mould the child's character, but he cannot take the place of the mother. After all, it is only a small percentage of the child's waking hours, about six, that are spent in school. The periods before and after school are the mother's. Through the child's lessons the mother can find the opportunity of inculcating the precepts enumerated above. As I write an instance comes up in my mind. It is most appropriate as illustrating the advantages a mother has over the teachers. During Empire Day celebrations, I wonder how many teachers have the hardihood to impart to their pupils the facts concerning the rise and development of the Empire. They are more concerned with drilling the children to make a good march past and in preparing their mind for the balderdash which is often given the children than in presenting the facts of the case as they really are. It would be asking too much to prevent a child from taking part in such celebrations; but after the function is over, the mother should ascertain what the "lesson" was and seek to correct the false impression by giving a true account of the case. She must tell the child of the benefits which we derive from being members of the Commonwealth; but, at the same time, she should not forget to remind him of the injustice under which we labour for no other reason than that of the colour of our skin. The recent and most glaring example of injustice is the treatment of the natives of Kenya on the discovery of gold in their reserve. With tact the mother can fire the child with a passion for justice without inculcating race hatred.

With regard to the influence of woman as wife, much depends on the type of man the woman is fortunate or unfortunate to have as a husband. I am not one of those who prefer to reform a man after marriage. If he proves intractable during courtship, the odds are that he will remain so ever after. Perhaps it is well to begin with a discussion on the type of man most desirable or on the influence of woman during courtship. Of course tastes differ, but speaking for the average of which I am one, a woman should prefer a man who is first and foremost a patriot. I am afraid we women will have to change our standard of values in this respect. The majority are still influenced by "the gold standard." But surely, the time has come when we should "go off gold" and appraise a man for his sterling character. Instead of having an eye on their bank accounts, we should demand of our prospective husbands an account of services of self-sacrifice to the race, failing which, we must make them understand that unless they are willing to participate in the fight for race upliftment, we shall have nothing more to do with them. During the war many a man had to join the colours just to please his sweetheart. If women can influence their men to commit murder (for war is murder, despite the euphemism by which it is called), why can't we influence our men for good? I know from experience that our men are not lacking in chivalry. The truth is that we women have not been demanding much of them. A few honeyed words from them and lo, and behold, the trick is done. But if they realise what type of woman they are up against, I am sure they will respond and show what a fine lot they are. I have heard many of them orating in the drawing rooms in England and America what great things they will do for Africa on their return home, and provided they could count on the support of the women, I have no doubt that they will endeavour to practise their ideals.

After the excitement of courtship comes the humdrum of married life. Here, again, the influence of woman is undisputable. Apart from running the home, which I hope every intelligent woman contemplating marriage should know how to do, there is the no less important task of being a helpmate to her husband. With the best will in the world, it is at this stage that many marriages are wrecked. Some wives treat their husbands as if they were still boys, and naturally, a man who is worthy of the name, resents such treatment. The right type of man welcomes criticism and advice from his wife. It all depends on the way in which they are proffered. The main task of the wife is to be a bulwark of moral support to the husband. However patriotic he might be, the rough and tumble of the work-a-day world, the scramble for places at the top tends to a depreciation of ideals. The plums of office are for "safe" men, and a patriot is never considered "safe" by the powers that be. Naturally, there will be the tendency on the part of the patriot to compromise and play for safety. Here is the wife's opportunity. Here she can exert her influence. Her duty is to keep the flag flying and to remind her spouse of the dreams of his youth. What is more, she should be prepared to forego the amenities which a "successful career" brings—wealth and social prestige—remembering that it is not how much a man gets out of life but how much he puts into it that matters. Situated as our race is, not one of our ideals can be realised without self-sacrifice. And who but the wife can give the necessary encouragement in times of disappointment to provide the impetus to succeed?

But it is not the lot of every woman to be a mother or a wife. What then? Are there not other spheres in which woman can wield her influence?

Assuredly, there are. Apart from the usual avenues of teaching, nursing, etc., the intelligent woman who is desirous of helping her race will find an outlet for her ambition. She need not believe in the hocus-pocus which passes muster as religion before undertaking the task of enlightening her less favoured sisters. A simple faith in the moral order of the universe is enough to create in her a "passion for souls." If she is a woman of means, she might become the Mary Kingsley of Africa to interpret the motherland to the world. Hitherto, such interpretation, rather misinterpretation, has been undertaken by foreigners, some of them knowing not even the language of the people they seek to interpret! Or is she interested in politics? In that case, she may become our Emmeline Pankhurst, the leading spirit of the Suffragette Movement in Africa. In any case, the woman who wishes to help her race can find out what she is capable of doing. My aim is to create in my sisters the desire to help. That done, then where there is a will, there is always a way. It is the women who have to set the pace; for no nation or race can rise above its womanhood.

Elizabeth Mgbeke Ezumah
CHAMPION OF TWINS

Nigeria [1998]*   Igbo

In the past, the Igbo of southeastern Nigeria associated multiple births with evil, appropriate for animals, not for human beings. Such births were viewed as an evil curse that had befallen the family and that threatened to bring chaos into the community. Twins were thus abandoned in the forest and left to die, and rituals cleansed their mother, the families, and the community.

Madame Elizabeth Mgbeke Ezumah provides a personal account as the mother and champion of twins. She recounts the death of her first-born twin at birth, and the subsequent attempts by fearful family and neighbors to remove the remaining child. Because she refuses to kill the second child, she is ostracized. While she attributes the cessation of the practice to the advent of Christianity in the Igbo-speaking areas of southeastern Nigeria, it is clear that as an Igbo woman, she had already begun to question the practice before the missionaries arrived. Her story also illuminates the anguish of Igbo mothers who used Christianity to buttress their challenge to the killing of twins.

Ezumah was a homemaker and a leader in the Methodist Church at Ngodo Isuochi. She passed away on 3 June 2004 at the age of 105, while this volume was in preparation. This text is part of an interview conducted in 1998, when Ezumah was eighty-nine years old, by her daughter-in-law, Dr. Nkoli Ezumah, a sociologist.

Nkoli Ezumah and Diedre L. Badejo

NKOLI: Greetings, I would like to have a discussion with you about the ways in which twins and their mothers were formerly treated.

MADAM ELIZABETH: Before I had my twins, the people of this area did not welcome twin babies. They did not bring them up before the advent of the Christian church. For instance, I was the first person who encouraged women to keep their twins and bring them up. Even before I had my own, I emphasized that killing of twins is murder. I remember a particular woman who lived near us. When she delivered her twins, they came and informed me of the birth and loss of the babies. That happened from time to time among other women. I asked about this issue of delivering and at the same time losing the baby. A particular woman became pregnant four consecutive times, all twins. The twins all died and it appeared as if they had died at birth. When she was pregnant again, I requested to be called during delivery, so as to witness the happenings. This idea of delivering and losing babies upset me greatly.

As time went on, I became pregnant. One day, while we were having a women's meeting here, I went out to urinate. I did not realize that I was experiencing labor. As I stood astride to urinate, I felt a severe pressure on my waist. Then as I was urinating a baby slipped from me, and fell on the ground. Hei! I shouted. Some of the participants in the meeting rushed towards me. They lifted the baby, but she was already dead. The women instructed me to get ready to receive a hot compress on my tummy. I told them that I was still feeling as if another baby was there. But they insisted that nothing was there, that it was only that one that came out dead that had been in my womb. After a while, when I delivered the remaining baby, they started screaming because they were not happy that I had had twins.

People called me "the champion of twins" because I was the person who encouraged them to appreciate their twins and to accept them as normal children. At that time people killed twins in the "bad bush." There were thick forests designated as "bad bush" in many Igbo communities. They were assumed to be the abode of evil spirits. People who died of infectious diseases or from circumstances that were mysterious were left to die in the "bad bush."

As time went on, as I was here at home, some people would come and tell me that somebody had been delivered of twin babies. I shouted and asked, "Why didn't you call me?" I was informed that the twins had been squeezed into a pot and moved to the "bad bush." I protested, insisting that we should hurry to the place to rescue the babies. I cautioned them, on getting to the "bad bush" where the pot was dumped, that we should be cautious while breaking it, in order to bring out the babies carefully. Eventually one of them died because they had been squeezed into the pot. Later the surviving baby was taken back home to the parents. Then I urged the women that I must be informed about anybody who was to deliver a baby. Actually they began to come to pass on the information. Whenever any woman was in labor, they came and informed me and I went to assist with the delivery. They were many. I did not count them. After all, why should I count them? If I had counted them, they would have been numerous. I was not the only person doing the job, even at Obulolu, at Umu-ada, at Uhuda, at Ihube, and even at market stalls.

NKOLI: At that time when you kept your own twin, what did people do?

MADAM ELIZABETH: They ostracized me. Some people who were my friends abandoned me. They started suggesting to me what I could do to kill the baby without letting people know what happened. I refused to comply with them. I said, "I am not going to kill the baby." Some people brought me concoctions to be used in killing the baby. When I was curious I unwrapped the packages and critically looked at the contents. They contained ground brown substances like tobacco. I wrapped them up again and kept them. After some time one of the women came. She began to ask me why I had not done what she had asked me to do. Then I discussed the matter with her, buttressing my points with references from the Bible. By then I was reading my Bible religiously. I cited Bible passages and discussed them with her. I told her that the message is in the Bible. She then replied and asked, "What about those people who are also church people but have killed their own twin babies?" I told her that was their own concern, that I could not answer for their deeds.

NKOLI: What about your parents? What did they do when you decided to take care of your surviving twin?

MADAM ELIZABETH: My parents? Ehe! My mother. She was not coming to my house. But whatever was traditional, to be done for a nursing mother, she did for me, although she never came to my house and did not see the baby. She endeavored to get as many gifts as possible sent to me through others. When the gifts were handed to me, I sent my greetings to her. The pots and baskets with which those things were brought were never sent back to her. After I completed maternity staying indoors, my mother and I planned to meet with each other. She came out in the Uhuolu Square. She went to the extreme end and waited for me. After eating my meal, I dressed up and went to meet her. She brought me a lot of gifts. We stayed there. She started crying. I asked her why she was crying. Ha! I threatened to go back to my house. Then she began to plead with me, asking me not to go. Because she loved me very much, she said, "My dear, pardon me." She said that she did not know that I would still be alive.

[After that] she used to come [to the house]. When she came we stayed here in the parlor conversing, while the baby would be inside the room. She would not see her. I was the person she was interested in seeing.

NKOLI: How did people relate to your surviving twin baby?

MADAM ELIZABETH: People nicknamed the baby Anyasogwaohu, The

One Whom People Abhorred, Yet Itched to See. Listen! When I was going to church with her, we passed Oye Ngodo [the big market square in Ngodo Isuochi]. Come and see. People who came to church from Ihube [a town about 6 miles from Isuochi] rushed to behold her and hugged me. The people from my village, on the other hand, threw away their baskets in disgust, running to spread the news to one another. They said, "Do you remember the baby who survived? Whose mother used to advise others to keep their multiple babies whether they are twenty or forty?" It did not take long for my friends and neighbors to all avoid me and my baby. They were concerned about what would happen to me after I cared for her. They were also concerned about the fate of their own children. So they tried to prevent their children from playing with her, but they could not. It did not take long before she started walking and running about. The other children started taking her out. They came and took her away from here. The parents of those children would then chase them outright from their homes. "Don't let that child come into the house," they would shout. They all put up short barricades in front of their doorsteps so that the children could not enter their homes with the baby. However, they could not enforce that because the children persisted in moving together with the baby. I went and bought earthenware bowls and plates from Isiagu, which I used to share food for them. After sharing, I got them seated and I would serve the food to them. They would begin to eat. If they requested more, I would give to them.

NKOLI: But by then how was it that you had a strong faith in the church?

MADAM ELIZABETH: It is the Bible. All the time, I was reading the Bible. I remember that there was a time I was invited to Obululo in Umuokpokocha, to a meeting of dignified and well-known people. They asked what they could do for me so that I would stop my campaign of saving twins. I said no to them, insisting that it is from the Bible that I got inspiration for whatever I was doing. It was not I who wrote the Bible nor was it I who said the things in it. It is the Bible that converted me. It is from the Bible that I see the teachings concerning everything.

NKOLI: What did they do when you refused their request?

MADAM ELIZABETH: What could they do? They dispersed in annoyance. In the end they agreed to watch one another and encourage mothers to rear twins. But how could they watch over one another? Were they not all very busy, so busy that they could not watch other people? Wherever I went people would be admiring me. If it were nowadays, there is nothing they could do to kill the babies. Hei, if it were now I would broadcast to the world what the people were doing over here, and also how we have fought against it. Hei! It was terrible. If you saw how they pointed accusing fingers at me, you would be wondering. "Hei!" Was there any place where I was not known? Was there any? Ewo! Jessy! She received and received money and gifts, including edible things. Once when we attended a meeting, a white official said that I should bring her along. When we arrived at the white official's house, he said to the baby, "Hello! Jessy, the beautiful, hello!" The white man lifted and lifted my baby and said "Olololo" and kissed her. The money realized after the meeting was counted and given to me. He also brought his own personal gifts of money and added to it. He said I should use that money to take care of the baby.

NKOLI: Were there some people who killed their own twins and now have no children? Are there some people who now regret what they did?

MADAM ELIZABETH: Oh, yes. Some have become childless because of their deed. One of our kindred in Obululo is now childless. At one point she started picking up abandoned babies, so as to have a child. But after raising such a baby, the parents came and took their child. Ha! Ha! Ha! How can I ever remember all that transpired between the people and myself in this matter?

Translated by Ifeyinwa Obionwu

Mariama Bâ
MY LITTLE COUNTRY
Senegal 1943   French

Mariama Bâ was born in Dakar, Senegal, in 1929. Her family was one of influence, and in 1956 her father became the first Senegalese minister of health. Her mother died when she was young, however, and she was raised by her maternal grandparents in a conventional Muslim environment that included attending Qur'anic school from an early age, a practice she continued during school holidays after she started formal French education. It is a matter of record that—contrary to the practice of the day for many women of her generation, and against the express will of her maternal grandparents—her father sent her to French schools for further education. She excelled at school and at fourteen entered the Teacher Training College in Rufisque. While at this school, she wrote the essay published here. She graduated with a teaching diploma in 1947, taught for twelve years, and then, apparently for health reasons, asked to take up an appointment as an inspector of schools.

Throughout her career, Bâ was an important writer and social commentator. She considered the very act of writing a political one for Africans and believed that writers should participate actively in the affairs of their developing countries. Her feminist essays and political writings were published in journals and newspapers during her lifetime and widely debated in Francophone African society. As much an activist as a critic, she participated in several women's organizations. Her pioneering cultural work was informed by the commitment to social equality that marks her two most famous works.

Her first novel, *Une Si Longue Lettre* (1979), published in English the following year as *So Long a Letter*, catapulted her to international fame when it won the inaugural Noma Award for publishing in Africa, presented to her at the Frankfurt Book Fair in 1980. It has since been translated into sixteen languages. Bâ, a divorced mother of nine, died after a long illness just a few months before the publication of her second novel, *Le Chant Ecarlate*, or *Scarlet Song*, in 1981.

This short essay, "Ma Petite Patrie" ("My Little Country"), is a rare gem written sometime after 1943, the year in which she entered Teacher Training College. A piece of juvenilia composed when she was fourteen, it has been preserved because it was reproduced by two different French colonial authorities as a wonderful example of the impact of French education on native girls, at a time when such an education was controversial among the French as well as the Africans in their domain.

The essay responded to an assignment signaled by its closing lines, "What a sweet memory I have / Of the pretty place where I was born." It became celebrated not only for its quality but more particularly because the issues surrounding the idea of education that concerned the whole society were presented so perceptively by one so young.

Although this work celebrates a traditional way of life, in it Bâ, quite remarkably, anticipates the major themes not only of her own later mature works, but also those of a whole generation of French West African writers, including such people as Camara Laye and Mongo Beti. These themes anticipate the major debates on culture and acculturation, tradition and modernity, African versus European civilizations—all her lifelong concerns, which were to culminate in the novels that brought her an international audience, and that continue to be discussed to this day.

Abena P. A. Busia

✦

I remember a time not so long ago, my childhood more pure than millet flour, more impassioned then the insects of the fields. Life was beautiful, and beautiful the light of the paths where the orchestra of the trades reverberated. In the compounds, women were pounding millet. The nourishing song of the pestle in the mortar, the black and brilliant beauty of the women filled my heart with joy. I was dreaming of couscous mixed with fresh milk . . .; pure milk . . ., the white milk in the gourds.

Yes, I remember days gone by, tender experiences, the bright sun that cast a spell on me, the Qur'anic school. It was a courtyard. But how big and stony that courtyard was with its bushy *bentenier*! A crippled, one-eyed toothless marabout ruled over us, and we called him, justifiably for that matter, by a name roughly equivalent to the word "monster." I can see myself in a small blue *pagne*, the slate resting on my semi-bare thighs. I can see the little girls of my age, most of whom are married now. Above all, I can see our excursions through the *filaos*. There were ferocious battles during which bodies became entangled and bruised. The strongest and most skillful threw their opponents mercilessly to the ground. I was always in the victorious group. There were also mad dashes to get a drink at the well of an old gardener who could hardly put up with us. He was continually chasing us, and we were continually coming to bother him at his work.

Yes, I remember tender experiences, the first rainy season of "my life on earth." The water dampened the earth; the ground beneath my feet became soft. Naked, I ran beneath the raindrops that crashed upon my back. What child of my race has not felt this joy or experienced the intoxication of drinking the water that falls from the sky, of feeling it caress the skin and run down to the ankles? The trees were shivering with the cold, the birds with fear. But as for me, *enfant terrible,* I continued to gambol about despite the menacing calls of my grandmother, who had a deadly fear of rainwater because she had lost my mother on a rainy morning.

I remember days gone by, festive days, the festivities of Tabaski. As soon as the day had dawned, I went out to wash my grandfather's sheep. I loved warm, grilled meat with pepper and a pinch of salt. It was in vain that my aunts chased me from the kitchen and hid the pieces. A crafty child, I always found some to put on the grill, with the help of my grandmother of course. In the evening, I was decked out like a queen. Gold medallions in my plaited black hair, jewels of brown coral on my neck, my henna-blackened feet in gilded slippers, and there I was running about the neighborhood in search of flattering compliments.

Toward 3 o'clock, a drum sounded. What emotion was awakened in me by the dances in which I myself was a dancer! The resounding tones of the *tabala* (no longer the "*tabala* for ordinary dances" but the *tabala* for great festivities) mixed with the cadenced singing and intensified the excitement. Agile and supple, I sprang forward like my sisters. The uncanny power of drums when music becomes movement, the movement of the music. The blood was boiling in my veins. I jumped, danced. I felt my stomach jutting forward or retreating toward the small of my back. . . . I was eight years old, and I was shouting, "drum, carry me off."

Then one day, my father came, and school; my free and simple life came to an end. They whitened my mind, but my head is black, and my unassailable blood remained pure, like the sun, pure, preserved from all contact. The blood in my civilized veins remains pagan. It revolts and rises up at the sound of black drums. Always I want to dance, to dance forever, to dance again. Today my little homeland is broken, molded, flattened, and transformed into a road that leads to the slaughter-house in Dakar, but my memories of it make my heart vibrate more rapidly than the finger of the diali can pluck the string of his *halem.* To relive for a moment the tender experiences. To relive and to retell, yes:

What a sweet memory I have
Of the pretty place where I was born.

Translated by Richard Bjornson

P. A. Itayemi Ogundipe
NOTHING SO SWEET

Nigeria 1947   English

Shortly after World War II, Phebean Ajibola Itayemi (later Ogundipe) won a British Council short story competition for the western region of Nigeria, coming ahead of the fledgling writers Timothy Mofolorunso Aluko and Cyprian Odiafu Duaka Ekwensi, both of whom became better known than she. With the publication of her story "Nothing So Sweet," she became Nigeria's first woman author in English. The story reflects the concerns of young educated girls during decolonization, an era in which social change marked every sphere of life. Benefiting from the drive for expanded educational opportunities for all young people, the girls also had a wider range of career choices. Many of them chose nursing, which by this time was being transformed from a male-dominated to a female profession all over West Africa, with attractive training programs and pay and enhanced career advancement. As the story illustrates, the youth of the period looked away from "traditional" values and longed to embrace "modernity."

Young women such as the story's narrator were inclined to exercise independence in their choice of marriage partners. Whereas their mothers and aunts would probably have capitulated to their parents' wishes with regard to becoming the wives of men of substance, and perhaps even considered it good fortune, the young modern women of the late 1940s and early 1950s wanted prospective husbands who were closer to them in every way—in age, in education, and in general outlook. Marriage by abduction, the focus of this story, had become outmoded in the urban centers of Yorubaland, if not actually illegal. The story also resonates with contemporary events of historical importance for Nigerian women, for it was written after the creation of the Women's Party in Lagos (1944) and during the prolonged protest of the Abeokuta Women's Union against a traditional ruler who shared some of Eso's attributes.

Born in 1927, P. A. Itayemi Ogundipe became a distinguished educator and civil servant. After obtaining her B.A. from the University of St. Andrews, she earned a diploma from the Institute of Education at the University of London in 1952. In 1960, the year of Nigeria's independence, she accepted an appointment as an education officer in the Western Region (later Western State) civil service, serving as principal of the Adeyemi College of Education (Ondo). Transferring to the federal service in 1966, she was promoted to the position of senior education officer. She oversaw the implementation of the harmonizing of the federal universal primary education scheme with that of the Western State. In December 1976, she retired as assistant director of education.

Since her retirement, Ogundipe has acted as a consultant for various national and international agencies. The themes of "Nothing So Sweet" have become current issues in recent U.N. conventions and platforms for action, which shows Ogundipe's historical foresight. She remains active as a writer but did not follow in the footsteps of her former male competitors. With P. Gurrey, she compiled a collection of folktales, *Folk Tales and Fables* (1953), but she is perhaps best known for her textbook *Practical English: A Comprehensive Secondary Course* (first published in 1965), which has been reprinted a number of times.

LaRay Denzer

✦

CHAPTER I

I never knew that he meant it, or that my parents meant it either. He was comparatively old—I think he must have been fifty-five at least—and I was only seventeen. Ever since I was quite young I can remember him coming to our house. He would take me on his knee and call me his wife, which word Yoruba people generally use to mean affianced wife as well as married wife. Whenever he called me his wife, meaning his fiancée, I used to think he was only joking. Many other men came to our house, and they would say, "Will you marry me, little girl? If you consent to marry me I will bring you meat every day from now on, because I am a hunter," or "I will bring you very big yams, as I am a farmer."

I always said "Yes," because I knew they were only joking. I regarded Eso, the fifty-five year old man in the same light, as I regarded those other men.

Eso was too big a man, too old a man, too important a man to be called by his name. So he had a nickname, "Ogongo," which is Ostrich, the king of the birds. His contemporaries called him this, and the women in his house called him the father of "this" or the father of "that" according to the names of his children.

We were all natives of a small, out-of-the-way village in the interior of Southern Nigeria, in Yoruba-land. There was a church with a school which boasted of Standard Four as its highest class. Everybody in our village, including the school teachers, had a farm. The school teachers found their salaries too small to save out of if they were to have enough left to live on comfortably, and so grew as much of their own food as they could, to help their salaries on. The pupils did most of the work on the teachers' farms. And so everybody living in our village, except the sellers of European cloth and other articles, who would stay a few days selling and then move on to another place, had at least a farm. Some people would work on their farms in the daylight and hunt animals at night.

Eso, or "Ogongo" as most people called him, was a well-to-do man with a large area in which cocoa was grown. He grew other crops also—cotton, yams, beans, peas, and maize. I can remember as far back as when I was five or six his occasional calls at our house. I would be called to come to him and he would look at me and say I would soon grow up. He gave me things— sometimes smoked meat, sometimes smoked fish, and sometimes honey in a little bottle—from his pockets. I believe I was shy at first, but my relatives would always urge me to take the present from him, until I came to look on him as a never-ending source of presents and native sweetmeats. As I grew older, however, I used to look suspiciously on his generous way of giving me presents, because most times he would in return want me to sit on his knee and be petted by him, and I soon came to resent this.

When I was nine I noticed that yearly gifts of yams and meat came from him for me. The few, earliest corn-cobs, the first crop of beans to be harvested, were always sent to me, or rather, to my parents. They did not tell me anything then; they would only say in our household that my "husband" had sent yams, beans, or whatever had come from him.

When I was eleven, he came to our house one day. As I grew up, his visits became more frequent than when I had been younger. When he came I was called to come to him as usual, but I soon left him and went away. I sat in the room adjoining the one which was used as "sitting-room." Here I overheard everything he, my "husband," said to my parents.

"Will you not send my 'wife' to school?" he asked in our language. My mother seemed surprised.

"To school?" she asked. "Surely you do not want her to be sent to school? If she goes to school she will soon grow to scorn you as an illiterate farmer, and an old one too."

"I do not mean that she should be sent to school to get up to Standard Six," explained "Ogongo." "I just want her to receive enough education to enable her to read the Bible (Eso had been baptised "Matthew" when Christianity was still new in our village, but he had never been to church in his mature years) and to read any letters that may come for me. She will also learn about weights, so that I can be sure that these Produce Buyers who buy my cocoa do not cheat me when they weigh it."

"You will be making a great mistake, 'Ogongo,' if you send this girl to school—"

"If the difficulty is about her fees, I will pay them, buy her uniform and all she needs at school."

"I am warning you, 'Ogongo,' that the girl will probably become unmanageable if you send her to school. She is obstinate and proud enough as it is. Besides, she won't be able to help me much at home," objected my mother.

"If he wants to send her to school, let him, as he is willing to pay all expenses," interposed my father in his gruff, scarcely-concerned way. "After all, she is his 'wife' and he can do what he likes with her."

So the matter was settled. Uniform, slate, pencils, books and fees came more promptly than they should have come from my parents. I was rather small for my age, which was eleven, when I started at kindergarten, but I soon grew rapidly.

When I was fourteen, and in Standard Two, my parents had asked him to take me from school, as I could now read and write. But my "husband" said he wanted me to write a good hand, which he knew, from his inspection of my exercise books, that I did not yet do. He also wanted me to be able to speak English fairly well so that he could show me off. He thought I should speak English quite well in Standard Four in the Elementary School. After all, he had money to spend on me, he said. Thus it was that I did not leave school until I was sixteen and in Standard Four.

I believe I had somewhat lost sight of Eso, who did not come to see me often now because he did not want to disturb my studies, but who came to see my parents, presumably to discuss me with them. If I had not lost sight of Eso, I should not have expected to go to another school for Middle I. But I did expect to be sent to a higher school. My parents gave me no answer. They did not tell me to take the entrance examination to any school, and when the beginning of the next year came, and school began everywhere, I stayed at home working until I realised that that was the end of my school career. I regretted it, because I often thought that after only two more years, one in Middle I and one in Middle II, I would have a Standard Six Pass which would enable me to be a nurse or a Pupil Teacher.

I asked my mother why I could not continue my education in another school. At first she impatiently said I had learnt enough already in school, but afterwards, when I insisted and tried to convince her that I was far from having learnt enough, she told me that Eso had said that I would not continue after Standard Four. In the earlier years she would have told me that my "husband" had done this or my "husband" had done that. I resented that word fiercely now. Mother would leave off and call him Eso or "Ogongo" and hint that a time would soon come when I myself would call him my husband.

In the meantime I had grown to dislike Eso. I resented the way I was always called to see him whenever he came to our house, as if I existed for him alone. More than that, I resented his proprietary way of treating me. He would take me to stand between his legs while he sat, because I would never now consent to sit on his knee. He would pat me all over and say his little "wife" was growing fast and would soon become marriageable. I took no notice of these words, which became more tactfully spoken as I grew older.

Eso came to see me very frequently in the year after I had left school. Whenever he was unable to come he would send a younger man from his family with compliments from him. When he came one night I asked him why I could not continue at school. He seemed surprised and answered that I had learnt enough surely, and he too had spent enough on my education. Besides, I was quite grown up.

This was in the year 1936. Day by day as I stayed at home and sullenly worked while longing for school and thinking of my Standard Four classmates who would in a year or two be working and be going about in shoes, hats and European dresses, while I settled down into being the wife of an illiterate farmer, my dislike for my elderly fiancé slowly grew into hatred. Sometimes I would refuse to see him when he came to see me, and if I had to go to him I would not speak to him. I scarcely ever remained more than five minutes in his company. A rebellious fire was being slowly kindled in my heart. But Eso and my parents thought my reluctance to be with him a good sign. So at last I understood—in fact I had taken a long time understanding—that it was settled that I was his fiancée, and having understood, I had to be as shy as other girls were with their suitors. This was their interpretation of my reluctance.

Actually there was no courting done. All the courting that was necessary had probably been done when I was a sturdy two-year-old. Since then I had been his fiancée, and between an engaged couple it did not seem that there was any need for courtship.

Sometime after my seventeenth birthday (I had insisted on the day of my birth being discovered when I was in Standard II) my mother began to hint that I should prepare for marriage.

"Whom am I marrying?" I asked rebelliously.

"Why, Eso of course," she answered.

"I am *not* marrying Eso," I said.

"In the first place, you shouldn't call him Eso," she corrected. "You can't call your fiancé by his name like that. It isn't done. You say you won't marry Eso? What nonsense! Who else would you marry, when he has spent so much on you? He has sent you to school, he has sent you yams, meat and other things every year, and he has already paid your dowry this year—"

"O-ho!" I cried. The "modern" ideas I had picked up in school were still fresh in my brain. "So you have received a dowry for me already. Well, you might have received it for me, but it was not given to me; so it is you, not I, who owes Eso. Give him anything you like in return for his money, but not me. Parents do not find husbands for their daughters these days. It just isn't done, at least in the modern places. Better find something else to give Eso for his money, or return the money if it is not yet spent."

My mother was alarmed at the spirit I had shown, and I believe mother, father and Eso had a private conference about me. I was left alone for a while, and I honestly believed they had left me alone forever. After some weeks, however, mother let fall another hint of marriage with Eso. The hint was a sort of feeler. But since they had left me alone for a while I thought I had won my point and would not be marrying Eso, and had only to press my point firmly to be left at rest on that subject. So no sooner had my mother hinted than I told her in no uncertain manner that I would not marry Eso.

After that everybody was silent, and how blind and deaf I was in my imagined victory. I rejoiced that I would have nothing to do with Eso any more, and did not know how premature my joy was. Nobody tried any longer to persuade me to marry Eso. Afterwards I found that a drastic measure had been decided on. My mother started buying me a show trunk full of Yoruba female apparel—wrappers, *bubas*, headties and *iboruns*. This fact should have been an eye-opener to me. I was not a good daughter since I had not obeyed my parents and consented to marry Eso, yet clothes were bought for me as if I was the best daughter that ever lived. The only time Eso's name was mentioned after that was when mother praised him to me one day.

"Do you know how rich Eso is?" she asked with just a shade too much indifference in her voice. "He has a very large cocoa farm, and cocoa has been selling very well this year, so I expect he has made a lot of money on cocoa alone. Cotton, too, has sold very well so far this year (this was true of 1936) and he has large fields of cotton. Palm oil has now risen to 13 shillings a tin and he has a big palm oil industry."

In our little village, where everything that was grown was very cheap, 13 shillings was an unusually high price for a tin of oil. When oil was cheap you could get a tin—four gallons—of very fine oil for 1/9 or 2 shillings. I was no longer interested in my ex-fiancé as I now thought of him, but I had to admit he was rich.

"He is of a very good family, too. He stands a good chance of becoming the king when the present one dies."

This made me more thankful than ever that I was now free of Eso. Whenever a new king was enthroned, hundreds of girls would be given to him to wife [marry] as presents from his subjects. Those subjects who had no grown-up unmarried daughters would give him girls of seven, eight, nine or ten years old. If your eleven-year-old daughter had an ulcer which was costing you much trouble and money you gave her to the king as his wife. In most cases these very young girls were treated as housemaids by the mature wives of the king. In most cases the ill-treated girls grew up to become the wives of the household retainers of the king. Everything about Eso, his fifty-five years particularly, made him an eligible candidate for the throne which everybody expected would soon be vacant. And I—well—I could not imagine myself as one of the scarcely cared for, much less loved, occupants of the women's quarters of the palace.

"He is descended from a long line of warriors, too," went on my tactful mother. "That is why his name is Eso. Only brave, tried warriors are allowed to be called Eso. The Esos boast of the fact that they never receive a battle wound in the back, since they never turn their backs to the enemy.

They either conquer the enemy or die in battle rather than return home conquered."

I acknowledged the truth of these things, and said I realised how Eso was, and the subject was dropped. His name indeed signified him to be one of a race of fearless warriors, who will either win a battle or die. This fact was to be responsible for what later befell me, though at that time I dismissed Eso from my mind altogether. I was too light-headed, too certain of my own victory. I had had my way. Soon how disillusioned I was to become.

CHAPTER II

"Subowa, come into the parlour," called my mother to me in the backyard.

My name is Olasubowa, which means "Honour clusters round us." I might sometimes adopt the I-know-better tone of a half-educated girl speaking to an illiterate mother, but I was fairly obedient. I therefore went into the parlour at my mother's call.

Whatever I thought I was called for, I could not have been more surprised than I was when I saw Eso in the parlour. I was feeling embarrassed when he beckoned to me to come to him. He had been returning home from the farm and had called at our place before going home. I stood looking at him. I would not greet him, I would not go to see him. He put his hand in a large, grimy bag which was hung at his side and brought out a large piece of smoked meat. He held it out for me to take. I shook my head without saying a word.

"Come," he invited, "accept it. It is a friendly present, no longer part of a dowry."

But nothing he could say would make me accept the meat. My parents urged me to take it, but I would not. Disappointment which I could not understand until later showed on all three faces. I left the room then.

"Subowa, come here, quickly," said my mother some time afterwards.

I went to her in the parlour.

"Quick! Eso has just gone, and he has forgotten to take his cap with him. Most probably he is still in front of the house. Take it to him." The cap was a special one known as "*akoro*," which only Esos can wear. It was dark outside but I did not fear to run a few yards from the house.

I ran, hoping to overtake Eso. I could not call to him to wait and take his cap, because I did not know what name to call him by. I had gone about 150 yards from the house and thought of going back with the cap when Eso spoke just in front of me.

"Is that my cap you're bringing? I was just coming back for it."

He had scarcely finished the sentence when out of the bushes nearby came about eight men. They had planted themselves in different places.

"Carry her," commanded Eso.

Instantly I was carried, struggling, shoulder-high by the men. One had a coarse, strong hand on my mouth. I struggled and twisted and scratched and kicked, all in vain. I was being carried along shoulder-high by these men.

I now understood. It was something commonly done. It was to be my wedding night. I was being carried to Eso's house to become his bride. He had never given me up. To him I was just a small battle, and he was an Eso, one who either conquers or dies. He had resolved to have me as his wife. I had caught his fancy when I was a tiny child, as one who might be his comfort when he was getting old. My parents had given me to him, and after he had spent so much on me and waited so many years for me to grow up I had become stubborn. I simply had to be subdued.

My parents had helped him in his schemes. It was not that they cared nothing for me, but if they had let me have my own way about not marrying Eso, Eso would have asked for a refund of the money he had spent on me since I was young. To refund the capital dowry alone would throw my parents into debt. Apart from the chief dowry there would be the yearly gifts, and all that had been spent on me at school. If he wanted to be hard on my parents he would reckon the price of the yams, corn, meat, and so on on a yearly average for fifteen years. When all was said and done the sum total would be a load of debt hanging around my parents' necks so heavily as to drag them down into ruin.

They knew this. They were not going to have it. Was it a bad thing they had done, then, in bringing me into the world? Were they to be thrown into debt because they had a stubborn daughter? Had they treated this same daughter worse than other parents treated theirs? No! Had they not fed and clothed me and looked after me, and also bestowed me on a rich man? Very well, then. Since other people did not get into debt because of their daughters, they, my parents, would not get into trouble because of me.

I now understood their disappointment at my refusal of the meat that night. It was the failure of a plot. I was to have taken the meat and, when Eso was going, I would have gone with him a few steps from the house to show gratitude. The plot failed when I refused the meat, but my mother's ingenuity contrived a new and almost infallible one on the spur of the moment. I realised how well it had succeeded as I was being carried along in the dark.

When we were out of earshot of our compound, the coarse hand was lifted off my mouth. We were passing in front of the house of a former classmate of mine. Her name was Bisi.

"Bisi's mother! Bisi's mother!" I screamed. "Come out and rescue me from Eso and his men!"

"What?" said a man sternly, "calling your husband by his name? What modern nonsense is that?" and clap came a hand on my mouth again. "Will you be sensible and walk, or shall we continue to carry you in this uncomfortable way?" asked one of the men, not explaining whether the way was uncomfortable to him or to me or to both of us.

"No," Eso said curtly before I could answer. "Carry her along. You don't know how clever she is. I suppose they teach them monkey tricks at school. But if she once had her feet on the ground she would escape."

When we were about a hundred yards from Eso's house, he left us. It is the custom that when a bride is being brought into the house, the bridegroom must not be in the house at the moment of her arrival. All the women in Eso's compound were in front of his house when we came to it. He had told them of his intentions before that time, and as soon as I was safely in the hands of his men, and on my way to his house, he had sent one of the men to tell the people at home that he had succeeded in getting me.

My captors now set me down in front of the door-step, and two of the strongest men there held me firmly. Eso's first and, therefore, oldest wife came forward with a calabash of water in her hand. She poured some water onto my feet as was the custom. I kicked the calabash from her hands with a wet foot and when the calabash broke on the ground consternation arose among those who were looking on. I even heard one say, "What kind of stubborn bride is this? Let her wait just a bit, though. Before two weeks are out her husband will thrash the devil out of her. Eso does not stand any nonsense from any woman."

Another calabash was brought with water in it. The eldest wife, standing out of reach of my feet this time, again poured some water on my feet, and handed the rest to a woman who had been Eso's latest wife until he decided to add me to the list. She threw the rest of the water on the roof. When this is done, the bride should be taken into the house so that some of the water coming down from the roof may fall on her head. It is the custom.

As soon as the water was thrown on the roof, I suddenly began to struggle so that the two men should not carry me inside under the water that was trickling down from the roof. My struggles took them unaware so that for a moment no hand at all was on me, but as I turned to fly I was seized very violently. The water had now all come down from the roof, except for one or two drops, but they couldn't go for water a third time.

I was carried across the threshold, some of those who carried me cursing under their breath and promising to take it out of me once I was in their power as their kinsman's new wife. I was taken into the innermost room of the house, a very small room, and was locked in with two of the women of the house.

For a man to seize his fiancée and drag her by force to his house and make her his wife is no rare thing in our village. If the man has paid the dowry and done all he should do for his fiancée, and the girl is so fond of her parents' house that she does not want to leave it, or if she favours another man's attentions, it is quite on the cards that her fiancé will come one night, lure her out and carry her off.

After some time in my little prison, I heard the voices of my relatives in the parlour. They had come to ask that I might be returned to them. All relatives always come with tears and supplications to take a seized bride back, though they very seldom succeed. I knew my parents were glad Eso had taken me, but if they had not come according to custom, they would have been accused of heartlessness. I heard my mother pleading tearfully— crocodile tears!—and talking of what a help I was at home and how I should be allowed to stay with them some months more. My sister was weeping loudly in real earnest. But soon they went away. They had not even been allowed to see me.

Some time later, when Eso appeared at the door of the room, the two women rose to go. I said that they should not go, and that if Eso came near me I should kill myself. I told Eso that he was getting into trouble by not letting me go with my parents, and sooner or later I would have the law on him for kidnapping me. Was not that enough trouble for him, I asked. Then I swore by one terrible god of war whom, as a warrior, Eso worshipped, that I would kill myself if he did not leave me alone and go away. The women still stood in the room listening.

"If the girl is giving trouble, two of us can come and help you subdue her," said one of Eso's kinsmen, showing his face at the door. I felt hot all over. There I was, standing, looking defiantly at Eso with two women and a man looking on. The latter guessed the situation.

"Shall I go and find another man?" he asked Eso.

Eso was deep in thought and he did not answer. I knew that if those two men came I was doomed. They would leave the way open next morning for me to go home if I wanted to, and expect me back within ten months with a baby in my arms. If that was the condition I knew I would not go back home. I should just stay and be a quiet wife. That was why my parents had been told to come for me in the morning if they wanted me back.

The man went away to fetch another. Eso turned to the women.

"You two can go."

They knelt in salutation before they went from his presence.

"Why don't you want to be my wife?" Eso asked me in a conciliatory tone, "I am rich and I can give you anything you want."

"I do not want your riches. I do not want to be your wife. Do you not yet have enough without me?"

"Oh! but come," he said a trifle impatiently. "You're mine, you know. Your parents gave you to me and received a large sum as a dowry from me. If I let you go, where will they get the money to repay me?"

"I don't know and I don't care," I said. He moved nearer.

"I tell you again, that if you come nearer, I will kill myself and you will be tried and hanged for murder," I said violently. "Better let me go," I said more quietly. "You know that European missionary who came to our school last year? He and his wife, a doctor, made friends with me. I have written letters to them and they know all about you. They said that if ever

I was in trouble I was to let them know, wherever they were. If you keep me here, sooner or later they will come and help me get you into trouble for kidnapping me. Do you know that in Lagos and places where Europeans are, people are not allowed to take wives by force?"

I got him there. All these village people are very much afraid of Europeans and European laws.

"That is certain future trouble for you," I went on. "But if you lay a finger on me then be ready for an ignominious death sooner or later. There are some things in my hand, which I have just taken from the pocket of my *tobi*, and I can easily kill myself now. I have a small sharp knife and a needle here. I have some red ink powder which is highly poisonous."

Eso knew nothing about ink powder, so I could easily hoodwink him in that direction.

"There are still about five paces between us. If you move one pace nearer, I will swallow the ink powder and then cut my throat with the little knife your blacksmith nephew gave to me. If I die, my European friends will see to it that you are not tried in this village where they may let you off very lightly, but in Lagos. The lands of your family and all your property will be confiscated and you will be hanged."

I then sat down on the mat, looking at him. When the man returned with another man, the position seemed to be less defiant than before.

"Shall we come?" asked the first man doubtfully at the door.

Eso pondered for a moment.

Then, "No, you can go," he said.

I took a very deep breath. He closed the door and I rose up at once with my fears and my determination renewed. But he lifted a screen which I had not noticed before and went into an adjoining room, where I soon heard him snoring.

I sat alone, sleepless, in the little room. In the middle of the night the oil in the oil-lamp was used up and the light went out. I got up and huddled first in one corner, then in another. A thousand fears were in my mind. At daybreak Eso came out of the room where he had slept and passed out at the door without greeting me, though he knew I was there in the darkness. As a matter of fact he had been doing some hard thinking as to how he should get himself out of the embarrassing position in which he found himself.

His position was thus. He, Eso, had not been able to subdue a mere girl, whom he had bought with his money. He could not reconcile himself to that. Yet, if he kept me with him, he feared he would get into trouble through my European friends, as I had assured him he would. But a more immediate difficulty was to be faced. When he went out at daybreak, his relatives would ask him, as was customary, if the bride had been virtuous. What would he say? Yet they must not know that he and his bride had spent the night in separate rooms. If they knew, Eso would be the laughing stock not only of the whole household but of the whole village. Such was Eso's position.

"Eso has just come out of the room," said somebody nearby. "He would have been the merest simpleton had he not subdued that girl. He has spent an awful lot of money on her. He wasted money sending her to school and after he had paid the dowry he had to give her mother some money to buy her clothes."

I now understood where the new things my mother had bought for me had come from. The more I discovered about how much Eso had spent on me, the more angry I was with the parents who had practically sold me.

However, Eso had answered the questions his relatives must have put to him about me; they all came and smiled at me. The one who had volunteered to come with a companion and help Eso last night now came and teasingly asked if I still wanted to go home. I said, "Yes," and he said I would be allowed to go if I actually did want to go. He laughed then and wondered whether my parents would like to feed another man's wife. He left me and went away.

Later in the morning my clothes—most of them the new ones paid for by Eso—were brought from my parents' house. They brought me a well-cooked breakfast after I had had a cold bath which I asked for. They had sent my small sister and many small cousins to be with me in Eso's house until the first seven special days' stay in my husband's house was over. After these seven days every bride is allowed to go and visit her parents for the first time after leaving them. Then she settles down in her husband's house and may have a small sister or two, or nieces, to stay with her and run errands for her.

The breakfast they brought for me had been specially cooked, but I refused to eat. I feared that they might have put some drug or other into the soup, as was the customary course adopted with stubborn brides. The whole household came to beg me to eat—some asked me not to be shy. Some thought I was being stubborn. But everybody did his or her best to try and make me eat. I would not eat.

Lunch time came, and still I did not eat. In the evening my supper was left in the room in the hope that I might eat it during the night when nobody was near. I did not eat it, but when in the night the oil in the lamp they left with me and my small companions gave out, I was glad to find that the meat in the soup brought me at supper time was good, fat pork. I washed the pieces of meat thoroughly in the water I was to have washed my hands in before eating. When I thought I had washed it enough to free it from the ingredients of the soup, especially salt, I separated the lean meat from the fat and left the former in the water. Out of the fat I squeezed as much water as I could, and put the fat in the lamp to melt and act as oil. The wick gave a sickly flame and the melting fat had a nasty smell, but it was better than no light at all. I did not sleep that night either.

I looked enviously at my little niece and sister and cousins sleeping soundly, fearing nothing.

In the morning one of Eso's younger wives came to clear away the food that had been left with me as my supper. When she saw the food apparently untouched, she began to grumble at having to cook for someone who would not eat the food. She interrupted her own grumblings with a loud peal of derisive laughter. She threw her head back and laughed.

"So" (the scorn in the voice which was purposely loud enough for me to hear cannot be expressed on paper), "So it is meat alone that our fine bride feeds on! Ha! ha! What an inexpensive bride to be sure! And she could easily get costly food to eat, since her husband is so rich." (She stressed the "her" as if Eso was not already the husband of fifteen women, including herself.)

"Living on meat when there's European diet to be had for money! What an inexpensive taste! Why doesn't she ask for sardines (pronounced "sandin") milk and cheese and bread and tea and wine?"

To simple village folk, everything imported seemed costly. Hence she thought tea, milk, cheese and sardines would be much more expensive than meat. She continued to laugh scornfully until she left the room.

She was telling another of Eso's wives, a woman of about her own age, about it all when they found the lean part of the meat in the water basin. Both of them laughed, jeered, and spoke with coarse loudness.

"Stranger and stranger!" they commented. "The bride who would not eat feeds only on fat. We had better tell the Lord of Creation (an impertinent term for their domineering and close-fisted husband Eso) to buy a herd of swine and get some swineherds, so that our fine educated lady can get fat to live on."

In the middle of the night that had passed, I had somehow thought of abandoning resistance and becoming Eso's wife. Lack of food for a whole day and lack of sleep for two nights were thus combining to weaken my will. But now, seeing what sort of women I should have to live with, and live under, as Eso's wife, my determination was again strengthened. I refused to touch my breakfast and treated my lunch in the same fashion. Everybody came to ask me to eat. Everybody asked me what I wanted. I answered the questions all in the same words: "I want to go home to my parents."

"But wait till the seventh day has come and you can do as you like. Meanwhile, eat."

I usually made no answer to them after that. In the evening I refused to eat an early supper they had brought. Everybody about the place was now grumbling about the food and labour I was wasting. They decided that my husband (in the eyes of all but myself and his frustrated self) should do something about it.

The men of the house called a meeting with Eso. They decided I was a very obstinate girl into whom they would very much like to knock some sense, but they did not want anybody dying of starvation in their house. I would get them into trouble. They decided that Eso should send me home that evening and later my parents would send me back if they found I was to bear Eso's child. I believe Eso valued his prestige more than anything else in the world, for he could not tell them that he was surely losing me and that they could not expect any baby of his from me. I believe he would not have told them to save his life. He pretended to agree with them in expecting me back within a year.

Eso was indeed losing many things. He was losing the money he had spent on me, because he knew he would now be unable to claim it from my parents, who had handed me over to him. He was losing the battle between me and him, between my stubbornness and his love of subduing stubbornness in anyone. Only he himself knew the full extent of what he was losing, and beside himself only I knew that he was losing anything at all. But his prestige was more to him than all these things he was losing. He would hate to be the laughing stock of the whole village. And so Eso let me go.

CHAPTER III

It was my fifth evening at home; the seventh evening and the sixth day of my "marriage." For all I was so weak through hunger and lack of sleep, I had walked briskly enough to my parents' house when I was released from Eso's, with two elderly women to come and explain the situation to my parents.

I could never feel safe unless I was out of our village, for Eso might be making other plans for securing me. The days I spent waiting for the reply to the clumsily respectful letter I had written were days of intense suspense. And now I held the reply in my hand. The boy to whom I had entrusted the letter, which I had written immediately after my return to my father's house, had not failed me. He was travelling to the town where my missionary friends lived, and had now returned. After a fearful pause I opened the letter with trembling hands. It was a gracious reply to my plea for help. The wife of the missionary was a doctor, and she ran a Nurses' Training Centre. Her reply was to ask me to come to her and she would train me as a nurse. At least that was enough plans for the next year (the training was a twelve months' training).

For me it was more than enough. I packed a few clothes into a little wicker portmanteau a school friend had made for me. The town I was going to was eighteen miles from my village. To me it was an easy six hours' tramp. The motor service between our village and the town was very irregular owing to bad roads. Besides, if I were to go by lorry, everybody would see me and I should probably be detained. I had done my packing secretly, or else my parents would have sent for Eso to stop me from "running away."

I could not sleep that night. I got up at about 3:30 a.m. and left the house at about 4:00, moving very quietly so as not to rouse anybody. My joy at the freedom that seemed so near to me was greater than my fear of the darkness.

I made my journey at morning-walk pace—an average of three and a half or four miles an hour. By 6 o'clock I was about seven miles from our village. I reached the doctor's at about 10 a.m., having had some minutes' rest at intervals on the way. When the doctor and her husband smiled at me and showed me where I was to live with the other nurses in training I felt that I would never experience a happier moment than that in my life. At last I was free and safe from all molestations.

There was "nothing so sweet" to me at that moment as my newly-gained freedom. I was free, *free*. . . .

THE MARCH ON GRAND BASSAM

Anne Marie Raggi, an Ivorian of Ghanaian and Lebanese parentage, was born on 8 October 1918 in Grand-Lahou and spent her entire life in Grand Bassam, the first capital of Côte d'Ivoire, approximately 30 miles from Abidjan, the country's major commercial center. Well educated, and a French citizen, she was one of the pioneers who committed herself to the fight against colonialism under the auspices of the Organization of African Democracy (RDA) (the Union of all the anticolonialist parties in French West Africa), and the local party, the Democratic Party of Côte d'Ivoire (PDCI). With other women, she was responsible for creating the women's branch of her political party.

In part of her life story, Raggi recounts the remarkable events of 1949 in which she took part. The conflict between Ivorian farmers and French colonizers after the Second World War led to terrible repression and detentions without trial of the militants of the PDCI and the RDA. The brutality of the colonial authorities prompted the women to take the lead in the anticolonial struggle, especially in an attempt to liberate their jailed comrades, who began a hunger strike on December 12, 1949, to protest their not being brought to trial.

The women's support of the strike action took two forms, one directed at their own husbands, the other at the French authorities. The action against husbands and lovers belonging to other opposing political parties, or otherwise not in favor of the hunger strike, took the form of all kinds of domestic noncompliance, including the withdrawal of sexual favors. Women whose husbands belonged to other parties bought RDA membership cards and put them "under their wrappers," that is, in their underwear. When their husbands attempted lovemaking, they were informed that that place of privilege was already taken—by an RDA member who was man enough to take a stand.

Furthermore, when one man had his girlfriend arrested for taking that kind of action, the women responded with another very West African gendered response. They invaded the court, and, when threatened by the police, began to dance and take off their clothes. A similar tactic had been used against British colonial authorities during the "Aba Women's War" in Nigeria in 1929 (see p. 169). In many African and Sahelian communities, the nakedness of women is taboo, and so this public undressing was, and continues to be, a powerful form of political resistance. An organized undressing to expose the body thus becomes an invocation of women's power, forceful enough to stop the malfeasance, as happened in this case.

At the suggestion of Anne-Marie Raggi, on 15 December 1949, the women began their action against the French authorities by boycotting products imported by French merchants. Then they decided to march on Bassam Prison, where their husbands were being kept. Two thousand women on foot and in buses from all parts of French West Africa joined the assault on Bassam Prison on 24 December 1949. The repression was gruesome: the French press as well as the French National Assembly spoke at length about it, and three months later the prisoners were judged and some of them released. This march is considered the first mass demonstration by West African women against the French colonial authorities. Anne-Marie Raggi was interviewed in January and May 1998 at her home in Grand-Bassam by members of the Women Writing Africa Côte d'Ivoire committee, Georgette Gina Dick and Claude Coffie. She died in 2005.

The second life story is that of Lucie Traoré Kaboré, wife of the RDA militant Dominique Kaboré, and a militant of the RDA herself. Her life reflects the fluid nature of affiliations and movements within French West Africa—movements that have been far more curtailed by postindependence national boundaries. Born in what is today Burkina Faso, she received her teaching diploma at the celebrated school for girls in Rufisque, now in Senegal, also attended by Mariama Bâ during the same period (see "My Little Country," p. 186). She held her first teaching position in Côte d'Ivoire, where, like Anne-Marie Raggi, she took part in the famous Women's March on Bassam.

Lucie Traoré Kaboré lives in Ouagadougou, in Burkina Faso, where she heads an association she created in 1974, the Association of Widows and Orphans of Burkina Faso (AVOB). When she lost her husband in 1972, Lucie Kaboré had to face the hard Mossi traditions concerning widowhood. These include shaving a widow's head and forcing her to choose a new husband from among the brothers of the deceased. The in-laws, furthermore, have the right to take over all that the deceased has left behind, thus putting into danger the future of the widow's children.

Like the interview with Anne-Marie Raggi, Kaboré's journal article comes from 1998. They have been placed together to highlight the context of 1949—the immediate postwar ferment that led to independence—in which these testimonies have the most meaning. The texts bring out the interconnectedness of the lives of the people of French West Africa in the pre-independence era. They also remind us of the pan-African dimension of the anticolonial and nationalist struggles in the former French West Africa and especially of the decisive role played by African women.

Aminata Diaw, Abena P. A. Busia, and Diedre L. Badejo

Anne-Marie Raggi, THAT IS HOW THE WOMEN WOKE UP

Côte d'Ivoire [1998]*   French

In those days [the 1930s and 1940s], the women had no right to say anything about anything. They did the house work, cooked the meals, went to the fields, and came back very late at night. In those days, very few women were literate; the majority did not go to school. But women, with their children, accompanied their fathers and their husbands during the periods of forced labor—and they wept. The blacks were ill-treated, especially those who came from the northern regions. They were beaten. Dead bodies were often found on the Moossou Road, where the gas and oil refineries were located. They were usually Korhogolese or Burkinabe men. We witnessed all that. Later on, when the war came, when they called up our men, a whole village would sometimes go to help those whose men had gone to war, because the women thought they'd never come back again. There were even women who killed themselves. But the women's story really started when our comrades in the Party were arrested, when we suffered repression directly at the hands of the colonial powers.

Our late president, Houphouet (Boigny), faced with the colonial situation, created the Planters' Trade Union (1944). The trade union was created in Grand Bassam, with the Dadiés, the Anomas, and a lot of people from Bassam. It's from the trade union that our democratic party (PDCI) was born in order to help people understand [the stakes]. I was among the members; I was young and a bit of a tomboy. When we saw that our Party was going to work, we went to Bamako [in April 1946]. And it was in Bamako that we created the African Democratic Union (RDA) on 18 October 1946. When the [colonial governors] saw that it was becoming powerful and was spreading everywhere in Mali and also in Guinea and Niger, they dissuaded some of our comrades from staying with us. The Chamber of Commerce succeeded in convincing others. So there was division. That's how the Progressive Party, the Socialist Party, and the RDA split from each other.

On 6 February 1949, there were three of us women at a funeral: Jacqueline Nouama, Rebecca, and I. We were told, "There's a war in Abidjan and all the members of the RDA are being arrested." Monday, 7 February, early in the morning, they [colonial police] came to fetch Mathieu Ekra at our headquarters and they arrested him. Then on 8 February in Adjamé they arrested Camara Lama, a Sudanese [Malian], and Vieyra because they were the leaders there. On 9 February, the others were arrested: Mockey, Paraiso, Sery, Koré, Jacob Williams, Bernard Dadié. It was then that Bernard Dadié wrote his first poem, "Hearses and Freedom," which imagined this country and the others as they are now. They were arrested the way they were found, almost naked. We women gave them our wrappers to cover up. If you look at the pictures, you will see Mathieu Ekra covered in a striped and spotted wrapper; that was Monique Adjoba's. All the women went home to fetch wrappers for all those who were not dressed. That's the way they were jailed.

We had to share the work. How to feed them? How to take care of them? Everyone was mobilized. The very evening [of their arrival in the Grand Bassam jail] we found mats and sandals we were able to give them. And then all of Bassam mobilized. The profits on everything the women sold were kept to help our prisoners. It was then that the women regrouped. When the husbands were arrested, the women joined the RDA. We created a women's section in Mory Keïta's compound with Mrs. Ouezzin Coulibaly, Marguerite Sacoum [Williams], Odette [Ekra], Georgette [Mockey], and all the wives of those who were arrested. Mory Keïta himself was among those who were dismissed from their jobs.

In those days there was an unshakable solidarity among people. We even heard that the women whose husbands or boyfriends were in the Progressive Party bought the RDA card and put it under their wrappers. When their husbands made certain suggestive gestures, the women told them "It was occupied by the RDA"—that was to force them to help free the RDA prisoners. And then, one of those men had his girlfriend arrested. She was very popular. She was called Sibo. She was taken to Bassam. Well, then, the women flew into a rage. They took cars and went to Bassam; Marie Kodja led the group. They all went to the court, where they were left to stew in a corner, so they started dancing and undressing. Such a thing had never been seen before. So the women were let go.

This is what the women said, "They lulled us to sleep, but now we've awakened to defend our children, to defend our families. We want our children to be like the children of France. We want to take things into our own hands." And the women truly joined the fight. Samba Ambroise's wife was arrested in Dimbokro; in Palaka, they shot at a woman who was following her husband who had been arrested. She had her baby on her back; she came later to the men's trial. That's how the women woke up. These are some of the incidents that motivated us. We held a meeting at the law court and decided to destroy the prison and save our jailed companions. That's how the Women's March on Grand Bassam [of December 1949] began to be organized.

Translated by Georgette Gina Dick and Judith Miller

Lucie Traoré Kaboré, MY NAME IS LUCIE TRAORÉ

Burkina Faso [1998]*   French

My name is Lucie Traoré, widow of Dominique Kaboré. I am in charge of the Association of Widows and Orphans of Burkina Faso (AWOB). I was born into a Catholic family of the Toussian ethnicity in Sidi in the province of Kénédougou (southern Burkina Faso), but I will not tell you when. My father was a veteran of the Second World War who, after his discharge, became a farmer. As for my mother, she stayed at home. I went to elementary school in Bobo Dioulasso. After receiving my school certificate, I went to Bingerville in Côte d'Ivoire for secondary education. After Bingerville, I moved to Senegal for higher education, or to be more precise to attend the best-known teacher training college, the Teacher Training College for Young Girls, in Rufisque.

It should be said that we were in the middle of the colonial era and that the colony of Upper Volta was part of the whole block of French West Africa. The weakness of the educational infrastructures forced one at the end of each cycle to move from one colony to another. When I finished my studies, I embraced the teaching profession and my first assignment was at a school in Treichville, a neighborhood of Abidjan. Before that, I had married Dominique Kaboré, who held numerous colonial administrative positions both in Côte d'Ivoire and in Upper Volta.

In fact, Dominique Kaboré was in charge of cabinet personnel in the governments of Côte d'Ivoire and Upper Côte d'Ivoire. In the wake of political problems, he was exiled to Guinea in 1949. This exile was to have repercussions on my professional career, since I had to follow him. He came back to Upper Volta where he was appointed postmaster of Zorgho. After completing his studies in Paris, he returned to Upper Volta as regional administrative commander in Bobo Dioulasso.

We had eight children, two boys and six girls, and by the grace of God they all have good salaries and positions. The girls are a pharmacist, a sociologist, a teacher, a dentist, a pediatrician, and an accountant. As for the boys, one is an architect and the other works in civil engineering.

Where politics are concerned, I became involved in the RDA in 1949. Why did I choose this party? It was the party of my father and then of my husband. I participated in the famous Women's March on Bassam in 1949 in Côte d'Ivoire to demand the liberation of RDA leaders who had been imprisoned by colonial authorities. Thanks to my political involvement and especially to my husband, I had the opportunity to be in close contact with well-known personalities such as Ouezzin Coulibaly, Modibo Keïta, Sekou Touré, Gabriel d'Arboussier, Philippe Zinda Kaboré, and so forth.

I should emphasize that being involved in politics during the colonial period was very difficult, especially for a woman. Not only did her social burdens work as a brake on her freedom of action, but a woman herself could not imagine that she might play a role in this domain. The great majority of African women were totally ignorant of their rights and their duties.

To return to my own involvement in the women's cause, everything began with the death of my husband in 1972. Where widows are concerned, Mossi traditions are harsh. When you lose your husband, your head is shaved. You must choose a new spouse from among the brothers of your deceased husband. I had a very difficult time during that ordeal. What finally results is the appropriation of your possessions and their redistribution, which leaves the widow and her children destitute. This trauma led me to create a space in which widows and orphans could meet and be counseled. That's how the organization of widows and orphans was born in May 1974 that would then become the AWOB, whose headquarters are located in Ougadougou. As its symbol, the association chose an illustration of the ceremony of shaving a widow's head.

The objective of the AWOB is to defend widows and orphans on the judicial level. In addition to that, and thanks to all the volunteering widows, it counsels and studies ways of finding solutions for their problems through training, through the creation of cooperatives for producing crafts, through education and literacy programs for both children and adults.

Translated by Marjolijn de Jager and Judith Miller

Mabel Dove-Danquah and Others
FROM THE "WOMEN'S COLUMN"

Ghana 1949, 1950   English

By the 1940s, the Gold Coast was home to a firmly established and vibrant literate culture suffused with anticolonial nationalism, especially visible in the columns of the burgeoning newspapers. While women constituted a tiny portion of the literate elite, they made significant contributions to nationalist newspapers of the time, including the *Accra Evening News*.

Launched on 3 September 1948 by Kwame Nkrumah, the first president of Ghana, the *Accra Evening News* featured in each issue a "Women's Column." The dominant voice of the columns was Mabel Dove-Danquah, writing under the pen name Akosua Dzatsui, a name that signified difficult times in need of endurance and fortitude. Dove-Danquah often assigned the column to other women political activists, and together they led the women's battle for emancipation from colonial rule, while at the same time challenging patriarchy by writing essays questioning gendered myths and attitudes. Two nationalist poems and a satiric essay testify to the variety of forms various writers used, often contributing anonymously.

"The Blackman's Burden," by Adjua Mensah, and "An Ode," by Akua Amaku, were featured in the column on 2 August 1949 and 29 June 1950, respectively. As in other cases, we cannot identify the two women, but it is clear enough that they are writing rather flippant satires rather than formal verse. In two different ways, each asks about economic inequality. Mensah challenges God about the paradox of Christianity's creating whites rich and blacks poor and suffering, and she questions the values of whites who seem to enjoy the suffering of blacks. Amaku addresses the "highly paid bosses" directly, ominously suggesting the breakdown of their system that seems imminent.

In "I Have Tamed My Wife," Mabel Dove-Danquah (writing under her pseudonym Akosua Dzatsui) offers a sharp response to men who assume that women are not interested in national liberation, much less in their own personal and professional freedom. For further information on Dove-Danquah, see "Satire from the Women's Corner" (p. 174).

Audrey Gadzekpo

✦

THE BLACKMAN'S BURDEN

Oh God who has't made the Europeans white
And willed that Africans be black,
Look down on us in our sad plight
Groaning under the white-man's sack
Was it for this we were created
Why didn'st thou give us hands and brains?
Or is it that men, with minds degraded,
Find pleasure in causing others pains?
By these self-same whites we were taught
That thou, O God, art Father of us all,
Yet by them cruel wrongs are wrought,
As if we were meant to relish gall.
"Thats the price for your heavenly ticket"
Says the whiteman when we complain;
If through want we pick his laden pocket.

Adjua Mensah

AN ODE

You waited too long our highly paid bosses
Of the Public Works Department

Lights for ever failing, water very short
Roads all lives imperiling,
Bridges the devils theatre
And for this neglected service,
Increments never halt
And from the shallow drains,
Mosquitoes become our guardian angels
Allowances, leaves and pensions rank priority in thought
A long past war they always blame.
For this and that delay
Yet those who work hard with hands and brains cannot make ends
    meet.

Akua Amaku

"I HAVE TAMED MY WIFE"

Talking to an intelligent gentleman the other day, my heart gave a decided jump when he gave out the above startling statement. In the course of conversation, I asked him whether he allowed women who might create the eternal triangle to enter his home.

He appeared somewhat surprised at the question; "Why not," he exclaimed with the usual male arrogance, "I have tamed my wife."

I must confess tough as I am, I had a shock. Was the wife a tiger, a leopard or a domestic animal?

I have mentioned this incident because many men these days complain bitterly that their women folk are not interested in this movement of Africa's liberation, that very few women of Ghana have daubed their warpaint, sharpened their claws and are using all that sweet feminine cunning and artifice so that with passion and ardour they can give the monster of imperialism the embrace of death.

Now my dear, dear lords of creation, how can women who have been tamed be able to cope with the diplomatic flatteries and imperialistic endearments. How can poor frail women say to thee magnetic monsters— Away with your gewgaw! Away with your sweet nothings! Away with the honey of temptation—I will not sip, I will not taste.

Tamed women are submissive women, they wear the chains of slavery, even a people who cow and tame the spirit of womanhood cannot fight as fiercely and as courageously as he wants the esteem and loyalty of the one woman.

Women of Ghana, we must ask of our men the laurels of brave manhood honour, justice, truth, and loyalty, not mansions, not cars nor the gold dust of the earth. And when we see them cast away their self-indulgences, and break our chains of servitude and call us to their side; then we will rise and go to them and follow them, even into the thick of the fight and we will conquer and stand together formidable and indomitable free men and women of Ghana.

I can just imagine a subtle alien say to one warrior woman "Your claws are too sharp my love, may I gently bite them off, and he will bite them off with such tenderness and after that if he complains—your embrace is suffocating me, my darling." What can a modest woman do? she has to relax and so the monster escapes the embrace of death.

But besides this sweet nonsense—and I hope, you have been amused— If the men of Ghana want their women to be brave, bold and hardy, they too must be men, not only men fearless and vigilant in a liberation movement but men worthy of the women who went down to the valley of death to usher them into the world and on whose bosom they rested in their tender years.

Men of Ghana, liberation movements come and go nations rise and sink if made of gold or diamonds they are still chains; they are servile, meek, seen but not heard, their master and lord's yea is their yea, his nay is their nay.

But perhaps, the men of Ghana are throwing the challenge not to their wives who are already too tame but to the untamed and irrepressible, the warrior women of Ghana, those bear the heat and burden of the day, those who toil, and delight in toil, those who live so that others might live more abundantly. Even then the imperialists are wide awake, they do not sleep the poor darlings (excuse the word darling—sleeplessness is no joke—mere woman's sentiment).

Akosua Dzatsui

MOTHER AND DAUGHTER

Adelaide and Gladys Casely-Hayford occupy a central place in the intellectual history of West Africa in the twentieth century. The mother-daughter pair made significant contributions to the evolution of a modern class of talented and politically active women on the continent, who adapted to new facts to articulate a broad understanding of the untapped possibilities of Africa and African womanhood. In the twin historical moments of decolonization and feminism, Adelaide and Gladys opened up new horizons of affirmation to reckon with oppressive colonial and patriarchal traditions. As the mother's "portrait" of her daughter selected for this volume illustrates, the two were similar in many respects, but the effort by each woman to radically redefine herself within her own generation accounts for significant differences.

Adelaide Casely-Hayford's life spanned two centuries, nine decades, and three continents. She was born Adelaide Smith in Freetown, Sierra Leone, on 27 January 1868, to a large Krio family of cultural aristocrats whose hybrid lineage consisted of West African, English, and ex-slave settler elements. Her father, William Smith Jr., moved the family to the Isle of Jersey, England, following his retirement in 1872, where Adelaide's mother, Anne Spilsbury Smith, died three years later. William Smith enrolled his daughters at the Jersey Ladies College, where they had the distinction of being founding students. At age seventeen, Adelaide left for Germany to study music, returning in 1888 as a confident and sophisticated young woman. She set sail for Freetown in 1892 but returned shortly after when her stepmother died in 1894. With her father's death a year later, Adelaide felt rudderless for the first time in her life. She fulfilled her father's wish that she and her siblings return to Africa, but once again the death of a family member brought her back to England. During this period, she established ties with the musical genius Samuel Coleridge-Taylor, a fellow Sierra Leonean who awakened Adelaide to the idea of forging links between Africa and the United States, since the latter was still largely ignored by Africans studying abroad. Adelaide also met and married the Ghanaian-born lawyer, activist, and writer Joseph Casely-Hayford. The couple went to live in Ghana, where Gladys was born in 1904. Her daughter's ill health forced Adelaide to go back to England for a while, and when she returned to Ghana, her marriage was practically over.

Adelaide arrived with her daughter in Freetown just as news broke of the First World War in 1914. This time she was determined to realize her dream of establishing a vocational school for girls. She rallied sufficient support for a trip to the United States, and at age fifty-two, accompanied by her niece, Katherine Easmon, she made the journey, in search of inspirational ideas and funding. Her visit was reported in local newspapers and black magazines and journals, including W. E. B. DuBois's *Crisis*. She visited numerous schools in over two dozen cities and met with black leaders in education and politics, including DuBois, Nannie Burroughs, and Margaret James Murray, Booker T. Washington's widow. She spoke before black and white audiences throughout the United States, sometimes breaking the color barrier. The Girls Vocational School opened in Freetown in 1923 with the dual purpose of building character and stimulating an African-centered consciousness. Adelaide revisited the United States in 1926 for another round of fund-raising activities. She was forced to close the school in 1940, however, due to recurring financial problems and her own failing health.

Rarely acknowledged by chroniclers of African history, Adelaide Casely-Hayford was a trailblazer with a distinguished record of achievement. Shaped by European colonialism, she saw the need to fill the ideological vacuum with respect to Africa. As the first African to be invited to the United States on a lecture tour, she laid the foundation for transatlantic relations between the two continents. She incorporated Africa Day into the roster of celebratory events in her school, along with Empire Day. She held various positions of leadership in women's organizations and in the West African branch of the Universal Negro Improvement Association (UNIA), Marcus Garvey's pan-Africanist movement. Her resistance to colonial ideology informs her fiction, as evidenced by her comic representation of the mindless imitation of English manners in "Mister Courifer" and her response to Aldous Huxley's denigration of Africans in "Savages." She was awarded the King's Silver Jubilee Medal in 1935 and the MBE (Medal of the British Empire) in 1949, when she was eighty-one. She died in Freetown on 24 January 1960.

Gladys Casely-Hayford was paradoxically a source of joy and disappointment to her mother. Like her parents, she was endowed with a prodigious creative intelligence, but a leg deformity incurred at birth and the fierce personalities of her parents engendered in her a desire to chart her own course. She staked out a different creative ground in poetry, adding music, drawing, and dance in her early years. Gladys began to generate a celebrity independent of her parents after publishing three of her poems—"Nativity," "The Serving Girl," and "The Souls of Black and White"—in *The Atlantic Monthly* in June 1927, at the height of the Harlem Renaissance movement in the United States, under the pseudonym Aquah Laluah. She was introduced in the volume as follows: "Aquah Luluah is a young African who studied for several years in Europe. She is a member of an ancient African family and the granddaughter of a native king." As Adelaide Casely-Hayford's biographer points out, "Neither grandfather was a native king." On the other hand, the description has an imaginative reach that served, in the era of the "New Negro," to harness readers' interest in the young woman. Countee Cullen's inclusion of her poems in his collection of Harlem Renaissance poetry, *Caroling Dusk* (1927), attests to her growing influence as a literary artist.

After schooling in Wales, Gladys returned to Freetown to teach in her mother's school, while she made plans to leave for further studies at Columbia University in New York. In 1929, she departed for the United States, but in London she joined a theatrical group headed for Berlin. While in Europe, Gladys suffered a nervous breakdown and was hospitalized for several months. After her recovery, she substituted for her mother at the International Conference on African Women in Geneva in 1931. She resumed teaching at the Girls Vocational School upon her return to Freetown in 1932. Despite her conflicts with her mother, the two remained intimate throughout their lives, including the period of Gladys's tumultuous marriage to Arthur Hunter. Gladys went to Accra in 1940 to give birth to her son, Kobe, and returned to Ghana in 1950 for what would be her final visit. She died in Accra on 23 August 1950 of black water fever.

Tuzyline Jita Allan

◆

Adelaide Casely-Hayford, PROFILE OF GLADYS
Sierra Leone 1940   English

We had quite a lot in common, my darling one *gial pickin* and I. We were both premature, utterly negligible, puny little infants causing our parents a lot of anxiety and trouble. We were both Wednesday's children—full of woe. At an early age we both learned to suffer, but we possessed such iron constitutions that we survived. When Gladys was only three, she contracted bronchitis, then pneumonia and ended up with whooping cough, without any cessation whatsoever. We both had a keen sense of humour. Even when she was about to be stricken down with her short fatal illness in 1950, she wrote us a letter which was full of jokes and fun, radiating her joyous personality. I received that letter a few hours after the cable announcing her death.

She was a lonely little girl and I fully realised how inadequate I was as a playmate. When we played "follow my leader," she was disgusted with my leadership and would ask whether she might not take my place. Sometimes, with her spade and bucket, we would go down to the seashore together and she would watch with envious eyes some practically naked little boys with whom she longed to play. When I allowed her to do so, keeping an eye on them all the time, it did make her so happy. In her childhood days in England she found great solace in her imaginary friend, Peggy, whom we were admonished to treat with the utmost respect. When riding a bus, we were cautioned not to sit on Peggy and to allow her plenty of breathing space, much to the amazement of the other passengers.

She didn't like textbooks and hated arithmetic; but she was a voracious little reader, devouring Kingsley's "Heroes" from cover to cover at the age of seven. I tried to teach her, but not very successfully. Some ideas stuck in her brain, however, because one evening we were watching a beautiful sunset and she said, "Oh, mother, do look at that lovely archipelago in the sky."

To a child of her temperament, loneliness may have been an asset. It gave her unlimited time for meditation and her talents plenty of scope to develop. It may also have been the means of increasing her love of companionship, making her a most amazingly sociable little girl.

At the age of fifteen, she left me to go to Penrhos College, Colwyn Bay. The Headmistress, Miss Rose Hovey, had been my school friend and was quite prepared to take her. "Ma," as she was affectionately called, once wrote to tell me that Gladys had written a poem on "Ears" which was the finest ever written by a Penrhos girl. It would have been greatly to her advantage to have remained there, but without my knowledge, her father made other arrangements which were just as expensive and not nearly so effective.

After some years in England and the Gold Coast, she came back to help revive our little school, which was in a critical condition, and between herself and our white American teacher, wonders were performed.

Gladys was no respecter of persons and some of her guests were downright disreputable. As long as you were a human being in need, you could count on Gladys for help. Invariably, she brought home these lame dogs and I, with my meagre income, had to extend hospitality—sometimes quite grudgingly. She insisted that whatever we had must be shared. This outstanding capacity for love and kindness swallowed up her many eccentricities.

One day, she was walking along the thoroughfare near the market when she saw a man lying in the middle of the road. She pulled him to the kerb and seeing that he was still breathing, rushed into a shop for brandy and milk to revive him. By this time, quite a crowd had gathered, and one woman shouted out, *"Nor make norbody tiff dah lili missis in poss oh! You nor see waitin e day do?"* Gladys then realised that she was carrying her bag under her arm, so she looked all round the crowd and spotted one man. "Oh," she said, handing it to him, "Please take care of it for me." After her ministrations, the sick man revived and an ambulance came to take him off. The crowd dispersed and Gladys suddenly realised that she had parted with her hand-bag. The man was still standing there and came up to her at once. "Missis," he said, "here is your bag." It transpired that this was a man, in and out of prison the whole time, but after the look of confidence and trust Gladys gave him, he admitted that he could not possibly steal from her.

Although there were times when I secretly felt that Gladys was inclined to be irreligious, I realise now how grossly I misjudged her. Whatever their appearance, she was everlastingly seeking for people's good qualities rather than condemning them. As Carlyle often pointed out, it is "this gift of tenderness and understanding sympathy that gives the measure of our intellects." Having definitely conquered fastidiousness, Gladys was a spiritual aristocrat.

It was only at her death that I realised what a place she had made for herself in the affections of the community. I went to my window about two hours after the radio had announced her death in Accra, and saw a group of market women looking up at the house disconsolately and utterly woebegone.

In spite of my help, she was in a chronic state of financial embarrassment, largely brought about by her marriage (without my knowledge), to a man I had never even seen, and who was never able to support her and their little boy. Consequently, she suffered untold hardships.

She had no sense of values and never could discriminate in any way, either with human beings or commodities. Then too, she utterly lacked determination and perseverance. These traits were a great handicap throughout her life. Yet on the other hand, she could sit down and in a short time, write a poem which was a joy and inspiration to read. Once she casually posted some specimens of her work to Columbia University and immediately received an invitation to migrate there without delay. She left me to go, but never reached America, because of financial difficulties. As usual, her lack of discrimination prompted her to join a coloured jazz troupe with headquarters in Berlin. She bitterly regretted her decision in after years.

Meanwhile, her considerable literary talents continued to develop by leaps and bounds. She expressed herself chiefly in poems. Knowing that

Cambridge, a suburb of Boston, was the supreme educational centre of the States as it sheltered Harvard University, with its Female section, Radcliffe College, I took some of her poems to a friend there. She was so impressed, that she sent them to the editor of the *Atlantic Monthly*. To our great surprise, three of them were accepted and immediately appeared in this very literary American publication. Their appearance resulted in an offer for Gladys to enter Radcliffe College at once, but through my dear daughter's own action, another splendid opportunity was lost.

Life did not seem quite fair to her somehow and I must take my share of the blame. She wanted both her parents. Had her father lived, I know she would have been his right hand. Her optimism however always came to the rescue as in this poignant little verse:

With Pa, I feel so lonesome, 'cause
  Mammy she ain't there.
With Ma, I feel like crying', cause of
  Daddy's empty chair.
Then when I start a-straining at
  the leash to go away,
Ma wants a savoury omelette—so I
  cook it and I stay.
Pa respects a person's feelings an'
  he up and says to me
That as an individual, I had certain
  rights you see,
And he'd not encroach upon them;
  Thus we struck a friendship true,
That will go on enduring so long as
  skies are blue.
And when he says quite casual,
  "Would you like some ginger beer?"
I just unpack my box again and say,
  "Yes, Daddy dear!"

She was a patriot through and through, as her poem "My Africa" will show. In this she was her father's own daughter, because undoubtedly, the Honourable Casely spent all his time, his talents, his energy and money on laying the fundamental structure of self-government in the Gold Coast, which is now almost an accomplished fact.

Sierra Leone 1950   English

Beat, Beat, Beat dears, beat the golden grain,
For food builds up the sinews, and stimulates the brain,
Just as you beat rice, dears, with your pestle in your hand,
You'll beat distrust and bloodshed out of Africa, our land.

Clean, Clean, Clean dears, clean the silver fish,
Drop its shimmering shining scales, then lay it on the dish;
'Tis destined in the future, little Africans, that you
Shall clean away the scales that hide true Africa from view.

Burn, Burn, Burn dears, burn the sweet palm oil,
And every mother's son, dears, will thank you for your toil;
For in the years to come, dears, while other nations shout,
You'll burn the heart of Africa, till all its dross burns out.

Grind, Grind, Grind dears, pepper ripe and red,
For there are many hungry, eager, strong, black lads who must be fed;
Your dear black hands that guide the stone will remain faithfull still,
To guide and comfort Africa, when passing through Life's mill.

Efua Sutherland
NEW LIFE

Efua Theodora Sutherland was born in Cape Coast, Ghana, on 27 June
1924. Her matrilineal roots were from royal clans in two Fante towns,
Gomoa Brofo and Anomabo. Having lost her own mother at the age of five
months, Sutherland was brought up in the family of her grandmother, Araba
Mansa, who, despite modest financial circumstances, maintained the dignity
of their illustrious ancestry.

Sutherland's academic career was assured by her performance at school and
by the support of Anglican nuns of the Order of the Holy Paraclete based in
Yorkshire, England. She acquired both her basic education and teacher train-
ing in institutions established and run by the nuns: Saint Monica's School in
Cape Coast and, on a scholarship, Saint Monica's Training College in Ashanti
Mampong. After five and a half years of teaching at the senior primary level
and the training college, she received support in 1947 to attend Homerton
College in England, where she received a B.A. She studied for one year at the

School of Oriental and African Studies at the University of London, where she specialized in English linguistics, African languages, and drama.

She thus returned home in the early 1950s as a member of a very small group of Ghanaian women professionals with university education, in the period leading up to the independence of the Gold Coast and its transformation into the nation of Ghana. Like many intellectuals and political activists at the time of independence, Sutherland had a profound sense of her identity as an African. Her awareness grew out of her experiences in England, her marriage to African American peace activist Bill Sutherland in 1954, and the pan-African orientation of the independence movement in Ghana in which they were both involved.

Sutherland joined the staff of the Institute of African Studies at the University of Ghana as a research associate in 1963 and worked there until 1984. She is most recognized for her work as a dramatist, which went beyond the writing of plays to the development of theatrical forms and institutions aimed at exploring the wellspring of indigenous texts and dramatic forms, which she discovered through her research on Ghanaian dramatic and literary culture. She is credited as a pioneer in the conception of African community theater as total theater, which she named *Anansegoro*, after the traditional storytelling tradition of the Akan.

Sutherland became a beacon throughout the continent as a pan-African cultural worker. In this regard she has left two lasting legacies of her vision. She was instrumental in the initiative to re-inter the bones of W. E. B. DuBois in the grounds of his last home in Ghana and establish a center for pan-African culture there. Second, the biannual Panafest, today the largest pan-African cultural festival on the continent, was born out of her vision for an African drama festival to be held in and around the World Heritage site of Cape Coast Castle, "the door of no return" for ancestors of countless millions of African peoples around the world today.

Sutherland wrote poetry, essays, and short stories, in addition to her plays. Many of these have been anthologized in a variety of languages. She wrote her plays in Akan and English. She was responsible for the establishment of many Ghanaian cultural institutions, including the Ghana Society of Writers in 1957 (now the Ghana Association of Writers); the Ghana Drama Studio, on whose site in the center of Accra the National Theater was erected and which is today at the School of Performing Arts of the University of Ghana; and the experimental theater project in the storytelling village of Atwia. Through these and other institutions, Sutherland worked to stimulate a core of creative Ghanaians to ensure that drama would function to educate and raise national consciousness.

Sutherland's belief in the cardinal importance of stimulating the minds of young people led her to establish Afram Publications Ghana Ltd., a leading indigenous publishing house in Ghana. She spent countless hours assisting young writers in honing their skills and the quality of their products. A preoccupation with nation building and the importance of tradition and transformation at the dawn of the independence of Ghana suffused all aspects of her work. Sutherland's foreword to the coffee-table book *The Roadmakers* (1961) is a piece of crisp prose. Sutherland provided the original concept for the book and its text, and also chose the subjects for the pictures taken by veteran photographer Willis Bell.

Foriwa (1962) dramatizes the state of a decaying town in the countryside mired in past ancestral glories, and then points in the direction of hope. Based on African legend, this play imagines a visionary woman, unable to contain her frustration with the comatose state of her people, who attempts to galvanize her society into action. Sutherland also reinterprets other motifs, including that of the marginalized person who emerges as the savior of a community. Set in southern Ghana, the town of Kyerefaso, in spite of its lack of progress, has a misplaced sense of superiority. A well-educated, hard-working young man with a high sense of social responsibility from the supposedly backward northern part of Ghana comes to visit. Labaran, as a social and political activist, pitches his tent on the rubbish dump and from this liminal location slowly begins to reach into the community to effect change.

The beautiful daughter of the queen mother, Foriwa, an earnest, well-educated young woman, wants to do something to lift her people out of their morass. When she meets the stranger-activist Labaran, she finds her soul mate. The deep comradeship between Foriwa and Labaran is meant to suggest a hopeful revitalization for Kyerefaso.

The text below is drawn from the play's climax, when the queen mother creates a crisis by delivering an epoch-making speech about the duty of the current generation, particularly men, to contribute to social reform so that they may be worthy of the heritage of their ancestors. In the extract from Act III, Scene 1, the queen mother is about to make the transgressive remarks that insist on breathing vitality into tradition, and that will eventually bring new life to Kyerefaso.

Esi Sutherland-Addy

✦

FROM THE ROADMAKERS

Ghana 1961   English

Ghanaians live in a time of construction and fundamental change. We are building new roads to our prosperity and creating the fabric and character of our national life.

Our fathers knew nothing of the new roads of technological advance and industrialisation with which we are concerned, but they left us excellent paths of human relations and wisdom which we intend to save.

This book pictures us as we are today, children of an ancient people with our roots deep in Africa's soil; converts and victims of the many human, ideological and material influences which have found their way into our country by land, sea and air.

We live close to the spirit of our ancestors in quiet villages they founded on our white shores and in our green forests. A wonderful spirit of community and adjustment to life prevails there which is one of the paths of human progress our fathers found.

We pursue our life of fishing, farming and craftsmanship under the leadership of our men of wisdom. But we want to see our land developed and our opportunities increased. We want motor powered fishing boats, more efficient tools and new skills for our farming. We want better houses and healthier villages. And if we are not to continue losing our children to the towns, they must get from their education the initiative for enterprise, the practical ability and the adjustment to the environment of their villages which are vital to their survival there.

We live also in the young towns near ports and mining pits, timber yards and factories. There are workshops and technical institutes where we can acquire new skills; schools, training colleges and a university college. There are increasing outlets for our artisans and professional men. The bustle and pressure of commerce and petty trading in commodities we do not manufacture is there. The least desirable tastes and values of the outside world reach us through films and junk we import. Life is expensive and lacks the security and stability that is a valuable characteristic of life in our villages. A problem of delinquency is arising. We are distressed to have Borstal institutions in a society which believes that the responsibility for children is a sacred privilege of the family.

We have also acquired too many confusions from history. Our task today is to reassess our views and our values, for only then can we choose a clear direction. Our choice is made very much harder by all the records of achievement and the material supplies that the twentieth century world has made available to us. But we are now making this choice.

All the skill and equipment we need for the material progress which will raise the standard of living for our people can be bought or acquired through hard work. What we cannot buy is the spirit of originality and endeavour which makes a people dynamic and creative. Wisdom has recognised this and raised a voice which might well save Ghana and all Africa from continuing the error of looking outside herself for inspiration in determining the road of her progress. That voice speaks of the African personality. It invites Africa to make her own original contributions to the cultural heritage of mankind.

Most of the world has spoken. In our age, we have yet to be heard.

FROM *FORIWA*

Ghana 1962   English

STANDARD BEARER [approaching the Queen with stylized movement]: Gently, gently.

[The QUEEN MOTHER rises, and steps down from the dais. The atten-
    dant who carries the stool spreads out the sheepskin rug for her to
    stand on.]
Spread skins of the gentle sheep in her way.
Lightly, lightly walks our Mother Queen.
Shower her with silver,
Shower her with silver, for she is peace.
[The fan bearers scatter silver stylistically around and retreat, their
    movements echoed by the girls on the foundation. The STANDARD
    BEARER takes up his position before the QUEEN MOTHER. The other
    members of the Asafo approach and take up a position behind him.]
Osee!
Osee to the manly men of old!
They crouched like leopards
Upon the branches of trees.
[FORIWA appears on the verandah and stands there watching.]
Before the drums beat
Before the danger drums beat, "BEWARE!"
Before the horns moaned
Before the wailing horns moaned, "BEWARE!"
They were upright. They sprang!
They sprang upon the enemy.
And now, blood no more!
No more thunder shot on thunder shot.
But still, we are the leopards on
the branches,
We are those who roar and cannot be
answered back
Beware! We are they who cannot be
answered back.
QUEEN MOTHER [quietly]: What news? What news do you bring?
STANDARD BEARER [wiping his brow stylistically, the Asafo members
    doing the same]: It is the Path-clearing Festival.
We come with dusty brows from our
pathfinding, Mother,
We come with tired thorn-pricked feet,
We come to bathe in the coolness of
your peaceful stream,
We come to offer our manliness to new life. [He stands aside for the
    Asafo men to lay down their guns at the QUEEN MOTHER's feet.]
QUEEN MOTHER: All is well, then. The gun is laid aside.
[The LINGUIST nods with satisfaction.]
The gun's rage is silenced in the stream.
[The LINGUIST nods more emphatically.]

Now hear me. What's going to be your weapon from now on?

LINGUIST [in a panic]: That is not the customary question. At this point in the ceremony, you step on the guns, and you ask . . .

QUEEN MOTHER: With my respect, Linguist, I'm aware of it. The meeting that I called now begins.

[Everybody there becomes visibly tense. The QUEEN MOTHER addresses the Asafo.]

Are your weapons from now on to be your minds' toil and your hands' toil? Is that the meaning of this dedication to new life? [She looks wildly around her.] Where are you, women all? Come, join the men in dance, for they are offering themselves to new life.

[All the women present stir, but they don't know how to behave. Uneasiness spreads to everyone. The QUEEN MOTHER scans the street for FORIWA, and sees her upstairs.]

Foriwa!

[FORIWA comes down with all eyes on her. The QUEEN MOTHER is intensely roused. She takes a few steps towards FORIWA.]

Come, daughter, will you not dance? The men are tired of parading in the ashes of their grandfathers' glorious deeds. That should make you smile. They are tired of the empty croak, "We are men. We are men." They are tired of sitting like vultures upon the rubbish heap they have piled on the half-built walls of their grandfathers. Smile then, Foriwa, smile. Their brows shall now indeed be dusty, their feet indeed thorn-pricked, and "I love my land" shall cease to be the empty croaking of a vulture upon the rubbish heap. Dance, Foriwa, dance.

[FORIWA feels a challenge in this strange appeal and quickly decides to join forces with her mother in this moment in which she senses a crisis. LABARAN, who has become very alert, is busily recording and watching.]

FORIWA [stopping abruptly in the middle of the street]: Mother, I do not find him here.

QUEEN MOTHER [not getting her meaning]: Who do you not find here?

FORIWA: Him with whom this new life shall be built. He is not here, mother. I don't see him in these empty eyes. I see nothing alive here, mother, nothing alive . . .

[She stops suddenly, and walks back to the entrance of the house. The whole place stirs. The QUEEN MOTHER is taken aback.]

QUEEN MOTHER [quietly, to the meeting]: Forgive this show of passion. A full heart, like a flood, forces a channel for itself. Sitting here, seeing Kyerefaso die, I am no longer able to bear the mockery of the fine, brave words of this ceremony of our festival. Our fathers earned the right to utter them by their deeds. They found us the land, protected it, gave us a system of living. Praise to them. Yes. But is this the way to praise them? Watching their walls crumbling around us? Failing to build upon their foundations? Letting weeds choke the paths they made? Unwilling to open new path ourselves, because it demands of us thought, and goodwill, and action? No, we have turned Kyerefaso into a death bed from which our young people run away to seek elsewhere, the promise of life we've failed to give them here. [Deciding to say no more, she returns to the sheepskin rug and addresses the LINGUIST.] Linguist, those are my thoughts. I knew no way of reaching my people better with such thoughts than to use this ceremony of our festival as my interpreter. Kyerefaso needs the new life of which we speak, and men to make it true.

LINGUIST [without much spirit]: You have all heard the Queen Mother.

QUEEN MOTHER: And now, I would like to request that the solemn rite be performed; the rite of purification, which, of all that we enact at our festival, means to us true faith and nobility.

[The HEAD PRIEST rises, ready to oblige.]

But these young men had something to say to me. We will hear them first, or anyone else, in case they harbour bitterness that might mar the spirit of forgiveness and of peace for which we will soon pray. Let the young man speak.

[She returns to sit on the dais. An attendant moves the sheepskin rug there.]

LINGUIST [to 1ST SCHOLAR]: The Queen Mother will hear you.

1ST SCHOLAR [very uncomfortable]: Em . . . em . . . er, in the light of present circumstances, we . . . er . . . [He looks helplessly at his friends.] We wish to postpone the presentation of our protest . . . until such time as . . . as . . .

2ND SCHOLAR [with difficulty, at the prompting of 1ST SCHOLAR]: We must adjourn for consultations through appropriate democratic channels . . .

SINTIM [shouting with irritation at the scholars]: O quiet there! Let's have the prayers, and seek in them some solace for our bewilderment.

[The QUEEN MOTHER rises. FORIWA turns delighted eyes at SINTIM and goes to stand at his side. The HEAD PRIEST walks up to the shrine. Everybody is drawn into a moment of quiet prayer, as he makes ritual gestures over the God-Tree with his hands. That over, he sprinkles a little white powder in everybody's direction. He climbs the dais, dips three fingers into the white powder and marks the QUEEN MOTHER on her arm. The tension breaks. The HEAD PRIEST returns to his position. The QUEEN MOTHER steps down from the dais, an attendant moving the sheepskin rug for her to stand on. The LINGUIST moves to left of her.]

QUEEN MOTHER [solemnly]:
And may it happen that we can, in future
meet at this festival and truly sing,
Osee!
There's blood no more,
Enmity no more

Our fathers bought the land with their blood,
We build it with our strength,
We create it with our minds,
Our fathers found the paths,
We are the roadmakers.
[To the LINGUIST] Linguist, tell the people when you speak for me,
    that I seek that all of us make these words live now, in our time.
LINGUIST: The Queen Mother has spoken her thoughts.
HEAD PRIEST [moving forward]: We have heard her.
[He looks round for reaction. There are only bewildered looks.]
    If anyone has anything to say now . . . Sintim?
SINTIM [coming to himself]: Well er . . . my thoughts were so far away
    . . . er . . . We need to get our breaths back as it were. [with sincer-
    ity] Hasn't she spoken as if the ancestors themselves have freed her
    tongue? Those were no simple words, were they? And, after all, we
    came here as representatives who should now return with our news
    before we er . . er . .
HEAD PRIEST [satisfied]: Quite right. We will go and deliver our news.
    No doubt, the council will decide on the proper method by which to
    speak our answering thoughts to the Queen Mother. But there is
    one confusion they would surely wish to clear at once. Tomorrow is
    the customary day to begin the public ceremonies of our festival. Are
    we going to keep the festival or are we not?
QUEEN MOTHER [with feeling]: I respect the festival itself, father. Tell
    that to my people.
HEAD PRIEST [pleased]: They shall be told.
QUEEN MOTHER [relaxing]: Let us go, then. With goodwill.
FORIWA [quickly coming forward]: Not yet, mother. Not before I, your
    daughter, have committed myself before my father here, and my
    friends. When the Linguist tells this story, he shall also say, that I,
    your own daughter answered to your call. Mother, I will stay and
    place my efforts here. I choose Kyerefaso and this new life.

Celestine Ouezzin Coulibaly
WE WOMEN OF THE UPPER VOLTA

Burkina Faso 1961   French

Celestine Ouezzin Coulibaly was born in the southeastern section of Upper Volta, today known as Burkina Faso. By profession a primary school teacher, and married to one of the founding members of the Organization of African Democracy (RDA), Coulibaly led the 1949 Bassam Women's protest march, in which Anne-Marie Raggi and Lucie Traoré Kaboré participated as well (see "The March on Grand Bassam," p. 203). Coulibaly was also the president of the RDA's women's wing in Côte d'Ivoire and, later, in Upper Volta (Burkina Faso). In Burkina Faso, she was the first woman senator, the first woman minister, and the first woman member of the National Assembly.

"We Women of the Upper Volta," one of the earliest newspaper articles to be written by a woman in Burkina Faso, appeared on 10 November 1961 in a weekly named *Carrefour Africain*. The issue celebrated the first year of independence and the third anniversary of republican status for Upper Volta. All of the other contributors were male politicians of high rank.

Clearly, Coulibaly is determined to write optimistically, and not to sound discouraged by the difficulties of a new state and a citizenry lacking educational opportunities. She insists that the nation cannot move toward greatness without the full participation of all its citizens.

Aminata Diaw

✦

Here we are on the threshold of the first year of our independence and our constant concern must be to take part in the weighty responsibilities resting on the shoulders of our Chiefs of State. The Voltaic woman, well aware of her multiple responsibilities as mother and educator, is, we submit, this generation's worker, a vital member of the nation. Not forgetting our many obligations in the home, we also anchor childhood education with an eye toward forming a new youth, the future of our country.

In our African societies, woman's awakening is not entirely well conceived, although society's progress requires it, and a country cannot develop without women's participation in different parts of our rapidly developing age. Indeed, in a short time, Africans have experienced radical transformations in political and social life. And in different regions of our nation, women have contributed to radical transformations and to the building of a new African society.

Woman, the companion of man, must work compellingly to help create a climate truly favorable to the full development of the nation. No longer does the regime in power keep women in inferior status. In those days, not so long ago, women were totally disregarded. She was considered secondary, as an object or a tool in the hands of her husband, whose actions she had no right to control.

We had no position in society and we had no political rights whatsoever. Legally, women were considered incapable and therefore unable to consent to their own marriage, so marriage was, rather, a bill of sale agreed upon by the future husband and her own family.

The dowry consisted of inconsequential symbolic gifts, rather than gifts of serious meaning for a family one was joining. The dowry became, instead, a display of wealth and false power, no more than a purchase price for a woman. Thus, a woman's safety after marriage was in no way guaranteed, since a husband could send her back at will. Today's marital code has changed this state of affairs. Even so, former African traditions have been forgotten: In precolonial Africa an African woman was never considered an inferior being.

Is there any need to recall also that our history has included many women rulers, among them some illustrious women? Who would deny that in our rural areas woman works as hard as man? Does she not go to the field, to the most remote marshland to get water? Does she not go into the brush to gather firewood, or walk long distances to market? In her home, does she not accomplish the hardest and heaviest task, the crushing and grinding of millet? Does not all of the family's social life rest on her shoulders?

The truth is that, with independence, women's real emancipation has begun. With independence, women can once again become full-fledged citizens in an African state. Every struggle fought since then aims at securing women's individual freedom, so long desired.

In African states that are already independent, women will defend the precious possession of our liberty with loyalty and love. For our flag to fly forever, and we want this to be perfectly clear, there will not be, there cannot be, any peace, justice, and liberty without the end of imperialism. We, Voltaic women, whatever our age or our situation and in league with our young people, will be an immense power born from maternal suffering. It is we who must form the links of the chain of a great African family.

In the Republic of Upper Volta, women's struggle for a better future has been closely connected to that of the entire nation. Voltaic women have been courageously active in our national party during the dark and difficult years of the struggle. They have suffered the same pain and the same deprivations as the men and have never given up, not even when faced with the ultimate sacrifice.

Since the beginning of 1960, Upper Volta has embarked with optimism and determination on a new phase of economic struggle for a better future. In this new period, women as citizens fully aware of the goals of Voltaic evolution, completely free of former complexes and constraints that weighed heavily upon us, now assume responsibilities as significant as men. We must actively participate in the work of human investment, in the struggle against illiteracy, alcoholism, malnutrition, and against all the other failings that constitute the sad heritage of the defunct regime.

Translated by Judith Miller and Marjolijn de Jager

Kate Abbam
ON WIDOWHOOD

In 1971, Kate Abbam founded *The Ideal Woman,* the first women's magazine in Ghana. The poem and two essays below appeared in the magazine, for which she has been publisher for thirty years. "We Were with You" was written on 13 June 1968 (but published in 1973) and dedicated to Ethel Kennedy, who was beside her husband, Robert Kennedy, when he was shot on 5 June. The poem expresses the anguish of pregnant women at the loss of their husbands and pity for the babies who will never know their fathers. Abbam expresses solidarity with a woman remote from her own life, using the terminology of Ghanaian women's mourning, as expressed in the words "*agyeeei*" and "*puei.*" The name *Antubam* is given to a child born after the father's death.

In July 1972, Abbam's own husband died, leaving her responsible for small children. In an editorial called "We Shall Overcome," she lashes out bitterly against Ghanaian's inhuman treatment of widows, a topic she had been vocal about for many years.

Twenty-two years later, in 1994, Abbam delivered a speech at a Methodist conference in Kumasi, Ghana. The speech indicts a church that has been in Ghana for more than a century, failing all the while to change evil widowhood practices even among the faithful, the majority of whom are women.

Kate Abbam wrote each of these pieces under a different name. When she wrote the poem in 1968, she signed it Ewura Ekua Badoe, her birth name. She signed the editorial Kate Abbam, using her married name and the Christian name given to her when she went to school. By the time she delivered her 1994 speech, she had been enstooled as Queenmother in her village under the name Nana Assanwa Ewudziwa Gyampafor II, and she signed the speech with that name.

Esi Sutherland-Addy

✦

WE WERE WITH YOU, DEDICATED TO ETHEL KENNEDY

Ghana 1968   English

Ei! We were with you when the doctors said his condition was grave.
When all hope seemed lost, we kept vigil with you.
Mmmmmm! when you held tightly to your seat and said—

"*Abba,* Father, let this cup pass from him; not as I will, but as Thou
   wilt."
God! we were with you when the doctors called you and the other rela-
   tives to Bobby's bedside during the remaining vital minutes.
We were with you when you clenched the hand of your eldest son.
When at the very last you cupped his head in your hands and seemed
   to scream his name, Bobby, Bobby, Darling!
"Agyeei"! We were with you.
As you held on to him as though you were holding on to his last breath
   of life.
Ah! we were with you.
How many a slip between the lip and the cup!
When his brother Edward steadied you as you collapsed into his hands,
Our hearts bled for you.
We were with you when you came round, pale and shaken, "*Puei, puei.*"
When you bravely saw to the funeral details, we were there with you.
When with lighted candles you laid him to rest, "*Agyeeei!*"
When you bade farewell to his mortal remains, "*Agyeeei,*" we were with
   you!
When Edward steadied your shaking shoulders in his hands,
When alas, the tears could not be held back.
When they chased each other down your cheeks.
When your very heart seemed to be wrenched from inside, we were
   there with you.
When the unborn child seemed to leap inside your body;
Oh! how our hearts bled as we tearfully said "*Antubam! Antubam!
   Antubam!*"
We were right there with you.
Oh! weep not, brave lady, weep not. God gave and he has taken away.
Weep not, brave lady weep not. We of your sex do mourn with thee.
Have heart, dear lady, have heart.
For God so made the heart of women with extra strings for griefs such
   as this to bear.
Thine unborn child "*Antubam*" must be named.
For surely, "O, Antubam, O, Antubam, O, Antubam," Farewell, dear lady,
Farewell. Remember that our hearts still bleed for thee.

We Shall Overcome

Ghana 1972   English

Kate Abbam the editor has always held strong views about the topics for the
essay competition. What she did not realize was that she would soon be a

victim of the very vices she was fighting against. She never thought for a moment that her husband's relatives—a few of whom belonged to the so-called "intellectual class" and most of whom she has helped to look after, would turn round in a chameleon fashion, and, hiding behind a mantle of what they called "tradition" would rush to her house soon after her husband's death and long before he was buried, to take inventory of his personal effects, whilst the man who worked hard to acquire those properties lay cold and lonely in a hospital mortuary.

She little dreamt that they would molest and abuse her in the process—thus adding insult to her injury—to her heartbreak over the death of her beloved husband.

Yes, just picture the man's relatives both male and female—filled with envy and avarice, ransacking the bedroom the couple had shared up till the time of death of the man.

To back up their shameful deeds they started spreading a series of false rumours as to the cause of the man's death to discredit the widow. This gave "busybodies" all over the country something to do—tongues of men and women began to wag. Stories were made up and spread like wild fire. Fantastic stories that could make the dead man turn and groan in his grave and say "A a a a a a h ! ! !"

Yes, these relatives, backed by some rapacious friends, constituted themselves into the law. They prosecuted, judged and condemned the Editor all in one breath. Her crime? For daring to become the widow of a philanthropist [who had been] the apple of the eye of the family. Her sentence? That she and her four children should be prevented from coming anywhere near the dead body of their beloved one and that nothing whatsoever in the form of burial things such as coffin, clothes, spices etc. should be accepted from the widow and her children. This happened in twentieth century Ghana—to a woman married to a man under the ordinance for fifteen years, and who has loved him in "sickness and in health."

And what did the church do, knowing the couple belonged to a Christian church and were married in a church? Well, have a guess ! ! The church sat and looked on with apathy. Meanwhile, the widow and her children were left at the mercy of merciless relatives. The widow is, however, undaunted because she believes in the law of Karma and she trusts in God. "Vengeance is mine, said the Lord. I will repay." Truth, like a cork submerged in water, will always pop to the surface. She only hopes and prays that something will be done to save future widows and orphans from cruelty. If this record-breaking ordeal that she has gone through could shock the conscience of the churches as well as the Law makers in Ghana to do all in their power to protect widows and orphans, then she would at least feel satisfied that she has been martyred for a good cause.

It is a well known fact of history that doctors and scientists who devoted their lives to the study of the nature of certain diseases often died of the very diseases they struggled to find a cure for. Therefore it is not insignificant that the Editor of *Obaa Sima* should suffer for what she has been fighting against.

Only the foolish woman would say "it happened to Adwoa, but it cannot happen to me." Let us admit that, in present day Ghana, it is a crime to become a widow. Do we all want things to continue as they are? Do you? This should be food for thought for all sensible men and women of this country. We on our part will do our best through the medium of this magazine—but it is up to the rest of you, women of Ghana, to play your part too.

CHRISTIANITY AND WIDOWHOOD RITES

Ghana 1994   English

There have been a lot of changes for the better in the living patterns of Ghanaians, but when it comes to changes in the treatment of widows, one can say without hesitation that the people's behaviour seems to be getting worse.

My own ethnic group are those who live along the coastal belt in the Central Region in the Southern part of Ghana. Among the Fantes, widowhood is bad luck. A widow is looked upon as a person carrying ill luck on her trail and is treated differently from other women. When her husband dies, even if she was living with her husband under one roof, a Fante woman has to be informed officially by the man's relatives that her husband is dead. She has no right to go near the dead body. Invariably, she is asked to submit all the keys to the man's trunks, wardrobe etc. The man's relatives will then ransack his things to select certain articles of clothing for the burial. It is only when the man is laid in state, that the wife will be allowed to see the dead body, that is, if she is lucky. Some widows are now allowed near their husband's bodies.

The widow has to provide all the burial things like coffin, bedding, spices, trinkets etc. for the decoration of the body as it lies in state. The higher the status of her husband in society, the more the widow will have to spend. If the children are grown, they will be called upon to provide the coffin, and the widow will provide the burial things. Often the relatives of the dead man may refuse the coffin or the bedding or the shroud after the widow has presented them, because in their estimation, the funeral furnishings do not befit the status of the dead man.

The widow considers herself lucky if her things are accepted and if she is allowed to sit by the body as it is laid in state. If she is banned from the dead body and all her things refused, there is a big trouble ahead for her. This kind of treatment is meted out both to a woman who was living happily with her husband prior to his death, and a woman who might have separated from her husband just prior to his death—so that one is at a loss to discover the criterion for such treatment of widows.

The widow faces other privations. The man's relatives will insist that she shave off her hair as a sign of mourning for her dead husband. In some cases, she is allowed to "redeem" her hair, by paying a certain amount of money to prevent her hair being shaved off. In some cases the relatives will shave off her hair by force.

The widow has to walk about barefoot, and she has to sit at a particular corner of the hall, on a mat or on a short stool, to receive sympathisers who call upon her daily. She is not to shake hands with any sympathisers who call on her daily, and she is not to speak during certain periods of the day.

In some areas, a widow is made to carry fire in a coal pot at midnight and to parade in the streets with shouts of, "Move off! move off! It is bad luck to meet me!" until she reaches the seashore, where she is cleansed by the washing of her body by her sisters-in-law. In most cases the relatives shower the widow with abuses and accusations throughout the period of mourning.

"She has killed her husband and has stolen the man's property" is a common assertion. Sometimes, even before the man is buried, and inventory of the personal effects is taken and an oath is administered to the woman to say whether there is any money hidden somewhere, or whether there is any of the man's property she is aware of.

All this is done to a woman who is in a shocked state of mind due to the death of her husband. It is often done under duress. Some women are known to have been beaten and manhandled.

After the burial, anything can happen to the widow. In some cases, she is allowed to stay in what has been her own home until the final funeral celebrations. In a few cases she is driven out immediately after the husband is buried. More often than not, long litigation follows the death of a man (unless he dies a pauper). If the man died without leaving a will, then unless the widow is able to resort to court action, she may lose everything. There is the Law of Intestate Succession, but many women are legally illiterate—they do not know their rights. Even in cases where the man leaves a will, the relatives have been known to go to the courts to contest the will. Often the relatives get the better of the case, because not many widows may have the strength and resources to fight legal battles.

It must be emphasised that the sort of treatment a widow receives depends on two major factors. The first is the sort of people who constitute the husband's family. Education has nothing to do with this, because the worst offenders are often the educated relatives of the man. Greed is more important in determining their behaviour. The second factor is the amount of courage possessed by the widow. If the widow is brave and is not superstitious and is able to challenge the man's relatives in one way or another and if she gets the backing of her own relatives, she will get less rough treatment from her husband's relatives.

It is a sad fact that the churches do nothing whatsoever to help widows at the time when they need comfort. The best that a church does is to conduct a burial ceremony either in church or at the graveside for the dead man—if they consider him worthy of a church burial. After that, what happens to the widow and her children is the business of the widow herself. It does not matter whether the couple were staunch members of the church or not. The widow is left at the mercy of the man's relatives, who, under the guise of "tradition" will do whatever they like to her.

In 1979, at a woman's leadership training seminar in Liberia which discussed the suffering that widows experience from these customs, Mrs. Maude Solarin, a Nigerian Christian Council Organiser, pointed out that the Church had a responsibility towards widows to let them know that somewhere they had someone to turn to for support. Women have held conferences in several parts of Africa to study their position under the law in different African countries and to plan together how to improve the lot of widows. Little has come out of these conferences to date. Until this happens, unhappiness, ill-feeling, and enmity will breed in our societies between the widow and children of a dead man on one side, and his relatives on the other side.

One may ask, but why don't men make wills, so that their widows will be spared lots of troubles after their deaths. Few African men make wills, the excuse being that they fear they might be poisoned by ambitious wives. Thus at their deaths, the children undergo a lot of hardships and the burden on the widows becomes heavier. Many African women have had to suffer a great deal of humiliation due to the absence of effective inheritance laws. What is the Church (Christianity) doing about widowhood rites? What are the priests and heads of Christian Churches doing about widowhood rites? What are the church women's groups doing about widowhood rites?

When a person dies, whether male or female, it is the women (usually the dead person's relatives) who take charge of the dead body right from the mortuary up to the time it is laid in state. Even though there are a few male "undertakers" around, the majority of Ghanaians have not yet come to appreciate services rendered by these men. A dead body is very precious to the extended family of Ghanaians. The women therefore take charge. They wash, dress, and adorn the body, and lay it in state for relatives and friends to pay their last respects. The women weep and mourn for hours on end, to make the funeral grand as we put it. People (women) travel hundreds of miles for funerals, especially if the deceased happened to be a prominent figure in the society. Yes, women, are indispensable at funerals.

The majority of church goers are women, and some women are leaders of churches and religious (Christian) organisations. Women support churches both physically and financially. Is it not a pity that the majority of widows do not get physical, moral, and financial support from their Christian churches, even though women form the majority of church goers?

Why can't Christian churches become Refuge Homes for women who lose their husbands?

Why can't the Christian Church formulate the Church's own guidance or laws with regard to the treatment of widows and orphans? Maltreatment of widows is a human rights violation.

Why can't the church preach the strict adherence to intestate succession laws to their members and thus protect their widows?

What stops the church from making couples sign some form of binding legal or moral laws (whatever you may choose to call it) before couples are admitted into the Christian fellowship before couples are married in churches where they call on Christ to witness the ceremony?

Constance Agatha Cummings-John
MAYOR OF FREETOWN

Sierra Leone [1995]*   English

Constance Agatha Cummings-John's remarkable career as an educator, a pan-Africanist, and a feminist reached a peak in 1966 when she was elected mayor of Freetown, becoming the first black African woman to run a city government. Her pathbreaking impact on modern West African politics began in 1938 with her election to the Freetown City Council, a historic achievement captured in a pre-election statement that appeared in the Lagos newspaper the *West African Pilot:* "If she wins, she will make history. The emancipation of West African women will no longer be a dream but a reality."

Born 7 July 1918 into an elite Krio family in Freetown, Constance Agatha Horton was educated at the Freetown Secondary School for Girls and at Achimota College in Ghana. In 1935, she went to England for further studies, at Whitelands College in Putney, London, and two years later she traveled to the United States to study vocational education at Cornell University. Infuriated by the racist treatment she received in the South and the damaging images of Africa reflected in conversations with nearly everyone she met, she "became politically conscious," as she writes in her *Memoirs.* In London in 1937, she became involved in the International African Service Bureau (IASB), an organization founded by the pan-Africanist pioneer I. T. A. Wallace-Johnson. That year she also married Ethnan Cummings-John, a member of the IASB, and returned to Freetown, becoming principal of the African Methodist Episcopal Girls' Industrial School. In May 1938, she cofounded the West African Youth League with Wallace-Johnson, a move that enhanced her chances for winning a seat on the Freetown City Council later that year.

During her second trip to the United States, Cummings-John joined the American Council for African Education (ACAE), an organization founded in 1944 in New York City to raise funds for African students' education in the United States. She met and worked with various leaders in black political and religious organizations, including Paul Robeson, then head of the American Council on African Affairs (ACAA). She also spoke frequently before church audiences to raise money for a school she planned to build in Freetown. The Eleanor Roosevelt Preparatory School, which opened on 2 January 1952, with an enrollment of 364 students, was named after Roosevelt in appreciation of her support for African and other black causes. A year earlier, in 1951, along with Mabel Dove-Danquah and Lottie Haxeley, Cummings-John founded the Sierra Leone Women's Movement (SLWM), mobilizing large numbers of market women. The founding members of the movement had a tremendous influence on women's political activism in West Africa during this period.

Cummings-John was elected to the House of Representatives in 1957, but her election triggered a court battle with her political enemies, who charged her with election fraud. She won the case on appeal and was reelected to the city council in 1958. After a brief stay in Liberia, where her husband had been sent as ambassador, Cummings-John was elected mayor of Freetown in 1966. A military coup in 1967 forced her to relocate to London, where she remained active in education and politics. She returned to Freetown in 1974, but due to political unrest there, she finally settled in London in 1977. She died on 21 February 2000 at age seventy-nine.

Tuzyline Jita Allan

✦

On my birthday, January 7, 1966, I assumed office as major of Freetown, thus becoming the first black African woman to govern a modern capital city on the continent. News of my election found me at home. When the City Council sent for me, there was much jubilation among my supporters who carried me shoulder high straight to the entrance of the hall. After the usual swearing-in ceremony, the Town Clerk, J. B. Jenkins Johnston, and the mayor's secretary, Mrs. Cecelia Parkinson, took me into the mayor's chambers where I was robed. Fully robed and wearing my chain of office, I returned to the council hall to conduct the remainder of that day's business. I briefly spoke about the importance of my election for the women of Sierra Leone. They had been left behind in our politics for some time, but now we would show them that we could hold our own with the men. After the meeting, there was much celebrating. Even my political opponents greeted me with cordiality and respect. Naturally, my friends were the most joyful. Mrs. Marie Nelson, Mrs. Edith Harry Sawyerr, Councillor Patience Hamilton and some other ladies planted their arms together and carried me to the mayor's car and saw me off.

When I had returned home, the news of my victory spread and hundreds of well-wishers gathered to celebrate with me. Innocently, I moved around the crowd, entertaining and chatting, but before much time elapsed, my security officers hurried me to my bedroom and warned me to stay only with my immediate family and friends. Being hustled off like that into private confinement disturbed me a lot. I am a good mixer and I enjoy being in a crowd, especially when I am involved in public affairs. It brought home forcibly what my new position was in political life. No longer could I be the happy-go-lucky councillor. As a public official, my movements had to be restricted and protected. Until the end of my term of mayoral service, I was saddled with security officers, one of whom was Colonel Juxon-Smith, soon to become the military head of state. Sometimes I ignored them, insisting on mingling with my people or walking to and from my house to the Mayor's Parlour. Why should I have to fear my fellow men and women when I had done them no harm? rather I had contributed to their welfare. Later, I would change my assessment of human nature to some extent, but I still believe that most people are helpful and well-meaning. . . .

One of my first official tasks consisted of appointing my mayoress. Traditionally, the mayor's wife held that position, but with a female mayor, a different arrangement had to be made. Since my husband remained in his post as ambassador to Liberia and Ivory Coast, he could not undertake the required duties. As a result, with the council's approval, I appointed my sister-in-law, Mrs. Oni Uel Cummings-John, to the position. She was my mate. Together we had been through a lot: school, Girl Guides, my first journey to England and SLWM. Her support and assistance during this time was really invaluable. . . .

I contacted the leading women in the city. Mrs. Lerina Bright-Taylor, Dr. Bankole-Bright's sister, agreed to head a committee of women instructed to explore ways and means of creating harmony in the city. Many Krio women, both Christian and Muslim, joined forces. . . .

Mrs. Bright-Taylor supported me very well in all the council projects. Her committee gave me a big reception to mark my assumption of office as a symbol of recognition for Sierra Leonean womanhood. Then it cooperated in establishing a number of self-help projects, initiated by the council, that aimed to persuade women from all walks of life, including the market women, to support. The most important of these was the clean-up campaign the committee launched in April, 1966.

The city needed a sanitation campaign because the residents had neglected their houses and compounds. They used drains as dustbins, abandoned cars at the sites of accidents, dumped construction materials on the street without regard to vehicular or pedestrian traffic. The council wanted to implement a clean-up policy, but lacked funds to finance a crew of its own, so the women's committee and I decided that the best thing would be to enlist the aid of the entire community. If the people pitched in and helped themselves, each individual in his or her own small way, then we could keep the city clean, hazard-free and healthy. Through the cooperation of the council, the Ministry of Health, the women's committee, and the SLWM, we developed a campaign to educate the community about its responsibilities. In July, we held a big demonstration with floats carrying anti-disease equipment and cleaning materials. We drove these through the streets, followed by a lorry playing music to get the public's attention. I gave a broadcast talk stressing the advantages of a clean city and hazards of a dirty one. After the parade, female volunteers went from house to house to discuss sanitation measures with the residents and to instruct them in the best ways of ridding their compounds of dirt and disease. They particularly emphasized the importance of clearing away areas that might form the breeding ground for mosquitoes.

A big part of this campaign aimed to improve hygiene in the markets. As I have pointed out several times in this account, my interest in market conditions continued throughout my career. Now that I was mayor, I was determined to do something concrete about them. Whenever I had brought up market matters before, the councillors always agreed that they were important, but stopped short of taking positive action on the grounds of lack of funds. True, during the 1950s things had improved somewhat, but mostly conditions remained unsatisfactory. The women's committee decided it should seek greater participation from the market women to ensure the success of the clean-up campaign. We called a mass meeting to appeal for their cooperation, taking care to assure them that we did not intend to raise their fees or touch their profits. We showed them the best ways to create a healthy environment for their families and their customers. Now that a woman was in charge of the city, contended the leaders of the committee, let women show the men that they could run the community in a better way. . . .

Another important thing we did during my term of office was to set up a Boys' Society. Juvenile delinquency began to concern the community. Many young boys of school age roamed the streets and lived in the areas near Government Wharf, Big Market and King Jimmy Market. They were loafers, waifs and strays, wandering around with no purpose, hanging about the markets, sometimes thieving, often getting into trouble with the police. They also congregated around the cinemas where they just looked at the pictures or harassed the customers. They lived just anyhow, with no one to care for them. Some of us thought that they were wasting their opportunities, so we decided to do something about the situation. The women's committee, the SLWM and several influential men, including Rev. Sammy Green of Bishop's School, Dr. E. O. Pratt of Fourah Bay College and H. E. Johnson, united forces to encourage these boys to attend a meeting at the Grammar School building at Oxford Street (now Lightfoot Boston Street). We provided food, speakers and films. The speakers highlighted the need for cooperation and good citizenship. The first meeting was successful, a good beginning. About two hundred boys came and thoroughly enjoyed themselves. To each boy we gave soap, a towel, a toothbrush, toothpaste, a pan and cup. After the meeting we provided food and entertainment. We developed a full programme of activities and frequent meetings. Staff members from Fourah Bay College, who won the boys' respect, became active in the organization. They divided the boys into groups and encouraged them to select their leaders. One project they undertook was to plant little flower beds along the road from the Cotton Tree to Parliament, each boy taking charge of his own bed. They took pride in this project. Frequently, we impressed upon them the need for good citizenship and personal responsibility in the community. It was really a kind of school for those boys who lacked money to pay fees at ordinary schools. The *coup d'etat,* however, interrupted the smooth running of the Boys' Society. The chairman left the country, the City Council disbanded, and other leaders ceased their participation. It continued to exist, but was no longer a strong organization. The number of waifs and strays increased in the city's streets.

Two other projects commanded my interest while I was mayor. The first was the Bomeh project; the second was the establishment of the municipal secondary school at Kissy. The Bomeh project represented an attempt to deal constructively with the problem of the municipal dumping ground in Ascension Town. The people called this place Bomeh. People took very little care in the disposal of refuse. As a result, the place stank and formed a breeding ground for all kinds of insects and pests, particularly large flies and mosquitoes. People nearby made many complaints about the situation. Dr. Nicol-Cole and Eustace Ashwood put the matter before the council, urging action before the situation led to an outbreak of epidemics. Something had to be done. I suggested that the place was ideal for the establishment of a market garden, and further, that such a plan would provide employment for a number of people. . . .

Our workers began to lay out their beds of vegetables, erected a water standpipe for use in the plots, and built a road. The place looked beautiful and there was much praise in the newspapers and from the residents in the neighbourhood. The harvested produce—cabbages, tomatoes, garden eggs and lettuce—was excellent in quality. Chellarams agreed to sell it for us. The councillors used to buy some of the vegetables for their households. . . .

The last accomplishment of the council during my tenure as mayor was to establish a municipal secondary school at Kissy. We decided to build it because so many parents had approached various councillors, including myself, about finding places for their children in the existing secondary schools. After independence, demands for education intensified, but neither the government nor the private institutions had funds for expanding the school system. Already, the council had set up several municipal elementary schools. Now, we felt that it was necessary to a take some responsibility for providing secondary education for the city's children. The Minister of Education, Salia Jusu-Sheriff, approved our plan. In the August (1966) meeting of the council I announced that we would open the school in late November. Eight hundred pupils applied for admission, but space existed for only 200 boys and girls. Mr. S. E. E. Taylor, a respected educationist, was appointed as principal. From the response to the new school in the Western Area, it became evident that the city needed more schools of this type. Immediately, the council urged the Ministry of Education to approve plans for a second one. Before the council could pursue this plan, my term of office had come to an abrupt end.

Olufunmilayo Ransome-Kuti
AFFIRMATIONS AND REMEMBRANCES

Olufunmilayo Ransome-Kuti was a significant figure during a critical era in Nigeria's history: the heyday of nationalist and anticolonial movements and the struggle for Nigeria's independence. No other woman was more important nationally, and only a few other African women of her time established comparable international connections.

Born in October 1900 in Abeokuta, Nigeria, of Christianized Yoruba parents, she was christened Frances. Later experiences with racism in England caused her to use only her Yoruba name, Funmilayo. In 1925, she wed Rev. I. O. Ransome-Kuti, with whom she had three sons and a daughter. The Ransome-Kutis ran a boarding school and also found time for political activities. Rev. Ransome-Kuti was one of the early organizers of the Nigerian Union of Teachers, a proto-nationalist organization of Nigerian educators. Olufunmilayo Ransome-Kuti participated in the founding of several women's organizations, most prominently the Abeokuta Women's Union (AWU). The objectives of the AWU included uniting women; promoting their social, economic, and political rights and interests; and cooperating with all organizations seeking economic and political freedom and independence for the people of Nigeria.

Her work as head of the AWU catapulted Ransome-Kuti into national prominence and subsequently into international work. The AWU challenged the taxation of women without political representation and ultimately mounted massive civil protests and demonstrations resulting in women's appointments to political bodies in Abeokuta and the resignation of the Alake Ademola, the region's traditional ruler. About this abdication, Ransome-Kuti would later remark, "I didn't really attack Ademola, I attacked imperialism. Those Europeans were using him against his people. . . . I was attacking Europeans indirectly and they know it."

A founder of one of the main nationalist parties organized after World War II, the National Council of Nigeria and the Cameroons (NCNC), Ransome-Kuti was the sole woman member of the NCNC delegation that went to London in 1947 to spur constitutional change in Nigeria. While in London, Ransome-Kuti met with many women's organizations, spoke at factories, and was contacted by the British branch of the Women's International Democratic Federation (WIDF), which had been founded in Paris in 1945. The WIDF promoted women's solidarity across race, nationality, religion, and class boundaries, and opposed apartheid, racial discrimination, and fascism. The WIDF set up a special commission to investigate the conditions of women in Africa and Asia, and Ransome-Kuti wrote the section of the report on Nigeria. Later, Ransome-Kuti's travels to WIDF conferences would result in the British government's revoking her passport and labeling her a "communist sympathizer." In 1959, the U.S. State Department refused to grant her a visa to attend a conference in San Francisco, because of her travels to WIDF conferences.

Throughout her adult life, Ransome-Kuti espoused a global perspective. She analyzed connections among gender, race, and class, as she worked to oppose colonialism, imperialism, and sexism. Ultimately, she considered herself a human rights activist and not merely a political activist. To that end, she championed the poor and disenfranchised of both sexes. Additionally, in a country and at a time when ethnic allegiances often triumphed over allegiance to the newly forming nation, she was among a handful of nationalists who struggled to organize across ethnic and class lines. Although she enjoyed the steady support of her progressive husband until his death in 1955, and later of her activist children (especially her well-known son Fela, an internationally acclaimed musician and cultural critic), she often felt herself alone, defending beleaguered positions. In many quarters, she suffered from a reputation for being headstrong and difficult.

Ransome-Kuti traveled throughout Africa, maintaining especially close links with women's organizations in Algeria, Egypt, and Ghana, and attending women's conferences in Dahomey (now Benin), Guinea, Liberia, and Togo. She remained active in Nigeria, although, ironically, independence and military coups circumscribed some of her activity. In 1965, the Nigerian government awarded her membership in the Order of the Niger for her contributions to the nation.

In February 1977, soldiers attacked the Ransome-Kuti family residence in Lagos, primarily to harass Ransome-Kuti's son Fela, whose music critiqued the military and ruling junta. Ransome-Kuti was thrown from a window and never recovered from the physical injuries and psychological trauma of the attack. A little more than a year later, on 12 April 1978, she died in Lagos. Her body was borne on a motorcade to Abeokuta, where all markets and shops closed for the day in her honor. Several newspaper headlines attested to her historical significance: "The Voice of Women Is Dead" was the banner of one; another, a month later, memorialized her as a "Defender of the Rights of Women."

The first document reprinted here was originally published in the *Journal of Human Relations*, a U.S.-based publication founded in 1952 and designed to "give voice to specific findings and reasoned opinions as well as to practical programs integrally related to the betterment" of Africa and its diaspora. That Ransome-Kuti was published in this journal is a reflection of her international standing among the progressives of her era. Although here she does not specifically name the British—and implicates all people with retrograde attitudes toward women's agency—the piece reiterates the biting critique of what had happened to women's lives under colonialism that she first controversially articulated in 1947, updating it with an agenda for the 1960s.

Later in that decade and, in the early 1970s, in response to a request from a young researcher, Ransome-Kuti wrote by hand the bits of memoir published here. The original document, twenty-two handwritten pages, is difficult to read; sections are crossed out, sometimes the handwriting is unclear, and the punctuation and spelling are not pristine. Nevertheless, it is invaluable for the history it offers and the information it provides about her remarkable political activities. Moreover, the family history that Ransome-Kuti recounts captures the determination of those whose lives were disrupted by the slave trade to reconstruct their families, offers insights into family associations, and illuminates the social links between sections of the precolonial elite and the Christianized elite.

Cheryl Johnson-Odim, Judith Byfield, and Diedre L. Badejo

◆

THE STATUS OF WOMEN IN NIGERIA

Nigeria 1961   English

It is highly gratifying that Nigeria is ripe for independence when her women are emerging from the corners of slavery and backwardness. Long ago our women in Nigeria were worse than slaves. The slaves could run away from their masters when they were not pleased, but the wives considered it immoral to divorce their husbands. The husbands, on the other hand, regarded the wives as their perpetual and life-long slaves. Therefore the more help the men needed on their land determined the number of women they married.

The status of women in Nigeria was abjectly subordinate. Husbands in some parts are happy when they have female children, not because they have any regard or love for womanhood, but they look forward to the dowry they can collect on each female child they sire. In many cases the babe in the womb is betrothed to a prospective husband and gifts are collected in advance. The child goes to her husband when she is barely old enough to start her life of slavery. She suffers in quietness. These conditions and others whereby dowry was paid enslave our girls and deprive them of their rights.

In the area where child betrothal was not practised, the man sometimes pawned himself to pay his fiancee's dowry; it being no hardship to him to serve his creditor because he was sure that that dowry was [the] purchase price of a woman who would work for him to purchase more and more women. This might be called indirect slave trade.

There were women weavers, potters, traders, and politicians; our mothers invented the mode of preparing our food, of spinning by hand the lovely fine yarns with which our clothes were woven. They contributed towards the development of our country in many ways along with their sufferings.

The women cooked, hoed, swept, bore children for their masters, and gave them all the comfort they needed. They were sent about by any inmate of their husbands' household; if they showed any sign of reluctance to work (perhaps because they were tired or indisposed) they were abused, insulted, and chastised without mercy; they dared not retaliate or grumble.

Once a man who wished to live a Christian life by keeping only one wife later found it difficult to get labourers for his farm work; his cocoa, kola and palm nuts were wasting; he therefore decided to get four strong wives. He paid dowry on these women and they came to live with him on his farm; they worked from dawn till dusk, so that his produce wasted no more. They had children for him in addition to the hard work.

If there were misunderstandings between husband and wife which resulted in divorce, the husband claimed back every penny he expended on the wife, be it dowry or gifts. The period they lived together will not be considered no matter the number of years. If she had issue an amount of 50/Shillings is deducted for each child from the total amount he reckoned that he paid. If a husband died, the dowry was also usually refunded to his family in the same manner. So there was no consideration for time of service for enslaved wives.

Now the old orders have changed; our women have been rapidly taking their proper places in the role of Nigeria. Our men are now learning that their women are no longer their slaves but their immediate associates. Our women try to pull their weights with men in all spheres of Nigerian life. It is our adage now that in some spheres of life, woman can do what man can do. We have now women doctors, police, athletes, lawyers, artisans, teachers, scientists, and many women are kept at key posts in many government and commercial offices.

But our women still have a strong battle to face. Our men feel much reluctance to accept the present condition. They still live in the past; they still wish to treat their wives as their forefathers treated their grandmothers. As a result, there are uncountable broken homes and cases of divorce in our courts all over the country. Men do not want women to take part in our legislation; they want women as mere voters, ordinary election tools. Similar conditions prevailed in other countries before ours; we must learn to overcome our own difficulties as they did.

With independence on October 1st, 1960, a new day dawned in Nigeria. Women must be ready to work and contribute to the progress and development of their country. One of our greatest tasks is to learn tolerance. We have to be silent at times when we have the right to talk for the sake of peace; not to be too firm in demanding our rights when dealing with our husbands. We should try to forgo our personal interest for our husbands. We should realize that our men are jealous, and are used to being called masters and lords; so that it is not easy for a master to take the position of equal. It should be realised that our Nigerian Independence could only be felt in every home where wives tolerate their men because we must try to build happy homes for our children. Many of us are still ignorant. We all must know our responsibilities and common domestic work. Our homes must be clean and healthy. Centres should be created where women, married and young, could learn house crafts.

The education of some women is ill-adapted. They follow fashions and like to come out every time in the latest vogue; it is not a sin to be fashionable, but women within an independent Nigeria must be reasonable in their dress, clean, simple, and attractive. Many of our children die owing to lack of proper care by the mothers. Poverty and dirt are the causes of these deaths in many cases; no good food for the mothers nor for the children. The babies are wrapped in dirty clothes and laid on wet floor uncovered and unprotected against mosquitoes. They die of malaria fever, diarrhoea, tuberculosis, malnutrition, and ignorance.

It is pitiable that some parents consider it a waste of money and indulgence to give a girl education because she ends it in the kitchen. They forget that it is the responsibility of the women to bear and bring up a new generation. They forget the wise adage that the hand that rocks the cradle rules the world. It is still more lamentable that even the few educated women look down upon the uneducated ones, instead of encouraging them to pull their weight and shake off their slavish ideas. They ignore and render no help to them to improve the condition of these unfortunate ones.

If we could read and write in our language half of our battle is won. When we visited a Chinese women's adult education class we were greatly impressed by the women's zeal; they were so absorbed in their lesson that they hardly took their eyes from their books. Every one of them was keen because they wanted to equip themselves with the weapon of liberty. There was to be a total eradication of illiteracy in their country within five years after their liberation and no woman wanted to be left behind. We Nigerian women should be ready to emulate them and set to work vigorously. We should ask for more maternity hospitals and clinics to be set up, for free medical aids. Centres where women could receive instructions in child production and rearing should be established. Doctors and nurses should be attached to these centres. Our women should be ready to learn and make good use of the knowledge imparted to them.

In the midst of plenty most of us are hungry; some do not have breakfast till mid-day; even then there is little nourishing food. Women's chief duty all over the world is management of the kitchen. God giveth us sunshine which contributes largely to the plenteousness of our vegetation; by this, we have different kinds of fruits; we are able to grow certain kinds of crops twice a year, the privilege of which many countries are deprived. In Nigeria we are blessed with a variety of climates and soil so that if the climate of [the] Western Region is not suitable for some crops they may be easily grown in the Northern Region. We have each group of food crops in a variety of species; we have different crops coming out at different seasons of the year; there is no time of the year that Nigerian people should be hungry or starved.

Our doctors should examine the vitamins contained in our different fruits and foodstuffs, and give directives as to how to so combine them that even the poorest person could get sufficient nourishment cheaply and conveniently; that our children may grow better; that our expectant mothers may suffer no more from malnutrition; that their labour may be easy and safe; that babies may be strong; and that death may be less in our midst.

The women should urge the government to encourage the farmers to start co-operative farming that introduction of mechanized systems may be used to our advantage. Many of our women are farmers and they should take an active part in food production; we need more food—we have the land, we have suitable climates, and the Government should gladly launch the scheme because good food makes a good nation. Women should be sent to other countries to learn the system of extensive farming. We need food and plenty of it, and we must stop indulging ourselves in eating imported food; we must take pride in our own food.

Our country produces cotton and silk freely for the production of our clothing. We have different kinds of fibres and other materials in our forests from which other kinds of materials could be woven, but we have not exploited them. We have women who are weavers, but their numbers are not adequate for our need and the quality of materials is not advanced enough to befit us as a free country.

We want our men and women to be sent to other countries to learn the art of spinning, dyeing, and weaving. Africans love bright attractive colours. We should be able to turn out sufficient clothing, woven from different materials for our need especially as we have the raw materials. Women are always good in this direction. Skilled men and women should also be imported to our country to teach us; big factories should be set up all over the country; and women should be ready to contribute to the advancement of this scheme; for we can turn out attractive clothes in cotton, silk, and other materials for our use if we only work intelligently.

Women in New Nigeria should work hard to remedy their short-comings that they may not lag behind in the midst of the women of the world. Educated ones should organise women's clubs in one form or other to enlighten the backward ones, and then strengthen the present Nigerian Women's Organisation. This Organisation is non-political, and should not allow our men to bias the minds of its members because that is the only organ through which our voice could be echoed throughout the world. It is only the Organisation that can make us brave alongside the other women of the Commonwealth of Nations.

Our Women's Organisation was founded in 1944 when oppression of the citizen, especially women, was becoming acute through the sole native authority system which was one man rule. This rule obtained in many parts of Nigeria when autocracy was at its highest point. Men and women groaned heavily under this yoke of political bondage. No one could sell his farm product or celebrate any festival freely. The poorest women had to pay tax. Women organised and broke down this power from its highest seat, and they demanded the eradication of the power all over the country. Before they could achieve this, many women had to be jailed for periods ranging from seven days to three months; they had tear gas thrown in their midst; they were beaten with batons; dragged on the ground. It was the beginning of our struggle towards our constitutional freedom. The women faced the struggle fiercely and courageously with their men folks and they were victorious. Many reforms have taken place in Nigeria since 1944, and we are happy that they have brought us our freedom today.

We should work very hard to have our marriage systems reviewed and reformed; laws should be made against payment of dowry on our girls in any shape or form. Our girls should be ready to take part in any work for the progress of our country from the lowest to the highest setup of employment. Their interest in all spheres of life should be the interest of government. By that we expect better mothers, homes, and better citizens.

We need women in all spheres of life in our Independent Nigeria and we can only have girls made fit for this position through Government Scholarships; for it is through that that we can have enough skilled men and women to man all our departments. Ten years after gaining our independence we should have advanced so much that we would no longer have to import skilled workers; we should by then have well-trained women in any key position.

Nigerian women should not forget their sisters in other parts of Africa. We should endeavour to take part in their struggle for liberation, for when any section of African people is still in slavery no independent section can be truly happy. We should contact these our sisters to know their problems and share in solving them so that with them we may march together to the land of Canaan.

Autobiographical Notes

Nigeria 1968   English

1/10/68 Sierra Leone

I wish to endeavour in a small manner to put down in words something about my life. The life which I attributed mostly to my mother who brought me up in a way to make me what I am today and also to my father who worked so hard to be able to give me the education which had backed up the home training my mother contributed.

My parents worked hard and lived a life that was worth emulation. They joined hands and their efforts together to make their lives worth living financially.

My father was born on the 27th of July, 1870. His father was the eldest son of one Sobowale who was taken in slavery by the Spanish during the slave trade. The ship in which these slaves were being taken away was captured by the British, who were working to stop the slave trade.

My great-grandfather with [the] other slaves were taken in their boat and were landed in Sierra Leone. These slaves were captured from different parts of Nigeria. They were men and women and youths as well. The British people arranged to have them converted into Christians and to learn to read. . . .

The British people sent Missionaries [to] Sierra Leone through the advice of Queen Victoria of Engl[and]. These slaves became quite happy. They started [to] get settled and tried to build up families for themselves.

My great grand father took a girl among the slaves to wife. She was a twin and her name was Taiwo. She was married to Sobowale in the Christian manner. . . . She had one son and [her husband] died. She married another man with whom she had three sons, Sowemimo Olufusibi and another son who later became a clergy man. Each man this Taiwo married was a Christian attached to a European whose name they adopted. The first man she married had the name of Thomas from his master, and the second husband had a master who was called Coker. Mr. Coker died and she married another gentleman called Wickliffe for whom she had a daughter.

It was from this Madam Taiwo that we got the name for our family Union organization "the Jibowu-Taiwo Union."

My mother was born on the 4 of October 1874 baptised on the 16th of May 1875 by Rev. W. Moore. She was given the name of Philis Lucretia. Her father was Mr. Isaac [Adesolu], one of the descendants of the early Christians brought back from Sierra Leone. Her mother was a daughter of Oba [left blank] of Ife [?] and sold as a slave to an Abeokuta Chief. Rev. W. Moore gave my mother to Rev. and Mrs. Wood to be brought up. She stayed until she was about to be married. She was one of their house girls. She was taught to read and write. She was also taught to sew to cook & gardening. I was very happy when my mother's baptismal certificate was found among her things after her death, because we were not quite sure of her birth-day.

I was born on the 25th day of October, 1900. I was nursed and brought up by my mother and father. My father lost his parents before he was fifteen years old. An Uncle took him up and sent him to the primary school. He was trained a carpenter. He married my mother on the 2nd of September 1897.

I attended St John Anglican Church School, Igbein in Abeokuta for my primary education. It was not easy in those days to get secondary for youths. So, my parents were faced with this difficulty until his friends Rev. M. S. Cole, the Principal of Abeokuta Grammar School through the advice of Rev. S. C. Phillips who was also the Vice Principal of Abeokuta volunteered to admit me into Abeokuta Grammar School, if they could persuade five other parents to allow their daughters to join; so that they would form a class of six girls in the Abeokuta Grammar School. Five other prominent gentlemen agreed that their daughters should be admitted. So, in January 1914 Abeokuta Grammar School became a co-educational school. We were in the same class with the boys, the same grade during the first and the second year. The girls were separated from boys at the beginning of third year because the number had risen considerabl[y] to about 40, and a small class room was built for the girls, in Igbein. In 1917, the girls school was shifted to Ake. The Principal Rev. M. S. Cole arranged with my father that I would be teaching the girls, and he would teach me after school to continue my studies. Father wanted me to have the best education possible, so he started to arrange for me to go to England to continue my studies. I left home in May 1918.

I was sent to Wincham College in Lostock Graham in Cheshire, North of England. I was there in 1920 to learn Cookery, Sewing, Fancy work, Millinery and Piano and elocution. I returned to Nigeria in 1922 to take charge of the Abeokuta Girls', as the school was then called. I taught for two years and got married on the 20th of January 1925 to Rev. Israel Oludotun Ransome-Kuti, the son of Canon J. J. & Mrs. Ransome-Kuti. We had four children, a girl Dolupo and three boys. The girl is a qualified Nursing Sister and the first boy Olikoye is a Pediatric Doctor. The second son Olufela is a Musician and the third boy is also a doctor of Medicine.

My husband and I left for Ijebu-Ode on the 20th January 1925, the very day we were married. He was the principal of Ijebu-Ode Grammar School. I organised the young ladies in Ijebu-Ode where I taught them sewing, handicraft and cooking. In 1928 on the 4th of February I [s]tarted a class of kindergarten for nine children. The children must not be as many as ten because it would then be a school. I was keeping them for two years before they were sent to the Primary School.

In 1932 my husband was transferred from Ijebu-Ode Grammar School to Abeokuta Grammar School.

THE CAUSES FOR REVOLT REMEMBERED

Nigeria 1973   English

It was not a case of Women Taxation.

It was on Tuesday the 25th of September 1973 as one big chief in Abeokuta and a Junior chief walked up to me through the heavy crowd of women in my compound. They came to me upstairs. I was not too surprised to see them, because they were all friends. I walked up to meet them, greeted them and asked what sort of wind . . . blew them to me. The elder of the two asked the younger one to deliver the message they brought from the Alake. The young chief got up and said, "We bring you greetings from Baka the Alake." He said, "The Alake said he begged me in the name of the Crown, because he learnt that many women are flooding to my house and paying one shilling contribution each to me, and that I should stop this collection of these shillings because it did not make men pay their tax for the year 1973/74." I told them that Alake is an intelligent Oba. I was sure, that he could never have sent such a message to me. I said, "What connection on earth have women's Olumos [shillings] contributions got to do with men's taxation?" I told the chiefs how our organisation had had the plan for the development of Olumo Rock in our mind for some time, and how we have been working towards it. I told them that the members of my Women's Union are peasant women, and they will not find it difficult to contribute one shilling towards the improvement of Olumo Rock, but because of the pride of every Egba woman, and one shilling from every member of the Egba Women's Union will give us at least L4000. which is N8000. to work with. I told the chiefs how our organisation had been discouraged in organizing "Self Help" schools for the improvement of various women's health and good living and to create good care for our babies and the public in general.

I took them to my store where I was keeping several of these 28lb. bundles of cotton yarns which we were using for weaving cloths, and we had to pack up the industry when we were being victimised by the members of our former civilian Government, when we women were heavily taxed for putting on clothes woven in the women['s] textile factory. I told them that we established a maternity centre where a pregnant member with her shilling membership card would receive free maternity care, free delivery, free medicine, the child would be registered in the Government's Baby Registry, and the baby would be looked after free until he was one year old. We were doing this to combat infantile mortality but we had to back up, through the victimisation our poor members were receiving from the members of our civilian Government. This Government had watch dogs all over the place that these people were after the poor women in particular. By this time peasant women were exempted from paying poll tax, so heavy income tax would be levied on any woman see[n] with the cloth woven in the women['s] weaving centre, or on any woman seen entering or coming out of the women's maternity centre. When the worries and the victimisation were getting too much for the women, we had to close our weaving centre; where we had two power looms, two power winders, . . . three hand looms, six winders . . . are still locked up. All our equipment also for our maternity clinic. Baby's food, baby's . . . syringes, injection tubes, and medicine, feeding bottles, medicines for babies, pregnant women and nursing mothers. All these materials are also locked up and wasting away since 1953. Now the women want to see Olumo Rock improved and modernised and to be made a centre of attraction for the tourists.

Then a chief said, "Please, Bere, don't be annoyed, I would like you to come to say all these you said to us to Alake and the chiefs. They will still be at the Afin (palace) holding their meeting." I agreed, and promised to come there. In about half an hour I took two of our women to the Alake's palace.

Before we left for Ake some of our women told me that they had noticed one or two police men walking up and down along our street, and that they saw the police land Rover driven along the street. I did not see these because I was busy in the house. But about three days before these chiefs came to me a friend came to tell me that it was being rumoured that I was asking the women to contribute one shilling each to fight against women['s] taxes. He said [the] police [were] being set up to watch. This action of opposition by the police or the chiefs did not discourage us to stop our collections.

WORK SONGS

GREETINGS AND PRAISE

Featured here are four forms of poetry that accompany different types of work in different settings: pounding, planting, milking, and grinding. The themes and purposes are varied. The Hausa Lugude is a lighthearted greeting chanted in the family setting, while the Diola song "One Single Measure" accompanies communal planting activities. Next, Fulfulde/Pulaar women of Guinea praise their cows and make an invocation before milking them. Finally, the "Praise Song" by Zebuglo of Loho is a solo improvisation accompanying the grinding of grain.

Lugude is a genre of work song commonly chanted by Hausa women, especially those in *purdah* (the seclusion of women from public observation). It is integrated into the processing of various foods by pounding with a mortar (*turmi*) and a pestle (*tabarya*). The song and the pounding form part of a rhythmic matrix in which the utensils are turned into musical instruments. As the pounders manipulate the pestle, they hit the inside and the topmost part of the mortar with their pestle. The matrix can be made more complex by other women and children sitting beside the mortar and tapping its base with a short rod. Though they carry out a major part of their lives within the confines of the family concession, women pounding in one compound may send out salutations to their friends and neighbors by raising their voices high enough to elicit responses. In one such song, "Greetings While Working," Hauwa, in one compound, calls out to the first wife of Mallam Audu, in the next. The singing can be so pervasive that rather than break its flow with a prosaic interjection, the third voice of a visitor joins in, integrating herself into the flow and spirit of the chant, which conveys goodwill all around.

The following song comes from the Casamance region of Senegal, where rice is the most important food crop produced. With the advent of the cash-crop economy, men left subsistence farming to women. Even though the steady fall in the price of cash crops such as peanuts has brought men back into the production of rice, it is still considered largely an activity of women. It is primarily organized through the establishment of jointly owned farms between cowives or the tending of farms on an individual basis. At different stages of production, a farmer can call on cooperative groupings of other women in the community to assist. This is usually a group of which she is a member and to which she pays the necessary dues. This team of fifteen or more women workers is called *Fapeulum*. Membership in the team guarantees a rebate in the charge for services. The group might also be a small one made up of four or five family members. Work songs like "One Single Measure" are sung in chorus by such groups working in the rice fields. Unlike other work songs, such as those that accompany pounding, these melodies are not accompanied by instrumentation or a strong rhythmic pulse provided, for instance, by a uniform movement of hand tools. This may be because most of the backbreaking work involved in sowing, weeding, and even harvesting of rice is done without implements. Coming through the song is the proprietary role and established expertise that Diola women have had in the growing of rice.

In contrast to the two communal pieces discussed above, the next two are solos: one a common invocation uttered by the Fulfulde/Pulaar women of northeastern Guinea when milking cows, the second a melancholy grinding song from the upper west region of Ghana.

The Fuuta Djallon mountains of northeastern Guinea have been the home of Fulfulde/Pulaar pastoralists since the seventeenth century. Animal husbandry is a passionate vocation, and cattle have a privileged place in the traditional Fulfulde/Pulaar worldview and the rich ritual and literary culture that is associated with it. While men dominate animal husbandry and the literary tradition, women are particularly involved with the milking process. This process begins with a ceremony to prepare the cow and to ensure that it will give as much milk as it can. Stroking the cow she is about to milk, a Fulfulde/Pulaar woman whispers poetic endearments and appellations to it as if it were a person. She praises the coloring of the cow and traces its genealogy. In the Fulfulde/Pulaar worldview, evil persons may cast spells that could interfere with the success of one's endeavors in animal husbandry. Hence, incantations are meant to counter these evil forces. Before actually taking hold of the cow's teats, the invocation ensures that no one with occult powers can take her cow's milk from her. The words *diouhou* at the end of line one and *diafa* at the end of line two are untranslatable phrases that are part of the formula for the invocation.

Women in northwestern Ghana can sing praise songs only as work songs, while they are grinding millet or churning shea nuts into butter. In *dannu,* the form they practice, women are expected to praise their husbands' families and ancestry, since the married woman becomes part of her husband's family. Not surprisingly, women have turned *dannu* to their own ends, adding social and personal commentary, about both life and death.

The most important performer of *dannu* in the Dagaare language is Zebuglo of Loho, whose compositions have been heard—since 1999—on Radio Progress, a station run by the Catholic church. Her life story is well known, for unlike many *dannu* performers, she breaks into her singing to speak about her life and about topics of the moment, so that these comments become part of her song. Her comments often subvert customary beliefs, for example with respect to childlessness, one of her major themes. Since she gave birth to ten children and none survived, she blames the "witches" or evil people in her husband's family. She understands well that life is made difficult for childless women, but she is nevertheless assertive about herself and her abilities.

When she sings of her childlessness, she makes clear that she is in deep mourning—see the line "this is not a soft xylophone," for example. Further, she suggests that the *kpeli,* a calabash drum usually played as an accompaniment to the funeral xylophone, should accompany her mourning. And yet, she can claim, "I built Loho—I produced ten children." Her tone speaks defiance about the fact that they are all dead.

Zebuglo sees herself as a *goba,* a master xylophone player. She says that she has not been "initiated" through the customary male ritual, and the defiance can be heard again as she announces her talent as God-given, since men do not allow women to play this instrument. Defiantly also, she punctuates her singing with refrain in vocal imitation of a xylophone.

The following excerpt includes the traditional element of praise-naming in attributes: *Mankanama*, for example, combines *mankana*, a tough swamp tree, and *ma*, a suffix meaning "mother of"; *Yelibaye* means "he who says"; *Ninbaye* means "they who say"; and *Hayelima* means "mother of 'I hate problems.'" At the same time, Zebuglo also describes her belief that she should have come into the world as a man but had her sexuality stolen from her and had to make do with being a female. As a man, she jumped into the water "*buu buu*," which is an expression meaning "swimming with foolish abandon." While there may be humor in this image, the sharp reality of pain follows in the image of "bangles on a leper."

Esi Sutherland-Addy, Patience Mudiare, and Edward Nanbigne

✦

Communal, YOU OF THE HOUSE

Nigeria 1979   Hausa

Call:
Hey, you over there, you over there
You people of Mallam Audu's house
Mallam Audu's first wife
And his favorite
The one with henna on the palms of her hands
Good afternoon
I wish you a very good afternoon
This is Hawa greeting you
Did you sleep well?

Response:
I greet you, too
How are you?
I send you greetings
A very good afternoon to you, too

A visitor:
Greetings, keep up the good work pounding

Response:
Oh, thank you, thank you
Welcome, welcome
Welcome, Aïsha.

Translated by Rabi Garba, Patience Mudiare, and Antionette Tijani Alou

Communal, ONE SINGLE MEASURE

Senegal 1998   Diola

One single measure and the earthen pot is full
One single measure of rice and the pot is full
One single measure and the earthen pot is full

I told Aissatou to prepare the rice seeds
"What sort of seeds do you want?"
I went to do plots when the rain came
I sowed, then the rice grew
I planted out the nursery bed for the pricking
One was white and the other was red
I pricked all the nursery beds

I went to the rice-field one Friday
To see if the rice was ripe
The stalks were coming out
The stalks were out
The rice was ripe
They then said, "so you are back, Dandene"
I said "Yes"
"You did well"

Translated into French by Souleymane Faye
Translated from French by Marjolijn de Jager and Judith Miller

Communal, INVOCATION AT MILKING

Guinea 1987   Fulfulde/Pulaar

In the name of God *diouhou*
God the merciful *diafa*
If God wishes it, if the Prophet wishes it,
As for me I do not covet anyone else's cream,
But let no one covet my cream either,
I will not take any one's cream
But let no one take my cream either.

Translated into French by Abdoul Sy Savane
Translated from French by Abena P. A. Busia

Zebuglo of Loho, PRAISE SONG

Ghana 1999   Daagare

Hi len lan, len lan len, hi len lan, len lan len
When I sing the truth of my story,
Accompanied by the *kpeli* drum,
Still this is no soft xylophone I play.
If the force of truth does not save me,
The trees and all of nature will.
I did not give birth uselessly.
Had it not been for death,
I would also have a few [children].
I built Loho. Am I dead?
Even I, I could have had ten living children, I.
What else could I do? Didn't I help build Loho?
I can't say witches should not eat them.
They should eat; it is their house they are destroying.
They are not killing me, they are not killing Nyensaala.
Hi len lan, len lan len, hi len lan, len lan len
They have thought I was nothing
What woman is pregnant for twelve months?
Haa! God!
Kin of my protector, oh! Death
Kin of *Yelibaye,* oh! Death
Kin of Jebuni *Ninbaye* of Kaleo, oh! Death
See Death, oh! Death, ahh!
And my husband won't bemoan Death?

Oh! Death, oh! Death
Oh! Death, kin of the knowledgeable one, oh! Death
Oh! Death, Oh! Death
Hee hee, hee hee hee, hee hee hee hee
Somebody's mother from the Bawaara of Kaleo
Sen lan len, len len, len lan len
Mankanama of the royal house of Loho
Sen lan len, len len, len lan len
My namesake, Zebuglo, mother of Jebuni
H'mm h'mm len len len, len lan len
They do not like me at all, *Hayelimaa*
Len len len, len lan len, len lan len. . . .

H'mm h'mm h'mm h'mm h'mm
Where there are many tadpoles, children come.
When they come give them a place. . . .

I'm a great xylophone player and nobody initiated me.
God gave me the talent
And I came to Dumbie's lineage with it.
H'mm h'mm h'mm h'mm h'mm h'mm h'mm
Once I was crying about a penis,
But they said why not have a swim,
And I put it down and
I jumped into the water, *buu buu.*
When I returned it was gone,
So I took a useless vagina
And I came to Loho, to live in destitution.
H'mm h'mm h'mm, hen ai h'm ai h'm h'm h'm
That is why my life has been a struggle to no end.
Oh! This thing pains me, like bangles on a leper. . . .

Translated by Edward Nanbigne and Abena P. A. Busia

SONGS OF MIGRATION

Seldom do rural women of the Songhai-Zarma area move from the frontiers of the desert, which appears desolate compared to the land to which they may be transported in their dreams. These three poems of young Sahelian women, chanted to accompany the pounding of grain, juxtapose fantasy and the dreary drudgery of daily life. They are all on the theme of migration. The pounding women dream of marvelous countries where they could escape the daily torture represented by the pestle and drawing rope. They dream of the near-mythical land of kola trees, which offer shade and the special nuts that lubricate all major transactions in a large number of societies in the region. They also imagine luscious mangoes and mango trees that contrast with the dry scrub of their surroundings.

This precisely is the theme of "The Beauty of Kumasi." The city of Kumasi, located in the dense and humid forest zone of Ghana, is the capital of the king-dom of Asante, which rose in the eighteenth century and remained an imperial power until the end of the nineteenth century. No doubt its situation on the frontiers of the savannah region of West Africa facilitated its intense trade with peoples of the savannah and the Sahel region. Coupled with its reputation for grandeur and wealth, Kumasi has attracted a mass migration of people from the Songhai-Zarma area over the years. Returning migrants tell of huge markets with consumer goods from England arrayed beneath the wide awnings of large stalls and shops, as well as of a legendary display of wealth. Each word in this short poem therefore evokes a network of images. The first two lines fantasize about the condition, while the last two come down to earth with a thump, invoking the burdensome drudgery of drawing water and grinding grain.

By contrast, "These West-Coasters Are Liars" is a lighthearted, wistful satire based on the lame excuses given by men who were unable to bring back the things of which the women dreamed. Those who strike it rich may be few. Returning with whatever possessions they have been able to acquire, they may also fall subject to many indignities, some of them at the hands of corrupt officials at national borders. Those who return empty-handed must face the scorn of young women, for the customs officer may also offer a convenient excuse for those whose journeys yielded no fruit.

In "The Non-Migrant's Song," a young woman sings a diatribe against the man who did not even make an effort to migrate. She has been not only deprived of gifts from faraway lands, which would raise her status socially, but also denied even the right to dream about her gallant husband in a faraway land of bliss.

Fatimata Mounkaïla

✦

Communal, THE BEAUTY OF KUMASI

Niger 1988   Songhai-Zarma

The beauty is in Kumasi
In the shade of the small shops
Far from the task of carrying water
Far from the horrid pounding [of grain]

Translated by Antoinette Tidjani Alou

Communal, THESE WEST-COASTERS ARE LIARS

Niger 1998   Songhai-Zarma

These people coming back from the Coast are all liars:
No Custom Officer has ever seen them,
But whoever comes home penniless,
It's the Customs Officer who stripped him clean.
These people coming back from the Coast are all liars:
No Customs Officer has ever set eyes on them.

Kando, Fado's father
Is on good terms with Customs Officers.

Gamatié, Yambo's younger brother, is back;
The Customs Officer didn't see him.

Sanda is back, he's become a real big-shot;
The Customs Officer didn't catch him.

The lucky ones got through
While the Customs Officer was taking his bath.

Translated by Antoinette Tidjani Alou

Communal, THE NON-MIGRANT'S SONG

Niger 1998   Songhai-Zarma

Go-nowhere, you're always sitting around,
Your ankles dry
Like a foal with white socks.

Lazy-bones, are you there?
Door-step, are you there?

What, are you speaking to me,
Are you crazy?

Am I your father?
Or your mother, who sat on you for nine months
And hatched you in the tenth?
Lazy bones, that's what you are!

Men travel to the land in the West, but *you* don't go West.
Men travel to lands in the South, but *you* don't go South.
They go to the east, but *you* don't go East.

Have last night's leftovers been heated up?
Let them bring it to you.
Is the millet porridge ready?
Let them bring it to him.
So, you wanted to spend the dry season here at home?
Wait and see!
Look at my cloth, it's going to pieces.
By the grace of God, you'll buy me a new one.
My father needs a new *boubou,* you'll buy it.
And you'll have to get some cloth for my mother!

So, you wanted to spend the dry season here?
Wait and see!

So, you feel like eating some nice couscous with sorrel-seed seasoning?
Go and fetch me the condiments!
Go and fetch me the salt, it's on top of the kitchen storehouse.
Go out and buy the ingredients,
After that, you can have your couscous with sorrel-seed seasoning!

Translated by Antoinette Tidjani Alou

SONGS OF INSULT

Three songs that fill the working space of women allow battles of varying intensities to be fought. They may be called "Songs of Insult." "*Tabardé*, or Blanket-Making" accompanies the making of the patchwork covers traditionally used in Tuareg communities against the biting cold of the Sahara Desert's night winds. This work has to be done by groups of women, who sing as they sew. In this case, there are three voices: two antagonistic potential mothers-in-law and the chorus. Each mother who sings wants to paint her child in the most positive light, even as she challenges the other mothers. The verbal duel depicted in the text is based on oblique innuendo. The mother of the girl depicts her as a kid, while the boy's mother calls him a buck, both precious images in a pastoral culture. The chorus functions as witness and arbiter, approving or disapproving of what is being said. The chorus maintains the rhythm of work and ensures a playful tone.

Two other insult poems illustrate how the context of work can, by the conventions governing it, provide the least powerful women in a family with opportunities to speak their minds. "The Sisters-in-Law Diedhou" depicts the tensions arising out of an extended family system in which a wife may live with her sisters-in-law. Saddled with the chore of pounding, the wife, who might normally be the inferior person in the family, sets the boundaries. Using a watch as a metaphor, she does not mince her words about the behavior of her sisters-in-law. She establishes herself as a no-nonsense personality by invoking her mother-in-law and another persona (Fanta Sane), both of whom have presumably developed respect for her. The reference to a signature in the last lines of the song alludes to the new Senegalese Marriage Code.

"*Seybata*, or My Backside—Insult Her!" accompanies the pounding of grain in the Zarma society of Niger. A more recent composition, estimated to have emerged around 1998 in the environs of the city of Niamey, the song's treatment of the young wife and her in-laws is bold, even brazen, and subversive. Taking advantage of the fact that a young wife and other young women of the concession would not ordinarily face their parents-in-law to do their pounding chores, the young women turn their backs on these elders, not as a gracious gesture of politeness but as a prelude to enacting a discourteous skit. The saucy young women with their backs to the venerable elders in the compound alternately take on the roles of new wife and father-in-law. The new wife breaks into sanctified areas such as the dysfunctional sexuality of her mother-in-law. She buttresses her stream of abusive language by extending and patting her own backside and those of the women pounding, which she personalizes and calls euphemistically *Seybata*. The power of expression lies in the gesture as the well-rounded bottoms of the pounders saucily bob up and down in rebellious defiance of the in-laws. With the exception of certain well-regulated and specific circumstances, a young Zarma woman who is not a *griotte* will not use scatological language or make obscene gestures in public. Hence, this song represents an evolution in social attitudes and a search for new parameters.

Fatimata Mounkaïla and Esi Sutherland-Addy

✦

Communal, *Tabardé*, or Blanket-Making

Niger 1999   Tuareg

As for me, my nanny-goat is better than a certain billy-goat,
The nanny-goat may be crafty but the billy-goat is honorable,
There is no doubt about it.
A she-camel's gait is elegant,
A donkey's gait is heavy and graceless.
May the mouth say whatever it wishes to say,
Should some camels become donkeys,
This would not surprise me one bit.
May God bless love!
May God turn you into a *tabardé* blanket,
So that we could prick you wherever we liked!
The *tabardé* blanket is sewn
So that we may sew your mouth.
The *tabardé* blanket is sewn
So that we may burst your eyes.
The *tabardé* blanket is sewn
So that we may block your ears.
The *tabardé* blanket is sewn
So that you may finally lose your power.
The *tabardé* blanket is sewn
So that God may unite people and preserve love among them.
The *tabardé* blanket is sewn
The way a *tabardé* blanket ought.
A *tabardé* blanket is sewn
With so many different pieces of cloth.
A *tabardé* blanket is sewn

With so many different types of thread.
A *tabardé* blanket is sewn
With so many different needles.
A *tabardé* blanket is sewn
By so many women's hands.
A *tabardé* blanket is sewn
Sew on, sew your blankets!

Translated into French by Manou Zara Villain
Translated from French by Christiane Owusu-Sarpong and Esi Sutherland-Addy

Communal, THE SISTERS-IN-LAW DIEDHIOU

Senegal 1994   Diola

Sisters-in-law Diedhiou,
If you are not courteous,
I will set you right like a watch.

Sisters-in-law Diedhiou,
If you are not accurate,
I will set you right like a watch.

If you are not courteous,
I will make you "run" like a watch.

Even if you are not right,
I will set you right like a watch,
My body is like soap.
My body is like soap.

Where might Mama be?
Where might Mama be? Go ask Fanta Sané.
Mama did sign.

Just ask Fanta Sané.
Mama did sign.
Just ask Fanta Sané.
Mama did sign.

Translated into French by Sarauni Bodian, Aminata Diaw, and Rokkaya Fall
Translated from French by Marjolijn de Jager

Communal, Seybata, or My Backside—Insult Her!

Niger 1999   Songhai-Zarma

The bride:
That cunning old woman,
Insult her!
Who pours oil on the fire,
Insult her!

That burning wild-fire,
Insult her!

You say you're out to break a marriage,
Insult her!
But she wants to preserve her own.
Insult her!
Insult her for me, Seybata,
Insult her!
Insult her, my bottom,
Insult her!

My strong black biceps,
Insult her!
Insult her! Insult her! Insult her!
She makes more babies than the bean fodder plant,
Insult her!
She makes more babies than a female locust,
Insult her!
Insult her!
She makes more babies than termites and mice,
She makes more babies than a watermelon,
Insult her!
That cunning old woman,
Insult her!
You never pay the griottes to praise me!
Insult her!
I who always bring dinner to you,
Insult her!
I always send you a calabash full of creamy millet for your lunch,
Insult her!

I always send a full pot of water for you,
Insult her!
Yet she refuses to praise me,

Insult her! Insult her! Insult her!

The father-in-law:
Why should she praise you?
Insult her!
Such a cunning young bride.
Insult her!
She makes couscous with the bran from her millet.
Insult her!
She throws away the millet water!
Yet, there stands my horse tethered to a post.
Insult her!
Yet, there stands my sheep tied to a stake.
Insult her! Insult her! Insult her!

The bride:
Kailou's father, I'm not addressing you.
I'm talking to Kailou's mother
Insult her!

She makes more babies than the grape tree,
Insult her!
She makes more babies than a date palm,
Insult her!
She makes more babies than ants and mice,
Insult her!
A whole host of baby boys!
A whole host of baby girls!
Insult her!
And she never praises me.
Insult her! Insult her! Insult her!
Your dear horse, Haaro, will not eat my bran,
Insult her!
Your dear horse, Haaro, will not drink my millet water,
Insult her!
I will make myself some couscous with my bran,
Insult her!
I will pound the grains and make myself some porridge,
Insult her!
I will throw away the millet water.
Insult her! Insult her! Insult her!

The father-in-law:
Who are you talking to, Laki?

Insult her!
You young shrew with a tongue like a razor-blade!
Insult her!

The bride:
Kailou's father, I'm not addressing you.
Insult her!
I'm talking to Kailou's mother.
Insult her!
I'm talking to that old hypocrite,
Insult her!
The little bit of millet bran I scrounge for here and there,
Insult her!
Has made my arms stronger than those who have sheaves galore!
Insult her!
The little bit of millet I scrounge for here and there,
Insult her!
Has given me more muscles than those who have barns full,

Insult her!
Rashida, hold baby Nayé for me,
Insult her!
So I can insult their grandmother, that old devil!
So I can insult her and tear her to bits.
Insult her!
Insult her! Insult her! Insult her!

The father-in-law:
Kailou's mother, insult her for me.
Insult her!
That shameless bride with a razor-blade tongue.
Insult her! Insult her! Insult her!

The bride:
Kailou's father, I'm not addressing you.
Insult her!
I'm talking to Kailou's mother.
Insult her!
The woman who's busy breaking people's marriages,
But who holds on to her own,
Insult her!

The mother-in-law:
Why call me "Kailou's mother"?

Insult her!
Go ahead, call me Bibata!
Insult her!
My name is Bibata.
Insult her!

The father-in-law:
Insult her for me, Kailou's mother,
Insult her!
Then, we'll send a letter to your son.
Insult her!

The bride:
Go ahead, send him a letter!
Insult her!
Let him repudiate me!
I'll find another man!
Insult her!
If I leave him, another woman will take my place,
Insult her!
She'll insult you and tear you to pieces!
Insult her!
Insult her for me, Scybata!
Insult her!
Insult her for me, my bottom,
Insult her!
Insult her for me, Baki's mother,
Insult her!
The thing that is hidden inside my wrapper,
Insult her!
Since you have the right to insult her,
Insult her!
She's my mother-in-law,
Insult her!
So I can't insult her.
Insult her!
Insult her for me,
Insult her for me,
Since you have the right to insult her:
Insult her! Insult her! Insult her!

Translated by Antoinette Tidjani Alou

THE 1970S AND 1980S
NEGOTIATING NEW SOCIAL
IDENTITIES

Selma Al-Hassan
TANOFIA

Ghana 1971   English

Selma Al-Hassan's "Tanofia" appeared in *The Cowrie Girl and Other Stories,* a 1971 collection by young Ghanaian writers still in secondary school. Al-Hassan, now known as Selma Valcourt, wrote the story at age fourteen, in the 1968–1969 academic year, as a member of the Creative Writer's Club in Achimota School, which she attended from 1966 to 1971.

The story depicts a relationship between two girls, one of whom insists that she is not really human but a gift from the river god Tano to a childless woman. The story blurs fantasy and reality and may be read as a way for young people to explain the inexplicable death of a young person.

In 1981, Valcourt entered the National Film and Television Institute in Accra, Ghana, and in 1986, two years after graduating, she took a position with Ghana Television as a broadcast journalist. She became a prominent anchorwoman and producer of news reports. Valcourt left Ghana Television in 1997 to live with her husband in the United States. Between 1998 and 1999, she was a regular columnist for the *Daily Dispatch,* a newspaper in Accra. She is now attending nursing school.

Naana J. Opoku Agyemang and Esi Sutherland-Addy

✦

Charlotte was the name she was popularly known by. She was my best friend. She was an only child and extremely beautiful, and yet kind to every one.

She was very good at swimming. She could stay under water for a long time; she really seemed to be able to breathe under water. She sometimes looked like a mermaid when she was swimming.

We were in our third year at Achimota School when it happened. One afternoon, she said to me, "Selma, do you know I'm not human?"

Of course, I didn't believe her. "How do you expect me to believe you?" I asked.

"Why don't you believe me?" she asked.

"Now Charlotte," I said, "you know you're human and I know you are, so shut up."

"That's what you think," was the reply she gave me.

"What are you then?"

"I'm the daughter of the Tano."

"Come on, be sensible. It's impossible."

"Do you want to perish?" she asked.

"Yes, I do," I replied jokingly.

The other girls heard us arguing. "Trust Charlotte to say that," said Theodosia.

"Look!" exclaimed Charlotte, "I think I have to prove it to you."

"Tell us about it," I said.

"Well, you see," she started. "When my parents couldn't have any children, they went to River Tano and my father gave me to them. That's why my earthly mother goes to the shrine every three months to offer sacrifice."

"Your mother doesn't go to any shrine every three months," said Josephine.

"She does!" answered Charlotte.

She went on and told us that her real father wanted her back [and] that was why she got ill so often.

"I don't believe you," I said.

"Okay, look into my eyes." I did and she opened them wide to make them look frightening.

"Please!" I almost shouted and fell back onto my bed.

"Do you believe me now?"

"No, I don't."

"Selma, you'll not live to see dawn tomorrow. You'll perish and die out like a candle tonight. The wrath of Tanofia herself, the daughter of the great Tano, can make her do anything."

"Who's Tanofia?" I asked teasingly.

"I," she replied.

"Trust you, Charlotte," I said.

"As I was saying, you'll die tonight of suffocation. I'll do it myself. Nobody'll hear us. I'll push you into that cupboard and lock you up there and take out your body when I feel like it."

"That will mean murder," I told her.

"That's true," she said. "Okay, I'll use another method. You'll die in your sleep, and come with me down into the depths of the Tano." I had been laughing, but I suddenly felt frightened. "Could it be true?" I asked myself. "No, but I am afraid. I'll tell her I believe her."

So I told her I believe her, but still she insisted on my perishing.

"Don't believe her," said Yaa.

"Kneel down fast and repent," said Charlotte, "or else perish with Selma." Yaa didn't, so she and I were the victims of Tanofia's anger. We had a very long argument over this story by Charlotte that day before we went to bed.

The school clock was striking twelve when I woke up to find Charlotte beside me, eyes wide open and grinning from ear to ear. My! Was I scared! She sat looking straight into my eyes. I covered my head quickly with my blanket and began to pray as fast as I could.

When I lifted up my blanket, she was gone, and I was glad. However, she came back presently, took my arm and flew with me over the whole town until we got to the banks of the river. It was a really large one, banks overflooded and with waves all rush[ing] around. It seemed to be annoyed.

Don't forget I was still as scared as could be. It was now time to dive in and we did, with me shaking like a leaf.

The depths of the Tano were very cool and inviting with many whirlpools around us. They made me very scared indeed. Their rooms, gates, windows, doors, everything down there was made up of whirlpools. I could breathe all right and could also talk to the fish and other creatures of water. Charlotte's father was a nice old man with a long beard. He didn't seem to have much time for us so we spent most of the time with her mother, a very beautiful and young woman with large black eyes and black long hair. She spent hours and hours with us, telling us stories of the river and how she became the goddess and so on.

We ate on plates made of tiny whirlpools and ripples. We dined mainly on minced octopus which was really delicious. I had a very happy stay there and I felt very very sad when I had to come back to the upper world. I cried when I said good-bye to the god and goddess.

The upper world looked the same old grey thing to me. I told all the girls about my stay down there. They did not believe me, but what did I care? The god and goddess had promised me anything I wished for. Theodosia, Yaa, Josephine against Charlotte and me, argued till we could argue no more. A few days afterwards, Charlotte felt terribly ill, and we all felt very sad. Gradually she got worse and worse. She was admitted into the hospital but no one really knew what was wrong with her. She complained of pains all over her body. One day, as we sat talking to her, she said, "Now I know how it feels to die. Good-bye friends, it's been so nice living with you. I'm going back to the Tano where I came from. I might see . . ."

That was all she said and was gone. I cried and cried because I was going to miss her terribly. But then I realized that she was going to her father.

Flora Nwapa
THE TRAVELLER

Nigeria 1971　English

Flora Nwapa was born in Oguta, to two staunch Anglican schoolteachers, on 13 January 1931. After completing primary and secondary school in 1948, Nwapa studied for the Cambridge Overseas Senior School Leaving Certificate and made Grade 2 in 1950. She started attending Queens College, Lagos, immediately, to take a postsecondary school course and study for A-level exams in English and history. In 1953, she was the first Oguta woman to enter the University College, Ibadan, as a matriculated student. Upon earning a bachelor's degree, with a concentration in English, history, and religion, in

1957, she traveled to Europe to study at the University of Edinburgh on scholarship. Upon returning from Scotland in 1958 with a diploma in education, she accepted the chieftaincy title *Ogbuefi,* which literally means "killer of a cow." In Oguta, unlike most other Igbo societies, a woman of means, integrity, and good standing in the eyes of the elders takes this prestigious title. Having attained great educational achievements, Nwapa made the Oguta community proud, and in return they honored her.

For a year, she worked as an education officer for the Ministry of Education at Calabar in Calabar State. Then, while teaching at Queens School, Enugu, from 1959 to 1962, she gave birth to a child, Ejine Olga Nzeribe, with the charismatic trade unionist Gogo Nzeribe, who came from a prominent Oguta family. They did not, however, marry. From 1962 to 1967, Nwapa worked as an assistant to the registrar at the University of Lagos in Apapa, Nigeria. In August 1967, at the start of the Nigerian civil war, she married Gogo Nwakuche, an Oguta man, and together they had two children, Uzoma and Amede. In the first Federal Government administration after the Nigerian civil war, Flora Nwakuche was the only woman cabinet member in the administration of Gov. Ukpabi Asika of East Central State from 1970 to 1975.

Nwapa's woman-centered novels, *Efuru* (1966), *Idu* (1970), *Never Again* (1975), *One Is Enough* (1981), *Women Are Different* (1986), *The Lake Goddess* (unpublished), and *The Umbilical Cord* (unpublished), define her as one of the world's best womanist writers in the second half of the twentieth century. She also published two collections of short stories: *This Is Lagos and Other Stories* (1971) and *Wives at War and Other Stories* (1975). Her biography of her parents, *Golden Wedding Jubilee of Chief and Mrs. C. I. Nwapa, April 20, 1930–April 20, 1980,* was presented at the opening ceremony of their new house in Oguta near the lake. Her only collection of poetry, *Cassava Song and Rice Song,* appeared in 1986. The author's deathbed plays, *Conversations* (1993) and *The First Lady* (1993), established her as a playwright.

In 1977, she launched Flora Nwapa and Company and Tana Press Limited, the children's wing of this publishing venture, which made her the first African woman to establish an independent publishing enterprise. Nwapa's *Mammy-water* (1979) was the company's initial publication, followed by several dozen other children's books. Flora Nwapa and Company published books by celebrated African writers, including Ama Ata Aidoo, Patience Ifejika, Leslie Ofoegbu, Abarry Abu, Peter Moneke, and Ifeoma Okoye.

Straddling two worlds, Nwapa westernized the skills her foremothers had passed on to her. Whereas Ruth Uzoaru, Hannah Onumonu, and Lady Mary Nzimiro, to name only three of the enterprising Oguta women who influenced her, traded in palm kernels and imported textiles, Nwapa marketed the books she wrote and published through Tana Press. Many of her books were also sold at book parties given in her honor, at conferences, and at feminist book fairs throughout the world.

The female characters in Nwapa's creative corpus reflect the spirit of the idyllic goddess of the lake, *Ogbuide,* a female deity whom the Oguta people worship. Oguta lore has it that the goddess bestows on women beauty, wisdom, power, riches, and peace. Bisi, the protagonist in "The Traveller," for example, is the epitome of a successful woman. She has a good job, a nice house with a maid, her own car, many friends, and quiet dignity. More importantly, Bisi valorizes the African woman by correcting the traveler's myth that urban women are "good-time girls." When Mr. Musa approaches Bisi as a former acquaintance from their school days, Bisi is hospitable and gracious to her visitor. But when he crosses the line by proposing an amorous relationship, Bisi remains morally correct. It is her extrasensory perspicacity and attendant empowerment that puzzles Mr. Musa. Upon leaving town after a tour of three days, he acknowledges defeat and dejectedly complains that Bisi has been most unkind.

In 1983, President Shehu Shagari honored Nwapa with the coveted Officer of the Order of the Niger Award for her service to the Federal Republic of Nigeria in Creative Writing and Publishing. Her illustrious career in literary production also earned her the University of Ife's Merit Award for Authorship and Publishing in 1985. She died in 1993.

Marie Umeh

✦

There was a knock at the door and Bisi went to open it.

"Good afternoon, please come right in."

"You remember me, don't you?" the stranger asked.

"I remember the face, but not the name," Bisi lied.

"We were together at College."

"Of course it was at College. Please sit down, and where are you now?" Bisi asked. It was obvious that she still could not place the man.

"I am in Lagos and have come to do some business here. I thought I should come and say hello to you. You were in Edinburgh last year, weren't you? I saw you for a brief time while in the company of Obi and his sisters."

"You are right," Bisi said remembering her holidays in Edinburgh, but she still could not place the man.

"How are you enjoying teaching?"

"I love it. I did not know I would enjoy it so much."

"I am glad to hear this. Many people get bored with it in no time, and look around for something more exciting."

"You are right. It all depends on the individual. Where do you work in Lagos?" Bisi asked.

"I work with a firm of experts. We give our expert advice to the public on buildings and so on."

"And you are enjoying it, aren't you?"

"It is exciting. I do a lot of touring. In December, I was in the Cameroons. After this trip, I shall come more frequently to the East."

"And how long are you staying here?" she asked.

"I leave for Ogoja tomorrow, Onitsha next tomorrow, and on Saturday, I go to Port Harcourt."

"That's grand. I like touring," Bisi said, getting up. "I am sorry Mr. . . . ."

"Mr. Musa," the stranger said promptly.

"Mr. Musa, I must go to my lesson now. The children are waiting for me."

"And I must be going too. Thank you very much. Are you free this evening?"

"Sorry, I am not free."

"You are free tomorrow afternoon then?"

"Yes, tomorrow afternoon, I am free, but you are going to Ogoja."

"I shall be back before lunch time. Can you come to lunch with me at the hotel?"

"That is very kind of you. But it is a shame that you should come all the way from Lagos and invite me to lunch. I should invite you to a meal in my house."

"Oh, that does not matter at all. Anywhere I go, I could ask as many people to meals as I want. It costs me nothing. The pleasure is mine. When do I come for you?"

"One thirty."

"I shall be here at one thirty, then. See you."

"Bye bye."

"My God, isn't he talkative?" Bisi said as soon as Mr. Musa's driver drove away. She wondered whether he was actually at College with her, and blamed herself for accepting the lunch appointment.

However, at one thirty the next day, Mr. Musa was in Bisi's house, Bisi came out and they drove to the hotel.

"How was your trip to Ogoja?"

"Fine. I am making headway, and I am very happy."

A taxi hooted and overtook Mr. Musa at a very dangerous corner, and stopped not quite thirty yards in front.

"These taxi drivers should not be given licences," Mr. Musa said.

"They know what to do. It is just sheer irresponsibility and lack of patience. What makes me mad is when they abuse you when they are wrong," Bisi said.

"I guess you just go your way when they abuse you," Mr. Musa said laughing.

"Of course I don't. I abuse them and talk to them in the language they understand. I am not a lady when it comes to that."

Mr. Musa laughed. "That's what I do too."

"Shall we have some drinks?" Musa asked as they arrived at the hotel. "What would you like to drink?"

"Babycham," she replied.

"That's good. I like Babycham myself, but I will have a small Star."

"Good afternoon, doc," Bisi greeted a man who came in.

"Hello Bisi, how are you?"

"Very well, thank you. How is the battle?"

"Still raging. Do you know the latest?"

"No, what are you up to now?"

"Well, we were there as usual. We sat down at our seats. Patients came, we took a full report, wrote everything down in long hand, took the patient in and examined him fully, and called in the next patient. In this way, by twelve o'clock no doctor saw more than three patients."

"Hello, doc."

"How are you, Musa, when did you come?"

"A couple of days ago."

"Nice to see you."

"Yes doc, you have a case," Bisi said.

"You mean private practice for doctors?" Mr. Musa asked.

"Yes, P.P. for doctors. They have a case, haven't they?" Bisi said.

"Yes, but unscrupulous doctors could easily abuse it."

"Excuse me," the doctor said and left.

They selected a table for two.

"Are you going to have pounded yam?"

"No, when I come here, I want to eat something different. And besides I am slimming."

"Women are always slimming. Oh that's good high life music. Do you like it?"

"I like it, but I don't like listening to high life music," she replied.

"Why?" he asked.

"I like to dance to high life music."

"That's a good one," he said.

When they finished eating, they went to his room. He tuned his radio, and waltz music was playing, very softly.

"Let's dance, shall we?"

"Dance?" she asked in surprise. "I have just eaten. I can't do any dancing now." He laughed and did not insist.

"By the way, I hear Dora Okeke is here. Can we see her tonight?"

"Oh yes, what time?"

"About nine o'clock."

"That's late, make it eight."

"You see, someone is taking me out at seven, and I guess I will be free at nine."

"All right, nine then. I must go now. I haven't had siesta."

"There are two beds."

"No, thank you," she said.

He came near her and put his hands round her neck. There was no response. He took her hands in his and squeezed them. The effect was the same.

"What is the matter?" he asked.

"With what?" she replied. He left her.

"I shall take you back now."

"That is thoughtful of you."

He drove her home.

Mr. Musa arrived at nine thirty full of apologies.

"Let's go now," Bisi said and called her maid who locked the door. "Helen," Bisi called, "please bring my wallet. I have no money on me and I may buy some petrol."

"Oh don't bother. It is all right," Mr. Musa said.

"No. Helen, please bring my wallet quickly. It is in the cupboard."

"I said don't bother."

"I can't find it," Helen said.

"I said let's go."

They arrived at a petrol station and Mr. Musa filled the tank for her, and got a receipt. When they arrived at Dora's school, she was not in.

"What do we do now? It is too early to go to bed," Musa said. "It is ten fifteen, you know I can't go to bed before midnight."

"All right. Let's visit a friend of mine."

"Who is he?"

"It is a she. You know Nwakama at College?"

"Okechukwu Nwakama?"

"Yes, Okechukwu. He is my friend's fiancé."

In five minutes they were in Sophia's house. They were introduced.

"And when is the lucky man coming home?"

"Next year," Sophia replied. "Can I offer you beer?"

"Yes, provided you share it with me."

"We don't drink beer here. We are bush."

"I know you are not bush. You will share it with me."

"All right. We will share it," Bisi said.

Beer was brought and the two girls had half a glass each which they did not enjoy. When they finished, they got up to go. Bisi drove to her house, and as she said good night to Musa, he drew her to him.

"Don't be in a hurry. Kiss me good night."

Bisi pushed him away. He wanted to come near again, but thought better of it and said, "I shall see you tomorrow at eight. We shall collect Sophia and have supper or drinks somewhere. Good night."

"Good night," Bisi said and shut the door.

The next evening at eight, Bisi collected Sophia. Mr. Musa was picked [up] from his hotel and they went out to have drinks. All the places they went to were interesting, and at about eleven o'clock they decided to go home.

"Take Sophia home first," Musa suggested.

"Yes, take me home first," Sophia echoed.

Bisi laughed and reversed the car. Sophia was seen safely home. She then drove Mr. Musa to his hotel.

"Good night," she said not turning off the engine.

"No, you must come in."

"No, it is late, and I must rise early tomorrow morning."

"I know. Come in for a few minutes."

"No," she said and shook her head vigorously.

"This is most unfair, Bisi. Please come in. You can go any time you want to go. I won't stop you."

"No."

He locked his side of the car, came to her side and took her by the hand. She allowed her hand to be taken, but she remained doggedly on her seat.

"All right. If you don't want to go in, let's go for a walk."

"For a walk, at this time of the night, not me."

"What do you want me to do now?" Musa asked in despair.

"Go to bed and let me go home."

"You have refused to come in?"

"Yes, I have refused to come in."

"What is your reason?"

"Reason, you don't do things always with reason." Musa went into the room and came back.

"What about this cocktail party tomorrow night?" he asked.

"I am not invited."

"Oh, don't be impossible. You said yesterday you will go with me."

"So I said. Can't I change my mind?"

"This is hopeless. We shall go, Bisi."

"I don't want to gate-crash," Bisi said laughing.

"The guest of honour and I were classmates. I saw him only yesterday and I assured him I would be there. Please Bisi, be reasonable." He opened the door of the car and went in. "Drive me to anywhere," he said. Bisi laughed and said nothing.

"Please, Bisi please."

"All right, I shall go with you. When is the party?"

"Come at four or five."

"For the cocktail party?" she asked in surprise.

"Can't you come at that time?" he asked.

"I shall come at seven o'clock. Good night."

"Look, Bisi, this is most unfair. Please just go into that room, then come out. I shall be here, I promise."

She shook her head vigorously. He took a deep breath, and sighed. "Good night then. I shall see you tomorrow."

At seven o'clock, Bisi was in Mr. Musa's hotel.

"Can I drive you tonight?"

"Oh, never mind. When you go back to Lagos, tell your friends you had a woman chauffeur in Enugu."

"You are going to eat goat meat," Bisi said to Mr. Musa.

"Goat meat at a cocktail party?"

"Of course, when there is no goat meat, the guests demand it by right. It must be brought."

It was not a bad cocktail. But it was the same pattern. One heard the usual questions asked at parties. "How is the car behaving?" Conversations on promotions. Nothing on the international or national level whatever. They called on one or two people, filled Bisi's tank again and drove to the hotel. When they arrived there, Mr. Musa came out and banged his side of the door. Bisi remained as yesterday, in her seat.

"Oh please, let's not do this all over again tonight."

She said nothing. She remained doggedly again on her seat and did not even switch off the engine.

"Come, Bisi, let's go in. It is only eleven thirty. When you want to go home, I shall not keep you."

"I am not coming out. What am I coming out for?"

"When you come out, you will know."

She laughed.

"After all, we are adults and responsible. Why are you behaving so childishly? Why are you doing this to me?" He opened the car, took her handbag and placed it on the bonnet of the car.

"When you want to go, go and take your handbag," he said laughing.

"You are clever, aren't you?" Bisi said.

Mr. Musa forced his way into the driver's seat. "Oh no, don't do that. You are hurting me. You know this seat is only meant for one person."

"The way you talk, Bisi, well, I must confess one thing."

"Go ahead."

"I am not in love, but I feel as if I am."

"And how many times do you feel like that in a week?" she asked laughing. She was not disappointed.

He did not say a word. That was not what he expected. For some time, they did not talk.

"Come on, let's go in, Bisi." Bisi shook her head.

"Why do you stay there shaking your head at everything I say?"

She did not of course say a word.

"Look, as I said before," Mr. Musa began again, "I am not in love, but . . ."

"I am not in love either, or do you think I should be?" Bisi said firmly. The cheek of him to repeat it.

There was a long silence.

"Will I see you tomorrow?" Mr. Musa asked.

"When does your plane leave?" Bisi asked.

"About twelve twenty."

"I shall come at eleven to drive you to the airport."

"Can't you come earlier than that?"

"No, I can't."

He came closer and kissed her. But she did not return the kiss. She switched on the engine, was about to drive off when he said urgently, "Wait." He opened the car and went in. Bisi looked at him in surprise. "Won't you let me go. It is one a.m."

"You don't seem to believe me. What I have been doing has been the accumulation of my feelings for you for a long time, even at College."

"Really?"

"You don't seem to believe me, Bisi."

"Does it really matter whether I believe you or not. I thought that what mattered was whether you yourself believe what you have just said."

She started the car again. Mr. Musa came out willingly and she drove off.

Bisi told her friend Sophia everything the next morning. Both girls went to see Mr. Musa. He was ready to go to the airport.

"You are lucky to have two beautiful women to see you off," Sophia said.

"Well, maybe I may not even have one after all. Your friend is unkind," he said.

They did not wait long before the plane took off. And as Bisi and Sophia were driving back home, Bisi began to laugh.

"Why are you laughing?"

"Musa, what kind of man is he? And what kind of woman does he think I am?"

Adja Khady Diop
TWO POEMS
Senegal 1975   Wolof

Adja Khady Diop was born in 1922 in Dagana, in the north of Senegal. Hailing from a religious Muslim family, she began Qur'anic school at an early age before being trained in sewing, homemaking, and dyeing. Marriage did not keep her from investing further in education. She opened her own Qur'anic school and later launched a political career. Never having attended Western-style schools, she writes not in French but rather in Wolof using Arabic script. Her profound sensitivity can nevertheless be seen in her themes, which touch on the everyday experiences of ordinary people.

Khady Diop has shown, especially during the celebrations of the international year of women, in 1975, that a poetic sensibility is not the province only of men or of Western-educated people. With her special elegance, she captures in hymn form, for example, the central place of the stream that waters her region. She has created in written form a repertoire of proverbs, which everyone can consult to be reminded of the rules that regulate social life. Her poems also catalog all the trades and activities that have always fallen to women. These activities do not result in monetary gain, money being nonexistent in early societies. Nevertheless, women profited mutually from a system of exchange. By reminding Senegalese women that the activities they still engage in have been inherited from their grandmothers, Khady Diop insists on the ingenuity of the older generation, which refused to be satisfied with homemaking and participated actively in business ventures, including the creation of different kinds of weaves, such as *jalam* and *deru*, which allowed women's families to make ends meet and have helped make Senegal famous.

In her poems, Khady Diop sings of the hidden treasure of Senegal and of the ancient ways it was used. Few women have explored this subject, but Khady Diop shows by doing so how important education is in encouraging women to reflect on all that might be useful to their country. In the two poems selected here, Khady Diop reflects on technology, initially presenting Senegalese women in conventional occupations, and then celebrating a key moment of collective joy at the sight of new technology, an airplane, likening it to both a flying train and a hot-air balloon.

Rokhaya Fall

✦

THE WORK OF SENEGALESE WOMEN

Hey you, woman, what's your job?
I'm a cotton spinner and a homemaker.
    And you, what's your job?
Dyer and homemaker.
    And you?
Hair braider and homemaker.
    And you?
Tattooer and homemaker.
    And you?
I'm a seasoned healer and homemaker.
    And you?
I help women give birth, I'm a midwife and nurse.
    And you?
Hairdresser and homemaker.
    And you?
Potter and homemaker.
    Let the world know: you are good workers.
Brave women; you're any man's equal.
Bravo to our ingenious great-grandmothers,
Who carded cotton into *jalam* and *deru*.
Who made distaff and ash from wood and clay.
    When they had no cash to use, they bartered,
Importing what they couldn't find,

Exporting what they had in abundance,
Trading, bartering, and doing all they willed.
Dressing in the Dahomean style,
In gold and beads and rich imagination.

THE YEAR WE LOOKED UP AT THE BALLOON

The year the balloon first flew above us,
We heard the noise and turned our heads.
When it flew low, children ran in its wake.
All raised their eyes to see more clearly,
Saying: This is the balloon we've heard about.
It's a flying train.
Look at the flying train!
Just look at the flying train!
Until it touched down at the Diala Wali runway.
Today so many people travel by air,
The country itself is a great flying balloon.

Translated into French by Souleymane Faye
Translated from French by Judith Miller

Aoua Keïta
CONVERSATION WITH MIDWIFE SOKONA DIAOUNÉ

Mali 1975   French

As a trade unionist, politician, activist, and midwife, Aoua Keïta has been a pioneer. She has left an indelible mark on the history of Mali. She was born on 12 July 1912 in Bamako, went to the first girls' school established there in 1923, and continued her studies at the Medical School of Dakar, where she obtained a diploma in midwifery in November 1931. She worked as a midwife in Mali and Senegal. She also worked in Benin, Tanzania, China, and Vietnam.

Keïta's political life began with the 1947 creation of the Sudanese Union of Democratic African Unity (RDA). She was an active member of this party together with Dr. Daouda Diawara, whom she had married in 1935. She was a founding member and secretary general of the RDA. She entered the party's political bureau in 1958 and became a member of the assembly in 1959. In July 1959, she represented her country in Bamako at the meeting at which the Union of West African Women was constituted and, in 1962, at the Dar es Salaam Conference, which saw the birth of the Pan-African Women's Organization. She was the only woman to take part in the drafting of the Malian Marriage and Guardianship Code in 1962. In her capacity as the first woman trade unionist, she presided over the Trade-Union Congress of working women of Mali. She died on 7 May 1980.

The excerpt below comes from her autobiography, *Femme d'Afrique* (An African Woman), published in 1975. In dialogue with her friend Sokona Diaouné, Keïta reveals the differences between the traditional African and the modern Western approaches to childbirth. The conversation also includes views of education and of the preparation of girls for marriage.

Diaouné is described as a *magnamagan*, that is, a woman belonging to an inferior caste who is responsible for preparing girls for marriage. She has acquired her knowledge from her own mother, who alone is traditionally entitled to transmit it to her. When she becomes menopausal, she will be entitled to become a midwife, just like her mother, and to transmit her knowledge as a *magnamagan* to her own daughter. This, in effect, is an esoteric form of power, which entails secrets scrupulously kept by the initiated.

The dialogue between Keïta and Diaouné introduces the cultural and social world of the Soninkés, an ethnic group who live on the borders among Senegal, Mauritania, and Mali. The dialogue reveals the beliefs and rituals linked to the sex education of girls and to their preparation for womanhood. The text includes the importance of herbs (such as *n'gongo dilli* and *goyé*) in those practices. Finally, the text depicts two types of knowledge without ceding the importance of either. The friendship between the two protagonists, Keïta and Diaouné, testifies to their mutual respect for the different forms of knowledge each holds. The selection begins during a conversation between Keïta and Diaouné.

Aminata Diaw

✦

Questioning Sokona, I asked, "What's the connection between menopause and the trade of birthing babies?"

"When a woman doesn't see her period anymore, when she's no longer busy at night [to be understood as no longer having sex—*KEÏTA*], she has all the time necessary to look after births, birthing mothers, and babies. In a few years, I, too, will go live in Goumbou in order to follow my mother as she goes from village to village taking care of the women in labor. That's how I'll finish my apprenticeship and be able to take over as efficiently as possible from my mother when she passes on—which I hope is a long time off."

"But why don't you learn this with me now, right here?" I said to her. "I've trained a lot of women in Kita, Tougan, and Gao and supplied them with equipment."

"No, *Gaffouré* [a term of respect—*TRANS.*] for us Soninkes the trade has to be passed down from mother to daughter. And that's not all of it. To do this work, there are magic words that help when you massage a woman's belly, words you *toubabs* [Western-educated people—*TRANS.*] wouldn't know and wouldn't be able to teach. I prefer to be initiated by my mother who will pass on at the same time all the charms and secrets I need, just as she did when she initiated me to my current trade, which I practice to the complete satisfaction of my female clients. Nevertheless, dear Aoua, I do have something I wish to confide, but I ask you to be very discreet about it. I'd be in a lot of trouble if the birthing women of Ouagodou knew I told you."

"I'm listening Sokona; you can be sure I'll keep your secret."

"Well, then, whenever the birthing women of my region are confronted with a breech birth, or a baby coming shoulder or face first, they predict that something terrible will happen. They go to pieces, praying God and all the saints to protect women against these fetuses whose role is to kill their mothers. Considered to be bad luck, these babies are neglected. No one takes care of them. Healers and charlatans alike give out holy water, amulets, and charms to protect the mothers' lives. You hear everywhere, 'It's better to lose the water than the jar that holds it,' or 'It's better to save the container than the contents.' In other words, it's preferable to save the mother, who has a chance of having other children.

"Unfortunately, this often means that both are lost. If an infant survives, it will die within two weeks of its mother. It's a rare family that looks after orphans properly.

"The loss of blood before birth or the umbilical cord that moves into the mother's vagina are also thought to foreshadow mourning. For us, every baby that presents itself bottom, arm, or face first, all those who show their umbilical cord at the very first moment of birth are meant to die. They often take their mothers with them. But, in town I heard that you know how to fix things so that both mother and child survive. The *griotte* from Goumba Faragaba whom you saved and whose daughter is named after you talks about this everywhere she goes. Other cases, in Nara, in Kabida, in Soninke, Kebane, and Timbedrane, have given you a sensational reputation. No birthing woman here can equal it. In the name of our great friendship, I want you to teach me the secrets that the whites taught you about how to deal with these situations."

After having shared with Sokona a few explanations about these abnormal birth positions which worry every midwife, I added:

"What I've just told you is usually learned after a long training period. One usually goes to primary school in Nara and then secondary school in Bamako. And for the technical training, which is what it should be called, you have to study and pass an exam either in Dakar or in France."

"*Gaffouré*, something's not clear in what you've just said. You're saying that you have to read and write in order to take certain courses in midwifery, yet a few minutes ago you said you'd formed women who birth babies. Have those women, that you call midwives, gone to school?"

"No, Sokona. They didn't go to school. I was talking about 'village midwives' to whom I've taught hygiene in order to limit the number of accidents. I also taught them the best care for newborns: how to section and cut the umbilical cord with sterilized instruments, how to clean out the eyes to prevent infection, how to clean the baby and treat the umbilical wound, how to bathe the mother and watch over both mother and child in order to alert a clinic in case of difficulty. These well-trained and conscientious women can play an important role in our rural areas: finding out who's pregnant, gathering them together for outside consultations, watching over the birthing, and gathering information for the midwife in case of complications."

Sokona, who was listening to me very carefully, sneezed at the end of my talk. She declared: "God approves the truth of what you've just said. You didn't even put snuff in my nose—and we only sneeze spontaneously when the truth has been told!"

After these words, my friend picked up her things and left for her house, where preparing dinner and other occupations awaited her.

Left alone at my place, I began to think about everything we'd just said, especially about my friend's occupation. Since my interview with Dagnouma Coulibaly, I hadn't had the chance to speak seriously about the work of *magnamagans*. In Gao, Kita, and Kayes, I'd tried to learn more about what they do. Unfortunately, it had been impossible for me to learn the slightest detail. Because of the difference in our ages, some *magnamagans* didn't take me seriously. They limited themselves to advising me to get married again. They told me, "If you have the experience twice, you'll know as much as we do. In any case our trade can only be inherited." Others categorically told me, "You don't need to know what we do. Our work is and will remain the domain of inferior castes, people like ourselves. You're a noble descendant of Sunjata Kéita, the founder of the Mali empire. What will you do with this knowledge? Neither your rank nor your age permits you to exercise our trade. Unlike Europeans, we don't teach our children everything."

I was therefore very pleased with the idea that Sokona might provide some explanations about what she did. After so many shared secrets had confirmed our friendship, I thought I had the right to hope. And, also, I was going to make Sokona understand that I wanted to know about her work for my own information and not to make use of it in any other way. At least she would accept a discussion, which all the other birthing women had refused. We'd had the chance to speak about a variety of problems. After a chat about our romantic lives, she'd said:

"Why do you stay alone, *Gaffouré*? You know that being single is severely condemned by our religion. You're a practicing Muslim, so you must get remarried. You have a fine choice: all the leaders of this canton, all the rich businessmen, all the bureaucrats would like to have you as their wife."

At the time, I'd told Sokona the following: "Yes, I know, dear friend. I know I'm somewhat disobeying Muslim law and that it isn't very nice for a woman to live alone in a town such as Nara. However, I have no intention of getting married here. Besides, I've given my word to a man I love very much. I want to marry him, if God wills it."

Because we'd been this intimate, I made the firm resolution to get as much information about her trade as I could from Sokona.

A few days after the festival, Sokona came to tell me she was leaving for her native village, Goumbou. She stayed there for almost two weeks, during which she told her mother about the latest troubles in her marriage. At the same time, she inquired about how many girls had come of age and what would be the dates for their marriage ceremonies. All the girls who had started menstruating that year were considered to be of age. Sokona's mother, who was responsible for initiating three-quarters of the girls of Goumbou, was beginning to be tired because of her age. And we mustn't forget that she was also the woman who did all the local birthings.

Sokona was anxious when she came to say good-bye. I wished her a good trip, an excellent stay in Goumbou, special good luck, and a little calm. I gave her several small presents for her mother and her daughter. The daughter was married to someone in a village a few kilometers from Goumbou.

When she returned, my friend came right to my house and we took up our lively conversation where we had left off. That's how we came, one Sunday, to speak about her visit to Goumbou, her new work, and her trade as *magnamagan*.

The trip to Goumbou had eased her mind. Her mother had offered her the same advice as I and had given her several charms. The marriage situation was developing in her favor. Her husband had stopped going so often to the Arab encampments. He was paying more attention to his business, his herds, and the upkeep of his properties. He was being exceptionally sweet to her, although she was still unmoved. "He gets on my nerves," she told me. "I won't abandon our home, as you and my mother suggested. However, I can't possibly share my man with that garbage. Even though she's disappeared, my husband still makes me sick. Besides, I hardly have time to look after him."

It was true that April and May were periods of intense activity for Sokona and her *magnamagan* colleagues. In the vast canton of Ouagadou, made up of more than forty villages, all marriages happened within the first few days of the month of June. Sokona, who had twenty girls and four women to initiate, had no time for boredom. In addition, she wanted to help out her mother, whom as I'd said earlier had started to lose some of her strength. This was possible as the wedding ceremonies of Goumbou and Nara, the most important towns of the Ouagodou canton, never took place at the same time.

On the last Sunday of May 1954, Sokona arrived at my house as usual between 12:15 and 12:30. Her normal baskets full of cotton or grain had been replaced by a brand new basket, in quite a different shape, and holding an industrial quantity of *n'gongo dilli* [very thin roots about thirty or forty centimeters long—*TRANS.*]. These roots are from a special grass that grows on the banks of waterways. The best ones come from the banks of the greatest rivers. *N'gongo dilli* roots from Bafoulabé, Kayes, and Segou are the most sought after for their quality: they're recognizable by their odor. *Magnamagans* roll them so that they stand up to boiling and to wear and tear. Sokona also had a huge spindle covered with thread, which she had manufactured. It was a soft, thick cotton thread that breaks fairly easily.

"What are you doing with all that *n'gongo-dilli*, my friend?"

"I'm preparing it for future brides. I have twenty-four to look after. Wouldn't you like to be the twenty-fifth and profit from my expertise? The wedding season is approaching and, according to the soothsayers, it's going to be a good year. The clarity of the morning star predicts happiness and prosperity for those who get married this year," she added, laughing good-naturedly.

"I'm all for being part of the group in such a propitious year. You can initiate me while we wait for my future husband to show up."

"That's not only difficult; it's impossible, Aoua! A *magnamagan* can't just do anything! First, you have to realize that what we do is different according to the region. To the east and the north of Mali, a girl's initiation begins the day of her wedding. During the first seven days, it consists only of telling her about the most sensitive parts of a man's body. You teach her some movements and caresses. But she is subject to no discipline whatsoever. To the south and in the center, that's to say in your part of the country, where there are Bambaras, Malinkes, Miankas, Bobos, and other ethnic groups, I'm told there isn't even that much preparation. The day after the wedding, the bride sinks or swims: housework, meals, washing. Preparation for marriage, or should I say love, is only practiced by the Pulaar people, the Kassonkes, and the Sarakoles. Naturally the Sarakoles hold the record. Everyone knows that Bamako's best *magnamagans* are either Sarakole, or from the Sarakole region, or trained by Sarakoles. If I tell you it will be hard to train you, *Gaffouré*, I do have my reasons. Because, when we do it right, marriage initiation is done in two separate phases."

Looking all around the dispensary, Sokona asked:

"Are we really alone? Can I speak frankly without worrying about being interrupted by a third person?"

"We are all alone," I answered. "Except for the women in labor and any relatives that might stop by without warning us, nobody will come in today."

Nevertheless, to be safe, I went to ask the cook to make sure that no one bothered us. She was living in one of the houses connected to the dispensary and from her doorway could see if anyone approached my doorstep.

"Just tell anybody who comes that I'm taking a nap, Kiberé."

Having taken those precautions, I went back to Sokona who, seeing that I had a notebook and pen in hand, said:

"I won't tell you a word if you plan on writing it down."

She took up her handiwork again and started braiding a handful of roots.

I quickly put my things down, went back to Sokona, and promised her to write nothing.

After a moment in which she seemed to assess the situation, she began again: "In the Sarakole tradition, marriage initiation is done in two separate phases."

The First Phase: "From the beginning of the cold season, which begins after the harvest, that is toward the end of November or the beginning of December, all the girls of around fourteen or fifteen who have a serious boyfriend—and they all do—must be initiated to love.

"That period when new things are flourishing everywhere corresponds to the rest period for farmers. Young people of both sexes take advantage of the time off to organize folk dances and singing every evening. At the end of all these festivities, the girls who are meant to marry in the course of the year gather together at their respective *magnamagans'* homes. You should know that the first visit of each young girl to her *magnamagan* is also chaperoned by an aunt. In the following days, knowing both the route and what they can expect at the beginning of the rainy season, they come alone but willingly. Of course you can guess that from December until March I have to chase away the young men who lurk near by. After that, the girls only come twice a month.

"This year's group of girls began their initiation in early December. Each morning, four large container gourds, made especially for the circumstances, are filled with fresh water. These containers, which you have certainly seen, are placed in a shed with a thatched roof that I have rebuilt each year. In the evening around six o'clock I make a porridge of flour and millet which I place in four wooden platters and leave out in the fresh air, either on the roof of the shed or somewhere else that is well-ventilated. As soon as the drums stop, all the girls who have the same initiator go to her house. That's usually around ten o'clock. Between ten and twelve, my students work for me: kneading cotton, separating grains, preparing indigo.

"When it is the middle of the night, I separate the girls into four groups. Seated in the middle, I make them take a cold shower. With the stems of a long grass which grows everywhere around here, I make brooms with very thick heads. I use one broom per group, and I dip the head in the fresh water I've collected, which I shake out in the direction of the girls. That's how they get a shower of cold drops which fall on their bodies like fine rain.

"These brooms have to be made by the *magnamagan* who must gather the grass for them while it is still green. She aligns the stems and then bunches them together while reciting magic words. The drops of water come from the containers that have been exposed all night long to the wind and are thus as cold as the water that comes from the doctor's machine [an oil-fueled refrigerator—KEÏTA].

"I keep this up until there is no more water in the gourds. As you know, it's excessively cold in Nara from December to March. So with the help of the wind from the north, all the girls start to tremble from their heads to their toes. In that state and without any clothing on, they eat the porridge, which is also very cold. They use their right index finger for eating. And exposed to the wind and frozen on the inside, they keep on trembling and rattling their teeth.

"We go through this every night until about one o'clock in the morning until the end of March. The process lasts about four months—or four moons. This is followed by another, which consists in the imbibing and then evacuation (as called upon) of n'gongo dilli, which the initiator begins to boil from the time of the call for the two o'clock prayer. My students only come twice a month for these lessons. We go through a trial period in which the magnamagan, playing the husband, fondles the student to make sure she has learned what she needs to from her five months of training. If it works as it should, the initiate begins to move as though she'd just been doused by a cold shower."

The Second Phase: "The wedding takes place on Thursday night, so from Monday afternoon, the future bride is purged and put on a special diet: only liquids morning and evening. At noon, she can eat grilled meat (chicken or guinea hen—no duck as it has too much fat). This diet is meant to purify and weaken. It seems that some twenty years ago, young girls were so strong that their resistance made the first attempts at sex very difficult. That explains the help that magnamagans used to bring to the grooms. But, with the way our country has evolved and the new under-standing of young people, that kind of help now seems scandalous and has almost completely disappeared in urban environments."

Sokona went on with her description: "So the day of the marriage itself, the magnamagan doesn't have a lot to do. One of the sisters of the groom, in charge of all the ceremonies, sets down a brand new woven mat on a portion of the earthen floor, which must be completely dry. The mat has to be placed on seeds, which must start to show growth by the end of the seventh day. The magnamagan covers the mat with a white cotton cloth, burns a lot of incense, and completes her work by placing white mosquito netting over the bedding. Everything must be new. Because the bride is usually very tired and not feeling very well after the first day's contact, the training she has had with the magnamagan only goes into effect in the following days.

"In Sarakole traditions, the young married couple doesn't sleep on a bed or a raised platform. They spend the first seven days on the mat I described earlier under mosquito netting. The bride keeps to her 80 percent liquid diet. For breakfast, she has a gruel of pounded millet with *goyé* and cooked with *n'gongo dilli*. For dinner, she eats almost nothing, just a little porridge. And from two o'clock, she drinks a huge amount of *n'gongo dilli* tea. This diuretic infusion contains a perfume that deodorizes urine. The bride is allowed to urinate all day and up until after the evening meal, which is eaten by Sarakole people at around 8:30. After that, she must not urinate, but she must keep drinking tea. When she has sex, she will then release in short streams what's in her bladder; this clear urine, as clear as stream water, is nothing like normal urine. On the morning of the eighth day, the sister who set up the wedding mat will pick it up. She should find that the seeds have begun to sprout. And in that case it means the *magnamagan's* training has been successful. If this isn't the case, the *magnamagan* loses her reputation. No family will ever give their daughters over to her again.

"The initiator should follow the brides during the first twelve months of their marriages—if they are all in the same village. If not, the initiator should go see her students as often as she can or send them the products they need: incense, *goyé*, rolled *n'gongo dilli*, charms for around her waist, etc.

"Among the presents offered to the bride by her parents, there should always be two or three pairs of thick silver bracelets. These hollow but noisy bracelets, which a woman wears to bed, play an important role during the sex act. The intense trembling of the body causes the bracelets to knock against each other and produces a noise that is tremendously exciting to Sarakole men, who really respond to it. In fact, I've come to think that men used to this kind of shaking, to teeth chattering, to streams of perfumed liquid and all the rest, might find it difficult to be with women from other regions who haven't been initiated to these practices. That's how I explain why our men hesitate to take wives from the east and center of our country."

Taking advantage of my friend's sudden silence, I said:

"One question, please, Sokona."

"What is it?" she asked.

"The four women who are part of the marriage group this year, must they follow the same rules as the young girls?"

"I only watch over them for the first three days. As you should know, they don't have a seven-day ceremony."

Continuing her account, she said to me pointing to her basket: "There's the *n'gongo dilli*. Today I must braid it. I need a large roll for each new bride. If the roots are of good quality, each roll can be used two or three times. If not, they'll need two or three rolls a day because the infusion gets made in enormous quantities. That's all the bride drinks."

Sokona started working again. Seeing her lips moving, I asked her: "Can you say aloud your magic words, so I can know them?"

"Oh, no, Aoua!" She answered vehemently, putting down the roll she had just finished. "Such things are only passed on from mother to daughter. I only have the right to transmit this to my own daughter when she'll be older than thirty-five. If I die before then, it's my mother who will teach her. If my mother dies before my daughter reaches the correct age, well, the secret will die for our family—as I don't have a blood sister who could teach her. You see, my friend, our trade is as tiring as any other and has its own secrets that we must know how to keep. Our luck is that we start in December and finish in June, leaving us free to work the fields. I also have to prepare incense for the wedding chambers. And to make a good incense, you have to have a mixture of products that aren't all that easy to find. Some come from Mauritania, others from Bamako, Kayes, or Nioro. The hardest to work with is *goyé*, which you have to pound after wetting it in order to remove the outside, then you have to sift it to separate the seeds from the bran, then turn this into very fine powder by crushing it between polished stones. I spend long hours at the market on fair days trying to locate all these products."

Sokona got up and said: "It's late Aoua. I have to go home; I still have a lot to do. I have to get dinner and take care of all those things I've just spoken about."

"Just one more question," I dared.

"I'm listening."

"Haven't you ever had an accident with those girls who have to undergo such rigorous treatment?"

"What kind of accident?"

"Fever, cold, cough, pneumonia, for example?"

"No, Aoua, this treatment, which you call rigorous, isn't so hard for a self-respecting Sarakole girl who wants to hold on to her husband. Naturally there are girls who fall ill and are cured during the initiation period. Some die. It's completely normal: everyone has her destiny. If it's written that a girl should go to God rather than to her marriage bed, then that's what happens. No one can do anything about it. Even the *toubab* doctors can't stop a girl from dying if she's been called by the Almighty."

Translated by Judith Miller

RURAL POEMS

Ndeye Seck and Khadi Diop are rural Senegalese women whose poems appear in a volume called *Hearts in Distress,* published by Tostan, an American non-governmental agency that works in Senegal to provide basic education to women in rural areas. Newly literate women, encouraged to express themselves, often write remarkable poetry.

Both of the poems reprinted here evoke the painful financial crises of the 1970s, when men were forced to leave African villages and cities to seek work in the cities of Europe and the United States, leaving women alone and struggling to provide for their families' needs. Not surprisingly, the women often had to seek employment and thus compete with the remaining men for paid work. In "Tribute to *Yaxa ma Jam* Women," Khadi Diop praises women who have managed during this difficult period to support their own families—without the help of men—by going into the fishing business. These women have chosen the Wolof expression "*yaxa ma jam*"—literally, "I have been pricked by a fish bone"—as the name of their business association. In the poem, Diop alludes to the possible return of their husbands from "America or Italy," and imagines that they will "respect" and "value" their wives' work. *Ndeysaan* is a conversational Wolof expression of sympathy. She also mentions *gongo*, incense that she imagines that these fisherwomen will use in order, once again, to seduce their husbands. *Ethmaloses* are bony fish.

In "Emigration Terrifies Me," Ndeye Seck writes of the painful process of separating from her husband when he emigrated in search of work. In the men's absence, beyond even the daily requirements of food, clothing, and shelter, women worried about the inevitable expenses involved in preparing for two of the most significant Muslim celebrations, the *Korite*, a ritual that ends the Ramadan month of fasting, and the *Tabaski*, the Festival of the Sheep, which commemorates Abraham's sacrifice. For these events, women prepare special meals and give gifts to their children. Both children and adults are supposed to wear new clothes and visit their relatives and neighbors. Although the expenses are high, the personal honor and dignity of women demand that they fulfill these responsibilities, even if their husbands have not kept their promises and have, in fact, sent no money. The untranslatable word "*Ndeketeyoo*" expresses this painful situation.

Aminata Diaw

✦

Khadi Diop, TRIBUTE TO *YAXA MA JAM* WOMEN

Senegal 1975   Wolof

Awakening early in the morning
On their way to work,
Nourished by their sweet [memories]
Fulfilling their needs,
They refuse the condescending sympathy
Of the *Ndeysaan*.

What a delightful sight to see them when the canoes reach ashore
Fighting with men for their catch,
Definitely the bony *ethmaloses* there,
And with their bleeding hands

Extracting fish bones.
Keeping on with their work
With courage and dignity,
Not going back home
Until the end of the day.
No woman ever surpasses them.
At times a firebrand would
Take away the fruits of their labor
And disappear with the wind
Toward America or Italy.

How brave you are!
And your men respect you.
They acknowledge your value
And your subtle fragrance of *gongo*.
How much I love you.
How much I admire you,
Women of *Yaxa Ma Jam*.

Ndeye Seck, EMIGRATION TERRIFIES ME

Senegal 1990   Wolof

Never will I forget the night
When my husband told me that
He's to emigrate.
I panicked when thinking about loneliness
And our young children.
Then he attempted to assure me that
He will just go and return
With invaluable riches
For our happiness rather than our life of misery.
What a heavy load is this exile for me!

Never will I forget
The day my husband said farewell to us,
The fateful moment of departure
When faith was my only rampart,
My flooding tears,
And kids weeping around me,
And him trying to reassure us with nice words,
"It will not last long," he kept saying,
"I will come back as soon as I get rich."

Then adding, "You, my honey,
Be courageous,
Keep your ears shut to bad omens,
Your eyes shut to temptations,
Just don't move, take care of the house,
It will not last long.
I will be back as soon as I get rich."
Ndeketeyoo, a turned head meant a turned page.
As soon as he left he forgot me.

Damned exile!
Here I am destroyed and my family disintegrated.
When will this suffering end?
Neither my letter answered nor my body remembered,
My man has forgotten me,
Forgotten my children,
And I am running here and there for lunch and for dinner,

For clothes and shoes,
Selling in all marketplaces during nights and days.
I have no energy, no patience left,
But I do not want to be dishonored.

No more sleep at night,
Turning over and over in my bed until the morning,
And the worst still comes during the traditional ceremonies
Of *Korite* and *Tabaski*
When kids long after white *boubous,*
Brand new shoes and the big horned ram
And Dad to slaughter it
Emigrated for my desolation.

Oh! I do not know about your life any longer
But whatever it may be, it is not unknown to Allah.
Neither is my desolation unknown to Him.
Those who are expecting and hoping for my shame
May God make them always be disappointed.
May He never let them trample me underfoot.
May God always keep me pure
Preserve me from any sin.

Translated into French by Souleymane Faye
Translated from French by Christiane Owusu-Sarpong and Esi Sutherland-Addy

Buchi Emecheta
A Necessary Evil

Nigeria 1977   English

A consummate storyteller who trusted her instinct early in her career to write about the lives of African women, Buchi Emecheta enjoys an international reputation as a prolific and gifted writer. She was born in Lagos, Nigeria, on 21 July 1944, to Jeremy and Alice Emecheta. Allowed few choices as a girl growing up in a male-dominated culture, the young Emecheta developed a strong sense of individualism that signaled a desire to defy traditional assumptions about women's subservient position in the society. Determined to receive a university education, she made a successful push to join her brother in elementary school and devised other creative strategies that won her a scholarship to the Methodist Girls' High School. Facing new obstacles, Emecheta decided to marry Sylvester Onwordi, a schoolmate who seemed to embody the promise of an enlightened and secure future. Pressing for an advantage in this regard, at age sixteen, she eloped with him to circumvent a high bride-price of five hundred pounds.

In 1962, Emecheta traveled to London to join her husband, who had left the previous year to pursue further studies. Four years later, the marriage broke down, leaving Emecheta with the biggest challenge of her life. Single, broke, and culturally alienated, she was hardly prepared to raise five children, the eldest only six years old, but she responded to this shocking jolt of reality with characteristic stamina and ingenuity, using adversity as a springboard for a writing career and advancing her education. In 1972, she published her first novel, *In the Ditch,* and two years later she received a Bachelor of Arts in sociology from London University. With the publication of *Second Class Citizen* (1975), which won the Daughter of Mark Twain award, Emecheta began to capture the attention of the literary world. *The Bride Price* (1976) and *The Slave Girl* (1977) reinforced readers' admiration of her work, but for her more fastidious critics, *The Joys of Motherhood* (1979) was the clearest indication of a superior artistic ability. Her corpus grew to include other well-known titles, such as *Destination Biafra* (1982), *Double Yoke* (1985), *Gwendolyn* (1989, published in the United States as *The Family*), and *Kehinde* (1994). *The Rape of Shavi* (1983), a feminist utopian novel, has surprisingly escaped critical attention, while the recently published work *The New Tribe* (2000) awaits evaluation.

As this chapter from *The Slave Girl* illustrates, Emecheta's fiction rightfully commands a respectful presence in feminist and postcolonial studies. Set in the turbulent years between 1910 and 1945 in Nigeria's Iboland, the novel approaches women's social value through the taboo subject of slavery. Courageously, Emecheta takes on the continuation of domestic slavery within Nigeria, long after it was officially abolished and prohibited by the British colonial masters. Equally important, her central goal is to explore the context for the domestic drama: an economy and society controlled by British and "Christian" colonial policies and interests that directly governed the fate of all Nigerians in the first half of the twentieth century. The excerpt's dark satire captures the narrative intensity with which the author records the neglected histories of women and the nation.

Tuzyline Jita Allan

◆

It was now past midday, and it was still very hot. The sun was shifting from the centre of the sky to one side. Okolie was thankful that when they had met Eze at Asaba he had at least given Ojebeta some food. She yawned and stretched like a tired cat, and he kept assuring her that their relatives would soon come. Thirsty, Okolie asked the girls for some water. One of them went to fetch a big green bottle which they kept under one of the benches away from the sun and poured some water into a white bowl with a blue rim for him to drink. He admired the smoothness of the bowl, rubbing his rough farm fingers all over it, then gulped down the cool liquid and asked for more. The girls started to giggle again; these girls laughed at everything, he thought. He could not, however, finish the second bowl so he gave the rest of the water to his sister.

Ojebeta noticed that the water here tasted different, as if something had been added to it. She was about to ask her brother about it when they heard a group of laughing female voices approaching. One of the girls called in a voice so low, so urgent and so sibilantly formed that Ojebeta thought something terrible must be about to happen:

"Chiago, Nwayinuzo—shh . . . shh . . . They are coming. They are coming. . . ."

At once heads were once more bent to work. The big girl called Chiago stood with the wooden cloth measure in her hand like a soldier on guard, almost behind Okolie and his sister. The owners of the jocular voices were still hidden by a stall that jutted into the middle of the passageway. Many other people came and went. Ojebeta was silent in expectation. Okolie's stomach started to rumble in apprehension.

They heard the leave-takings and farewells; and then a very big lady appeared from around the corner—a lady who was tall of bearing, a lady who was very proud. She had a large, very sensuous mouth, and the laughter was still on her lips. She was also the most well dressed person Ojebeta had ever seen. She was wearing a brown *abada* with fish patterns on it, a yellow blouse, and silk scarf on her head. She walked with easy steps, saying hello to this stall and how-do-you-do to that person. She seemed to know everybody and they responded to her warmth.

"There she is," said Chiago unnecessarily under her breath, while keeping a straight face and not looking in the direction of the woman who was their owner.

At last Ma Palagada strolled into her stall and greeted them fulsomely.

"Oh, oh—have you been waiting for me long? Why did you not tell the girls to come for me? I was at a meeting with the U.A.C. people. Welcome!

Welcome! Have they given you something to eat? Is this the little sister you talked about? Welcome. Oh, my! She is just a baby. For her to have lost everyone. . . . Still, God knows best. Welcome!"

A velveteen cushion on a bench was plumped up for her to sit on. Okolie watched and answered her in monosyllables, indicating that, no, they had not eaten anything: the girls had not known who he was.

At this Ma Palagada laughed; it was not a very loud sound but it had a mellow richness in it. It was the laughter of the well fed, the laughter of someone who had not known for a very long time what it was to be hungry. "We shall soon take care of that. These thoughtless girls should have given you something."

She looked down again at Ojebeta, appraising her from head to foot, then called her to come to her.

Ojebeta did not want to go and she clung to her brother. It was not that she did not like her relative but that the whole show was just too sudden for the poor child. What did this woman want with her? She might be a relative, but Ojebeta had never seen her before; moreover, she did not look like any relative she had ever seen before. All this cloth on her stall and the amount she had on herself, and her way of speaking the Ibo language—Ojebeta was overwhelmed. No, she did not want to go to her.

It was at this point that she had the first clue of what was in store for her, for here something like suppressed anger escaped from her brother. His voice was direct and businesslike, almost as if he were someone who did not know who she was, a stranger to her. Ojebeta was so startled that she burst into tears and called out:

"My mother, please come to me, I am lost!"

Ma Palagada was moved and told Okolie to be gentle with his sister. "Come," she urged Ojebeta, "I only want to greet you. You haven't even said a single word to me. Come. I am your relative, you know. Come. You mustn't be frightened of us. We are not bad people. Just come here. . . ."

Okolie pulled and half carried Ojebeta to the lady who, with a smile on her face, felt her arms and peered into her eyes, then smiled again and asked, "Are you hungry?"

Ojebeta was a child brought up with so much love and so much trust that it never occurred to her to distrust a smiling face. Her tears had been a reaction to this new voice she heard her brother whom she had known all her life use to her; now the voice had stopped. She nodded her head vigorously up and down like a mad lizard. Yes, of course she was hungry.

She heard the other girls giggling again. Now what had she done? Ojebeta wondered in bewilderment, hating the smallest girl who sniggered the most. She felt like fighting that girl, for she was not much bigger than herself, but she ignored her and kept on nodding.

"You shall have some food," Ma Palagada said. "Chiago, go to the food stalls and buy Ogbanje—is that your name?—buy her a piece of *agidi* from those people from Accra. Have you eaten their *agidi* before? It is very nice."

Ojebeta nodded once more; she had tasted "*agidi Akala*," as her dead mother used to call it. On the days her mother used to go to Onitsha she would buy one large piece, and Ojebeta and all her friends and her father would sit up and wait for her to come home from Otu, just to have their little bits of Accra *agidi*. In those days it had been a real delicacy for her; and now she was once more going to have some to eat, her mouth watered like a dog's. Ma Palagada gave some money to the big girl Chiago, who ran among the other stalls, turned a corner and disappeared into the market. They all waited. More customers came. Okolie and Ma Palagada talked blatant nothings to gain time. Sitting away from her brother, apart from the other girls, Ojebeta thought of her mother, her father, of the "*agidi Akala*" she was going to have.

Chiago soon arrived with the corn dough steaming. It was the first time Ojebeta had seen it hot, for the *agidi* her mother used to buy was always cold by the time she reached home from the market. She watched Chiago peeling the wrapping leaves off and putting them into another white bowl.

"Do you want pepper on it?" asked Chiago then.

Ma Palagada, who had seemed to be unaware of the goings on, intervened: "Let her do it the way she wants. Give her the pepper and salt. She can spice it herself."

So Chiago handed Ojebeta the whitest and the best *agidi* she had ever seen in her life. At first Ojebeta did not know what to do. Should she eat it all, or share it with the others, her brother in particular?

Okolie saw her dilemma and said, with his mouth watering, "Eat it, it's all for you."

Ojebeta could not believe her ears. The other girls did not even look as if they were at all interested. Why, in her home five people would have shared this, for *agidi* was regarded as something special, not heavy enough to be everyday food. She did the only thing that she felt was right: she scooped one big handful and gave it to her brother. The latter looked this way and that way, felt ashamed and said with little heart:

"No, my sister, you eat it. Your relative bought it for you."

That was strange, thought Ojebeta. But if Okolie had gone off his food, what of the new relative she had just acquired, who had been kind enough to buy all this hot *agidi* with fresh pepper and salt? She walked up to her with the innocence of a child who had never been taught to fear adults and said, "Have some, it's nice." Ma Palagada smiled, called her a good little girl but said that she had eaten; they had had their midday meal before she went to the meeting. So Ojebeta could eat it all. She hurried back to the bench and, sitting with her head bent to one side, busied herself with her day's good luck—a whole piece of *agidi Akala* to herself.

Ma Palagada and Okolie talked and talked in voices so low that Ojebeta did not bother to make any attempt to find out what they were saying. It was too much of an effort, and besides what did it matter at the moment. So immersed was she in the *agidi* that she scarcely heard her brother announce:

"I am going to the food stalls to eat some pounded yam. I shall not be long."

Ojebeta looked up and nodded.

"I will show you the way," Ma Palagada said casually to Okolie. "Chiago, take care of the stall. I shall not be long."

"Yes, Ma," said Chiago.

Ojebeta went on scooping the *agidi* into her mouth, showing it off as she did so to the youngest girl, whom she had heard them refer to as Amanna. But Amanna did not even seem to envy her, and instead laughed each time Ojebeta scooped the food up. The urge to fight this cheeky girl was becoming strong, though once more she managed to ignore her while polishing the bowl with her fingers, at the same time making a great deal of noise with her mouth. It had been a delicious meal and Ojebeta was now full; though the last bit had been cold and not as tasty as when she first started it, she finished it all.

Now she looked about her, pleased with the world. The other girls still giggled, but she had decided to take no notice of their foolish behaviour. She sat perched on the wooden bench by the edge of the stall so that she would be the first to catch a glimpse of her brother and Ma Palagada when they showed up eventually. She watched people come in and out of the stall and was fascinated by the fast method the girl Chiago used to mend torn clothes, for she had never before seen a sewing machine. She wished she too could have a go at the black monster with yellow patterns on it. When Chiago wound it, it made sounds as if it was singing, and after it sang on each piece of cloth they came out stitched together so well and so quickly. This way, she noticed, it was not necessary to use needles like her mother had used for sewing tears in her cloth.

After Ojebeta had watched this for a while, the longing for her brother and for them to be going home from the market began to increase. She could see that some other people were already starting to leave. Yet Ma Palagada's girls sat there, doing their sewing, intermittently singing scraps of song, but looking as if they were willing to wait the whole day if necessary. Ojebeta was fed up of waiting. The sweet sensation the hot *agidi* had given her was fast evaporating and giving way to a kind of boredom, tinged somewhat with rebellion. Not wanting to ask the permission of these unfriendly strangers, she scrambled up from her seat, determined to go and find her brother. Had he not promised Uteh's husband that they would be back home before the evening meal? Well, it was fast approaching sundown and she knew they had a very long trek ahead of them. She then realised how tired her feet were, but the urge to go home was far more pressing than her need to give in to fatigue.

As she took a few steps from the stall, the girls looked at her and all of a sudden stopped their endless chatter. Chiago was the first to find her tongue.

"Where are you going, little girl from Ibuza?"

"I am going to look for my brother," came the unpolished reply.

For once the other girls did not laugh at her. Only Amanna made a slight tittering sound but was quickly hushed by Chiago's stern glance. The latter was thinking fast to herself: *Poor parentless child. They probably did not tell her. She probably does not know she may never see her brother again. Poor girl.*

Aloud she said, not without pity, "Come back, little Ibuza girl. Your big brother will soon be here. Come back, or you will get lost in the market, and the child-catchers from the coast will take you away in their canoes. Come back."

Ojebeta stood and looked at her for a moment, wondering why the child-catchers should want to take her away. She had, it was true, heard stories of people going missing even in Ibuza, but that such a fate could befall her was beyond belief. After all, she was only going to get her brother, over there round the corner. She would run faster than any child-catcher in the world, and once she had found her big brother Okolie who would dare catch her?

"Will my 'little father' be here soon?" she asked, seeking further reassurance.

"Of course he will. What have we been telling you?" replied Chiago, her eyes averted.

Ojebeta did not know what came over her then, except that it was connected with her having been brought up by simple people who looked you straight in the eye because they had nothing to hide. The way this big girl spoke to her, the way the others all at once seemed to be made of mechanical wood, working without feeling at their work and not daring to look at her, made her uneasy. She did not want to wait to find out what they were being so cagey about; all she wanted was her brother and for them both to go back home to Ibuza, where her aunt Uteh would be waiting for her with pounded yam and palm soup and little crabs from the Oboshi stream. All the girls were seemingly engrossed in their sewing, and she told herself that they were not watching her. She knew where her brother Okolie was—just round the corner, at the stalls of the food sellers. If she ran that way she would surely find him, still sitting there eating yam and stew. She would find him, before these girls ever caught up with her. She would find him. . . .

And just like a hunter's arrow that had been quivering impatiently in its bow while the hunter covered his prey until the opportune moment to let fly, so did Ogbanje Ojebeta dash out of the Palagada cloth stall. She ran, almost flew like an arrow, her little legs like wings, her heart beating fast in fear and anticipation, going as she thought to her brother—her brother, the only person she knew in this market full of strange people, the only person who would take her home to their town, the only person who had brought her here. She made music with her metal charms and cowries as she ran to meet him. She was an unusual sight among the sophisticated, rich, fat mammy traders who formed the backbone of Onitsha market.

"If I can't find him, my big brother," she said to herself as she ran, "I shall go back to Ibuza to the hut of my big mother and wait for him."

But it was to be an abortive attempt at freedom.

At the end of the line of cloth stalls was a very big one belonging to a fat mammy called Ma Mee, who was one of the richest Onitsha marketwomen at the time. She, like Ma Palagada, had a double stall, but her twin stalls curved into the pathway, almost blocking the way from the riverside. Hers was a corner site, and the fact that she occupied this privileged position had been the cause of a great deal of backbiting and bickering among the other cloth traders, particularly the smaller fry who had only a single stall. They said that it was because of Ma Mee's advantageous placing that she sold more cloth than the rest of them put together. They said that her situation made it possible for her to see prospective buyers coming up from the canoes; they said that very few customers passed through her stalls without buying anything. But, as often happens in like circumstances, no one could bring themselves to tell her to her face. Ma Mee had been in the selling business for a long time. She knew that people talked among themselves, for from time to time some of the hurtful things others said about her did reach her ears. But she reasoned to herself, "If I go about challenging all the things people say about me, who will be my friend? For whoever I challenge about spiteful things they are said to have said about me, that person will deny it, and I will only have added one more enemy to the list I already have." So she behaved as if the gossip did not exist, and this spirit endeared her to many other traders who consequently came to regard her as having great maturity. In fact in avoiding the trouble of having open enemies, she was simply being prudent, for there were occasions when each trader needed the goodwill of the others, for example when robbers—well aware that the cloth stalls contained valuable materials and belonged mainly to a few wealthy and privileged women—would organise themselves for raids. But if one stall could raise the alarm and the thief was seen, God have mercy on his soul. These were women who did not have time for the police; they could not afford to lose a day's trade by going to a court or going to see a chief. They invariably dealt with the culprit in the way they themselves thought fit.

The same fate awaited any runaway domestic slave. Many of the market women had slaves in great number to help them with the fetching and carrying that went with being a full-time trader—and also in the vain hope that one day the British people at the coast would go and some of these house slaves could be sold abroad, just as their fathers and grandfathers had done, so profitably that the abundance of capital and property they had built could still be seen in many families round Onitsha and Bonny and Port Harcourt.

On this hot afternoon, a tiresome and very hungry Igbo beggar of a fisherman had caught a sizeable thorn fish which he had brought to the prosperous cloth sellers. He had expected to sell it at a higher price than

Ma Mee was offering, and because he was anxious for the extra money to take home to the hinterland to feed his needy family he stayed on and was haggling and haggling. Ma Mee was really beginning to pity him and the unfortunate fish that was still alive, wriggling its body and fighting desperately for air. Although its protective thorns could be deadly to an enemy and were all spread out in its fruitless struggle to free itself, the fisherman did not want to kill it outright for he could show prospective buyers that it had just been caught and, better than just fresh, was still alive. The fisherman became more despondent as Ma Mee would not agree to the price he wanted and as he saw that the fish's resistance was growing more feeble, whether because it now realised it was fighting a losing battle or because of the effects of having been out of the water for so long on such a hot afternoon. He stopped dangling the fish on the powerful wire which he had strung through its open mouth, and was summoning up the courage to touch its slimy body, at the same time as Ma Mee was beginning to feel compelled to buy it from him, when they all—the fisherman, Ma Mee and the girl slaves who had been passive throughout the preceding argument—heard the cries of alarm of the girls at Ma Palagada's stalls.

Everyone's first involuntary reaction was to look for a club, a knife, even the wooden measuring stick, to arm themselves with ready to fight to protect their own territory, as it were. They all dashed out, led by the poor fisherman who wanted to play the role of a gallant man preserving the women from robbers.

Ma Mee was a big woman, so big that she never stopped perspiring. But there were certain happenings which appeared to make her weightless: happenings such as market thieves and runaways. For if you did not help your neighbour in such a situation, the day the same trouble befell you, people would turn a blind eye rather than offer assistance; it was an unwritten law among the traders on the banks of the Niger. So, tightening her voluminous *lappa* round her substantial posterior, her breasts heaving in unison to her great haste, she rushed forward prepared to do battle with and if necessary maim this market thief causing the outcry, if she could lay hands on whoever it was, for daring to go into her absent colleague's stall.

However, it was not a market thief that they saw; it was a sight so peculiar that people simply stared bemused as it sped past their stalls—Chiago tearing along the pathway chasing a small, helpless and terrified child: a little girl festooned with bells and cowrie shells, just like a slave prepared for sacrifice! They stared, and did not understand.

Chiago's cries soon put them in the picture.

"Hold her! Please hold her for me, she is new—hold her!"

But she did not look at all like any slave girl Ma Mee had ever seen before, this little creature who more or less ran into her arms for protection and cried out:

"Oh, my mother, I am lost."

For a split second, Ma Mee held her, as she would have embraced her very own child; then she let go of the fugitive but still barred her way with her great bulk.

"You are not lost, little girl with pagan charms," she replied. "You are just a domestic slave."

Almost fainting with that kind of disappointment and sense of unfairness which is sometimes inexplicable, Ojebeta the only living daughter of Umeadi cried out once more in despair, this time to her dead mother:

"Save me, Mother, for now I am lost."

Unable to go forward past Ma Mee, she had no alternative but to allow herself to be caught by her pursuer.

"Let me go, let me go!" Ojebeta screamed as she wriggled violently in the hands of Chiago, the biggest of the Palagada girls.

Chiago would have held Ojebeta gently except that she knew it was likely to have resulted in real trouble for herself. So she gripped her tightly, masking her pity for this parentless child by explaining unnecessarily to the crowd, and especially to Ma Mee, that Ojebeta had only just arrived that very afternoon.

Ma Mee did not envy her neighbour for having four girl slaves; and this new little one would bring the total number of Palagada slaves to seven, since they also had two male slaves who had been bought or captured—she was not quite sure of the story—from among the people called the Urhobos. It was said that Pa Palagada had bought the men from some Potokis who were leaving the country and returning to their own land. The two, who were young boys at the time, could not remember where they had originally come from, so they were given Ibo names and were put to work on the Palagada farms. Sometimes Ma Palagada would bring to the Otu market the big yams that these two hardworking and now hefty men had produced. So as far as Ma Mee was concerned the Palagadas already had as many slaves as they needed; after all, one couldn't sell them abroad as in the old days. However, she kept all these thoughts to herself.

Chiago thanked Ma Mee in the way she had been taught to greet important ladies like her, with a curtsy, and half pulled, half carried Ojebeta back to their own stall, knowing that the eyes of all the other women were following her. As she tried to lessen the shock for the poor girl, Chiago too was near tears, remembering how it had come about that she herself had been sold.

That year had been a bad one for her family. Where exactly her village was to be found was now shrouded in obscurity, though she knew she came from somewhere not far from the rivers where Pa Palagada went to sell palm kernels to some foreigners near Bonny. But she could remember that she had had a mother who was forever bearing children, and who was always carrying a baby on her back, held there with a tiny piece of cloth which was all she had. Then came a year when the rains were so heavy that almost all the vegetation, except the oil palms, was carried away. Her father had brought her to this dark bearded, overblown and formidable-looking man, who told her that his daughter was getting married just like the white people did. Her father told her that they needed a little girl to wear white muslin and to carry flowers for this man's beautiful daughter. Having done that service, she would be well paid, and her father would be waiting for her by the river, with the very canoe with which they had come. She had believed her father, especially when it was explained to her that the money she would earn would be used to pay the native doctors who would make her mother well again. And then their life would be back to normal. They would live in their house on the boat, and come to land to sell the fish they caught, and when it became too wet to live on the water, they would come to land and plant and eat cocoyam, *ede*, and sometimes yam. . . .

Chiago remembered that she had had to cross another river, and they had walked what seemed endless numbers of miles. For days they had walked and they were so tired that for part of the journey Pa Palagada had to be carried by local bearers in a hammock. At a town called Arochukwu they had stayed for days, and it was here that she had a bitter taste of what life held in store for her. She did not see the so-called daughter of Pa Palagada; in fact she seldom saw him at all. She was thrust into a small room at the back of the house with other strange people, who all seemed unhappy and, like her, scantily dressed. They all ate together, and had to go to the stream to fetch water, and she had to help in the large cooking place they called the "kinsheni," or something like that. She had stayed there with Pa Palagada and his entourage for just five days, and then they had set off again walking and walking and only resting at occasional drinking and eating places. They crossed another fairly small river in a canoe, and by this time Chiago had not even been able to remember from which direction she had originally come.

She had thought about it constantly since, and had finally decided that she had no choice but to accept things as they were. Her family would certainly have starved had she not been sold to this man, Pa Palagada, who had later handed Chiago to his wife. It was a blessing that at least her stomach had been sold with her, so her parents would no longer have to worry about how to feed her; and perhaps the money her head had fetched had helped her family for a while.

The picture of her family, however, had dimmed after eleven years with her mistress and her husband. The long stay had taught her a great many things. The most important was that a slave who made an unsuccessful attempt to run away was better off dead. Such a slave would be so tortured that he or she would be useless as a person, or else might be used for burial.

She had watched one such horrible burial when she had been about twelve and was travelling with Ma Palagada in the Ibo interior. The chief wife of the master of the house had died, and it was necessary for her husband to send her to the land of the dead accompanied by a female slave. The one chosen was a particularly beautiful slave, with smooth skin and black closely cropped hair, who was said to be a princess captured in war from another Ibo village; she had made attempts to return to where she came from, but unfortunately her new owner caught her and she lost her freedom of movement. On the eve of the burial she was brought and ordered to lie down in the shallow grave. As might be expected, she resisted, but there was no pity on the faces of the men who stood by watching, amused by her cries. She made appeals to the gods of her people to save her, she begged some of the mourners to spare her life, saying that her father the chief of another village would repay them, but to no avail. One of the sons of the dead woman lost his patience and, maybe out of mercy and a wish to have it all done with as quickly as possible, took a club and struck the defenceless woman hard at the back of her shaved head. The more Chiago thought about it in later years, the more convinced she was that the woman slave must have had seven lives. She did not drop down into the grave she was later to share with her dead mistress as was then expected. Instead she turned to look at the chief, who was calling on his son to cease his brutality, and she said to him, "For showing me this little mercy, chief, I shall come again, I shall come again. . . ."

She was not allowed to finish her valedictory statement, for the stubborn young man, disregarding his father's appeal, gave the woman a final blow so that she fell by the side of the grave. But she was still struggling even when the body of her dead mistress was placed on her. She still fought and cried out, so alive. Soon her voice was completely silenced by the damp earth that was piled on both her and the dead woman.

Chiago never quite recovered from this early shock, not even when sometime later she heard Ma Palagada talking to another woman trader about it and ending up by saying that one of the chief's younger wives now had a baby daughter very like the slave princess who had been buried alive; to clinch the resemblance, this little girl was born with a lump on the back of her head, in the same place as where the slave princess had been struck. . . .

Chiago had seen, too, many slaves who had become successful, who had worked so well with their masters that they themselves became wealthy traders at Otu market, given their freedom when their masters grew old. The majority of them, particularly the male slaves, did not wish to go home, if they could even remember which part of the country they had come from originally. Some of them stayed because they could not return to their region as a result of some atrocity they had committed. One of the Palagada slaves was born a twin and her people, somewhere among the Efiks, did not accept twins; her mother had nursed her secretly and later had her sold, simply to give her a chance in life.

If only Chiago could have communicated all that passed through her mind to this struggling little girl. She wished she could tell her that the only course left for her was to make the best of everything, by being docile and trouble-free. She had stopped holding her too tightly but had her arms round the girl's naked waist, looking at her with pity as if she were her own sister. In fact they would soon be like sisters—did not the same fate await them?

"I shall tell my father of you," Ojebeta whimpered in between exhausted hiccoughs. In her confusion after the long, wearying journey and her escape attempt, she imagined her father was still alive and well in Ibuza. She stared at everyone in front of the stalls they passed, hoping that one of them would be her brother.

If the girls felt like reminding Ojebeta that her parents were long dead, they restrained themselves. They had seen scenes like this played out before their very eyes too often, and they knew from experience that to indulge in a little fantasy would do her no harm at all; if anything, it would do her good. So they let her wallow in her own world of wishful thinking. She went on repeating that she would tell her father, her mother and her big mother Uteh, until she was completely exhausted.

Ma Mee soon strolled round to their stall to find out how they were coping and whether Ma Palagada was back. Chiago replied that she was sure she would be back soon, and this statement awakened in Ojebeta a last, futile hope to gain sympathy.

"Please, kind mother, can you bring my brother back for me? He only went there round your stall to eat pounded yam."

"Yes," Ma Mee replied in a soft voice, "I shall bring your brother back. But do you want me to buy you anything to eat? Do you want honeyed meat balls from the Hausa people down the coast?"

Ojebeta shook her head vigorously as though she would snap it off from her body. She did not want anything, not anymore, not from these people who had tricked her into letting Okolie out of her sight because of some hot agidi.

"I don't want anything. I only want to go home." She little realised in what circumstances and how long it would be before that going home took place.

Ma Mee walked back to her stall telling herself that buying and selling people could not be helped. "Where would we be without slave labour, and where would some of these unwanted children be without us?" It might be evil, but it was a necessary evil.

Daughters of Divine Love
TWO SONGS

Nigeria 1977   Igbo

From 1967 to 1970, Nigeria was engulfed in a civil war known as the Nigerian-Biafran war. The Biafrans of eastern Nigeria, predominantly of Igbo origin, seceded from Nigeria and declared an independent state of Biafra on 30 May 1967 to protest the injustices, violence, and discrimination perpetrated against its people in other parts of Nigeria. The Nigerian government termed the secession a rebellious act and, in order to crush the move, declared war on Biafra. That war was fought on many fronts. As it went on, and as various parts of Biafra were overrun by Nigeria's military, with support from some foreign countries, life and property in the affected areas became extremely unsafe, especially for women and girls. Hence, on 16 July 1969, the late Bishop Godfrey Mary Paul Okoye offered some young girls at Ukpor, in Anambra State, shelter and protection from the continuing violence and atrocities. These young girls later became the founding members of the order of the Daughters of Divine Love. Since the cessation of the war, the order has blossomed, and their activities have since spread beyond the borders of Nigeria to various parts of the world. Their activities can be seen not only in the Motherhouse in Nigeria, but also in Kenya and Gabon, in Italy, Germany, and the United Kingdom, and in the United States, Cuba, and the West Indies. The order now numbers seven hundred.

The songs below were written by two of the Igbo nuns who founded the order. "How the Daughters of Divine Love Congregation Started in the Year 1969" describes the reasons for the formation of the order of the Daughters of Divine Love. The song also depicts the nuns' immense joy and satisfaction at the founding. It particularly notes the contribution of Pope Paul VI, who gave his blessing to the formation of the congregation and who suggested a list of names, from which Bishop Okoye eventually and prayerfully selected the name "Daughters of Divine Love."

The second song is an anthem of the order that was composed upon the death of Bishop Okoye in 1977. While proclaiming love for Christ, the song expresses the deep sorrow and helplessness that the death of Bishop Okoye brought to the sisters. In the song, they seek solace, comfort, and solidarity in their faith in Christ. The song also affirms their optimism and determination to forge ahead as witnesses for Christ despite the sudden death of their founder.

Nkoli Ezumah

✦

HOW THE DAUGHTERS OF DIVINE LOVE CONGREGATION STARTED IN THE YEAR 1969

A new congregation is founded.
It is called Daughters of Divine Love.
It means Daughters of Divine Love.
It was in the year 1969,
In the midst of the Nigerian-Biafran war,
That Bishop Okoye started this congregation.
Think of the air raid,
Think of the hunger,
Think of how much these girls suffered.
But one good thing

Is that God in His mercy and love
Sent us the grace for founding this order.
Please tell me how it happened!
Since I cannot imagine anybody
Able to start a congregation,
Amid the suffering of days and nights.
My dear sister, please wait, I have a song.
Wait, because the founding of this order is miraculous.
One thing I know, it was the will of God.
The bishop gathered these women at Ukpor
To protect them from the war.
It was not his intention to begin a congregation.
When the bishop was in Rome,
He thought of a new congregation.
He went and told Pope Paul VI about it.
This pleased Pope Paul VI.
He listed possible names
And asked the bishop to choose one
The bishop prayed for ten days
That he might choose the good name
The one to please our heavenly father.
The bishop chose Daughters of Divine Love!!!

WE LOVE YOU JESUS

We love you, dear Jesus, remember
We Daughters of Divine Love,
We cannot cry without reason,
The Lord is my shepherd and king.
We hail thee, O Christ our hope.
We hail thee, O Christ our hope.
A man appeared sent from God.
You know his name was John.
He was sent by God to bear witness.
Chorus: That all mankind should believe
Thy throne, God, endures for ages.
Thou art a friend to the just.
The daughters of kings shall acclaim thee.
Chorus: The lord is my shepherd and king.

Translated by Sister Maria Trinitas Keke

Hadjia Barmani Coge
ALLAH IS THE LIGHT IN THE DARKNESS

Nigeria 1979   Hausa

Hadjia Barmani Coge was born in 1944 or 1945 in Rafin Dinya, near Funtua in Katsina State, Nigeria. She was born Salamatu Ahmadu and received the name "Coge" from her performances of the dance of that name, which resembles the walk of a lame person or *cogele*. She started her musical career as a child by taking part in litanies and Sufi religious ceremonies in a style known as *Kidin Amada*, performed by groups of women in *purdah*, involving devotion through the invocation of saints.

Early in Barmani Coge's career, one of her relatives noticed her gift for singing and encouraged her to perform at a marriage ceremony. She initially opposed the idea, fearing that such public performances would take her away from strictly religious performances. But in the end, the persuasion was successful. She was so powerful a singer that she immediately gained influential patronage for her artistry.

Remarkably, Barmani Coge managed to secularize what was initially a sacred, ritual style of singing. As with the Bori ritual singing, she tends to sing at night, accompanied by a chorus of women and *kwarya*, upturned calabashes floating on water and played with the hands. Both her material and her style are common to traditional Bori performances; however, in the performance itself, she stretches the limits of respectability through her body language and gestures. Barmani Coge uses her public voice for transformation: she sings in support of women's work, skilled and unskilled, commenting on social change and the need for empowerment.

A successful housewife as well as performer, she has twelve children and over twenty grandchildren, and has managed to support herself and her household. Although she was her first husband's only wife, one of her most successful songs is about resistance to polygamous marriages. After her husband's death, as an elderly and independent woman, she became the fourth wife of another wealthy man, but at the time she composed this song, she was not in a polygamous marriage. She composed it to highlight the difficulties of women in such marriages and to enable women to talk about the problems of polygamy.

Hausa women, when speaking directly to their husbands, accord them the deference that authority is due. Consequently, in the song, the husband and the person to whom she turns for help are both addressed as *mallam*, meaning "teacher." In the Islamic societies of West Africa, some of these teachers become spiritual advisors who acquire reputations for helping to resolve all manner of difficult human situations. In this instance, the *mallam* seems to be suggesting that, should the husband wash his face before prayer with the offered potion, he will be cleansed of the other woman and enabled to see his wife anew. What makes this a subversive text is that Allah, through the *mallam*, helps to frustrate a second marriage. The song exists in many forms with many situational variations. In each version, the woman refuses to take the arrival of a cowife without comment and acts in some manner to resist. The version published here was recorded in 1979.

Ousseina D. Alidou

✦

I was living with my husband,
A really pleasant existence,
An enjoyable life with no quarrelling.
    Allah is the light in the darkness.
One day my husband said to me
He wanted to take a second wife.
I said, "*Mallam,* that's all right,
I will have someone to live alongside me."
    Allah is the light in the darkness.
He did not know I had my own plans.
If I am the one in charge of this house,
There is no way I will allow some bitch
To come in as my cowife.
    Allah is the light in the darkness.
As night fell,
I told my husband, "I am going out somewhere."
And I went straight to a *mallam*
Who welcomed me.
    Allah is the light in the darkness.
I said, "*Mallam* I want your help,
My husband is bringing in a second wife."
    Allah is the light in the darkness.
The *mallam* said, "I already knew,
And I want to tell you that
This marriage will definitely go ahead,
Nothing can stop it,
But there is one small thing I can do
To help you if you want.
After this marriage has taken place
You can try to destroy it."
    Allah is the light in the darkness.
The *mallam* gave me a potion
And said to me,
"Sprinkle this potion
Into his religious ablution kettle!"

Translated by Graham Furniss and Sulaiman Ibrahim Katsina

Afua Kuma
JESUS OF THE DEEP FOREST

Ghana 1980   Akan-Twi

Madame Afua Kuma, a nonliterate farmer, wife, mother, and traditional midwife, was also a member of the Church of Pentecost, which provided opportunities for her creative energies. Many communities, hearing about her abilities, invited her to pray at Christian meetings in towns during Christmas conventions, retreats, and Easter rallies.

Kuma's prayers and praises, rendered in the Akan court-praise poetry style, are significant for several reasons. In Akan society, praise poetry is a restricted literary form performed by men chosen from particular lineages and trained from youth to recite pieces dedicated to their prospective patrons. Kuma's use of praise poetry in Christian worship introduces the form to a new audience, even as it bespeaks the transgression of traditional norms forbidding women to participate in the subgenre. Furthermore, the text provides a quintessential record of a growing phenomenon, the use of indigenous languages and ideas in Christian worship and the involvement of nonclerical members in spontaneous prayers.

While Kuma's prayers and praises may use the syntax and diction of the subgenre, she adapts them for her new audience. She alludes to biblical stories and introduces English words that have been assimilated into Akan. We have kept praise names in the original Akan. These are only partly translatable, because they belong to a class of honorific words that are meant to convey—through profound sounds—the importance of the person being praised. Here, however, we have indicated—using brackets or a colon—an approximate translation of the Akan word of praise.

Kono is a type of basket. *Adwinasa* is a variety of the richly colored, hand-woven kente cloth fit for royalty; the word comes from *adwene* (creative mind) and *asa* (end) and means "my very last invention." *Kofi* is the personal name given to a loom, as is quite customary in Akan society, in which instruments of creativity—looms or drums—may be named.

Kuma draws on imagery from the forest, farm, river, and marketplace, as well as the home, the kitchen, and local institutions and customs, to paint a rich tapestry of the God-force. The aesthetic value of the text lies in the sheer exhilaration it evokes through the piling up of high-sounding phrases, praise epithets, and appellations, and the effective use of hyperbole, contrast, and allusion.

The selected verses have been drawn from the published collection. They should not be seen as a fixed sequence, however, for in practice Kuma would use them creatively as a repertoire to suit the occasion and her own religious sensibility.

Esi Sutherland–Addy

✦

We are going to praise the name of Jesus Christ.
We shall announce his many titles:
They are true and they suit him well,
so it is fitting that we do this.

All-powerful Jesus
who engages in marvelous deeds,
he is the one called Hero—*Okatakyie!*
Of all earthly dominions he is the master,
the Python not overcome with mere sticks,
the Big Boat which cannot be sunk.

The great Rock we hide behind,
the great forest canopy that gives cool shade,
the Big Tree which lifts its vines
to peep at the heavens,
the magnificent Tree whose dripping leaves
encourage the luxuriant growth below.

Wonderworker, you are the one
who has carried water in a basket
and put it by the roadside
for the travelers to drink for three days.
You use the *kono* basket to carry water to the desert;
then you throw in your net and bring forth fish!
You use the net to fetch water and put it into a basket.
We ride in canoes on the water's surface
and catch our fish!

Lightning, you who lay low our cities,
we encourage you, "Come on, come on!"
with the firing of muskets.
Master of Wisdom,
who have set a trap to catch the wind,
who bundled it up with lightning,
and tied the load with a rainbow!

Great and powerful Jesus, incomparable Diviner,
the sun and moon are your *batakare* [sacred armor].
It sparkles like the morning star.
Sekyere Buruku: the divine tall mountain,
all the nations see your glory.

You weave the streams like plaited hair;
with fountains you tie a knot.

Magician who walks on the sea:
He arrives at the middle,
plunges his hand into the deep and takes out a whale!

The spider's web is his fishing line.
He casts it forth and catches a crocodile.
He casts his fishing net, and catches birds.
He sets a trap in the forest and catches fish.
Holy One! . . .
Jesus: you are solid as a rock!
The green mamba dies at the sight of Jesus.
Iron rod that cannot be coiled into a head-pad:
The cobra turns on his back, prostrate before you!
Jesus, you are the Elephant Hunter. Fearless One!
You have killed the evil spirit, and cut off its head!
The drums of the king have announced it in the morning.
All of your attendants lead the way, dancing with joy. . . .

Weaving-loom-Kofi, you give us our woven cloths.
You give us *Adwinasa* to wear in the morning.
He gives plenty, even in excess, and to everyone!
We don't receive your gifts in our left hand,
Great One, *Katakye;*
But because of your bountiful blessings,
our right hand is full!

Mmpowmmeahene and *Gyaasehene*:
Chiefs of many small villages
and steward of God's household,
Jesus, who walks on gold dust—
with great strides he reaches this place,
while gold-nugget stars lead the way.
Powerful and wealthy Chief:
With golden blocks you fashion a wall;

precious beads are your corner-stones. . . .

Chief among chiefs, when you stretch forth your hand,
widows are covered with festive beads
while orphans wear *kente!*

Chief of Lawyers, to whom we bring our complaints;
you stand at court and defend the poor.
Chief of Police, a big rifle stands at your side!

Jesus! You are the greatest warrior among the soldiers.
Jesus, you are on the right and on the left,
where the sun rises, and where it sets!
You are the Chief of the rear-guard!
You are *Korobetoe*, who lives for ever:
chief of defense and chief of body-guards,
a friend to old men and women!

A great and shining nation belongs to Jesus;
The rainbow protects its rampart
while lightning marches round.
Signs and wonders open its gates,
for these are the keys of his kingdom. . . .

Translated by Father John Kirby, SVD

Toelo
LISTEN TO ME, CHILD OF A *GRIOT*
Burkina Faso 1981   San

In San, the land of the Sànan people of Burkina Faso, the *kuma* (people who invent the word) are renowned singers. Toelo, a singer known for the strength of her language and the pertinence of her themes, often sings at funerals, where *kumas* can demonstrate their talent and compose songs on various themes, not necessarily on death.

"Listen to Me, Child of a *Griot*" was composed and performed during a funeral ceremony on 3 November 1981 in the village of Toma, located in the Nayala province. Toelo sings of the suffering of orphans and affirms her delight in being a woman.

Fatoumata Kinda and Denise Badini-Folane

✦

Listen to me, child of a *griot;*
I have a secret to tell you!
If I were to be born again
If I, Toelo,
Were to be born again,
I would want to return
Always as a woman!
To be a woman . . .

Is the best all conditions!
A woman . . .
As bad as she might be,
Will always find a man.
It's the bad man
Who will never find a woman!

You see, Oh *griot*,
Even if a woman is blind,
Even if a woman is limping,
Even if she has a dead arm,
Even if she has a dead foot,
She will always find a husband . . .
It's the bad man
Who never finds a woman!
I tell you, child of a *griot*,
If I Toelo,
Were to be born again,
I would want to return
Always as a woman!
I tell you, child of a *griot*,
To be a woman . . .
Is the best of all conditions!
Even if a woman is deaf,
Even if she presents herself as an incomplete woman,
Who does not know how to spin cotton,
Nor how to perform the other duties of a woman . . .
She will always find herself a husband
I tell you,
It's the bad man
Who never finds himself a woman!
If I were to be born again,
I would want to come back
Always as a woman!
To be a woman . . .
Is the best of all conditions!
You see, my *griot*,
I only have my words
To console me!
My stomach is heavy with words
And my heart is filled with suffering!
The family members I have left are running away from me,
And my mother is no longer alive!
Tell me, child of a *griot*,

Who is my family?
Who is my friend?
Who is close to Toelo?
Who is close to Toelo,
Toelo who goes from one man to another?
I have only my song!
Child of a *griot!*
My song to comfort me,
To relieve me of my sufferings!
My song is my only relative!
My song is my only friend!
You see, child of a *griot,*
My mother is now beneath the ground!
My mother is forever under the ground!
And every time I see the "motherless"
I am frightened,
And I am cold!
You see, child of *griot,*
The real enemy of a woman
Is death!
My mother is forever under the ground!
And every time I see the "motherless"
I am frightened,
And I am terrified!

Translated into French by Andre Nyamba
Translated from French by Christiane Owusu-Sarpong and Esi Sutherland-Addy

Shaïda Zarumey
LOVE POEMS FOR THE SULTAN

Niger 1981   French

Shaïda Zarumey was born in 1938, in Mali, to a Malian mother. Her father
was a clerk in the colonial administration of Niger. Zarumey lived in Niger,
during her early school days, and then in Mali, where she attended secondary
school. She earned a doctorate in Paris in 1970. From 1970 to 1975, she taught
at the Institut de Développement et de Planification Économique of Dakar;
then, until her retirement, she worked as an international civil servant specializing in women's rights in several countries of Africa, Asia, and Europe.
    The two poems selected here were first published in a collection entitled

Interchanges for the Sultan, one thousand copies of which were printed in 1981, at the author's expense, by Quantics, in Paris. It is the first collection of poems known to have been published by a woman from Niger. The voice is that of a mature woman—a mother, a daughter, a citizen of her country angered by injustice, a citizen of the world, and a woman in love. Its unifying metaphor is the "Sultan," the beloved of the "last springtime of the heart," the singularly privileged listener to whom she speaks.

"Incense"—as a complex essential oil, an aphrodisiac heat, a perfume of fire that envelops and emanates from the woman who knows the art of love—evokes the sensual ritual of female seduction. A rite of intimacy, the burned perfume also evokes a domestic rite: It spreads the fragrance of well-being throughout the house.

In "Taka," love and religion meet in an amalgam that may be shocking to some. *Taka* is the abbreviation of *can taka,* which, depending on the kind of beads and the national language, is also and variously called "*niamese*" (coming from the name Niamey), "*jigida*" or "*zigida,*" or else "*kofi.*" They are the beads used for belts known all over Africa. In Niger, a *Gadbi,* which originally and without any negative connotation meant a woman who knows how to be seductive, often wears a belt made of incense around her waist. In this poem, the belt of beads, here made of crystal, is considered the equivalent of the Muslim prayer beads (*tabji* in Hausa). On this chain of beads the Sultan will "recite" his "verses" of love. *Sura* is the word used for verses of the Qur'an.

In these and other poems, Shaïda Zarumey elicits "the thing hidden," the *hijhab* that is usually covered with a veil of discreet silence. The mature woman who speaks openly of love and desire challenges the ideals of modesty and restraint valued in Niger.

Antoinette Tidjani Alou

✦

INCENSE

It is incense that warms me
When you go away
And incense that fills the house with fragrance
When you are here and when you go away

Incense too that warms our wild embrace
In the dark night, when you go away
It is incense that keeps me warm
It fills the house with your presence
Your presence, when you go away

TAKA

A row of Czech or Slovak beads
A row of crystal beads awaiting your prayer

A row of crystal beads for the Sultan
Awaiting his recital of the *sura* of love
While his fingers play on my row of crystal beads

Translated by Antoinette Tidjani Alou

Nawa Kulibali
NAWA'S LAMENT

Côte d'Ivoire 1986   Senufo

Among the Senufo in Côte d'Ivoire, an individual's ties with her mother's family are determinant: the mother's brother, who is her children's uncle, is the "owner" of all members of the family. Nawa Kulibali was a member of a family of ten (including stepbrothers and -sisters). As a young girl, she refused to marry the man her uncle had chosen for her. Instead she fled with her boyfriend, Salifu, to the cotton-growing zone, 120 miles away from her home, Korhogo, in northern Côte d'Ivoire.

Until recent years, the Senufo lived on subsistence farming, but early in the 1970s, cotton became a favored cash crop. Growing cotton, one could make enough money to build a house made of concrete or buy a motorbike. Still, the risks were great and the work difficult. For the sake of an abundant harvest, some farmers worshipped many gods; others consulted diviners, who might recommend the appropriate sacrifice to produce material success. Salifu, Nawa's husband, reportedly consulted a *Kalamoho*—a marabout—and agreed to pay the highest price possible, the life of his wife, in exchange for material wealth and success in cotton growing.

The marabout had finished his job before he realized that Nawa was a kind woman who did not deserve the fate her husband had determined, but all he could do at that late hour was to inform her of her husband's treachery. It was too late, he said, to undo what had already been determined. Nahua was a mother of two when she died in May or June 1990. As for Salifu, he had already taken another wife.

It is important to note that, although Salifu chose to sacrifice his wife as the most rare or most valuable treasure he had to offer—and that such acts are being increasingly reported—they impinge directly upon the Senufo's ancestral customs. Since an individual is the "property" of her mother's family, a man may offer a marabout, as a person of value, only his sister's son, his own nephew. Fathers are not regarded as having such authority over their own sons, and certainly not over their wives, who come from different families. In this case, the distance that Salifu and Nawa had put between themselves and their families allowed Salifu to offer the only "thing of value" in his life to the marabout.

People believe that Nawa sang her lament in order to inform her extended family about what was to happen. She asked her elder brother, Lacina, to make a recording of her singing so that she might leave a testimony and to inform her mother, sisters, and brothers of her impending death.

In the late 1960s, with the advent of the tape recorder in the Senufo region, women began to record their songs. Cassette dealers record songs or simply duplicate and sell original recordings. The tape of "Nawa's Lament" was provided by Soro Sohelo, who worked in the area where the tape was recorded. At first, the recorded song was a family secret, but eventually cassette dealers smuggled it out, lengthened it by copying and repeating bits, and made it commercially viable. Hence, on tape the song is not finely structured, for there are many repetitions and false starts. We have selected portions for this volume.

Sassongo Silue

✦

LIFE IN THE COTTON FIELDS

Mother, thank you for bringing me to life but it is now without any
    purpose.
Mama, thank you for bringing me to life but it is now pointless.
I am being trapped among vultures.
I am being insulted by those good-for-nothings.
I am among those good-for-nothings.
Mother, thank you for bringing me to life but it is now without any
    purpose.
Mother, thank you for bringing me to life but it was without any
    purpose.
Mama, thank you for bringing me to life but it proved pointless.
All these vultures go gossiping against me.
I am being insulted by those good-for-nothings.
Mother, thank you for bringing me to life but it was without any
    purpose.
Mama, thank you for bringing me to life but it proved pointless.
I've been trapped among snakes.
I've been trapped among pythons.
I wished Mother were not informed of that.
I wished Mother did not hear about what is happening to me.
I am experiencing a lot of hardship in the cotton fields.
I wished Mother did not hear about that.
I suffer from hatred in the cotton fields.
I wished Mother did not hear about that.
Dear cotton, keep growing, cotton of the cotton field, keep growing.
I shall tell my mother all from the beginning.
I think I should also tell my father all from the beginning.
I think I should really tell Toritcha how this may end.
Ah! In these cotton fields!

There is so much suffering in the cotton fields!
There is so much quarreling in the cotton fields!
There is so much hatred in the cotton fields!
We are so beaten and so beaten down in the cotton fields!

DISAPPOINTED LOVE

I suffered a lot, just for you,
But you did not take that into account.
I accepted being insulted.
I offered myself as a solution to your loneliness.
I experienced being insulted just to find a solution to your loneliness.
I accepted being insulted by everyone.
Mama, you see, life with my love is impossible.
Life with my darling has turned impossible.
Mama, you see, life with my darling has become impossible.
I offered myself as a solution.
I offered myself as a solution to your loneliness.
I accepted all the bad names.
Mama, you see, my love has turned away.
My love has been ungrateful.
Life with my love is hard.
Mama, you see, my love has turned away.
The people of Korhogo insulted me and I took it.
The people of Kagbolo insulted me and I took it.
Everyone insulted me and I took it.
I did not know my darling had no respect for people.
My darling has no respect for people.
Mama, my darling has no respect for people.
Life is hard with my darling.
Mama, look, life with my darling has become hard.
I did not know that my lover was ungrateful.
I did not know that Salifu was hard to live with.
Jeneba, I did not know that Salifu was hard to live with.
Darling of my early and young days,
Why should you exhibit me like that
In the open?
Long ago, when I was visiting you at home
I would slide through to your place
Thinking that you were a good person.
Early in the morning as soon as the morning cock sang
I would slide through to your place,
Thinking that you were a good person.
Early in the morning when some husband shouted at his wife

I would slide through to your place
Thinking that you were a good person.
So, darling of my early and young days,
Why should you exhibit me like that
In the open?
Why should you exhibit me like that
And leave me crying?

MESSAGE TO MY FAMILY

You, Lacina, who is operating the tape recorder,
You, Lacina, the tape recorder operator,
When you get to our home village,
Tell my mother that I greet her,
And say hello to Lacina,
And say hello to Madu,
And say hello to Brahima,
And say hello to Natogoma,
And say hello to Lohonyon.
Tell my mother that I greet her.
Tell Jeneba that I greet her.
When you get there
Tell Lacina
When he finishes his trading activities on market day
Let him look for a diviner.
Living conditions have turned very troubling.
The living conditions in the cotton fields have turned hard for me.
The working conditions in the cotton fields have become unbearable
    for me.
I will send the letter to Lacina.
When he knows the contents, let him come so that we can talk. . . .

MISFORTUNE AND DEATH

Hold up your sorrow tightly,
Mother, hold up your sorrow tightly.
Mother and father, when they hear of my death
Let them refrain from crying.
When they hear of my death in the cotton fields,
When they hear of my death in the cotton-growing area,
Let them hold up their sorrow tightly.
Mother, hold up your sorrow tightly.
Uncle, hold up your sorrow tightly.
You are as easy crying as a monkey.

Brahima, you are as easy crying as a monkey.
Lacina, you are as easy crying as a monkey.
Jeneba, do not cry.
Nawa, do not cry.
Toritcha, do not cry.
Hold up your sorrow.
You must dominate your sorrow.
Do not make things worse by your cries.
Nagaluru, do not cry.
Hold up your sorrow.
Do not make things worse by your cries.
When they hear of my death in the cotton growing area,
You must dominate your sorrow.
Do not make things worse by your cries.
Tell Toritcha that
I'm just trying to know how all this came about.
I'm just trying to know who is at the beginning of all this.
If I know who is at the beginning of this process
I shall comply with the recommendations of the fortune-teller.
I am waiting for a note from Mama.
As soon as I get her note
I shall comply with the recommendations of the fortune-teller.
I am waiting for a letter from Mama.
As soon as I get her note
I shall settle this matter.
We used to get on so perfectly.
How can you believe that we have come to quarrelling?
This is the reason why.

I Ask You My Darling

When the time comes to "catch" me
Do not do it in the open.
I am waiting for a letter from Mother.
As soon as I get her note
I shall settle this matter.
I'm just trying to know who is at the bottom of all this.
When I know who is at the bottom of all this
I shall deal with it.
Do go and consult a diviner,
Mother, my Mama, do go and consult.
Father, my Papa, do go and consult,
Go and consult.
I am suffering from starvation.

I am suffering from misfortune.
I am suffering from the *sandoho.*
I am suffering from the curse of spells.
I am suffering from love.
Go and query the diviners.
Rid me of evil spells.
Rid me of misfortune.
I am being tormented by love and I feel lost.
Do go and consult.
Do go and ask my fate.
Do go and consult the *sandobele.*
Query God to learn what is happening to me.
I am being tormented by love and I feel lost.
Tell the *Kalamohos* that I just want to save my head.
Tell the *Kalamohos* of Jelige district in Korhogo that I just want to save
   my head.
Do tell the *Kalamohos* that I just want to save my head.
Tell the *Kalamohos* of Kapele that I just want to save my head.
Tell the *Kalamohos* that I just want to save my head.
Tell the *Kalamohos* in Abidjan that I just want to save my head.
I shall ask someone to go and see my mother.
And ask her if I have become worth nothing.
I shall ask someone to go and see my father and ask him
If all that is happening to me was bound as early as my birthday,
If all that is happening to me is part of the family inheritance,
If I have become worth nothing.
I shall ask someone to go and see Toritcha and ask her
If all that is happening to me is part of our family's inheritance.
I shall ask someone to go and see my mother and ask her
If all that is happening to me was bound as early as my birthday.

Translated by Sassongo Silue

Ellen Johnson-Sirleaf
PRESIDENT DOE'S PRISONER

Liberia 1985, 1987   English

Born in 1938, Ellen Johnson-Sirleaf married immediately after leaving secondary school. In 1962, at the age of twenty-two, and with four children, she left
Liberia to earn a degree in accounting in the United States. On returning to

Liberia in 1964, she worked as an accountant in the Department of the Treasury, where she was soon made accountant-general and later special assistant to the secretary of the treasury. In 1968, at a National Planning Conference, she detailed the many policy and political shortcomings of William Tubman's administration. A consulting team from Harvard University that feared for her safety as a result of her report facilitated her departure for a study tour in the United States. She thus took leave in 1969, first to study economics at the University of Boulder, then to earn a master's degree in public administration from Harvard in 1971.

Immediately upon her return to Liberia in 1972, she was appointed assistant Minister of Finance and began a series of prophetically critical speeches. At a commencement speech for the College of West Africa in 1972, she cautioned that Liberia was laying the seeds for its own destabilization and could face a coup d'état, as had happened to other countries in the region. The following year, she accepted a position with the World Bank in Washington, D.C., as loan officer first for the Caribbean and later for Brazil. In 1977, she returned home to assume the position of deputy minister of Fiscal and Banking Affairs, a post she held until her elevation to minister in 1979, when the finance minister, James Phillips, was relieved of his post following the Rice Riots of 1979. Dozens of Liberians were killed during the riots, and several leaders of the progressive groups were jailed. The government was weakened and exposed.

In April 1980, the virtually unknown staff sergeant Samuel Doe staged a coup in Liberia, killing President William R. Tolbert and removing all government officials, including Johnson-Sirleaf, from power. For the next five years, she worked for the World Bank and then for Citibank, in Nairobi.

On her return to Liberia in early 1985, she cofounded the Liberia Action Party (LAP), which was initially denied registration by the military government. She then proceeded to the United States, where she delivered a speech to the Union of Liberian Associations in the Americas, at a meeting in Philadelphia on 26 July 1985. In this speech, given barely three months before the proposed elections, she expressed strong criticism of Samuel Doe's then-transitional government.

On her return to Liberia later that month, Johnson-Sirleaf planned to campaign for the LAP. Instead, she was charged with sedition and placed under immediate house arrest. Despite widespread appeals that she be tried in a civilian court, her case was heard by a military tribunal. Doe, then a self-appointed general, was on record as having said he had executed thirteen members of the government he overthrew, and Johnson-Sirleaf should have been the fourteenth. The widespread interest in her case, particularly on the part of U.S. agencies and the U.S. Congress, led to her being sentenced to ten years at hard labor in Bella Yellah prison, rather than being executed. In addition, as her sentence was delivered, she was invited to address the court, in order, as she explains it, to give the government some basis for pardoning her. She made a conciliatory statement and was released after nearly two months with a conditional pardon.

The proposed elections did take place in October. The LAP had been permitted to register during Johnson-Sirleaf's imprisonment, on the condition that they not carry her as their vice presidential candidate. The regime had wanted a guarantee that she would leave the country, but her family refused to commit to that on her behalf. Instead, on the insistence of the LAP, she was carried as a senatorial candidate. She won her seat.

She refused to sit in the assembly, however, on the grounds that so doing would make legitimate an illegitimate government. After incidents of disappearing and burning ballots and the intervention of an illegally appointed governmental special panel to take charge of the vote tabulation, Doe was declared winner with 50.9 percent of the vote and duly became president. The blatant rigging of the October 1985 elections plunged the nation into a repressed state of tension, which exploded on 12 November, shortly after the declaration of Doe as winner. A coup attempt was launched, the invasion was crushed by forces loyal to Doe, and Johnson-Sirleaf was imprisoned for alleged complicity and once again formally charged with treason, on 10 January 1986. In the end, she was pardoned and released at the beginning of June 1986, and she returned to the United States to work for political change in Liberia.

When Charles Taylor launched an armed attack against the Doe regime from Côte d'Ivoire on 24 December 1989, many inside Liberia, and many exiled political leaders, including Johnson Sirleaf, welcomed the insurgents and supported their leader in the hope that Doe's forcible removal from office would pave the way for the restoration of democracy. But as the insurgents rapidly made progress toward the seat of Doe's power in Monrovia, Taylor began to demonstrate that he was just as murderous. He killed all key political figures who fled for safety to his occupied territories. Johnson-Sirleaf and others soon withdrew their support, since he had abandoned his rebellion's avowed democratic and liberating objectives. In 1997, after seven years of his ruthless dictatorship, when more than 200,000 people had been killed and more than a million people made refugees or displaced, the country once again held an election. Seen as the only credible challenger to Taylor, Johnson-Sirleaf came in second in a race that over time has been challenged as being not entirely free or fair. In the ensuing years, Johnson-Sirleaf has become a household name in Liberia and throughout a subregion that is still not at peace. Her political activism continues, and there are renewed calls for her to seek the presidency again.

The first text below is an extract from the unpublished speech that Johnson-Sirleaf gave in Philadelphia on July 6, 1985, to the Union of Liberian Associations in the Americas and that led to her first arrest. There she called for a four-point agenda: economic recovery; strengthening the new social contract; participatory democracy; and *"yama yama,"* a colloquial term found in many West African languages meaning "this and that," or, as Mrs. Johnson explains, "some things which are small in importance but big in implications." We include here her preliminary remarks and selections from the sections on economic recovery and participatory democracy.

The second text below is taken from a published interview granted to Jeremy Harding in New York on Johnson-Sirleaf's return to the United States. It is Johnson-Sirleaf's own history of her political ordeal following her second arrest, in November 1985.

Medina Wisseh and Abena P. A. Busia

Speech, Philadelphia   6 July 1985

I have just spent the immediate past three weeks at home and I can say to you that I once again feel a strong sense of destiny in the making. On the one hand there is a growing tenseness so reminiscent of the 1979/1980 environment that it can do no less than scare even the brave among us. Yet, on the other hand, there is a beautiful kind of excitement. For the first time in our lifetime (and for me that is saying quite a bit) there is a political consciousness perhaps unequalled in a nation's history. It has gripped almost every man, woman, and child—in the village, town, slum, estates, settlements, and capital. Never before have the workings of government been so discussed and laid bare. Never before has the appreciation for the effect of the workings of governments on the welfare of the people been so intensified. Never before has the shortcomings of government been so placed under a microscope and ridiculed. Never before has the desire of the people for participation in the running of government been so pronounced. It is exciting, and although you officers and members of ULAA are not there, there is full knowledge of and appreciation for the role you have played and continue to play in furthering the cause for participatory democracy. All but the very young will remember your efforts in the 1970's and all but the bigotted will applaud your efforts in the 1980's. In this respect I commend you for a consistency in principles, which has led you to challenge and expose injustice and impropriety from whichever government it has come.

Contrary to what we had read and been told, Liberia has neither bountiful fertile soil nor a satisfactory resource endowment. Our harsh and inhospitable climatic conditions—including heavy rainfall—not only means an eroding topsoil but major impediments to the development of both physical and social infrastructure. This also makes for high investment cost in the development of other types of infrastructure such as minerals and energy.

For years we were able to mask these economic constraints because the prices for our two primary exports, rubber and iron ore, remained sufficiently high. We showed total disregard for these limitations by wanton milking of the public purse. Bad enough in the days of the past, this exploitation is today at an unprecedented level, although the economic pie is considerably smaller and national capacity considerably weakened.

Recognize then that Liberia's economic development must rest largely on the judicious use and management of our scarce resources, the first action on the economic agenda is to halt the corruptive hemorrhaging toward the end. Government must reduce the level of its intervention in the economy, and resultingly the level of bribery and kickbacks to a long line of civil servants.

Next on the economic agenda is an improvement in overall management capability. I look at the cross-section of Liberians in this room today. I look beyond this room to several cities in several countries. I look at the many walking the street of Monrovia or sitting quietly in an unbusy office (in low profile they call it) and then I look at the many idiots in whose hands our nation's fate and progress have been placed and I simply shake at the tremendous cost which we pay under righting the wrongs of the past. If we were talking about the short-term sacrifices of waiting for a young, committed and capable technician to gain the necessary experience in managing an operation—I would have no serious problems. But most times than not we are faced with placing an important function of the economy in the hands of a corrupt and incompetent functionary whose only qualification for the position is a family or friendly connection to those who walk the corridors of power. Let me repeat what an International Monetary Fund (IMF) officer said on national television in response to a reporter's question regarding possible solutions to our economic problems. I believe he said, "There is nothing wrong with the Liberia economy which corrections in corruption and mismanagement will not cure." That statement may not cover some of the structural problems to which I earlier referred but in a nutshell he has summarized the action imperative for arresting the increasing deterioration.

They tell us that democracy is a luxury in Africa; that a multi-party political system is inappropriate to our traditions, that the electoral process is foreign to our heritage and that participatory politics is potentially exploitative of our masses. Such rubbish is repeated in one for[m] or fashion by even some of our renowned continental leaders. But we know and can see clearly through their attempts to halt the development of political institutions merely to perpetuate themselves in power. This is the African legacy which has led to succession only through the barrel of a gun—a legacy which now threatens us with two political forces—the military and the civilian, the latter with no means to exercise full political choice or expression. Add to this a growing disguised military rule in the form of a civilianized soldier and we will realize how much behind Africa is falling in this important aspect of national development. But we are reminded by the words of former U.S. Ambassador to the United Nations, Jeanne Kirkpatrick, "A Government is not legitimate merely because it exists." It must belong to the people, respond to the people, acquiesce to the wishes of the people. Any Government which refuses to be and to do these things must be removed by the people.

The Liberia agenda calls for resistance on the part of all of us to any attempts to reverse the clock or hold time still in the participation of the people in the selection of political leaders, in the exercise of political choice and in the expression of political views. Let me hasten to add that this process is possible only if we have a free (but responsible) press which is neither owned nor manipulated by, nor is the mouthpiece of government. Our agenda must insure and safeguard the vital machinery of democracy and accountability. The majority of Liberian people have shown an unmatched and unwavering courage for indeed their eyes are open and the time of the people has come.

INTERVIEW May 1987

On 6 January 1986 the second Republic of Liberia was born. A new constitution which guarantees basic fundamental rights including due process of law, freedom of speech and association went into effect. A multi-party system assured by the constitution but labouring under the denial of representation because of the October 1985 electoral fraud, was to get a new lease of life.

I and other political leaders detained in the aftermath of the abortive 12 November 1985 *coup d'état* were still in gaol. We had been lucky. Hundreds of other citizens had not survived the brutality and viciousness which followed the coup attempt. All that seemed behind us.

I started the New Year with hope. The US delegation to the inauguration of General Doe had been allowed to visit me in prison on Inauguration Day, 6 January. They brought high-sounding words of due process, justice, reconciliation, peace.

On 10 January I was called to the Office of the Commandant of the Military Barracks Prison, the infamous Post Stockade, and told that I should gather my personal belongings as I was being released. Hoots of joy and excitement by the other prisoners filled the air as I bundled my scanty worldly goods for what I thought was a short ride to freedom. On return to the Commandant's office, I was confronted by a group of Security men headed by the nation's Chief Security Intelligence Officer. He slapped me on the back and announced that I was under arrest, charged with treason for complicity in the coup attempt. I was then promptly driven off and incarcerated at the Central Prison, located on a nearby beachfront. At Central I was placed in confinement, which meant I had to stay behind bars in the main building of what was called the Women's Cell. At 6 p.m. I went into solitary confinement—a double locking of my room door until 8 a.m. the following morning. This meant no toilet facilities—forcing me to exercise control or to resort to old-fashioned methods.

Within a day, my family found out about my transfer and came quickly to the rescue with mattress, pillow, buckets, dishes, towels, utensils, clean drinking water, and all the other essentials for survival. I settled to life in a civilian prison which provided a little more comfort, with armed soldiers less in evidence.

A week later I was called to the Prison Superintendent's office, who happened to be an Army Colonel, and told that I should gather my personal belongings . . . again as I was being released. This time I refused to budge until I was told the full story.

As expected, I was transferred back to the Post Stockade—no explanation, no indication of what was to follow. Those I had left behind at the Stockade welcomed me back. They were not surprised. Word had spread that, having established himself firmly in the presidential seat with American connivance, General Doe was set to move against his primary political foes.

Life at the Post Stockade returned to normal. The investigations of prisoners at the Ministry of National Security continued but, with growing international pressure, several political prisoners had been released, most of them on 6 January. The rest of us prepared mentally for the long haul of, at best, uncertainty and, at worst, extermination.

On 6 February I was summoned to the Commandant's office again, this time to be hustled into a van full of armed soldiers and driven to the police station near the Temple of Justice which housed the city's courts. In the cell into which I was ushered, I learned that I was to appear in the magisterial court for a preliminary hearing into my case but had been taken to the police station to allow time for dispersal of the thousands of supporters who had thronged the courtyard anticipating my arrival. Jackson Doe, the presidential candidate of our opposition Liberia Action Party, had preceded me.

The crowd stood their ground and waited. After an hour, I had to be brought to the court amidst their thunderous applause. The courtroom remained packed as the judge heard the arguments. It was now 55 days since I had been detained.

On 13 February, the magisterial court brought in its verdict. Jackson Doe was released. I had to face a Grand Jury.

Following the court's decision, I was whisked back to Central Prison to await the outcome of the Grand Jury's review. By the middle of March, it was clear that something was amiss. Word reached me that the Grand Jury had found no evidence of my involvement in the attempted coup and had issued a "Bill of Ignoramus" which would have resulted in my immediate release.

When it was taken to him by the Clerk of Court, the presiding judge seized the Bill, refused to read it in court as required by law, and immediately had the jury sequestered. This was the same judge—Eugene Hilton—who had deserted the court rather than read a Not Guilty verdict brought by the jury in the case of James Holder and Robert Phillips, who had also been charged with treason for alleged involvement in the coup attempt.

Charged with treason

After reported pressure and bribery by the government through Justice Ministry officials, the Grand Jury reversed its opinion. On 2 April, the judge issued a Bill of Indictment charging me with treason. The Bill was served on me in prison by the Sheriff of Montserrado County. Thus, 113 days after my arrest, the government had finally succeeded in justifying the containment of my political activities.

I remained incarcerated throughout the month of April while my lawyers sought desperately to have the case placed on docket for the May term of Court. Justice delayed was justice denied, they pleaded. Finally, in the first week of May, the trial started—but surprisingly the government had called the case to request the court to grant official sanction to a petition for a change of venue from Montserrado County where I resided and from where the coup was allegedly attempted. The basis for the petition was that "the government would not receive a fair trial" in the county (Montserrado) where I had won a Senatorial seat. The fact that it was I, and not the government, who was on trial was lost on the Justice Ministry solicitors.

The Presiding Judge, Jesse Banks Jr., proved to be a man of honour and integrity as he refused to be intimidated by the government and, a few days later, ruled against it. He then called for a hearing of the case to commence the following week of 13 May. The Supreme Court, the highest body of last legal resort, immediately intervened, with a Writ of Certiorari which stopped Judge Banks from hearing the case. It was an open secret that the Executive Mansion through the Justice Ministry had ordered the Supreme Court to bring its lower court into line with the government's objective. At about the same time, the lawyers for defendants James Holder and Robert Phillips were courageously battling with the Supreme Court to compel Judge Hilton to return to the court. International observers concerned with human rights, the rule of law and African political development were by that time on hand in Monrovia. These included the American Bar Association, the International Human Rights Law Group (US), the Lawyers Committee for Human Rights, Amnesty International (UK), and the International Red Cross (Geneva).

The international press kept vigilance. Other specialised bodies such as the Interparliamentary Union kept a steady flow of communication. The US Congress grew increasingly weary of a dependent ally who showed so little respect for constitutional democracy and due process of law.

The international outcry proved so intense that by the third week of May, all trials, civilian and military, ground to a halt. We once again settled to the uncertainties of what would happen next. It came soon enough. A number of the police and Immigration officers who were also incarcerated at the Central Prison went through several transfers without explanation— first to the Post Stockade, then back to Central, then to the notorious rural military prison at Camp Bella Yellah, then back again to Central.

On Friday, 6 June 1986, the ordeal ended abruptly. In a nationwide broadcast, President Doe granted unconditional "Executive Pardon" to all those allegedly implicated in the 12 November coup attempt. The Minister of Defence and several high-ranking army officers proceeded to the Central Prison to effect the release. The crowds gathered outside the prison gates were held at bay. Press coverage was denied. Representatives from the official radio and television station were told that General Doe had ordered an official blackout of the event. Private journalists who stood their ground had their cameras and notebooks seized. On release we were told that to avoid any intermingling with the crowd, we would be driven to our homes in a tarpaulin-covered Army lorry.

The weekend following my release, I was requested to take the Senate seat which I had won during the October 1985 elections. My acceptance of the seat would have represented a change in my personal position and the position of my party (LAP) which had refused to accept legislative seats in protest at the blatant electoral fraud which placed the Doe government in power. I stood by my original position and refused the Senate seat, thus spurning overtures by private emissaries and through a public appeal by the Superintendent of Montserrado County. This refusal, well publicised by the BBC Focus on Africa, set in motion a fresh wave of censorship of my movements and restrictions on my civil liberties.

On 9 June, I applied to the Immigration Bureau for an exit visa to enable me to leave the country for medical reasons. The Commissioner of Immigration refused to grant the visa with the comment that I did not deserve an exit visa since I had not thanked Mr. Doe for releasing me from prison. Other released political prisoners faced similar comments from government officials. Within a week, the government announced an official ban on the travel of all those who benefited from the executive pardon. Round-the-clock surveillance of my activities then commenced. I was followed by security officers in various car—taxis, unmarked, unlicensed—as I went about my daily activities. At night, cars without lights stalked my neighbourhood. Army trucks and police cars frequented the area. I learned to live with this heightened form of intimidation.

During this period the opposition parties were engaged in an intensifying tussle with the government over their desire to combine their efforts under an umbrella organisation, the Grand Coalition. The Supreme Court subsequently ruled the body illegal and fined the heads of the three opposition parties $1000 each. The ruling arose out of what legal scholars are calling a landmark case involving a court taking upon itself the role of litigant. It seemed lost on the court that the constitution which went into effect on 6 January guaranteed citizens the right of association and of peaceful assembly to petition for the common good.

Wives' protest

Events moved very quickly after that. The opposition leaders refused to pay the fine and were incarcerated at the Central Prison. We condemned this action through public statements and asked the High Court for a review of its decision. The government responded by having the leaders transferred from Central Prison to the rural Bella Yellah military camp, although the court's detention order clearly stated that they were to be held in a prison in Montserrado County.

I then joined wives of the detained men in mobilising the women of the country to protest against the detention. A series of meetings were held to plan for a massive show of dissent through a demonstration. Government reaction came quickly. Armed soldiers kept constant surveillance of my home and those of the detainees' wives. I was contacted by a high-ranking official of the National Legislature who is a tribesman and friend of President Doe and told that "if the so-called concerned women proceeded with the planned demonstration they would really become women of concern." The threat to our personal safety was hardly veiled.

The final threat came on 16 August, preceding the planned demonstration by the women. The chairman of Mr Doe's party, accompanied by armed soldiers, visited my home and in the presence of my family warned that if the demonstration went ahead and anything happened to me, no one would be responsible. Similar threats were made against other women.

On Monday, the day of the demonstration, thugs of the notorious ruling National Democratic Party of Liberia (NDPL) task force visited my home around mid-morning. I was fortunate to see them approaching in taxis and was able to throw them off by pretending that I was not at home. It was clear that they had instructions to move against me. I immediately went into hiding.

After finding me absent from the demonstration, the thugs returned and terrorised my home and that of my elderly mother nearby. I remained in hiding, avoiding being seen during the day and sleeping in a different place each night. Meanwhile, the NDPL thugs roamed my neighbourhood in an effort to locate me. This continued until early September when I was able to escape from the country.

SONGS AND TALES OF SOCIAL NEGOTIATION

Nyano Bamana
THE MAN WHO DUG UP YAMS

Senegal 1971   Tenda

Marie-Paule Ferry, born in Angola and a researcher at France's National Center for Scientific Research (CNRS), recorded the tale "The Man Who Dug Up Yams" in 1971, in the Senegalese village of Iwol. The storyteller, Nyano Bamana, hails from the Bedik people. Ferry's research took her to the region of Kédougou, in eastern Senegal, where she studied the Bedik and Beliyan (Bassari) peoples. Both the Bedik and the Beliyan form part of the larger Tenda group. The Bedik, an ethnic minority, are considered to be in danger of extinction: There are only about 1,500 Bedik left between the Niokolokola Park in Senegal and Guinea. The Bedik people still practice initiation rites and religious ceremonies and live according to their traditions.

The Bedik people came to the eastern region of Senegal from the Bambara areas of Mali during the thirteenth or fourteenth century. The Bedik have never been centrally organized into realms or states, as were the ethnic groups in the north of Senegal. They are patrilineal, like the Malinke- and Pulaar-speaking peoples who live on all sides of them. They are primarily farmers, but on a scale too small to support them fully; they supplement their income by producing crafts such as baskets, bamboo mats, pottery, and sculpted wooden benches. The Bedik tell their stories at night, at festive periods of dancing and singing, during the dry season, when agricultural activity is at a low point and the villagers stay at home. The tales' words are supposed to be extremely powerful. As is the case throughout West Africa, stories are not just told for sheer pleasure but often provide an opportunity for the group to solve problems or educate the youth. Living precariously and traditionally, and totally dependent on the amount of rain that falls during the rainy season, Bedik farmers scrupulously respect the popular belief that attributes the power of making the rains stop to stories told at night.

The Bedik tell different types of tales representing the Tenda world. One category of tales takes place in the wilderness, and its protagonists are animals that act like humans; another category is set in the village, and humans are central to the story. The wilderness is a metaphor for the unknown, the mysterious; hidden forces and unknown beings dwell there. Women generally stay away from the wilderness and remain in the village, where social life is organized. The Bedik tales set in villages are known especially for their focus on daily life, their humor, and their brevity.

The language used by the best storytellers is not only metaphoric but also poetic and rhythmic. Storytellers suggest meaning indirectly, using onomatopoeia and ideophones, such as the invented word *bodobodobodo* in this story. When the husband says "*bodobodobodo*" after stumbling, the word evokes the sound of his near fall and suggests that, as he fell, he forgot the real word and replaced it with a word recalling the fall that caused his forgetfulness. The word and its implications all underline the man's stupidity.

In this tale, Bamana takes her theme from the Bedik people, the seasonal rhythms of their agriculture, and their necessary focus on the yam, a root vegetable and a key food. Using contrasts and opposition and involving her audience in the tale, the storyteller underscores the didactic function of storytelling in a Bedik world still almost untouched by modernity.

Aminata Diaw

✦

It was a time of famine.

The men went out to dig up yams.

One of them, more gluttonous than the others, told his wife that if she couldn't recognize the yam he dug up first, she wouldn't eat. Nor would any of the other women.

When he came home, she washed the yams, prepared them, and when she served them, she said:

"Syaro, here are the yams."

He said to her: "Well, come see if you can pick out the one I dug up first. Then we can eat! But if you don't know it, none of the women will eat, including you!

"Is it this one?"

"No, it's not that one."

"Is it this one?"

"That's the one I dug up last, just before coming home. It's not that one!"

"Is it this one?"

"Forget about it. You don't know!"

And thus he sat down and ate all the yams.

The next day he left again. He left to dig, then came back and said: "Nyano, here are the yams."

She washed them, and once they were clean, she started cooking them. When she served them, she said: "Syaro, here are the yams!"

He again said to her: "So come look!" She went over to him.

"Is this the one?"

"No, no!"

"This one?"

"That's not it at all. That's the one I dug up last just before coming home."

"This one?"

"No, not at all. You don't know. You might as well give up."

As she didn't know, he ate everything again.

The next day he left again. He dug and he said to her: "O.K., let's try again."

When the yams were cooked, she served them and called Syaro: "Syaro, here are the yams."

"Come see if you get it right today, then you'll eat."

She began: "Is it this one?"

"No. No."

"This one?"

"No, give up, you don't know!"

"This one?"

"That's the one I dug up last."

So he ate them all up again! And Nyano had lost so much weight! She spoke to her mother about it.

"Nyano, hunger is making you skinny. Don't you have anything to eat?"

So Nyano loaded up her things and left for her mother's house. She spent a week there. She took, she pounded, all she needed. They had cassava there. She took, she pounded, then she went home.

When she prepared the meal, she said to her husband: "Syaro, they gave me flour over there. And that flour that they eat over there, well, if a person can't recognize it, the women in the house won't let him eat it."

He said, "That flour there? It's just *bodobodobodo*. Who's never seen that? It's *bodobodobodo*."

"What? You think that's *bodobodobodo*?"

"Well, maybe it's beans?"

"What? beans? That's not beans!"

"Well, maybe . . ."

"Oh that's weak, that's not it! You don't know!"

And so she ate everything. And her husband got nothing.

The next day she cooked again. That day, too, she told him to come have a look. He tried a name. It wasn't that. He tried another name. It wasn't that. So she ate everything up again.

He ran to the diviner called "Red Forest." Once he was there, he said to him, "Red Forest, I'm upset. Nyano makes our porridge. And if I don't know what flour she made it with, I don't get to eat. Now I don't know what to do. She cooks, she eats, and only she knows what it is."

Red Forest told him, "In this season, it must be cassava. It's called 'cassava.' She's cooking with cassava flour. You must say to her it's cassava flour."

As soon as he left Red Forest, he started repeating "sassava, sassava." He got home, but before reaching the shelter in the fields, he stumbled. Bang! And out popped "*bodobodobodo!*"

"Hey, Nyano, don't you want me to guess again? It's *bodobodobodo*. Who wouldn't know that! It's *bodobodobodo!*"

"It is not *bodobodobodo!*"

So she ate everything up that day too.

He returned to Red Forest. "Red Forest, I don't know what to do, she said that wasn't it."

"Did I tell you to say '*bodobodobodo*'! I said 'cassava,' so what is this *bodobodobodo*?"

So Syaro left reciting "sassava, sassava!"

When he got home, he stumbled and, bang! out popped "*bodobodobodo.*"

"It's *bodobodobodo,* who wouldn't know that!"

"It is not *bodobodobodo!*"

He went back to the forest. "I told you 'cassava,' why are you saying '*bodobodobodo*'? I said 'cassava.'"

So he went home. But before arriving, he stumbled, bang! "*bodobodobodo.*"

When he arrived, his wife said to him: "Syaro, come eat this porridge. It's called cassava flour. I didn't have to go to the diviner. We're in a famine. When it's a famine, you have to think about each other. If somebody goes out, everything he finds should be brought back and shared by all. You dig up the yams every day. I cook them and I don't get any to eat. Every day! That's why I wanted to see if you could recognize the flour my mother gave me. A woman and a man aren't the same thing. I could have finished all the flour, cooked it all without your getting any. But come and eat!"

From that time on, when he went out for yams, he wasn't stingy with his wife.

And that's how it is.

Translated into French by Marie-Paule Ferry
Translated from French by Judith Miller

Communal
NAME POEMS

In West Africa, poems woven around personal names are common. Some are exclusive to particular families, while others may be used and embellished upon for different purposes. This is particularly true of poems composed for first names. Such poems are typically short and laudatory in nature. They praise positive character traits and physical beauty. They may also implicitly condemn negative tendencies. Name poems are often used by mothers and grandmothers in their daily discourse to praise children who have done their chores well. They are likewise aimed at encouraging the next generation to grow up into adults upon whom their families and society can depend. Name poems are also declaimed by women in praise of a brother, other family members, or close family friends.

In "Hasan," a mother paints a picture of a happy, popular, and successful man in the Songhai-Zarma community. The hyperbole of its images conveys grandeur. In "Sîta," a mother sings of the dilemma of nomadic families who may perceive the advantages of education but fear cigarettes and alcohol. They worry that if their children lose the skill and respect for herding, they will have to sell their precious herds, which are their only heritage. The poem sounds the nostalgic tones of a person denying the changes apparent in her society. In the last two lines, she evokes the idyllic image of the shepherd

guiding the most precious of the "beautiful browns"—the large cattle with
horns like lyres.

Fatimata Mounkaïla

✦

HASAN

Niger 1972   Songhai-Zarma

Hasan, the twin, master producer of pure white cassava.
For the twin, a skimpy serving of creamy millet is not enough.
What he enjoys is a calabash full to the brim
With the spoon floating and bouncing on the top.

Hasan, the twin, master producer of pure white cassava,
Arrives in the village
Carrying his lance, carrying his shield.

When Hasan walks into the village, powerfully armed,
The daughter exclaims: "He has come to see me!"
The mother exclaims: "He has come to see me!"
When Hasan arrives, powerfully armed.

Hasan does not have to flatter the mother of his beloved.
Whether the mother likes it or not, he'll marry her daughter.
Hasan does not take his wife's name from house to house.
He does not throw dirt in her face.
He doesn't say to her: "Come on, let's fight!"
Hasan is not an ant of a man.
The ant-man harasses his wife.
He harasses her on the sly.

Hasan is not a couscous-cooker of a man.
Whenever the couscous-cooker goes out,
A trail of criticism about his wife follows him.
Hasan does not say to his wife: "Come on, wife, let's fight,
If that's what you want, let's go!"

A helpful son, a handsome and powerful stallion,
Hasan does not go to Gurunsi without thinking about his mother.
He brings her, from afar, gifts of the richest clothing.
Clothes for grand occasions: short tunics, long tunics, layered tunics;
Barazza, Dan Kura, to be worn over the *Dan Zabacci.*

The twin, master producer of pure white cassava,
Master of the fig-tree, he is himself a fig-tree.
The prestigious Chief of Say.

When Hasan rises,
When Hasan rises to leave after a courting visit,
A quarrel breaks out:
The mother says, "It's for me that he came!"
The daughter says, "It's for me that he came!"
They quarrel with each other over my baby.

Translated by Antoinette Tidjani Alou

SÎTA

Niger 1984   Fulfulde

Sîta does not like cigarettes.
Sîta does not drink alcohol.
Sîta does not like going South to Kourmi.
Sîta won't study at the Western school.
All that Sîta will be guiding
Are the beautiful browns.

Translated by Salamatou Sow

Communal
EYIDI, OR NAMING

Côte d'Ivoire 1979, 1982   Abe

In the Abe language of southern Côte d'Ivoire, *eyidi* means the art of naming. A specific women's genre, *eyidi* poetry, declaimed rather than sung, identifies and redefines a conflict, allowing the speakers to reframe a difficult
social situation. Characterized by terse expressions, allusive phrases, and a
moral message, an *eyidi* often takes the form of a proverb and can even
become a proverb in its own right.

Women resort to this particular speech in order to challenge a specific
individual when ordinary channels of communication have completely dete-
riorated. An offended party might, for example, seek to resolve a dispute by
enlisting an ally who will help her create an *eyidi* in the style of a brisk dramatic exchange. Wherever the offended party encounters her ally, and
whether or not the offending party is present, she voices her challenge in the

first phrase of the poem. Her ally completes the *eyidi*'s proverbial intent by declaiming the second phrase. The next verses, spoken in turn and often improvised, comment on the conflict.

Aggressive and offensive, an *eyidi* can nevertheless deflect the anger and tension underlying the dispute through the laughter it provokes. Resulting in the best of cases in a generalized catharsis, an *eyidi* encourages social tolerance and integration. The author of an *eyidi* can hail from any social sphere. The creative flexibility of the genre permits some women to become genuine artists whose pungent phrasing acts on the consciousness of their villages.

Eyidi poetry exists in many areas of Côte d'Ivoire. The following examples come from the Abbey people. Each refers to a different type of situation. The first refers to a backstabber, the second to a quarrel between lovers. In the third, the offended party charges the offender with being inattentive, quarrelsome, and meddlesome by comparing him to an "ear going to Gabon," a Central African country far from Côte d'Ivoire.

Helen N'gbesso and Chantal Ahobaut

◆

Offended Party: If I leave for a moment . . .
Ally: . . . I'm stabbed in the back
Both: When we're together, you speak sweetly to me.
But if I get up to leave during a conversation
You proclaim, "This Leeno girl is really insignificant."
After that, you strip me naked.

Offended Party: I love the man . . .
Ally: . . . but the man does not love me.
Both: If I love you
And you don't love me, I shall cease to love.
What's so fine about you that your refusal to love makes me suffer?
So you don't love me. . . . I love myself!

Offended Party: The ear that is determined to go to Gabon . . .
Ally: . . . doesn't care about the distance one has to travel to get there.
Both: If somebody over there is speaking in the street while we are
    speaking here
His longing for a quarrel will make him strain his ear to catch what's
    being said over there.
If the person speaking is at the other end of the village, he who's standing here will turn his ear there.
He doesn't catch what we're saying here
Because, wanting a quarrel, he hears only what's being said there.

Translated into French by Chantal Ahobaut
Translated from French by Judith Miller

RECITATIVES FOR DRUM AND DANCERS

From Niger, Mali, and into the Senegambian area, it is common for women to invite well-known drummers in their communities to play for them at various gatherings, including weddings and baptisms, or, in recent times, those organized by such institutions as political parties. The invitation may also be issued by an informal neighborhood group of young women who wish to have an evening of entertainment. Dancers may use the occasion to air private matters; to affirm their family, caste, or status; or to preen themselves for their beauty. At the same time, the occasion may also express solidarity among groups of women.

Dancers and drummers develop a special relationship in these sessions. The drummers are there to do the bidding of dancers. Drumming is done in rounds. Those who wish to request a round of drumming (rather like a cross between a live jukebox and karaoke) must be able to express their feelings in the form of rhythmic poems, which they recite as they enter the ring.

"Play for Me, Drummer-Man," from the Songhai-Zarma area of Niger, portrays a variety of attitudes that might be taken by the dancer. First, the singer confirms the intense relationship between the drummer and the dancer. Second, she establishes her status, physical attractiveness, and skills. Third, she speaks as a bully who intimidates the weak or those thought of as weaklings, here skinny women.

Taasu is actually the generic name for a specifically satiric form in Wolof (Senegal) culture. Mareme Seye, of the village of Mboss, sings this song about her husband, who has taken on a second wife. She takes advantage of a large crowd to cut him to the quick by praising another man in the village, Seex Kasse. The *Taasu* poem is structured as an effective verbal retaliation and a public humiliation for the husband.

"The Gazelle" joyously defies social norms. The poet champions the cause of both slender and plump women, and submits that a balanced view of womanhood would consider qualities beyond physical appearance. In defiance, the slender Songhai-Zarma woman can recite a poem such as "The Gazelle" and be joined by all those who have the same build or are sympathetic to her position.

Esi Sutherland-Addy and Fatimata Mounkaïla

◆

Sadi Habi, PLAY FOR ME, DRUMMER-MAN

Niger 1999   Songhai-Zarma

Dance back and forth, player of the *cimba,*
Play for me.
Let me dance a few steps around the dance circle.

My tongue never falters and my dance steps are unique.

Even as a child, I never spoke nonsense.
I knew what was good and I knew what was bad.
My parents gave me everything good and a sound education.

My father would kill cows.
I would break the bones and suck out the marrow.

Player of the cimba,
Beat your drum.
While I do a few steps around a dance circle.

Woe is the skinny woman
Whose words cannot be taken to the mosque,
Whose words cannot be repeated before the saintly Mahaman Jobbo.
My father is well versed in Islam
He has read the Qur'an a hundred times.

Drummer-man, player of the cimba,
Beat the drum for me.
So I can dance a few steps around the dance circle.

Short am I and fleshy
Short, with hips as round as a calabash.
Low tree surrounded by tall trees,
Your shade is cooler than all the others.

The kapok and the fig tree do not grow just anywhere.
Happy are those who have such trees in their yards.

They grow in the courtyards of kings
They grow in the courtyards of princes
They grow in the homes of lucky men.

Translated by Antoinette Tidjani Alou

Mareme Seye, TAASU

Senegal 1979   Wolof

Seex is certainly not a "cheating husband"!
Tell me! What's a cheating husband?
A velvet gaze
Always focused on your *pagne*

He makes you dizzy
Then . . . he burns you like an ass.

Translated into French by Cherif Thiam
Translated from French by Antoinette Tidjani Alou

Communal, THE GAZELLE

Niger 1972   Songhai-Zarma

The gazelle is strutting around,
She's magnificent,
A beautiful creature is strutting around,
She's magnificent.

When she grows plump,
She remains a gazelle,
And when she gets thin,
She's still a gazelle.

Whether plump or slender,
She's a gazelle.
Whether plump or slender,
She's magnificent.

The gazelle advances,
Lithe as air.

The gazelle strides forth,
May God preserve her!

Translated by Antoinette Tidjani Alou

Salle-ka-ma-kani
TYPES OF WIVES AND HUSBANDS

Niger 1992   Songhai-Zarma

These two texts belong to the repertoire of the Zarma *griotte* Salle-ka-ma-kani.
Her name literally means "The wholly happy one." She is often commissioned
to perform such songs at weddings and baptisms, both occasions on which

women gather in large numbers. The "typologies," which list stereotypical flaws and misdemeanors in marriage, constitute social parodies, meant to be both didactic and entertaining. Such texts may function in part as thinly veiled criticisms of persons present, who must accept the adverse observations with dignity, knowing that one cannot make a public scene with a *griotte*.

Fatimata Mounkaïla

◆

FIVE TYPES OF WIVES

Among women, there are five types.

The first type is the cumbersome.

The cumbersome is the wife who sits by the doorstep as soon as the sun rises. She lies by the door to enjoy the fresh morning air, her mouth open; the doorstep is her pillow. When her husband comes home from work, he says: "Get out of my way! You've been sleeping at the doorstep since this morning. Other women have already done this and that, but you just lie there snoring." She lifts up her little head, stretches out her scrawny neck, and answers: "Leave me alone! I won't do anything! I won't do anything!" And back she goes to sleep. She's of no use whatsoever in this world.

The second type is the sleepyhead.

This is a very troublesome sort of woman, a harpy, a shrew, who is always harassing her husband. Their neighbors often interfere to calm them down. They look on in amazement: "Good heavens, what a difficult woman!"

The husband says: "Get out of my house!" She answers: "I am not leaving!" Whether he likes it or not, it's the husband who will have to leave the house. As soon as his back is turned, it's back to sleep. This type of wife is a real sleepyhead.

The third is called: I feel I'm going to get sick.

This woman is always saying: "I'm going to get sick." When the housework gets heavy, that is to say when her husband has guests, she tries her best to find some balm. She rubs it all over her forehead. That day, the husband's guests will have to go to bed without dinner. She's going to be sick. She's sick!

The fourth type is called: What did I get out of this?

This is the woman whose husband brought a low bride wealth and who has not given him any children. If the husband tries to bother her, she replies: "What did I eat or drink that belonged to you? You married me for very little and I have no children for you." Before the husband realizes it, she's already gone.

The fifth type is called: The woman who's as strong as iron.

This is the real woman! No matter what fortune befalls her husband, if she has the means to do so, she will help him. If she has the means, she will not stand by and allow her husband to lose face. Whatever she owns belongs to both of them. If a guest comes to see her husband while he is out, she will serve him food just as her husband would have done. The guest goes away contented and very happy. Yes, this woman is as strong as iron. She's the real wife!

THREE TYPES OF HUSBANDS

As for men, there are three types:

The first type is called the impregnator.

He has so many children that he cannot feed them. When he sees the sun setting, he says to his wife: "Hey, don't you see that it is getting dark? Why haven't you been to your family's house to find something to eat for your children?" The wife will say: "Yesterday, I was there; they gave us some food. Day before yesterday, I went there, I got some food. Is my family the father of these children?"

"All right, stay there. You're the one they're going to cry on anyway." Upon this, the impregnator pulls up the hems of his boubou and off he goes to town. When someone invites him to eat, out of politeness, he sits down and gorges himself till he's quite full. Then, he goes back home, knowing that he has eaten while his children are there crying on his wife. This is the impregnator for you.

The second type is called the famished one.

Yokojonjon's family suffers from chronic malnutrition and is always under pressure. Even when there's food in the house, they are always under surveillance, and get the strict minimum. Besides, he's always spying on everyone and his poor wife is never in peace.

The third type is called the provider.

In Yokolla's house, even the guest who happens to come by eats his fill and is satisfied. And even if the devil causes trouble between him and his wife, he keeps on providing for his family's needs. A quarrel does not cause him to change his behavior in this regard. This man is the only one who deserves to be called a husband.

Translated by Aïssata Niandou and Antoinette Tidjani Alou

Nana Yaa Tiakaa
THE POOR ORPHAN: A FOLKTALE

Ghana 1995   Akan-Twi

The Akan "spinner of tales" (*anansesem tofo*) creatively retells stories that his audience generally already knows; his dramatic performance belongs to what have been described as "total creative intercourses" in which each verbal and nonverbal element becomes meaningful.

This type of tale, often called "The Two Girls" or "The Two Daughters," is widespread in West Africa. Its performance served the purpose of encouraging girls to conform to the model of the exemplary, submissive woman—the only type of woman her society would tolerate and integrate. In two parallel sequences, progressing in opposite directions, the same "initiatory" story is thus told—the first sequence ending with the successful entry of the heroine into her cultural world, the other leading to the social death or marginalization of her rebellious sister.

Nana Yaa Tiakaa, the seventy-two-year-old storyteller of Wenchi (in the Brong Ahafo region of Ghana), is the Queenmother's older sister; she has lived all her life in the royal home (*ahenfie*). Her own life story is filled with the very images that her tale employs: thick forests inhabited by ferocious animals, such as "the mighty Elephant" or "the Leopard and his claws," known only to hunters and to mysterious beings such as the legendary dwarf Adape Akua Taa Ben Sini (whose name means "Adape Akua and her half-broken tobacco pipe"). Her memory abounds with images of festivals, such as the nubility rites for girls that take place by the riverside, the place of purification. At the back of her mind, undoubtedly, are many painful images that recall the fate met by women living in a Brong rural environment in a matrilineal and, during her childhood, still strongly polygamous society. The story also vividly represents the tragedy of the "poor orphan" the storyteller was herself when, much too early in life, she lost both her parents and was left with the responsibility of raising her siblings alone.

Nana Yaa Tiakaa's version of a well-known West African tale, then, is rooted in the natural and social environment of a Brong village, and in the circumstances of her own life. In order to survive, she had to learn the painful lesson proverbially expressed at the end of her story: "If you act insultingly in public, sticking your thumb out at people, you are sent off with slaps." A certain amount of submissiveness and conformity to Akan social norms was a prerequisite for remaining part of a communal order still ruled by men. Nana Yaa Tiaaka's profound existential sadness nevertheless infuses the whole text, as she makes us empathize with Ataa Kumaa's fate. The tragedy of Ataa Kumaa's life as an orphan and the difficulties of her entry into adulthood are summarized in the tale-song (*dwom*), a lament she repeats four times as she moves along the road that gradually takes her to her "initiator," Aberewa, the old woman who lives in the most remote part of the forest. Ataa Kumaa will come back to the village liberated from childhood but not from the burden of womanhood to which she surrenders, while her rebellious and callous sister will meet her untimely death for refusing to play the game.

Telling a tale is, of course, an occasion for letting one's imagination and fantasy loose in their dalliance with a web of words. But to tell a tale (*anansesem to*), among the Akan, is not mere child's play; the artistic performance of such pluri-coded poetic texts, in which elements of the "real" social and natural environment are rhythmically intertwined with mythology, proverbs, and songs, affects both the teller and the audience in their cultural representations and beliefs. The inner movement of the tale, its profound motivation, the issues it raises, all open up questions and lead the participants either to continue or to cease trusting in and complying with well-established social norms. The audience will, in any case, be shaken by the symbolically unfolding drama—the many dangers of this passing world, the awaiting silence of death, and the cruelty of social tensions and of family relations are laid bare. Human beings seem to be thrown into the game of life with, as their sole defense against destiny, the power of their poetic language—a power to accept or to contest and alter the disorders of an unhappy social life.

The storyteller raises questions; the audience is free to think and act. Before the drama unfolds, the teller announces: "We are entering the world of make-believe," symbolically detaching it from the "real world." And when it ends, the storyteller neatly concludes: "Whatever you think of my tale, whether you like it or do not like it, do not let it end with you. Spread it and let someone else tell another good tale." And so the "storytelling" act of provocation goes on . . . without constraint.

Christiane Owusu-Sarpong

✦

A man once lived with his wife. They had two daughters: Ataa Panin, the elder twin, and Ataa Kumaa, the younger twin. Soon after their birth, their father died. A year or so after their father's death, their mother also died. But before she died, she called Ataa Panin to her and said:

"Ataa Panin, I am very ill. I doubt whether I will ever get better. I am dying. Therefore I leave Ataa Kumaa in your care. Take good care of her. When she grows up, give her hand in marriage to a good man. When she bears children, take good care of her and her children. Treat her children as if they were your own and bring them up well. Use all that I have and all that I bequeath to you in looking after Ataa Kumaa and her children."

"Yes, Maame, I will do exactly as you have told me," Ataa Panin promised.

Because of this promise to her mother, Ataa Panin took very good care of her sister. The days went by. Then came the day of the great festival, the day of the *Afahye*. For the occasion, Ataa Panin strung gold nuggets and beads together, twisted it into a serpent-like necklace, and asked Ataa Kumaa to wear it for the *Afahye*.

As part of the celebration, she went to the riverside with other young girls. During the rites at the riverside, the necklace that Ataa Panin had strung together for her tore from her neck and sank to the bottom of the water. "The necklace that Ataa Panin strung for me is lost," Ataa Kumaa told her friends. "Please help me to look for it." For over three hours Ataa Kumaa and her friends searched for it but they did not find it.

"Let us go home," her friends urged her after their fruitless search. Ataa Kumaa cried all the way home. She was afraid of what her sister would do to her so she stayed outside the house and cried.

In the meantime, Ataa Panin was very worried about her younger sister's long absence from home. "Ataa Kumaa should have returned home by now," she mused. "She should have been home by now. I am going to look for her." When she stepped out of the house to look for her sister, there was Ataa Kumaa, standing there and crying her heart out! "Why are you crying?" Ataa Panin asked her. "You said you were going to the riverside, and yet you stayed out so long. Your eyes are swollen from crying. What happened to you? Did someone beat you?"

"No," Ataa Kumaa replied.

"Why are you crying then? If anyone has beaten you let me know so that I can go to that person's house and give him a piece of my mind," urged Ataa Panin.

"No one has beaten me," Ataa Kumaa insisted. "However, the gold and beads necklace which you strung together for me tore, and I have lost it in the water."

"What?" exclaimed Ataa Panin. "Have you lost the valuable piece of jewelry that my mother bequeathed to me on her deathbed, and which I lent you, in the water? Go back and look for it, and return it to me, otherwise you will not enter this house today! Return to where you lost it and search for it again!"

Poor Ataa Kumaa!

"My dear sister," Ataa Kumaa pleaded with her elder sister, "my friends and I searched for it for a very long time, but we could not find it."

"I don't care a fig about how long you searched for it," Ataa Panin told her sister. "Go back and look for it again. If you are unable to find it, I will demand from you the eyelash of an elephant. If you don't find it, I will demand from you the claws of Etwie, the leopard. If you don't find it, I will demand from you the leaves of the sacred tree Ahum ne Aham. I am demanding from you half of the dwarf Adape Akua Taa Ben Sini's pipe. I am demanding from you the crust of dirt on the back of Aberewa, the old woman!"

"Where am I going to find all these things?" Ataa Kumaa asked her sister.

"I don't care at all where you find them," Ataa Panin replied.

"All right," Ataa Kumaa told her, when she realized she had no choice. "I will go." She set out on her way. She traveled a very long distance before she saw an elephant. "Little girl," Elephant cried out to her. "This place is where no human being ever comes. Why have you come here? Any human being who ventures here never returns. What are you looking for in a place like this? Now that you are here, you will certainly die! You will never return home! Tell me, why have you come here?"

The girl plaintively sang her reply:

"Mother died and left behind Ataa Panin and me,
"Father died and left behind Ataa Panin and me.
"Ataa Panin strung together gold beads and twisted them into a neck-
    lace for me.
"Now it is torn and lost under the water.
"Ataa Panin says all she wants . . .
"All she wants is the eyelash of an elephant.
"All she wants . . .
"All she wants are the claws of Etwie the leopard.
"All she wants . . .
"All she wants are the leaves of the sacred tree, Ahum ne Aham.
"All she wants . . .
"All she wants is half of Adape Akua Taa Ben Sini's pipe.
"All she wants . . .
"All she wants is the crust of dirt on the back of Aberewa, the old
    woman.
"Where on earth am I going to find Father Elephant's eyelash?
"The great and mighty Father Elephant!"

"It is all right," Elephant consoled her. "Continue your search. If you
find any of these things, on your way back I will give you my eyelash."
    "Thank you," Ataa Kumaa replied.
    She then met Leopard and told him the story. He also promised to help
her on her return journey. Soon after she left Leopard, she met the sacred
tree Ahum ne Aham.
    "Little girl, this is a forbidden place," he told her. "What are you doing
here?"
    Then Ataa Kumaa sang her song to him too, just as she had done before
to the elephant and the leopard:

"Mother died and left behind Ataa Panin and me.
"Father died and left behind Ataa Panin and me. . . ."

"Go on your way," he said to Ataa Kumaa. "There lies the way to Adape
Akua Taa Ben Sini. If you find what you are looking for, on your way back
I will give you some of my leaves."
    The way to Adape Akua Taa Ben Sini was through a very thick forest!
And this little girl had to walk all alone through it until she met Adape
Akua. She was busy cutting her tobacco into little bits just like a cigar. She
loved to chew these bits of tobacco. "Little girl, this is a forbidden place.
What are you doing here?" Adape Akua also asked her.
    Then Ataa Kumaa sang her song again:

"Mother died and left behind Ataa Panin and me.
"Father died and left behind Ataa Panin and me. . . ."

"Ah, little girl, you poor thing! Your story is very sad indeed. Go, this is
the way to Nana Aberewa's place. If she gives you what you are looking for,
I too will give you what you are looking for," Adape Akua promised her.

Ataa Kumaa cried all the way to Aberewa's house. It was dark now, and
she was walking through this fearsome forest all by herself. She sang her sad
song along the way. Then she met Aberewa, the old woman. "Why are you
here?" Aberewa asked her. Then Ataa Kumaa sang her sad song, saying:

"Mother died and left behind Ataa Panin and me.
"Father died and left behind Ataa Panin and me. . . ."

"This is a very sad story," said the old woman. "However, this is a forbidden place; no one has been able to get out of it."

"Nana, please help me," pleaded Ataa Kumaa.

The girl looked for Nana Aberewa's house. When she had found it, she
took a broom and swept the whole place clean. She washed all the dishes,
and set the house in order. She even removed all the cobwebs in the house!

"Ahaa!" exclaimed Nana Aberewa, when she discovered what Ataa
Kumaa had done. "Under normal circumstances, you would be unable to
leave this place. However, your story is so sad. Because of the good you
have done me, I also will help you."

She turned her back to Ataa Kumaa. The old woman had not had a bath
for a very long time because it was so cold, and there was a thick crust of
dirt on her back. She asked Ataa Kumaa to scrape some off. Then she tied
it up in a parcel, and gave it to Ataa Kumaa. She also gave her a ring. "Take
this ring too as a reward for all the good things you have done for me.
Wear it on important occasions." Ataa Kumaa thanked her and set off on
her journey back home.

Soon she met Adape Akua Taa Ben Sini.

"My child, did you find what you were looking for?" she asked Ataa Kumaa.

"Yes," Ataa Kumaa replied. Adape Akua broke off half of her pipe, tied
it up in a parcel, and gave it to Ataa Kumaa.

On her way from Adape Akua's house, she met the sacred tree Ahum ne
Aham. He gave her what she was looking for. She then met the leopard,
who removed some of his claws for her. When she had left Leopard, she
met Elephant; he too removed his eyelash for her. She set off for home.

As soon as she got to the outskirts of her village, her sister saw her coming.

"Ataa Kumaa, is that you?" Ataa Panin asked. She eyed Ataa Kumaa's
ring with particular interest. Ataa Kumaa kept it in a safe place. Not long
after Ataa Kumaa returned home, it was time for the celebration of the
Afahye once again.

"Ataa Kumaa, can I wear your ring today?" asked Ataa Panin that day.

"Yes, you can," Ataa Kumaa replied. "Go and take it." Ataa Panin did. During the day's celebrations, she lost her sister's ring!

"Ataa Kumaa, I have lost your ring," said Ataa Panin to her younger sister.

"Go and look for it then," said Ataa Kumaa to her sister. "Otherwise, bring me exactly what you demanded from me!"

"Where did you find these items?" Ataa Panin wanted to know.

"No one told me where to find them when I set out to search for those impossible items," Ataa Kumaa replied. "Therefore, go; you will find them if you search diligently enough!"

Ataa Panin had no choice but to set off on her search for the same items that she had demanded from her younger sister. The elephant was at home when she arrived there.

"My child, this is a forbidden place," Elephant told her. "What are you doing here?"

"I have lost a valuable piece of jewelry that belongs to my sister who was here recently," Ataa Panin explained. "Now she is demanding from me exactly what I demanded from her. Therefore I want some of what you gave her, so that I can pacify her. Give me some so that I can be on my way!"

"This is the way to Leopard," Elephant told her. "If Leopard gives you what you want, on your way back, I too will give you what you want."

She met Leopard just as Elephant told her she would. "My child, this is a forbidden place. What are you doing here?" Leopard asked her. "I have lost a valuable piece of jewelry that belongs to my sister," Ataa Panin replied. "Now she wants it back. Therefore, give me some of what you gave her so that I can pay back what I have lost."

"Go," Etwie told her, and showed her the way to the sacred tree Ahum ne Aham, Adape Akua Taa Ben Sini, and Aberewa the old woman.

"Good morning, Nana Aberewa," greeted Ataa Panin when she came to the old woman's place.

"A very good morning to you too," responded the old woman. "This is a forbidden place. What do you want here?"

"Well, I lost Ataa Kumaa's ring," Ataa Panin explained, "and she is asking for so many things in exchange."

"Where are you going to look for them?" the old woman asked.

"Why, right here on your back. Turn around so that I can scrape off some of the crust of dirt," Ataa Panin rudely demanded of Aberewa. "Turn around!"

Aberewa sat very still and looked at Ataa Panin. She was dumbfounded by her insolence.

"Aberewa," shouted Ataa Panin, "didn't you hear what I said? Give me what I want so that I can be on my way."

"I don't have what you are looking for," Aberewa replied.

On hearing this, Ataa Panin pushed Aberewa over and scraped off some of the crust.

"How could you do this to me?" Aberewa asked the girl. "I have nothing to say to you. Go, and you will reap the consequences of what you have done on your journey back home."

On her return journey, she met Adape Akua Taa Ben Sini. She was just as insolent with her as she had been with Aberewa. She even fought with her. "I do not have what you are looking for," Adape Akua told her. Ataa Panin would hear none of it. She broke off a piece of Adape Akua's pipe and went her way.

"Go. I have nothing to say to you," said Adape Akua bitterly. "You will see what happens to you on your journey."

Her encounter with Ahum ne Aham was no different. After a very long struggle, she plucked off some of his leaves and took off. Then she met Leopard. "Little girl, how was your journey?" Leopard asked her. "Were you successful?"

"Well, they would not give me what I asked for," she told Leopard. "So I simply took what I needed from them. Now it is your turn to give me what I want so that I can go home."

"Aha, so you are not afraid to play games with me, are you?" Leopard snarled at her. Leopard pounced on Ataa Panin and beat her to death.

Ataa Panin never returned home.

This is why our elders say that if you act insultingly in public, sticking your thumb out at people, you are sent off with slaps. Therefore, whatever you think of my tale, whether you find it interesting or not, don't let it end here with you; spread the moral lesson and let someone else tell another good tale.

Translated by Frederika Dadson

BODIES AND BABIES: THREE SONGS

Depending on the situation, individuals or small groups of women may sing about birthing and sexuality. These songs are not restrained by ritual status and form a pool of lyrics that mature women may draw upon in a variety of informal leisure and work situations. Such songs, which are performed without instrumental accompaniment, may be sung in praise, thanksgiving, lament, or satire. The themes range as widely as the experiences and emotions of the women who sing them and may be adapted by each singer to suit her personal circumstances.

The selections that follow came from three different cultures—Diola and Sereer, from Senegal, and Hausa, from Nigeria. Each provides a radical reading of childbirth, childlessness, and aging, respectively. In "The Torments of Labor," sex and childbirth are stripped of their glory and presented with loathing, amplified by the insensitive behavior of the birthing mother's father and husband. By contrast, "I Have Hope" sounds the pain of the childless woman whose husband is also insensitive to her suffering. "Did You Say I Am Old?" sung by Kataf women in the south of Kaduna state in northern Nigeria, is representative of Kuku songs used to taunt ungrateful, oppressive husbands.

Esi Sutherland-Addy, Nkoli Ezumah, and Christine Ohale

✦

Communal, THE TORMENTS OF LABOR
Senegal 1998   Diola

Call: Oh, the signs of labor had started.
Response: All I wanted was delivery.
Call: Oh, the signs of labor had started.
Response: All I wanted was delivery.

Call: When the warning signs of labor started,
I went to see Bourama.
From his door-step, the good man asked, "What's the matter?"
Response: All I wanted was delivery.

Call: I went to lie down on my bed,
But I was afraid of delivering alone.
I got up, went to sit by the door.
I sent for my Aunt Sadiya to assist me.
I sent for my father, I sent for my mother.
Response: All I wanted was delivery.

Call: So Aunt Sadiya arrives.
She says: "What's wrong with you, girl?"
I tell her: "I'm going to die."
She says: "But, if you die, people will say you're a witch."
Response: All I wanted was delivery.

Call: At long last, the baby was there.
I say to her: "I don't want this child."
My Aunt Sadiya is childless. So she says, "I'll take it."
I tell her, "Before you take it, ask me why I don't want the child."
Response: All I wanted was delivery.

Call: When my labor started,
I saw my husband leave his room dressed like a king.
He said he was going to a sacred ceremony.
Response: All I wanted was delivery.

Call: Then when the child took his first steps,
Back came my husband, to solicit me, on his knees.
I knew it was starting all over again,
And later he would abandon me.
Response: All I wanted was delivery.

Call: If only I had thought this through before,
I would have gone to my father's,
So he could find a key
To lock up my private parts.
But my father didn't think of this either.
Response: All I wanted was delivery

Call: Maybe, that way, I would have had four years of relief.
Response: All I wanted was delivery.

Translated into French by Souleymane Faye, Aminata Diaw, and Rokheya Fall
Translated from French by Antoinette Tidjani Alou

Communal, I HAVE HOPE

Senegal 1998   Sereer

Oh, you men, I still have hope!
Sterility shouldn't prevent marriage,
But a woman isn't free to choose.

Men say a sterile woman
Has no future.
She brings bad luck.
She mustn't speak to her husband.
What could be worse?

Life is too short.
Let's enjoy it!

How can I go on living with our mothers
When I'm not myself giving birth?

I place myself in God's hands.

Translated into French by Souleymane Faye, Aminata Diaw, and Rokheya Fall
Translated from French by Judith Miller

Kunak Bonat, DID YOU SAY I AM OLD?

Nigeria 1970   Hausa

Do you say I am old? I am old?
Am I old only from the waist up?
Am I old only from the waist up?

You say that I am old?
What of the work I do in your house?
What of the children I have produced for you?
What of the farm work I do for you?
Are they not from this same body?

So you say, I am old, I am old.
Am I old from the waist up?
Am I old from the waist up?

You say I am old?
You know I am old, eh?
So why did you look for me last night?
What did you do with me last night?

So you say I am old? I am old?
Am I old only from the waist up?
Am I only old from the waist up?

Translated by Zuwaqhu Bonat and Diedre L. Badejo

Bohintu Kulibali
I AM NOT A COW

Mali 2000   Bambara

On Fridays in Bamako, Mali, a women's peer group, most of whose members are in their early thirties, meets to talk, eat, share problems, and offer support to one another. The women all pay a small amount weekly, and when a sum has been saved, it is given to one of them, who is then able to start a business. While storytelling was not at first part of the women's meetings, they began to tell stories when a friend offered to record and translate them.

The women's stories are *nsiirin*, a category of Bambara folktales also known as *ntalen*. While *nsiirin* storytelling usually occurs during the dry season at night within one's home, these stories were told in daytime during the rainy season. Three of the eight stories featured the theme of the evil cowife and the orphaned stepchild, apparently a favorite for women in their thirties, since they may soon have to face the dreaded prospect of a second wife. The women clearly identified with the deceased wife.

The storyteller speaks in phrases, interrupted by a response from the audience, ordinarily the interjection "*naamu!*" meaning, "Carry on! It is the truth!"— impossible to translate literally into English. The word affirms the prowess of the storyteller and the veracity of her tale. As in this story, the rhythmic pattern of statement and response tends to fade away as the story proceeds. The core of the story uses repeated ideophones, or invented sounds and syllables that vividly invoke and describe the narrator's feelings—in this case, *kololo* and *nyangasi*, which refer to the narrator's sensations as she grows horns on her head and sprouts hair on her skin.

Sven Ehrilich

◆

This is a story about two women.
 Naamu!
They were co-wives.
 Naamu!
One of them,
 Naamu!
She died and left her child in the care of the evil one.
 Naamu!
Now, every day she would cook food and give it to her children.
Then she would cook cow-dung and give it to her cowife's child.
Now, the child grew up eating cow-dung.
She ate it and ate it and ate so much of it,
That little by little she changed into . . . into a cow.

Her skin was covered all over with cow hairs.
Cow horns grew out of her head.
So she set off in search of her aunt,
For her mother had an older sister
Whom a certain king had married and taken to his village.
The girl did not know where this village was.
As she set off she said to herself:
I am going to look for my older mother's village.
She took the road and walked and walked till she came to a well by the side of the road.
 Naamu!
The people there ran away, saying:
"Ee! Did you see the cow, the cow, did you see her?"
She responded, saying:

"I'm not a co-how!
"I'm not a co-how!
"My mother died and left me with her cowife.
"Millet-pap is cooked and given to the other children.
"Cow-dung is cooked and given to me alone.
"Horns grew out of my head, *kololo!*
"Cow-hairs grew out of my skin, *nyagasi!*
"Horns grew out of my head, *kololo!*
"I am on my way to Nya, at Gala,
"To my older mother, Nya, at Gala."

They said: "Go, and peace be with you on your journey."
Again she walked and walked till she came to another well.
The people there also ran away from her, so she sang her song.
She set off once again till she reached the village where her aunt lived.

Indeed she reached this village.
When she got there, the people began to run away from her once more,
But when sang her song, they said:
"Ee, this cow speaks human tongue!
"Let her come back so that we can listen to her song."
So she came back to them
And sang once more:
"I'm not a co-how!
"I'm not a co-how!
"My mother died and left me with her cowife.
"Millet-pap is cooked and given to the other children.
"Cow-dung is cooked and given to me alone.
"Horns grew out of my head, *kololo!*
"Cow-hairs grew out of my skin, *nyagasi!*
"I am on my way to Nya, at Gala,
"To my older mother, Nya, at Gala."

They said: "Ee, peace be on your journey,
"And let there be peace where you come from."
It happened that a certain slave of her aunt was at the well.
She said: "Ee, she has mentioned the name of Nya, we should go and
    call Nya."
Others said: "Ee, she speaks of the wife of our king."
They said: "What are we going to tell her?"
They said: "How can we tell her about the thing that has become a
    cow?"
They said: "What are we going to tell her?"

They said: "We should go to her father."
These people did not know him.
They ran to call the wife of the king.
The king's wife said that she would come down,
She herself would come out to meet her little niece.
She did not recognize her, since her niece had been changed.
She came down to the well.
When she arrived, she said:
"Cow, who are you looking for?"
The cow said:
"I'm not a co-how!
"I'm not a co-how!
"My mother died and left me with her cowife.
"Millet-pap is cooked and given to the other children.
"Cow-dung is cooked and given to me alone.
"Horns grew out of my head, *nyagasi!*
"Cow-hairs grew out of my skin, *kololo!*
"Horns grew out of my head, *kololo!*
"A tail grew out of me, *kololo!*
"A cow-tail grew out of me, *kololo!*
"I am on my way to Nya, at Gala,
"To my older mother, Nya, at Gala."

The aunt ran to her niece and took her in her arms.
And said, "This is my little niece! This is my little niece!
"Who has dared do this to her?"
Women came and began to heat water.
They took her and removed the cow hide and parts.
She dressed in beautiful garments and went up to the house.
From where I took it, there I leave it.

Translated by Sven Ehrilich, Hamidou Kante, and Nene Ramata Sissoko

THE 1990S AND THE NEW CENTURY

Werewere Liking
ECLECTIC CONNECTIONS

Born in 1950 in the Bassa country of Cameroon, Werewere Liking now runs an arts village and school in Côte d'Ivoire. Writer, painter, singer, composer, choreographer, researcher, designer, theater director, and educator, Liking ranks among the great African artists of her generation, one of the few women to have garnered international recognition. *It Shall Be of Jasper and Coral: Journal of a Misovire and Love-Across-a-Hundred-Lives,* the best known of her five innovative prose texts, rewrite some of the fundamental myths governing the West African imagination. These novels foreground exceptional women figures, just as many of her poems and theater pieces celebrate the strength of African women.

Her theater and operatic pieces—some fifteen in all—adapt the ritual structure of the Bassa people's healing rites to questions of contemporary social and political concern. Known for its elaborate costuming, drumming, and dancing, her theater work uses all the languages of the stage to involve the audience in the pulse of the performance. In *Singuè Mura, Given that a Woman,* for example, Liking explores, through puppetry, dance, and mime, the consequences of women's oppression, especially the complex repercussions of abortion and sterility on the health of an African village and on Singuè Mura, the remarkable woman who animates it. In the excerpt included here, the eponymous heroine has just learned that her beloved mother-in-law has betrayed her by convincing her only son to take another wife, who is younger and supposedly fertile. Unable to have children because of botched abortions that followed a series of sexual abuses when she was a child, Singuè Mura confronts the terrifying fact that women always suffer mutilation in one form or another.

The interview that precedes the text was conducted by Judith Miller in Madison, Wisconsin, on 15 March 1995.

Judith Miller

✦

INTERVIEW WITH WEREWERE LIKING
Côte d'Ivoire 1995   French

JM: Werewere Liking, will you help me understand how you have become one of the only Francophone African women theater producers and directors, and the only one I know of to tour internationally? How, in the space of thirty years, you have not only written poetry, novels, and theater, but have also designed costumes and jewelry, composed music, launched a singing career, become a director and choreographer, done some filmmaking, written books on African marionettes and statuary, and set up a structure to teach all of this to young Africans from all over the continent?

WL: Well, I think it began in the beginning. And by that I mean I was born into a culture where the verbal arts—poetry, philosophy, declamation—are part of a general initiation to life, called by the Bassa people the *mbock*. Bassas believe that one can arrange and rearrange the universe through words. When I was little, we had wonderful evenings in which my grandfather brought the greatest of the Bassa storytellers to our village in central Cameroon. They sang; they played musical instruments; they danced; they mimed. They were complete artists. And my great aunt was a teacher of our initiation rites; she was one of the last sources for our knowledge of the *kiyi*, or "ultimate knowledge."

JM: Can you explain more about initiation rites?

WL: You know it's Westerners who invented the term "initiation." For us, it's just a question of the school of life. Everyone was initiated in a particular direction in order to be able to master certain skills, tasks, and ideas and in order to transmit them one day. You could, for example, be an initiate of the healing arts, or of the art of dialoguing—with which you can resolve a maximum of problems—or you could be initiated as a woman in how to give life as efficiently and with as much joy as possible and also in how to find a certain autonomy from your man. You could also be initiated spiritually—to become someone who would help others. We had these "initiations" at specific points in our lives. As we evolved and what was special about each of us became apparent, we were oriented in a particular way. (Sometimes we were oriented to help control what seemed to be a dangerous tendency.) The goal was always to maintain harmony within ourselves and within our society. Of course, now all of this is starting to disappear because of both religious and political repression.

JM: Do you mean Christianity?

WL: Yes but Islam, too; and today even our postcolonial leaders are afraid of the strength people derive from initiation.

JM: So, you would say that you always knew you were destined to become an artist, to be, in your own way, someone who initiates others to forms of knowledge that are being lost or repressed?

WL: It didn't exactly happen like that! In fact, it all really got launched because I ran away from home when I was sixteen. My parents were divorced and my mother had become a Jehovah's Witness. She wanted me to marry one of the parishioners from her church. (You know I already had my two children by then; but that's a long story and I won't tell it here.) Anyway, I wasn't going to marry this man. So I jumped a train and got picked up by a compulsive liar who took me home to his family in Bafia. They were great to me, but I had to keep out of this guy's hands. And given that my great-aunt had always told me that if I accepted what people offered, I'd have to pay them back, I decided to run away again. So I found a bus driver who said he'd take me to Yaoundé if I slept with him for two nights. I said "O.K.," and he didn't even wait for more passengers. When we got to Yaoundé, I practically flew off the bus and ran into a crowded neighborhood, where he chased me, yelling, "Thief." There were hordes of people after me: dogs, kids, everybody. When I saw an open door, I ran into a room and hid under the bed. The boys who were there thought I actually had stolen some money, so they kept quiet when people came looking. When I told them I'd only stolen "two nights," they were pretty disappointed.

JM: Who were these boys? What happened next?

WL: They were guitar players and they had a small band. And as it happened, they were looking for a singer. They wanted to know what I could sing, did I know Sylvie Vartan, Sheila, Françoise Hardy, etc.? Of course I'd never heard of those singers and I knew only some hymns from the Jehovah's Witnesses. So they taught me what I needed to know, and they bought me a red mini-skirt and sneakers and a shirt with a little round collar—I'd never worn anything like that before. I guess it worked. People liked me on stage, even though I was so nervous I almost died of shame. But that's how I became a singer.

JM: Where were your kids? How long did you live like that?

WL: My children stayed with my grandparents. And eventually I went to Douala where I got a gig in a nightclub. I sang with a band called "The Red Devil." In Douala, I met some really good people who told me I had talent, who encouraged me. I learned to distinguish classiness from vulgarity. I'd been so naive; I hadn't even known that vulgarity existed. I think that's what saved me—my naïveté. There were so many girls in Douala who sold themselves. It seemed to me then, and I remembered what my great aunt had said, that the worst thing a woman could do would be to get paid for making love. All the time I was at the nightclub, I worked things so that the manager thought I was with the band leader and the band leader thought I was with the club boss. I was able to keep away from all of them. But because I wasn't sleeping with the band leader, he never let me rehearse. I had to learn Ella Fitzgerald phonetically. I never knew what I was singing.

JM: I know you started to write and to paint when you weren't much older than eighteen. How did that come about?

WL: Among the people I was starting to spend time with and learn from was a newspaper man. He first taught me how to write articles. So I started to write; then I did all kinds of things: publicity, sales. I left the nightclub. But I had also met someone who told me I looked like I could do anything *except* sing in a nightclub. He gave me an arts course: "The ABCs of Drawing" and that got me started. You know, it's really funny because the only thing I could never do in elementary school was draw. I got into all kinds of trouble because of the stick man. I couldn't ever get him right. Sometimes I put his feet on his head. My art teacher spent a whole morning trying to help me trace the stick figure. And when I put his feet *and* his arms on his head, my teacher hit me so hard out of frustration that I fainted. When I came to, he told me I should go out to the playground when it came time for art class.

JM: That sounds like a major gesture of revolt, a complete refusal on your part. Or maybe the playground was a brilliant premonition, after all.

WL: I don't know what it was. But I know that when I started reading the art course materials and I read that most people don't draw what they see but rather what they know, I realized I'd better learn to *see*. And from then on, I've been painting.

JM: What happened to the man who got you started?

WL: He wanted to marry me; but I knew that somehow I'd find the father of my children again. He understood, but I've seen him since then. He was transferred to Gabon and when I had a show in Libreville, he came to see my work. He was ecstatic about my canvases. I think I really learned from him how thrilling it is to find talent in a young person and encourage it.

JM: And your dream of refinding your first love?

WL: Well, I refound that man I'd been carrying around in my head all those years; and we did get married. It was a great, great love story. He was wonderful in a lot of ways: he told me I had enormous promise as a thinker and a writer and that I'd waste my time in the kitchen. I sat in on all his classes at the University of Yaoundé. I learned everything that he learned. I even started researching his courses at the library. That's also when I became passionate about poetry. We'd have these incredible evenings with other students, with professors. We'd refashion the world with our words. There were nights when we'd recite our poems while we walked our friends home, and when we'd get there we'd turn around so they could recite theirs. We'd walk and recite until 4:00 or 5:00 in the morning. That was 1969. I was nineteen years old. And we were crazy. My husband had such energy. It was fabulous. And the professors started celebrating our own cultures and talking about history in another way. They got us interested in our heritage. You know, of course, that all those years of French colonization had almost succeeded in making us totally passive. At least 80 percent of what was taught to us about Africa by the colonial education system wasn't true. I experienced some of this firsthand when I saw how we were taught about the Cameroonian resistance movement. I can remember talking to the independence fighters in the bush when I was about five. I remember the women's songs we sang in our own language at night, songs composed to keep us in touch with what was going on in the bush after the French soldiers had isolated the local populations. I remember, most of all, my twelve uncles being shot in the head by the colonial army, their bodies left to rot and be eaten by vermin. We lived through those things, but they never showed up in any schoolbook I read. The professors asked us to search out these kinds of experiences. They taught us to record storytellers from home, to listen to our traditions, to look at things differently. I decided to return to my great-aunt's teaching when I realized that not far from Yaoundé there were healing rites going on exactly like those I'd witnessed in my childhood. I started to study them.

JM: And that's what moved you into theater!

WL: Finally, yes, but not before I got into trouble by criticizing the kind of theater my friends were doing. I thought it was too Western. So one of them said to me: "If you think you know what theater is, why don't you do it?" I started to see what could be theatricalized from the rituals I knew and wrote *The Devil's Tail* in 1976. We produced it, but not without trouble because some authority thought I was making fun of the president, who was rumored to be "illegitimate." What I thought I was doing was standing up for single mothers who refuse to write on their children's birth certificate "father unknown." I had had that experience and I told the bureaucrat who was making me fill out the forms that I knew very well who the father was! But he told me it was just my "opinion"!

JM: With things so exciting in Yaoundé, why did you leave for the Ivory Coast?

WL: It all changed around 1975. Our first "president for life" got scared and decided to break the intellectuals. The professors were ridiculed. The government lackeys started playing up publicly how privileged professors were. Then the government slashed their salaries, took their rent perks away, made them look like opportunists to the guys in the street, even to their students. The intellectuals didn't fight back. They couldn't deal with what was happening, even if they realized that most of it had to do with the economic crisis. So they closed down, gave in, shut up.

JM: And you decided to leave.

WL: I never thought about leaving my country. My ambition wasn't to become internationally known. I wanted to stay with my husband. In fact, I started to write, really and truly, in 1975—hundreds of poems, a lot of which I used later in my novels: *Orpheus of Afrika*, 1981; *It Shall Be of Jasper and Coral*, 1983; and even in *Love-Across-a-Hundred-Lives*, 1988. And I wrote another play, *The Sleep of the Unworthy*, 1980, about a megalomaniac president. I used excerpts from presidential addresses from all over the world. I exposed all the hollowness. I almost got arrested because of it, but luckily a childhood acquaintance who worked in internal affairs warned me that the police were coming, so I hid all my manuscripts at a friend's house. My husband couldn't take it. He was nervous. He told me maybe I'd better go away.

JM: Wasn't this about the time you met Marie-José Hourantier?

WL: Right. She'd been trying to get in touch for a couple of years, and when I ended up in the hospital with a serious kidney infection, she found me. I'd been trying to avoid her because I thought she was just another white woman trying to patronize me and find out what I'd learned. But she, in fact, helped me out of a horrid situation.

JM: What was that?

WL: Well, you know, I tried to kill myself. I think I took too many pills. It's still a blur in my mind. It seemed like hell. It was all happening because of the pressure from my in-laws. Today, I think that my husband and I were too far ahead of everyone, that we had a marriage nobody could understand. Normally, it's the husband who gets pushed ahead. But I had a man who encouraged me. Members of his family, even some of my cousins, started to say that I was the man of the house. It was pretty insidious. They ended up convincing him he'd been emasculated by me. Little things, you know, wearing him away bit by bit. So with the suicide and my ongoing kidney problems, he decided, with Marie-José's assistance, to evacuate me for treatment to France. When I was released from the hospital, all I knew was I didn't want to return to Cameroon. I asked my husband to come and join me, or at least to pick a neutral place, somewhere where we could meet and negotiate and not have to deal with his family—with all those people. But having become "the man" he'd never been, he insisted I come back to Yaoundé. He threatened to end our marriage if I didn't come back immediately. Well, I couldn't. And so, he took another wife. And I suffered. It took us four years to get a divorce. I think he always thought I'd come back. And I kept writing to ask him to meet me somewhere else. But he never wanted to.

JM: Is that when you went to Mali with Marie-José to do fieldwork?

WL: She'd been posted there and invited me to come along. It was incredible. The research healed me. I went everywhere to see marionettes, women's rites, all kinds of rituals. In Mali, people are closer to their traditions, closer to something fundamental. For example, the marionettes are wrapped in the most beautiful cloth: they wear costumes not even a village chief could afford. Each villager has to contribute something in order to dress the marionettes. When I asked an old woman how she could justify it, she answered: "Daughter, we may be poor in material goods but we're not poor in spirit. We can dream about beauty. And maybe it will happen. If we're weighed down by misery, even to the depth of our souls, how do you expect us ever to get free of it?" That set off something in me. People need to have access to the sublime, and African arts have always offered that. Mali made me sure of what I know today. I had experiences with certain Dogon priestesses, which felt like a personal revolution. And all the more so because my great-aunt had called me back to Cameroon to initiate me to the *kiyi*. She spoke to me of the origins of our people, of their migrations, of the kinds of questions that advance you to another plane of existence. That's when I understood what I had to do—and not necessarily only with Bassa people, but on a much larger scale. What I learned in Mali increased my desire to keep associating knowledge with knowledge, to build a pan-African network.

JM: How did you end up in Abidjan?

WL: Because of all the writing I'd done. Marie-José and I had already published a book on Bassa ritual, *From Ritual to Stage Among the Bassa People of Cameroon*, 1979, under the patronage of Professor Jacques Scherer of the Sorbonne. I was offered a contract at the Institute for African Ritual and Aesthetics. Marie-José got a position at L'École Normale. And off we went. For about six years, I published about two texts a year and quite a few articles.

JM: But I know that it wasn't all that easy for you and that the Institute didn't turn out to be a haven.

WL: A lot of the colleagues there fought me tooth and nail. They didn't like my creative work. They didn't appreciate the theater I was doing with the students. They were annoyed with how much I was publishing. For example, my study of Hampaté Ba's *Kaydara, An Interpretation of Kaydara by Hamadou Hampaté Ba*, 1984, was selected by the publisher of the Nouvelles Editions Africaines to represent the Institute, who didn't discuss this choice with many Institute members, and they hated me for it. I figured when my contract was up, I wouldn't ask for another one, all the more so because one of my students said to me, "If you really think one can live as an artist, why are you still at the university, instead of doing your art?"

JM: And that was the beginning of the *Kiyi* experience in 1983.

WL: The first phase of it, yes. Marie-José and I opened a small house, the Villa Kiyi. We started to do theater there. But we kept running into the same problems we'd always had.

JM: What were those?

WL: There was something about the way she saw things, or, rather, the way she talked about her vision that shocked me.

JM: Did you think she was too Eurocentric?

WL: That's right. I always thought she saw like a European—even today. Maybe I was wrong. She always told me I was wrong. It had led to some pretty animated discussions. Some of them show up in *Towards a Meeting with . . .*, 1980. It was always very stimulating: She didn't let me get away with messy thinking. I really learned to defend my ideas with her. And she made me see Africa from a critical perspective, even when it hurt.

JM: But in 1985 it was time for you to go separate ways: You became a theater professional, an arts promoter, a gallery owner, a teacher, and all the rest.

WL: It was my chance to work toward a pan-African aesthetic, to try to explode all our mental borders, to liberate a kind of energy that can contribute to a healthier Africa, to make being an artist an honorable profession—not just the praise-singer a powerful man brings out when he wants to hear what's good about himself. I wanted to establish a different image of Africans than the one even we see all the time on television: massacres, famines, war. I wanted to show young Africans that they're capable of creating, that, above all, they're free but that they're also *responsible* for their choices. At the Villa Kiyi, we combat the sense that everything is going wrong "because of colonization, because of God's wrath, because we're damned, etc." We always try to say we're responsible for everything that happens to us, that we can change if we want to, that we're free to open ourselves up to the world. I look to initiation techniques to convey this sense of responsibility to my young people.

JM: Do you use these techniques in your theater work?

WL: My actors need to know, as initiates do, how to find emotions in their bodies—which muscles are connected to which feelings, where to place an emotion physically so it can be communicated. And I help my actors know themselves, situate their lives in terms of life in general, understand that we're all connected.

JM: That's the practice of the *kiyi*, isn't it? And that's how you're continuing the work of your great-aunt.

WL: That's what I'm trying to do, with my actors, my musicians, all my people in the Villa Kiyi. We share this energy with the public, all the spectators who come—European and American tourists, well-off Africans, students, and especially the people from our neighborhood who come with their stools and set themselves up just outside the paid places—because, of course, they can't pay.

JM: Do you think you're changing the way people think about African women?

WL: I can't say that. But it's true that at least in early times African women were really pretty independent. Even today, I'd say it's women who hold Africa together and make things work. But it's also true that women were left completely behind during the colonial period. They were almost totally kept out of what then passed as "education." And the men who are governing Africa today are the ones who got that kind of education. I'm teaching something else.

Translated by Judith Miller

From *Singuè Mura*, or Given That a Woman

Côte d'Ivoire 1990   French

VII. Fifth Movement: The First Flux

When in the distance the din of the hunters grows quieter, the marionette representing the Mother-in-law—which had remained suspended from the wall of the sanctuary—advances timidly from behind the curtain, You inhabit it, Singuè Mura. You aren't able to imagine another refuge than this breast that has so often warmed you with tenderness! You're still astonished at your gaping wound, the source of so many memories. The song of complicity with your Mother-in-law bursts out of you, taken up and swollen by the voices of Village Chorus. Your face surges out of the belly of the marionette, a brutal birth to new suffering.

Singuè Mura: What is it that fatally condemns the confidant to betray the friend? Husband and wife turn their back on each other, daughter and mother split apart? Who would have believed it could happen? Oh you, dear Mother-in-law, my own Mother. You sacrificed your mind and your reason for a home quickly deserted. You found yourself with an only son and no possibilities for your future. So you know the price a woman pays when she becomes solely a reproductive machine. The ambitions she denies, the enthusiasms she curtails! The agony of being raped in her heart and her body, the fears she hides, the bitterness that accumulates, and the screams she silences. The nearby goals pushed farther and farther away so as not to distance the man and appear too big, too far away, because then she panics and flees. Remember the threats held out, Mother, the vision of permanent solitude, an empty home, a nervous breakdown. . . . And the constant ongoing duty of all women, mothers and wives, to keep reinventing the man.

Songs and memories of women's efforts to convince their sons, their husbands, that they're more than a pile of flesh and bones, but, rather, images of divinity. Flattery and faith. Initiation to motherhood, conjugal tests, patience, love's victory. All of that is in your song, your dance.

How strongly linked we were by that fundamental desire to transmit the flame, enlarge and prolong the dream. Do you think I didn't want it, I didn't try?

Feverish with impatience, tired of waiting, I collected children. Don't they weigh as much as the child I would have carried in my belly? Would the gift of my life to one child count more than what I have given to all I adopted? Lies!!!

A man can pass himself off as father to any foundling. But a woman has to go through hell simply because nobody saw her stomach balloon! After all the battles I fought and sacrifices I agreed to, must I still share my husband and my love? And what's more, with an idiot, who's never done anything with her hands or her mind—simply because she has what it takes to be a baby machine? There's not even any choice in the matter! It's unfair! Does it always take several women, or worse, several parts of different women, to please a man? Oh Mother, you've abandoned your daughter, you've condemned a woman to a lifetime of mutilation!

No! Within the effigy of the Mother within the breast of your beloved Mother-in-law, you can no longer take refuge; she can no longer be the center of your life. You're struggling for breath. You're losing your mind and your faith. You tear yourself from her, you empty her of love, you spit your hate at her.

I've had enough! To go on putting up with this village of ungrateful sorcerers who wallow in injustice. To continue accepting a society that wants to impose as the only possible model a woman without brains, with no personal ambition. Never! No longer! Do you hear me, Mother?

You empty poison out of a vial and quickly swallow it—as if you were afraid of losing your courage. The song coming from the Village Chorus communicates all your physical and emotional pain, all your thwarted love, your deepest unknown self. You fall down. You hear your Mother-in-law's voice call you desperately, but you no longer have the strength nor the desire to answer.

Translated by Judith Miller

Bernadette Dao Sanou
A DECENT WOMAN
Burkina Faso 1992   French

Bernadette Sanou Dao was born in Baguinda, in Mali, and at age twelve, she went back to her homeland, Burkina Faso, to continue her studies. She also studied at the universities of Dakar and Ohio and at the Sorbonne. She entered the civil service of Burkina Faso in 1977, and for twenty years she remained at the Ministry of Education. From 1986 to 1987, she was the minister of education for Burkina Faso. In 1997, she became responsible for international cooperation, and in 1999 she became the minister for regional integration. In addition to carrying out her official functions, Dao created the Association for the Survival, Protection, and Development of the Child, in 1988, and the Common Fund for Women, in 1991.

Dao has also won many literary awards for her books. In 1986, she received first prize for a collection of poems written in Dioula, one of the languages spoken in Burkina Faso. She was awarded the National Grand Prize of Arts and Letters for *Childbirth,* an adult collection, and for *Emeralds,* a collection of poems for children. For *Quota* and *Symphony,* published in 1992, she was awarded the French Jean Cocteau Prize in 1995. In 1997, she published *The Last Wife.*

In "A Decent Woman," from the volume *Quota,* using an ironic, nearly corrosive style, Dao describes gender relations in Muslim society. In such a society, the man, in the manner of a *kalifa,* or master, holds the keys that will open the gates to heaven, and his wife, therefore, must be entirely submissive to him. The voice of the woman reiterates, with feigned innocence, all the stereotypes held by the society about women. Nevertheless, the last three lines of the poem introduce contemporary social transformations, through the reference to the code, a judicial text for the protection of the rights of women. What makes this text particularly interesting is that it underlines

the need for men to wake up to these very changes of which women are
already fully aware.

Aminata Diaw

✦

Kalifa told me:
"A decent woman
    Must love her husband
Must find him more handsome than any other,
Bless him each day
For having made her into a person

"She must say YES when he coughs
    WELL DONE when he burps
    And AMEN when he farts!

"She comes running at the slightest gesture
    Of his pointed finger
    She does this and she does that
According to his will, good or bad!

"She makes him food
    The way he likes it
Her own taste matters very little
She serves him desserts he likes
    Her own taste matters very little
She serves him dessert at one in the afternoon
And so flatters his palate
    His belly and below
Whether she wants it or not!

"A decent woman
    Listens to her husband speak
    She says: YES to his dubious talk
    WELL DONE to his silly laughter
    And AMEN to his crude words!
She gapes admiringly at him
    And puts him on a golden pedestal!

"She dresses to his taste
    Her own taste really doesn't count
She does her hair up to his taste
    Her own taste really doesn't count
She lets him choose perfume for her

And is wildly delighted
Whatever its scent may be!

"A decent woman
   Quickly forgets 'paper and pen'
   And the school which taught her that
   From her husband she gets
   All learning
   And all discernment
From him too!
She sees the world through his eyes
And her own life, both joys and tears,
Are seen through his eyes too!

"A decent woman
   Must love her husband,"
   my husband, *Kalifa*, told me
Love him deeply and bless him forever
   Find him handsome and very bright
   At every turn
   Leave everything to him
   To him alone
   And wait
   Enraptured
   For him to bring life
   And the world to her!
Between my hands
   I have this code, curious to say the least,
     And dare say nothing of it
     For fear of provoking *Kalifa*.

Translated by Marjolijn de Jager

Ama Ata Aidoo
SPEAKING AS A WOMAN

Ghana 1992   English

Christina Ama Ata Aidoo was born in 1940 in the small village of Abeadze Kyiakor, in the central region of Ghana, where her father was the ruler. She was a child prodigy, and having gained admission into a prestigious girls secondary school in Ghana, Wesley Girls High School, proceeded not only to win academic prizes but also to write. Her first publication was a short story entitled "To Us a Child Is Born," which won a prize in a 1958 competition organized by the national daily newspaper *The Daily Graphic*.

In 1961, she entered the University of Ghana, where she won a prize for her now much-anthologized short story, "No Sweetness Here," in a literary competition organized by the Mbari Club of Ibadan. This award enabled her to attend a writers' conference in Nigeria, where she met Wole Soyinka and others and turned to writing plays, including *The Dilemma of a Ghost* (1965) and *Anowa* (1969).

Other books followed, in several genres: *No Sweetness Here*, a collection of short stories (1970); *Our Sister Killjoy*, a poetic novel (1977); two volumes of poetry, *Some One Talking to Sometime* (1985) and *An Angry Letter in January* (1992); a highly successful novel, *Changes* (1991); and another collection of short stories, *The Girl Who Can and Other Stories* (1997).

"The African Woman Today," published in 1992, spans centuries and geographical space to (re)place African women in an historical narrative while simultaneously marking the ironies and obstacles affecting their lives. "A Young Woman's Voice Doesn't Break. It Gets Firmer," also published in 1992, is one of several poems dedicated to Aidoo's relationship with her daughter Kinna.

Aidoo has taught English and African literature in universities in Ghana, eastern and southern Africa, and the United States. She has held director-ships of various Ghanaian corporations and councils and was the country's minister of education from 1982 to 1983. Since 1995, she has lived perma-nently in Ghana, where she has established an organization called *Mbaasem* (Women's Affairs), dedicated to supporting women writers in various ways, including the creation of a physical space for their use.

Esi Sutherland-Addy

◆

THE AFRICAN WOMAN TODAY

"In most countries of Africa whole sectors of the economy, such as internal trade, agriculture, agro-business and health care are in the hands of women."

West Africa (15 September 1991)

It might not be fair to blame as well-intentioned an event as Bob Geldof's Band Aid,[1] which was staged to raise awareness of the plight of drought victims in Ethiopia, and even raise funds for them. But there is no doubt that since then the image of the African woman in the mind of the world has been set. She is breeding too many children she cannot take care of, and for whom she should not expect other people to pick up the tab. She is hungry, and so are her children. In fact, it has become a cliché of Western photojournalism that the African woman is old beyond her years; she is half-naked; her drooped and withered breasts are well exposed; there are flies buzzing around the faces of her children; and she has a permanent begging bowl in her hand.

This is a sorry pass the daughters of the continent have come to—especially when we remember that they are descended from some of the bravest, most independent and innovative women this world has ever known. We speak of the Lady Tiy of Nubia (ca. 1415–1340 BCE), the wife of Amenhotep III and the mother of Akhenaton and Tutankhamen, who is credited with, among other achievements, leading the women of her court to discover make-up and other beauty-enhancing processes. Her daughter-in-law was the incomparable Nefertiti, a black beauty whose complexion was nowhere near the alabaster she is now willfully painted with. Again from the pharonic era, we evoke Cleopatra, about whom "more nonsense has been written . . . than about any African queen . . . mainly because of many writers' desire to paint her white. She was not a white woman. She was not Greek . . ." says John Henrik Clarke with the impatience of painstaking scholarship.[2] According to C.W. King, of Julius Caesar, Mark Antony, and Cleopatra, the last was "the most captivating, the most learned, and the most witty." Among the many languages she spoke fluently were "Greek, Egyptian, Latin, Ethiopian, and Syrian." Yet Shakespeare, heralding Western racism, could only dismiss Cleopatra as a "Strumpet."[3]

Collisions

Modern Africa came into collision with Europe with the journey of Vasco da Gama from Portugal southward to find Asia. He passed what became known to the West as the Gold Coast (Ghana) in 1492, and the Cape of Good Hope in 1496. Since then Africa has never known peace. First there was the slave trade. Then the end of the slave trade was celebrated with the conquest and colonization of Africa in the mid-nineteenth century. From then on, various Western groups considered Africa their happiest hunting ground. The energies of the people, the wealth on and in the land, everything that could be taken was taken by European powers, with complete abandon. The people resisted—to the best of their abilities. But it could not have been an even match, since one side fought with spears or bows and arrows, while the other used guns.

Less known is that in response to Europe's insistence on conquering the continent, Africa over five centuries produced countless women soldiers and military strategists, many of whom died in the struggles. A famous example was Nzingha (1582–1663), who tried to prevent the Portuguese from overrunning Angola. She died without achieving her objective, but only after showing them what she was made of. For their part, the Portuguese demonstrated that they had not come to Africa on a mission of chivalry. They fought Nzingha with uncompromising viciousness. When she suffered serious setbacks in 1645–1646, they captured her younger sister Fungi, beheaded her, and threw her body into the river.

In fact, in precolonial times, fighting women were part of most African armies, a well-known example being the all-female battalions of Dahomey (ancient Benin, early nineteenth century), who sought to protect their empire against invaders and internal treachery.

The Nzingha/Portuguese pattern was to be repeated in several areas of the continent over the next centuries. Queen after queen rose against the invaders. In the last years of the nineteenth and early twentieth centuries, Yaa Asantewaa, an Asante (Ashanti, Ghana) queen led an insurrection against the British. Although her armies were defeated, "it is safe to say that she helped to create part of the theoretical basis for the political emergence of modern Africa."

True, all these women were reigning monarchs who found it relatively easy to organize armies against foreign occupation. But history is also replete with accounts of insurgencies organized by women from non-monarchical traditions. One example is the women of Aba in Eastern Nigeria, who in the 1920s so successfully harassed the British that the colonial administration had to move its headquarters from Calabar to Lagos. Around the same time in Rhodesia (Zimbabwe), Mbuya Nehanda (Nyakasikana) was accused of fomenting an insurgency against the British. In the end, the conquerors decided that the only way to get rid of this frail woman was to hang her. And they did.

Struggles for Independence

After the Second World War, many women stayed in the forefront of the agitation for independence. Some, like General Muthoni (of the Mau Mau Rebellion) became guerrilla leaders whom the enemy feared even more than their male counterparts. Others, like Mrs. Ramsome-Kuti of Western Nigeria, were mainly nationalists of bourgeois and petit-bourgeois backgrounds. But then, so were the majority of the men who were their companions in such struggles.

Today, we know that the story of South Africa's fight against the institutionalized horrors of conquest would be different if women had not been prepared to get actively involved. And they paid the price. They were killed, maimed, incarcerated, and exiled. For instance, Sibongile Mkhabela was a student leader at the time of the Soweto riots. The only woman charged in the June 7th (1978) trials, she was jailed for three years and then banned after serving the sentence. Countless others like Winnie Mandela, Albertina Sisulu, and Zodwa Sobukwe survived the hounding of their men, only later to show an awesome readiness to assume leadership with all the sacrifices such decisions entailed.

Given such a heroic tradition, it is no wonder that some of us regard the docile mendicant African woman of today as a media creation. But if she does exist, she is a result of the traumas of the last five hundred years' encounter with the West, the last one hundred years of colonial repression, the current neocolonial disillusionment, and of a natural environment that is now behaving like an implacable enemy.

In 1992, the African woman must cope with a "structural adjustment program" imposed by the International Monetary Fund (IMF) and the World Bank that is removing subsidies from her children's education, from health care, from food. Transportation to and from vital areas of her life have either broken down or never existed.

In 1992, there is a drought and the world is phenomenally hot. And the African woman has already given up on the season's crops. She is now wondering whether there will be enough water to last her and her children through this year for drinking, for cooking nonexistent food, and to keep the body minimally clean.

In 1992, the African woman is baffled by news of a "plague that has come to end all human hopes."[4] And she is afraid that she and her children might not survive this disease whose origins no one seems to know, and for which there is yet no cure.

Africa is the second largest continent, covering an area of over thirty million square kilometers. In spite of centuries of exploitation by its conquerors, it is still, potentially, the richest piece of earth in the world, with 60 percent of all known exploitable natural resources. And in spite of the vicious campaign about an African population explosion, Africa is not the most populous place on this earth. China is. In fact, given its size and its current population of around five hundred million, the continent is *under-populated*.

Burdens and Riddles

Three major factors have influenced the position of the African woman today. These were indigenous African societal patterns; the conquest of the continent by Europe; and the apparent lack of vision, or courage, in the leadership of the post-colonial period. "Leadership" in this context does not refer to political leadership exclusively. We speak of the entire spectrum of the intellectual, professional, and commercial elites in positions to make vital decisions on behalf of the entire community.

From ancient times, the majority of societies around the world were either matrilineal or patrilineal. It is now clear that most African societies were matrilineages lasting millennia, from the prepharonic period all the way down to a micronation like the Akans of Ghana. What changed the pattern in some areas were, first, Islam and, later, Christianity, since both religions were obviously patriarchal in orientation. The African societies that retained vestiges of their matrilineages were also the ones that met both Islam and Christianity with the greatest resistance. These areas—for instance, coastal West Africa—are also where one finds some of the least oppressed women.

Today, it is not all easy to imagine the *coastal* West African woman bearing with any equanimity even the thought of the heavy black veil, the burden of purdah, circumcision, infibulation, and so forth. But even for the West African Moslem woman, the veil is no more than a couple of meters of an often pretty gossamer fabric. This she normally and winsomely drapes over the back of her head and her shoulders. Indeed, the effect of this type of veil is to make its wearers look more attractive and decidedly unhidden. In this, West African women seemed to have more in common with Islamic women in faraway places like the Indian peninsula and the rest of Asia than with their "sisters" to their immediate north.

What seems to separate the woman "south of the Sahara" from the Arab-Islamic woman of the north is not so much the latter's "closeness to Europe" and "civilization," as the former's relative freedom to create herself, economic and political dynamics permitting.

But then, according to Nawal El Saadawi, "There are many misconceptions [in the West] about the identity, character and diversity of Arab woman." This Egyptian writer asserts that although the North African–Islamic–Arab woman *is* veiled and circumcised, to know nothing more than that about her "borders on racism." Maybe African women share more commonalities than we are aware of.

In any case, some tenets presumed to be "Islamic" may not sound so strange to women in Southern Africa who have had nothing to do with Islam. For instance, in precolonial Zimbabwe as well as in colonial Rhodesia, the woman was regarded as a permanent minor, first her father's ward, than her husband's. If she outlived her husband, then as a widow she became the ward of some male in either her husband's home or her own home. Sometimes a woman became a ward of her own son(s)! This meant that she could never own property or be granted a bank loan. The situation was so bad that a conscientious and sensitive ZANU (PF) government (in Zimbabwe) attempted a corrective measure by passing the Legal Age of Majority Act in 1982. This law stipulated that at age eighteen a young woman became an adult, with all the attendant rights and privileges.

To a certain extent, African women are some sort of riddle. This is because, whether formally educated or not, "traditional" or "modern," they do not fit the accepted notion of them as mute beasts of burden. And they are definitely not as free and equal as African men (especially some formally educated ones) would have us believe. In fact, they fall somewhere between those two concepts.

To some West African men, the way West African women struggle to be independent "is really quite bad." They think that "these women are all over the place." Wherever men meet, you can be sure to hear jokes and stories about women, all of which are supposed to show how "terrible" we are. One solid piece of "advice" any growing boy is likely to pick up along the coast of

West Africa is: "Fear women." And if there really is a Fon (Gabon) proverb that translates as "Woman is the root of all evil, only our souls can save us [from her]," then women have been in trouble for a long time in Africa!

The colonial period did not help women either. It is true that some of the "civilizing" missions did not want their policies to run counter to any patterns in the "natives" that were tolerant of women's development. So they gave a few girls some opportunities for formal education. Some of the girls' secondary schools in the area go as far back as 1837. But the missions came with their own ideas on how females should be educated to be "proper women." While the boys in colonial elite schools were being prepared to go to England to become professionals (mostly lawyers), girls in the equivalent schools were being taught needlework and needlepoint, crochet, and baking. This was to make sure that they became wonderful wives and great mothers. And many turned out exactly as programmed. Even they were only a few women from either traditionally royal or nouveaux riches families. For the great majority of West African women, colonialism meant unmitigated suffering.

A few women managed to squeeze some advantages out of the neocolonial era, and excelled in areas where women would not normally be expected to. The emphasis is on "few," because educational policies in Africa have never been democratic. Today, the pyramid is a symbol of what is happening to young women in the educational systems of West Africa: a massive base and a needle-thin top. At the primary levels, girls and boys get equal opportunities to enter the system, or almost. But by the time a given age group gets to the universities, the ratio of girls to boys is as low as one to ten or worse. Apart from impossibly poor environments, this is a result of a number of negative forces in young women's lives, such as becoming pregnant and getting expelled from school, while the offending male—whose identity no one cares to know—is left free,[5] or receiving discouraging career counsel from sexist teachers and school authorities as well as schoolmates and well-meaning but reactionary relatives.[6]

High-Powered Tokens

Given the chance, a number of young women show their independence and courage in choosing careers, and in most cases do brilliantly, but women in high-powered positions are still hostages to tokenism. Certainly as "tokens" many of them have attained the top of their professions. Some even got there as early as other women from some of the most technologically advanced regions of the world. So that for a long time some countries in Africa have produced women doctors, lawyers, judges, university lecturers, and professors. There have been women in "rarified" professional areas such as imaginative writing, publishing, geology, architecture, engineering, transportation ownership and management, and music conducting. When we talk of African women today, we speak of over two hundred million people, some of whom are commercial and air-force pilots, engineers (electrical and mechanic), primary and secondary school teachers, telephone operators, and nurses. These professional African women are the exception rather than the rule—but that is how it is throughout much of the world today.

However, there is one group of women almost peculiar to West Africa. These women are in trade and commerce. Mostly, such women are referred to as "market women" or "market mammies" by non–West Africans. But of course, not all of them actually work from the markets, although the great majority do. Their activities range from gem dealing and high finance to "petty" trading. Therefore, their workplaces also range from highly sophisticated modern office complexes to the pavements of the cities where their kiosks stand.

For these women, the market is both a business arena and a home away from home. From early morning when they occupy their stalls they conduct their commercial business and their business as homemakers, including the day's cooking for husband and children. Indeed, many people who grew up in urban places (for example, in Ghana, Nigeria, Togo, and Benin) could confirm that much of the time they went after school straight to the market to be with their mothers. The market was where they ate lunch and supper, did their homework, and had their baths from buckets and bowls. Such people recall, often with a great deal of nostalgia, that during the weekday, home was the market: a house was only for sleeping in. Meanwhile, these women make money to feed, clothe, and educate their children, and sometimes support their men.

For most West African women, work is a responsibility and an obligation. This idea is drummed into us from infancy. We could never have fought for the "right to work"—a major concern of early Western feminists. In West Africa, virtually no family tolerates a woman who doesn't work. So that today, there may not be too many homes in the region, including traditionally Islamic areas, where girls are encouraged to think they needn't have ambitions because one day they'll grow up to marry and be looked after by men.

Yet, Africa's women farmers may get the rawest deal of all.[7] Although it may now be fashionable to admit that women have been the backbone of the continent's agriculture, that is a very recent trend. Earlier on, their existence was not even acknowledged. Governments never mentioned women in agricultural policies. So the burden of constant poverty, of working on the farm from sunup to sundown and then coming home to take on dozens of other roles, was added to the deprivation of being invisible to policy-makers.

Debating Feminism

Currently, the debate about African women and feminism is hot. It is common to hear feminism dismissed as a foreign ideology, imported into

Africa "with . . . crusading zeal" (A.N. Mensah, 1990) to ruin good African women. It is also easy, and a trap we all fall into every now and then, to feign a lack of interest in this discourse, or to airily maintain that "we don't need feminism" because we had strong women for antecedents. Many of us have declared at one time or another that "African women were feminists long before feminism." Certainly from the male camp, the cacophony is that African women do not need "feminism." Even though in many modern African states grown-up women are expected to crawl on their knees to offer food and other services to their husbands, their in-laws, and others in authority generally, most men still maintain that in their county, "women are not oppressed. There are roles which women and men have to play"— including crawling, obviously. The latest and most interesting front in the discourse was opened by Alice Walker, when she proposed that we substitute the term "womanist" to describe the global African woman's particular concerns.

When people ask me rather bluntly every now and then whether I am a feminist, I not only answer yes, but I go on to insist that every woman and every man should be a feminist—especially if they believe that Africans should take charge of our land, its wealth, our lives, and the burden of our own development. Because it is not possible to advocate independence for our continent without also believing that African women must have the best that the environment can offer. For some of us, this is the crucial element in our feminism.

On the whole, African traditional societies seemed to have been at odds with themselves as to exactly what to do with women. For although some of them appeared to doubt gender and biology as bases for judging women, in the end, they all used gender and biology to judge women's capabilities. Otherwise, how was it that men ruled by proxy for women from those nationalities, like the Akan of Ghana, among whom inheritance and succession, and therefore power, were vested in the matrilineage and not the patrilineage?[8]

Some of us are convinced of something else: that much of the putting down of women that educated African men indulge in and claim is "African culture" is a warmed-up leftover from colonization. European colonizing men (especially Victorians) brought with them a burden of confusion: first about their own women, and then about other women. All of which was further muddled up by the colonizers' fantasies about the sexual prowess of both African men and women.

In the meantime, no one wants to hear African women discuss their problems. In Harare, a journalist recently wrote an incredible outburst that began with "Women, women, women, will they ever stop moaning?" He then went on to ask "whether [our] women will ever stop weeping to find solutions to their problems so they won't weep again?" He ended by declaring grandly that "it serves no purpose trying to convince each other that women are oppressed. *There are better issues to focus on.*"[9] (Emphasis mine.) A full comment on this piece could make a sizable book.

A way to appreciate some of the contradictions in the position of African women today is to adopt a bifocal mode of looking at them. One view would be from inside their own environments. This would reveal that in relation to their men, they were just as badly off as women everywhere. But viewed from outside, internationally, the picture changes somewhat. "For years, some of us have been struggling to get the world to look at the African woman properly. Hoping that with some honesty it would be seen that in actual fact, vis-à-vis the rest of the world, the position of the African woman has not only *not* been that bad, but in some of the societies . . . she had been far better off than others."[10] And this should include the self-congratulatory West.

This much is evident about the majority of African women today, from the Cape of Good Hope to Cairo. They live in the rural areas of the continent and its urban shanties. They have had only the most minimal education or none at all. They are married, monogamously or polygamously. They have had between two and six children. They are involved in peasant farming and petty trading. Their lives are ruled locally by men who speak in languages they do not understand and from abroad by alien men who speak languages they could not possibly understand.

All this should be enough to make the African woman want to fold her arms, keel over, and just die. But she is doing anything but that. She is still pushing. The African woman today is a real heiress of her past. We need to intensify our struggle. For instance, instead of letting ourselves be "lulled into a false sense of security through tokenism and processes of 'de-feminization' which in most cases is a prerequisite for performing certain functions," we need to be able to challenge "gender and class oppression, imperialism and exploitation" and seek "access to policy-making positions, legal reforms, equal rights in education, employment and credit facilities."[11]

In the meantime, if, like men around the world, African men harbor any phobias about women moving into leadership positions, then they had better get rid of them quickly. After all, men have monopolized leadership position in Africa over the last five hundred years, and still overwhelmingly do. If they alone could save us, they would have done so by now. But instead, every decade brings us grimmer realities. It is high time African women moved onto center stage, with or without anyone's encouragement. Because in our hands lies, perhaps, the last possible hope for ourselves, and for everyone else on the continent.

NOTES

1. Also sometimes referred to as Live Aid, it was organized by Geldof in 1985. It galvanized the world. Among the honors Geldof received was an honorary knighthood bestowed by the Queen of England, and the 1986–87 Third World Prize. The Western media fell over itself paying him well-deserved homage, calling him "Santa Bob," "Sir Bob," and "St. Bob."

2. See, among others, Cheikh Anta Diop, *Cultural Unity of Negro Africa* (1980); Ivan Van Sertima, ed., *Black Women in Antiquity* (1981), and any of the volumes in *The Journal of African Civilizations* series by the latter.

3. In Act One of *Antony and Cleopatra*, Shakespeare was unbelievably crude about Cleopatra. But then the Bard's racism is a great source of acute embarrassment. See *The Tempest, The Merchant of Venice,* and *Titus Andronicus.*

4. Line from my poem: *These Days: II.*

5. The story is so heartbreaking that no aspect of it bears telling. *The Herald* (Harare, February 20, 1992) reports the most terrifying example of this to have come to the continent's notice in recent times. In an incident between boys and girls in a co-educational secondary school in Kenya that left *"19 female students"* dead, and during which, according to doctors, "71 girls were raped," *"only two schoolboys were charged with the offense!!!"* (Emphasis added.) Some of us keep talking about the problem, albeit to deaf ears. For example, "Profile: Remembering Tomorrow—A Conversation with Ama Ata Aidoo," by Sarah Modebe, *Africa World Review* (October 1990–March 1992), London; *African Woman* (Autumn 1991), London.

6. One stock advice to a young schoolgirl who plans on having higher education is that she should be careful. Otherwise she would never find a husband. The harm done is never less because such "advice" is often well-meant or based on the common knowledge that "men are scared of smart women."

7. According to Anthony Yudeowei of West Africa Rice Development Association, "over 80 percent of the small holder rice farmers of West Africa are women."

8. Of course, this shows why it is dangerous to assume that because a society is matrilineal, it is also a *matriarchy*. Certainly, the Akans are one very good example of a people with a matrilineal base and an obvious patriarchal superstructure. (Freudian symbols unintended.)

9. Cephas Chitsaka in the *Sunday Mail,* November 24, 1991.

10. Quotation from my letter to Mineke Schipper to explain why I felt unhappy at the title and subtitle of her book, *Source of All Evil—African Proverbs and Sayings On Women.*

11. Page 176, *West Africa* (3–9 February, 1992). Bisi Adeleye-Fayemi was reacting to a letter from K. Asare in a previous issue of the weekly. From my rather brief experience as cabinet minister (Education in Ghana, January 1982–June 1983), I fully endorse the view that in order to function as tokens women defeminize. Or we fall into the trap of being overly feminine. But then either way, we are rendered ineffective. Because on one hand we alienate the public (?) and on the other, our male colleagues refuse to take us seriously.

A Young Woman's Voice Doesn't Break. It Gets Firmer

—for Kinna IV

I remember
you at four
seven or
eleven,

your baby voice:
both real and pretend
telling me
(or rather whining slightly)
how you missed me, and
who had done what to you or said,
while I
had been away . . .

Now
your voice
comes briskly along the wires,
through the air waves and
over the earth

reporting
how alright everything
at home is, and
ordering me to
just relax
and be about the business
I travelled
all the way here for.

And clearly,
if you missed me,
you were not half about to let on.

Young woman,
—for I dare not call you "Child" anymore—
may be
when we are into
our normal existences with
their needs and their tensions,

I do not notice the
changes that
take place in you.

But when
I am away and
the phones permit,
I do.

The measures of your growth
knock confidently at the
    doors of my perception
announcing themselves in
more than certain terms.

Of course,
we only speak of a data of
one.

But
if yours
is anything to go by,

then surely,
as she grows
from child into woman,

a girl's voice doesn't break:
it gets firmer.

Deborah Nazi-Boni
THE UGLIEST GIRL IN THE KINGDOM

Burkina Faso 1994   French

In Burkina Faso, as is true everywhere in West Africa, tales were essential to
the process of socializing young people. Generations of storytellers carefully
sought to preserve the educational function of their art. In the contemporary
period, nevertheless, the transformations that have occurred in the hearts of
traditional African societies have not spared expressive forms, including
tales. In experimenting with the form of the tale, Deborah Nazi-Boni is
among those writers who have, in fact, enlarged and diversified their public.

A teacher by profession, Nazi-Boni is the daughter of a major political figure and writer in what was once known as Upper Volta, now Burkina Faso. In 1994, after founding and running two in-house newsletters, she published her first book, *Mulatto Tales,* which strives to draw from both the author's traditional education and her acquired Western culture. She creates a blended world in which the educational and moral goals of the African tale exist alongside elements of the European fable. Often, the tales plunge the reader into a world of fantasy.

"The Ugliest Girl in the Kingdom," however, has close ties to an African world, with its emphasis on social stratification and a female's customary passage into society through an arranged marriage. But by subverting the values that she also makes explicit, and by refusing to reinforce the stereotypical categories of traditional tales, Nazi-Boni means also to disconcert readers and thus invite them to reflect and question.

Aminata Diaw

✦

This is the story of N'Koma and Kandé. It happened long ago in the distant kingdom of Makunda.

The counselors were already seated on wooden stools when Kandé, the King, appeared. Tall, slender, with sculpted, one might even say aristocratic, features, he had the very dark complexion of the sons of Makunda. He folded his red *boubou,* which was very starched, behind his back.

"Peace be with you," he said, by way of a greeting.

"Peace be with you too!" the counselors answered in unison.

Then he sat in a wooden armchair and was thus in higher position than the four counselors. "You wished to meet me, I am listening!" Without being taciturn, the King did not like making long speeches.

The oldest counselor spoke first. "Your Highness, the time has come to look for the Guardian."

"That time had to come," the King replied, as laconic as usual.

"We need your permission to start the search," the second counselor interjected. "And we are asking for a prompt answer from you, because it is time!"

The King took a deep breath and said, "Let the custom be carried out. May the spirits of the dead ancestors favor us."

Kandé's face was calm. It was a programmed ordeal and the time for it had come. The room fell silent, meaning that the counselors had no more to say. After the period required by protocol, the first counselor spoke again, "If your Highness doesn't have any special orders to give us, we will leave."

"So be it!"

The four counselors rose together, bowed quickly, each moved three steps backwards, turned, and went out. For a brief moment, Kandé remained in the Council Chamber, a room with rust-colored walls. He realized, then, that he was the least free citizen of the kingdom. Indeed, he'd always known it and hadn't made any effort to look for a wife: the custom was going to provide him his first wife, in any case. He had been prepared from birth to submit to the custom of the Guardian. That was what constituted the ordeal; that was what constituted the foundation of the kingdom, not the entire foundation because no one would be foolish enough to entrust all the secrets of the fathers to the same person.

He left the Council Chamber, signaled his groom, who saddled his horse. The ride invigorated him; it reconciled him with himself and the world. He went for a long ride, and stopped to take a few steps alone into a grove of trees.

His thoughts returned to the custom. "Was it so terrible? Who was the ugliest girl in the kingdom? How ugly could she be? Was she so frightening or repugnant? You'd think that these deformed girls, whom the Diviners struggled to find, did not have human parents!"

The Guardian was meant to be the incarnation of ugliness. The King had to stare with wide open eyes at this ugliness and transform it into a woman. She wouldn't be the mother of his first child. Another woman, the one whom his heart would choose, would be his true wife and the mother of his children. But he had to wait for two years. Two long years with that unknown woman to whom heaven had forgotten to give any gifts. Two years during which she would be initiated, trained, tested, two years at the end of which she would become "the Guardian."

He would then have the freedom and the right to love! The Guardian would join the old women, and would only rarely come to the Palace when necessary. She would be accorded the respect due the greatest woman healer in the kingdom. She would then be counselor, almost a mother, to the King. Could one really say that fate was unjust? To take the ugliest girl, who was often of poor background, and make her a queen of knowledge, a woman accorded respect and attention.

The Diviners set to work. The counselors had asked them to act. Before the full moon, they had to find the ugliest girl in the kingdom. In the case of a tie, their aptitudes would then be taken into consideration. The one most receptive to learning would be chosen. Using his own formula, each of the Diviners consulted the kingdom's secret forces. It would be full moon in three days; they had to decide. The Council of Diviners took place in a mud house solely reserved for that purpose. All five sat down.

"I have been told that N'Koma is the right candidate."

"N'Koma it is," the second Diviner also said.

"My fetish also confirms it. N'Koma is the ugliest girl in the kingdom."

"It is certain that N'Koma is the right candidate," the fourth Diviner agreed.

They fell silent. On the whole, the Diviners were unanimous, for the kingdom was not, after all, inhabited by gnomes.

"As for me," the Fifth Diviner said, "I had two very different answers.

One was positive: N'Koma was definitely the girl revealed to me, but the second test was negative. The third consultation didn't yield anything. No other person was revealed to me. I swear that this is what I saw!"

They were all equally knowledgeable. Postponing the decision-making to the following day wouldn't serve any purpose. They had inquired. They had an answer. They should not bother the forces any longer. For the first time, the Diviners were not unanimous. What should they do? The double answer the Fifth Diviner had received was like a warning, but the name of N'Koma was also mentioned for the fifth time. They agreed that N'Koma would be the Guardian, but there remained a small doubt.

With the proper ceremony, they asked for N'Koma from her parents and she was taken to the women's quarters in the palace. She was a virgin. On the night of the full moon, the most senior woman would take her to the door of the King's bedroom. She would go away after announcing N'Koma's presence. The King and the future Guardian would meet for the first time. Kandé turned his back toward the door.

"Your Highness, N'Koma is yours!"

"Let her come in," he said.

He delayed the moment of shock by keeping his back turned to the door. He wanted to discover the creature whole, to face her immediately and totally, to hasten the ritual and get through the ordeal. Sensing the silent presence of N'Koma, he turned. Beauty and ugliness would be revealed in that instant. A drooping mouth, lips . . . such lips—inside-out flesh stretched tight and teeth so far apart that one wondered how many there really were. She lowered her head sharply.

"Look at me," Kandé said softly. He had to look at her; that was an important part of the ritual. He raised her chin with his finger as an adult would do to a child. He was neither filled with fright nor disgust, but with immense pity for the human being facing him. Sometimes, nature had a good laugh at human expense. How was that sight possible? He was searching for an ounce of beauty to cling to, even if he only found it in her hands. He found none. Everything was deformed, there was no harmony in that puny little body. He raised his eyes to the face of the girl. He looked her in the eyes. The girl lent herself to yet another examination. Her eyes were infinitely sad. One felt her complete resignation, her acknowledged powerlessness in light of her fate. He hung on to her distress. He shared her pain. He passed the ordeal. Thus did she become Guardian.

N'Koma lived in a room close to the King's. She regularly left that part of the palace at the same hour, veiled and flanked by two of the most senior women. They often didn't come back until evening. Kandé would call her, sit her down, and question her about herself and her people. He would make her his friend and thus pass more easily the two years to come.

They ended up laughing. She would hide her face to laugh or turn away to smile. And Kandé found in her a sharp mind, and a philosophy which was different from his, a very different worldview, the wisdom of an old woman. He only looked at her eyes, trying to find deep inside them what she did not say. Are eyes not "the mirrors of the soul"?

The counselors came occasionally to inform the King about the training of the Guardian. N'Koma had the requisite abilities. She would be a great Guardian. Two years went by. Kings generally looked around during the two years of the ordeal. Kandé's father got married the very day following the last day of the second year. An understandable haste! Kandé, on his part, went about his duties as usual. The counselors thought it useful to remind him. They said, "Your Highness is free henceforth to choose his real wife."

"I am obviously thinking about it," Kandé replied.

In actual fact, he thought very little about it, since he was divided between the affairs of the kingdom, his rides, and his discussions with his friend N'Koma.

Six more months went by and the King was still not talking about getting married. Nevertheless, he went regularly on long horse rides and everyone expected something; but nothing happened. Diviners and counselors consulted one another. The Guardian had to make way for someone else. The King's not being in any hurry was suspicious. The Diviner confirmed that the King was not "put off" by N'Koma. He was acting of his own free will. That's what was most disturbing. They remembered the double message of the Fifth Diviner. What if they had all made a mistake? The training and the preliminary tests confirmed that they had made the right choice.

"What if the King doesn't want another wife?" The Fifth Diviner dared to suggest. One of the Counselors laughed a long time. From time immemorial, as all *griots* knew, it had never happened. It was inconceivable, and moreover, it was not allowed. Nevertheless, they considered the issue from that angle, and decided that they had to watch the King more closely.

The meetings of the Guardian and the King were frequent, longer than necessary, in their opinion, given that thirty months had gone by. They had to act, or the kingdom would be shaken to the core. They had to get rid of the Guardian without telling the King. Only water and waves could carry away the secrets she knew. She had to die by drowning. One of the most senior women would replace her. It was a less effective solution, but that was what the custom made provision for in extreme cases. Consultations were made and it was agreed that in two days, at high tide, N'Koma would be tied up and thrown into the sea.

The young woman didn't meet the King that afternoon. He didn't see her the following day either. When she was asked, the most senior woman lied, saying there was a ceremony to prepare for; N'Koma was officiating and was not able to meet the King. Kandé had his doubts. His counselors were coming into the private part of the palace more often than usual. Under one pretext or another, they were walking around looking worried.

Something was brewing! Besides, his heart was not at peace. He had a premonition. He spent the morning scrutinizing the town from the top of the ramparts. The usual hustle and bustle put his mind a bit at ease. Three horsemen suddenly appeared and surrounded a fourth rider who seemed all bundled up. Kandé understood: they were going to kill N'Koma.

The King wore dark robes and wrapped his head in a turban. He allowed the convoy to go ahead. He mounted his horse and followed cautiously in order to stay out of sight. They were going toward the sea. So that was where the greatest secrets were buried? He hid his horse and continued. One of the riders kept pointing toward the waves, and, like a sleepwalker, the girl moved forward. A big wave enveloped her and she disappeared out of sight. The horsemen mounted their horses and galloped rapidly toward the town. The King threw his turban on the ground and entered the water. The waves were strong and overwhelmed him at times. He was, however, quite strong. Veils were floating at a distance from him. The body of the young woman resurfaced.

Kandé swam further and further into the water with his arms wide open. Risking his life! Did he realize it? He was risking his life for N'Koma! And the miracle happened. Her hands were freed. Their hands met.

Without ever understanding how, he carried the tiny body in his arms to the shore. She was unharmed. He put her on the sand and collapsed. The sun was setting when Kandé regained consciousness. A very beautiful young woman was bowing over him. She was wearing N'Koma's veils, but she was quite obviously not N'Koma.

The unknown woman started crying. "Be it known to you that you have saved me twice: from death, and from the evil spell that a sorceress, an avowed enemy of my father, King Xénou, had cast upon me. When I was a child, she transformed me into a deformed and repugnant being. I was given to another family who made me their real child. The secret had to be kept. A man had to love me so much," she continued, "in this hideous form that he would risk his life for me. You have done it and I am thus transformed into the person heaven had given to my parents, the King and Queen of the N'Guza kingdom. My real name is indeed N'Koma."

He looked into her eyes and recognized her. It was true! It was getting dark when a turbaned rider and a very pretty young woman entered the doors of the palace. "I have found my wife," the King proclaimed. And he introduced the beautiful creature who was beside him. The only thing left was to celebrate the wedding.

The Diviners and the most senior women hid what they were feeling, but they were extremely worried. They were unable to transfer the powers to the most senior woman. Had the Guardian died, that would have been an easy task. They resolved to confess their crime to the King. After all, it was permitted, a crime provided for by law.

"Let the Diviners get busy and let them give a prompt answer to all these questions!" the King thundered.

They became more and more feverish. The Fifth Diviner was the one who finally had the revelation. N'Koma and the new wife of the King were one and the same! The Guardian was indeed the ugliest girl in the kingdom and the King had a new wife. The custom was saved!

Translated by Judith Miller, Cosmos Badasu, and Tobe Levin

Afua Kobi
A TRADER CAUGHT IN ETHNIC VIOLENCE
Ghana 1994   Akan-Twi

Long-distance traders like Afua Kobi have been a central feature of economic life throughout West Africa, once linking the deep forest areas, such as the Ashanti region in present-day Ghana, to North Africa by Saharan caravans long before shipping began along the southern coast. Such traders still bring in the daily foodstuffs and consumer goods for large cities like Kumasi, the regional capital, which has a population of nearly one million. In the bustling wholesale yards and congested lines of retail stalls in Kumasi Central Market, some twenty thousand traders meet daily to distribute food to urban shoppers and to traders from the smaller markets of city neighborhoods and other towns in the region.

Asante matrilineal culture allows for women's autonomy in trading and farming. Women have secure farming rights in their lineage land and secure property rights to the income they earn from selling and trading crops or any other work. Asante mothers are expected to contribute substantially to the support of their children and work hard to provide for them. Like their brothers and husbands, they aspire to expand their businesses, educate their children, build houses, and pass on property to their descendants. This is why Afua Kobi mentions the fact that her friend has put up a building at Tafo Zongo—it is a measure of her success. So many women engage in market trading throughout southern Ghana that the whole marketplace is considered a female location with female leaders. Very few Asante men trade in local foodstuffs, partly because other male-dominated occupations usually bring better incomes.

People in different regions of the country prefer different foodstuffs. In the coastal areas, for example, corn-based foods such as the *kenkey* mentioned in the text are the most common staple foods. *Kenkey*, made from fermented corn dough the consistency of stiff dumplings, is precooked, travels even better than bread, and is commonly eaten with pepper and canned fish, thus making it a good food to take on journeys or eat in haste. In this context, it is a "fast food," as opposed to yams and other tubers, which require elaborate preparation. For yams, the starchy roots that are a favorite staple food throughout the country, particularly in the tropical forest areas in the middle of the country, Kumasi is the center of national distribution.

The leader of the Kumasi yam traders is the senior *ohemmaa,* or market queen, in Kumasi Central Market; she also leads a national coalition of yam traders' groups. These white-fleshed tubers are massive (a single one can feed a large family) and look like cords of firewood when stacked by the hundreds on the farm or in the market. One or two dozen trucks line up each day at the Kumasi wholesale yard, each unloading thousands of yams brought in from farming districts. Like many other food crops, yams actually grow best in the border areas between the forest and grassland zones to the north of Kumasi, in the areas between Salaga and Tamale where Afua Kobi does her trading.

During the twentieth century, the wholesale trade between Kumasi and these farm districts was one of the most lucrative trading specializations in the marketplace system, requiring considerable capital. The growing incomes from commercial yam production and distribution created tensions between local communities, especially in the northern areas at the heart of the story. In Gonja and Dagomba, tensions also intensified between chieftain elites and the commoner farmers, who often identified as Konkomba. The new wealth in yam farming led commoners to resist financial and other dues that ruling elites had collected since before colonial times. Sporadic rebellions and repression sometimes brought considerable loss of life and property. Furthermore, during the year 1995, head of state Flight Lieutenant J. J. Rawlings was seen as partisan in these disturbances. His regime extended price controls from imports and manufactures, such as cloth, to local food-stuffs, such as yams, and demolished markets and beat traders around the country. He was also perceived as promoting the interests of decentralized ethnic groups (those that historically had not had chiefs), such as his mother's Ewe group and the Konkomba, through policy and favoritism. At the time of the disturbances Afua Kobi describes below, it was widely rumored that Rawlings had promised the Konkomba land rights of their own in an autonomous district or region.

Afua Kobi was born in a farming village in the central Ashanti region in the late 1940s. Her mother was a farmer who fed ten children and also sold her food crops in Kumasi, as Afua's youngest sister still does today. Afua got married and had two children in her home village, but when she got divorced she moved to Kumasi to avoid her ex-husband. She lived there with a cousin and eventually remarried and had three more children.

In Kumasi, Afua Kobi traded full time, selling cloth and then children's clothes, but with little success. Finally, a friend told her that her brother's wife had a yam stall and was looking for someone to sit there and retail the yams that she brought in from various farming districts. Sometimes her friend also brought her yams, so she was making a steady income.

When I first met Afua Kobi in 1978, I was spending a lot of time with a yam-trading family in the stalls just opposite. She was a compact, energetic, and cheerful person, always friendly and attentive to her business. Only a little older than my graduate student self, she carried a round-eyed son on her back while a charming preschool daughter amused herself in the stall.

I moved back for a year in 1994 and was shocked to find her in a bad situation. She had become sick with guinea worm from drinking infected water when she was on the road buying yams, and now several long worms were eating their way out of her legs. She was suffering so badly that she could hardly walk from her house to the street. She was living in a tiny room added onto the back of her ex-husband's house, perched precariously above an eroded gully. The herbal medicines she had tried on her leg did not seem to be working, so I convinced her to come in my car to one of the public clinics, where she knew there was a doctor specially trained in removing guinea worms. This delicate and excruciating process took several days, after which the doctor had to be brought to the house daily to clean her wounds.

She now had the time to tell me about a disastrous road trip she had taken nearly a year earlier. Not only had it left her with the worms, but she had lost her trading capital, which belonged to someone else. Until she paid back that money, no one else was likely to lend her more to return to trading. She seemed bewildered and demoralized by the misfortunes that had piled up on her one after the other. Those were the stories she wanted to tell when I asked about her life.

Gracia Clark

✦

I started selling yams three months after my daughter Monica was born. At that time, the price of yams was not like today. At that time, with a small amount of money you could trade. I was at the market then. I had rented someone's stall. When I went to the wholesale yard to buy some, I would bring them into the stall and retail them. At first, I used to sell behind Kobokobo gate [near the railways], where the Breman people are. . . . At that time, Monica was a baby on my back. Then a woman went to buy [for me], and in those days a hundred yams might cost twenty-five pounds or thirty pounds. Maybe in one day she could buy two hundred for me, and I might be able to sell them all. When they were all sold, I might get two of the yams, and the woman also would give me a little of the little money we made. It was like that, little by little.

Sometimes, my sister would say, "I don't want to go on the road," and that friend of mine, she would go. She got somebody to give her money. And I also said, "When I get someone to give me money, I will go with you." I didn't have anyone to give me some, which meant I was always in the market. Even that sister of mine, her brother buys cocoa, so her brother helps her. Now she has put up a building at Tafo Zongo. That is where she lives now, that friend of mine.

Later on, a woman said that she would give me a loan so I could go on the road too. She brought too small an amount of money. If you don't have enough money on the road, you will take out transport fares, the children will eat while you are away, and if the money is not enough, when you come back and go sell the goods, you will not get anything. . . .

When I had done it for a while, I earned a little and added to it. That day, I went to Kintampo with a friend who is now dead. We bought yams together. One day we stopped at the wholesale yard. When we got there, there were already plenty of yams. While we were there we ran up a debt of about thirty thousand cedis. The little money I had got, I lost again. Then the problem left me thinking and worried me. After some time, I said, "No, I will find someone who will really give me money to go to the north, to go far away to Salaga, Beeyi, and Yeiji." A certain Auntie gave me a small loan. It was small, but I went with it anyway. We went and walked around, and when I came from there, I did not lose money. Then I observed and it later got better. That means it was moving forward when those things happened, the fight which made me lose the money again.

So it was a friend of mine who invited me to sell, explaining that it was a nursing mother's work. Before my mother died, whenever I came back and had some yams, I put them in a sack and sent it to her. If a friend is passing by and she greets me, I can give her some, to go and boil when she is leaving. It doesn't cost me anything. And when I am going home, I will have some to take along. In the same way, I get some for my loved ones, for my sisters, when they come. So that means that the yam business is a nursing mother's work. When you do it, nothing can bother you, you will not be hungry. At my age, yam work is what I like. That is what I do. That is what I have sold and found that it is good for me. . . .

In 1979 I was lucky that someone gave me money to work with little by little. I went to the north, where the fighting was last year. When we arrived and finished buying all our things, we were turning back to find a truck. So we were going to a village, and as soon as we arrived there, a woman who sells drinks (she even lives here at Suame) said, "And where are you going? Haven't you heard about the fighting which is coming?" One sister and I said, "Eh! We've got this far, and where in God's name are we going to get a truck to take us back to Kumasi?" Then, my sister, it was a serious problem. While we were standing there, we saw a truck coming. Even when we tried to stop it, it did not stop. So when a smaller one arrived, we stood in the road and begged and begged and begged. Right there he stopped. He said, "You can climb in." By that time, I was so tired, I could not climb up. There was someone in it who held on to me and pulled me into it.

When we arrived in Salaga, the trouble had become serious. There were so many people crowding around, saying, "Our sisters, we thank God that you have found us alive." During the troubles, they said that some people were killed in some of the villages, but as for us yam traders, none of us were killed. The Konkombas, Dagombas, and Gonjas who have been killed and scattered over there, it is not a small affair. People said that the fighting was about to arrive there in Salaga town. We should try very hard so that by tomorrow we might have a truck ready to leave town. We went to see a watchman at the bus station. If we could take one, we would get to Tamale and get another truck there to come to Kumasi. At midnight, the watchman came and called us, and we boarded the bus.

Right away, men in battle clothes with their bows and arrows came to remove all our bags from the bus, and they would not allow us to leave. The people from around there, the Gonjas and Dagombas, were saying that we had been there for a long time. It had been a long time that we had been coming to stay there to buy yams. Now that fighting has come and they are going to fight, instead of us following them to go fight, we are running away. So they wouldn't let us go home, and we began to cry. We were crying. Then, as soon as we went back to our house, the watchman came to say that we should be quiet. Even the women who were from around there wanted to run away to Kumasi here. He said that we should not fall asleep, we should sit down, and he would come to call us. If the women from there came to board the bus, we wouldn't have any place to sit. Once the bus left, too, they wouldn't let any more cars leave there. So we were there when the man came again to call us, about one in the morning, and we went to board it.

Then, as soon as we boarded it, the men came again. "Where are you going? Where are you going?" We didn't answer. Then immediately they noticed two boys, some of the boys from there. These children had learned Twi, they had come to live in this region and learned to speak Twi. So the men said that these boys should get off. One boy said that he was from Mampong, the other said that he was from Offinso. Then another one said that he was in a college in Accra, and one said he was attending school somewhere I have forgotten. The men said, "You lie, we live here with you." So because they speak Twi, they could not speak the men's language. The boys were desperate. If they got down, the way things were, and went to fight, they would be killed, for they didn't know how to fight. We told the men right away that they should leave the children alone. "You know that schools have reopened. Today, school fees are high, mothers are to be pitied. When you pay, and they reopen and your child doesn't go, then it means that you have worked for nothing, and [the boys] got down and came back." The men were very, very serious. We pleaded and pleaded and pleaded, and finally they stopped. The bus filled up and we left.

After we left, when we were coming back, we came to one town, maybe the third town, and it was completely burnt. You would find some of the people burnt, and a body lying there. Another person they have burnt with his things. Then when we went a little past that town, we found some people running away. They had filled up the road and they stopped the bus, because they said the driver should pick them up. And the driver said, "We have left some of the people behind, and people are already standing inside the bus. So they won't have a place." It meant that little children were left behind. Sadness and weeping, my sister!

Slowly, we arrived in Tamale. When we arrived there, they said the Kumasi bus had already come and gone, so we told the bosses our story. They said, "You have a problem like the one that happened in Abidjan, so you should wait. When the bus for Accra comes, I will let you go by all means." After a while, it came and he collected money, and we sat in it. Much later I was told that when we left, some of our sisters came just after the bus left.

They say that when they arrived there, on the streets of Tamale, just while you are walking along, a cutlass might go bam! and cut off a head. A young woman told me when she came, "Auntie, as for you, you saw nothing. As I was coming along just like this, there were some people in front of me. I suddenly saw them being beheaded with a cutlass. They fell, and their heads were on the other side, bouncing. O Lord, and the blood, wherever you passed there was blood." She said, "I left my shoes there, just look at the blood." Eventually, she made it to the station and entered the room of the men in charge there. They said, "Be patient. The way things are, only at night will a bus come." When it came, she got on it, and eventually God brought her here to Kumasi. That's how I know the story.

In the end, the government had to go and make peace. First, he sent this person, oh, I have forgotten who. It seems to me one of the soldiers. He was nearly killed at Bimbila. Only God helped him to come safely back. Rawlings himself said that he would go, but he could not go, he could not land. They would have killed him. They said that he was the one they wanted, for he was the one who asked them to vote for him, and after the voting, he would give them a paramount chief, and he would give them a share of the land. When we voted for you, you did not come to give us a paramount chief, and you did not come to share out the land. That means it has become a serious issue, and if it is like that, they will start fighting. So they were waiting for him to come to make peace, and his flesh would have been torn to pieces and scattered everywhere. What was done was that he selected soldiers and policemen from Accra, Sunyani, and elsewhere, and they were placed in Salaga.

So when we heard that soldiers had gone there, we were afraid to go and collect the yams we had left behind. Our elders, the market leaders, told us that if that was the case, we should collect money, those of us who usually go there, and buy rice, sugar, and salt and take them with us as a peace offering. So we bought six bags of rice, and we bought two bags of salt, and we bought three bags of sugar and gave them to some people to go first to give them to the chief there in Salaga. He and his elders should take them, because as a result of the fighting their foodstuffs have been burned. They have run short of food, and they should take these and give them to their children. So after some time, they accepted them. "Soldiers are here, so they should go."

Some of us were afraid. If I myself say that I was not afraid, I would be telling a lie, my sister. Even the soldiers were not living in the town where we live. They were living in a place like a barracks. So even if something happens in town, before a soldier hears about it to come, you would be killed by then. On the day that we were going, we arrived in the evening. As soon as we arrived, we went to the soldiers and they said, "Where are your things?" We told them the town where they were. They said, "Tomorrow we will go with you." When they are going with you, too, they take money from you. "So you should come here in the morning." So we got up early in the morning to bathe and ran to meet them. These soldiers and the policemen alone were twelve, with their guns, and they pushed us in their midst. We were shaken, and they had smoked marijuana and cared for nothing. When we arrived at the village where our yams were, they said that they were going to Bimbila. We got down, because they said that they were going and would come back. We should go and find where our things were, if they were there. When they got back, they would pick us up.

We went to meet the Konkomba people that we know. Even when we were going there, we were no longer afraid. We were afraid where we were in Salaga. The Konkombas said, "Mother, they have come to burn this town, so your yams, which you put in the house, have all been burnt. They have also come to steal some away to sell, so let us go to the countryside." They put us on bicycles to go to the farm. When we went, the yams had sprouted. The unspoiled ones had sprouted so high! What we bought, we have stored there in a shed. When you pick it up, you find it rotten, rotten, all of them! My body was trembling. Should I throw it away, or is it better that I leave it? We went on to examine all of them. Maybe when you count out a hundred, you may have about ten yams, and the rest are all rotten. After examining them, we returned with them to the house. By the time we came, the soldiers had returned to Salaga, leaving us behind. Then we said, "We are afraid to sleep here with you." They said, "As for us, we will not harm you. If the soldiers had not come to burn this town, the fighting would not have spread to this place." The soldiers went to burn it and killed two people there. Are they in their right minds?

We stayed there for five days. No car came when we woke up, except for those soldiers' cars. No car passed through and none came. Then, on Wednesday, we saw more soldiers' cars coming. When we begged, one Auntie and I, they passed by. When we begged, they passed by. We saw one coming, and some big soldiers who were wearing clothes with stripes like leopard skin were coming, and I begged so hard. When they were about to reach me, one of them pulled a gun and aimed at me. I said, "Lord Jesus!" He passed by. When he passed, he turned around to look at me and laughed. I immediately started to cry. The Auntie who was with me said, "Auntie Afua, it's nothing, leave everything to God. He can't kill you." And I said, "When this fighting first came, a woman was stopping a car like that and a soldier killed her." There in the north like that. When he kills you, he just kills you straight away. Who is going to ask him anything? We sat there like that, and then we went back to bed.

The next morning, a young woman came to pick up goods. She came with a truck to load her goods. She came with some soldiers' cars. When she came, we pleaded with them. The soldiers' car followed the truck that came to load the yams. I mean, when a driver comes and there are no soldiers with them, they refuse to come. And we pleaded with the soldiers. They said, "You have stayed here for a long time. Why are you so stubborn? Is this the only place you can work? They have not stopped fighting here. When they get any of you, they will kill you. It is said that you buy guns and bullets for them." Me, I don't even know where guns are sold, or where bullets are sold. When I even see a gun, I get afraid. Eventually, they picked us up.

We arrived at Salaga, and after three more days we got a truck. We went to look for these soldiers again, and we arrived with them at the farm. One soldier looked angry all the time. Then we bought *kenkey*, canned fish, and pepper and prepared food for them. We were in the truck with this soldier and he didn't talk to anyone. They had their bullets, which brought fire when you shot them, and big long guns from here to there. We arrived in one village and collected some goods and were returning. On the way back, it began to rain, so we mostly rode in their car and the truck carrying the yams followed.

Then we reached a place where there was a pothole, but during the dry season it was filled in with earth. When it rained heavily like that, by the time our car reached there, the soil filling the pothole had sunk in. The soldiers' car was moving fast. It managed to stop somewhere and he told the driver carrying the yams to stop. The driver did not hear and fell into the hole. These soldiers got down, with some policemen from Manhyia whom I knew. They were all there and some were among these ones and got down. They went to collect sticks and soil. That one soldier stood there unconcerned. He said, "I won't get down. When we move this truck, we won't stop anywhere, we won't pick up these things again." Then the Auntie and I felt frightened. They got down from the car, leaving us behind, and we quickly got down from the car. As I got down, "My knees! The rain has beaten us. Eh, rheumatism, that has killed my sister." That is what he said to us, and he left, and gradually the car moved.

When we picked up one Auntie's things and we were about to get mine, the driver said that he would not go for those things because of the rain. I was crying. Then the policemen who knew me said, "We will go there with our small car, so you stand at the junction and let us go with him. The landlord has brought the yams to the roadside, and we can go and bring them into the truck." So when they were going, the one I went to buy yams with was in another car, and I was calling for her to get down. They said that I should wait, because one young man said he knew where the farm was. They went, and after a while she returned. Why? The car is coming. When we got there the man had not brought the yams there. I burst into tears. I cried and cried and cried. We came to the man's house. As soon as I arrived, I got down and said, "Father, why have you done that?" He said, "Ah, the things are there." The young man didn't know where the farm was, and by then the day was over. They said that I should go and tell the man to let the children bring the yams home the next day. It had rained, and they were going to sprout. He would not let the children go.

At this, the soldiers said, "Is that so? You let us go, and when we have gone, then tomorrow, God willing, we will come and take the rest of your things. So the yams we have already taken, we will go and put them in your office and bring back the car." When we reached home, they demanded forty thousand *cedis.* "You should bring forty," and then, I won't say much, but do you see? We should bring forty so that they will go with us the next day. I begged and begged and begged, but they refused. What we had to do was to pay them the money. We paid it to them, and at least I knew that once we had paid it they would not charge us more the next day. In the morning, we went to see them again, and when we finished unloading the yams, we went to see them and went out with them again.

We did the trading with them like that. When we went out, we didn't eat some of the food and gave it to them. Then, when we gave it to them and went to collect all the goods, and came back to the town where we stayed, one Auntie said she was going to the house where she stayed to say goodbye to her landlord. But she did not tell the soldiers when she was going, so we could not find her. We said, this Auntie, she should come back and let us go. After a while, we saw her coming. One soldier drew a gun. He said, "Why don't I shoot you?" And a policeman hit him, and he asked "Why?" He said, "You didn't call us to go with you when you were going, and now he is going to fire a gun. If you had been killed when you went off alone, we would have been in trouble." He said, "You are walking with your elderly mother, isn't it so? You frighten them like that. They themselves are already afraid and that is why they say we should walk with them, and you are frightening them with a gun. As for a gun, we don't play around with it. If that gun had gone off when you pointed it at her, you would have killed someone's mother." And then they went on and on, and all of us were crying. The policeman was angry with the soldier.

We climbed into the car. Then all of the soldiers went to stand somewhere laughing. When they came, they said, "Give us money for the days we came with you." "Eh! Yesterday you collected money from us, and are you going to take money from us again?" "Bring as much as you gave yesterday." I said, "Brother, I don't have that much." We talked and talked and talked, and he said, "Twenty thousand. If you don't give it to us, we will not move the car and go with you. If the lorry carrying the yams moves, we will shoot it." In the end, we had to pay them the money. Now, we went two times to take goods, making sixty thousand. We paid them the money and eventually we arrived. It was a terrible business. All our money had gone. We did not even have any to pay for our tickets, my sister. The next day, we got a loan from someone to buy tickets, took the Salaga truck, and came to cross the river, eventually.

One day when it rained, the car we were traveling in nearly had an accident. After we arrived in Kumasi, it was about three days before we unloaded the goods. When we were unloading the yams, my sister, any yam that we picked up was bad. They were all rotten. After counting out a hundred yams, maybe you might get thirty good ones out of it. The driver is only after his money. When we finished unloading the yams, if you had loaded three thousand yams, you might get fifteen hundred in the end, and what you had left behind in the bush also might have exceeded fifteen hundred. And for all that, even to this day, some people who had bought some have still not paid for them.

The whole thing left me thinking, I say.

People came back, and those who had money went out again. Those who could come and go like that got a lot of money. But I said, "The money is locked up. The money is lost." I stayed like that, I didn't go anywhere. Just recently I asked someone to loan me a small amount. I made three trips, and the money was all gone. Only last Friday, I went to buy goods and I came to unload them this Friday. I lost about fifty thousand, and it has all become a debt. Now, I have not gone to the market yet to collect the money and see what is left. I would like to return it, little by little, and then tell the person to take it, so that I will know what I still owe. I will sit down for God himself to show me the way.

Translated by Gracia Clark with A. K. Yeboah

Amma Darko
RUSSIANS UNDER ACCRA

Ghana 1996   English

Amma Darko was born in 1956. While attending the University of Science and Technology in Kumasi, she became involved with a student drama group, where she made her first attempt at creative writing. After graduating from the university in 1980, Darko worked at a technology consultancy firm but found it unsatisfying. Hard economic times and a tight labor market in Ghana impelled her to seek work abroad. At the time, Germany was recruiting workers for its growing economy, and Darko had a German pen pal, so she decided to try her luck there. She was shocked when she arrived and found that the only jobs available to African women were in menial service and prostitution. The obligation to send money home to relatives made Africans' work situation in Germany even more desperate. Darko's bitter experiences as a domestic worker, a far cry from what she had been trained for, provided the emotional material for her first novel published in English, *Beyond the Horizon* (1995). She returned to Ghana in 1987 and developed her career as a tax inspector in Accra, married, raised three children, and become a prolific writer who works daily on her manuscripts while always seeking ways to perfect her craft.

Darko's publishing history is unusual in that although she writes in English, the official language of her country, her reputation was initially made in Germany, the setting of her first novel. Her German publisher, Schmetterling Verlag, has produced all of her published works and sponsored speaking tours; therefore, she may be more widely known in German than in English. Only three of her works are known and read by an English-speaking audience: *Beyond the Horizon, The Housemaid* (1998), and *Faceless* (2003), although three other works (*Webs, In Excess,* and *A Cross of a Kind*) have been published in German. As a prolific African writer and astute critic of the social scene, Darko deserves to be widely known by an English-language audience.

Darko's childhood formed the basis of a semiautobiographical work, *Webs* (available in German as *Spinnweben*); the excerpt below is from the unpublished English manuscript. In "Russians under Accra," Darko describes the tumultuous times just prior to the military overthrow of Kwame Nkrumah's government in 1966. She compares her learning the ways of the world from older girls with the "education" of the "Ghanaman" on the street, whose knowledge of politics came primarily from rumor, at a particularly turbulent moment in the new nation's history.

"The Man" is Kwame Nkrumah. Educated in the United States in the 1930s and 1940s, and deeply influenced by African American writers and a vision of pan-Negro solidarity, he returned to Ghana to form the Convention People's Party (CPP) in 1947. The CPP was aimed at the common man and advocated immediate self-government for Ghana. Through Nkrumah was imprisoned for calling a general strike, the British eventually released him and asked him to form a new government. Nkrumah's charismatic and strategic work led to Ghana's being the first African nation to gain independence, in 1957. Anxious to make Ghana the "black star" of Africa that would lead the continent in the pan-African movement, Nkrumah began ambitious and expensive public-works projects. Influenced heavily by Marxist writings, he focused the economy on state-run enterprises and hired Russian consultants as he sought to follow the socialist model of development in Ghana. Growing inflation, a dramatic drop in the world price of cocoa, tax increases to cover the country's rapid modernization, and a corrupt government that relentlessly suppressed opposition views all resulted in increasing public dissatisfaction with Nkrumah's government. Food shortages—the first ever—in 1964 represented a major turning point for the Ghanaians in the street, who had been the strongest Nkrumah supporters.

Darko's satirical treatment, which emphasizes the role of gossip and innuendo in creating events in this heavily oral culture, uses linguistic patterns in a way that will resonate with anyone who has spent time in West Africa. Conversations in the marketplace and at roadside food stalls show the interplay of national, tribal, and personal concerns. Meanwhile, as Ghana's inflation affects a young girl's friendships and her pocket money, Darko's work becomes a coming-of-age story for the girl and the nation.

Yaa Tumu is the narrator's first best school friend, an older girl with whom she can discuss matters forbidden at home. *Fufu, kenkey, tuozafi,* and *akpene* are starchy staples of the Ghanaian diet: they are boiled, then some of them are pounded with a mortar and pestle; they are thereafter shaped into balls and usually eaten with soup or a stew.

Louise Allan Zak

✦

The rumour, like all rumours, started suddenly and from nowhere; gradually seeping into people's ears and entrenching itself onto their minds. And soon it became the major "*talk talk*" matter: Nkrumah has brought in the Russians so the colonial masters are very angry with him.

This was in 1966.

I had sat for the common entrance and was looking forward to passing and entering the prestigious Akwapim Girls Boarding School in the eastern highlands of Ghana, which was noted for her iron discipline and excellence; and I didn't know nor could understand who the Russians were exactly; why the President had brought them in; and why the colonial masters were unhappy about it.

Age and school advancement, plus my appointment as the school's bell girl, all combined, earned me a total of three pennies more pocket money, which therefore increased my daily school pocket money to nine pence. Inflation had so far, then caught up only with Mami Adele's crabs and Mami White's roasted corn and groundnuts, which each took additional pennies off my newly additionally earned three pence, but which still left me with a penny for my bus fare. So my friendship with Fatima Atia had been severely curtailed. She was still walking to and from school, barefooted; and I was still sandaled and gone regularly busful. So I ventured to make new friends and closely befriended another classmate of mine; a funny and sharp headed girl who bore the most curiously un-African name I ever heard—Ruby Bartholomew. And it was she who first brought to my notice, the rumour about the Russians.

My aunt's husband never talked politics or anything near it, with us. But Ruby's father was a medical doctor; attended medical school at a college in London and passionately looked down upon any colleague of his who studied his medicine in Russia or any of the former eastern bloc countries.

Ruby was a spoilt child and very fat. And she told me straight in the face that she considered me an ugly girl but made friends with me only because I was the bell girl. I tolerated her because I found my next *Yaa Tumu* [best friend] in her, albeit in politics; and so overlooked the insult she meted out to me and held onto our friendship. And through her, learnt more about the Russians that Nkrumah had allegedly brought in.

Like me, many that heard about the Russians didn't know where they came from. Ruby first told me she heard they were a tribe from north Africa; returned following day to say they were from a place called South America; then decided two days later that indeed, the Russians were actually from the big country called China. However, she appeared to be at a loss as to where Nkrumah assembled them and brought them down to Ghana.

The tone of the rumours left no one in doubt that the presence of the Russians in the country was something very negative. Where exactly they came from, didn't seem to matter anymore to many. All that mattered was that they were in the country and it wasn't good news that they were in the country.

Ruby's father, apparently spurred on by his dislike for anything Russian, was more open about political issues than my aunt's husband was; and had openly been discussing issues with friends, most of which Ruby overheard. So she came up to me one morning and said, "Yesterday I heard that Nkrumah had built bungalows under Accra. It is called underground bungalows."

"Under Accra?"

"Yes. They say maybe there are even some too here under our school."

"You think so?"

"No . . . yes . . . ah, maybe. Who can really know? Only he knows where they are."

"And why would he build bungalows under Accra?"

"To house the Russians. That is where he has hidden them. They live there."

I became confused. I didn't understand why if the Russians were brought in by, and were thus the invited guests of the whole big President himself, he wouldn't put them up in some fine buildings at say, the Airport residential area or the Ringway estates, but go hide them under Accra. But Ruby had no direct answer to that except to add that, "They say they are hiding under Accra to prepare to do bad things in Africa." The average Ghanaian had, around this time, never heard of a thing called *coup d'état* before. Where foreign affairs was concerned, he only knew that: some white people came to his country several years ago to lord over him. They made him understand that he was a primitive man and needed to be civilised. They asked him to stop worshipping his rivers and rocks and to start worshipping a certain white man called Jesus. Then they took away his gold and his diamonds and told him the very next minute that this man called Jesus was strictly against stealing. Then a certain strong Ghanaman called Nkrumah, who had studied plenty books in a wonderful school in that country called America, where they say, the big God above in the skies lodges when he visits Earth, fought with them and sacked them from Ghana and made himself president.

Period!

But coup d'etats? What was that?

And yet, the rumours.

So the "they say . . . they say . . ." continued and most of what reached my ears, I got from Ruby Bartholomew. And one morning at school, she said, "They say the only one entrance to the bungalows under Accra, where the Russians are hiding, is inside the Flagstaff House."

"Where Nkrumah lives?"

"Where Nkrumah lives. In fact, they say you even have to pass through his toilet to get to it."

"How amazing," I thought.

Yet, while the rumours persisted, and while no one also seemed to like it that the Russians were lodging beneath the very grounds upon which the soles of our feet treaded daily, Ghana-man on the street didn't panic.

Well, okay, he had heard about these mysterious people living underground in Accra and knew he either didn't like it for whatever reason he himself was not too sure of; or knew he was expected not to like it and so didn't like it. But his concern was not so much because the mysterious people were said to be Russians, but because he was not clear about what they were up to and was anxious about whether what they were up to could affect or interrupt for the worst, his daily routine life.

So he waited.

Ghana-man waited; and when he waited and waited and the rumours persisted and he saw no dramatic change, for the worst, in his daily routine life being attributed to the Russians hidden under Accra, the curse of apathy stepped in and he began to shrug disinterested, to new rumours.

And why not?

He was still getting his corn and cassava to chop; and so long as he set a good trap, could still end up with some fine bush meat for some fine weekend soup; so why should he worry?

He also knew that Nkrumah did him good by risking his neck to kick out those white men who came talking about Jesus to him; and he knew that, if nothing at all, for that alone, he had to show an everlasting gratitude by never talking evil about this man Nkrumah.

Never mind if his thoughts were full of evil about him.

He also knew that Nkrumah was governing with others, all who together, formed something they called the C.P.P.

It stood for the Convention Peoples Party.

Ghana-man also felt that, whether the whitemen who came and lorded over us some time ago liked it or not, the Russians had come; so it was up to them to leave us alone with our Russians and contend themselves with this Queenmother of theirs they said was never sad and was always smiling and wearing neat white gloves.

After all, what change did the presence of the Russians under Accra bring to the tastes the white lords craftily introduced us to and which we too headlong readily acquired?

No change!

Russians or no Russians, we were still craving for our tins of "Peak milk" and "Lipton tea" and we still didn't give up on our "Tate & Lyle" cubed sugar and our sweet sweet "Heinz baked beans."

So where laid the worry?

But whoever it was that was behind the rumours, it seemed, had a lot to worry about.

There was talk about systems, political systems, which was the grounds for the discomfort of the past overlords and their cronies, about the presence of the Russians under Accra. But the rumour brewers also realised too soon too that the language they were using about the systems, were too complicated for the complacent Ghana-man, who was still getting his cassava and corn and bushmeat. So they changed strategy.

They started talking the kind of language that the complacent Ghana-man would understand vividly enough to compel him to begin to worry. So very soon, the "they say . . . they say . . ." no longer covered the issue of the Russians living under Accra, but more precisely, about Nkrumah's want to have Ghanaians live like the Russians.

That was "Point One." And it hit home.

So then came the next inevitable question: How did the Russians live?

The answer was "Point Two;" and it came in the form of the next batch of rumours that followed Point One, the question.

. . . they say . . . in Russia, all women wear the same dress and all men wear the same shirt and same trousers. And at the end of every two weeks, all Russians then form a long line to go and get another clean set of dresses and trousers and shirts; and to hand in the dirty ones for washing!

Agh! Now that was something. One pair of attire for two whole damn weeks? And handed over to be washed? To be washed by whom? Well, in Russia . . . they say . . . that one group of Russians do all the dirty washings for all Russians. Another group does all the cooking; another group, all the ironing; another, all the dish-washing; another all the this and another, all the that! And shitting? What about shitting? Who does all the shitting for all the Russians?

Silly! Don't be silly! That and eating and urinating, are about the only things individual Russians do by themselves, for themselves. Apart from that, even the sweeping of rooms, one group of Russians do for all Russians.

And medicine too?

Oh come on! Who drinks medicine for a sick man? But if you mean medical care, well, yes . . . they say . . . in Russia, one group of intelligent people learn the science of medical care to take care of all the Russians who get sick!

Oh dear! Ooooooooooh!!!! dear !!

And who gets paid most in Russia?

Most? Who gets paid most? No one gets paid most. No one gets paid in Russia.

WHAT?

Yes! In Russia . . . they say . . . that everybody works for everybody and all are answerable to only one big boss: a certain big Russian man called Mr. K G B!

K G B?

Did it maybe stand for something like: Kenneth George Biney? Or did Mr. KGB have some African roots, in which case he could sound like say: Koku Gama Bodobodo?

So the Russians lived like Mr. KGB wanted them to?

Exactly!

. . . they say . . . that the Russians, they have no right to decide what food they wanted to eat at any particular time. Mr. KGB decided everyday at dawn, what all Russians would eat, what all Russians would drink, what all Russians would wear—which wasn't much, it you asked me; what all Russians would . . .

Cut!

Shit!

Hell!

Did he also decide when Russian men must sleep with their wives too?

Of course!

Good God! And when all Russian men must impregnate their wives too?

Sure!

Hey! Then who the hell want to live like the Russians? Any wonder then that they were so happy living under Accra?

And the rumour brewers hit their jackpot. All complacent minds and apathetic souls got jolted into active thinking. The man on the street no longer just shrugged when he heard about the Russians. He began to worry about them; about their presence down there under Accra and about the undesirable prospect of ending up living like them. And the more he worried, the more questions he asked. And his tone was changing, because the questions got more daring and more unfriendly; and Ghanaman's worry gradually but steadily bred with him, animosity of unequalled proportions.

"Well, do the damn Russians have tribes?" many were said to have screamed during one of the many meetings that started to take place at workplaces and drinking bars; on campuses and at the market places; and on the streets and corners of Ghana, to discuss the daunting issue of the

Russians under Accra. And the discussions and arguments went on heatedly and unabated.

"Well, hell! Why don't someone tell those confused balls of rotten *kenkey* that here in Ghana, we do have tribes! What the hell did this Mr. KGB think he was doing, deciding daily what all of Russia must eat? And what the fucking hell did this confused President Nkrumah think he was doing, deciding that the Russians must come and live under Accra and teach Ghanaians to live like them? Teach what anyway? How to wear one dress for two weeks or how to impregnate to the beat of someone's baton? And this Nkrumah, did he want to throw Ghana into an unending tribal war? Asantes against Ewes? Fantis against Dagombas? Did Nkrumah think that when his appointed Mr. KGB à la Ghana decided on one particular day that all Ghanaians must eat the Ewe tribe's *akpene*, the Asante tribe would look on peacefully and nod their acceptance without a fight?

And what was to happen if on one Wednesday dawn, the order should come that it was *kenkey* day. Apart from the Ga and the Fanti tribes, who else would rejoice and sing hallelujah? The Asantes perhaps? Or the Dagombas up north, who are used to their daily intake of their *tuozafi* balls?

And who the hell did Nkrumah envisage would pound all that mountainous heap of *fufu* when Mr. KGB à la Ghana, decided on an Asante day? The Asante chief perhaps?

And had Nkrumah sat down at all in that bloody lazy chair of his at the Flagstaff House to consider how the proud Asante chief would feel, being ordered by this "made in Russia" Ghana law, to eat the staple food of one of his servants?

Was the President out of his mind?

And with such talks and reactions, it became apparent that the brainwashing of Ghanaians was complete. The creation of anti-Nkrumah sentiments, had been marvelously accomplished.

The carpet of doom was gingerly spread out.

The time fast neared, and the stage for Ghanaians to receive the news of their first ever *coup d'état* with joy and relief, instead of with shock and confusion, was grandly set. So that, even the market women, once Nkrumah's staunch supporters, also started grumbling.

". . . what the hell was this foolish Russian life Nkrumah was wanting to bring to bear on Ghanaians at all? Did the Nkrumah they trusted so much, mean to say he wanted to place the market mummy and the doctor and the lawyer on the same footing as the housemaid and houseboy and even the latrineman? Was this all that the freedom and justice screamed at the colonial master about? Was this all that Nkrumah meant when he removed his big white handkerchief on independence day and wept and sneezed into it and proclaimed that Ghana was free forever?"

And the rumours persisted, reaching dizzying heights.

It was 1966.

A nervous January passed peacefully and uneventful. But the air was thick with tension. Something was going to happen. Everyone was expecting it to happen, yet, no one knew for sure what it was that was going to happen and how it was going to happen.

My aunt's husband began to lament on how if he had enough money, he would have sent all of us out of the country.

Who wanted to sit and wait till his head was delivered on a golden platter to the Russians? Yet, where was the cash with which to flee?

And with these unfulfilled wishes and desires of Ghanaians, frustrations and despair stepped in. People didn't give a damn anymore.

Ruby Bartholemew came up to me one afternoon while I was eating my rice and lentil sauce in Mami Adele's shed, audacity in it's raw form written all over her face. Not giving a damn about who will hear or who will not hear, she slumped down beside me and proclaimed rather loudly, "Do you know what I heard yesterday? They say that in fact, Nkrumah our president, he doesn't like Ghanaians at all!"

"He doesn't what?" I glanced nervously around me.

What was this palaver that Ruby Bartholemew was coming to bear upon me? I thought. What palaver at all was this eh? Discussing Nkrumah by force with me under Mami Adele's shed?

"I said they said he doesn't like Ghanaians!" she repeated audaciously. And all heads turned sharply in our direction. But all remained sitting.

Months ago, before the onset of the ". . . they say they say . . .," everyone in that shed who heard the mentioning of Nkrumah's name by Ruby, would have gotten up soundlessly and wordlessly and left, to save his neck. But then, that situation wouldn't have arisen at all in the first place because Ruby wouldn't have dared in the first place, to come and mention the name of Nkrumah in the context that she did, in the shed anyway. But now, all who heard what Ruby said, remained fearlessly seated, to listen to more stuff and if possible, also participate. Ghanaians it seemed, were ready; had been made ready by the "they say they say;" so ready to wish the downfall of Nkrumah. And all were anxiously waiting.

"Why?" I asked Ruby, "why did they say Nkrumah doesn't like the Ghanaians?"

"Yes, why, Ruby?" another added, "Who said that?"

"Or is he not Ghanaian?" a third asked.

"He is. But he doesn't like Ghanaians!" Ruby replied, "He only likes living in Ghana because he is the President!"

"Eh, is that true?" a fourth burst in, eyes ghastly widened, "Why?"

"Why? Look at his wife!" said Ruby.

A moment of thoughtful silence elapsed.

"His wife? What about his wife?"

Ruby sneered, "Do I have to tell you? Can't you see for yourself what it is about his wife? Does she look like a Ghanaianwoman to you?"

Another thoughtful silence elapsed. Then girl number two hit the jackpot!

"Of course she doesn't look like a Ghanaianwoman to me. How can she look like a Ghanaianwoman to me when she is . . . aaaaagh! It is true!!"

"Fiiii . . . fi tii tii! Are you now seeing it? Why should he go and marry an Egyptian woman when there are so many unmarried Ghanaian women around?"

"Aaaaah yeeees! It is true!" in unison, "It is very true!" And petty anger stepped in.

"Agh, but he, he doesn't like us but he wants to remain our president. What is that eh?" burst in someone.

And another supported her, screaming, "It is cheating! Big big cheating!"

And by the time we all left for Mami White's shed for our roasted corn and groundnut, our minds had staunchly been entrenched with the picture of Nkrumah and his Egyptian wife. Why the hell should he fight with his life to get rid of the white colonial master only to go in for a wife who was a near duplicate of the white woman?

And we too became ready to see him down.

My aunt and her husband still did not talk politics with us, but they started talking more openly about someone they referred to as: The Man. They naturally assumed that we had not the slightest idea who the subject of their conversation was. But I did, thanks to Ruby. So even without their knowledge, right there in the living room as they discussed "The Man," I learnt more about Nkrumah.

And January passed. No event; no nothing. Just heightened rumours.

Then came February.

As the days slipped past the mid-month period, all began to assume that that month too would eventually pass away without any upsetting event.

But it was not to be.

Nkrumah apparently miscalculated and underestimated the desire of Ghanaians to rather remain "colonial-master" Ghanaians, than "Russian" Ghanaians.

Like my aunt's husband once said in the living room, "Better a Ghana without her gold and diamonds than a Ghana fighting tribal wars per the power of a law that compelled the Ga chief to eat *tuozafi* and the Asante to eat *akpene.*"

Nkrumah was graciously delivered to the slaughterhouse on a golden platter, by Ghanaians.

The task of the "they say they say" was duly accomplished. It's perpetrators headed towards the victory platform in glee. Nkrumah did not see the month of February to its end.

On the dawn of February 24, 1966, while on his way to China for an official visit, anti-communist insurgents in the army marched to the

Flagstaff House; fought a ten hour battle with the Presidential Guards, defeated them and stormed the President's residence and headquarters.

Nkrumah received the news of his overthrow en route to Peking. He never set foot in Ghana again.

He ended up in the welcoming arms of Sekou Toure in Guinea. The "they say they say" brewers congratulated themselves on a job well done.

The Ga tribe sighed with relief. They wouldn't have to eat *tuozafi* by law.

The Asante tribe too sighed . . . whew! That was close. Their omnipotent chief very nearly ate *akpene* by law. What would Okomfo Anokye have said to that?

I also sighed with relief. How could I have been made to wear the same dress and shoe and eat the same food with Fatima Atia. That was real close.

My thoughts centered on my impending common entrance examination to Akwapim Middle Boarding School.

A hell!

REGRETS FOR RWANDA

The frequency, violence, and extreme horror of the conflicts on the continent of Africa in the last decade of the twentieth century have provoked many African writers. The writer and poet Tanella Boni, a philosophy lecturer at the University of Cocody, Abidjan, was president of the Association of Writers of Côte d'Ivoire from 1991 to 1997. She has published poetry, novels, and stories, including *Labyrinth, Grains of Sand, There Is No Suitable Word,* and her two novels, *A Crab's Life* and *On the Other Side of the Sun.* The three poems that follow appeared in *There Is No Suitable Word.*

Véronique Tadjo, of French and Ivorian origin, is also a poet and novelist. After teaching English for many years at the University of Cocody, Abidjan, Tadjo moved to London, where she lives with her family. Her novels include *The Blind Kingdom, As the Bird Flies,* and *Fields of Love and Battle.* She received the UNICEF prize in 1993 for *The Lord of the Dance* and *Mammy Wata and the Monster,* both children's books. In 1998, Tadjo took part in a writer's retreat on the theme "Writing as a Duty to Memory," held in Kigali, Rwanda. Out of this experience was created *The Shadow of Imana—Voyages into the Depths of Rwanda,* a book in which, using both fiction and fact, Tadjo portrays the horrors of the Rwandan genocide. "The Story of Consolata" and "Anastasio and Anastasia" are extracts from her observations, by way of which the author concludes that despite the experiences of prison and rape that characterize genocide, life is stronger than death.

Aminata Diaw

✦

Tanella Boni, FROM THERE IS NO SUITABLE WORD

Côte d'Ivoire 1997   French

WHERE TO FIND THE PROPER WORD

Where to find the proper word
To the door of silence . . .
To open the story's dance
Close to my woman's skin
Which the good Lord created
As an instrument of unpublished music.

SILENCE CAME RELUCTANTLY

Silence came reluctantly
And crossed our separate paths
At the intersection of life and death.
Power has stolen the key to our hearts
And sold us as spare parts
To the kingdom of the amnesiac sun,
Of the song of our most lunatic dreams.
But we no longer dream you say:
We buy our lives on a silver platter.
Here survival's law is etched in letters of fire:
Be silent and eat!
Quiet everyone, we're shooting!
Sing if you want,
But gauge the truth of your words
And long live Unrivaled Thought!

THOUSANDS OF SPECKS OF DUST WERE WE

Thousands of specks of dust were we
Pulverized where night began.
The camp of refugees were we.
A rapture of trinkets affixed to the site of the heart
Brightened the rocky path of our earthbound lives.
Our ancestors were drinking our evanescent words
To the beat of wines and dances from other lands.

Translated by Marjolijn de Jager

Véronique Tadjo, FROM THE SHADOW OF IMANA

Côte d'Ivoire 1997   French

THE STORY OF CONSOLATA

Consolata's face is astonishingly sweet. Her skin shimmers with copper and ivory and her graceful body moves in harmony with each step she takes.

She loves the rain when it falls in her garden and waters her flowers, turning time into liquid.

Her eyes are velvet and her smile tastes of mangoes.

If sometimes she turns away very quickly, her silhouette forms a powerful arabesque. And then, there is the small of her back that makes one think of a love that smells of the earth.

Consolata pronounces words quietly, but they come out of her mouth with such clarity that they make you shudder. She doesn't impose herself; she speaks without emphasis.

Her father is dead, her mother is in prison, her brother also. Her two sisters are somewhere in the city. Her country is an exile without end. She's there but she has been gone for a long time, since the war and the genocide. She doesn't recognize the land that betrayed her and that continues to reject her because she finds nothing to anchor her. And yet, she has again taken up the gestures of daily life, reborn gestures that have lost their flavor. One senses that she is alone and that she will stay alone for centuries.

She goes to visit her mother in prison. She brings her clothes, soap, a little food. The old woman is in a crowd of other women prisoners. She cannot get near her, touch her. They speak from a distance. The distance that separates them is too enormous. She raises her voice to be heard, tries to communicate her feelings over the roar, over the despair. But her words disappear in the tide of bodies that flow into each other.

She no longer recognizes her mother on the other side of the invisible barrier, that broken, destroyed woman who doesn't look like anything anymore. She thinks that she won't come back to see her, that they both hurt too much. In this place, there are no mothers and daughters.

There's no date for the trial, no time limit to the jail sentence. All her efforts to get her out have failed. The unstoppable machinery has gone into motion. So Consolata tells herself that she has already lost her mother, that it's just a matter of weeks, of days. The old woman has lost too much weight, become too fragile on her withered legs. It seems as though she wears a mask of pain on which wrinkles carve long gashes. She'd like to find signs of the past in her mother's eyes, but a shadow covers them, an opaque screen.

So Consolata has already mourned the future. It no longer exists for her. Her days are but a long burning wait, a desire to leave for somewhere else. The world exists on the other side of the hills, far from death, far from prison, from her memory, captured, stuck, stopped in time.

Consolata approaches the cat that has just had her first litter. The kittens suck hungrily and the animal purrs, her eyes closed. Consolata finds it wondrous, but by the way she bends her head you can feel that the mystery of life is breaking her heart. She can't take her eyes off this animal happiness, off the intertwining of soft little bodies burying themselves into the warm fur of the contented cat.

ANASTASIO AND ANASTASIA

Anastasia woke up abruptly when dawn called; she felt invaded by the memory of her rape. The sun might well try to show its smiling face, she didn't see it. She was walled up in the prison of her flesh. Her mouth was like cotton wool and kept her from saying one word. Her wants had been worn away like rocks lashed by furious seas. She no longer recognized the insides of her body; she felt foreign to that heavy mass which was crushing her mind. She felt exhausted before the day had even begun. She would have liked to be able to sleep longer, close her eyes more tightly. Disappear into forgetfulness, navigate softly, allow herself to be carried away by subterranean waves. Close the door to the cries and whispers of life, to life's groaning turnstile. A slow slipping. A loss of consciousness. It was much better in the folds of her bed. Quieter, more reassuring. She could return to her favorite places, re-create the special moments when, an unencumbered little girl, she scrambled over the paths that led down the hill. There wasn't a tree, a bush, a hiding place she didn't know.

Does tomorrow always lead to pain? She felt it in her brother's face, in his despair, his clouded eyes, his already bitter lips.

Anastasia was bolted to the darkness, her eyes open to hostile dreams, asking herself if the morning could erase from her memory those years that had been emptied of honey.

Daylight existed only to keep her alert until she slept again.

Despite the years, she carried the wound in her flesh, in her hair, in her smile. She felt fragile, vulnerable. What was she going to do with all those bad feelings tossing around in her head and leaving so little place for anything else?

What frightened her the most was the way her mind wandered, keeping her from concentrating on anything. Deeply felt terrors came back to haunt her. And so she cried out:

"I won't have anything to do with you. I spit you out! I vomit you up! You betrayed me. You ruined my future."

Just think that Anastasio had dared write to her, tell her that he was thinking about her, that he'd never stopped thinking about her, and that he asked her forgiveness for having hurt her. "Answer me, I beg you," he said. "Break this silence I can't stand."

Anastasia held the letter in her trembling hands. She had read and reread the words but she couldn't stop the pounding in her chest. How did he dare write those lines, think that they, together, could still have something in common? Her throat was dry and she felt as though she'd been slapped in the face. She was afraid. Was she going to be able to find her way out of this labyrinth? Would she be able to find herself again? Doesn't he understand what awful thing he did to me? Doesn't he know he's destroyed me?

Out of the shallows of her sleep came despair. Her eyes closed and her mind escaped to fly over the entire universe, but she still had the sensation of slowly drowning. She sank and sank until she lost the rhythm of her breathing. Then she woke up with a start, opened her eyes on total emptiness, completely compelling.

She knew that from now on Evil lived in her body. There was no room in her life for lightness.

Immobile, Anastasio stood in the hall to listen to the noises of the house. It was two o'clock in the morning. Everything seemed calm. He could barely hear the regular breathing of Anastasia and the more rapid breaths of his two little brothers in the next bedroom. He closed their door and listened some more. No sound was coming from below. His parents were sleeping soundly.

He entered his sister's bedroom on tiptoe. He approached the bed where she was sleeping, stretched out on her back. By the light of his flashlight, he could see that she was wearing a white T-shirt and that she'd pushed the sheets down to her waist.

Anastasia woke up with a start when the coarse light hit her face. She tried to cry out but Anastasio was faster. He put his hand over her mouth to stop her. With his other hand, he held the tip of a knife against her neck. "Shut up and don't move, otherwise I'll hurt you! I'll cut your face. Do you think I haven't seen you slink around the boys? You act like a whore!" Feeling Anastasia struggle, he increased the pressure of the blade on her skin. He heard her muffled shout.

Now his sister, frightened, had stopped moving.

Anastasio let her go for a few seconds and grabbed a wrapper hanging near the bed. Then, using it like a large blindfold, he covered her eyes and her mouth. He tied the cloth so tight that Anastasia thought she was going to be smothered. "Don't move," he repeated, "or you'll be sorry!" When he spread her legs apart and entered her violently, she couldn't believe anymore that what was happening was real. It must be happening in another life, another time. She didn't even have the strength to cry. Her mind had stopped working.

Anastasio left her on the soiled bed.

She remained inert, terrified.

She was ashamed. She felt dirty, repulsive. She no longer existed.

How was she going to get up? Face the others?

Her mind left her body, floated in the bedroom, and knocked into the ceiling.

That was the first time she died.

Translated by Judith Miller

Nana Adwoa Anokyewaa
KAPRO, THE ROYAL GIFT

Ghana 1998   Akan-Twi

"Kapro, The Royal Gift" records a rare type of traditional female voice that speaks with pride as a repository of the history of her lineage, and is a traditional ruler in her own right. Nana Adwoa Anokyewaa, a seventy-year-old mother of ten children, a onetime politician extremely active in the women's wing of the Convention People's Party headed by Ghana's first president, Kwame Nkrumah, is now the Queenmother of Kapro. In Akan culture, a Queenmother is a political and social leader who presides over the succession to thrones and leads the women of her community. She is respected as the "wise old woman" of her people as a source of knowledge about the community's traditions and history.

Kapro is a tiny village about twelve miles northeast of the city of Kumasi, in the Ashanti area of Ghana. The village itself does not claim any pride of place among the better-known Asante villages either for great landmarks or for any spectacular development. However, its history is an integral part of ancient and modern Asante history. As a Queenmother of Kapro, and by virtue of her position as the "wife" of the Asantehene, the King of Asante, Anokyewaa has close and intimate political, social, and cultural knowledge of the Asante kingdom. She comes from a lineage that has always had these important ties to the kingdom. Without any formal education, Anokyewaa has walked carefully and wisely all these years in the paths that her ancestors trod to earn them the royal gift of Kapro. She was pleased that her knowledge would be set down in written form for posterity.

Frederika Dadson

✦

I am going to tell you about my origins. I, the narrator of this history, before I succeeded to the stool, was known as Adwoa Kakraba, but according to Asante custom, I had to take a stool name. So my stool name is Nana Adwoa Anokyewaa, chosen from the names attached to the stool of an ancestor whose appellations one finds meaningful. There are names that denote courage, and others cowardliness. The following narrative explains how I became the Queenmother of Kapro.

My ancestors came to Asante from Denkyira. When they were in Denkyira my mothers were not Queenmothers. Rather, the men of my matrilineal line were the ones who directly held royal responsibilities as chiefs. They held the position of Twafohene [head of path clearers] of the King of Denkyira.

The King of Denkyira made a law that, whenever he traveled out of his royal town of Dwukwae, whoever met him on his arrival at his destination would be killed. One of my ancestors, Nana Essuman, who was then the Twafohene [path-clearer] of the King felt the law was too cruel, so he and some elders decided to speak to the King about it. Before the discussion could take place, the King heard about it and angrily threatened to fight Nana Essuman. Advised by their god Konsi, that very night Nana Essuman and his family gathered all their belongings and moved out of Denkyira. Only a few family members who were too old to travel stayed behind.

Nana Essuman's younger sister called Nana Serwaa, who was in the prime of her adolescence at the time of their flight from Denkyira, was carried on the shoulders of the men—they found her too delicate for the rough journey. They traveled a long way for about forty days and nights until they came to the River Pra, which in those days marked the boundary between Denkyira and Asante. Once they had crossed the Pra they were out of immediate danger; Denkyira had no jurisdiction over them.

They were very tired, yet they had to move on, traveling for ten days until they arrived at a place called Essumeja on Asante soil! The Essumeja-hene was very hospitable to them, even giving them permission to bury our head of family (who had died then) on his royal grounds. He had wanted them to stay with him, but Nana Essuman had sworn an oath to serve only the great Osei Tutu, the Asantehene [the King of Asante], so my people moved on.

They finally arrived in the Asafo suburb of Kumasi where once again they enjoyed the hospitality of the chief of that area, Asafohene Asare Boakye. They got the chief to formally present them to the Asantehene, to whom they pledged their loyalty.

Before my ancestors left Denkyira, they lived near the chief's palace where Nana Osei Tutu had lived when he was in Denkyira and he knew Nana Serwaa very well; they were very close. The Asantehene requested Asare Boakye to give them a place to settle at Dontuaso; then Nana Osei Tutu married Nana Serwaa and they all lived peacefully together.

So we were not sent to Asante as slaves captured in one of the Denkyira wars with Asante: neither was it a war in Denkyira that sent us running away to Asante.

After we had settled down, a quarrel arose between the Asantehene and the Dormaahene, Kyereme. Okomfo Anokye, then in the service of Nana Osei Tutu as high priest, was responsible for preparing the Asante nation for war. In those days, the Twafohene of the Asantehene was the chief of Anwoma. Therefore when Okomfo Anokye had prepared the nation and the symbolic seven guns for the war with Kyereme, he summoned the Anwomahene to formally herald the war with the shooting of the guns, as it was his duty to do. Anwoma could not perform his part of the rituals.

So Nana Osei Tutu called Nana Serwaa to him, "Which one of your brothers do you say was the Twafohene of Denkyira?" he asked. "Nana Essuman," she answered. "Tell him I want to see him," he requested. Nana Essuman went to see Nana Osei Tutu, and the Asantehene introduced him to Okomfo Anokye. The preparatory rituals for war—a well-kept secret—were very grave and momentous events nevertheless, when Nana Essuman was told what he had to do, he accepted the task. We were victorious and after the war, the Asantehene, impressed with the performance of Nana Essuman, gave the Twafo stool to him and his descendants. That is the responsibility of preparing the Asantes for war—clearing the "war path" for the Asantehene. My ancestors played a crucial role in all the great wars during Nana Osei Tutu's reign.

After Osei Tutu's victory over the Dormaahene, he said to his wife Nana Serwaa, "My wife Serwaa, I want to preserve your name for posterity. So I will give you a stool that shall stay in your family. It will be the special stool for the wife of the Asantehene. Only your descendants within your clan shall occupy that stool.

"As the occupant of that stool, you shall be responsible for the ritual bathing paraphernalia of any occupant of the Golden Stool of Asante, of any Asantehene, in his preparation to visit the stool house every Akwasidae [festival day]. You shall provide his sponge and his food. Since he is not supposed to eat pepper on such occasions, you shall give him a meal of fruit. You shall give him oranges, bananas, and pineapple. When he has finished his meal, you shall descend to the kitchen and wait for him."

According to our custom, a chief's wife is not allowed to enter the kitchen where the chief's meals are prepared. But the occupant of my stool is the only person who is allowed to do that, and yet I have never been boastful about this special role.

When the King descends from his apartment on such occasions, he goes to the kitchen to inspect and commend our efforts. Then he gives the servants their stipend; and gives me my stipend even before he gives the Queenmother of Asante, the Asantehemmaa, her stipend. After that we prepare his meals at the *sodoo*, which is the traditional name of the enclosure where the Asantehene's meals are prepared.

Therefore we are totally responsible for providing these domestic services for the Asantehene. I am the one and only enstooled "wife" of the Asantehene.

Now after the Asantehene's victory, all the families within the clan that had run away from the Denkyira were given a place to settle. The Twafo group was given a place called Adumanu, but Nana Serwaa was not satisfied with the arrangements.

"I am now your wife," she told the Asantehene, "and you have created a stool for me. Why do you let me live among my family? As a Queenmother in my own right, should I not be given a place of my own? According to our custom I, your wife, am to be protected from vulgar eyes. Therefore give me a place of my own."

The Asantehene saw the wisdom in Nana Serwaa's demands and gave her a new place called Kokoben. She and some of her family members moved to settle there and renamed the place *Kyekyewere,* or "the comforter." The Asantehene had "comforted" his wife with this piece of land. She sent her brother, Adesi, to scout this new area. He came upon a river, Eduosua, which was naturally divided into lagoon-like portions with all kinds of fish in it. Adesi made a receptacle from palms to carry some of the fish. Then he put the rest into a hole that he dug on the bank of the river and covered it. He said, "Come for them the following morning."

When he returned home Nana Adesi called out to his sister Nana Serwaa, "You will not believe what I discovered today!" he told her. "I found a river with all kinds of fish in it. You would find it hard to make a choice."

They were unable to go to the river the following day as planned, but on the third day when they uncovered the hole, the rotten fish sent forth a very bad stench. They took some more fresh fish from the river and returned home.

"Nana, the ones I stored in the hole were all rotten when we got there," Adesi explained to his sister on his return.

"I never dreamt that there could be such an abundance of fish that some would even rot," she observed.

But there was more in that area beside fish. The land was very fertile. Therefore Nana Serwaa sent a message to Otumfuo the Asantehene that they would like to move to this new place. Another reason why Nana Serwaa wanted to move from Kyekyewere was that a son of the Asantehene called Mumuena ("an ugly person is a rare phenomenon") lived there with his attendants. He was so sensitive to his ugliness that his executioners killed any person who dared to make fun of him. So Nana informed the Asantehene that she was afraid for her people who might be tempted to laugh at this man. The Asantehene gave them permission to move to any place of their choice. So Nana Serwaa and her people moved to settle beside the river.

"This is where we will live," Nana Serwaa told her people, "right beside the place where the fish, *enkaa,* rotted." The name of the river changed from Eduosua to Kapro, a blend of the name of the fish that rotted in the hold on the river bank, *enkaa,* and the Asante word for rot, *pro.* Thus the name of the large piece of land that the Asantehene bequeathed to us changed from Kyekyewere to Kapro.

In giving the gift of Kapro to my ancestor Nana Serwaa and her descendants, the Asantehene stressed that he wanted to keep her name alive forever because she had shown great resourcefulness in his time of need. She was a woman who would make any marriage a success. She was the great symbol of womanhood who would stand beside her husband in his time of need and help him on to victory. She was indeed a woman! This is why he created the special *Aheneyere* (or "the King's wife's") stool for Nana Serwaa. And she served him faithfully in the duties that were attached to the stool. They are still the duties that I have to perform for the Asantehene. This is why I can lay claim to Kapro and say that it is mine.

When I was growing up I tried to pay attention to everything about my heritage that the elders of my family talked about. I saved what I heard in my mind. If I had not done that, I would have known very little.

Initially, my lineage was hidden from me. It was not until I was an adolescent that my matrilineal grandfather, Nana Kwabena Takyi, informed my father that I was in direct line to succeed to a stool in my family. But I was not enstooled immediately. Nana Takyi encouraged me to have children because, since my lineage had almost died out, and I was quite alone, they thought it wise to wait until I had as many children as I could to replenish my lineage before I was thrown into the frenzy of public life. I was protected and encouraged; they were afraid that, if they enstooled me too early in life, I might die and leave the stool vacant. I had ten children in all.

One day, Nana Takyi asked permission from my father to take me to the family home where, according to Asante custom, appropriate rituals were performed to prepare me. Nana Takyi and I went to Kwadaso and during the week we spent there, he told me more of my history and answered all my questions. He told me that the settlers at Kapro at that historical time were not part of my family, and proceeded to explain how each family had come to settle there, and about their lineage. I stored all this information in my mind. I never discussed it with anyone.

My father, however, gave me the most information about my people, because Nana Kwabena Takyi had advised my father, who was educated, to record my origins for the time when I would be mature enough to learn it. Before my father died, he showed me the notes. The sheets of paper were very old and one could hardly read the writing. I even attempted to paste the torn portions together but that did not help much.

After the ceremony enstooling me as Queenmother of Kapro, the Twafohene formally presented me to the Asantehene as the current occupant of the *Aheneyere* stool of Kapro. For a long time, because the stool was vacant, the Asantehene had been deprived of the services that my stool was created to perform. That is why I sent my ninth daughter, Yaa Anokyewaa, when she was six years old, to live with, and serve, the Asantehene, Nana Opoku Ware. This gesture was to let him know that the stool was fully occupied now. He nurtured her until she was an adolescent. Then he sent her back to me.

I am the present occupant of the *Aheneyere* stool. I nominate and install the head of family. I nominate and install the chief of Kapro. I have the power to destool them too. I was born and nurtured to preserve my heritage. I am an authentic source of the history of my people. In Asante tradition we are a people protected in times of trouble because of the assistance Nana Serwaa and her people gave to the Asantehene, Nana Osei Tutu, during the war with the Dormaahene, and at other times. If it were not for my knowledge of this history, there would be an unbridgeable gap in the knowledge of these matters. If my uncles and my father had not entrusted me with this knowledge, it would have been lost forever. Since then I have used it responsibly. No one knows better than I do the history of the stool that I now occupy and how it is related to the Asante Golden Stool. There have been times when the traditional court in Asante has had to move to my house to take crucial evidence to support or reject succession claims and land disputes. You are therefore recording my history for posterity.

Translated by Frederika Dadson

Adja Dior Diop
THE IMPORTANCE OF WORK

Senegal 1998   Wolof

Starting practically from scratch because her education never got beyond grammar school, Adja Dior Diop has made her way in the entrepreneurial trade sector. Her promotions came slowly but surely. Today she holds a seat on the Economic and Social Council of Senegal, representing Senegalese businesswomen and entrepreneurs and expressing advanced views about women's access to positions of power.

In addition to demonstrating her recognized talents in the development of African women in business, Diop has also been a devout follower of Islam. She has presided for many years over the largest Senegalese women's organization, which makes pilgrimages to Islam's holy places, such as Touba in Senegal, the center of Mouridism, and Mecca.

Aminata Diaw

✦

I was born on Thirteenth Street, in the Medina [the indigenous neighborhood in Dakar under colonialism]. My mother's name is Anta Manga, and my father was Amadou Hady Diop. I took up my mother's trade, which was weaving and dyeing. In those days, Ndiago woven wrappers as well as Tukuler wrappers were in style. My father, for his part, was a transporter, but he died early. I didn't stay long in school and when I left, I got married.

At the time I started working, not many women could travel abroad. I imported goods to Dakar and resold them. My *marabout*, Serigne Cheikh Mbacké, helped me understand that work is really important in life. Whether a woman travels or not in the context of her work is not the question. The essential thing is her determination. That's how I started to buy handicrafts, bags, pouches, statuettes, etc., that I sold in France where I would buy goods to bring back and sell in Dakar. It was very difficult for a woman then to go abroad. To get an exit visa, you had to have your husband's permission. I was one of those who fought against this kind of permit, which was required by Senegalese authorities.

In those days, married women who traveled were considered to be too free, too independent. People said that they were the ones who "wore the pants" in the home. In spite of this, I persisted. We never imagined that we'd get to where we are today! In the beginning, I had some problems with my husband, but my religious guide talked to him. I, too, told him everything I was doing, and when finally he understood that my work could only help him, he gave me his support. As you know, every beginning is difficult but, little by little, my business began to take off.

In 1995, we created the African Network for the Support of Women's Entrepreneurship (RASEF) in Dakar while preparing for the International Women's Conference in Beijing. The Dakar meeting brought together some fifty-two countries and was difficult to organize. In Dakar, we decided to put in place a structure that could assure the organization of future meetings. That's how the RASEF came to be. After that, we asked each group to form a national board when it got back home, which allowed us to hold a General Assembly in Beijing and elect an international board. We Senegalese were the first to create a national office. I was elected president of the National Board of the RASEF and vice president of the Economic and Social Council of the entire organization.

In the RASEF, there are women who have been successful in their work and others who have just begun. RASEF includes urban as well as rural women. The latter are more numerous and have the greatest problems getting access to loans. Because of that, we thought it necessary to create a Savings and Loan Cooperative to be able to help them, without exhausting all of our own funds. Most of the women are in agriculture, fishing, and seafood processing. Others are in dyeing or weaving. They're the ones we've funded. In addition, we are trying to help those who produce but can't find a way to sell their products. It's a major problem. We buy their products to protect them from exploitative middlemen. Right now, we're working on a project to train and inform women.

Since we created the RASEF, only the British Council has helped us organize seminars, for example, and to set up our banking cooperative. The RASEF gets no subsidies, even if the Ministry of Women's Affairs gives occasional support. The RASEF for the moment runs on its own funds. I donated the space for the RASEF office and the banking cooperative. But if outside help is at a minimum, we haven't lost hope, for the "Senegalese Plan of Action for Women" takes our association into account. I hope that the RASEF will eventually have all the support it needs. In the meantime, we're working for the cause of women.

Our banking cooperative finances the fisherwomen of Yarakh and they've reimbursed their loan. The same is true of the women from Bargy who are in the processing business, or those from Richard Toll who are in agriculture, or those in Casamance who grow rice, and the women of Mbacké who are in weaving and dyeing. These are the five groups that we've funded with the only conditions being paying one's dues to RASEF and the banking cooperative.

The financing of the project follows the same pattern. A request for a loan is sent to the cooperative's bank director, then it's sent to the Credit Committee who gives its opinion to the Board of Directors, after examining the request. The board then states its opinion. Sometimes we receive a project that's not well conceived so we work on it to improve it to be able to fund it. We monitor and follow the loan beneficiaries also so that they can get to work and pay back their debt in a normal period of time.

We also tour the country to meet women and tell them about the RASEF and how useful the organization can be for them. Our hope is to create a sense of solidarity among all women. Things having so profoundly changed, women want to take full charge of themselves. The RASEF members, with help from the British Council, have even organized English lessons to make their trips abroad easier and more successful.

Translated into French by Rokhaya Fall, Aminata Diaw, and Marietou Diongue
Translated from French by Judith Miller

Adja Mariama Niasse
TEACHING THE QUR'AN
Senegal 1998   Wolof

Adja Mariama Niasse is the daughter of the late El Hadj Ibrahima Niasse, also known as Baye Niasse, a renowned religious leader and great scholar who had disciples in Senegal and throughout Africa, especially Nigeria, and even elsewhere in the world (notably in the United States). A woman of exceptional spiritual dimension, Adja Niasse pursues with dignity her father's mission by devoting her life to instructing children in the Qur'an.

The originality of Niasse's career is less in her mastery of the Qur'an than in her appropriation of the field, which had belonged only to men. Her merits are not limited to being involved in this field. Most importantly, she has brought a new vision to it by starting an educational complex whose goals and ambitions equaled those reserved for either the French school or the Christian Confessional schools, a majority of which benefit from institutional support linked to Senegal's colonial past. The school she leads today has about a thousand students, most of them very young. Students that graduate from her school are the pride of Senegal at national and international levels in Egypt, Iran, and Saudi Arabia, where they are often invited to participate in Qur'anic recitation contests.

Aminata Diaw

✦

My name is Seyda Marieme, Cheikh Marieme for some, others call me Seyda or Marieme Ibrahima Niass. I was born in Kaolack, in a village called Cosi. I am the daughter of Aladji Ibrahim Niass and Astou Sarr. I was born in 1934, on December 24. My father, who went to Mecca when I was five, taught the Qur'an to all his daughters.

When he went to Mecca, he put my sister, my brother, and me in Qur'anic school, first in the care of Ahmadou Lawadani, then Mouhamadou Kabani, and then his son Abdoulaye—all Mauritanians. At the time, every candidate for the pilgrimage left a *wasiiya*, a sort of will. We were meant, then, to study until his return and then we were to keep on going until we had perfectly assimilated the Qur'an. When around 1947, I had fully learned the Qur'an, my father organized a big party and invited the dignitaries of the time. He gave me a horse and some gold. After that he continued my lessons in Arabic and in the Qur'an, and for the *xam xam* [esoteric knowledge], in addition to what he had taught me, he sent me to the *marabout* Omar Thiam.

My father is one of the pioneers who decided to teach the Qur'an to their daughters. That's why in his will he had expressed his wish to have his daughter learn the Qur'an. I have even heard him say that man would see himself overtaken in every domain in which he'd be in competition with woman. We can see that today: if you have children, you will see that each time a boy competes with a girl, she will get ahead of him. Baye decided to teach the Qur'an to his daughters because he saw how intelligent they were.

My father loved me very much. At the end of the day's lessons, we would usually go home to eat, but he didn't always let us go home. We were sometimes kept at school where we'd eat our noon and evening meals. We'd be awakened at 4:00 in the morning to read our Qur'anic tablets. At the time there weren't any electric lamps. We studied by the light of a fire. After reciting, we had *fediar* (dawn prayers) and after a small meal, we went back to sleep until the morning, when we'd eat breakfast. Then we went back to studying until the noon meal or sometimes even the hour of the early afternoon prayer. Everything depended on what we had learned and assimilated. Those who had learned the lesson recited; otherwise we were in trouble.

When we got back home, Baye had our meal brought to us and we ate together. You should know that he respected me very much, and took me everywhere with him. He liked his children a lot, especially his daughters. We'll never forget the atmosphere. We had wonderful moments with our father. He truly admired me and I am forever grateful for it. He always favored me and didn't try to hide his preference.

At the age of seventeen, I married and I went to Dakar to live in Thierno Omar Kane's home. Upon my arrival, my husband entrusted me with the Qur'anic instruction. Thus I took care of the education of the very youngest children, beginning with his own sons. Eventually, everyone put their children in my care. Since I began teaching the Qur'an, I have taught many individuals who, in turn, have become teachers. I never stopped because children's education is my passion. What pleases me the most is molding the children, taking care of their moral education. I'm drawn to children because I think of them as God's gift.

I spent thirty-five years on Malick Sy Avenue, in Thierno Omar Kane's home. An important Algerian official, having seen the talent of some of my students, asked to see me so that he could visit my school. I had to explain to him that he *was* in my school. "How do you manage to get such brilliant results?"

I answered, "Just by being here."

"Here under such difficult conditions?" he went on.

"Yes," I replied. "When it feels a little tight, we move to the living room and then to the mosque—there is a mosque in this house."

"You deserve encouragement for all of this!" And, upon his return to Algiers, the Algerian government bought me this house I live in and even helped finance my activities.

Because the children are becoming more and more numerous, I had to rent another house in this neighborhood in Sacré Coeur. President Diouf also gave me 34,000 square meters of land where I've already done some building. That's how I keep busy: educating, training the children. And I can say that about 1,000 disciples are under my tutelage, and their food and all the rest depends on me.

Truly, a woman is obligated to participate in the life of her society because every time that God refers to man, he refers to woman too. To cite from the Qur'an, he always says, "Men and women Muslims" or "You men, you women." God said that men and women are completely equal. It's just that women should not be extravagant in their behavior and dress. Today, you see women engineers, women doctors; there are women in every job

that only men used to have. And I've even noticed that women often surpass their men colleagues! I don't say that because I'm a woman. Men
themselves know that women are more competent! Right? For that we
praise the Lord! We women must be involved in business, especially when
we know women to be determined and courageous.

Translated into French by Aziz Diaw
Translated from French by Judith Miller

Oumou Sangare
A WASSOULOU SINGER

Mali 1998   French

The singer Oumou Sangare comes from Wassoulou, a region in southern
Mali on the border with Guinea. Unlike many other Malian singers, Oumou
Sangare is not a *griotte*. In this region, dominated by Bamana and Peul cultures, singing is not the prerogative of *griottes*. She started singing like her
mother, whom she accompanied to family events. Her grandmother was a
well-known Wassoulou singer.

In 1987, she created her own *Kamalen n'goni* (six-string guitar) band, but
her career really began in 1989 when she recorded her first cassette, *Moussoulou*, in Abidjan. This first cassette became a bestseller in Mali in 1990
(100,000 cassettes were sold in West Africa). With *Songs of Young Girls
Going to the Riverside*, she entered the realm of world music. Together with
the Latvian violin player, Gidon Kremer, she won the UNESCO International Council of Music award for the year 2001.

The Wassoulou tradition from which Sangare takes her inspiration is that
of the hunting societies. This music is usually played by men for men,
accompanied on the *Kamalen n'goni*. Sangare appropriates this male genre of
Wassoulou music, modernizing it and introducing such new themes as love
or the problems of young girls searching for freedom.

The following are excerpts from "Oumou's Voice," an interview with
Amadou Chab Touré, for *Tapama*, a cultural magazine published in Mali in
December 1998. We include also the last stanza of her famous song "Mous-
soulou," in its English version.

Aminata Diaw

◆

My maternal grandmother was a great singer. My mother also sings, but certainly not as well as her mother did. And as for me, I actually was steeped in
music right from childhood on. . . . My mother used to take me by the hand

and I used to follow her from one festive occasion to another. . . . My mother has a beautiful voice and she loves singing. But she did not want to make a living out of show business. . . .

When I first started singing, my mother used to tell me that my voice reminded her of her mother's voice. My voice was my grandmother's voice. My mother found my voice beautiful. She often would call me and ask me to sing for her, just for the sake of hearing my voice, of dreaming, and of seeing the image of her own mother standing in front of her. . . .

I never studied music. The voice I sing with is my natural voice. I never trained my voice . . . neither did my mother. I believe that my voice, that our voices are God's gift to us. It is Him one needs to thank for that. . . .

Because my mother is with me in Bamako, I have Wassoulou beside me. My grandmother was always singing songs about this marvelous land of Wassoulou. . . . With my mother, from morning to evening, I do nothing else but talk about the Wassoulou in Wassouloukan. It is to my mother and to my family background that I owe my knowledge of my homeland, of its language, of its sounds. . . .

The first time I went on stage, it was with Ami Koïta, Kandia Kouyaté, and Tata Bambo. This was in 1987. I was small and the youngest among the performers. That night I was very scared. I was so scared of this extraordinary event during which I was going to sing, side by side with the greatest voices of the country, in front of three thousand people, including the then President, Mr. Moussa Traoré. But when I went onto the stage, after the other performers, I got a tremendous applause from this huge audience which had fallen in love with me. I have never forgotten this incredible evening. This was the evening which made me. . . .

When I am sick about things in my life, I sing. When I have a problem, when something bothers me profoundly, I need to get it out of me . . . and so I sing.

I am very attached to tradition. I am not against the modernization of music but I cannot accept the distortion of traditional music from Wassoulou. I want to keep certain sounds alive, in particular those that are distinctive. . . .

I cannot really tell you how I compose. This process is not very clear in my own mind. But I can tell you why I compose. Generally I work on traditional songs and pieces from our folklore. But I only borrow the rhythm. The rhythm becomes the basis of the song I start composing because I do not want to create something to which the ear is not already accustomed. Thereafter, I put my own words into the chosen rhythm, words from my heart. So, my work as a composer consists of feeling the things that are important in life, of carrying them and transforming them into songs. The rest is just technique. The music of the songs is made collectively, by the musicians, the technician, and myself. . . . More and more, I work at the piano, searching for my own melodies. . . .

You can really find the land of Wassoulou in my music, as you can find Mande in Salif Keïta's music. I pay a lot of attention to the original rhythm. What matters most are the sounds and the emotions they carry. I try to keep the sounds as unadulterated as possible. The *kamalé n'goni* instrumentation constitutes the basis of my music. We do not tamper with it. All the other instruments are tuned to it. . . .

When I started making music, I loved rasta music. I used to listen to reggae at home. A lot of people, then, were confusing rastamen and their music with drug addiction. Reggae, for them, was a kind of drug. And that confusion used to upset me, because I liked reggae but not drugs. So I sang "Bamba Niarté the Rastaman" to tell people that they could and should all love reggae and rastamen, instead of rejecting them, because I believed that they stood for the progress of mankind. . . .

The experience of the Women of Africa Project. It was a meeting of African women musicians—Sali Nyolo of Cameroun, Anitra of Madagascar, Tibigui de Kuamolo of South Africa, and myself. I went to that workshop with my *kamalé n'goni* player, two dancers, and my *djembé* drummer. Each of the three other participants came along with a musician. We worked for two weeks in Swaziland, and for three weeks in London. Then we went on a tour for a month. I learned a lot during this encounter. I felt things I had never felt before in music. And I am eager to have another such experience. . . .

I love my work and I love my family. Both are precious to me. So I need to compromise in order to save them both. I am very lucky, I must say, to have an understanding husband. This gives me courage. . . .

Women can only improve their lot if they open up to the world, if they go to school, if they learn more about their rights. Right now, they know only about their duties! The fact that girls are not in school is a big problem that women have to deal with. Each one of us must, in her own small way, help solve this problem. . . . For that is how we, the women of today, will become the actors of tomorrow's world.

Translated by Christiane Owusu-Sarpong and Esi Sutherland-Addy

Moussoulou

Women of Africa! Work for your country is good.
Women of the Ivory Coast! Work for your country is good.
Women of Africa! Work for your country is good.
Women of Senegal! Work for your country is good.
Women of Africa! Work for your country is good.

Anna Dao
A Perfect Wife

Mali 1999   English

I was born in Paris and spent my childhood in a number of countries with my father, who was a diplomat, and my grandmother. I completed my education in Canada and for several years afterward lived in Mali, working for various United Nations agencies. During the same period I produced and hosted a public-affairs talk show for Radio Klédu and wrote a column for the weekly newspaper *Le Républicain.* I left Mali for the United States at the end of 1993 and am now living and working in New York.

"A Perfect Wife" is part of a collection of short stories I am working on titled *From Africa to America.* The story was inspired by my grandmother, who is the most influential person in my life. She taught me everything I know about our ancestral customs and traditions, from the myth of creation to the role of humankind in the universe. She told me with great pride about her family, their life during colonization, my great-grandfather's participation in the war, the humiliation, the resentment during French occupation, the fight for liberation, the lost lives, the "few good white people" who helped their cause, and the "few black traitors" who betrayed them. Nothing was really black or white. Each side had its "rotten apples."

My grandmother told me that the future comes from the past. She told me the same stories again and again so that I would know and remember who I am and where I came from. What my grandmother told me could not be found in books, so I decided to write about it. Both women in "A Perfect Wife" have a little of her in them. Astou has her strength, Sira her generosity. "A Perfect Wife" is a tribute to my grandmother, who helped shape the adult that I am, and my great-grandfather, whom I never knew but heard so much about.

Superstition held that women "with elongated necks" were looking toward their husbands' graves, and that those who laughed uncontrollably lacked discretion. The expression "had her neck promised" meant she was engaged.

In Malian tradition, the natural parents of children are consulted in private by other family members but have no right to organize their offspring's wedding. The child's paternal uncles and maternal aunts organize the wedding. In Malian society, a child belongs to the entire community. Before deciding to accept or refuse a suitor's offer of kola nuts, families customarily request a period of several days or weeks to discuss the offer among themselves. The *griot* brings on three separate occasions, which constitute the three stages of the official proposal, three very large kola nuts, so that each father can take a bite. The third kola nut serves to confirm the proposal, as well as the bride's family's consent. Only after the family has accepted the third kola nut will they officially inform the young daughter that she is now engaged.

Upon the death of a husband, his sisters untangle the widow's hair, and while doing so, they console the widow, reminding her of all her good deeds. They vow to take over from their deceased brother and promise to assist and help the widow as he would have done. Of course, this only happens if there is a good relationship between the wife and her husband's family. A widow's mourning garb is made of a "mini *boubou*," which is a long halter top; and a large scarf that completely covers the head. The clothes are made of cotton, dyed a shade of blue used only for widowhood.

Anna Dao

◆

The word had swept in without warning. It took everyone by surprise, creating and provoking curiosity, torment, consternation, confusion, excitement, and commotion everywhere. In the beginning it was confined to hushed whispers late at night over pillows, intended only for the ears of one's loving mate, and given with the firm recommendation to keep it under wraps.

Without anybody knowing how, the word had flown out and was found down on the market road where it was exchanged in veiled terms only for a vigorous promise never to let it out. Then it arrived and wandered under the shade of mango trees, to the edge of the well where the conclusion came after a firm assurance that it would never be peddled. It traipsed over family thresholds, and made its way into kitchens. Always in the end were the sworn intentions never to allow the slightest peep or leak. Tired at last, it was seen crawling under the palaver tree where it was whispered somberly and then it died at the sight of unidentified shadows.

Like spring rain, it had crossed the entire country. It was meted out prudently, parsimoniously, and always with the same never-ending imploring exhortation: "Above all, keep it to yourself. Never let it out." Yet, it had spread like smoke, undermining and disturbing the life of the people in town, in the whole community. And now, after months of tension, deliberations, presumptions, suppositions, and speculations the word was finally going to lose its illegitimacy, it would be publicly proclaimed and officially become the latest news.

With loud bugles of fanfare and tam-tam the occupying French force announced to the gathered crowd that in countries far beyond the salty waters, talk of powder and fire had just begun. And in order to defend his threatened territory, the good people of the occupied land would have to give up the courageous young men that were helping them work the land.

War! The word had now become official. From now on, war was a reality. Fear hung like a big rain cloud in the sky, ready to burst wide open. It slammed down upon their faces. A unified silent prayer rose and spilled over everyone's lips as a rumbling groan: "War! *Soubahanalai!* God save us! Protect us!" The elders knew, the women understood, and the youth would soon find out.

Sira was twelve years old. Married for only two months, she could not imagine the upheaval that this declaration would bring in her life. Chosen by Astou Kone, Idrissa Keita's first wife, Sira had been married to him in an attempt to bring what fifteen years of happy marriage had not brought: children.

A year earlier, Astou had sent for the *griot* Sekouba Kouyate. She asked him to scout among the honorable neighboring families and find the young girl who, though no longer a child, had not quite reached puberty, to become her co-spouse and share her space in Idrissa's bed. To carry out the difficult task entrusted to him, namely to find a young lady that would not only be the perfect wife for Idrissa, but would also know how to set aside Astou's "due share of water," respectfully. Sekouba Kouyate decided to follow secretly and spy on all the girls of an age to be married. In the ensuing days, the *griot* would "accidentally" run into them early in the morning on the paths to the market when they went to buy condiments, or by the rivers where they washed the family linen. By ten o'clock he would head into their homes to quench his thirst, share a cola nut, and discuss the latest gossip with one of the elders of the house, while furtively observing every gesture and movement of the girl helping with household chores.

Thus, one by one, he eliminated the lazy girls, the girls who walked with their faces to the ground, those with elongated necks, those with uncontrollable bursts of laughter, those with irascible fathers or quarrelsome mothers.

One by one, the *griot* narrowed down the potential candidates, and soon held a small list of girls, among whom was Sira. Sekouba Kouyate liked her not only because she was sweet, docile, and reserved, but also because her father, Oumar Keita, was a well-known and respected man in the community. Her mother, Mariam Coulibaly, everybody agreed, was a kind, affable, and helpful woman, whose tongue was like a needle always used to patch conflicts between members of her family as well as problems with neighbors. There was also the rather important fact that Sira had a wide mouth, itself a sign of good luck.

Furthermore, the two families knew and respected each other, as they were both descended from the Keita ancestry with an illustrious warrior ancestor in common, Soundiata. Therefore, nothing stood in the way of the union between their households.

Sekouba Kouyate reported his research and selection to Astou, who in turn repeated the *griot*'s words to her husband, Idrissa. He approved and consented to ask for Sira in marriage.

And that is how, one evening after having said his Safo prayer, Sekouba Kouyate made his entrance into the home of Sira's father. After the greetings and customary chatting, the patriarch Oumar Keita asked him to explain the reason for his visit. Sekouba Kouyate revealed that he was the messenger sent by Idrissa Keita, first born of the now deceased Abdoulaye Keita and Sali Traore, who had sent him to raise his voice and inquire if the lovely and coveted gem named Sira already had her "neck promised" or if he could request to become a candidate and bring cola nuts?

Oumar Keita smiled and replied that he was not the right person to be asked that question. The *griot* should refer to his young brother Fatogoma, the father of the child. Then, he called one of his sons and ordered him to take the *griot* to his brother's doorstep.

Fatogoma invited the *griot* in, listened to him, and then explained that because he was not Sira's only father, he needed time to think and also consult with the others about what answer to give to the present request.

One month later, a nervous Sekouba Kouyate entered Fatogoma's hut for the second time where, to his great relief, he was told that he could inform his master Idrissa to bring the cola nuts.

Once they had been accepted, and the dowry had been ascertained and presented, the marriage between Idrissa and Sira was celebrated in style.

To the blaring brass band and the drums they (the subjects) had been told about the necessity of their participation, however coerced and forced it might be, in the saber rattling, which felt completely foreign to them. "They," the people, who had practiced hospitality and welcomed "visitors" only to wind up intruded upon, disposed of, shunned, and set aside, were being called out and forced to defend the now anxious and nervous colonizer. The colonizer, who was afraid of the same fate he had once inflicted, now demanded "their" assistance to help drive away and keep out a new intruder who was threatening to invade and take away his homeland, his history, and his lady love. To make them accept what was being offered, to simply consent to go out and get killed far away from their land, the "ungrateful visitors" sent some of their own.

The good people were visited by their *griots,* their fathers, their chiefs, their elders, their wise men, and their men of God.

The conqueror had ordered the *griots* to remind the people of their glorious past, so that once flattered, incited, and galvanized, they would only think and dream of fighting. The wise men and the men of God were ordered to reassure them and persuade them that their daily prayers, along with their families' sacrifices, would suffice to guarantee their safe return home.

The elders and fathers were herded together to hear talk of bonuses and the meager benefits to be granted to their families; and the honor and prestige awaiting those whose sons would go off to fight for such a noble cause.

Answering the calls of the conqueror (temporary master of their lands), and of their *griots,* fathers, chiefs, elders, wise men, and men of God, the young brave men answered "present" and then departed.

They departed with their ears still ringing with the *griot*'s chants and speeches about the exploits of their ancestors: heroic deeds that forbade all fear, desertion, or mutilation.

They departed full of pride and happy to serve, even if it meant aiding some unknown land that, they had suddenly been informed, was also part of their home.

They departed because they were good sons who didn't know how to disobey their fathers.

They departed because all their life, they had been taught to respect, and never contradict, their elders, their chiefs, and their wise men. Those who did not volunteer were kidnapped and conscripted. Sometimes in broad daylight on the roadside, sometimes in their villages, or sometimes simply sitting at home and accused of vagrancy, they ended up, in spite of themselves, as soldiers. Whether they volunteered, were conscripts, or were simply rounded up in due course, they all appeared before a group of men responsible for testing them and determining the ones worth mobilizing. The test weeded out the weaklings, the sickly, the scrawny, and the puny. Some of them, indignant at having been refused on such slim grounds, protested and even swore to commit suicide if they were not enrolled.

Idrissa Keita enlisted voluntarily and, after having passed all the imposed tests, was placed in the group of privileged men who were going to wage war to protect and defend those who had made them captives in their own land.

When the news came about Idrissa's imminent departure to strange shores across the sea, his wives, sisters, and brothers all got busy praying for God's mercy, to ensure his safe return among them. They consulted the stars again and again, and they asked cowry readers and geomancers to find out which offering or sacrifice would bend the will of the invisible forces that gave him protection.

Idrissa unflinchingly drank the sometimes sweet, sometimes bitter, potions his sisters brought, gulping down their strong-smelling and colorful concoctions without question. He patiently daubed his skin with all of the lotions his brothers gave him and, without coughing, he burned and sprinkled himself with the many powders and roots his two lovely wives placed before him. His body was adorned with the talismans that each had obtained for him. Great platters of food were prepared and given to the less fortunate. In his neighborhood mosque, special prayers were said for him and for all those like him who were being "confiscated" to be sent away.

A few days before his departure, Idrissa called his brothers Lamine and Jabril to his bed chamber for one last talk that went on into the small hours of the morning. That night, he assigned each of them the roles they would have to take on in his place. Lamine, the brother closest to his age, became the acting head of the family; the one to make all the decisions and ensure that the family needs were met. Jabril, the youngest, could read and write a little and his duty was to pick up Idrissa's monthly pay, which he would then turn over to Lamine, who would give half to be split between Astou and Sira, and keep the other half for household expenses.

Afterwards, Idrissa went to say goodbye to his five sisters. Then, he sat down before his wives, asked them to "give him the road," and made them promise to look out for and take care of one another. With tears in their eyes Astou and Sira agreed to everything he said. Finally, he went to the homes of those who had seen him come into the world. And there, he bade his mothers and sisters farewell, then knelt before his fathers to receive their blessing. While bowing before each elder, a choked-up Idrissa felt their rough hands tremble as they laid them upon his head. Their voices quavered with emotions as they recited the *baraka,* or good luck benediction and safe return wishes, while something deep inside them, like a scratched record, kept on repeating that they would never be gathered together again.

The dreaded hour came. Festivities were held so that the banging tam-tam, accompanied by the singing and dancing, would cover up all the sighing and heaving footsteps of the budding warriors, muffle the mournful chants of the women, drown out the crying of abandoned children, and provide a distraction from the raspy sobbing of elders, who would crush the stubborn drop of water that refused to leave their eye-corners by nimbly taking up the end of their sleeves from time to time.

The beat of the tam-tam followed the soldiers to the camp where they were taught some of the basics of military life. More celebrations took place along their route to the station where a train took them to their next destination—a port. There, they were crammed into a ship, a thousand or two at a time, for their passage across the salty waters. The voyage ended ten days later when Idrissa and his companions landed on the shores of the land they now were to defend.

When they arrived, the sons of the desert were issued uniforms identical to those worn by their hosts. Instead of helmets, though, each man received a lovely brightly colored fez, which was supposed to remind him of his home. They were also given huge, oversized shoes that had been made especially for them, but their poor little feet slid around in them.

Since they had been warned that long daily walks caused the arriving troops' feet to swell, after a great deal of thinking and consideration, the fine shoemakers had concluded that if running could widen the foot, it most certainly had to lengthen it too. Blinded by the irrefutable logic and good sense of their deduction, the good men set to work and manufactured immense cloddish combat boots that paddled the soldiers' slim feet. All decked out, the children of the tropics were sent to the front where they endured the deadly combination of the cold weather and cannonball fire.

Even with the head of the family gone, life resumed its rhythm of births and deaths, sowing, harvesting, and cooking days. In addition, the arrival of the monthly allocation came, the information-propaganda selected and spread by the occupying force, the rumors that could not be contained, and, of course, letters from Idrissa.

Like most of his illiterate comrades, Idrissa took his correspondence to one of the young educated soldiers who, during his free time, became their letter-writers. Each letter began the same way: "I am writing to you to give you my news. I'm fine and hope that this letter will find you fine too. Nothing wrong here." And then a blank—a total blank. What else was there to say? Where could he start? What words could he possibly find to describe the daily horror that their lives had become? Shipped in by the thousand from all parts of the African continent, they were the pawns, the disposable and dispensable, used as sacrifices in order to avoid shedding the blood of the "better men"—those other humans whose useful, precious existences deserved to be spared, preserved, and saved.

Condemned to endless hours of toil in the trenches, they spent days in the icy rainwater with swollen and chafed feet confined to boots designed just for them. They did their best to face and resist the devastating, exterminating assaults of the enemy who wiped out a good number of them each day. To escape flying bullets, they piled up dead bodies as barriers and hid behind them. There were so many bullet-ridden, mangled bodies, as well as the bodies of those who had let themselves go and had been eaten by illness: the last remains of poor souls whom they hadn't had time to bury and whose outrages would come back later to haunt them and prevent them from sleeping.

To keep their sanity they would gather and huddle together whenever they could. To keep from shivering, they would sit tightly bunched, pressed against each other for hours, warming their bodies and their hearts with talk of their countries, their families, and of all the things they would do if they ever made it back home.

Jabril would read to the family the few lines that usually made up Idrissa's letters. Reassured, Astou and Sira spent night after night spinning cotton and talking about him. Astou talked endlessly, and Sira listened tirelessly, drinking up everything she was told. Distrustful at first, not knowing what to tell and what to keep to herself, Astou had grown fond of Sira, who was a cheerful, sweet girl who never got tired of keeping Astou company even when she really didn't want to. Sira, the girl recommended by the *griot,* whom she had pushed Idrissa to marry. Astou was certain that Sira, her co-spouse, would always give her her due share of water even when she would have Idrissa's children. Little by little, Astou opened up to her attentive rival Sira who, without realizing it, was learning to better know and love the man who was also her husband.

While unveiling her past and narrating to Sira, Astou went back in time and relived how she had become Idrissa's wife. Idrissa had been part of the household, a son of the house, a childhood friend of her older brothers who had "put on pants" at the same time they did. Just like them, she had known him all of her life. He had always been there, quick to support her and to smile at her. Every time their paths crossed as she walked past the group of boys, her brothers and the others would wink at each other and burst into laughter. They would yell out, "Hey guys, outta the way! Here comes Idrissa's wife." They'd crack up, holding their sides, while an embarrassed and silent Idrissa kicked the dust or some imaginary stone. A flustered Astou would look down, hasten her steps, and rush to disappear.

As time went by and Astou grew up, her figure changed and took on new curves. When she reached the age to be requested, Idrissa, ready and impatient to get married, went to see his favorite father. He begged him to hasten the *griot* with cola nuts before anyone else beat him to it and stole away his beloved forever. Amused, the father of the impetuous lover nevertheless took the time to consult other family members before sending his emissary to ask Astou's parents for the release of their daughter for his son Idrissa. Permission was granted, and the union was sealed with joy.

The two women talked about war. Sira was afraid she would never again see the man she had discovered and come to love through her co-spouse's words. Although she was worried and shared the same anxiety, most of all, Astou was jealous that her rival could speak so freely about her feelings. "The nerve!" she thought. "How dare she be as apprehensive as I am about my Idrissa?"

Days, months, and years passed, punctuated by the return of a few insane and mutilated men, the mournful wails of parents who had their sons reported "dead" or "missing in action," and the growing love of two women for the absent Idrissa.

And then suddenly, from out of nowhere, the rumor landed, headed inland, and spread like wildfire. Confirmed, the rumor became truth: the war was over. The men were coming home. Some in one piece, but many only half human with ravaged faces and atrophied bodies. Others, beaten by the multiple forces quarreling within them, had become disturbed and deranged. They were all going to be reunited and once the euphoria of the homecoming would be over, many would find it hard to readapt and fit in among those who had learned to get by and managed without them.

One morning, Astou and Sira cleaned and incensed Idrissa's bedchamber together. They laughed and sang as they cooked, ignoring the exchange of their brothers-in-law's knowing smiles, and their sisters-in-law's looks of innuendo. They overlooked the whispering of their uncles and aunts, and the grins on the faces of the elders and neighbors, all of whom had come for the long-awaited arrival of Idrissa. Lamine, Jabril, and a few close friends had already gone to the train station to greet him.

As the hours passed by, the joyfulness and excitement were replaced by anxiety, doubt, aggravation, and irritation. A premonition that something was wrong germinated, but was immediately suppressed by excuses invented by exasperated minds that stubbornly wanted to believe that nothing could have happened.

Then out of nowhere he came, appearing before them—the Imam entered the yard followed by a few wise men. Their grave faces brought shattering silence. They were quickly seated and given water to drink so that they could say the words they had come to deliver. Sira sat down. Astou, with shaky legs and buzzing head, stood immobile. The man of God drank, gave thanks, cleared his throat, and looking at the ground declared: "What God gives, He takes back when and where He wants."

Astou's mind clouded, emptied. She slid. Hands grabbed her and sat her down on the mat next to Sira. Men grasped their prayer beads. A murmured *"A ka dogo Allah yé"* (Everything that happens is tiny compared to God) could be heard, while Idrissa's sisters and the neighborhood ladies let out their first screams of disbelief, despair, and devastation.

Dead! Gone! Idrissa, without their knowing it had eaten his share of salt, drank his share of water. And while they were preparing for his welcome-home festivity, he had gone to rest in peace. Numb, Sira listened, and understood. Slowly, tears streamed down her face. Like a wounded animal, Astou shrieked, heaved, and choked. Their pain was fanned and kindled each time they heard the keening of the sisters-in-law and the other women.

Having announced the news, the Imam and his followers got up and left. Astou and Sira were taken to Idrissa's bedchamber, a room they had so lovingly arranged a few hours earlier and in which they were now going to be isolated for the next 132 days. They were placed side by side on two mats laid on the ground. Then, according to tradition, their sisters-in-law sang their praises while taking out their braids. After the ritual, Astou and Sira were bathed and given their mourning clothes.

Idrissa's companions came to express their condolences. Some of them were speechless; stricken to the soul. Their whole being refused to grasp and accept what had happened. But there were the others who tried to articulate and let out the words of what had happened, knowing how his family hungered for details and thirsted for knowledge. They developed and described, wove words interspersed with long silences, for they knew neither when nor how to stop. It was through their words and explanations, jealously collected and preserved, that the family came to understand the irony of Idrissa's tragic end.

The war was over. Idrissa had not been hurt. Along with many wounded infantrymen, he had embarked on a boat for a two-week voyage that brought them closer to home. Idrissa was anxious to be back; anxious to see Astou and Sira. He longed to see Astou, to whom he would tell his ordeal, and recount his moments of fright. Astou, against whom he would snuggle up to ward off and cast out his harassing, hounding demons. Astou, who would find ways to appease his soul and liberate him from his invisible persecutors.

And then there was Sira, who would revive and invigorate him with her youth, allow him finally to experience the joy of fatherhood.

Idrissa had made it to the tropical shores and the nearby station. A train was to take him back home two days later. On the eve of their return to their birthplace, Idrissa and his comrades went out one last time to admire the immensity of the salty waters and to fill their lungs with its special air. With eyes closed, and trembling with gratitude, they thanked the heavens and the hidden forces that had watched over them. Then, like children, they tossed off their army boots and dug their toes into the wet sand. The sun was setting when they decided that they had enough and that it was time to head back.

They had walked for a short way away from the water when a shrill call ripped through the silence causing their feet to turn around. They ran back, their fiery eyes aglow as they scrutinized and searched the stretch of ocean. Then one of them hollered out as he pointed his finger toward the horizon where something was moving. The thing appeared, rocked, bobbed up and down, disappeared, then reappeared again. Forgetting that he didn't know how to swim, Idrissa rushed towards the struggling, slapping hand that was blindly, frantically searching for something solid to grab. He reached the desperate man, who seized him and curled his arms round him. The man hugged Idrissa tighter and tighter against him until Idrissa choked. Then, arms flailing, they started swirling and rolling over. They popped up, jostled by the flow of water, and then sank. Over and over, they rose to the surface, and were carried further and further away by the furious sea that held them as prisoners. When the waters finally calmed down, gentle waves separated the two men, and then brought Idrissa back to the shore, abandoning their hold and depositing his drowned, lifeless body at the feet of his petrified friends.

Later that day, unknown hands washed and anointed him, then enshrouded him in seven meters of white percale, the gift of some compassionate soul. Thus prepared, Idrissa was carried by his friends to the cemetery where he was laid to rest.

Those who had gone to the train station to pick him up were stopped on their way and taken to the mayor who, having been informed, had the bitter task of breaking the news.

The Imam, his followers, and the repatriated soldiers came back in the afternoon to pray with the community for the eternal rest of the deceased. The man of God asked Idrissa's wives and all those who had known or had come close to him, to forgive the man who had left them.

Furious, they forgave.

Helpless, they forgave.

Filled with grief, they forgave.

Angry and bitter, they forgave.

Days became weeks and weeks became months.

During that time, the two women lived together, cut off from the rest of the world. Their friendship blossomed as never before, and their dependency on each other grew. They rolled in pity, whined, and got mad. They shared the mourning, the food, the questions, the resentment, the emptiness, and the loneliness. When Astou sobbed, Sira consoled and calmed her. She pulled her close to her, held her, and rocked her until Astou fell asleep finally worn out.

For four months and ten days with the streams of visitors coming and going, with the old times to recall, the fits of laughter together with the tears and regrets it provoked, Sira comforted and cared for Astou. She watched over her co-spouse, forcing her to eat, to remember and to talk. And little by little, Astou relived and came to tell Sira the last part of her life with Idrissa. The years of joy and longing when they had tried everything to conceive and have a baby. She told of the diets, the prayers, and the alms-giving—and always nothing. Astou's uterus remained barren. Finally she gave up hope of bearing Idrissa's child and learned to tolerate the idea of sharing him. Idrissa was reluctant at first. Even after she had accepted the idea of a co-spouse to give Idrissa children, he still wanted to wait and try. Finally, on her insistence, he agreed to take on a second wife on the condition that she, Astou, would choose the one who would become his bride. Feeling awkward and not knowing how to go about it, Astou in turn had called upon Sekouba Kouyate to help her out.

After the four months and ten days, Astou and Sira left their mourning clothes for the new outfits that were gifts from Idrissa's family. Then they went to visit all the family members and close friends who had come to assist and comfort them during the mourning period. Then, Astou and Sira each went to her father's home "to bury the last tears for the death."

When they came back, the family held a meeting to decide on their futures. Lamine, Jabril, and Idrissa's five sisters wanted them to stay. They were part of the family. Lamine had two wives, but offered to take Astou as the third. Jabril had only one wife and wanted to marry Sira. Astou wished to remain, but without remarrying, and Sira consented to start a new life with Jabril.

Nine years later, and after five false starts where "the babies had fallen" (in miscarriage), a delighted Astou was watching over an exhausted, confined Sira, drained by seven months of imposed rest and the stranger that continually moved and wiggled inside her. Astou joked that she was pretty sure that the expected happy event would be a girl.

"If that were the case," Sira replied, "everybody would know whom to name the baby after."

Astou feigned offense and asked what Sira meant. Was she referring to her?

Sira quickly replied, "No, no," and then muttered under her breath, "who else in this house is almost as difficult?"

"I heard that," yelled out Astou. Then they laughed.

Astou didn't wait. She went away a few days later, tiptoeing out so as not to disturb anyone. She passed away seated on her rug at the end of the morning prayer, after having been reassured by the one calling her that Sira no longer really needed her. She was told that Sira would know how to manage, and how to go on without her from that point on. Astou smiled, let out a relieved sigh, and then went up to join the one who had come for her: Idrissa.

Two months and three days later, a girl was born. A fulfilled Sira smiled.

To keep her promise and honor their friendship, as well as to perpetuate her memory and to give the newborn an identity, Sira and her kin decided that the child could only have one name. Thus, each time one of them would call her, all would remember the one who had left them. Later, Sira would tell baby Astou about her other mother, who had loved her and watched over her, but couldn't stay long enough to wait for her arrival. She would lovingly describe Astou in detail, so the child would adopt Astou's qualities, and make them her own.

On the seventh day after her birth, old Sekouba Kouyate took the newborn in his arms and with tears in his voice whispered three times in her right ear and then three times in her left ear: "Your name is Astou. Your name is Astou. Your name is Astou."

Isatou Alwar Cham-Graham
CHILD SOLDIERING
Gambia 1999   English

"Child Soldiering," a poem by Isatou Alwar Cham-Graham, appeared in a newsletter entitled *Child Labour in Sub-Saharan Africa* in October 1999. At the time, Cham-Graham was an intern at the African Centre for Democracy and Human Rights Studies in Banjul, Gambia. The newsletter was dedicated to the rights of children, specifically to the evils of child trafficking, female ritual slavery, and child soldiering. The phenomenon of the child soldier has taken on horrific proportions in the civil wars of West Africa, especially in Liberia and Sierra Leone. Apart from the traumatic effects on individual children, their involvement in the wars will guarantee that the effects of conflict will be felt for generations to come.

Cham-Graham now works as the principal investigation officer in the office of the ombudsman of the Gambia, where appeals can be taken by citizens in cases of abuse of power and corruption on the part of state officials. She is also a poet and composer.

Esi Sutherland-Addy

✦

Oh! Mother dear; come quickly to my call.
Swiftly like a falling star, come to my aid.
My pain is indelible and my eyes are misty.
Here I stood one legged; blinded with fear, insane with hunger.
In this debris of human suffering, the rebel camps of brutal crudities.
Who lured me into their snare, when I was a godly eleven-year-old.

I pray thee, Mother dear, not to loathe my acts.
For they are collusion to evil, like a virgin they've defiled me
With hate, drugs, rifle and ammunitions.
Like them, I've killed, maimed, raided and scorched,
But now I have caught up with the atrocities I've inflicted on others.
A single bullet has made me one legged, rejected by my comrades
Whose feet are swift like those of deer's.

Oh! Mother dear, come quickly like a falling star.
The sores of the amputation are festering with maggots.
Your milk has spilled before it ferments
Like the fig tree never to be fruitful.
Yet today is my first spring; a teenager, mother.
For I am thirteen years—but the sweetness of a rose
I will never know, nor the adulteration of manhood.
For this time next year I'll be folded with mother earth.
Like the Hands of a clock, death ticks slowly.

Yet today is my first spring, but a spring that would not bloom to
    summer
For I am thirteen, but there are no loved ones to wish me many more
    to come.
But a wish I have all the same.
A pen to write my plight, an earthen privacy.
Oh! I pray thee, not a mass grave.
May my tomb be embellished with flowers.
Like the fallen heroes of Flanders Field
The Lord's prayer, to atone the ills and evils done by me.
A beaming moon; Cherubs to sing me home,
And God's speed.

Nagbila Aisseta
THE HUNGER PROJECT AWARD SPEECH

Burkina Faso 1999   Fulfulde

At an awards ceremony in New York on 9 October 1999, the thirteenth
annual Africa Prize for Leadership for the Sustainable End of Hunger was
awarded to the women farmers of Africa. Nagbila Aisseta, a food-crop
farmer from Burkina Faso, accepted the Africa Prize from Jury Chair Javier

Pérez de Cuéllar on behalf of her sisters across the African continent. That Africa Prize award ceremony marked the official launch of the Hunger Project's African Woman Food Farmer Initiative, "designed to make the African woman an economic player, a decision-maker, a planner, an entrepreneur, and a power in her own life and in the life of Africa."

This strategic initiative, which was designed by African women activists, is aimed at providing the opportunity to create lasting change in the social status and well-being of Africa's 100 million rural women who grow 80 percent of Africa's food, for they are the key to ending hunger in Africa. Throughout Africa, as in much of the rest of the world, women still carry most of the burden of immediate, daily survival. However, though they are indeed the major providers of food crops, their vital role in the national economy is not reflected in the decision- and policy-making bodies, on local, national, or continental levels, that govern their economic lives. In particular, they have little input into the allocation of resources, from national and international sources, into the agricultural sector in which they are the principal laborers. The aim of the Hunger Project's initiative is to transform this reality, one country at a time.

Because the project was launched in Burkina Faso, Aisseta was chosen to represent all women farmers in Africa. In the light of the kinds of transformations the project aims to achieve, it is worth noting that the first woman chosen could not get permission from her husband to make the trip to New York; hence Aisseta came in her stead.

On her first trip out of her home, Aisseta delivered her acceptance speech, reprinted below in English, in Fulfulde, her native language. While she prepared her speech herself, more important is the significance of her having *written* it. In many countries across the continent, the languages inherited from European conquest, in the West and the Sahel—principally English and French—remain the main languages of instruction, often even at the primary level. Furthermore, a spoken fluency in native languages, such as Aisseta clearly already had, does not guarantee written competence in that language; even today, that remains rare. The Hunger Project, like many other literacy programs of the last few decades, teaches literacy in indigenous languages, creating a cadre of people with little formal education who have literacy skills in their own tongues, while highly educated elites in the same country, fluent in English and French, are likely to lack literacy skills in their mother tongues.

Since returning to Burkina Faso, Aisseta has become an active spokesperson for the woman farmer and the literacy program. She has twice been named "woman of the year" in her country, which is an unusual honor for a rural woman of limited formal education.

Naam is a literacy program that began as a traditional cooperative association of young persons (Kombi-Naam) in Burkina Faso.

Abena P. A. Busia

✦

I would like first of all to express to the Hunger Project my profound gratitude for giving me this great opportunity of my life, to travel from so far away from Burkina Faso to be with you here in New York. On this auspicious occasion, allow me to tell you, in just a few words, something about my modest person.

I was born in 1962, in a village of Burkina Faso named Zincko. My village is about 100 kilometers north of Ouagadougou, the capital city of my country.

I come from a very poor polygamous family. My father and my mother are both farmers. I am the eldest of nineteen children.

In accordance with the traditions, I got married at the age of fifteen. I gave birth to seven children of whom two died very young. Since at that time girls were not sent to school, I did not go to school. Nevertheless, thanks to the Hunger Project–Burkina Faso, other women and I were able to take literacy courses in our national language. And I am proud, therefore, to read my speech myself before you this evening.

Most part of my adult life, as a wife and mother, my work consisted of feeding and taking care of my husband and children. Indeed, every day I get up at 5:00 a.m. and start my day by cleaning up the house. After that, I serve breakfast to my family. Around 7 a.m., I fetch water for our daily needs. Around 10 a.m., I go to the bushes to gather wood for fuel. It is only around 12 p.m. that I will begin grinding the millet grain for the main meal of the day. After that, I go back to fetch more water. Between 5 p.m. and 7 p.m. I bathe the youngest of the children, give food to the family, and put the children to bed. It is only around 9 p.m. that I can take a bath, eat something, and then go to bed. To these daily domestic chores, the fieldwork comes in addition, especially during the rainy season. This is truly the typical life of all the women in Zincko, and perhaps of all the women farmers of Burkina Faso.

Like all my sisters in Burkina Faso, I have no right to the land, nor do I have access to financial loans. This make me dependent on the goodwill of my husband, who himself is poor. Since the establishment of the Hunger Project in my village two years ago, I can tell you that many things have changed for us women. For example, in addition to literacy courses, health and nutrition programs, and access to credit, training in food processing and income generating activities, the Hunger Project's Vision, Commitment, and Action workshops taught us how to analyze and solve our problems in dignity and with self-reliance. Even our husbands are very proud of that. The consequence of our regained dignity is that today more young girls are sent to school.

I thank the Hunger Project for this new initiative for the African woman food farmer. Yes, I am proud of this honor that recognizes the contributions and the value of the African woman. But above all I am proud that this special initiative that is launched this evening will indeed support and encourage the African woman farmer to persevere in her struggle to eliminate poverty and malnutrition. As this evening testifies clearly, we know that from now on we are no longer alone in that struggle.

We will tell our governments in Africa that this initiative of the Hunger Project is a strong appeal to them to take seriously into account the vital work of the African woman food farmer in the social and economic development of our countries, and give her the consistent support she deserves.

I cannot conclude without expressing once again my profound gratitude to the Hunger Project for honoring through me all the women food farmers of Africa for our outstanding contributions to feeding our families, our villages, and our whole nations. As soon as I return to my country, I commit myself to sharing this honor with all women of Burkina Faso and in particular with the women of the partner villages of the Hunger Project in Zincko, Nagreongo, and the women of the Naam movement and indeed in other parts of Africa.

Thank you.

Translated by Michel Coclet

Mariama Ndoye
EN ROUTE TO THE TWENTY-FIRST CENTURY

Senegal 2000   French

Mariama Ndoye was born in Rufisque, Senegal. She holds a doctorate from the University of Dakar and worked there from 1978 to 1987 as curator of an African Museum. Then she moved to Côte d'Ivoire to teach at the Sainte Marie French Secondary School of Abidjan. She also worked as a consultant for the African Development Bank. Today, she spends all her time writing and running her boutique.

Ndoye has published several novels, including *On Paved Ways* (1997); *Soukey* (1999), for which she received the 2000 Vincent de Paul Nyondo prize; and *Like Good Bread* (2001). She has also won a literary competition in Senegal in 1982 for the short story "Sisters in Memory."

"En Route to the Twenty-First Century" was published in *The New Senegalese—Text and Context* in June 2000. The story is interesting because of its realistic, humorous, and even cynical tone. Ndoye approaches the myth of the year 2000, which nourished the ideologies of the independence era and its promise of development, through the metaphor of the "rapid car," thus portraying the socioeconomic realities of Senegal and of many other countries of this subregion. All these countries have experienced bad governance, economic crisis, and structural adjustment programs, and in all these countries, men and women have had to develop their own daily strategies of survival.

Aminata Diaw

✦

Here we are in the private domain but in a vehicle destined for public transportation. It's a broken-down wreck from a car lot that closed down a long time ago. Who cares? The mechanics are really ingenious and always find a way to produce replacement parts by mucking about with the originals. The gear box and the newest wheel rims are at least ten years old.

The Office of National Public Transportation has put the key under the mat. Since independence, successive malcontents—workers and students on strike—have decimated its fleet, resulting in the perennial and uncontested triumph of what we call "the rapid car." As irony would have it, this rapid car can't go any faster than sixty kilometers an hour or it risks finding itself belly up with four wheels in the air. But it goes to every corner of the capital. You can even, sometimes, negotiate the price. It looks like a small blue and yellow van. Inside, you squeeze in as many seats as possible, some of which can be moved around. Two along the sides form a sort of narrow corridor. The driver's mate squeezes past to collect the fares. In the middle, two other rows face each other. Here space is even tighter so that passengers' legs intertwine whether they like it or not. On the body are painted the names of a venerated *marabout* and his sons: his benedictions and slogans as well. You can read, for example, *"goor yombul"*—It's not easy to be a man—or *"Kanaan fankul mur"*—Jealousy won't change your luck—or even "Super Jet," "Air Touba," or "Air Tivaouane." But let's return to the guts of our wreck.

No sooner has the motor sparked than the driver's mate demands cash on the barrel head. The last passenger has barely tickled the bench with his behind when he hears himself hailed, *"Gnewel boy!"* literally, "Come on, boy," but understood as "Out with the fare and pronto!" The youth in question seats himself weightily, poses two muscled hands on his thighs, and flexes his arms as if to take flight. His biceps are bulging, his eyes are red, his hair resembles a bush. Sweat pearls at its roots, on his sideburns, on the down of his mustache. He looks the driver's mate in the eye and says, "I'm going to pay with what, man? My teeth?"

The passengers hold their breath. Here we go again: another messy discussion. Is this person drunk, strung out? He answers the mute questions of his traveling companions. "I'm not crazy and I'm not high. I just don't have anything to pay with, that's all. I'm unemployed. I've crisscrossed this town all day long, every day God made me—for weeks now. I've used up all my nest egg and my legs just won't carry me any more."

Spurred on by the inquisitive glances of some and the frank accusation of others, he continues, "You want me to steal the money? Tell me where? Where should I steal it from, huh?"

So they lower their eyes, embarrassed. He spews out his complaints against the state and its lackeys: the lying, thieving, raping, and those other "-ing" politicians. The mate, caught off guard, mutters, "Boy, we're not finished yet and don't forget it. I can handle you anytime. You'll pay me before you get out of this car."

The mate is a big, strapping, uncombed boy. He inherited his girth from his wrestler ancestors. A phony muscle man? Probably, because a regime of bread and peanuts, or sweet potatoes baked under the ashes for lunch, doesn't make for a diet of champions. All the same, the hustlers who go after clients in the bus stations and the driver's mates are reputed to be stubborn brawlers. There are plenty among them on parole. You've really got to be out of your mind to take them on. This explains why the passengers are beginning to twist in their seats.

The mate now hails a rather obese lady, "Hey, auntie!"

"I'm not your aunt. I'm no older than you are."

"O.K., Sister! Your fare! You're taking up two good seats, right? You pay double!"

The girl is corpulent. Her wrapper barely covers her thighs, which form big hilly mounds when she sits. We catch a glimpse of the undergarment supposed to be seen only by her lover. Luckily, her *boubou* guarantees the decency Islam requires. It's more or less transparent as the girl's young age and outside temperature dictates. Her opulent chest rises intermittently. She's made a major effort just to reach the car—it always stops several meters farther away than one would like. And after such trouble, to be treated like this!

She's outraged. And here this lout has drawn everyone's attention to my weight. How awful! Everybody's looking at me now!

She stutters and the tears start. A true gentleman comes to her defense, "Hey, Mate, leave her alone. Are you the one feeding her? Even in an airplane a single person doesn't pay for two seats. You can't make her do that in this motorized tomb. Mademoiselle, don't pay any attention to him. You're the kind of woman we Africans love. What do we want with those slippery fishes and skinny minnies on display in fashion magazines?"

Everyone guffaws. The tension goes down a notch. An older person offers to pay for the young man we mentioned earlier.

"Don't be discouraged, son. Your time will come. Don't lose so much confidence in God that you commit a crime. This mate, too, has to live from the bit of money we hand over. Your misfortune isn't his fault. Nor is ours. We wobble through life like zombies. Our bodies are empty drums. We come and go as though we were obsessed in order not to appear apathetic to our wives. What is life but movement? If there's nothing in the pantry, shake your sieve all the same. A few grains left over from more prosperous times will still be there, sticking to the sides."

The young man, touched by the old man's intervention, doesn't dare answer. Lowering his head, he murmurs. "Thank you, father, I know you're right."

The old man stands up to extract his used wallet. He opens it slowly, respectfully and parsimoniously so as not to expose its contents to the gaze of fellow passengers. He takes out a 500-franc bill that looks like the last person to hold it was a charcoal seller. What a mess these 500-franc bills are! So beautiful new and so disgusting used! The central bank made a mistake with them. You can't give them to a pretty woman, dirty as they are. They say the government plans to take them out of circulation and replace them, but the government says a lot of things it never does. They'll change the money when chickens grow teeth. Nonetheless, the mate grabs it. For him money has no color provided it will pay for a monthly sack of rice.

A mother asks the philanthropist, "What's your name?"

"Ibrahima."

"Ibrahima what?"

"Ibrahima Sy."

"Sy is Tukuler. You're truly a *torodo,* a real noble! May Allah reward you a hundred times for this good deed!"

"Amen, amen," the passengers chant.

Suddenly an abnormally high voice interrupts the wave of benediction. "Ibrahima? Ibrahima! Leave my Ibrahima alone. He's tired. He's just a fish seller, who's got to feed one, two, three, thirty mouths." She counts on her fingers. "We owe money to the storekeeper, the landlord, even the charcoal seller. No more rice; I have to run all over the place, from morning till night. I can't let my daughters manage by themselves: the pimps would get them. Ibou is courageous but Ibou is dead. Ibou is a walking cadaver. He's on his feet but he's lost his mind."

The woman talks and talks, and suddenly bursts into tears. Everyone understands she's a victim of overwork or depression. She's got too much weighing her down and it's starting to overflow. The mere mention of Ibrahima's name sets her off again. A few passengers leave the car. They haven't reached their destination, but they can't take it any more. So much pain in such a short time. All these snapshots that capture the malaise of our age. And yet it's December, 1999. We've been waiting for decades for the year 2000, *attum nataange:* the year of joy and prosperity, as a popular song would have it.

Translated by Judith Miller and Tobe Levin

Aminata Traore
AFRICA IS NOT POOR: AN INTERVIEW
WITH DEBRA S. BOYD

Mali 2000   French

Sociologist, researcher, writer, artist, businesswoman, and powerful orator, Aminata Traore was born in 1947 in Mali, where she lives today. During the presidency of Alpha Oumar Konare, she served a term as minister of culture.

She is responsible for establishing several cultural centers in Bamako, and was a founding member of the African Women's Association for Research and Development (AWARD). Her recent book *Rape of the Imagination* (2002) attests to her commitment to and passion for Africa. She holds the French Chevalier de l'Ordre du Mérite National medal. She is also the founder of the multifaceted Amadou Hampaté Bâ Center in Bamako, Mali, which encourages and implements artisanal, cultural, and educational development.

Debra Boyd filmed the following interview in August 1995 at the Hotel Djenné, one of Traore's businesses and her home in Bamako. The interview appears in Boyd's 2000 film *Santoro Story: A Portrait of Aminata Dramane Traore*. Boyd's provocative questions, which do not appear in this text, sparked Traore's vigorous and perceptive responses.

Aminata Diaw

✦

It is quite difficult to retrace the path of one's life, not because it is a particularly complicated or rich life story, but simply because remembering is not always an easy task. There certainly is a link between the family and social environment in which I grew up, on the one hand, and the choices I have made and the stands I have taken today, on the other.

In the family I grew up in, all women were involved in manual activities. My mother, who is still alive, was an excellent dyer. The woman who raised me, the one I call my little mother, spun cotton and I used to take her cotton to the weaver. When their fabrics were ready, I helped them to sell them. All this later made me realize the importance of the industry of dyeing and weaving. I was a little girl then and was attending school but, like most African girls, I was also helping my mother. Very soon, though, my studies took precedence over this type of activity. One must not forget that I am a product of a certain Mali, the Mali from the 1960s. That was the first republic and I was in secondary school. Like everywhere else in Africa, our people were full of hope for the future, and we were carrying within the vision of a new society. Later on, like most African countries, Mali was faced with more and more inextricable problems. I came to realize that the answer to this multidimensional crisis (at the same time an economic, a financial, and an identity crisis) lay in what you call "self-image" or "self-confidence."

I also believe that Africa needs its diaspora. You know, African countries that are most successful in their efforts today are those that rely on their diaspora. I think we have not yet found the space, the time, and the determination necessary for this cooperation between Africa and all her sons and daughters. This cooperation is not merely doing things together, but a will to live, a will to overcome the hardships of history, the bad hand that history has dealt us—be it slavery, colonialism, neocolonialism, or even, today, forms of dispossession which continue to impoverish our continent.

It is clear that a new awareness must come to be, a new collective awareness which will go beyond the limits of the continent—this is the strength of Africa. When I say that Africa is not poor, I mean that Africa is not poor because of the richness buried below its surface. Africa is not poor because of its people's determination to live here, to live here with dignity, but also because of its people's intelligence and of the talent and the energy of its sons and daughters who have built the rest of the world. If the so-called developed world has something to brag about, its pretensions to grandeur are, in a large measure, owed to the strength it drew from Africa.

I believe that those who left have helped to build America. Our resources have helped to build Europe. Today, Europe can boast of having accumulated physical capital, infrastructure, and a social welfare system. I am not saying that Europe itself did not work toward what it has become; what I am saying is that Europe was able to strengthen itself through over a century of colonialism and five centuries of various types of slavery. It is our wish that this twenty-first century will be the one to put a definite stop to unacceptable international and interracial relationships developed on the basis of arrogance and dishonesty.

Africa needs businessmen and -women. And actually, we do have our businessmen and -women. We have always had them. There are even businesswomen's associations. And I think that Mali is one of the African countries known for its business. This, in the eyes of Americans, is gratifying: It is important. Honestly, I do not believe that I became a business-woman because I was motivated by the desire to create an enterprise, by the fact that I knew how to sell commodities. This was and is not the basic reason behind my endeavors, even though it is important. What happened, I think, is that the initiatives I took turned, on their own, into forms of enterprises. In 1983 I started this whole adventure, and, truly, this has been a great adventure.

In all modesty, I am happy to have been able to achieve certain things, to have been able to offer employment to dozens of young people, to craftsmen, and women. I am happy to have been able to establish special relationships with weavers, with farmers in the villages. . . . We live in a country where 80 percent of the active population is rural and engages in manual activities. Our people manufacture quality products as well as foodstuffs. I have always found it difficult to understand why we hardly ever take ownership of these products, draw pride from them, and improve upon them. I have come to the conclusion that the African response to marginalization, to exclusion, lies in her capacity to invent the present and the future. This had been just talk until 1983, when I came to realize that it was not enough to talk, that it was not enough to be a consultant (and, in my capacity as a researcher, I have been a consultant for several agencies). It was not enough, I realized, to produce reports that would end up in drawers. One had to demonstrate that it could be done.

I actually had no space in which to do what I needed to do, but I was helped by my extended family to achieve my goal. I decided to transform my father's compound, and my whole family believed that it was the right time to attempt this transformation. So we started by trying something new: We built a mud house, created objects in a traditional manner, created a communal space—places where people could meet and drink, eat *fonio*, *dégué*, and grilled chicken while listening to Malian music. I wanted to live in this kind of atmosphere. I did not intend to create an industry, but it turned out to be an industry. I am not the one managing it. I just continue to conceptualize, and once a product or an idea is born and begins to take shape, I lose interest in it. There are marvelous people around me upon whom I can rely; they take up my ideas and bring them to life; then I can start thinking of something else.

Without any false modesty, I believe that we have quality products to offer, such as the now world-renowned paintings of Ismael Diabate, Abdoulaye Konaté, and Kossi of Togo. This is so because, in a way, we operate from a pan-African perspective. All the objects we have are authentic ones. When you are purely business-minded, when your assumptions are based on the profit motive, then you cannot put expensive objects on the market in a restaurant, for instance. But we are first of all concerned with the beauty of the object; we do not start off by thinking of profit. And this is what has made us successful. All the time, we have been thinking that the space we offer must be beautiful, that people must feel good when they come to us; and, mind you, eventually, everyone who comes to visit us starts contributing to this really convivial family atmosphere.

The Djenné was the first cultural enterprise I created. At that time, I was traveling a lot. I was living in Côte d'Ivoire and spending my vacations in Bamako. And I came to realize that there was no place in existence where Malian culture could be appreciated, where visitors could be taken to discover the richness of this country—and I often came home with friends. I used to take them from one restaurant to the other, yet I could never find a good restaurant where one could eat a proper African or Malian meal. Really, it is through these kinds of simple realizations that the whole idea was born. I thought to myself: "You must really persist." In this country, we have real treasures which we do not see, and we must do something about that. This was the basic idea—the desire to go beyond the discourse on culture; the desire to live culture. So we slowly started building. To tell you the truth, this was not based on the availability of funds. At the beginning, I did not have a dime and no banker was prepared to believe that a high-class African restaurant with no alcohol served could become profitable. I had to work very hard, and, each time I had some money, I sent it to my family. It took us five years to build the Djenné and to develop the concept, but as soon as the place was opened, we had an extraordinary response, from Malians, from expatriates, and from foreign visitors. Gradually, this first experience with the Djenné helped us to make progress. We learned how to improve on interior decoration, on the use of local building materials, on cuisine, on textiles. We learned a lot in fifteen years.

Djenné, of course, is a very symbolic name. We are sitting here in one of the first individual mud houses ever built in modern Bamako. We looked for this name, we considered different names with our friends, but Djenné seemed to be the most appropriate, because it is such a strong historical symbol, both from the architectural point of view as well as that of social organization. We wanted to offer ourselves the luxury of creating, in a small space, what we felt, even though this was not meant to be an exact imitation. What really counts is the suggestive power of the word Djenné, which, together with Timbuktu, is so important to me in the history of our country.

The first structure we built was the Santoro, a bit like what we have here. The proprietors were friends of ours, and they liked what we were doing; they offered their space to us, so that we could create the Santoro. What had been used to decorate the Djenné was so interesting to people that they thought that a gallery should be created where one could buy what one had seen in the restaurant. The idea of the Santoro, of the restaurant gallery, was born out of this desire to make the products we had created for the Djenné accessible.

Santoro: Toro is a fig tree. As in many localities, we have a myth of origin which retells how the ancestors would arrive at a certain place, and discover something or other of use to them, which would convince them to settle there. So, it is often a tree, or a hill, or a river to which one pays homage. In "San," the place my father comes from, it is said that the "Toro" saved our ancestor who had gone hunting and got lost. He was going to die, when his dog returned with wet feet; the dog had discovered a river, and that is where he found the "Toro." The river gave him fish, a well, water, and the tree gave its fruit. God knows the importance of environmental issues. Nowadays, these are vital matters in a country such as ours, which is undergoing desertification. In all such stories, I found something fantastic which brings out the fact that Africans are sensitive to ecological matters. Their sensitivity to the environment should be studied, exploited, and analyzed in the light of the difficulties with which we are confronted. The fact that the desert is starting to invade the lands is the true nightmare of our day, particularly for rural areas. At the time, we were preparing for the world conference on the environment and I was involved in its preparation. This is the context in which the Santoro concept saw the light of day.

After that, of course, I continued to travel, but I needed to settle down, to work as an independent consultant. That is when I created the Amadou Hampaté Bâ Center, which constitutes our backbone. That is where all the thinking is done and the concepts created, during seminars and workshops. We have offices and a library. The center is here to carry on what we began. We try to function at two different levels: We need to continue to think, to question Mali, and to discover the essence of this country. We need to find out what can help us remain true to ourselves and, at the same time, remain open to the world. This is because we would be worth nothing to others if we simply tried to imitate them. You only begin to get recognition from the moment you are able to offer the world something new; and that something you can find only in your history, in your culture, in your perception of life. So, it has become imperative to me to continue thinking, to continue writing, and to continue encouraging young people to read, to write, and more particularly to dare.

We needed to search in ourselves, we needed to plunge into our memory, as Malian men and women, in order to find what is essential for us to make our own place in this world, which, unfortunately, on a global scale, is becoming more not less chaotic. I personally believe (and many other people share the same view) that, although Africa is said to be poor and more and more impoverished, Africa is not poor. I believe that this must be said loudly and clearly, that this must be heard. Most of the time, one considers poverty as a material state of being. This means that one looks around and discovers a certain amount of material poverty. But we forget to question the perception we have of ourselves; we forget the considerable opportunities this continent has to offer and which make our region a much-coveted one.

What makes our region attractive is not openly discussed. In the political debate, it remains at the level of the unsaid; nobody talks about it. Everybody chooses to present the region as the poorest region of the world, destined to become poorer still in the twenty-first century, "unless it is better managed, unless neo-liberal reforms are put in place," etc.

Yet it is much more complicated than that and this is what we need to look at in order to find a way out of a descent into the inferno. For over two decades we have attempted a certain type of development, development as perceived and required by others. It is time for us to make a go of ourselves and to claim our right to make our own mistakes. Africa is not poor; it has been impoverished. As such, and despite the monumental difficulties people are confronted with, there is an enormous potential for hope, a will to live that is absolutely resistant to all odds. And that is why I believe in the power of culture. I believe that culture has the power to generate transformation from within, to negotiate, to renegotiate our destiny as African people. Nobody can teach us what we should aspire to become in the twenty-first century, in the third millennium. We need to know exactly, in light of the present global situation, where we are going, how we can get out of our present situation, and how to prepare ourselves for the future.

Translated by Christiane Owusu-Sarpong and Esi Sutherland-Addy

Biographies of Editors

Tuzyline Jita Allan is associate professor of English at Baruch College, CUNY. She is the author of *Womanist and Feminist Aesthetics: A Comparative Review* and co-editor, with Thomas Fink, of the anthology *Literature Around the Globe*. She has published numerous articles on the fiction of women writers, including Ama Ata Aidoo, Buchi Emecheta, Alice Walker, Virginia Woolf, and Nella Larsen. Allan is currently writing a book on black transatlantic feminism and editing, with Helen Mugambi, a collection of essays titled *African Masculinities in Literature and Film*.

Antoinette Tidjani Alou is associate professor in French and comparative literature and literary criticism at the Université Adbou Moumouni de Niamey, Niger, and a founding member of an interdisciplinary research group on gender, literature, and development in Niger. She is translator of *Anthropology and Development: Understanding Contemporary Social Change* by Jean-Pierre Olivier de Sardan, and editor of *Niger: Emerging Literature and Modern Orature; Voicing Identities*, a special issue of *Tydskrif vir Letterkunde*. She is currently working on a book called *Myths of a New World in Francophone Texts and Contexts*.

Diedre L. Badejo is professor of African world literatures and cultural histories and chair of the Department of Pan-African Studies, Kent State University, Ohio. She received a Ph.D. in Comparative Literature and an M.A. in African Area Studies from the University of California, Los Angeles. Her areas of emphasis are African and African American literary criticism, oral historiography, gender and cultural studies, especially Yoruba and Akan oratures. She is the author of *Òsun Sèègèsí: The Elegant Deity of Wealth, Power, and Femininity* (1996). She has published numerous articles and book chapters including "Methodologies in Yoruba Oral Historiography and Aesthetics" in *Writing African History* (2005); "Authority and Discourse in Orin Odun Òsun" in *Osun Across the Waters: A Yorùbá Goddess in Africa and the Diaspora* (2001); and "Womenfolks: Race, Class, and Gender in Works by Zora Neale Hurston and Toni Morrison" in *Black Identity in the Twentieth Century: Expression of the U.S. and U.K. African Diaspora*, (2002). She is currently working on a collection of her essays.

Abena P. A. Busia is associate professor of literatures in English and of women's and gender studies at Rutgers, The State University of New Jersey. She has published widely on black women's literature and colonial discourse and has read and performed her poetry at universities, churches, and poetry and jazz festivals. She is co-editor of *Theorizing Black Feminisms: The Visionary Pragmatism of Black Women*, with Stanlie James, and *Beyond Survival: African Literature and the Search for New Life: Proceedings of the Twen-*

tieth Annual African Literature Association Conference, with Kofi Anyidoho and Anne Adams. She is also author of a volume of poems, *Testimonies of Exile*.

Aminata Diaw is professor of philosophy in the Faculty of Arts and Humanities at the Université Cheikh Anta Diop, in Dakar, Senegal. She has participated in collaborative works such as *Senegal, the Trajectory of a State; Contemporary Senegal*; and *Governance in Senegal*, and is the author of the monograph *Democratizaton and the Logic of Identity in Africa*. She is currently the public affairs director of the Centre for Cultural and Scientific Programs at the Université Cheikh Anta Diop, the secretary general of the Senegalese Council of Women, and chair of the subcommittee on humanities and social sciences of the National Commission of UNESCO.

Rokhaya Fall is professor of history at the Université Cheikh Anta Diop, in Dakar, Senegal, and a researcher at the university's Institut Fondamental d'Afrique Noire, where she is working on a project about *lieux de mémoire* in Senegal. Her main research interests revolve around the question of cultural diversity in Africa.

Florence Howe is emerita professor of English at the Graduate Center, City University of New York, and emerita director/publisher of the Feminist Press at the City University of New York, founded in 1970 and responsible for the rediscovery of scores of "lost" women writers in the U.S. and in many countries of the world. Since 1994, she has been co-director of Women Writing Africa. In April 2005, she left retirement to become interim executive director of the Feminist Press. She has written or edited more than a dozen books and more than a hundred essays. Her books include *No More Masks! An Anthology of Twentieth-Century Poetry by American Women* (1973 and 1993), *Myths of Co-Education: Selected Essays, 1965–1983* (1984), and *The Politics of Women's Studies: Testimony from 30 Founding Mothers* (2000). She is writing a memoir.

Judith Miller is professor of French and chair of the French department at New York University. She is a specialist in French and Francophone theater, text and production. Her books include *Theatre and Revolution in France since 1968, Françoise Sagan*, and *Plays by French and Francophone Women Writers: An Edited Anthology*, and she is currently writing a monograph about theater director Ariane Mnouchkine. She has recently translated plays by Cameroonian playwright Werewere Liking and by French playwright Hélène Cixous.

Fatimata Mounkaïla is professor of comparative literature at the Université Abdou Moumouni of Niamey, Niger, and coordinator of a working group that is researching Songhai-Zarma-Dendi society and culture. She teaches classes on folktales, the epic, and French literature, and specializes in oral tradition, especially in Nigerian women's sayings and literary creations. She is the author of *Mythe et histoire dans la geste de Zabarkâne*.

Christiane Owusu-Sarpong is associate professor in the Department of Languages at the Kwame Nkrumah University of Science and Technology in Kumasi, Ghana. She is a specialist in ethnolinguistics and literary semiotics, with a focus on Akan oral literature. She has edited two trilingual volumes of Akan folktales and published a book on Akan funeral texts, *La mort akan: Etude ethno-sémiotique des textes funéraires akan*. Currently living in Paris, she is married to Ghana's Ambassador to France and has participated in several exhibitions and lectures focusing on Ghanaian culture, in particular *Ghana Yesterday and Today* at the Musée Dapper in 2003, for which she co-edited the catalog.

Esi Sutherland-Addy is senior research fellow and head of the language, literature, and drama section at the Institute of African Studies and associate director of the African Humanities Institute Program, both at the University of Ghana. She has published widely on African theater, film, and music; mythology; and the role of women in African culture and society. In addition, she has held portfolios as deputy minister for Higher Education and Culture and Tourism of Ghana, has conducted studies for UNESCO, UNICEF, and the governments of Ghana, Namibia, and Ethiopia, and has acted as rapporteur general at several world conferences on education. In 2004, she was awarded Honorary Doctor of Letters by the University of Education, Winneba, in Ghana.

Permissions Acknowledgments and Sources

For previously published texts not in the public domain, sources and rights-holders, to the extent possible, are indicated below. Original texts published with permission for the first time in this volume are copyrighted in the names of their authors. Unless otherwise noted, English-language translations commissioned for this volume are copyrighted in the names of their translators. Headnotes contained in this volume were commissioned for this edition and are copyrighted in the name of the Feminist Press. Archives and libraries that provided access to rare texts, or gave permission to reproduce them, are acknowledged below.

In the case of oral materials such as interviews and songs, every effort has been made to locate and gain permission from the original speaker(s). In the case of written materials, every effort has similarly been made to contact the rights-holders. Anyone who can provide information about rights-holders who have not been previously located is urged to contact the Feminist Press. Those seeking permission to reprint or quote from any part of this book should also contact the Feminist Press at the following address: Rights and Permissions, The Feminist Press at the City University of New York, Suite 5406, 365 Fifth Avenue, New York, NY 10016.

Ede Court Historians, **OYA OR THE WIND BEHIND THE LIGHTENING**
Text copyright © 2001, based on a 2001 performance in Germany. English translation copyright © 2005, published by permission of Omofolabo Ajayi.

Olorisa Osun, **PRAISE POEM FOR OSUN**
Text copyright © 1981. English translation copyright © 1996, reprinted by permission of Diedre L. Badejo from: D. L. Badejo. 1996. *Osun Seegesi: The Elegant Deity of Wealth, Power, and Femininity.* Trenton, NJ: Africa World Press.

Beatrice Djedja, *MAÏÉTO*, **OR THE BATTLE OF THE SEXES**
Text copyright © 2000, recorded in Abidjan, Cote d'Ivoire, in 2000, collected and published by permission of Hélène N'gbesso. English translation copyright © 2005.

Communal, **THE PLUMP WOMAN'S SONG**
Text copyright © 1972, recorded by Moussa Hamidou for IRSH (Institute de Recherche en Sciences Humaines), Naimey, Niger, published by permission of of IRSH. English translation copyright © 2005.

Young Women of Kong, **DYULA SONGS**
Text copyright © 1976, collected by, translated into French by, and reprinted by permission of Jean Derive from: Jean Derive. 1986. *Les Fonctionnement Sociologique de la Literature Orale, L'Exemple des Dioula de Kong* vol. 3, 999–1019. Archives of the Groupe de Recherche sur la Tradition Orale (GRTO), Abidjan, Cote d'Ivoire. English translation copyright © 2005.

Communal, **HAUSA SONGS**
Text copyright © 1979, collected by Fatima Othman and published by permission of the Department of Nigerian and African Languages, Ahmadu Bello University from: Fatima Othman. 1979. Unpublished BA Honors thesis. Department of Nigerian and African Languages, Ahmadu Bello University, Zaria, Nigeria. English translation copyright © 2005, published by permission of Ladi Yakuba, Rabi Garba, and Patience Mudiare.

Dior Konate, **SHE WHO DESTROYS HER HARP**
Text copyright © 1998, collected by and published by permission of Rokhaya Fall. English translation copyright © 2005.

Communal, *XAXAR*, **OR SATIRICAL SONG**
Text copyright © 1998, collected by and published by permission of Rokhaya Fall. English translation copyright © 2005.

Communal, **WELCOMING THE BRIDE**
Text copyright © 1997, collected by Aissata Niandou. English translation copyright © 2005.

Communal, **WHERE IS IT FROM?**
Text copyright © 1986, collected and translated by Helen Chukwuma from: Helen Chukwuma. 1986. Unpublished Paper, "Feminism and Fecundity in Igbo Birth Songs."

Communal, **IF NOT FOR CHILDBIRTH**
Text copyright © 1987. Translation copyright © 1987, reprinted by permission of Zed Books (Zedbooks.co.uk) from: Ifi Amadiume. 1987. *Male Daughters, Female Husbands: Gender and Sex in an African Society*. London: Zed Books.

Binta Bojang, *KANYELENG*, **OR CHILDLESS**
Text copyright © 2000, collected by Aminata Deme and published by permission of the author and of the collector. English translation copyright © 2005, published by permission of Aminata Deme and Judith Miller.

Afua Siaa, **NYAAKO**
Text copyright © 1955. English translation copyright © 1969, reprinted
by permission of J.H. Kwabena Nketia from: J.H. Kwabena Nketia. 1969.
Funeral Dirges of the Akan People. New York: Negro Universities Press.
Revisions to translation, made with the consent of the author, copyright ©
2005.

Manhyia Tete Nwonkoro Group, **WE OFFER YOU CONDOLENCES**
Text copyright © 1994, from a 1994 performance in the Assante region,
Ghana, collected by and published by permission of Akosua Anyidodo.
Translation copyright © 2005, based on a translation by Akosua Anyidoho
from: 1994. *University of Ghana Journal*. Legon-Accra.

Anonymous, **DRY YOUR TEARS, LITTLE ORPHAN DOE**
Text copyright © 1998, published by permission of the Archives
Cultúrelles du Senegal, Dakar. English translation copyright © 2005.

Nanahemmaa Ampofo Tuaa III, *NTAM*, **AN OATH**
Text copyright © 2000, reprinted by permission of the author and of
L'Harmattan from: Christiane Owusu-Sarpong. 2000. *La Mort Akan.
Etude éthno-sémiotique des Textes Funéraires Akan*. Paris: L'Harmattan.
English translation copyright © 2005.

Communal, **TWO SONGS FOR SUNJATA**
Text copyright © 1993, collected by, translated into French by, and
reprinted by permission of Adama Bâ Konaré from: Adama Bâ Konaré.
1993. *Dictionnaire des femmes célèbres du Mali*. Editions Jamana. Bamako,
Mali. English translation copyright © 2005.

Communal, **ELEGY FOR INIKPI**
Text copyright © 2000, collected by Helen Bodunde. English translation copyright © by D. L. Obieje

Madlena Van Poppos, **LETTER OF PETITION**
English translation copyright © 2005.

Nana Asma'u Bint, **POEMS**
English translation copyright © 1997, reprinted by permission of
Michigan State University Press from: Jean Boyd and Beverly B. Mack.
1997. *The Collected Works of Nana Asma'u*. East Lansing, MI: Michigan
State University Press.

Fassouma, **HINDATOU**

Text copyright © 1998, collected and published by permission of Fatimata Mounkaïla. English translation copyright © 2005.

Mariam Gaye, **WHO DID MY BABY WRONG**

Text copyright © 1950. English translation copyright © 2005.

Communal, **I'D LIKE TO STAY**

Text copyright © 1974, collected by, translated into French by, and reprinted by permission of André Nyamba from: André Nyamba. 1991–1992. "L'identité et le change sociale de Sanan du Burkina Faso." Thesis. University of Bordeaux, Bordeaux, France. English translation copyright © 2005.

Communal, **AN OLD MAN AND CARRY ON AND HAVE FUN**

Texts copyright © 1997 from: Oger Kabore. 1997. "Les Chansons d'enfants Moose: Signification socio-culturelle d'un mode d'expression des jeunes filles en milieu rural" in Junzo Kawada, Ed. *Cultures Sonores D'Afrique*. Tokyo, Japan: Institute for the Study of Languages and Cultures of Asia and Africa (ILCAA), Tokyo University of Foreign Studies. English translation copyright © 2005.

Communal, **CIRCLE SONGS**

Texts copyright © 1998, based on recordings made in Ghana. English translation copyright © 2005, published by permission of the Estate of Kofi E. Agovi.

N'della Sey, **A MOTHER'S PLEA: TWO LETTERS**

Texts from: Archives Cultúrelles du Senegal, Dakar. English translations copyright © 2005.

Women of Passoré and Ladre, **THE WHITE FOLK HAVE COME AND POKO**

Texts copyright © 1988, recorded in Passoré, Burkina Faso, in April 1988, collected, translated into French, and reprinted by permssion of Samuel Salo from: Samuel Salo. 1991. "Les Moosé Du Passore Face Au Régime Colonial (1904–1946)" *Cahiers du CERLESHS* no. 7. University of Ouagadougou. English translation copyright © 2005.

Women of Passoré and Ladre, **BAMAKO**

Texts copyright © 1988, recorded in Ladre, Burkina Faso, in April 1988, collected, translated into French, and published by permission of Samuel Salo from: Samuel Salo. 1992. "La Chanson Populaire Comme Elément D'Illustration De L'Histoire Coloniale De Moaga." Direction des Presses Universitaires. English translation copyright © 2005.

Mabel Dove Danquah and Others, **FROM THE "WOMEN'S COLUMN"**
Texts from: *The Accra Evening News*, Accra, Ghana, 1949–1950.

Adelaide Casely-Hayford, **PROFILE OF GLADYS**
Text copyright © 1983, reprinted by permission of Kobina Hunter from:
Adelaide and Gladys Casely-Hayford. 1983. *Mother and Daughter: Memoirs and Poems*. Ed. Lucilda Hunter. Sierra Leone University Press, 1983.

Gladys Casely-Hayford, **AFRICAN SCHOOLGIRLS' SONG**
Text copyright © 2005, published by permission of Kobina Hunter, son of Gladys Casely-Hayford.

Efua Sutherland, **THE ROADMAKERS**
Text copyright © 1961, published by permission of the Estate of Efua Sutherland from: Efua Sutherland. 1963. *The Roadmakers*. London: Newman Neame.

Efua Sutherland, **FROM *FORIWA***
Text copyright © 1962, published by permission of the Estate of Efua Sutherland from: Efua Sutherland. 1971. *Foriwa*. Accra: Ghana Publishing Corporation.

Celestine Ouezzin Coulibaly, **WE WOMEN OF THE UPPER VOLTA**
Text copyright © 1961 from: *Carrefour Africain*. 10 December 1961. Ouagadougou, Burkina Faso, 42. English translation copyright © 2005.

Kate Abbam, **ON WIDOWHOOD**
Texts copyright © 1968, 1972 and 1994, reprinted by permission of Mrs. Kate Abbam from: 1968/1972/1994. *The Ideal Woman*. Accra, Ghana.

Constance Agatha Cummings-John, **MAYOR OF FREETOWN**
Text copyright © 1995 from: Constance Cummings-John. 1995. *Memoirs of a Krio Leader*. Ibadan, Nigeria: Bookman Publishers.

Olufunmilayo Ransome-Kuti, **THE STATUS OF WOMEN IN NIGERIA**
Text copyright © 1961, reprinted by permission of the Center for African Studies, Central State University, Ohio, from: Funmilayo Ransome-Kuti. "The Status of Women in Nigeria." *Journal of Human Relations* vol. 10, no. 1 (Autumn 1961), 67–72.

Olufunmilayo Ransome-Kuti, **AUTOBIOGRAPHICAL NOTES AND THE CAUSES FOR REVOLT REMEMBERED**
Text copyright © 1995, from: Ransome-Kuti Papers, box 1, file 9. Special Collection. The Kenneth Dike Library, University of Ibadan, Nigeria.

Communal, **YOU OF THE HOUSE**
Text copyright © 1979, collected by Fatima Othman, reprinted courtesy of the Department of Nigerian Languages, Ahmadu Bello University, from: Fatima Othman. 1979. BA Honors thesis. Department of Nigerian and African Languages, Ahmadu Bello University, Zaria, Nigeria. English translation copyright © 2005.

Communal, **ONE SINGLE MEASURE**
Text copyright © 1998. English translation copyright © 2005.

Communal, **INVOCATION AT MILKING**
Text copyright © 1987. Translation from Fulfulde/Pulaar to French copyright © 1987, used by permission of *Notre Librairie*, revue des littératures du sud (www.adpf.asso.fr/notrelibrarie) from: Abdoul Sy Savane. "La Poésie Pastorale Peulhe au Fouta-Djallon." *Notre Librairie* 88/89 (July–September 1987). English translation copyright © 2005.

Zebuglo of Loho, **PRAISE SONG**
Text copyright © 1999, based on a 1999 performance, collected by Edward Nanbigne and published by permission of Zebuglo Sonaama Charia of Loho and Edward Nanbigne. Translation copyright © 2005, reprinted by permission of Edward Nanbigne from: Edward Nanbigne. 2001. "The Role of Women in Dagaare Oral Poetry: An Indicator of the Changing Status of Women in the Society." M. Phil thesis. Institute of African Studies, University of Ghana, Legon.

Communal, **THE BEAUTY OF KUMASI**
Text copyright © 1988, published by permission of CEHLTO (Center for Linguistic and Historical Studies by Oral Tradition), Organization of African Unity, from: Boubou Hausa. 1988. *L'Essence du Verbe*. Niamey, Niger: CEHLTO, 135. English translation copyright © 2005.

Communal, **THESE WEST-COASTERS ARE LIARS**
Text copyright © 1998, based on a 1998 performance, collected by and published by permission of Sadi Habi and Fatimata Mounkaïla. English translation copyright © 2005.

Communal, **THE NON-MIGRANT'S SONG**
Text copyright © 1998, based on a 1998 performance, collected by and published by permission of Sadi Habi and Fatimata Mounkaïla. English translation copyright © 2005.

Communal, *TABARDE,* OR BLANKET-MAKING

Text copyright © 1999, based on a performance and transcribed by Manou Zara Villain, collected by and published by permission of Fatimata Mounkaïla. English translation copyright © 2005.

Communal, THE SISTERS-IN-LAW DIEDHOU

Text copyright © 1994, collected by and published by permission of Rokhaya Fall. English translation copyright © 2005.

Communal, *SEYBATA* OR MY BACKSIDE – INSULT HER!

Text copyright © 1999, based on a performance by a group of girls, collected by and published by permission of Fatimata Mounkaïla. English translation copyright © 2005.

Selma Al-Hassan, TANOFIA

Text copyright © 1971, reprinted by permission of the author from: Selma Al-Hassan. 1971. *The Cowrie Girl and Other Stories.* Accra: Ghana Publishing Corporation.

Flora Nwapa, THE TRAVELLER

Text copyright © 1992, reprinted by permission of Africa World Press from: Flora Nwapa. 1992. *This is Lagos and Other Stories.* Trenton, New Jersey: Africa World Press.

Adja Khady Diop, TWO POEMS

Text copyright © 1975, published by permission of the Archives Cultúrelles du Senegal, Dakar, from: Adja Khady Diop. 1975. *Le Senegal d'hier et ses Traditions.* English translation copyright © 2005.

Aoua Keïta, CONVERSATIONS WITH MIDWIFE SOKONA DIAOUNÉ

Text copyright © 1975, reprinted by permission of Presence Africaine from: Aoua Keïta. 1975. *Femme d'Afrique: La Vie d'Aoua Keïta raconteé par elle-même.* Paris: Presence Africaine. English translation copyright © 2005.

Khadi Diop, TRIBUTE TO *YAXA MA JAM* WOMEN

Text copyright © 1975, reprinted by permission of Tostan pour l'Education Non Formelle en Afrique from: 1990. *Hearts in Distress.* Dakar, Senegal: TOSTAN. English translation copyright © 2005.

Ndeye Seck, EMIGRATION TERRIFIES ME

Text copyright © 1990, reprinted by permission of Tostan pour l'Education Non Formelle en Afrique from: 1990. *Hearts in Distress.* Dakar, Senegal: TOSTAN. English translation copyright © 2005.

Buchi Emecheta, **A NECESSARY EVIL**
Text copyright © 1980, reprinted by permission of George Braziller, Inc. and Harcourt Education Ltd. from: Buchi Emecheta. 1980. *The Slave Girl: A Novel*. New York: George Braziller, 1980 and Oxford, England: Harcourt Education Ltd.

The Daughters of Divine Love, **TWO SONGS**
Text copyright © 1977, reprinted by permission of Rev. Sr. Maria Trinitas Keke for the Daughters of Divine Love Congregation. English translation copyright © 1977, reprinted by permission of Rev. Sr. Maria Trinitas Keke.

Hadjia Barmani Coge, **ALLAH IS THE LIGHT IN DARKNESS**
Text copyright © 1979, English translation copyright © 1996, reprinted by permission of the Edinburgh University Press (www.eup.ed.ac.uk) from: Graham Furniss. 1996. *Poetry, Prose and Popular Culture in Hausa*. London: Edinburgh University Press for the International African Institute, 144–45.

Afua Kuma, **JESUS OF THE DEEP FOREST**
Text copyright © 1980. English translation copyright © 1980 by Father Jon Kirby, reprinted by permission of Asempa Publishers, Christian Council of Ghana, Box GP 919, Accra from: Afua Kuma. 1980. *Jesus of the Deep Forest, Prayers and Praises of Afua Kuma*. Tr. Jon Kirby. Accra: Asempa Publishers, 1980.

Toelo, **LISTEN TO ME, CHILD OF A *GRIOT***
Text copyright © 1981, based on a live performance by Toelo, collected, translated into French, and published by permission of André Nyamba, from: André Nyamba. 1991–1992. "L'identité et le change sociale de Sanan du Burkina Faso." Thesis, University of Bordeaux, Bordeaux, France. English translation copyright © 2005.

Shaïda Zarumey, **LOVE POEMS FOR THE SULTAN**
Text copyright © 1981, reprinted by permission of the author from: Shaïda Zarumey. 1981. *Alternances pour le Sultan. Paris*: Quantics. English translation copyright © 2005.

Nahua Kulibali, **NAWA'S LAMENT**
Text copyright © 1986, from cassette recording of a performance. English translation copyright © 2005, published by permission of Sassongo Silue.

Ellen Johnson-Sirleaf, **PRESIDENT DOE'S PRISONER**

Text of extracts from unpublished speech copyright © 1986, published by permission of the author. Interview copyright © 1987, reprinted by permission of *Index on Censorship*, the international magazine for free expression (www.indexonline.org) from: "President Doe's Prisoner." Interview with Ellen Johnson-Sirleaf, edited by Abena P.S. Busia. *Index on Censorship*. May 1987.

Nyano Bamano, **THE MAN WHO DUG UP YAMS**

Text copyright © 1983, reprinted by permission of Karthala Editions from: Marie-Paule Ferry, ed. 1983. *Les Dits De La Nuit: Contes Tenda Du Senegal Oriental*. Paris: Karthala. 98–101. English translation copyright © 2005.

Communal, **HASAN**

Text copyright © 1972, reprinted by permission of the Centre Nigerien de Recherche en Sciences Humaines (CNRSH) from: Jeanne Bisilliat and Dioulde Laya. 1972. *Les Zamu ou Poems Sur Les Noms*. Naimey: CNRSH. 121–127. English translation copyright © 2005.

Communal, **SITA**

Text copyright © 1984. English translation copyright © 2005, published by permission of Salamatou Sow.

Communal, *EYIDI*, **OR NAMING**

Texts copyright © 1979 and 1982, recorded in those years in Agboville, collected by and published by permission Hélène N'gbesso. English translation © 2005, published by permission of Chantal Ahobaut and Judith Miller.

Sadi Habi, **PLAY FOR ME, DRUMMER MAN**

Text copyright © 1999, based on a 1999 performance, published by permission of the author and of the collector, Fatimata Mounkaïla. Translation © 2005.

Mareme Seye, **TAASU**

Text copyright © 1979, published by permission of the Assesseur de la Faculté des Lettres et Sciences Humaines, University of Cheikh Anta Diop, Dakar, Senegal from: Cherif Thiam.1979–1980. DEA Memoir. Dakar: UCAD, Department of Modern Letters. English translation copyright © 2005.

Communal, **GAZELLE**

Text copyright © 1972, recorded in 1972 by Moussa Hamidou for the Institute de Recherche en Sciences Humaines (IRSH). Published permission of the IRSH. English translation copyright © 2005.

Oumou Sangare, **A Wassoulou Singer**

Interview excerpt copyright © 1998 by Éditions Donniya, reprinted by permission of Editions Donniya from: "Oumou's Voice," Interview with Oumou Sangare by Amadou Chab Touré, *Tapama*, December 1998. Editions Donniya, Bamako, Mali. English translation copyright © 2005. Excerpt from lyrics to "Moussoulou" copyright © 1991, published by permission of World Circuit from: Oumou Sangare, *Moussoulou*. World Circuit/Nonesuch. 1990 Samasso Productions/1991 World Circuit.

Anna Dao, **A Perfect Wife**

Text copyright © 2005, published by permission of the author from: *From Africa to America*, unpublished short story collection.

Isatou Alwar Cham-Graham, **Child Soldiering**

Text copyright © 1999, reprinted by permission of the author from: "Child Labour in Sub Saharan Africa" (newsletter), October 1999.

Nagbila Aisseta, **The Hunger Project Award Speech**

Text copyright © 1999, translated by Michel Coclet for the Hunger Project and published by permission of the Hunger Project from: Acceptance Speech, Thirteenth Annual Africa Prize for Leadership for the Sustainable End of Hunger, 9 October 1999.

Mariama Ndoye, **En Route to the Twenty-First Century**

Text copyright © 2000 from: *The New Senegalese: Text and Context*. Xamal. June 2000. English translation copyright © 2005.

Aminata Traore, **Africa Is Not Poor: An Interview with Debra S. Boyd**

Text copyright © 2000, published by permission of Debra S. Boyd from: 2000. *Santoro Story: Un Portrait de Aminata Dramane Traore*, a film by Debra S. Boyd (Genius of the Sahel Series of documentary films). Distributed by Cultural Encounters, Winston-Salem, NC.

Authors Listed by Country

BENIN

Sarah Forbes Bonetta, Victoria Davies, Madlena Van Poppos

BURKINA FASO

Communal, Nagbila Aisseta, Deborah Nazi-Boni, Celestine Ouezzin Coulibaly, Toelo, Lucie Traoré Kaboré, Bernadette Dao Sanou, Women of Passoré and Ladre

CÔTE D'IVOIRE

Communal, Tanella Boni, Béatrice Djedja, Nawa Kulibali, Werewere Liking , Anne-Marie Raggi, Véronique Tadjo, Young Women of Kong

GAMBIA

Binta Bojang, Isatou Alwar Cham-Graham

GHANA

Anonymous, Communal, Kate Abbam, Ama Ata Aidoo, Akua Amaku, Selma Al-Hassan, Yaa Amponsah, Nana Adwoa Anokyewaa, Amma Darko, Mabel Dove-Danquah, Akosua Dzatsui, Efwa Kato, Afua Kobi, Odarley Koshie, Afua Kuma, Manhyia Tete Nwonkoro Group, Adjua Mensak, Ola Bentsir Adzewa Group, Afua Siaa (Fofie), Efua Sutherland, Nana Yaa Tiakaa, Nanahemmaa Toaa Ampofo Tua III, Zebuglo of Loho

GUINEA-CONAKRY

Communal

LIBERIA

Ellen Johnson-Sirleaf, Malinda Rex

MALI

Communal, Anna Dao, Aoua Keïta, Bohintu Kulibali, Oumou Sangare, Aminata Traore

NIGER

Communal, Fassouma, Sadi Habi, Maman Ibrah Hinda, Salle-ka-ma-kani, Shaïda Zarumey

NIGERIA

Communal, Nana Asma'u, Hadjia Barmani Coge, Kunak Bonat, Sarah Forbes Bonetta, Ede Court Historians, The Daughters of Divine Love, Victoria Davies, Buchi Emecheta, Elizabeth Mgbeke Ezumah, Nwanyeruwa, Flora Nwapa, P. A. Itayemi Ogundipe, Olorisa Osun, Olufunmilayo Ransome-Kuti

SENEGAL

Anonymous, Communal, Mariama Bâ, Nditi Ba, Nyano Bamana, Adja Khady Diop, Houleye Diop, Khadi Diop, Adja Dior Diop, Mariam Gaye, Dior Konate, Adja Mariama Niasse, Mariama Ndoye, N'della Sey, Ndeye Seck, Mareme Seye, Samba Tew Sew

SIERRA LEONE

Adelaide Casely-Hayford, Gladys Casely-Hayford, Constance Agatha Cummings-John, Mame Yoko

INDEX OF AUTHORS AND TITLES